THE SECOND WORLD WAR

VOLUME 1

Henri Michel

THE SECOND
WORLD WAR

Translated by Douglas Parmee

VOLUME 1

PRAEGER PUBLISHERS
New York

Published in the United States of America in 1975
by Praeger Publishers, Inc.
111 Fourth Avenue, New York, N.Y. 10003

First published in France under the title
LA SECONDE GUERRE MONDIALE by Henri Michel

Printed in the United States of America

Contents

Book One   The War in Europe (September 1939–June 1941)

PART I   THE PRELUDE IN POLAND AND SCANDINAVIA

Chapter 1   The Obliteration of Poland from the Map of Europe

Chapter 2   The Phoney War

Book Two   The World War
(June 1941–January 1943)

PART I   THE GREATER REICH

Chapter 1   The Break Between Germany and Russia

Chapter 2   The Wehrmacht's Victories in the USSR

Book Three   The Defeat of Italy

VOLUME 2

Book Four   The Defeat of Germany

Book Five   The Defeat of Japan

Book Six   The World at the End of the War

List of Maps

List of Tables

Preface

Has the time come to attempt a synthesis of the events of the Second World War? The vast number of books and articles on the subject, from all over the world, would seem to suggest that it has. In fact, the sheer quantity of works sets the historian well-nigh insoluble problems; it is no more possible for one man to read everything than it is for him to avoid leaving important gaps. The quality of these publications is most uneven; memoirs and accounts of spying and battles abound, but the sources are not always disclosed and in most countries the archives are not available for research. In short, the historian is gorged with details but the essential nourishment is often lacking.

The variety of languages in which these publications appear gives rise to further difficulties which are not always solved by the existence of a translation, more readily obtainable, incidentally, as a commercial publication than as a work of scholarship and all too frequently presented in mutilated form, generally shorn of its critical apparatus.

It must be added that historical research on the subject has reached different stages in different countries; some of the belligerents—Japan, for example—are only now beginning to make their voices heard. In other countries, political events have more than once changed the trend in historical writing—for example the repercussions of 'destalinisation' in the Soviet Union have enabled Soviet historians to inquire into an event of such major importance as the German-Soviet pact although not as yet to study it from the original documents. We can only form some idea of it through German documents. Finally, in every country, the younger generation sees the events from a different angle than those who lived through them.

It is obvious that, in such circumstances, any attempt at synthesis must be tentative and provisional. It is equally plain that it cannot be the work of one man but of teams who often have not yet completed their task. Thus *La Commission d'Histoire de la Résistance en France* has given itself ten years in which to draw up an exact chronology of the underground

French Resistance movement, with some 150,000 index cards to deal with.

This book could not have been contemplated without the work accomplished during the last twenty years by the research team of the *Revue d'histoire de la deuxième guerre mondiale*,[1] which I am privileged to direct. The reader is requested to refer to this periodical to complete the selective bibliography placed at the end of the book. Through the specialists working on the *Revue* I have been able to acquaint myself with works which, either because of their technical nature or the language in which they were written, would otherwise have been inaccessible to me. It gives me pleasure to express my gratitude to them and I have been glad to quote them in my bibliography on every possible occasion.

It is obvious that the study of a conflict that set most of the world ablaze demanded a modicum of international co-operation. The *Revue d'histoire de la deuxième guerre mondiale* has often had occasion to devote special numbers to particular subjects, the result of co-operation of historians from various countries.

The recently created International Committee for the History of the Second World War[2] will no doubt lead to an increase in the exchange of books and documents which is so essential; it will enable various research organisations throughout the world to exchange information and, primarily, to make each other's acquaintance; it will help to bring to a successful conclusion the systematic card indexing of the sources of the Second World War, started by the French Committee for the History of the Second World War, and intended to gather together bibliographical information with card indexes providing guidance on the material held in archives.

In such a changing picture, the present work cannot claim to do anything but offer a provisional record of our present knowledge, an attempt to clarify rather than to explain, a factual account which poses more questions than it answers. No one will be surprised that a book written by a Frenchman and first published in France should lay stress on France during the war; certainly not with the intention of exaggerating the role of France, because everyone knows that it was a secondary one, but because it is plain that a French historian is most likely to produce something worthwhile when writing about France, even though he will find it more difficult to be impartial than on other matters. On the other hand, in the present state of historical research, it seemed necessary to stick close to the events and give an account of how they happened as well as how they were connected. I hope nonetheless that I have given the reader a picture

1. Published by the Presses Universitaires de France.
2. With its Offices at 32, rue de Léningrad, Paris VIII.

of the Second World War that will enable him to understand its main features and follow its development.

Although the Second World War ended with the defeat of Germany and Japan, it began with successes for them on such a scale that, at the time, it seemed these could be decisive. The first part of this book tells the story of the first half of the war, the success of the Axis powers.

From 1943 onwards, it seemed uncertain what course the war would take: the Wehrmacht had been checked, had indeed even begun to retreat, both in the USSR and in Africa, but deadly and destructive fighting was still taking place thousands of miles away from German territory. As for Japan, although she had not succeeded in extending her conquests, she still remained out of reach in her archipelago and could exploit 'Greater Asia' without let or hindrance. Of the three Axis partners, Italy had proved the frailest; her armies had suffered great setbacks, her fleet no longer dared emerge from its bases, her war economy had revealed its shortcomings and the Italian people were becoming more and more reluctant to fight.

On the Allied side, the USSR had made an extraordinary recovery, thanks to her vast resources and territory, the efforts and sufferings of her people and, finally, Stalin's iron fist and the solid structure of the Communist party; her successes had earned the Red Army the admiration of the occupied peoples; they had banished to oblivion the German-Soviet pact and Soviet imperialism. Everywhere the Communist parties, with unswerving loyalty to their ideological fatherland, were playing an increasing role in the secret Resistance or in the exiled governments. Britain had successfully extricated herself from the dramatic situation and isolation into which she had plunged after the defeat of France but her war effort had now reached its ceiling and would not be able to increase without American aid. The great event of the end of 1942 was the entry into the lists of an American army, as yet inexpert, of course, but possessing unequalled resources of war potential. The United States was struggling virtually alone against Japan; she was providing the Allies, including the USSR, with their lifeline of convoys, tanks, aircraft and dollar loans; through her industrial production and the expedient of lend-lease, she had become the arsenal of the Allied coalition. Thanks to the success of the convoy system, her munitions and men were reaching their action stations in the Pacific, Africa and Europe.

Up to now, the struggle had been on land and at sea; the air force had done no more than provide support for the army and the navy, often a decisive support; but it was not autonomous. Thanks to the massive American output of planes, the air force was from now on to play a strategic role, perhaps a major one, through its raids. Italy, Germany and Japan were

to be ravaged long before the armies of their enemies approached their
frontiers. One after another, the neutral powers—led by the South
Americans—descended into the arena. The origins of the war were becoming lost in the past; were they still fighting for Poland or was she to be
sacrificed to the Allied entente? What is more, since Roosevelt and Stalin
openly displayed their anti-colonialism, was not the British Commonwealth
itself under threat? The conflict had not only expanded beyond all
measure, it had changed its directions and aims.

One thing which was however becoming certain was that victory would
go to whichever of the two camps could manufacture the largest quantity
of arms or discover soon enough irresistible new weapons. To invent or to
produce these the belligerents strained every nerve and mobilised all their
resources. Whatever their political régimes and ideologies, all the great
fighting powers were transformed into 'companies for waging war'. Behind
the strategist and the soldier and supporting or preparing their impetus,
the scientist, the engineer and the working masses sustained their hopes
of holding out and winning. Propaganda was still stifling any production
of disinterested literary or artistic works; writers and artists were enlisting
on both sides; research workers were being sent for, formed into teams and
briefed; in every country the war really was becoming a total war; but in
this unprecedented effort, it was the scientist who from now on was to
play the primary role. He was, of course, working for war and destruction
but each of his discoveries was equally full of promise for peace and the
post-war period.

For the moment, at the beginning of 1943 soldiers and diplomats were
still occupying the front of the stage. When things began to go wrong,
would the Axis partners tear each other to pieces or would they manage to
collaborate? Would the Allies produce a common strategy, and, if so,
what? Would their alliance, forced on them by a common enemy, stand
the test, and to what kind of post-war conditions would they lead? While
ruin piled upon ruin throughout the world; while endless misfortunes,
old and new, descended upon hundreds of millions of men and women;
while hunger and disease were ravaging countries once rich and healthy;
while millions of Jews were finding their way to gas chamber and
crematorium; while further millions of human beings were being up-
rooted; while young people all over the world were sacrificing themselves,
the whole planet was being shaken and convulsed. The power of nations was gradually falling into a new order and a new hierarchy; peoples
who had been subjugated for centuries were feeling that the time had
come for nationhood; those who had been defeated in the first round
were preparing to reorganise themselves and, by fighting on, achieve

freedom and rebirth; above all, in their laboratories, scientists were bringing forth the world of tomorrow, pregnant, if it should so wish, with the
real victories of mankind over its real opponents: natural forces, famine,
cold, ignorance, social injustice and poverty.

INTRODUCTION

The Forces Involved in September 1939.
Strategic Plans

On September 1, 1939, at 4.45 a.m. the German Army crossed into Poland. On September 3 at 11 a.m. Britain, and six hours later France, in fulfilment of their pledges to Poland, declared a state of war to exist with Germany. The Second World War had begun. What were the forces involved and what were the motives, aims and plans for bringing them into action?

I THE ANTAGONISTS: THEIR HUMAN AND
ECONOMIC POTENTIAL

Superficially at least, the war was starting as in 1914: Germany was to have to fight on two fronts. In fact, however, on her eastern front she was protected by the German-Soviet pact and was faced, not as before by the Russian colossus, but by weak little Poland. To the west she had the same opponents as before: France and Britain, whose armaments, state of readiness and morale were, however, very different from in 1914. In addition, France had been forced to split up her armed forces; although not required to cover the defence of her frontier with Spain, as had once been feared, she still had to keep watchful guard against the blustering claims of Mussolini.

In human and economic terms, the democratic countries' potential was vastly greater than that of the Axis powers. It is true that by annexing Austria and Bohemia the Reich had increased its population from 70 to 85 million; with the Italians, the Fascist states were roughly equal in numbers to their opponents in Europe. In theory, the Third Reich could raise some 12 or 13 million soldiers and the Fascist propaganda machine had always boasted of the 8 million bayonets brandished in support of the Duce. But the democracies had at their disposal the limitless resources of manpower from vast colonial empires. In the event, apart from some reluctance on the part of South Africa, the Commonwealth showed no hesitation in faithfully following the mother country's lead into war; it was the same for the countries 'protected' by France.

At the outset, the Wehrmacht were able to deploy 54 first-line divisions and to reinforce them within a space of days by 59 reserve divisions. The French had 35 divisions, increased by mobilisation to 86 within a period of a few weeks; Poland had 30 divisions that could be brought up to 42; but Britain, which had recently reintroduced conscription, was able, a month after the declaration of war, to send over to France only two divisions. The French and Polish armies thus had to bear the brunt of the first attack alone. But even after leaving considerable forces on their Alpine frontier, in Corsica, in Tunisia, in the Near East and in Djibouti, the French army had a good chance of achieving numerical superiority on its north-eastern border. If the Poles were obviously going to be forced back on the defensive, the French army could, in theory, come to their help by taking the offensive. Did not the Franco-Polish convention of May 15 provide for a French attack a fortnight after mobilisation?

But mobilising large armed forces is not enough; you still have to provide them with officers, equipment and modern weapons. The democracies clearly had ample means to do this; their economic superiority was as striking as the weaknesses of the Axis powers were obvious from the statistics.

Although Germany had enough coal for her needs, she had to import iron ore from Sweden, in summer via the Baltic but in winter through the port of Narvik and via the more hazardous Norwegian territorial waters. On the other hand, despite the development of *ersatz* materials, synthetic rubber and petrol were far from meeting the needs of the war machine and though rationing had already been in operation for a number of years, massive imports of foodstuffs were required to feed the population. The Italians were in an even more parlous plight; they had no crude oil or iron whatsoever and their coal was imported—from England!

On the other hand, Britain had recovered from the economic depression; in 1938 her production was almost 20 per cent greater than in 1929. Though France lagged somewhat behind, the fact remained that the two allies together produced more steel than Germany. True, they were considerably dependent on imports, but the resources of raw materials in their empires were inexhaustible and their gold reserves would enable them to purchase anything they needed anywhere in the world, particularly in the United States.

II THE NAVIES

The shipment of men and materials presented few problems, since the democracies held complete command of the seas.

When Germany rearmed, she deliberately neglected the Navy. After the naval treaty signed with Britain in 1935, by which the tonnage of the German fleet was fixed at 35 per cent of that of the Royal Navy, Admiral Raeder had drawn up an ambitious programme of naval construction, providing for the launching over a period of twelve years of 13 battleships, 20 cruisers, 2 aircraft-carriers and 250 submarines. But by September 1939 this programme had barely started and its implementation had been greatly delayed. The naval strength of the Reich was only 3 pocket battleships, 2 heavy and 6 light cruisers, some 30 torpedo-boats and 57 submarines; 2 battle cruisers, the *Scharnhorst* and *Gneisenau*, were undergoing trials; 2 heavy battleships, the *Bismarck* and *Tirpitz*, were still being built and nearing completion.

What is more, when there were differences of opinion between the Kriegsmarine and the Luftwaffe, Hitler had come out in favour of Marshal Goering, the Air Force Commander, so that all naval air forces, be they land- or sea-based, remained subordinate to the Luftwaffe. Admiral Raeder had not even been allowed to have the reconnaissance aircraft which he wanted; in short, he had failed to obtain recognition of the necessity for all sea operations to be under the control of one single commander, in charge of both air and naval forces. The German Navy was thus in danger of being deprived of air support at the critical moment, the more so as Goering was convinced that command of the sea could be achieved by aircraft alone and land-based aircraft at that. 'I shall seek out the English fleet with the Luftwaffe,' he declared, 'and I shall drive it from one bay to the other all round the British Isles until it doesn't know where to find shelter next.' Good understanding between the chiefs of the services concerned could have reduced the gap between their two conceptions, but Raeder and Goering were at daggers drawn.

The Italian fleet was also of recent growth and possessed a number of very fast ships, but it, too, was not complete; its building programme had been based on the assumption of a war coming in 1942, so that in 1939, four 35,000-ton battleships were still under construction. The Italian Navy had been on a war footing since 1935 and this had resulted in premature wear and tear of material. Above all, fuel-oil stocks were completely inadequate; in September 1939, they amounted to some 1,600,000 tons against a monthly consumption of the order of 200,000 tons. Finally, as in

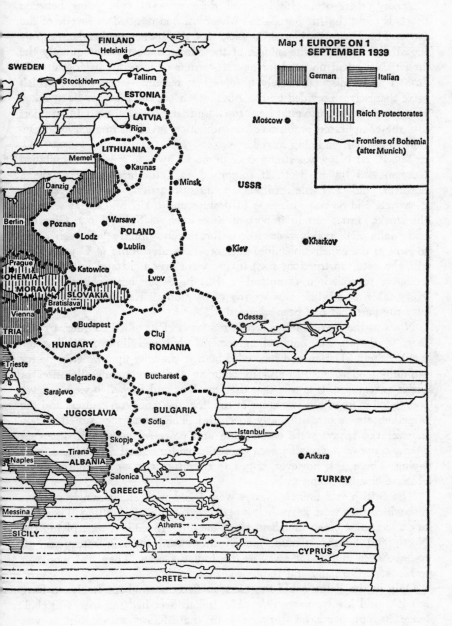

Map 1 EUROPE ON 1 SEPTEMBER 1939

German | Italian

Reich Protectorates

Frontiers of Bohemia (after Munich)

Germany, there were fundamental differences of conception between the Navy and the Air Force—and Mussolini had decided in favour of the latter. The Duce considered, in fact, that the Italian peninsula was 'one big aircraft-carrier in the middle of the Mediterranean'; consequently the Italian Navy had no need for aircraft-carriers or torpedo-carrying aircraft. It had at its disposal merely a few slow reconnaissance planes which were themselves provided by the Air Force; were the Navy to be attacked by enemy aircraft, it would have to call on land-based aircraft for support and the complicated problems of co-ordination involved in such an operation were far from being solved.

The Royal Navy was strong enough, on its own, to crush the combined German and Italian fleets. It comprised 12 battleships—many of them, however, old—3 battle cruisers, 7 aircraft-carriers, 64 cruisers, 200 destroyers and 60 submarines; 9 battleships and 6 aircraft-carriers were on the stocks. True, certain important bases such as Scapa Flow, Gibraltar and Malta were poorly protected; unfortunately, priority had been given to guns at the expense of mines and torpedoes. According to Captain Roskill, the battle instructions then in use were over rigid and left too little initiative to squadron commanders. But in September 1939 the Royal Navy taken as a whole was worthy of its glorious tradition and ready to play the part that had been assigned it.

Nor was the French Navy a pale reflection of its allied counterpart—far from it, despite international agreements that had limited its development, Admiral Darlan had succeeded both in drawing up a programme for building modern vessels and in securing the appropriate allocation of funds as required. It is true that the *Jean Bart* and *Richelieu* were not yet completed in 1939 but two ships of the line, the 7,600-ton cruisers and the torpedo-boats, were particularly successful. The submarines varied widely in size: the largest were ocean-going and powerful enough to intercept enemy convoys; the smaller ones were suitable for coastal defence and mine laying. There was, however, only one aircraft-carrier, apart from a single obsolete 'floating seaplane base'.

The British and French Navies were faced with an extremely onerous task which they were nevertheless perfectly capable of fulfilling. They had to protect some 7,000 merchant ships totalling 18 million tons plying the North and South Atlantic, the Mediterranean in both directions, all round Africa and as far away as the Indian Ocean. They had moreover to blockade Germany and Italy.

Only in the Baltic could the German fleet move about freely; to have left it would involve grave risks. The Italian fleet had the means to challenge its opponents for supremacy of the Mediterranean, but it was particularly vulnerable. Neither side had attached sufficient importance to aircraft-carriers; the Allies did not suspect that the most formidable battle-ship would be easy prey to air attack. Above all—somewhat surprisingly since the unrestricted passage of ships at sea was the prerequisite of an Allied success—the French and British Navies lacked escort vessels and long-range land-based strike aircraft; the techniques of attacks on sub-marines from the air had been overlooked. Meanwhile Admiral Raeder, though fully appreciating that the way to fight Britain was through the destruction of its merchant shipping, did not have a sufficient number of submarines available to undertake effective action; there were just 57, only 22 of which were ocean-going, whereas Admiral Doenitz, the submarine-warfare expert, considered that one thousand would have been required on the outbreak of hostilities. But if the Allies seemed in no danger of losing the war at sea, they could not win it there either. And the fact is that in September 1939, they were far from possessing on land and in the air the superiority they enjoyed at sea.

III THE LAND FORCES

The modern British Army was still in the throes of being born, the Polish Army's equipment antiquated. On the other hand, the reputation of the French Army, victorious in the First World War, was immense, even in Germany. But the reality did not match up with the memory. Individual infantry equipment was reasonably good and the basic artillery weapon was the well-tried 75-mm gun, but anti-aircraft defence was quite inade-quate. The most serious deficiency, however, lay in the tanks. It is true that the manufacturing programme drawn up in 1936 had been largely completed. Provision had been made for 50 battalions equipped with light tanks and 12 with heavy tanks. In all, out of the 2,500 tanks that had been ordered, by September 1, 1939 the Army had received 1,770. These tanks were well armoured but, on the whole, rather lightly armed; for lack of radio equipment, their intercommunication was poor. Only the heavy tanks were powerful both in weapons and armour, with the accompanying drawback of low speed and high petrol consumption which reduced their range of action; above all, the Army had only 385 of them.

As for anti-tank weapons, the artillery's 47-mm gun was capable of penetrating the heaviest armour, but their manufacture had begun only in 1937, and out of the thousand ordered, only 411 were ready by Sep-tember 1939. These guns were entirely unprotected against air attack and being horse-drawn they required a long time to set up, in contrast to the enemy's motorised and armoured equivalent.

All in all, when one considers that a German armoured division comprised some 350 tanks, it is plain that the French Army had the means to equip several armoured divisions, but in fact she was unable to raise even one against the six Wehrmacht divisions.[1] What was the reason for this discrepancy? After all, there were Frenchmen who had preached mechanised warfare; following General Estienne's lead, Colonel de Gaulle had conducted, in print and in conversation with political leaders, a campaign in favour of forming an armoured battle corps. It had been in vain. Hardly anyone had supported him, with the exception of Paul Reynaud who was clear-sighted enough to recognise that an offensive arm of this sort would enable France to fulfil its obligations towards her allies in Eastern and Central Europe. De Gaulle had caused dismay amongst other leading politicians by proposing to man this armoured corps by means of a professional army, the mere mention of which raised spectres of the Pretorian Guards or the Grenadiers at the time of the 19th Brumaire. Above all, at the technical level, he had failed to convince the military leaders, his superior officers.

Yet French military intelligence (the *Deuxième Bureau*) seems to have given fair warning to the French general staff. As early as 1935, it had pointed out the Germans' great innovation in using autonomous armoured units as a battering ram and it had described the composition of these units and their use of air co-operation. It had emphasised that hostilities might begin with a sudden attack; it had drawn special attention to the steady increase in the Wehrmacht's offensive strength. The articles by General Guderian, the German expert on tank warfare, had been translated into French.

Perhaps even the most intelligent people had been stultified by the precedent of the 1914–18 war and the prestige of its great—and victorious —military leaders. The French general staff listened more readily to the opponents of Guderian in Germany itself—Lieutenant-Colonel Boentsch, for example, who did not believe that a defensive front, solidly held, could be broken through by tanks alone. The Supreme Commander, General Gamelin, still convinced of the truth of the axiom that 'in battle, the infantry reigns supreme', had expressed the view of all his colleagues when he laid down in his directive of December 15, 1937: 'Tanks alone are unsuited to seize possession of any terrain or to occupy it for any length of time.' Consequently, 'their sole task is to act for the direct and immediate benefit of the infantry.' This is why, in September 1939, the French Army was not short of tanks but had only two light mechanised divisions; there was thus absolutely no possibility that France would attack the enemy

1. France had two light mechanised divisions, which is not at all the same thing.

in order to relieve Poland. But were the Allied air forces at least in a position to undertake effective aggression over German territory?

IV THE AIR FORCES

Between the two wars, the use of aircraft, a new weapon with unknown possibilities, had been the subject of passionate debate. Amongst all the military experts the Italian Douhet had stood out by reason of his coherent, indeed dogmatic, doctrine. According to him, as the aeroplane would in future make trench warfare impossible, the Army as well as the Navy would now have to step down in favour of the Air Force. Long-range bombers seemed to him capable of destroying the military and economic structure of an enemy so extensively as to paralyse its armed forces and demoralise its civilian population. Douhet used the metaphor of an eagle whose eggs are smashed by destroying its eyrie. All offensive operations would be the exclusive prerogative of the bomber aircraft; they would secure mastery of the skies not by air combat but by the destruction of enemy potential on the ground. As a result the Army and Navy were restricted to a purely defensive role; in Douhet's words, 'in order to put the full weight of attack in the air'.

In every country, there were three schools of thought. Some experts adopted Douhet's thinking, but they experienced great difficulty in imposing their revolutionary views on such powerful and traditionalist groups as the Army and Navy. Moreover, there had been no conflict to test the soundness of 'Douhet's doctrine'; in the Abyssinian war or the war between China and Japan, the superiority of the Italians and the Japanese had provided an immediate solution to a problem that would be posed in quite different terms in Europe; in the Spanish Civil War, the destruction of the enemy's potential was not to be contemplated. Other experts supported close participation in the ground fighting by the Air Force acting as a sort of long-range artillery or providing protective cover for the advance of armoured units. But there were many old-fashioned theorists who thought that an air force could never be anything more than an auxiliary service complementing the other two.

In Germany the Luftwaffe had enjoyed the benefit of unlimited funds since 1935; it had been provided with an organisation and material based on the most modern techniques; it had never been hampered by the need to preserve or adapt old, existing equipment. Although the air industry had been set up hurriedly and hastily equipped—mass production had not started until 1938—in 1939 the total production of the German aeronautical industry had nonetheless reached 885 aircraft per month and in

September the Luftwaffe possessed more than 4,000 aircraft, including one thousand fighters and 1,800 bombers.

Plans had been worked out for the close co-operation of aircraft with tanks; thus 450 bombers—Stukas—had been organised and equipped to dive-bomb enemy positions. The Germans had given priority to fast, light, twin-engined bombers, capable of carrying only one ton of bombs. These bombers were admirably suited for combined army/air operations, although they were not out of the range of enemy fighters. Their drawback was that Britain lay practically beyond their own range. Also they had been produced at the cost of neglecting the heavy four-engined bomber.

In general, the upper echelons of the German Air Force still lacked professional knowledge; many of them had come to it from the Army. Their supreme commander, Goering, had only had experience as a junior air force officer and former fighter pilot from World War I; he thought of the heavy four-engined bomber as a sitting target. The result was that the Reich possessed a powerful air force for waging a war of limited duration over a relatively restricted area; but it had no strategic aircraft.

The Italian contribution to the strength of the Luftwaffe was some 1,600 aircraft; they had been tried out over Spain but their quality was generally inferior and only 40 per cent of them were new.

France's industrial weakness was particularly noticeable in aircraft production. The aircraft ordered before 1937 were based on prototypes dating from 1934 and already out of date. In 1939, mass production of fighter aircraft had not yet started; there was no light bomber prototype and no dive bomber, although the *Deuxième Bureau* had drawn attention to the importance of this type of aircraft in the Luftwaffe. The most recent plan, called Plan V, called for the production of 4,700 aircraft which would provide a modern force of 2,600 front-line aircraft. In order to launch this programme, it had been necessary to purchase armament and equip new factories. By these means, the scheduled production had been maintained and starting from a monthly total of barely 35 aircraft in 1938, it had risen to 220 in 1939 and almost 300 at the end of the year. But the general staff had asked for absolute priority to be given to the fighter arm; bombers took second place and what was more, there was no good prototype.

To sum up, according to the files of the *Direction du Matériel aérien militaire*, on September 3, 1939 the exact situation was as follows: out of a total of 1,407 aircraft, 708 of the 1,157 fighters and 125 of the 175 bombers were with their squadrons, that is to say available for operations. Only part of these aircraft were equipped with the latest technical devices: variable pitch airscrews, superchargers, retractable undercarriage, radio and so on. Clearly, such an air force was incapable of attacking the military and industrial installations of the Reich; they would be at a disadvantage even over their own territory against the German Air Force. Could they at least expect the co-operation of a powerful British Air Force?

As the British had devoted their main efforts to the RAF, it was, after the Navy, their best service. Out of a total of 1,700 aircraft based in the UK, 1,100 of them were modern, more or less equally divided between fighters and bombers. The originality of the bombers lay in their variety. While most of them were medium bombers of limited range, there were also four-engined heavy bombers. Finally, by developing a theory that had been put forward by a Frenchman, Camille Rougeron, the British had begun manufacturing light bombers—Mosquitoes—which were as fast as fighters, so that defensive armament could be dispensed with; with this saving in weight, they could carry a payload of one ton for long distances—as far as Berlin. Britain was thus the only belligerent which by September 1939 had tried to provide herself with a strategic Air Force capable of carrying the war into enemy territory while still using the best of her Air Force in defence of her own territory. The question was whether there was anything left over to support the armies in the field.

For the moment, the French and British Air Forces together barely came to half the size of the Luftwaffe. But this figure was meaningless, for the whole RAF, planned basically for the defence of its national territory, would be needed to be deployed in France and the French general staff would have to find the best way to use the French Air Force. In any case, the planes of the Allies would no more be in a position to rush to Poland's aid than would their tanks, despite their promise of protection. It seemed likely to prove an empty promise.

V CAUSES OF THE DEMOCRATIC COUNTRIES' SHORTCOMINGS

The democratic countries were thus in a position of inferiority on land and in the air. What was the explanation for this discrepancy between potential and reality?

Since 1936, Germany had been preparing for war. The Four Year Plan had set up an economy based on the principle of autarchy and imposed austerity on the living conditions of the population. In the metallurgical, chemical and electrical industries, Germany had, beyond any doubt, a technical lead; a lead that was equally marked in scientific research, theoretical as well as applied. From now onwards, Czech industry—and in particular the firm of Skoda—would be adding its own contribution. It was true that progress was sometimes slow, whether in the field of artificial silk or rubber production, industrial oils extracted from coal, the exploitation of ore with low iron content or, most important of all, in petrol production. But the Reich's political and diplomatic efforts had now succeeded in making available for use the Hungarian wheat lands, copper from Yugoslavia, crude oil from Romania and manganese from Turkey. The USSR could supply all the rest, even if it might have to come via the Trans-Siberian railway. Thus the whole of Germany's national effort had been controlled and disciplined with warlike determination. It was true that there were some parts of the machinery which were creaking and that economically the Reich was still vulnerable. But for the moment it had made maximum use of its potential. This was not true of the democracies.

In the case of Britain, the reason for this was simple. After the 1914–18 war, she had disarmed and reverted to a professional Army. Next, she had pursued a policy of conciliation towards Germany, which was reinforced by suspicion of France, who was accused of suffering from chronic germanophobia and inveterate imperialism. The British political leaders, above all Neville Chamberlain, had been slow to become aware of the danger of Hitler, despite Winston Churchill's warnings. Subsequently, in view of the protection from immediate German attack afforded by that impassable anti-tank ditch, the English Channel, Britain had looked first to her own defence at sea and in the air. The Royal Navy took charge of the first, and the fighter aircraft, which had been given priority, were responsible for the second. To fulfil her obligations towards her ally, France, Britain had reintroduced conscription, mistakenly perhaps, since the formation of armoured units doubtless deserved higher priority than the creation of a large Army. But although it was plain that hardly any other possibility existed and that action was proceeding as quickly as possible, there seemed every chance that, in time, a vast rearmament programme could gradually be implemented. But there was one condition: the enemy must not be in too great a hurry.

But why had France, whose Army had won the 1914–18 war, who had frequently viewed the intentions of the Weimar Republic with such a suspicious eye, and who had not really disarmed after 1918, why had France not rearmed in earnest after Hitler came to power? Was it the fault of her politics, her diplomacy, her lack of money, the short-sightedness of her general staff, the shortcomings of her economy—and, most important of all, of her industry? Or were all these things to blame? It is indeed surprising, to say the least, that the very same French government which on April 17, 1934 had refused to sign an international pact for the limitation of armaments, thus leaving entire responsibility for her defence to France alone, should at the same time have cut back its expenditure on armaments. On later occasions, it is true, the amount of this expenditure had been steadily increased and the French Parliament had never failed to approve it. The fact remains that, at certain moments which were decisive for the country's security, financial considerations—the stability of the franc or devaluation—did hamper French rearmament and that, in the ministerial discussions preceding the presentation of the Budget to Parliament, the French Treasury often cut down the amounts requested by the Defence Ministry.

It is equally true that the War Minister had taken a long time to work out production schedules and set up organisations capable of putting them into effect. Hesitation over which orders to place, rivalry between various organisations and the lack of flexibility in certain financial regulations no doubt explained the fact that, although complaining of being starved of funds, the War Ministry often found it impossible to spend even the resources which it had been granted, so much so that 60 per cent of the allocations for 1935 had had to be carried over to 1936; hardly the way to encourage the Finance Minister to be more open handed.

However, once the programmes had been drawn up, the prototypes chosen, the funds made available and the orders placed, if excessive delay then occurred in the production of guns, tanks or aircraft, it could no longer be blamed on the civil service or the government or the military but fairly and squarely on the armament manufacturers. The nationalisation of these industries, decided on by the *Front Populaire* more for political and moral than military reasons, had given rise to passionate debate; it had probably led in the first instance to confusion and further delay before achieving a streamlining of the industries, and later on it was not able to remedy all at once shortcomings which were common to much of French industry: antiquated plant, shortage of trained technicians, insufficient quantities of machine tools. In addition, the liberal economy was ill adapted to undertake the planning, authoritarian decisions and price control required for a proper mobilisation of industry.

Furthermore, the general staff, whose task it was, after all, to place the orders, needed a coherent theory of warfare and clear and stable ideas as to its needs. In fact, at no time did the military authorities ever work out an overall plan of rearmament; of course, they wanted to break new ground but, lacking precise aims, their discussions of prototypes were inconclusive. 'Not one single army man,' Minister Dautry told the Parliamentary Commission of Investigation, 'realised the extent of the industrial problems that the country would have to solve.' How did the country itself view the matter? Were the French fully aware of the threat from Hitler and did they really have the will to fight to dispel it?

VI MORAL FORCES

A professional army draws its strength from its professionalism. But a national army finds its justification and fighting spirit in the nation from which it springs. On this point, too, the situation was very different in the two camps.

In Germany the Nazis had fully imposed their harsh régime. The whole population had been drafted; public opinion was rigidly controlled; the civil administration was under close observation by the Party or else replaced by the Party's own officials. Never had a great people been more completely brought to heel or so powerfully coerced to follow its leaders with unquestioning obedience. It is true that the Führer's supreme authority, the strange ascendancy that he exerted over the masses, the blind obedience that he both demanded and received from all, did not prevent personal rivalries, sectarian strife or conflicts between competing branches of the armed forces. But nothing of this showed to the outside world and nothing was to show until after the first setbacks. To all appearances—moreover, in fact—the German nation was solidly behind its heaven-sent leader; they were grateful to him for what had been accomplished, the successes that had been achieved and a new-found sense of greatness.

The Weimar Republic now belonged to a discredited past; in any case, democratic ideas had never penetrated to more than a section of the German middle classes. Economic self-sufficiency had, of course, led to severe restrictions on everyone but it kept the wheels turning and it had got rid of unemployment. The higher ranks of industry were thankful to the Führer for having put an end to economic stagnation and the mass of the workers were grateful to him for having once more ensured them steady employment. As for the general staff, the reluctance and misgivings of some of its members at the time of the remilitarisation of the Rhineland, the annexation of Austria or the Sudeten affair, were now nothing but a memory. Hitler had put a stop to the humiliation suffered by Germany in 1918; he had managed to wipe out a large part of the Treaty of Versailles; he had given the Reich a powerful army once again and revived a sense of national duty in the people; in a word, the generals had gained too much from being obedient not to become submissive.

Did this mean that the whole of the German people were going to war with lively step and a song in their hearts? Goebbels' propaganda machine said so and the cinema cameras recorded it. All the same, foreign observers noticed more resignation than enthusiasm. But if there were qualms, they were not obvious, and the opposition said nothing. It is true that it had been roughly handled: Communists, Socialists, trades union leaders and sometimes Christian Democrats had been thrown into the concentration camps—Buchenwald or Dachau—that had been opened with them in mind; the police were keeping a watchful eye on those who for the moment had been left free. And the Churches, Roman Catholic or Protestant, were suspicious of Nazi paganism, all the more so since the Pope had condemned it. But the clergy who spoke out against euthanasia or the Nazis' ideas on education would then go on to ask the faithful to pray together for the Fatherland and its Führer.

The only possible active opposition would have to come from outside, from those who had emigrated. But the fact is that they were too dissimilar to unite or even to make contact. Communists and Socialists might be brothers but they were hostile ones and the German-Soviet pact had for the moment reduced the German Communists to silence, especially those who had taken refuge in Moscow. There was no common ground between early National Socialists who were followers of Otto Strasser and politicians like Brüning from the Weimar Republic: the latter, incidentally, had taken refuge in Switzerland and was lying low and saying nothing. The exiles wanted Hitler's downfall but they could not accept the only prospect that made this downfall seem possible: the defeat of Germany, their Fatherland.

Even the Jewish exiles showed little unanimity. Their desire to be assimilated and their sentimental loyalty to Germany amazed their coreligionists in the countries in which they had taken refuge. Some of them tried to settle down in their new homeland; others had thoughts of going to Palestine; nowhere did they form a coherent, active opposition group.

Willingly or passively, with enthusiasm or resignation, the German people were following their Führer on the path to war, and they would continue to follow him as long as that path led to victory. Did the same state of mind prevail amongst the population of Britain and France? In Britain there was a current of feeling that was anti-war, represented in Parliament by Lloyd George, but the traditional good citizenship and patriotism of the British was too strong for this trend to appear openly, except in certain circles. It was true that in the government itself, even if Churchill's determination was well-known, Neville Chamberlain's seemed less certain. But in fact, although the British faced up to their obligations with calmness and resolution, they did not consider themselves as being fully involved as yet; neither the fate of the British Commonwealth nor their security were at stake. In the first round, France versus Germany, they were rather like spectators.

On the other hand, the French knew that they were immediately and directly concerned. Mobilisation had taken place in an orderly manner according to plan, but instead of the enthusiasm of 1914 there was resignation, as is painfully plain in the films showing the expression on the faces of those leaving from the Gare de l'Est. In the French Parliament, no one had seriously questioned the necessity of declaring war; an end had to be put to the series of surrenders that had only encouraged Hitler's aggressive intentions. But the spirit of Munich had still not disappeared, nor its corollary, the attempt to find a diplomatic compromise that might avoid bloodshed.

From this and from other points of view, the German-Soviet pact assumed exceptional importance. For the traditionally anti-German right wing, it reinforced the militant anti-Communism aroused by the *Front Populaire* and led to the firm belief that the war would benefit only the USSR and international revolution. This point of view was represented by Pierre Laval.

As for the Left, its unity had already been compromised by the defeat of the *Front Populaire,* which was now only part of history. The Communist party had shown the most determined opposition to Nazism, both at the time of the Spanish Civil War and of Munich; it was certainly true that the disclosure of the German-Soviet pact had surprised and dumbfounded it; so much so that it voted in support of the military estimates shortly afterwards. Later on, its leaders had tamely knuckled under to the Comintern's instructions; as at the time of the occupation of the Ruhr the party had become pacifist once again, or at least, neutralist.

As a result the *Confederation Générale du Travail* was split from top to bottom. The mass of workers remained torn, obsessed by the cares of day-to-day existence and the desire to improve their standard of living in accordance with the splendid promises of the *Front Populaire,* or else imbued with deep feelings of pacifism. Despite Léon Blum's urgings, the Socialist party had not yet completed the swing which was to bring them round, after refusing to vote for the military estimates, to support, if not to request, a coalition government to set about the task of waging war in earnest. Even those intellectuals most strongly opposed to Fascism often disliked the thought of a conflict the first effect of which would be to restrict freedom in France. And in the minds of every Frenchman the new war aroused thoughts of the holocaust of 1914–18, the futility of which had been so frequently condemned and a repetition of which probably even more horrible than before, seemed in no way necessary. In a people that twenty years earlier had lost more than a million of its young men, there was a biological reflex to avoid further bloodshed. The result was a rejection of war, implicit rather than explicit, which took the form, for example, of trying to find 'special assignments' which in 1914–18 would have been called quite bluntly 'funk-holes'.

This firm belief in the absurdity of war was expressed by Albert Camus in his Diary. He condemns war as 'revolting, an inexcusable massacre'. He finds it difficult to excuse the conscripts who accept 'their obligation to go yet feel remorse that they were not brave enough to stay behind'. He refuses to let himself be caught up in the machinery of war; he states that 'this war is not inevitable' and concludes that 'there are means of stopping it that can be tried'. Many Frenchmen thought as he did and many conscripts wrote back to their families in similar vein.

In a country where economic stagnation had slowed down the production of armaments, where units had not received their proper complement of equipment, where the population were trying to persuade themselves that mobilisation did not mean war, how could the government and the general staff fail to favour a long-term strategy, defensive in the first instance, with the object of minimising the sufferings of the French people and avoiding unnecessary bloodshed, in short, with the object of letting them off lightly?

VII STRATEGIC PLANS

The strategies worked out by the antagonists were based not on abstractions but on the heartfelt feelings of the various peoples as well as on the actual possibilities allowed by their economies and armed forces.

Although partly protected from the hazards of a long war by his agreement with Stalin, Hitler wanted a short war so that the Reich should not be exposed to the danger of running out of steam; the armoured divisions and the Air Force intended to support them were to be instrumental in the rapid breakthrough into the enemy's positions and a total disruption of its forces. Having the advantage of the initiative and of short internal lines of communication, the Wehrmacht could choose its own time and place to attack. Hitler's plan was thus to crush Poland as quickly as possible; the Siegfried line and Belgian neutrality would provide a solid barrier in the west to any French counter-moves. What would happen next was not yet clear to the Führer but he could not fail to hope that, faced by a *fait accompli*, Britain and France would once again bow to the inevitable and, rather than become bogged down in a prolonged and costly war, of uncertain outcome, they would abandon Poland to its fate just as they had previously abandoned Czechoslovakia and Austria.

On the other hand, the democracies were anxious to gain precious time. Thus, while the blockade would be progressively weakening the German effort, the mobilisation of the unlimited resources of the two empires, which nothing could prevent in view of their command of the seas, would one day give them irresistible superiority in arms and men. The lesson of 1914–18 was surely quite conclusive. So why launch out on an offensive that could only be premature and bloody and for which, in any case, they lacked the attacking spearhead? Such an offensive could in any case reach enemy territory only by going through Belgium and Belgium refused to accept this at any price.

So a defensive strategy was essential, thus satisfying both the military mind that could not see beyond the lessons of World War I and the civil population for whom the greatest crime of all was the sacrifice of human lives. Fundamentally, Britain and France were without war aims; the former's colonial empire was not threatened by Hitler's ambitions and the latter no longer had to win back Alsace-Lorraine. More than one politician was inhibited by a guilt complex, the legacy of the 'Versailles Diktat'; after all, how could you fail to recognise the rightness of some of Hitler's claims, which had already been voiced by the Weimar Republic, such as those concerning the former German colonies, access to raw materials or the return of German minorities to the Reich? Was the destruction of the Nazi régime sufficient grounds for sacrificing millions of men? Surely it was the Germans themselves who had opted for that régime and it was the blunders committed by the democracies—French intransigence, thought the British, British weak-mindedness, thought the French—which had greatly facilitated Hitler's coming to power.

So the defensive strategy of the French supreme commander had the approval of the French and British politicians—Daladier and Chamberlain —as well as of the military pundits like Pétain and Weygand. A few heretics—Churchill, Paul Reynaud and de Gaulle—had spoken up strongly on the other side and warned that the democracies could not remain passive without falling into the danger of sluggish indifference. They were lonely prophets preaching in the wilderness. So we find Marshal Pétain accepting 'Douhet's doctrine' but not pursuing it beyond the first stage which required armies to remain on the defensive.[1] So the instructions of General Gamelin, the supreme commander of the Franco-British forces, laid down the principle that a sound defence 'must await the enemy and contain it on a continuous front of fortifications and trenches impossible to break through'. That was why priority had been given to the fighter arm in order to defend French airspace whilst no priority had been given to heavy tanks to lead an offensive.

Such notions were perfectly logical and coherent. They were based on glorious historical precedent and they corresponded to the will of the people. For the present, however, they left the initiative for the conduct of

---

1. See preface to Colonel Vauthier's book *La doctrine de guerre du Général Douhet*, Berger-Levrault, 1935.

operations entirely in Hitler's hands and they condemned Poland to isolation and thus to disaster. The Allies were going to face the Germans in extended order; but in this sort of single combat, they ran the risk of throwing away all the advantages that accrued, on paper, from the numerical superiority of their forces. For basically the Allies could only achieve victory in three stages. First of all, their defences would have to be sound enough to withstand the enemy's first onslaught that would be intended to be decisive. Once this stage had been surmounted, the democracies would still need to maintain their lines of communication, increase their armaments on a massive scale and prevent the destruction of their convoys, harbours and factories, so winning the war at sea, in the air and in the arsenals. Only then would the time be ripe to take the offensive; the war would be carried into German territory, although no one knew exactly how; but in his heart of hearts, everyone was hoping, in fact, that Germany would admit defeat as a result of the blockade and the bombing before this stage was reached.

How many years would be needed to reach this successful outcome? Would the agreement between the Allies stand the strain for so long? Would the morale of the fighting soldier, so dubious from the very beginning, hold out long enough? And above all, should Germany win the 'first round', that is should the French front be breached, would the French consider that the fate of France and of the war could be decided beyond its own frontiers—as they had imagined it could be in the case of Czechoslovakia and Poland—by means of the protection afforded by those 'big ditches', the Channel and the Mediterranean—perhaps even the Atlantic?

VIII ITALIAN NON-BELLIGERENCE

Such remote prospects seem never to have been examined, either by the governments or by the general staffs. But since, by definition, a defensive strategy leaves the time and place of attack to the adversary's choice, the Allied strategists were forced to draw up plans to allow for every possible contingency—a dangerous approach since it could only lead to a dispersal of forces that were weak enough already.

At first, one possible burden had, however, been removed, the entry of Italy into the war in the Alps and Tunisia. King Victor Emmanuel was not in favour of it and the Italian military leaders had warned Mussolini of the inadequate preparation of the Army and the Navy, both of which had been forced to make good the losses they had suffered in Abyssinia and Spain. The Minister of Foreign Affairs, Count Ciano, if he is to be believed, had been extremely irritated that Italy had, without any warn-

ing, been faced by Hitler's irrevocable decision to attack Poland. Although
Mussolini was greedy for military success, as being the indispensable basis
for his prestige and future ambitions, he acquiesced in his advisers' views.

The Italians' pretext to avoid entering the war was to make any such
entry dependent on receiving very considerable quantities of arms and
supplies from Germany, and Hitler found it difficult to meet this request.

So Hitler cut his losses, sent an 'understanding' letter to the Duce and
declared in the Reichstag on September 1 that in the coming struggle he
did not wish to call on any foreign power for help. 'This is our business,'
he said 'and we shall settle it ourselves.' Italy invented a new diplomatic
concept by declaring herself a 'non-belligerent'; Ciano explained to Hitler
that it was not 'a strictly neutral attitude' but merely meant that Italy
'would not take the initiative in the west', thus complying with Hitler's desire to confine the conflict to the eastern front; in any case, had Italy gone
to war, she would have been exposed to attack from Britain and France in
the air, at sea and in her colonies, and the psychological effect might have
been catastrophic. So Hitler agreed to restrain his irritation and recognise
that this was all part of a 'subtle game between Germany and Italy'.

Italy's defection had, moveover, in fact provided Germany with the consolation of making the Allied blockade less effective; nor did it enable
France to avoid keeping hundreds of thousands of troops immobilised in
the Alps and Tunisia. As far as the French general staff was concerned, it
had, however, removed two strategic possibilities: one was the not very
formidable one of an Italian frontal attack, the other a violation of Swiss
neutrality in order to link up the German and Italian armies. But it also
destroyed a possibility that had appealed to one or two French generals:
the chance of carrying the war into the Plain of Lombardy and putting
the weaker of their opponents out of action.

IX THE INSOLUBLE PROBLEM OF BELGIUM

Since any attack against the French fortified lines on the Rhine and in
Lorraine was improbable, the likelihood was that, as in 1914, the French
and German armies would first join battle on the plains of Belgium. This
had probably been thoroughly considered by the French high command;
every possible contingency had been carefully examined and solutions
drawn up to meet each of them. The fact was that the military and political problems were so inextricably intertwined that no single solution could
be completely satisfactory.

The attitude most consistent with the general defensive approach that
had been adopted was to await the German attack on French territory. But

the Maginot line stopped short at the Ardennes and only improvised field fortifications could ever be built between the Ardennes and the sea, a fact which made the 'impregnable front' implied in the supreme commander's instruction a highly problematical affair. Militarily, to allow Belgium to be crushed meant depriving the Allied armies of valuable manpower at a time when British divisions were unlikely to appear on the Continent in strength for some considerable time. Diplomatically, leaving Belgium to her fate, after Czechoslovakia, would have had a most unfortunate effect on the neutral countries. Morally, such a course would be unworthy of France; it would amount to a confession of weakness and harm the morale of the troops.

So Belgium would have to be helped: but how? General Gamelin had indeed realised what the ideal solution would be: move the French armies as far forward as possible into Belgium, right up to the German frontier, on the line of the Albert canal where the Belgians had built good solid fortifications. In this way the Belgian Army, completely intact, would in due course be assimilated into the Allied defences; the Allied lines would thus be both shortened and more solidly held; the enemy threat to the northern industrial area would be largely averted; and Britain would not need to fear air and submarine attacks from aerodromes and bases set up in nearby Belgium. The possibility of aggression on Holland would also have to be taken into account and helping the Dutch would run the risk of overtaxing the strength of the Allied armies. In addition, there was an unfortunate gap between the Belgian and Dutch defences. But whatever these minor drawbacks, the 'Albert canal plan' provided a nice combination of the best immediate prospects of defence with considerable opportunities for future offensive action.

The Belgian authorities also shared these beliefs and desires. But by an extraordinary paradox they refused to consider taking the concerted measures required by such a plan of action. On September 3, King Leopold proclaimed Belgian neutrality, a decision taken by a national coalition cabinet and approved by Parliament and public opinion, with hardly one dissentient voice. It was the logical consequence of the policy adopted at the time of the remilitarisation of the Rhineland and described either as 'independent' or 'the policy of the free hand'; for Belgium, to start military talks with the Allies would have meant giving up her neutrality and provoking Germany.

Although the reasons behind King Leopold's decision and those of his very influential military adviser, General van Overstraeten, are not always very plain, it would seem that Belgian policy can be explained primarily by internal consideration and the desire to maintain national unity at all costs. It is true that the vast majority of the Belgians were ill-disposed to

Nazi Germany; the German ambassador in Brussels estimated it at 90 per cent of the population. But a very active minority was violently anti-French: the *flamingant* group, representing the commercial element of the Flemish Nationalist movement, was the source of serious strain in Belgium's political and social structure. In order to assert their language and culture and obtain equal, or even larger, representation in the upper echelons of government with the Walloons, the Flemings, apart from a cultivated French-speaking minority, were almost unanimous in spurning French language, culture and influence in Belgium. Any attempt in peacetime to establish military links between Belgium and France would assuredly have inflamed Flemish nationalist feeling and given rise to unpredictably violent reactions. A policy of complete neutrality between the two camps thus seemed the only way to guarantee that Belgium would remain relatively united.

Perhaps the King of the Belgians and his government also imagined that they had some hope of saving Belgium from invasion. In fact, they were fully aware that the peril would come from Germany, not from France. But they were anxious not to arouse Hitler's wrath in any way whatsoever. It is also likely that the way in which the democracies had repeatedly given in to Hitler had not helped to inspire the Belgians with any confidence in their strength or determination; consequently any attempt to call in the Allies as a preventive measure would amount to inviting a crushing German counter-blast, the immediate result of which would be the invasion of the country followed by the destruction of its unity. In consequence, the Belgians refused to accept any secret military pact or technical agreement with the French. They recognised that, should the Germans violate their neutrality, the only source of help would be the French Army; they were prepared to agree to its crossing over into Belgian territory but only at their own request and at that time. Meanwhile, they refused to make any active preparations for such a contingency; they merely agreed to keep in touch, have discussions and exchange information on a limited scale.

The exchanges of views had been concerned with the time the Allied troops would require to reach the Albert canal after the Belgians had called them in. The Belgians wanted them to be in their positions, beside their own troops, within forty-eight hours. They were demanding the impossible. The French high command estimated that it would take at least five days but was very doubtful whether the Belgians, left to themselves, could hold out that long, in which case the Allied armies would find themselves having to fight a pitched battle, something which General Gamelin was anxious to avoid at all costs since he knew full well that they were totally unprepared for it. So Belgium's internal problems prevented the

Belgian authorities from drawing up the plans which they recognised as being the only ones capable of protecting Belgium from invasion.

There was, of course, another possible solution: the Allies could take preventive action by advancing into Belgium in the hope that the Belgians would confine themselves to making a purely formal protest. Admiral Darlan was the only person to advocate this ruthless move, none of the consequences of which would impinge on himself. But no democracy, whose stated war aims were to defend the independence of small nations against that ogre Hitler, could possibly begin hostilities by violating the neutrality of their nearest small neighbour. Moreover, in such an event, one of the advantages of the manoeuvre—the incorporation of the Belgian and perhaps the Dutch armies into the Allied forces—would have been rendered very unlikely.

Thus any idea of moving the Allied armies up to the Albert canal had to be abandoned. The French strategists now had two alternatives: either to let Belgium be invaded in accordance with the defensive strategy that had been adopted—with all the unfortunate military consequences implied by such a passive attitude; or else to find some position in Belgium which the Belgians could hold long enough to enable the Allied armies to have time to come to their help, a position, in short, that would have the advantages of the Albert canal line without its drawbacks. The French drew such a line on the map: it joined the middle Scheldt to the Ghent canal and the sea. It had its advantages: the large urban industrial centres in the north would cease to be an embarrassment in the rear of the armies and the operation would only require part of the Allied forces to be committed; in addition, the Scheldt was quite a formidable barrier.

It was true that, in such an eventuality, a large part of Belgium would suffer invasion. And it would also require the Belgians to resign themselves to accepting such a situation, for their troops to withdraw in good order to the prearranged position, for a solid line of defences to be set up in good time and for the French troops not to be placed at risk by a more rapid enemy advance than was anticipated, and thrown into a pitched battle which would probably be disastrous from every point of view. All these were problems which, it was hoped, would be solved willy-nilly when the need arose. But would the Wehrmacht make its main effort in central Belgium, as in 1914? Nobody seemed to question it.

So in September 1939, the Franco-British Allies had unlimited economic and human potential at their disposal; their mastery of the seas was undisputed. But they were still ill-prepared for war—Britain even less well than France. They possessed sufficient quantities of the most effective weapons: tanks and aircraft; as for their use, they were still relying more on the lessons of the 1914–18 war than on the possibilities of new techniques. The will to fight was there; but it was not very keen. Thus the defensive strategy adopted was the least bad, in the circumstances; but in Belgium, its application was subject to special needs that made it difficult, if not unworkable. To sum up, in the face of Hitler's determination, backed by the discipline and even the warlike mood of the German people as well as by an army entirely planned for a swift and decisive victory, France and Britain found themselves in the awkward situation of facing an onslaught that might well overpower them, and of being forced to make last minute improvisations whose outcome would be quite unpredictable. But in the first instance it was only Poland, left entirely on her own, which was to bear the brunt of the attack by the formidable war-machine of the Third Reich.

BOOK ONE

THE WAR IN EUROPE

(September 1939–June 1941)

THE PRELUDE IN POLAND AND SCANDINAVIA

CHAPTER 1

The Obliteration of Poland from the Map of Europe

THE Polish campaign allowed the Nazi Reich to show, at its very first attempt, its mastery of methods of warfare; the surprise and ruthlessness of the onslaught shattered the enemy's armed forces; terror paralysed the civil population; the 'Fifth Column' caused its opponent to disintegrate from within. These methods were to change but little in future operations.

The architect of victory on the ground was the armoured corps; the German Army had succeeded in solving the most awkward problems involved in its use: the difficulty of having thousands of motorised vehicles strung out over many miles; overall control combined with the independence of the constituent elements; direct communication with units which become dispersed in the course of the fighting. The Panzer division had already become a small army in its own right, combining speed and strength. Its reconnaissance groups, with their machine-gun carriers, anti-tank gun and pontoon sections, were sufficiently powerful in themselves to overcome any minor enemy obstacles placed in their path. The main body consisted of two brigades, one of tanks—between 250 and 320 per division—the other of motorised light infantry. The heavy tanks had the task of demolishing the enemy force as soon as it had been detected, assessed and located; their job was to break through the front. The medium tanks were to open up the breach, both to some extent on each flank to protect the advancing army, and above all in depth, to enlarge the breach in the enemy lines. 'They tear into the flesh of the defending force,' wrote Bauer, 'like the fingers of a steel gauntlet.' The rifle brigade with its artillery, its AA and anti-tank weapons, its guns, howitzers and trench-mortars, would mop up the isolated centres of resistance by-passed by the tanks. The rear sections, also completely motorised, could provide petrol supplies and repairs with minimum delay.

The Panzer division moved forward under the protection of the Air Force, which preceded it, bombing the opponent's positions as required. It would drop paratroops behind the enemy lines to capture and hold any

Map 2 DEFEAT AND PARTITIONS OF POLAND

- - - - Polish Frontier on 1 September 1939
───── German troop concentrations on 1 September 1939
➤ The Wehrmacht's Advance
⊲─ The Red Army's advance
━━━ First partition of Poland and Lithuania into zones of influence
─── Second partition of Poland into occupied zones
▨ Polish territories occupied by the Red Army
▧ Soviet annexations after the Polish campaign

0   300 km

important point; during the attack itself, the aircraft would attack the enemy tanks, force any reinforcements coming to their aid to disperse and pound the defender's strong points with bombs. With his mobile command post, the Panzer division commander, equipped with two-way radio link could, in the thick of the fighting, give orders instantaneously according to the course of the operation.

This combination of tank and aircraft ensured the success of the German armies. But the Air Force had other roles. At the outbreak of hostilities, it could achieve command of the air by surprise attacks on enemy airfields, thus destroying its aircraft on the ground. It could paralyse any communication centres that might have enabled the enemy to re-group its forces. It could cause havoc and spread panic in defenceless towns: although Warsaw had been declared an open town, bombs were dropped on it as early as September 1, and it was bombed thirty-seven times within the week.

The Nazis' third weapon of the war was the 'Fifth Column'. As early as May 1939, thousands of young Poles of German extraction from the district of Poznan and Upper Silesia had gone to Germany to receive special training; hundreds of others, when called up for military service in Poland, deserted *en masse*. At the same time, German propaganda was loudly denouncing the 'persecutions' being inflicted on the German minority in Poland. The decisive phase was begun even before the end of August by German activities, described as 'Polish provocation': ss disguised as Polish soldiers set fire to buildings housing German organisations; after September 1, commandos of Polish 'German patriots' attacked radio stations, industrial establishments and even single Polish units.

On September 2 in Bydgoszcz (Bromberg) the Poles reacted by shooting 150 Germans in order to put down an actual uprising. As soon as the town was taken by the Wehrmacht, the ss retaliated by the mass execution of thousands of Polish civilians. The result of this initial subversive activity and subsequent terror was not only to increase the alarm and despondency of the civilian population, already sorely tried by the extent and sudden-ness of the tribulations that had overtaken it; it also heralded the important part that the ss was going to play in the territories conquered by the Wehrmacht, by working apparently independently of this but in agree-ment with it and, when necessary, with its help.

Hitler had always thought—as he wrote in *Mein Kampf*—that a Polish state which had the impudence to cut into German territory and had annexed German territory offered unforgivable affront to the German nation. As early as April 1939, he had decided to smash Poland. At that time, it is true, he was convinced that the western democracies would show the same lack of response in Poland's case as they had for Bohemia and later on for Czechoslovakia.

When France and England had then pledged themselves to come to Poland's aid, Hitler had hesitated momentarily as to which course to take: should he attack first in the east or in the west? In any case, as he had specifically stated at a high-level conference of generals in May 1939, his war aims in Poland went far beyond the obliteration of the last clauses of the Versailles Treaty: 'Danzig,' he had emphasised, 'is not the real issue; the real point is for us to open up our *Lebensraum* to the east and ensure our supplies of foodstuffs.' Poland was condemned with no possible reprieve: 'she would not resist Soviet proposals'; she was 'a doubtful obstacle to Russia'.

In the end, it was Hitler himself who had failed to resist discreet approaches by Stalin. Ribbentrop's talks in Moscow had decided on 'concrete action' by the USSR in Poland. The German-Soviet pact signed Poland's death-warrant. It also finally decided in which direction Hitler would strike: Poland would be the Wehrmacht's first victim. Of course, should the western democracies come to her aid, the ultimate decision would have to be reached in the west and Hitler had not disguised from those close to him that it would be 'a fight to the death' and that a 'swift victory in the west was a matter for conjecture'.

This was not the case in the east. Leaving just sufficient forces in the west to man the Siegfried line, Hitler, gambling successfully on the hope that the Anglo-French forces would take up their positions ponderously and slowly, launched the main weight of his attack against Poland: sixty-three divisions, including five mobile army corps—with six armoured divisions, supported by 2,000 aircraft.

The German plan was to launch converging attacks from Prussia and Silesia, from each side of the Polish Poznan salient; General von Rundstedt's troops were to join up with those of General von Bock roughly on the Vistula–Nareth line, after disrupting the Polish forces.

The latter should, in theory, have amounted to some forty divisions; but at the request of the French and British ambassadors the Polish government delayed their mobilisation for twenty-four hours. Léon Noël has written that his British colleague and himself had suggested a delay of a few hours and that it was the Polish general staff which had decided on a whole day's postponement. General Anders is no doubt exaggerating the importance of this action when he says that it hastened the Polish defeat by a fortnight. In fact, it was the swiftness of the German advance, facilitated by the confusion created by this delay, that reduced the available divisions to twenty. The Polish Army had twelve cavalry brigades but only one of them was mechanised; out of 600 aircraft only 300 were modern; 500 AA guns, mainly old ones, were in service whereas the plans for the modernisation of the Army, which were not yet complete, provided for 2,000. The concentration of armaments factories in Warsaw made them particularly vulnerable. A few extra tens of thousands of badly armed conscripts would hardly have remedied such an inherent weakness.

The Polish defence also suffered from the country's geography: the immense plain did not lend itself to fortification but did offer great possibilities for the movement of motorised units: the tributaries of the Vistula opened up the road to Warsaw for any invader. Above all, the occupation by the Germans of Slovakia meant that Poland had to defend a frontier some 1,000 miles long.

Marshal Smigly-Rydz, the Polish Supreme Commander, had refused to shorten his lines of defence by withdrawing them towards the centre of the country; apart from the unfortunate psychological effect of a deliberate withdrawal of this sort at the very beginning of the campaign, it would have meant abandoning to the enemy the most fertile parts of Poland and the industrial area of Silesia. He decided, therefore, to make a stand on his own frontiers and even in the 'Polish corridor', which involved a dangerous dispersal of the meagre forces under his command.

III BLITZKRIEG IN POLAND

The ruthlessness and suddenness of the German attack made any concentration of Polish troops impossible; apart from a few squadrons camouflaged on secret airfields, most of the Polish aircraft were destroyed on the ground. Very soon the channels of communication were put out of action as well. As the Polish Army had no intermediate link between the Supreme Commander and his subordinate generals, from the start the fighting could not be controlled from above. Although the Polish troops were cut to pieces in every sector, there was no panic retreat. The Tenth German Army in the south, which advanced most rapidly, reached the outskirts of

Warsaw on September 8 and was momentarily repulsed. No order for a general withdrawal of the Polish troops had been given until the 6th; but it was too late. Better news was a Polish counter-attack on September 9 in the central sector, towards Lodz, on the Bzura; but despite initial success and dreadful slaughter—Polish lancers were seen charging tanks—this attack was smashed.

The struggle continued in great confusion: large pockets of encircled Polish troops at Kutno and Radom resisted for some days before surrendering. In the battle area, the Polish state completely disintegrated—officials abandoned their posts and the civilian population fled in disorder. On September 5, the government itself decided to leave Warsaw. The capital was invested by the armies in the central sector and outflanked to the east by two pincer movements from north and south of the city; by September 14 it was completely cut off from the rest of the country.

On September 17, Soviet troops invaded Poland in their turn, meeting no resistance. The Russians seem not to have had time to prepare their intervention. They announced their intention to the Germans on September 9 but stated that they still needed two or three weeks to organise the invasion. They feared that the Wehrmacht might encroach on the zone allotted to them by the German-Soviet pact and Ribbentrop had to give full reassurance on this point. They were anxious to make the exact pretext for their intervention very plain and they disagreed with the Germans as to the wording. Now that Poland had collapsed, in order not to appear as aggressors, the Russians wished to base their case on 'the need to come to the help of the Ukrainians and White Russians threatened by Germany'. Ribbentrop objected that the two partners would then run the risk of appearing to be opponents. The Russians dug in their heels; they asked the Germans to make allowance for their embarrassment; 'up till now, they had shown little concern for their minorities in Poland'. At the end of the day, the Russian communiqué was a joint production; the Germans pledged themselves not to grant the Poles an armistice which would have the effect of making the Russian intervention seem pointless; they were eager for it to take place since it would obviate their having to pursue the remnants of the Polish army too far or too long. Every precaution was taken to avoid accidents or incidents.

Minister Potemkin, either through embarrassment or cynicism, justified the invasion by the Red Army to the Polish ambassador in these terms: 'The Polish state and its government has ceased to exist. Such a situation constitutes a threat to the USSR and makes it impossible to remain neutral any longer.' According to General Anders, the first result of the Russian intervention—which the Polish government seems not to have anticipated

—was to prevent large numbers of Polish officers and men from escaping into Hungary and Romania.

From now on, the struggle was confined to a few isolated points, and the main thing now at stake, if not indeed the only one, was Warsaw. The city had been fortified in great haste, thanks to the short respite afforded by the Polish counter-attack on the Bzura. Any attempt to defend the suburbs was abandoned for lack of resources; in the city's historic centre barricades were put up, anti-tank ditches were dug and barrels of turpentine were set on fire when the German army approached. Hitler hoped to capture the town before September 21, on which date the American Congress was due to meet; he was very disappointed. So that troop movements should not be impeded, he ordered that none of the civil population should be allowed to leave. From September 24 onwards, Warsaw was without gas, light or water; it was becoming impossible to fight the fires caused by air raids; the food supply would hardly last a week, the ammunition two days. On September 26 German tanks and infantry launched their attack. That afternoon, the Poles asked for an armistice which was not granted until the following day; but during that time the Germans made little progress. The Polish general Rommel was captured with all his troops and granted military honours. On October 1, the German 10th Division entered Warsaw. A few days later, Hitler went there to review the victory parade.

Gdynia, the last Polish town to offer any resistance, capitulated on October 2. The Poles had lost 450,000 prisoners to the Germans and 200,000 to the Russians. On March 8, 1940, Hitler put the German losses at 8,400 killed, 28,000 wounded or taken prisoner and 3,000 missing. The German victory was complete.

IV FRENCH INACTION. THE SAAR OFFENSIVE

While this victory was being achieved the French remained almost completely inert, although the Germans had left no more than forty-three divisions in the west, only eleven of which were regular divisions, concentrated mainly on the French frontier. And yet France was solemnly pledged to help her Polish ally, as was Britain, though in September there were as yet no British troops on the Continent.

The protocol drawn up in May 1939 between the Polish Minister of War, Krasprzynski, and General Gamelin, provided for immediate action by the French Air Force, followed without delay by a limited attack by the first available forces as soon as Poland found herself too hard pressed by the German offensive; in any case, not later than the sixteenth day of the war. In fact, on July 24, the instructions of General Georges, the commander of the French North-East Army Group, had stated that progressive action should be taken against the German system of fortifications between Hardt and Mosel.

As a result, on September 8, the Fourth French Army made a small advance from Sarreguemines; on the 9th it made contact with the forward approaches of the Siegfried line. This line was several kilometres deep in parts; more important, it was studded with small concrete defenceworks and the French troops did not attack it. Instead, they confined themselves to methodically clearing the Warndt forest. On September 22, the attack planned by the Third Army towards Sarrelouis was called off because of the bad news from Poland. On October 1, when the Germans had started to bring back reinforcements from the east, the French advance came to a halt. On October 16, at the first German attack, the French troops withdrew to beyond their initial starting point and gave up Forbach.

Why did the French troops confine their activity to this futile demonstration against the enemy, in flagrant violation of solemn pledges? Liddell Hart put the blame on the slowness of the methods of French mobilisation, which he called 'obsolete'. But the French military leaders knew very well how long it would take when they pledged themselves to help the Poles in the formal military convention. Perhaps they had hoped for longer resistance on the part of the Poles. If such a calculation had been made, it would prove how greatly the French general staff were mistaken as to the Wehrmacht's fighting capacity and methods. If not, why was the date of the French intervention fixed for the sixteenth day following mobilisation when it was obvious that this was a promise that could not be kept? We are thus justified in wondering whether the French general staff had pledged itself to help the Polish army for psychological rather than military reasons—scared, in fact, that, if they did not know that their allies were supporting them, the Poles would give in to the German demands without a fight?[1]

Whatever may be the reasons for all this, the consequences of Hitler's decisive victory were plain to see on the map. As long as the German-Soviet pact lasted, Hitler was relieved of any concern in the east and of a war on two fronts. After having allowed Austria to be annexed and Czechoslovakia dismembered, France had proved incapable of preventing

---

1. After the war an argument arose on this point between General Gamelin and the Sikorski Institute in London. General Gamelin declared that in the absence of a political agreement binding France and Poland, France could have refused to carry out the military protocol. In that case, why sign it? It is true that the political agreement had *followed* and not preceded the military agreement. M. G. Bonnet, in his memoirs, acknowledges that he completed the political agreement *after* the declaration of war! Why not before?

her brave Polish ally from being crushed or even delaying it; worse still, she had failed to keep her word. What a confession of weakness or pusil-lanimity! In the eyes of the world, Hitler's victory greatly increased his prestige; it placed central and eastern Europe at his mercy. The initiative was now his—whether he wished to proclaim his desire for peace or to launch his full strength against his western opponents. At the first crisis, cruel proof had been given that France's army was inadequate to meet her political obligations. Would it have improved sufficiently by the time the enemy turned its attention to her? And should some breathing space still be given, would she be able to take advantage of it?

V THE PARTITION OF POLAND

What would become of Poland now that she had been conquered and completely occupied by her two large neighbours? The first problem for these to settle was the careful marking out of the limits of their respective portions, a difficult task since their troops had overlapped in the course of the fighting; it was made even more laborious by Stalin's pettifogging and suspicious attitude during the preliminary talks. Once again, Ribbentrop had to go off to Moscow.

The difference of opinion concerned the extent of the territories due for partition. The Germans were inclined to the view that after each had taken his cut, there should remain a residual Polish state with 12 to 15 million inhabitants, all Polish—a sort of Grand Duchy of Warsaw. Such a state, the German ambassador Moltke considered, might provide the basis for discussions with France and England and facilitate a return to peace. Could such a Poland reasonably do anything but put itself under Ger-man protection, if only in order to obtain German help in recovering one day the territories the Russians had annexed? Moltke was already suggest-ing as the head of this rump state the name of General Sonskowski, who was known to be cool towards the USSR.

It seems that, though Hitler had quite firm ideas as to his aims in Po-land, he was much less clear in his mind how to put them into effect now that victory had made their realisation possible. Had he not told von Brauchitsch on September 7, after the first brilliant successes, that he was ready to conclude peace with the Poles, thus assuming the survival of Poland?

But Stalin, at first agreeable, quickly detected the hint of anti-sovietism concealed by the plan for the creation of a Polish rump state. He was at pains to emphasise how important it was 'to avoid anything liable to create friction between Germany and the USSR'. During the discussion over the exact line of demarcation, he invoked the will of the Ukrainian people—who had never been consulted—and vehemently opposed the idea that the Germans should keep a small area of territory allegedly inhabited by Ukrainians. Stalin's major argument was that it would be unreasonable to partition the Poles between the two states. He suggested an exchange: Lithuania would be joined to the Russian zone whilst the province of Lublin and part of the province of Warsaw would be included in the German zone. If agreement were reached, he did not disguise the fact that 'the USSR would tackle the problem of the Baltic states without delay'.

It is probable that Hitler was most anxious at this time for a good understanding with Stalin. In the short term, he saw it as offering the immediate possibility of exerting strong pressure on France and England to induce them to make peace. Should they refuse and the war continue, the economic co-operation of the USSR would be indispensable. But by September 17, no start had yet been made in implementing the economic clauses of the pact and the German experts noted little eagerness on the part of the Russians to honour their contract. It was better not to irritate Stalin.

That was why in Moscow Ribbentrop in the end accepted all the Soviet's conditions. The German-Soviet treaty of 'delimitation and friendship' of September 28 partitioned Poland definitively in accordance with Stalin's proposals. It provided that Germans living in the zone of Russian influence[1] as well as the Ukrainians and White Russians living in the German zone would be free to emigrate from one zone to the other. Anxious to establish 'a solid basis of friendly relations' between themselves, the two parties pledged themselves 'not to tolerate any Polish agitation in their territories that might be liable to affect the maintenance of law and order in the other's territories'—a euphemism which condemned the Polish Communists who had taken refuge in the Russian zone to remain silent, if not to be interned. A programme of exchange of trade satisfactory to the Germans was drawn up. Ribbentrop achieved a small personal triumph: an area specially reserved for his hunting activities was left in Reich territory! On October 4, an additional agreement approved the line of demarcation drawn with the greatest accuracy by a mixed German-Russian commission.

VI POLAND'S MARTYRDOM BEGINS

Hitler despised the Poles. He used one word to define the reasons for their defeat: it was because their organisation for war had been *Polish*. He ex-

1. That is, those living in the Baltic states.

plained the 'dreadful opinion' that he had of Poland and of the 'wretched lot of the Poles' by quoting the silting-up of the Vistula as an example of Polish incompetence! However, even after the agreement with Stalin, he persisted for some time in his intention of allowing a residual Polish state to continue in existence and he explained to Count Ciano on October 2 'that the form [of that state] would depend on the way pacification would be achieved politically'. He could not yet say if Poland would be an independent state or a protectorate.

But when France and England refused to rise to the bait, Poland's fate was settled in accordance with the Führer's real feelings on the subject. By an order dated October 8, Hitler decided on the straightforward annexation by the Reich of the Polish territories that had formerly been German before 1918, i.e. east Prussia and the province of Poznan and Silesia, which now became 'the incorporated Eastern Territories'. Four days later he made the rest of the German-occupied zone into the 'General Government' of the occupied Polish territories, under the rule of the Third Reich's legal expert, Dr Frank—a bargaining counter for later developments, perhaps, but meanwhile an amorphous state in which the victorious Germans could exercise completely arbitrary power. In a letter to Mussolini dated March 8, 1940, contradicting what he had said to Ciano five months earlier, Hitler explained to the Duce that, had he not assumed control of the 'General Government', Poland would have fallen into 'appalling chaos'. The country would have starved; 'the priests would have had their heads chopped off'—by the basically Catholic Poles presumably? 'The Poles could consider themselves lucky to have had to deal with the good-natured Germans!'

And here are the blunt terms in which this 'good nature' was expressed at a conference held on October 2, when Hitler met Bormann, Frank and a few minor aides. Hitler uttered one or two peremptory judgments on the Poles: the Pole was really made for dirty work. . . . You could not turn a Slav into anything but what nature had intended him to be. And the Pole was lazy by nature and had to be forced to work. As a result, there must be no question of mingling German and Polish blood; and the Poles should be given inferior status: 'Every chance of promotion should be given to the German worker but the Poles should be given no chance of this; it was, indeed, necessary for their standard of living to be low or kept down.'

Thus the 'General Government' would become a reserve of manpower for the Reich. It would be entirely under the control of 'a strict German administration'; it would not form a 'tight homogeneous' economic region, equipped with industrial plant. It would provide the Reich with 'cheap labour', which would be summoned to Germany for seasonal requirements and then sent back to live in Poland once the work had been completed. The 'General Government' would, in short, be 'one vast labour-camp'. The Poles would benefit 'since the Germans would look after their health and see to it that they did not go hungry'; but 'they must not move up in the world' and the Roman Catholic priests' task was to 'keep them in a state of ignorance and stupidity', in the interests of the Germans.

It is unlikely that the exploitation of slave-labour had ever been so systematically planned and cynically expounded. But beyond this exploitation there loomed an even more atrocious plan. It followed from the assumption of the inferiority of the Poles that they could have only Germans in control of them. As a result, Hitler said 'it was absolutely essential to ensure that no Poles remained in positions of responsibility; wherever this was the case, they would have to be executed, however brutal this might seem.' A little later on, Hitler stated that 'all the Polish intelligentsia must be executed'.

Experts in this field were already on the spot, following in the wake of the Wehrmacht and with its agreement, *Einsatzgruppen*—special action groups—of the Reich security police had moved into Poland. Their role was to 'counter any elements in the occupied territories that were hostile to the Reich'. They began by 'taking care of' the Jews. The latter were expelled from the territories annexed by Germany and forced to go back into the 'General Government' where, by the beginning of October, they were already being gathered into ghettoes. The same meeting on October 2 arranged that Viennese Jews should be transferred to the 'General Government', which was thus fated to become the 'Jewish reservation' of Europe.

Poland's martyrdom was beginning and the calvary of the Jews was already plain to see. Racialism was being confirmed as the most powerful motive force behind Hitler's policy.

CHAPTER 2

The Phoney War
(October 1939–May 10, 1940)

THROUGHOUT the Polish campaign, Hitler had instructed the Wehrmacht to exercise the greatest caution in the west, to remain indeed completely on the defensive. In his directive of August 31, 1939, he ordered that 'any hostile initiative should come from England and France'; in a further instruction, issued after some days of success in Poland, he allowed the Navy and Air Force to engage the enemy if necessary, but reiterated the injunction that 'any opening of hostilities must be made by the enemy'. The Führer was endeavouring to reduce to a minimum the disadvantages of a war waged on two fronts: his first and most urgent objective was rapid victory over Poland.

The manner in which this was achieved filled Hitler with optimism; by September 12 he was confiding to his aide, Colonel Schmundt, that he felt certain that France could be quickly conquered and England then persuaded to come to terms. On September 27, he made known his plans to the commanders-in-chief of the three services at a meeting in Berlin. Pointing out that time was working against Germany, he announced his intention of attacking in the west very shortly. Otherwise, the favourable impression created on the neutral countries by the triumphal success of the Wehrmacht in Poland would quickly fade; in addition, the industrial regions of west Germany which were particularly vulnerable had to be protected—according to Halder, Hitler was afraid that Belgium would enter the war. In addition, Italy could be brought into the war. Von Brauchitsch ventured a few timid comments which the Führer brushed on one side.

However, it was always possible that the democracies might climb down; anyway, it was worth trying. By occupying, under the terms of the agreement with the USSR, the whole area of Poland inhabited by Poles, Hitler had a trump card which he could play against the democracies, independently of Russia. So, on September 30, he made it clear to the

OKW (*Oberkommando der Wehrmacht*) that the restrictions applying to air warfare in the west were still operative.

Hitler and Goering received the Swedish industrialist, Dahlerus, probably in order to see how the land lay and told him that, if the present situation in Poland were accepted, Germany was ready to guarantee the *status quo* in the rest of Europe. A meeting with an English VIP was contemplated but nothing came of it. On October 2, Hitler suggested to Ciano that Mussolini might undertake 'an important mission by bringing the neutrals together'—keeping them well under control. But Mussolini was anxious to be a non-belligerent until something better turned up and he was irritated at being called a neutral. On October 3, Chamberlain firmly rejected any possibility of negotiation.

Next, Hitler called the world to witness his peaceful intentions. On October 6, in the Reichstag, he offered peace to his opponents, in vague terms. He did not put forward any concrete proposals and implied that the German conquests in Poland could not be challenged; in fact, he tried to put the blame for continuing hostilities fairly and squarely on the democracies. On October 10, Daladier declined the invitation, as did Chamberlain two days later: France and Britain could not accept any peace recognising an act of force.

Next the neutral countries, feeling themselves in jeopardy, were spurred into action. In the course of October and November, many offers of mediation were put forward by the sovereigns of Holland, Belgium, Norway, Sweden and Romania; Spain and the Vatican did the same. Nothing came of these offers.

Meanwhile Hitler did not halt his preparations for an offensive in the west; he confirmed his intentions in a minute of October 9, even before France and Britain had replied to his approaches of October 6! What is more, he revealed his real war aims: what was at stake was 'the destruction of the predominance of the western powers in order to leave room for the expansion of the German people'. Lifting the veil still more, on October 23, he told his generals that the object of the war was not 'to achieve the triumph of National Socialist Germany but to decide who should dominate Europe'. His peace proposals had thus no other purpose than to beguile his enemies and if possible to obtain the advantages which he so earnestly desired without having to fight for them.

The Führer's directives for the conduct of the war provided for two stages: first, the Franco-British army would be beaten in a straight fight; then 'an offensive would be launched against England's *economic power*', with submarines, mines and aircraft—there was no question at any time of contemplating a landing of any sort in the British Isles.

Hitler was now keen to attack. But autumn had come, with its rain and

mud and low cloud, unsuitable for the movements of tanks or the operation of aircraft. Eleven times Hitler gave the order to attack and eleven
times the weather forced him to cancel the order. And so, against Hitler's
wishes, a truce set in between the belligerents and, as the sound of the guns
died away, diplomacy and propaganda moved into the centre of the stage.
How would the opposing parties use this lull before the storm?

II RELATIONS BETWEEN GERMANY AND THE USSR

And most important of all, how would the German-Soviet pact stand the
test of time, in view of the fact that it had been concluded under the
pressure of urgent needs on both sides: Hitler's desire to avoid fighting a
war on two fronts, and Stalin's to channel the German onslaught away
from the USSR? On the whole, both parties were showing a common desire
to iron out difficulties so as to draw the maximum advantage from their
agreement. But suspicion was rife on both sides and it was sometimes increased by mutual ignorance. The scope of the agreement was threefold:
military, diplomatic and economic.

The Führer had been keen to keep the military credit for Poland's defeat for himself alone. He had been at pains to point out that at no time
had the Reich requested military assistance from the Russians—sure proof
of the vanity of a victor quick to take offence. Hitler had also made known
to his generals his firm belief that the USSR would respect the conditions
of the pact only as long as it suited their interests; but for the moment the
weakness of the Red Army was a reassuring factor. Thus there had at no
time been any question of a military alliance, however limited in scope.
However, certain civilities had been exchanged, above all in naval matters.
The Russians had asked for German ships to supply their submarines in
the Baltic and this had been granted; the Germans had asked for and
obtained the use of Soviet dry-dock facilities. The German Navy would
have liked more: supplies for their cruisers and submarines in Russian
ports, the possibility of acquiring Soviet submarines, the exchange of
military information. The German documents published on this subject
do not reveal what was the Russians' reaction to these requests.

Diplomatically, joint action had been taken against Turkey, to dissuade
her from signing any agreement with the democracies. The Reich had
recommended Japan to improve her relations with the USSR. At Germany's
instigation, the USSR had protested against the British blockade. However,
some friction had arisen in the occupied territories, particularly as the
Germans had on several occasions gathered thousands of Polish Jews together close to the demarcation line and secretly smuggled them into the

Russian zone. The Soviet authorities had confined themselves to pushing the poor wretches out again.

But it was primarily in the economic sphere that misunderstandings had emerged, although everything seemed quite straightforward, since the economies and needs complemented each other. But both sides were building up their armaments; as a result, the Germans needed the same machines or industrial products as the Russians and the latter were consuming a great deal of the raw materials that the Germans were hoping for. Above all, the Germans were hoping to obtain more than they handed over and wanted to pay off what they owed by staggering their deliveries of industrial products over a period of seven years. The Soviet government had other ideas. On the other hand, the Germans were growing impatient at the leisurely manner in which the cumbersome Russian bureaucracy was scrutinising their requests. And so, at the end of October, two months after the signing of the pact, nothing had yet been settled, even though a Russian purchasing commission had been roaming all over Germany showing an indiscreet curiosity that caused Keitel some concern.

The Russians had promised one million tons of grain, 900,000 tons of oil (including 100,000 tons of aircraft fuel), wood, manganese and 100,-000 tons of cotton. They had authorised goods intended for the Reich to be transported via the Trans-Siberian railway, pointing out that such permission was quite exceptional. But they refused to hand over any iron or chrome.

In exchange, they asked for the delivery of the *Prinz Eugen*, the hulls of two cruisers, a training ship, the plans of the *Bismarck*, the most modern types of torpedoes and mines, Messerschmitt aircraft and 'more recent machines that they had not been shown', aircraft engines—they suggested that they should build them and sell them back to the Reich—AA equipment, in a word, almost exclusively equipment needed for modern warfare.

Goering, who had been put in charge of the Four Year Plan, was of the opinion that the Russian requests should be met. But on examination, the German experts discovered that the Russians were asking for twice as much as the Germans were prepared to offer, over a considerably longer period. Keitel was unwilling for the Wehrmacht to part with certain weapons which, to his mind, it could not do without. Ribbentrop himself, who had negotiated the pact, recognised that the Russian requests would need cutting down by half or even two-thirds. As he told the Soviet ambassador: 'It must not be forgotten that Germany is at war.'

The discussions now degenerated into something like a haggle between a couple of tough horse-dealers. Each protested that the other was not keeping to the terms of the pact. The Germans complained that the Soviet

Purchasing Commission 'was poking its nose into everything' and behaving rather like the 'Interallied Control Commission during the years immediately following the First War'. Molotov upbraided the Germans for 'the exorbitant cost' of their aircraft. He recalled the promise that Ribbentrop had made on September 28: 'Germany would supply her *friend* the USSR with everything she wanted from her'. In short, there was deadlock.

However, no hint of these squabbles leaked out publicly. In the Soviet press, the attacks on Germany had ceased, even though, according to the report of the German ambassador in Moscow, public opinion remained suspicious. Above all, the Communist parties all over Europe had now stopped denouncing Nazism as the scourge of the age and were describing the current war as a conflict between imperialist powers which was of no concern to the people. Germany and the USSR had made a joint declaration laying all the blame for the conflict on to the democracies. On October 31, Molotov made a statement affirming the complete solidarity of the two states. 'The ideology of Hitler's Germany', he said, 'could not be destroyed by war,' and he spoke with a straight face of 'Germany's peaceful aspirations'![1]

Hitler accepted without a murmur the 'reorganisation' that the USSR was carrying out in its zone of influence. While the former Polish subjects, of White Russian or Ukrainian origin, were joined to their appropriate ethnic group in the Soviet Republic, Stalin forced 'mutual assistance pacts' on to Estonia, Latvia and Lithuania and made them grant him bases, while assuring them that he had no political ideological designs on them. Although Hitler had been bound by agreement ever since June 1939 to assist these three Baltic states, he made no demur. The USSR offered a friendship pact to Bulgaria, which King Boris declined; nor was it Hitler but Mussolini who was troubled by this Soviet approach and Ribbentrop had even informed Boris of Germany's assent. The spirit of the pact was being observed, therefore, on both sides and it was being implemented, albeit with some difficulty. Would the unexpected conflict between Russia and Finland raise new problems?

III THE FINNISH–SOVIET CONFLICT

The USSR wished Leningrad to be better protected; in other words, they meant to control that part of Finnish territory commanding the access to

---

1. German news films had shown pictures of 'fraternisation': Guderian reviewing a parade of Russian tanks, German and Russian troops skiing together at Zakopane, etc.

the city. Molotov simply summoned the Finnish Foreign Minister to Moscow; he did not go. And Finland discussed the Soviet 'proposals' word by word. In the course of talks held in Moscow with the Finnish Minister to Sweden, Stalin demanded that the Finns should hand over the Hankö peninsula and some islands in the Gulf of Finland as well as moving the Finnish frontier back in the Carelian Isthmus, receiving some Soviet territory in compensation. In addition, Finland was to destroy its fortifications in Carelia and the 'agreement' would form part of a treaty of mutual aid—the customary euphemism to disguise the status of protectorate imposed on a small power by a large one.

Finland was isolated; Sweden ignored her appeals and Hitler turned a blind eye. The appointment of a Socialist, Tanner, to the Ministry of Foreign Affairs hastened Russia's decision despite the fact that he was ready and willing to negotiate. Tanner was the epitome of the 'social traitor' loathed by the Bolsheviks; he had, moreover, committed the enormous indiscretion of reminding Stalin, in front of witnesses, that they were both old Mensheviks—which was, incidentally, not true as far as Stalin was concerned and was considered by him as an insult. Molotov did not mince his words: 'The Soviet government' he stated, 'expects nothing of any value to come out of the Tanner government.' Sweden and Norway made vain attempts to mediate; the Kremlin decided not to accept their communications. Roosevelt sent a message to Kalinin, the USSR President, and received from Molotov the friendly advice to apply his mind to Cuba and the Philippines.

On November 30, without declaring war, the Red Army began to move. Following a procedure that was to become standard practice, Stalin pretended that the only official Finnish government he now recognised was the one formed, at his instigation, by the Finnish Communist party representative to the Comintern, Kuusinen. Despite the great discrepancy between the two forces, the war lasted for three months. The Russians had probably underestimated their opponents and were using low-grade troops; they had made the mistake of starting the campaign at the beginning of winter and the bad weather soon cancelled out the overwhelming superiority of their tanks and air force. On the other hand, the shortness of the Carelian frontier prevented the deployment of large numbers of troops; and, finally, the vast areas of lake, marsh and forest hampered any military movement.

In short, all the Russian attacks in the Carelian Isthmus had foundered by December. Under the command of Marshal Mannerheim, a former Czarist guards officer and the 'liberator of Finland' in 1918, the Finns even went over to the offensive and carved a Soviet division to pieces north of Lake Ladoga; the Russians were also forced back on to the defensive in the extreme north. In the course of February, by dint of great efforts in the Carelian Isthmus, they overran the Finnish defences holding the 'Mannerheim line', thanks to the ice on Lake Ladoga which was thick enough to support the weight of tanks. On March 2, they were at Viborg.

Contrary to the diehard reputation which Soviet propaganda had been trying to pin on him, and which had led to his vilification by the whole Communist press in Europe, Tanner wanted to negotiate. On three occasions he went surreptitiously to Stockholm to meet the Soviet ambassador, Madame Kollontai, herself of Finnish origin. Marshal Mannerheim considered that it was no longer possible to continue fighting. The Soviets were less eager to stop but after Finland had accepted all their terms—those of the ultimatum of the previous November, plus the surrender of Viborg—the peace treaty was signed on March 12, 1940.

Stalin had given Hitler no warning of his intentions regarding Finland but the Führer refrained from embarrassing his partner in the tight corner in which he had been caught. However, Blücher, the German ambassador in Helsinki, was outspoken in his support of the Finns whom Mussolini had decided to help by sending arms; and Ribbentrop was subjected to loud expostulations from Molotov for this. But Hitler did not lift a finger; he withdrew the German ships from the proximity of the Finnish coast, persuaded Sweden not to go to her neighbour's help, rejected any suggestion that he might act as mediator, advised Finland to come to terms directly with her opponent—that is to say, to give in—and encouraged Sweden to offer to mediate discreetly.

The fact is that Hitler had absolutely no desire for the Finnish-Soviet conflict to spread, as the democracies were hoping (and their plans were an open secret), since this would open up a kind of second front at a time when he was concentrating his forces for a decisive attack in the west. Militarily therefore, Germany's interests coincided with those of the Soviet Union. But Russia's lack of success finally convinced Hitler of the deep-rooted weakness of the Red Army. The German delegates were able to exploit this during the difficult economic negotiations.

As a result, the Russians scaled down their claims; they had been asking for 26 two- or three-gun turrets: they now settled for 10; instead of 600 machines for making shells, they agreed to take 34; some requests they gave up altogether. Perhaps they were afraid of being deserted by their partners. In any case, while Hitler remained in the wings, Stalin was taking a direct part in the discussions and amazing the German negotiators by the extent and accuracy of his knowledge in his answers to their queries. The atmosphere was improved by certain conciliatory Russian statements: one from Stalin himself, who emphasised that it was not merely a question of 'a normal commercial treaty but of mutual aid'; another from Molotov who mentioned 'the *political* significance of the economic agreement'. At a critical moment when the talks seemed bogged down, Ribbentrop pointed out to Stalin on February 3 that 'the Soviet government had been able to realise its ambitions regarding the former Polish territories thanks to the German victory in Poland'. This 'represented a fairly considerable advance on the part of Germany' and 'a justification of her desire to obtain help'. He ventured 'to suggest to Stalin that he should reconsider the matter in the light of these factors'.

Stalin took the point at once and the commercial treaty was concluded on February 11, 1940. The Germans received satisfaction on the question of the time schedule for payments. They would be paying over a period of twenty-seven months for goods that would be delivered over a period of eighteen months. The Russians were to supply more goods than previously contemplated for a total overall payment of 1,000 million marks: copper, nickel, tin, molybdenum, tungsten and cobalt as well as the grain, crude oil and cotton as already agreed, but, in addition, the iron ore that had hitherto been withheld. Finally, the USSR granted a 50 per cent reduction on the freight charges for goods on the Trans-Siberian railway and agreed to make purchases on behalf of Germany from other countries and settle the accounts directly with them. The German negotiator Schnurre concluded that 'the USSR had pledged herself to provide Germany with far more goods than was justified merely from the economic point of view and that she would be doing so at the expense of her own supplies'.

On their side, the Russians also received satisfaction on a good number of points; rather than large quantities of plant, however, they were to obtain smaller amounts of high-quality specimens (armour-plating, boiler tubes, periscopes, mines and torpedoes, acoustic equipment, tanks, aircraft, samples of various types of ammunition, types of engine, equipment for the oil industry, locomotives and steel tubes). The Germans were providing them with a sort of scientific and technical object-lesson.

The interests of the two countries were now plainly closer together; in Finland the Russians had discovered by bitter experience certain grave military shortcomings which they must remedy without delay; and seeing that the war was going to be protracted, the Germans had a most urgent need of Russian foodstuffs and raw materials. Schnurre expressed this point when he noted that 'the effects of the British blockade have been *decisively* mitigated'. According to certain of Ribbentrop's statements, one of them made in Rome on March 10, the agreement had been extended to include co-ordinated action by various 'special services'.[1]

1. Ribbentrop had jokingly said that 'a number of the clandestine Communist newspapers circulating in France are printed in Berlin'. This was doubtless a mere figure of speech of which there has never been the slightest shadow of proof.

Certain points of friction still remained; the German negotiators complained of the 'continual distrust of the Russians'. Frequent incidents took place on the demarcation line in Poland, and sometimes even gunfire was exchanged. Each party reproached the other over delays in deliveries. These were minor blemishes; before committing himself in the west, Hitler was staking everything on agreement with Stalin; he wanted to be certain that his rear was covered and he was now doubly reassured, both by the evident goodwill of the USSR and by the weaknesses revealed by her setbacks in Finland. So the gamble of the German-Soviet pact, achieved despite a massive history of past antagonism and despite its unnatural character ideologically speaking, was turning into a durable agreement, beneficial to both parties, so much so that Mussolini, feeling himself rather left out in the cold, was taking umbrage.

IV MUSSOLINI'S HESITATION

Hitler had been irritated by Italy's decision not to join in on August 26, 1939. Although he had made the best of a bad job, he had not concealed his view that Italian neutrality could only encourage France and Britain to urge the Poles to further resistance at the expense of the Reich. Later, while in the euphoric state caused by his victories in Poland, Hitler had come to realise to the full that keeping the Mediterranean out of the war and surrounded by neutral or friendly powers, would ensure that the clash between Germany and Poland could take place in isolation and the stronger quietly crush the weaker without interference. But once it had been decided to go over to the offensive in the west, it was clear—and the OKW was convinced of this—that Italy, whose military—and especially her air and naval—power were overestimated by Hitler, would, by entering the war, be useful in tying down French forces in the Alps and in Tunisia, thus reducing the forces available on the north-east frontier with Germany. But when the OKW approached the Italian high command to arrange for the necessary co-operation, they received no reply.

The fact was that Mussolini had not yet decided on active belligerence. His Minister of Foreign Affairs, Ciano, was urging him to take the lead in establishing a sort of neutral alliance, and become, as it were, 'the prince of peace'. Discreet feelers were coming in from Belgrade, Bucharest and even from Budapest and Sofia to do something of this kind. The Duce was, moreover, not happy about the German-Soviet agreement; 'it had,' he said, 'created an unfortunate impression'; he feared lest the USSR might encroach on central Europe, which he considered an Italian preserve. The fate of Roman Catholic Poland had caused anger among the Catholic

Italians. Finally, the police were reporting unwelcome agitation on the part of the Germans in the South Tyrol, where the German victories were hardly conducive to encouraging the German-speaking inhabitants to leave their country.

So on December 16, to Ribbentrop's fury, Ciano made an important speech in which he emphasised the differences of opinion within the Axis. After which, the Pope, when receiving King Victor Emmanuel, openly expressed the wish that his country should continue to be neutral. On January 3, 1940, Mussolini took the liberty of offering Hitler some un-solicited advice to show moderation in Poland. He condemned the 'catastrophic repercussions' of the agreement between Germany and Russia 'where Germany would find her *Lebensraum'*. When asked for an explanation by Ribbentrop, Attolico, the Italian ambassador in Berlin, replied that 'should the war last five years, Italy will be unable to take any part in it before the second or third of them.'

The Germans' reaction to all this was not long delayed; in February 1940, Italy was informed that 'owing to the icy weather' they could not deliver more than 370,000 tons of coal; subsequently, the needs of the German economy would restrict further supplies to only 500,000 tons per month. And Italy was asking for 12 million tons of German coal a year! In his refusal, Ribbentrop stated, not without a hint of irony, that 'there was no difficulty in mining the coal'.

Had the two partners reached a critical stage in their relations? Whether or not they were aware of this, the British were working towards a rift between Italy and Germany by the use of sticks and carrots. In February, they asked Italy to sell them guns and aircraft; should Italy refuse, she would not get any English coal. This blackmail must have irritated the Duce. He flatly refused the bargain. Britain then decided to apply her blockade to the Italian ships loading German coal in Holland. Mussolini made a 'vigorous protest' and the moment of truth for Italian policy had come.

As if by magic, Germany promised Italy the 12 million tons of coal per year for which she had been asking, although expressing some doubts as to the possibility of shipping them to her. On March 8, two months after he had received it, Hitler replied to Mussolini's letter of January 3. He emphasised the fundamental solidarity of Nazi Germany and Fascist Italy; in spite of everything, 'fate would force them to fight shoulder to shoulder'. He minimised the Bolshevik peril because he said the Soviet Union was motivated more by a kind of 'Russian nationalism' than by Communism. When he went to Rome on March 10, Ribbentrop por-trayed Stalin as a sort of modern Ivan the Terrible and promised that the USSR had no ambitions in central Europe. Although expressing scepticism and reiterating that 'for him the enemy was still Communism', Mussolini promised that 'Italy would enter the war at the appropriate moment and would fight on the same side as and parallel with Germany'. 'Parallel' implied that Italy meant to achieve her own ends, in her particular and limited sphere. But the pledge was made.

All the same, when Mussolini met Hitler on the Brenner on March 17, he still showed some scepticism as to the likelihood of Germany's beating the Allies before the end of the year. He reminded the Führer that Italy could not take part in a long war and that he still needed several months to make preparations for it. Hitler was very conciliatory: 'the final decision rested with the Duce'. At that time the latter had no knowledge at all of what Germany had decided; he knew that orders had been given for an offensive in the west but he did not know when or where it would take place. Imagining it to be imminent, he issued a memorandum on March 31 making known his final decision. While stating the principle that 'Italy could not remain neutral without putting herself beyond the pale, abandoning her rule and becoming a kind of larger version of Switzerland', when he tried to be more precise regarding Italian strategy, he found himself compelled by the weakness of his forces to decide to remain on the defensive everywhere except at sea and in Ethiopia.

So it was the Duce alone who took the decision to launch Italy into the fray. His pride had overcome both his caution and his certain knowledge of Italy's unreadiness for war. Had he not said to Ciano 'that he did not want to be the laughing-stock of Europe'? The Axis now seemed more closely knit than ever: the democracies had failed to detach Italy from Germany. Had they at least used the respite to make proper preparations for the inevitable and imminent confrontation?

The British and French had, in fact, in the first place co-ordinated their action and increased their forces; secondly they had tried to solve the irritating problem of Belgium; thirdly, they had planned a grand strategy of peripheral operations in Scandinavia and the Near East; and finally they had attempted to weaken Germany both by reaching an understanding with the opponents of the Nazi régime and by the use of the blockade. Was this going to be sufficient?

V FRANCO-BRITISH DETERMINATION

For the overall control of their coalition the British and French had set up a Supreme Inter-allied War Council which met for the first time on September 12. On November 17, this Supreme Council created a co-ordinating committee to pool the economic resources of the two countries;

missions were to endeavour to negotiate group purchases abroad, but no real joint war production was agreed upon or even contemplated. The Reynaud-Simon agreements merely provided that one-third of the expenses of the war should be paid by France and two-thirds by Britain.

The British Expeditionary Force had taken up its positions on the Franco-Belgian frontier in the course of October. By January 1940 it consisted of five divisions. Its commander, Lord Gort, came under the Supreme Commander, General Gamelin but, as in every coalition, he had the right of appeal to his own government against any orders he might receive. He was sandwiched between two French armies of the First Army Group, but at Field Marshal Ironside's request he was not subordinated to that group but directly to General Georges. The RAF was under strictly British control.

How strong was Great Britain's determination in fact? A Wilhelmstrasse document leaves some doubt on the subject. In the course of October the Soviet ambassador in London met some British leaders. Butler, who was certainly not speaking for himself alone, is stated to have suggested that the British government would agree to making peace if they could be assured that it would last for twenty years. If a guarantee on the part of the USSR and the USA offered some hope of this, then the British government would be prepared to make considerable concessions in the matter of colonies. On his part, Chamberlain made no secret to Sumner Welles of the fact that, in the final settlement, Great Britain would not prove completely inflexible on the question of Poland and Czechoslovakia.

It is true that Churchill, who had joined the British government as First Lord of the Admiralty, and was supported by Eden, was criticising Chamberlain for his lack of vigour. He was advocating that the democracies should take the initiative in the air and at sea and, to start with, should lay mines in the Rhine. In France, Daladier's government had fallen on March 20, 1940, because it had failed to 'make methodical and energetic use of the resources of the nation'. Daladier had been succeeded by someone whose energy was notorious, Paul Reynaud, but who was merely the head of a coalition, not the leader of a team. Although powerless to bring about the changes that he would have liked to see in the high command and to give the armed forces the weapons they needed, the new Premier took every opportunity to assert his determination in the well-turned phrases for which he had a special gift: 'Victory is salvation; defeat, annihilation'; and 'We shall win, because we are strongest.'

Without consulting the President of the Republic or Parliament, Paul Reynaud persuaded the English to sign a declaration saying that 'Great Britain and France pledge themselves not to negotiate or conclude any armistice or peace treaty except by joint agreement.' It was a way of making Britain give public confirmation of her will to fight.

But armament production was getting under way slowly and with difficulty; in January 1940, there were still only 21 heavy tanks coming out of the factories as opposed to the 75 that had been planned. The fact was that mobilisation had reduced the amount of skilled labour and this had had to be put right by giving the status of 'reserved occupation' to highly skilled factory workers. In May, the number of heavy tanks coming out of the factories had gone up to 50 per month; this was still not enough and did not help the formation of the armoured divisions as decided by the high command in the light of the lessons of the war in Poland. This decision had, in any case, not been taken until January; and the formation of these units from scratch was very hurried; petrol supplies were badly organised for lack of storage tanks; the three proposed armoured divisions were short of tracked vehicles, repair units and liaison cars; radio communication links were either antiquated and clumsy or else non-existent.

VI ALLIED RELATIONS WITH BELGIUM AND HOLLAND

The game of blind man's buff had gone on for seven months. Belgian political leaders knew full well that Beligum could only be attacked by Germany and defended by France and Great Britain, yet they turned a blind eye by obstinately refusing to agree to the talks without which any co-ordinated action was impossible. The declaration of war caused them to withdraw slightly more into their 'policy of independence'. King Leopold issued a message reiterating his 'firm determination to keep the country out of war'. His influential military adviser, General van Overstraeten, the real army leader, although not in name, interpreted this imperative into terms of time: 'Gain time in order to arm ourselves to the hilt without compromising our position.' The fear of calling down Hitler's wrath on Belgium was so great that the numbers of troops and obstacles (the latter could impede only the progress of friendly forces) on the Franco-Belgian frontier were constantly changed; in order to give the impression of impartiality between the two opponents, these forces and obstacles were reinforced according to circumstances. Some Belgian leaders—the Ministers Devèze and Spaak—were, indeed, more clear-sighted and made some slight moves towards the French and English; but they had no effect on the rigid attitude of other Belgians haunted by the fear of jeopardising national unity and completely blind to the serious danger from outside.

On the Allied side, General Gamelin considered that Belgian neutrality was completely playing into the enemy's hands. He shrewdly weighed up the advantage to be gained by advancing into Belgium and offering determined resistance to the Germans (after incorporating the Belgian Army into the Allied defence positions) against the immense danger of a pitched battle where German superiority in tanks and aircraft would have full scope. But unless agreement had previously been reached, the Allied advance would depend entirely on how soon the Belgians asked for help. There was serious risk of losing this fight against time and the real fight that would then ensue.

So, after a further refusal on the part of the Belgians to engage in talks, even under the pledge of absolute secrecy, Gamelin adopted a plan of 'safety first': he would wage a defensive war in France on his own line of fortifications and their advanced posts; he would cross into Belgian territory only in response to a Belgian request and if adequate forces could be moved up, as and when required, to the chosen defence positions. It was the wisest thing to do until the Belgians showed a trifle more co-operation; there was little doubt on the French side that this would come willy-nilly through force of circumstances once the German threat became urgent. Meanwhile, no forcible entry into Belgium should be attempted, even though it seemed certain that the Belgians would offer only token resistance.

In October, the concentration of German troops in the Rhineland left no doubt as to the Germans' intention of launching a broad offensive. The Belgians realised this and concentrated the bulk of their forces on the Albert canal and along the Meuse. In his correspondence with Spaak, the Belgian Foreign Minister, Daladier confirmed that France 'would respond to any Belgian request' whilst emphasising the danger of being forced to improvise; he did not think that France would have a great deal of time. Gamelin in fact, with great shrewdness, considered that the German onslaught against Belgium would be ruthless, if not devastating. In consequence the French government and high command once again suggested general staff talks with the Belgians. Spaak turned down the idea, probably after consulting King Leopold. He believed that the emergency leading to German military action would last long enough for co-operation between the Allies and Belgium to be worked out. Everything suggested that the lessons of the Blitzkrieg against Poland had not been grasped in Belgium. Thus the directives of the officer commanding the north-eastern armies, General Georges, provided for the Allied troops in Belgium to advance only as far as the Scheldt. They were to advance further only if they had time to reach a prepared position where they could regroup. Meanwhile the weakness of the Allies can be deduced from their decision not to bomb the Ruhr for fear of German reprisals and not to

Map 3 THE SCHELDT AND DYLE – BREDA
OPERATIONS

Scheldt operations

→ Movement of the
Allied Armies

Dyle-Breda operations

➡ Movement of the
allied armies

〕 Position to be taken
up at the end of the
operation

--→ Movement of the
French Reserves

⬡ Fortifications

0   100km

attack the German ground forces from the air in order not to risk their small force of vulnerable bombers.

But in November, interest shifted from Belgium to Holland. The British were in fact greatly worried by the latter's situation; they feared that the Germans might set up submarine and air force bases and threaten the British Isles. An attack on Holland would also enable the Wehrmacht to outflank the Belgian defences on the west. It was thus important to be able to go to the help of the Dutch, that is, to advance as deeply as possible into Belgium.

Consequently the initial French plan of 'safety first', based on defence combined with a limited advance up to the Scheldt, was progressively abandoned in favour of bolder, even reckless, operations. As a result of a string of directives, it was finally decided that the Allies would make a double advance into Belgium. On the left wing, the Seventh Army would move beyond Antwerp to link up with the Dutch. While the Belgians were protecting the 'national strongholds' of Antwerp and Ghent, the British would be covering Brussels and the bulk of the French forces would move on to a line running from Antwerp to Namur along the course of the river Dyle and the Gembloux 'gap'. On November 17, the Supreme Interallied Council approved this new plan, called the 'Dyle plan'.

Such a plan was more than rash. It was based on a series of assumptions, and the successful outcome would be little short of miraculous. It assumed, in fact, that the Dutch army would be able to offer continued resistance to the Germans, that the Belgians, left to themselves, could retire in good order to the Dyle without having been too badly mauled on the Albert canal and that a good solid defence line would be established in time between Antwerp and Namur—and it could only be set up by the Belgians with their limited resources. In addition, this grand plan seemed completely to ignore the overwhelming shortcoming of the Allied strategy, i.e. its lack of large armoured units and the failure of the French and the English on the one hand and the Belgians and the Dutch on the other to work together to achieve the essential co-operation.

The immense danger of these 'large-scale operations' had not, however, escaped the notice of the French generals faced with the task of carrying them out. General Giraud, responsible for linking up with the Dutch and certainly not lacking in pugnacity, had emphasised that the Seventh Army could arrive at Breda in advance of the Germans only if it had three motorised divisions, if the requisite destruction of communication centres had been carried out in good time by the Belgians and the Dutch and if two Belgian or Dutch divisions were able to join up with the French immediately. In other words, the 'Breda operation' required a Franco-

Belgian-Dutch co-operation that was non-existent and which the Belgians and the Dutch did not want. General Blanchard considered that the First Army would only just have time enough to position itself in the Gembloux gap. General Georges, the officer in charge of the whole operational theatre, had made no secret of his misgivings; he had vainly suggested that the Seventh Army's mission on the left flank should be confined to occupying the Scheldt seaboard, as General Giraud wished. The English military leaders also expressed reservations.

General Gamelin dug in his heels and took a large measure of the responsibility. He even called a meeting of the army commanders at Arras on November 23, unknown to their GOC (General Officer Commanding) General Georges. General Gamelin's attitude here is so unlike his previous perspicacity and caution that it is difficult not to suppose that it was forced on him by the Allied governments. It would thus seem that the 'Dyle operation' was political rather than military. By agreeing to it, Gamelin was surely showing meekness rather than character. At least he tried to reduce its risks by once more attempting to reach agreement with the Belgians, the only thing that could minimise the effects of failure even if it would not ensure success; but with a persistence worthy of a better cause, the Belgians still shied away from any such agreement.

Van Overstraeten had stated that the invasion of Holland would be a *casus belli* for Belgium, but this statement had not led to any agreement to link the two neutral countries, both equally threatened. Worse still, the Dutch Supreme Commander had decided to withdraw the bulk of his forces to the north of the main rivers, a decision which, by widening the gap between the Belgian and Dutch defence positions, made the Wehrmacht's attack all the easier.

It is true that in January 1940, after a German plane had been forced to land at Mechelen on the Meuse, and the German plans for the invasion of Belgium had been revealed, the Belgian authorities were extremely scared. 'Extracts' from the captured documents were communicated to the French. And the principle of neutrality was bent, if not broken: the obstacles facing towards the French side were removed! King Leopold declared his readiness to call in the French, not at once, despite the imminent danger, but merely after any invasion. Moreover he took the precaution of demanding that the Allies should guarantee Belgian frontiers and Belgian property in the Congo and grant financial assistance. The French troops were put at the ready; if Georges still had reservations, because of the Allies' shortage of aircraft and tanks, Gamelin was in favour of 'seizing the opportunity'. But there was no request from the Belgians; when the alarm had died down, they merely put back the barriers protecting them against an Allied advance into Belgium.

Henceforth the Allied requests, however discreet or trivial they might be, fell on deaf ears in Belgium. Yet these requests left aside the thorny questions of political and military co-ordination and were concerned only with technical problems of execution: the evacuation of the civilian population, the routes to be followed by the Allied troops or liaison with the local Belgian authorities. The Belgians even refused to disclose their demolition plans.

Nonetheless their attitude was changing slightly. They admitted that on the Albert canal they could at best undertake delaying action; they started to build an anti-tank defence line from Wavre to Namur, with little positive result, since its course was altered on a number of occasions and bad weather held up the work. On their side, the Dutch were contemplating defending Walcheren and Beveland islands jointly with the British and Breda and Tilburg with the French. But it was all rather vague; nothing cut and dried really emerged. The Allied command was merely kept informed of troop movements and picked up hints as to the Belgian plans through contacts between officials, and from the fact that the French military attaché was able to move about freely, in mufti, all over Belgium.

One of the lessons of military history is the weakness of any coalition, however impressive the sum total of the forces of its constituent member states. In any case, though on the eve of waging a joint war, the French, British, Belgians and Dutch did not even form a coalition: they were not ready for anything, except to fight in extended order. Clearly, the failure of France to resist Hitler's demands since 1936 had hardly been conducive to inspiring confidence in potential allies. But on the other hand, everything pointed to the fact that the storm would break first on the Belgians themselves—and on the Dutch as well, although they had some faint hope of escaping it. The German troop concentrations seemed to forecast this, just as areas of low pressure forecast rain on a weather map; refusal to make the necessary contacts with France could not avert the danger for Belgium because she was the only door by which the Wehrmacht could enter France; but such a refusal was certainly signing her death warrant. Such arrant short-sightedness cannot be explained merely by worries connected with internal politics, however great.[1] It is probable that Belgian leaders had failed to gauge the speed of the German advance accurately; they thought that the overriding pressure of events would cause everyone to be both clever and co-operative and that all problems would be solved on the battlefield. This miscalculation seems to have been shared by Gamelin; as late as March 1940 he was still contemplating advancing as far as the Albert canal, after an initial 'leap forward', should the Belgians

1. On April 25, 1940, the Pierlot cabinet resigned in Belgium. The Liberal party had refused to approve the Education Budget as a result of language squabbles.

still be 'holding out'. In fact, once again proof was being offered that in 1940, as in 1936 or 1938, France had neither the military force or ideas required to fulfil her pledges. Nevertheless her army chiefs and the leaders of her government were not without aggressive intentions, as they were going to demonstrate by dreaming up vast hare-brained schemes.

VII ALLIED PLANS IN THE BALKANS

The French generals, particularly, were obsessed by the lessons of the First World War, because many of them had worked in close collaboration with the great commanders who had led France to victory. Hence the idea close to Weygand's heart and accepted by Gamelin, of creating a second front in the Balkans, based on memories of Salonica. In July 1939, Gamelin had envisaged it as a front of vast dimensions stretching from Poland to Turkey and Greece by way of Romania and Yugoslavia. It was with this prospect in mind that the 'Near East Expeditionary Force' was brought into being, under the command of Weygand with the ambitious title of 'Commander-in-Chief of the Eastern Mediterranean Zone of Operations'.

This vast scheme had its wings clipped by the German-Soviet pact. Henceforth, for the states forming the Petite Entente, the Red menace was either added to or replaced the threat from Germany. Poland's defeat removed any possibility of a really coherent second front. At best it was important to prevent central Europe from falling too quickly under the German or Italian yoke.

In the unfortunate situation now existing, Turkey seemed, if the most distant, at least the most solid sheet-anchor. The Anglo-French-Turkish treaty of October 17, 1939 provided for co-operation between the three countries 'in the case of aggression by any European power leading to war in the Mediterranean area'; but a separate agreement stipulated that Turkey could not engage in war with the USSR; thus Italy was the only country affected. In another agreement Turkey was granted a loan in order to purchase French or British war equipment; cautious to the point of inertia, the Turks had made it clear that they would not fulfil any of the pledges until they had received this equipment. This was the first brick, not very firm but still the most solid one there was, in the protective wall that the Allies wanted to build up in south-east Europe.

Yugoslavia was more afraid of Italy's ambitions than Germany's. At the outbreak of hostilities, it had mobilised 500,000 men and the unity of the country had been reinforced by an agreement with the Croat leader Macek. But it was tempting for Prince Paul, the Regent, to go to Berlin for protection against Rome, the more so as most of Yugoslavia's trade was between her and the Reich. Though the Army Chief of Staff, General Simović, made no secret of his hostility towards Germany, General Nedić, the War Minister, was at least prepared to wait and see.

As for Romania, she was more afraid of the Russians, the Hungarians and the Bulgarians than the Germans; would a guarantee from France and Britain be effective against this danger? Would it not be sensible to work for a counter-guarantee from Italy?

Nevertheless, at the Belgrade conference in February 1940, after Sarajoglu, on behalf of Turkey, and Metaxas on the part of Greece, had insisted on formulating a joint defence plan, Romania and Yugoslavia did not express their misgivings too openly and a joint plan was, in fact drawn up; but it was still necessary to prevent it from becoming a dead letter and this implied considerable help from France and England.

Weygand would very much have liked not to haggle over this support. His scheme was at the very least to create bridgeheads at Salonica and Constanza in order to exclude the Germans from the Mediterranean and the Black Sea. The best scheme of all, he wrote, would be 'to go as far as Vienna' and hold the Save-Danube line 'in order to break out and attack when the moment came'. And he went on into fancies of 'one hundred Balkan divisions'!

But there was no co-ordination or even liaison between the countries concerned. On the other hand, the British were showing little enthusiasm; they were anxious to handle Italy gently and so the idea of a bridgehead at Salonica was abandoned for the moment. The Turks were asking for nine dozen 75-mm guns as well as tanks and aircraft. Where could they be found? Thus everything pointed to the conclusion that they would remain neutral. There were certainly splendid Allied plans on paper: in March 1940, it was suggested that command in the proposed operational theatres should be shared: Salonica would be a French responsibility and Thrace, Turkish, in order to neutralise the Bulgarians, while the British suggested taking over a theoretical front running through Afghanistan, Iran and Iraq, although it was difficult to see how the war would reach that far.

In any case, the spearhead of the operation remained the French army in the Near East. Although on paper it was inflated—each brigade was called a division—it never consisted of more than 80,000 men of whom 50,000 were to be in the Expeditionary Force. But this force had only two tank battalions and one fighter and one modern bomber group; since it had no motorised transport, it was without any strategic mobility; it possessed neither AA nor anti-tank guns. As for its transportation, for lack of shipping, three months were considered necessary to move three divisions from Beirut to Salonica. If the speed of the Polish campaign was anything to go by, should the Danubian countries be attacked by the Wehrmacht, they would cease to exist long before that time. The 'Weygand plan' in the Balkans was thus at best a psychological operation to boost the morale of friendly countries somewhat dismayed by the course of events. Yet even broader horizons were to be opened up.

VIII THE PROPOSAL TO ATTACK OIL SOURCES IN THE CAUCASUS

Allied success in a long war demanded that the Wehrmacht should be deprived of that sinew of modern motorised warfare, oil, and Germany had taken over the Romanian oil, where joint German-Romanian companies were intending to increase the rate of flow for the Reich's benefit. In view of the Allied control of the Mediterranean, Romanian oil could only be shipped to Germany up the Danube. The Allies had thought of sabotaging the drilling and refining installations but as the effect would probably have been to push Romania completely into Germany's arms, these plans were never put into operation. There still remained the theoretical possibility of blocking the Danube. In April 1940, British experts disguised as sailors were supposed to sail up the Danube in boats laden with dynamite which they would then sink at the right spot; but the experts were detected and arrested by the Romanian authorities.

Even had this audacious plan succeeded, the Reich would still have had the oil from the Caucasus accruing to them by the trade agreement with the Russians. In January 1940, Daladier asked for various schemes to be investigated: the possible interception of oil-tankers in the Black Sea, direct intervention in the Caucasus and a liberation movement on behalf of the inhabitants of the Caucasus. It was finally decided to bomb the oil wells; this scheme seems to have been approved both by the British and the French, including Daladier, Reynaud, Gamelin, Weygand and even Vuillemin. But the execution of the plan was to be entirely in French hands.

Since Groznyy-Maikop was too far, it was decided that the raid should be made on Baku and Batum and include refineries, storage-tanks, harbour installations and railway lines. The first problem was one of distance; take-off airfields could certainly be found comparatively nearby, in Turkey and Iraq, but the chances of being able to use them were slight. This would mean that bases would need to be built from scratch in the 'duck's-bill' of Jezireh, in Syria, 400 miles from the targets, an area of sweltering heat in summer. The second problem was, of course, the question of aircraft. Since the American bombers which were going to equip the Near

Eastern Air Corps had a maximum range of rather less than 900 miles, it would be necessary to convert French transport aircraft.

Once these preliminary tasks had been completed, what could the operation be expected to achieve? According to General Chassin not only were the most whimsical calculations made, they were actually accepted. The raid was to take place at night, at 16,000 feet, and, despite the absence of aerial photographs, it was assumed that the concentrated nature of the target would enable every bomb to hit its mark. Thus with 117 aircraft—which, by the way, had not yet arrived in the Near East by April 1940—carrying 325 tons of bombs of just over 100 pounds apiece, it was hoped to stop the flow of oil from Baku within a fortnight. It was estimated that it would take the Russians six months to make good the damage. Even Douhet would hardly have been so optimistic.

However, there were other problems, this time of a diplomatic nature; the aircraft would have to fly over Turkey, who was determined at all costs not to come into conflict with the Russians: so Turkey's airspace would have to be violated, thus arousing her animosity at the very moment when she was the keystone of schemes for a Balkan front.[1] As for the USSR, a neutral power which would be suffering attack without warning in one of her vital regions, nobody seemed to be worried about her possible reactions, not even if they were to take the form of bombing in the Near East. The pleasant assumption seemed to be, on the contrary, that having received this sharp warning, Russia would withdraw into her shell and abandon Germany to its fate.

The 'Caucasus operation' never even began to get off the ground; one single French reconnaissance plane flew over Baku! Yet it was the most significant of all the hare-brained schemes in which fantastic targets were going to be struck at by the most pitiful means. It revealed the firm belief in the inherent weakness of the USSR. It was also evidence of the mixed feelings of hatred for the Russians and the Germans, prevalent amongst the French political leaders since the German-Soviet pact, feelings supported in part by public opinion.[2] The Finnish war provided the opportunity for another manifestation of the same attitude.

1. Turkey also controlled the railway line leading to the Jezireh 'duck's-bill'.
2. According to General Larminat (*Chroniques irrévérencieuses* p. 37–40), General Weygand said to him, after the German-Soviet collusion: 'Now all the swine are on the same side.' Germans and Russians both took the projected operation seriously: even today Soviet historians attribute far greater manpower and strength to the Near East Expeditionary Force than it ever possessed.

IX ALLIED PLANS IN SCANDINAVIA

Just as petrol was needed to keep engines running, so steel was necessary to manufacture armaments. And the Reich produced very little more iron ore than oil. Its ore was obtained from Sweden and it was of particularly high quality. The iron magnate Thyssen who, after helping Hitler to power had quarrelled with him and was now living in France, was confident that without Swedish iron, Germany was doomed to lose the war; he said that he had warned Hitler and Goering of this. Coming from such a pundit, such a categorical statement commanded respect and called for action: the 'iron-supply route' must be cut as well as the oil-supply route. This time the British showed greater keenness than for their allies' Balkan or Caucasian schemes; the point was that in winter, when the Baltic was frozen, the Swedish iron ore was shipped by rail to the Norwegian port of Narvik, which was clear of ice. From there, it was taken by freighter to Germany via Norwegian territorial waters, something which was anathema to the British who wanted complete control over the whole of the North Sea. As early as September 1939 Churchill had proposed laying mine-fields along the Norwegian coast—but the danger was that Norwegian boats would be the first to suffer. Next, the British government had put pressure on Sweden to stop exporting iron ore via Narvik. They promised Britain's help should the Germans turn nasty and had suggested preliminary talks which the Swedes had declined, being anxious to preserve their neutrality.

The attack on Finland threw a new light on the matter. The Soviet Union was banned from the League of Nations and vilified by world opinion everywhere; certain French right-wing newspapers attacked her as if it was she who had become the true enemy of France. In France the Communists had to pay the price for the popular outcry; the party was dissolved, its press shut down, its leaders arrested or interned. Anxious to keep public opinion happy, Daladier saw that help to Finland could be the means of proving his aggressiveness and determination as well as of 'cutting the iron supply route'. It might be thought that it would be difficult for Norway and Sweden to refuse to help Finland; moreover, they would legally be covered by the League of Nations decision.

On December 19 Daladier prevailed on the Supreme Interallied Council to go to Finland's help, with the co-operation of Norway and Sweden. In fact, at the beginning of January, Sweden agreed to allow free passage over her territory of war materials intended for the Finns and even of 'technicians' provided they were volunteers travelling privately. But she refused to take any part in the conflict.

On March 2 the situation of the Finns seemed desperate. A further Franco-British approach was made to Oslo and Stockholm. If Finland were to ask for troops, the Allies would be prepared to send her them. Since the consent of Sweden and Norway was taken for granted, the Allies promised that they would support them against any possible German threat. Daladier told the Consul General Nordling that France could send 50,000 men to help Finland, via Narvik. The operation would begin on March 15, timed to coincide roughly with the bombing of Baku. The French even thought of landing in Finland, at Petsamo, but the British were opposed to this as it would certainly bring about a complete break with the Soviet Union. It was clear that as far as they were concerned, helping Finland was an excuse and an opportunity to obtain a solid foothold in Scandinavia.

Both Norway and Sweden were agreed in not accepting the Allied proposals. But Norway hinted that, while protesting in principle, she would put up only token resistance to any initiative the British might take on her territory. The Swedes' refusal was firmer. On March 12, the British made one final attempt to be granted right of passage; but on that same day, Finland accepted the Soviet terms.

The Allies had adopted a peripheral strategy that was logical in view of their inferiority: in doing this they would divert the enemy's effort from the one field of operation where it might be able to force a decision: France. But their Finnish operation was just as makeshift as the air raid on the Caucasus. Had not one British transport expert who went out to Sweden pointed out that Norway's and north Sweden's railway links could easily be cut, thus rendering the situation of any expeditionary force advancing into Finland completely untenable? In northern Europe, as in the Near East, the Allied plans had been dictated by the desire to weaken the German economy. Surely this was the only way for them to take the initiative in the only operational theatre where their superiority was obvious, namely at sea.

X THE WAR AT SEA. THE BLOCKADE

Franco-British naval co-operation had been worked out as early as May 1939, on a very flexible basis. The oceans and the seas bordering on Europe had been divided into operational zones depending on one or other of the two Admiralties. But these zones were not rigidly fixed and on several occasions they were modified by joint agreement. In addition, forces of one or other of the two countries passed under the command of its ally—the French 'X Force' of Admiral Godfroy in Alexandria, for example, under the command of Admiral Cunningham. Finally, any joint operations were handled by the two Admiralties concerned.

The Allied navies faced an immense task. They had to try to maintain a blockade of Germany and they had to protect their own merchant navies against enemy pirate ships and submarines.

The British government, overestimating the needs of the German war effort, anticipated that the enemy stocks of fuel and raw materials would be rapidly exhausted. As a result, they attached great importance to the naval blockade which would prevent these stocks from being replenished. However, during the 'phoney war', the methods adopted were still based on the experience of the 1914–18 war. Attempts were made to prevent Germany's neutral neighbours from becoming German warehouses by persuading them, in a friendly manner, to agree not to import produce that might be intended for Germany in greater quantities than usual. But the neutrals were only relatively amenable; Holland showed herself particularly recalcitrant.

On the other hand, apart from the fact that the German-Soviet agreement had opened a large gap in the blockade, the British were handling Italy gently in order to keep open a chance of wooing her away from Germany. As early as October 1939, they agreed to let her make considerable purchases abroad; they even supplied her with coal and raw materials. Even more, Italian violations of the blockade were dealt with very half-heartedly; in March 1940, 82 per cent of the cargoes held on suspicion were returned to their owners and big Italian firms were granted permission to increase the size of their purchases.

In these circumstances, the blockade could hardly be very effective. On March 4, 1940, Goering boastfully assured Sumner Welles that there would never be any famine in Germany; 'many school buildings and halls were piled roof-high with grain'. He did, however, confess to a slight shortage of raw materials—until such time as they could be obtained from the newly-won former Polish provinces or bought from the European countries which Germany now had in tow, after her victories. At roughly the same time, for Mussolini's benefit, Ribbentrop was painting in Rome a picture of the inhabitants of Berlin 'who had been shivering with cold during the winter'. But for the moment these difficulties were not producing any discontent on the part of the people or any fall in industrial production. If the blockade were going to prove effective one day, that day was still far off.

For its own part, the German Navy was not dealing Allied shipping any devastating blows, either. It is true that its pirate ships had caused some losses: the *Graf Spee* had sunk nine ships in the south Atlantic before three British cruisers had forced her to scuttle herself off Montevideo. In the spring of 1940, the German Navy despatched nine raiders, including six auxiliary cruisers, as far afield as the Pacific and the Indian Oceans to undertake operations which met with varying success—the *Hipper,* for example, sent sixteen ships to the bottom in the area round the Azores but was damaged and had to return home. More than by the losses they were inflicting on the British Merchant Navy, these pirate ships were a nuisance to the Royal Navy by obliging it to hunt them down and thus disperse their ships all over the world.

There were few German ocean-going submarines in September 1939: barely twenty-seven, of 500 to 700 tons. Lurking on the sea-routes which converged on the British harbours each side of Ireland meant covering vast distances, since the Straits of Dover were closed by an anti-submarine barrier; so they found it difficult to sail further than the fifteenth meridian and were never able to operate in force. The British Admiralty was content to operate as in 1918: convoys were escorted slightly beyond the fifteenth meridian. The submarines were located by means of ASDIC,[1] a device transmitting an ultra-sonic wave under water and picking up the echo sent back by any object: it was an accurate instrument but only up to a distance of ten miles. The anti-submarine weapon was a depth charge of some 300 pounds.

But the British were short of escort vessels and aircraft equipped with radar capable of dropping depth charges. Here again, they were relying on their experience of 1914–18, when aircraft rarely sank submarines; some had even been shot down by them. The advantage of aircraft was, however, in making the submarine exhaust its oxygen supply by forcing it to remain submerged. The British started to use their aircraft-carriers and this led to the first duels between aircraft and submarines. German submarines damaged a battleship in Scapa Flow, a great feat, and sank almost 410,000 tons of merchant shipping in 1939—a smaller number than the British naval shipyards built over the same period; in retaliation, only nine submarines were sunk.

But the chief innovation in naval warfare during this time was when, from November 1939 onwards, the Germans started dropping magnetic mines by parachute: when a ship passed over the mine, lying at a depth of some five to eight fathoms, the mass of metal caused the mine to explode. The Thames was soon dotted with them. Their secret came to light when one of them was recovered from a mud bank, and ships' hulls were then

1. Allied Submarine Detection Investigation Committee.

demagnetised. Here again the Germans had shown the initiative. This
new device cost Allied shipping some 200,000 tons in 1939.

If we add that the German aircraft attacks on shipping forced the British to concentrate their naval forces and Merchant Navy off the west coast
of the British Isles, we are forced to the conclusion that, even at sea, where
they were indisputably stronger, the Allies had not succeeded in establishing a clear advantage during the seven months following the defeat of
Poland.

XI THE PHONEY WAR

These seven months had been nicknamed the 'phoney war'[1] because the
French civil population had the impression of a long period of waiting
for nothing to happen except a few private skirmishes in the No Man's
Land on the north-eastern frontier and a large number of futile air-raid
warnings. It had been a hard winter and if the nation's wealth seemed un-
affected, a large number of families where conscription had taken its toll
were financially embarrassed—only civil servants were having their pay
made up. The population was living in fear of air raids which, as a result
of a great deal of intense pre-war propaganda, either from pacifists or to
boost the Air Force, were expected to cause a holocaust; the air-raid warning system was working badly and the sirens often dragged urban dwellers
out of their beds for nothing. Cellars had been fitted up as air-raid
shelters under the direction of *concierges;* works of art had found refuge
in country houses; monuments were sandbagged; people walked about
with First World War gas-masks slung over their backs. More as a warning
than as a necessity, rationing of certain commodities had begun. In order
to maintain production in the armament factories, certain skilled jobs had
been made into 'reserved occupations', whereby the workers continued to
exercise their trade, at their normal rates of pay, often working at home;
the discrepancy in comparison with men who had been mobilised, as
well as the fact that some 'reserved occupations' were unjustified, bred
jealousy and bad feeling. Between fear of the future and the drab empti-
ness of the present, an insidious feeling of resignation or irritation grew
up, instead of a will to action.

The public were thirsty for news and they wanted it to be sensational.
So wild rumours spread. In the press there was strict censorship, every-
one listened to foreign broadcasts and, particularly, to 'the traitor from
Stuttgart', Ferdonnet, the spokesman of the skilful German propaganda

1. In French, *'la drôle de guerre'.*

machine, with the plausible leitmotif that France had been dragged into war by perfidious Albion and that the English would fight to the last Frenchman. The French government had formed their own propaganda machine, led by the subtle diplomat and novelist Jean Giraudoux, surrounded by a team of brilliant men—rather remote perhaps from the simple ideas and language of the mass of the people.

In the armed forces, the state of permanent inactivity relieved only by futile training exercises was slowly undermining morale. The commanders were aware of this and very properly attached great importance to the fair allocation of leave and to sport, theatre or film shows to alleviate the enforced leisure. Gradually, however, everyone was beginning to wonder just how necessary this war was, especially as, although it had been declared, it had not yet broken out. People were hoping against hope that, by some kind of miracle, it might come to an end before it really began perhaps by their opponents being starved out by the blockade or collapsing through internal dissension. Every night aircraft were unloading, not bombs, but tons of pamphlets on the sleeping Germans.

It was impossible for the politicians not to be infected by this feeling of lassitude and uncertainty amongst the people. Thus there grew up, not a peace *party* but a trend towards peace, unorganised yet heartfelt, with Pierre Laval as its spokesman in the Senate. The ambitious schemes in the Caucasus and in Finland had been partly conceived to whip up public opinion, and give the impression that the war had really started without disturbing anyone's peace of mind, because the operations were both remote and relatively trivial. Another facet of this disappointing Allied strategy was the attempt to disorganise the internal authority of the Nazis.

The fact is, the British believed in this more strongly than the French. On two occasions at least, Chamberlain stated solemnly that Britain was not waging war on the German people. He is reported as having said to his biographer, Sir Keith Feiling: 'What I am hoping for is not a military victory—I doubt very much if it is possible—but the collapse of the German home front.'

Thus numerous attempts were made to approach what was assumed to be the opposition to Hitler. The fact that no one ever really discovered what it was only made people try harder, so to speak, to invent it. Contacts were made in Berne, in Arosa (with the ambassador Ulrich von Hassel), in Lausanne-Ouchy (with the former Chancellor Wirth) and in the Vatican. The only semi-official contact took place by an indirect exchange of letters between the Secretary of State in the Foreign Office, Sir Robert Vansittart, and the Mayor of Leipzig, Goerdeler. The British government declared, almost in so many words, that it would be prepared to make concessions over colonies to a new German government but not to

Hitler. But the 'German opposition' proved rather shadowy. After all the successes that he had achieved, Hitler had quite definitely rallied the German people behind him.

XII THE NEUTRALS

Hitler's successes, added to the confession of failure shown by the lack of activity on the part of the Allies, could only arouse fear, or even admiration, for the Nazi Reich in the hearts of the neutrals. It was true that they all felt that no final decision had been reached as long as the Wehrmacht and the French Army had not come to grips. But meanwhile Romania, Yugoslavia, Turkey, Norway, Sweden, Belgium and Holland clung desperately to neutrality, thus playing into Hitler's hands.

A few dissentient voices could indeed be heard in the camp of the natural friends of the Axis. Hungary, through its regent Horthy, had been troubled by the German-Soviet pact: 'If Germany were to weaken, the way would be open to revolution.' The German decisions as to Slovakia had deprived the Hungarians of any hope of expanding in that direction; the German desire to avoid any disturbance in south-east Europe provided a curb on Hungary's eagerness to regain Transylvania from Romania. So the Hungarians were dissatisfied and Count Teleki made no secret of his mistrust of the Reich. But Henrik Werth, the chief of general staff, was openly germanophile. In any case, if the worst came to the worst, the Hungarians might try to come to some arrangement with the Italians but never with the Allies.

Similarly, since the German-Soviet pact Japan seemed to be taking a malicious pleasure in falling in with British wishes concerning the blockade, so much so that the German ambassador in Tokyo wrote that Japan was offering better terms to England than to Germany. But the first round that everyone was waiting for would not be fought in the Far East.

In Europe, the only current theatre of war, the hint of a crisis between Germany and Italy had been overcome; but in April 1940, Serrano Suñer, Franco's Foreign Minister and strong man of the régime, informed the German ambassador, von Stöhrer, of his belief that 'the moment Italy entered the war, Spain would also have to decide on her attitude'. And he was already hinting at what might be the possible spoils of such an intervention: Gibraltar and Tangier.

As for the United States, she was slowly beginning to emerge from her inertia and indifference to European problems. True, Roosevelt, whom his Secretary of the Treasury Morgenthau called the 'keenest and boldest democrat of his age', could clearly see the danger which the Nazis presented for democracy and civilisation in the American sense, but he knew that he could do nothing without the support of public opinion. His advisers were themselves divided: Morgenthau and Ickes were thoroughly anti-Nazi and were doing all they could to facilitate the purchases made by the French mission in the United States. But the Secretary of State, Cordell Hull, although also an anti-Fascist, was unwilling to appear to be provoking the totalitarian states. The Secretary of War, Woodring, was a confirmed isolationist.

Overall, the Americans certainly wanted Britain to win but most of them failed to assess or realise the extent of the danger facing her. Some of them were even inconvenienced by the measures necessitated by the blockade: American ships had to put into British ports in order to be checked and this gave rise to complications and delays in their business dealings with Europe.

The United States had as yet no European policy and did not associate her lot with Europe's in any way. The war seemed to her the logical result of blunders committed by Europe, above all by France, after the First World War, amongst the first of which was the failure to pay war debts. Some sectors of the population of Jewish or Polish origin had indeed been roused by the Nazis' anti-Jewish measures and the subjugation of Poland; there were numerous refugees, some of them completely destitute. But these stirrings had not as yet made any impact on the collective consciousness of the American people.

However, as early as September 1939, Roosevelt had declared a state of pre-emergency. In November, he persuaded Congress to pass the 'Cash and Carry' bill allowing belligerents to buy equipment from America on condition that they paid for it and took it away themselves. Only France and Great Britain were able to do this. It was a first infringement of neutrality and acceptable because it kept business turning over; but it was stripping the Allies of their gold reserves.

CHAPTER 3

The War in Norway

THE Allies could not hope for very much from a blockade riddled with gaps; so, if it could hardly be expected to shut off the flow of Caucasian oil, might it not at least be possible to cut the supply route of Swedish iron? As for Hitler, the Finnish war had revealed to him the strategic importance of Scandinavia. The stage was set for a race between the opposing sides: the goal was Narvik.

I THE OPPONENTS' PLANS

On the military level, there is a striking parallel between the German and Allied preparations for a Norwegian operation: each wanted to forestall the other.

On March 28, the Allied Supreme Interallied Council decided to demand that Sweden stop exporting iron ore to Germany, to lay mines in Norwegian territorial waters and to send an expeditionary force to Norway which it was hoped to land without difficulty with the tacit agreement of the Norwegians. Churchill and Reynaud had engineered this decision and even carried Chamberlain with them since, according to Churchill, the latter suddenly became an enthusiastic supporter of the offensive.

All the same, the French and British did not quite see eye to eye. The French primarily emphasised the importance of the iron traffic via Narvik, the British were more interested in the Baltic theatre of operations. Now that the Baltic was about to thaw out, the British would have liked to bomb the shipping concentrated in the German Baltic ports; but the French were afraid of bombing reprisals which would hinder their rearmament effort.

On April 5, similar notes were delivered by the two Allies in Oslo and Stockholm; they showed obvious embarrassment because they had to justify the violation of a neutral state; this is why the arguments put forward may seem surprising. Attention was drawn to the possibility of a further attack by the Soviet Union on Finland, in order to obtain bases in Norway—no doubt the Allies wanted to exploit the feelings aroused in Scandinavia by the Finnish-Soviet war but for the Scandinavians their enemy seemed the Soviet Union, not Germany. On April 8, another note informed Norway of the mine-laying in her territorial waters, an operation that had started three days earlier.

In theory, the Allied Expeditionary Force was ready: it was the one that had been intended to go to the help of the Finns. There should have been no problem about shipping it since the Allies had command of the seas. In fact, there was a shortage of specially equipped units and the British had to call on one of their BEF divisions in France. According to the French commander, the whole thing was a makeshift operation; there was poor co-ordination between the Allies.

As a result, there were delays which the Germans were able to turn to advantage. In concentrating on his scheme for a decisive offensive against the west, Hitler had over a long period been determined to respect the neutrality of Scandinavia. The Kriegsmarine, the service most closely involved, were divided on the subject. Admiral Raeder was convinced that a British action was imminent and must be forestalled but the 'Operations Division' feared that unilateral action on the part of Germany, which would make Norwegian territorial waters an operational area, might result in greater difficulties for German shipping in using them as extensively as it was now doing under cover of their neutrality—a practice which had become universally known when the British Navy challenged the tanker *Altmark* which was carrying British prisoners of war. According to the German admirals, it was this incident that convinced Hitler of Anglo-Norwegian connivance and made him decide to act.

But he had taken his decision for three reasons which he confided to Mussolini on April 18. Militarily it was necessary to prevent Britain from spreading the war into the Baltic; should she succeed in doing this, it would be impossible for Germany to continue her counter-blockade of the British Isles in the North Sea and the Atlantic. On the other hand, large bases could be set up in Norway which would enable the Luftwaffe practically to exclude the Royal Navy from using the North Sea.

Economically, it was impossible for Germany to manage without a regular supply of Swedish iron ore; and if British power were established in Norway, how long would Sweden be able to withstand her pressure? Moreover, depriving Britain of Danish foodstuffs and Scandinavian raw materials was a counter-blow of some importance.

Finally, there were ideological considerations. Rosenberg, the upholder of Nazi philosophy, was the 'patron' of a 'Nordic Association' intended to bring together all pure Aryans. He had under his wing a Norwegian by the name of Quisling, leader of the *Nasjonal Samling*, a tiny Norwegian Fascist party which wanted to link Norway and Germany in a large 'German-Scandinavian community'. Quisling had received funds from

Rosenberg, large enough to publish 25,000 free copies of each number of his paper; his party had sympathisers in the Norwegian Army and administration; he had set up an intelligence organisation which was working for the Reich, and the Germans had thereby discovered how useful it was, as the ambassador Brauer emphasised, 'to be collaborating with a political movement whose members are acting for reasons of conviction rather than with paid agents who are more easily detected'; and who cost more, anyway. Hitler had thought Quisling interesting enough to be worth meeting in the autumn of 1939, although he had made no promises nor disclosed any secrets. But on December 15, 1939, Hitler, backing up Rosenberg, dictated a minute emphasising the need to create 'a Greater German Federation of States'.

However, Hitler's conceited statement to Mussolini that 'he had left the Allies at the post' because he had learnt of their intentions through Churchill's and Reynaud's indiscretions and that, thanks to his outstanding qualities of mind 'the outcome of the war had perhaps been settled within the space of ten hours', was merely a boast. In fact, he had ordered the possibilities of operations in Norway to be investigated as early as January 1940. On March 1, he had issued his directives for the 'Weserübung operation', the occupation of Denmark and Norway, and on April 2, he ordered their execution. The Germans were the first to arrive in Norway because they had a start of a few days. But this short start was to upset the Allied plans completely and put them in an unexpectedly awkward situation.

II THE OCCUPATION OF DENMARK

Both for the Wehrmacht and Wilhelmstrasse the occupation of Denmark passed off without a hitch; it took place in the twinkling of an eye. Launched on April 9 before sunrise, four hours later the operation was all over. Whilst one armoured column crossed the Jutland frontier, paratroops were being dropped and ships were landing commandos at various strategic points, even in the very centre of Copenhagen. As he got up that morning, the King was handed the thirteen-point ultimatum from the German minister, von Renthe-Finke. At 6 a.m., after a dramatic session, the Danish Cabinet accepted the ultimatum and the King ordered his guard, which had been resisting the German patrols, to lay down their arms. At 8 o'clock, the bewildered Danes heard a German officer reading out on the radio an appeal from Hitler—written by the officer himself since by some mistake he had been handed the message intended by the Führer for use in Norway.

The Danes had been completely taken by surprise. It would seem that the government, made up of a radical-socialist coalition, although anti-Nazi in its views, had given no heed to the alarming reports emanating from their naval attaché in Berlin. In any case it could hardly have done anything, except prolong the fighting in order to save face—but at the sacrifice of human lives.

Under protest, the Danish government therefore agreed to 'place its neutrality under the protection of the Germans'. The Germans had thus completely achieved their aim, which was a peaceful occupation. Their troops were ordered not to interfere in the administration of the country, except in case of dire necessity; strict measures had been taken to ensure that there would be no looting or even excessive purchases of commodities on the part of the soldiers. The German government guaranteed the integrity of Danish territory; consequently, the German minority in Schleswig had been strictly advised not to indulge in any action of a provocative nature or in any victory celebrations and to behave with complete propriety towards the Danish authorities—they were not yet 'liberated'.

The Danish economy was to be entirely integrated with that of the Reich, which would supply limited quantities of coal and fuel. It was agreed that Danish industry should work 'indirectly' for the Reich, in 'friendly co-operation'. The maintenance of law and order and stable prices was declared to be 'highly desirable' by the two parties. In Denmark the German authorities seem to have perfected the methods adopted in their occupation of the western European countries which they conquered, with the one exception that on this occasion the occupation costs fell on the Reich, although the Danish National Bank did agree to advance the necessary amount in kronen. But the occupation soon showed its other face—the face of the Nazi Third Reich; as in Poland, from May onwards, ss units started to move into Denmark, following in the footsteps of the Wehrmacht 'in search of volunteers so as to interest them in the idea of a Germanic community'. A 'Danish National Socialist Party' immediately asked for representation in the government. For the moment it was not included in the unified coalition cabinet formed by the King from the four main traditional parties. So Denmark would still be running her own affairs, at least in appearance. Anxious to appear willing, the government even announced its 'full understanding and co-operation'. But Nazi Germany was holding other cards up its sleeve—*Volksdeutsche* in Schleswig, local Nazis—which she would be able to play when the need arose.

III THE OPERATIONS IN NORWAY

Events followed a very different course in Norway because the German troops landed there had to fight a force composed of French and British and also because the Norwegian authorities preferred fighting and exile to submission.

The speed of the Germans took the Allies by surprise. Whilst the first mines had been laid on April 5 and the British began embarking their troops on the 7th, on that same day the squadron under the command of Admiral Lutjens, whose movements had escaped detection by the RAF, put detachments ashore in the chief Norwegian ports. The German forces were not very considerable: seven cruisers, fourteen destroyers and about 10,000 men; at no point were more than 2,000 men landed initially. A parachute battalion had seized the Oslo and Stavanger aerodromes. But the decisive factor was the German Air Force, which terrified the Norwegians and was to paralyse the Allied counter-attacks.

Although lagging somewhat behind, the Allies had at least partly achieved one of their aims: they were engaging German forces in a remote theatre of operation. Were they going to take advantage of this to seize the initiative in Belgium, the main scene of operation? Admiral Darlan strongly supported this idea and suggested that the Allied troops should cross into Belgium if possible with the agreement of the Belgians but, if necessary, without it. But the government could not agree to violate Belgian neutrality. On April 9 another urgent appeal was thus made to the Belgians emphasising their 'weighty responsibilities'. General Gamelin pointed out that, given time, he could still move the bulk of his forces up to the Albert canal. He emphasised that it was a suitable moment, since the Luftwaffe was tied down in Norway. But once again the Belgians replied in the negative, and the Dutch followed suit. At this point, the French government's short-lived desire for action faded. Gamelin's only decision was to go to the aid of the Dutch, should they be attacked, whether the Belgians agreed or not. For the moment, the only result of the emergency was that, once again, Belgian troops manned the frontier facing France, since it was from that side that danger of invasion threatened!

It seems likely that the Allies had thus relinquished their last chance of taking the initiative and conducting the defensive battle that they desired in the most favourable circumstances: they were now reduced to conducting their first military operations in Norway but not in the circumstances they would have chosen. For one thing, instead of landing unopposed, they were forced to attack an enemy already established; for another, they were obliged to modify their plans; whereas they had intended to operate only in Narvik, they had to come to the help of the Norwegians, now under attack, and had to move the bulk of their landing forces into central Norway.

Nor was Allied co-ordination very good. The coalition lacked a permanent controlling body that could make decisions and ensure that they were carried out. Each government made known its views to the other at meetings of the Supreme Council, which were inadequately prepared and too infrequent. All that had been arranged was that, since the Norwegian sea area was the preserve of the Royal Navy, the expedition was under British command, overall control would thus be in the hands of a British admiral and, consequently, the expeditionary force would be under an English general.

It would seem that, at the start, the British Admiralty committed the blunder of seeing the whole operation with blinkers. It was obsessed by the idea of destroying the German squadron that had incautiously ventured within its reach. While the main British force was off Bergen, instead of trying to make a landing which at that time might have enabled the town to be recaptured, the Admiralty gave the order to seek out and destroy the enemy cruisers—thus losing the opportunity of intercepting the troop-carrying vessels, which were of minor importance in their eyes. This decision, which involved abandoning a military expedition that had been carefully prepared, was taken, according to Mr Derry, by the British Admiralty alone, which probably means by Churchill.

In fact, the only major naval battle took place in the north, in the Narvik fjord, where on April 13, the battleship *Warspite* pursued and disabled ten German destroyers. It was a good beginning but a shortlived triumph. Later, the English learned by bitter experience one important new lesson of this war, namely that the best armed warship was an easy victim for aircraft and that it was pointless to have mastery of the seas if you did not have mastery of the skies at the same time.

To avoid endangering its ships, the British Admiralty abandoned the idea of a landing at Trondheim and replaced it by landings to the north and south at Namsos and Aandalnes, points not occupied by the Germans; however, they had to be abandoned a fortnight later as a result of heavy Luftwaffe attacks, against which the troops which had been put ashore had no defence.

The struggle in Norway, wrote Admiral Barjot, became one between 'Britain, a maritime power almost without aircraft and an air power supported by weak naval forces'. The British had too few planes—their heaviest raid comprised a hundred aircraft whereas the Germans had sent a thousand to Norway. Their planes often proved inferior to their opponents', with the exception of the Hurricane fighters. Above all, the conditions were uneven: the German Air Force was home-based on well-equipped Norwegian aerodromes; the British aircraft had to come from at least 300 miles away; providing them with intelligence required many hours of flying time with the result that the intelligence (when it reached them) was often out of date. Moreover, the area covered was immense. It was a task that only naval aircraft could have undertaken successfully but all aircraft-carriers except one were in the Mediterranean.

Until they arrived, it was necessary to make do with makeshift airfields in Norway. But no provision had been made to protect the engines against the cold, the only remedy being to keep them running all the time; the aircraft had to be refuelled with jugs and buckets and as a result, patrols could not always take off when required. When the *Ark Royal* and the *Glorious* arrived from Alexandria on April 24, the Luftwaffe had been established for fourteen days. Thanks to the long period of daylight, aircraft were able to fly almost continuously but the aircraft-carriers proved vulnerable when they kept too close to land. The *Courageous* was sunk; the Royal Navy had now lost two out of their five aircraft-carriers since the beginning of the war.

To sum up, the RAF destroyed a few ships; it damaged a hundred or so aircraft but it lost many more itself; it failed to interrupt enemy communications; it proved unable to protect the expeditionary force that had been landed at Namsos, whose equipment was partly destroyed by Heinkels while it was still on the quayside. Reluctantly and with great difficulty, the force had to be taken off; it was a pitiful failure.

IV THE STRUGGLE FOR NARVIK

In the extreme north, however, the fight had gone better for the Allies, although not without providing some awkward problems. The first of these, unlikely as this may seem, was the rivalry between the naval and army commands of the Allied Expeditionary Force, despite the fact that both were British. They had received different orders! General Mackesy was instructed not to attempt a landing if the risk was too great; Admiral Cork, on the other hand, had been ordered to seize Narvik quickly, without counting the cost.

The first plan, hastily worked out by the Admiral, was rejected by the General, who pointed out that naval guns, with their flat trajectory, would be unable to reduce the German machine-gun nests and that since there were no proper landing craft, his men would have to be landed in open boats without protection. What is more, the ground was covered in snow and the British soldiers had not been provided with skis or snow-shoes.

French *chasseurs alpins*, better equipped, arrived at the end of April. Their commanding officer, General Béthouart, had the dual advantage over his British colleague of knowing Norway and being familiar with mountain warfare in winter. He suggested landing on the peninsulas to the north and south of Narvik. Two battalions of the Foreign Legion and two Polish battalions having arrived at the beginning of May, it proved possible to launch the attack in the night of May 27–28. At the spot chosen, the German machine guns were not protected from the British naval guns. The operation was successful; Narvik was captured and its German defenders pushed back eastwards.

But the situation in France had by that time become catastrophic. As a result the victorious troops were taken off from June 2 to 7. The operation went off without hitch, thanks to air cover helped by bad weather. But it was nonetheless a retreat. The expeditionary force had at last succeeded in providing itself with a well-equipped airfield, with wire-mesh landing strips and camouflaged shelters! But these efforts had all been in vain.

V THE NORWEGIAN RESISTANCE

The German victory was, in fact, complete. Contrary to Paul Reynaud's clarion call, the 'iron-supply route' had not been cut. But their military victory had not solved the problems of the occupation and administration of Norway for the Germans.

Although Norway was economically and sentimentally linked to Great Britain—'public opinion', so ran a telegram from the German ambassador Brauer, 'is entirely on the side of the British'—nevertheless, before the German attack the Norwegian government had decided not to relinquish its attitude of neutrality. According to Brauer, the Norwegian Minister of Foreign Affairs, Koht, was irritated by Churchill's alleged offensive preparations and he called him bluntly 'an inconsistent demagogue'. All the same, it was probable, in Brauer's estimation, that merely passive resistance would be made to a British landing. But the Germans had arrived first. How were the Norwegians going to react?

It was a hostile response, above all because of Hitler's psychological error in allowing Quisling to come to power, despite the continual warnings of Brauer who had long been emphasising that Quisling's party had no great following and its leader no political influence. On the morning of April 9, Brauer handed the Norwegian Premier an ultimatum; the latter took his time in replying and finally rejected it. In the ensuing confusion in Oslo, Quisling seized power, made a broadcast appeal denouncing all resistance to the aggressor and tried to paralyse the mobilisation of the Norwegian army to the best of his ability. Militarily, he had thus rendered good service to the Germans, even if the German military blamed him for some of his rather muddled measures—he had not been informed of their intentions. But politically he was a failure; he had formed a makeshift and inexperienced government, some of whose members had not even been consulted; most of the civil servants considered him a traitor to his country and refused to recognise his authority. King Haakon, who had left Oslo, also refused to recognise him or have any contact with him.

Realising that the Germans were barking up the wrong tree, Brauer took energetic action; he too withdrew his recognition from the Quisling government; he even had guards posted in front of the Ministry of Foreign Affairs to prevent Quisling from entering. But Hitler himself, not wishing to have anything to do with 'Marxist politicians'—the Norwegian cabinet was socialist—gave instructions from Berlin that Quisling was to remain in power and Brauer was forced to obey. As a result of his actions, he was relieved of his post.

King Haakon was certainly greatly shocked by the 'Quisling manoeuvring'; what is more the Germans had tried to kidnap him and use him as a hostage. From that moment, his decision was irrevocable and unanimously approved by his government: Norway would resist invasion; and Norwegian troops did, in fact, fight side by side with the French and the British, particularly in Narvik. As for the King, when his position in Norway had become untenable, he left with his government for Sweden and then London and a large part of the Norwegian Merchant Navy took refuge in British harbours. Norway was an example both of the legal government of a small country refusing to submit to the right of conquest and of an illegal government of collaborators trying to hold power against the will of the people, with the backing of foreign troops. The name of Quisling became synonymous with this sort of behaviour.

But this did not solve the problem of governing Norway. Seeing Quisling's inability to assert himself with his compatriots, General von Falkenhorst declared himself unable to support him, as did even the special envoy sent by Ribbentrop. As a result of this, Hitler decided to appoint a 'Reichskommissar for occupied Norway', Gauleiter Terboven, a Nazi of long standing. Contrary to what they had done in Denmark, contrary to their intentions and their own interests, the Germans had been forced into the position of governing Norway directly.

A bitter power struggle now ensued between Terboven and Quisling. As his authority was steadily being eroded, Quisling appealed to Berlin. He was ill-advised to do so, for Hitler, although offering him bouquets, turned against him. He decided that Quisling should not take over the government again until his party had become stronger; in a word, the Norwegians were being advised to become collaborators in order to put an end to the direct control of the Reichskommissar. Meanwhile, Quisling was made commissioner for demobilisation—a pure sinecure, since there had been no mobilisation. The Germans then set up a 'Directory' with the 'Norwegian Supreme Court'; but they were forced to admit that, for the Norwegians, their legal government was in London. Their political failure was patent for all to see.

Economically, however, Hitler was pleased at having brought the whole of Scandinavia into his orbit. Sweden had done nothing to help Norway; her co-operation with the Reich, under cover of neutrality, was more complete than ever. The Reich would not go short either of iron or timber.

VI CONSEQUENCES OF THE GERMAN VICTORY IN NORWAY

Diplomatically, Germany benefited from her military success; the small countries had been shown that it was inadvisable for them to oppose the Führer of the German nation. Romania took the hint and agreed to let the Germans have more and cheaper oil. The Soviet Union was glad to see the disappearance of any Franco-British threat to the northern regions of her immense territories.

Above all, although kept in the dark as to his partner's intentions until the very last moment, Mussolini showed effusive approval. He immediately cast his eyes on Croatia. Ciano refused to accept a 'special French envoy'—Pierre Laval—and on April 27 Mussolini made a very tart rejoinder to a letter from Paul Reynaud. Better still, the Duce wrote to the Führer that 'the Italian fleet had been put on a war-footing'. He called up the 1916 class on May 15; by the summer, he said, Italy would have 'two million men under arms'. In his metaphorical style, in tune with what he considered his mission, Mussolini stated that 'he could not stand by with his arms crossed while others were making history'. The defeat of Norway was the invitation to go into the kill against France.

The fact was that once again Hitler had achieved complete success in a Blitzkrieg. Another area of Europe had come under German control. Their failures had taught the Allies what were the chinks in their armour: their co-ordination was faulty; their plans were makeshift ones; they had been unable to conduct combined operations where success depended on the close co-operation of the three services; above all, their equipment had been shown to be inadequate in quantity and in quality and their air force grievously inferior. This was why the British Admiralty decided not to send naval surface units into the Skagerrak or the Kattegat, although that would have been the only way to halt the flow of German reinforcements into Norway.

The Allies had shown aggression disproportionate to their limited means and a lack of skill in using them to the best advantage: but although their failure left them rather discomforted, the final result was not entirely disastrous. The Norwegian Merchant Navy would enable them to increase both the number and the frequency of their Atlantic convoys; Iceland and Greenland, now separated from Denmark, would provide valuable sites for naval and air force bases. Above all, the German Navy had suffered such losses that it was practically impossible for it to expose its surface ships to further risk. Yet the immediate need was that the now imminent German offensive in the west should not lead to another complete victory for Germany. The replacement of Chamberlain by Churchill gave British policy a determination which had been lacking but it did not increase the size of the Allied armed forces. How would they stand up to the German onslaught? And how were they deployed to meet it?

PART II

THE DEFEAT OF FRANCE

CHAPTER 1

Plans and Forces of the Antagonists in May 1940

WE know Hitler's ideas concerning France and England because he confided them to his generals and to Mussolini. He made no attempt to minimise his personal role, which he described quite simply, 'without any false modesty, as irreplaceable'. He was 'fully aware of his gifts of intelligence and decision that were, he supposed, not to be found anywhere else. Nobody had yet achieved what he had achieved. He had led the German people to its apogee.' Having said his piece, Hitler had proceeded to give an accurate analysis of the situation and reached the conclusion that present circumstances were exceptionally favourable for a German offensive. Nothing need be feared from the USSR 'for a year or two'; Italian support was certain 'as long as the Duce was alive'; the weakness of the British Army made it 'a token force'; the superiority of the German over the French forces was indisputable, in personnel, AA, aircraft, armoured corps, anti-tank guns, artillery and the 'quality of the men'; Hitler had confided to Mussolini 'that it had been easier to boost the morale of the men than of the generals'.

But though the balance of forces was for the moment in Germany's favour, this might not always be the case. What worried Hitler was not France but 'the steadily increasing power of England—a tough opponent'. So the attack must be made at once, remembering that 'wars have always ended by the total destruction of the adversary'. Pompously Hitler delivered himself of the statement that, given the choice 'between victory and destruction, he preferred victory'. Once this decision was taken, the direction of the offensive could be seen from the map: since Germany's Achilles' heel was the Ruhr, the French and British must not be allowed to approach it; for that reason it was important to forestall them in Belgium and Holland. When Germany had won, nobody would worry whether it had violated Belgian and Dutch neutrality. At the end of these singularly cynical monologues, Hitler placed the fate of Germany firmly 'in the hands of Providence'!

Neither Mussolini, to whom Hitler had imparted some of his doubts (which he kept from his generals, particularly those concerning the hypothetical importance of the role devolving on the Luftwaffe), nor the German general staff were entirely convinced. Still impressed by the memory of the tenacity of the French and British Armies in the First World War, the commanders of the three German Army Groups in the west, von Leeb, von Rundstedt and von Bock, had expressed reservations, not to Hitler but to von Brauchitsch. Von Leeb's judgment was particularly pessimistic: 'it was impossible to hope to break England's and France's military power in such a way as to make them sue for peace.' Hitler does not appear to have been directly informed of these reservations. Von Brauchitsch timidly tried to give him some idea of their gist but retired into his shell when Hitler expressed in violent terms his dislike of being contradicted. The German generals followed their Führer.

II THE GERMAN PLANS

It remained to be decided how Belgium and Holland were to be invaded. The first plan drawn up by the OKH (*Oberkommando des Heeres*) went back more or less to the Schlieffen plan of 1914. The main role devolved on the German army's right wing, von Bock's Army Group B. After breaking Belgian resistance on the Albert canal, forty-three divisions, nine of them armoured and three motorised, would pour through towards the Somme. The limited objective was to destroy as many as possible of the enemy's armed forces to ensure a broad base for action against England whilst providing better protection for the Ruhr. But the possibility of totally destroying the whole of the French Army in one single battle never entered the German generals' heads. As von Leeb had written, France was not Poland—and, moreover, even in Poland, despite the final triumphal victory, some disturbing weaknesses had been revealed in the leadership and training of the German troops.

Barely was the plan drawn up than the critics began to let fly: some said that the French would not allow themselves to be taken in by the Schlieffen plan a second time; others pointed out that the Belgian Army was stronger than in 1914. Hitler himself, when he studied the plan on the map, was struck by the large number of natural obstacles in the way of Army Group B north of Liège. His conclusion was that it was necessary to break out both north and south of Liège; the main weight of armour could then be directed in accordance with the development of the fighting.

This modification opened up fresh possibilities. For example, as Hitler suggested to General Jodl, why should not an armoured detachment be

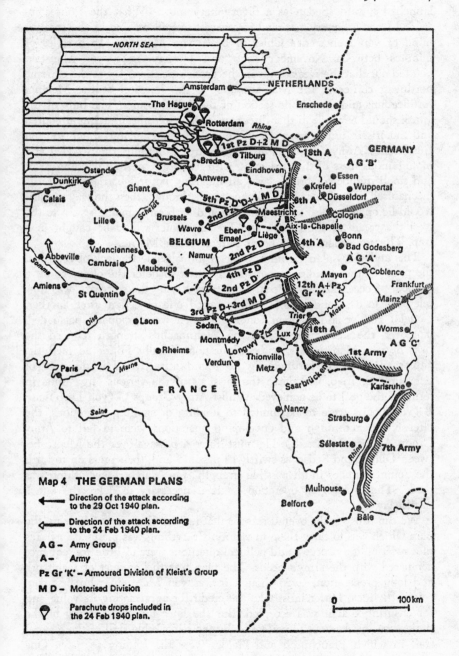

Map 4   THE GERMAN PLANS

← Direction of the attack according to the 29 Oct 1940 plan.

⇐ Direction of the attack according to the 24 Feb 1940 plan.

A G –   Army Group

A –   Army

Pz Gr 'K' – Armoured Division of Kleist's Group

M D –   Motorised Division

Parachute drops included in the 24 Feb 1940 plan.

0   100 km

launched towards Sedan as a diversionary move? What the Führer intended to be a diversion turned into a vast overall scheme in the creative mind of von Rundstedt's Chief of Staff, von Manstein. In a series of minutes between November 1939 and January 1940, von Manstein pointed out that the weak point in the French positions lay at the extreme northwest corner of the Maginot line, at the junction of the Maginot fortifications and the mobile section of the Allied armies. The bulk of the attack should be made in that direction. This would mean taking armoured and motorised units away from von Bock and giving them to von Rundstedt's Army Group A in the centre. Naturally the wooded and mountainous mass of the Ardennes, with its gorges, narrow winding roads and small number of bridges was an imposing natural barrier; but if the mechanised strike force could manage to get through, then the way to Paris would lie open—or else to the Channel and with an immense sweep to the west the cream of the British and French armies would be caught in a trap. This time there would be no miracle of the Marne.

This audacious plan would have been unrealisable for lack of time had the poor weather conditions not forced Hitler to defer the offensive on a number of occasions. Von Bock, who, from having the star part, was now relegated to a secondary role, vainly raised one objection after another. General Halder and General von Brauchitsch were gradually persuaded; moreover, the steady increase in the Wehrmacht's strength reduced the risks of von Manstein's proposed operation. Finally Hitler adopted the latter's plan, which instinctively he found attractive. His directive of February 18, 1940, laid down the missions of the various large units in terms of the goal to be achieved. Whilst Army Groups C (von Leeb) and B (von Bock) were to be limited to holding or spoiling operations, the offensive breakthrough and enveloping operations were to fall to Army Group A (von Rundstedt). He must 'force a passage over the Meuse between Dinant and Sedan as swiftly as possible' and 'then press on towards the Somme estuary in all possible strength'. On March 7, everything was ready. The Norwegian operation made it necessary to delay the attack until May 10.

We can thus see the overall reasons that led the Germans to draw up the plan which was to carry them to victory. Everything was planned in terms of a swift military success and political questions were of little consequence compared with the army's needs. The plan was the product of teamwork and long preparation. Even though it was von Manstein who first conceived the idea, Hitler must take the credit for appreciating its value and for ensuring that it was accepted. But the later intricate gearing of the project was worked out to perfection by the remarkable skill of the general staff in which Brauchitsch and Halder were the leading partners. One consequence of this sharing of tasks was that henceforth the Führer imagined himself to be a strategist of genius; the unfortunate effects of this were not to be seen until later.

The Allies had no premonition of the enemy plans whatsoever. The French Intelligence Service had certainly detected movements of units from the north to the south as well as bridging operations in the region of the Middle Rhine, measures which hardly seemed consonant with a repetition of the Schlieffen plan; but this information was submerged in a welter of other intelligence leading to different conclusions. It did nothing to make the French general staff alter its plans. On the other hand, the German command had had little difficulty in identifying and locating the French units by listening in on the communication links and decoding the French messages, since the French general staff was incautiously relying on transmission by radio.

III THE ALLIED PLANS

The Allied plans were given their final form on March 12, 1940. In theory, every eventuality was covered; the advance of the French armies would vary according to whether Belgium and Holland were attacked together or singly, while another variant depended on the speed of the enemy advance into Belgium. One thing was certain: the Allied troops would not stay in their positions to await the enemy attack; for psychological and diplomatic rather than military reasons, they would move out to meet their foe in such a way as to absorb the retreating Belgian army. It makes no difference that this scheme had been decided on by the government and imposed on the high command: the supreme commander, General Gamelin, and General Georges, the GOC on the north-eastern front, had agreed to it—the latter with some reluctance—and prepared for it after very little discussion. It was, however, a very risky scheme, first in its conception and even more so in its execution.

It had been agreed, in fact, that on the probable assumption that Belgium and Holland would be invaded simultaneously, the British forces with the Ninth and First French Armies would move up to the line assumed to be fortified by the Belgians and running from Antwerp to the Meuse via the Dyle and the Gembloux gap. The Seventh Army on the left wing was to advance much further to Breda and Zeeland, or even as far as Tilburg to provide the final link in a theoretical Franco-Belgian-Dutch front. However, the distance that this army would have to cover was 150 miles, much further than the mere 65 miles that the Germans

would require to reach the same objectives. The winner of this race therefore seemed obvious before it started.

The movements involved had indeed been carefully analysed and exact
details of the routes worked out on paper. But success depended on factors
which had not been fully assessed and on circumstances difficult to foresee. In the first place, information was lacking as to the Belgian plan of
operations—their troops, timetables and routes. Above all, the phasing of
the operation was very critical: everything depended on how long the
Belgians could hold the Germans on the Albert canal, how many troops
would be able to withdraw and how fit they would still be to fight. In any
case, the incorporation of the Belgian and Dutch forces into the Allied
coalition was bound to be a makeshift affair. Finally, the Allies were going
to risk sending their strongest forces into the plain of Belgium almost on
trust, over unknown, inadequately prepared terrain and on the assumption that it was there that the decisive battle would be fought, whereas the
von Manstein plan envisaged this as a purely secondary operation. The
Allied armies were going to be like a tree loosening its own roots in order
to fall more easily to the storm. They were going to advance towards the
enemy so as to be more rapidly encircled. In any case, for an army to
launch an offensive when it was planned and equipped for defence was, to
say the least, a wager. Did the Allies have sufficient forces at their disposal
—or did they think they had—to have any chance of winning?

IV THE GERMAN FORCES

For any valid comparison of the forces involved, we must consider not
only their total strengths but also their deployment and how it was proposed to commit them.

On May 10, the Germans had mobilised 5 million men, 3½ million of
them under arms. They had 157 front line divisions, including 12
armoured, 7 motorised and 3 ss divisions (one of them motorised). Included in this number were 2 incomplete armoured divisions armed with
captured Polish equipment and 37 infantry divisions as garrisons in occupied territory, fighting in Norway or under training. There were only
10 divisions on the ussr frontier, consisting for the most part of reserve
troops; this gives some idea of the significance of the German-Soviet pact
and of the Germans' confidence in their Russian partners.

The bulk of the German forces were thus concentrated in the west. On
May 10, the situation was: 114 divisions (this was going to rise to 137),
including 10 armoured divisions, 6 motorised divisions and 46 regular
divisions. It was far from being an entirely motorised army; it had only

120,000 lorries and, according to General Halder, it was due to receive only 1,000 lorries per month. It had been recognised that it would require the addition of 180,000 horses and the general staff deduced from this that each operation would have to be followed by a long pause, unless, of course, the armoured and motorised units were able to achieve success on their own.

The supreme commander was the Führer as head of the Wehrmacht, assisted by the *Oberkommando der Wehrmacht* (OKW), a combined services general staff under General Keitel, with General Jodl as his deputy. The ground forces were under the command of General von Brauchitsch and General Halder was in charge of its general staff, the *Oberkommando des Heeres* (OKH).

On the western front, there were three Army Group commanders. In the south, the troops manning the Siegfried line opposite Lorraine, Alsace and north Switzerland were in Army Group C, commanded by General von Leeb and comprising only 20 infantry divisions. In the north, facing Holland and north Belgium, was Army Group B, under General von Bock, consisting of some 30 infantry divisions and 3 armoured divisions.

The main striking force was thus concentrated in the centre, in Army Group A, under General von Rundstedt. He was commanding roughly 50 infantry divisions and, most important, 7 armoured and 3 motorised divisions. As we have seen, it was he who had been entrusted with the task of breaking through towards Sedan; it had been arranged that, as the fighting developed, further powerful units would be brought under his command.

V THE ALLIED FORCES

France had mobilised 5,700,000 men, 5,100,000 of whom were French. In 1939–40, 1,400,000 were allotted to 'special duties' (reserved occupations). Army units and ancillary services absorbed 2,700,000 men, plus some 100,000 foreigners—the embryonic Polish and Czech Armies. Of these, 2,240,000 were engaged in the defence of the north-western front. Every attempt had been made to avoid any dispersal of forces. There were 7 divisions guarding the Alps, 8 in North Africa and 3 in the Near East, while 3 others were still fighting in Narvik; this still left 94 divisions, plus 10 British divisions, massed against the Wehrmacht.

On paper, the Germans were thus only slightly superior in numbers; if one adds the 22 Belgian and 9 Dutch divisions to the Franco-British forces, the German numbers were even numerically inferior. But one disturbing difference was immediately visible: 3 French armoured divisions—a fourth was in the process of being formed—as opposed to 10 German Panzer divisions. Another disparity lay in their 35 regular divisions as against the Germans' 46.

The French infantry was well armed but certain units were not yet fully equipped. The artillery lacked shells heavy enough to destroy concrete defence works; half of the AA equipment was old; as for the transport, it consisted mainly of requisitioned private vehicles and its heterogeneous nature was matched by its inadequacy in numbers; horses were still the main means of locomotion. A number of large units were under strength because training had been held up for want of modern equipment. Finally, the 'B' series of units were made up of older conscripts, rather like the 'territorial' divisions in 1914. In short the 'phoney war' and the time which it had gained had been insufficient to make good the fundamental shortcomings of the French Army.

In May 1940, the English had only 1,500,000 men mobilised. The discrepancy between the French and British war efforts was blatant. The British Expeditionary Force was certainly in no way able to compensate for the inadequacies of the French. Its troops were insufficiently trained—some units had even completed their training at the front. Their equipment was incomplete and inadequate; they were short both of AA and of anti-tank weapons and of motorised and armoured units—there were only two tank battalions. The British had despatched practically all their officers and all their equipment to France, with the exception of one armoured division being formed. It was understandable that their government should be particularly concerned about its expeditionary force—it was the only force it possessed.

How were the Allied troops commanded? Even the French forces had no single supreme commander-in-chief. General Gamelin was in command of the land forces; in addition, as chief of the national defence staff, his duties were confined to co-ordinating the general staffs of the three services; the Navy under Admiral Darlan, and the Air Force under General Vuillemin were practically autonomous. Combined operations were worked out by regular but slow liaison between the widely dispersed command posts of the three Commanders-in-Chief. The Supreme Commander, General Gamelin, had four areas of operations under him, although, in fact, only the north-eastern one had any real importance. He had put General Georges in command of this, together with the appropriate general staff; however, the logistical services that he needed did not come under him but under the chief of staff of Gamelin's GHQ. The net result was a tangled web of responsibilities and a dilution of authority.

Unlike the Germans, the Allies thus had no really unified command, combining authority and responsibility and clear thinking with swift execution. Moreover, as the Allies were waiting for the Germans to attack, they were obliged to take various possibilities into account and run the risk of tying down large numbers of units in areas of secondary importance at the expense of the main operational area, which would only become clearly identified after the enemy's offensive had been launched. So we find fifty-nine divisions concentrated opposite Switzerland, along the Rhine and behind the Maginot line; this Third Army Group, under General Besson, and Second Army Group, under General Prételat, were confined to a purely defensive role and were intended, in part, to be transferred as the battle developed.

The First Army Group, which had the task of advancing into Belgium, and was commanded by General Billotte, contained almost all the powerful and mobile Allied units, that is 4 out of the 5 cavalry divisions, the 3 light mechanised divisions and one of the 3 armoured divisions. But his force totalled only 41 divisions in all, 15 of them regular divisions—*fewer in fact, than those stationed behind the Maginot line*. They were far from being the equals of the German strike force intended for the breakthrough.

As for the Sedan hinge against which the Germans were proposing to exert their pressure, it was very badly defended. The solid Maginot line had been extended just short of Montmédy onwards with defensive outposts of light concrete bunkers protected by barbed wire and anti-tank ditches. At this point, which was to prove decisive, the French forces were particularly badly placed, since the French military leaders had seen the Ardennes as providing an insurmountable barrier; thus General Huntziger had stationed three divisions, one of them a regular division, at Montmédy, which was a moderately well fortified sector, but only one division, and a B class reserve division at that, inadequately equipped with anti-tank weapons, at Sedan. This was, in fact, a badly fortified sector where the bunkers which had been hastily built during the winter months were often still without any doors or firing-slits.

It is true that, once the fight was on, the Allied command could always in theory bring up reserves to plug any gap at critical points or to support any massive strategic advance. In fact, there were 25 infantry divisions (4 of them still being formed), as well as 2 armoured divisions in reserve, dispersed over a vast area extending from Rethel to Saverne and Besançon. It was intended that they would be moved to any sectors that might be threatened, but only by rail. It had been calculated that it would take four days for a unit of division-size to be assembled, entrained, transported, detrained, regrouped and brought into the line. Did not this show a complete disregard of the speed of the enemy's armoured and motorised forces and of the destructive effect of the Luftwaffe on the French rear transport communications? In other words, what were the respective resources of the antagonists in tanks and aircraft? What provisions had the French command made for resisting the battering-ram effect of the German Panzer divisions, whose success in the Polish campaign had shown that they were no figment of the imagination but a formidable war-machine?

VI ARMOURED VEHICLES

There has been passionate argument in France concerning the number, quality and method of use of armoured vehicles. As far as total numbers were concerned, the French and German experts are now more or less agreed: the quantities were roughly the same on each side; the French and British could put up 2,280 modern armoured vehicles; the Germans 2,800. But in fact in Belgium, the main operational theatre, the Wehrmacht could throw 2,600 tanks and 720 self-propelled machine guns against the Allies' mere 1,520 tanks and 750 self-propelled machine guns.

Between Dinant and Sedan, the odds were everything to nothing, because the French had no armoured vehicles facing von Rundstedt's seven Panzer divisions.

The quality of the tanks was also roughly similar in the two camps; each of them was using some old and some recent models. The Germans had four types; Marks I and II were faster than the French light tanks but inferior in weight, armament and armour. At a conference called by the Führer on February 18, 1940, it had been agreed that this type of armour could be used only against a demoralised enemy. The German Mark III was more or less the equivalent to the French D type medium tank; but the French Somua, although slightly less well armed than the German Mark IV, was faster and had a wider range of action. Finally, the French army had the B model battle tank, very heavily armoured and armed, of which the German army had no real equivalent.

So each command could bring to bear armoured vehicles roughly similar in numbers and quality, with the reservation, however, that their battle order was different; but on the other hand—and this was the crucial point —the conceptions of the use to be made of armoured vehicles were miles apart. The Panzer division was thought of as a sword, sharp as well as heavy, to be used to slice through the enemy front and turn a tactical success into strategic victory. Consequently, it enjoyed considerable autonomy in action and the other units were subordinated to it. To achieve a breakthrough, several Panzer divisions would be grouped into an armoured corps and concentrated on a narrow front; they were supported by motorised divisions and equipped with all the combat resources necessary to hold on to essential positions until the arrival of the infantry. This had been amply demonstrated in Poland.

But the French general staff, blinkered by the lessons of World War I, had not succeeded in conceiving modern warfare in this way; they had not fully come round to it even after the defeat of Poland with all its obvious lessons. It is futile to try to allocate and assess individual responsibility in this matter. Pétain and Weygand showed the way through the weight of their immense prestige, but this was no reason for Gamelin or Georges or anyone else meekly to follow their views. And Gamelin had said to François-Poncet in 1935: 'Armoured divisions are too heavy and clumsy an instrument. They may break through our lines but the lips of the wound will then close up behind them and we shall smash them with our reserves. We have a more judicious approach. *We shall use tanks as an auxiliary for the advance of the infantry.*' And he added: 'When we want to form armoured divisions, we can always collect our tanks together and make them into units.' Since that time Gamelin's ideas had not greatly changed.

So the French Supreme Commander, like his colleagues, was living in a different age from the present, which was the age of machines and speed. Whether it was a question of advancing into Belgium, moving reserves or forming armoured corps, he always thought he would have time to spare. What is more, he failed to understand the complexity, or even the real nature, of tank warfare.

The French armoured division was, in fact, conceived as a *defensive* weapon, a sort of blunt instrument to knock out any adversary who had put himself at a disadvantage, to plug a gap and to make a local gain of no great consequence for the general outcome of the battle—which, it was thought, could only be really definitely won by the infantry. So the armoured division was at the service of the infantry; it could only be committed in the framework of an army corps, on a limited terrain. It had no means of reconnaissance, no AA or anti-tank defence adequate for it to exploit its success; such a task, in the battle instructions of the French high command, would fall on the light cavalry divisions, with their self-propelled machine guns and light tanks. So the creation of armoured divisions was vitiated from the start, in its very conception; what was more, they were not ready.

At the Parliamentary Committee of Investigation, this lack of readiness was denounced again and again. General Dufieux asserted that there were no proper instructions as to their operational role and that neither their transport nor their use was properly organised. They had been assembled with elements taken from all over the place and their cohesion left much to be desired. They were refuelled by unprotected tank lorries which were unable to 'stick close to the tank' on the battlefield. The anti-tank guns were drawn by old tractors which were slower than the tanks. Radio transmission quickly became impossible as the batteries in the tanks ran down; as a result, the unit commander soon found himself unable to command his unit.

So, in tank warfare, men and ideas from 1914–18 were fighting against opponents thinking in terms of 1940. What was the situation in the air?

VII THE AIR FORCES

Here the disparity between the forces was, of itself, catastrophic. The French hoped to be able to have 1,500 operational aircraft by May 1940, 1,300 of them modern ones; but they had barely more than 1,000, of which 600 were fighters and about 100 bombers. Certainly, some of these aircraft were based on excellent prototypes, particularly the fighters; but their numbers were dramatically inadequate. Britain might have remedied much of this shortage because she had, in fact, 1,500 aircraft, most of them modern; but only 350 of them were based in France. The British government and the British high command, having despatched all their ground forces on to the Continent, intended to hold back the greater part of its air forces for the defence of the homeland. The French knew this and had accepted the situation.

On the other side, the Luftwaffe could call on more than 4,000 combat aircraft, more than 3,600 of which were on the north-eastern front—1,500 bombers, 1,000 fighters and 340 Stukas.

This potential and real disparity of forces was matched by very different ideas on how they should be used. The Luftwaffe was organised into large units—air fleets and air divisions. Part of it, entirely autonomous, had the task of seeking out and bombing enemy targets in its home territory, at the head and fount of its operations. But the tactical air force was at the disposal of the Commander-in-Chief of the armed forces to make possible close collaboration between the two services; so the armour, with tactical and other intelligence provided by air reconnaissance, could quickly receive help from fighters or dive bombers. On the other hand, the extremely powerful German flak was brought right up into the front line so that defence groups could be set up rapidly at strategic points, where there was tank fighting or a position to be held. However, the method of using the Luftwaffe was exposed to great risks; in order to achieve quick success, in accordance with the conception of the Blitzkrieg, the German Air Force was thrown into the attack against ground targets before they were sure of having complete control in the air.

The battle order of the French Air Force was, superficially, not very different from that of the Luftwaffe; one part was kept in reserve under the orders of the Commander-in-Chief of the Air Force; the other part was allotted to the various operational zones, each corresponding to that of an Army Group. But because of the obvious German superiority, the French Air Force commander was primarily anxious to avoid too rapid a wastage of his forces. Thus, day bombing was severely restricted. On the other hand, even though the British Air Force based in France, while retaining its autonomy, worked in close co-operation with the French Air Force, the larger forces stationed in Britain came under the RAF. It took longer to call on it for help, and refuelling was more difficult; consequently, its action was less effective and more spasmodic. Above all, the dispersal of aircraft between army groups made it difficult to achieve the concentration of aircraft that the course of the fighting might require; it was entirely understandable that generals commanding armies on the ground wanted nothing better than to cling to the air forces that had been allocated to them. Finally, the armoured divisions and the air force had no theory or practical means of co-operation.

The question is whether the Wehrmacht could have been beaten in May 1940. General Halder pointed out certain disturbing factors: in April 1940, only 50 modern tanks had been manufactured, while for the whole of 1940, only 3,600,000 tons of steel had been allocated for the use of the Army instead of the 6,800,000 that had been requested. For Christmas 1939, the Führer had granted, as an exceptional treat, one pair of stockings to every German woman and a tie for every German man. Future economic prospects were gloomy.

But at this moment of time there existed a German war-machine under unified command, with modern equipment and organised in such a way as to ensure inter-service co-operation, which could launch a fierce offensive whose risks and effectiveness had been carefully assessed, against an enemy coalition inferior in numbers, in tanks and, above all, in planes. This coalition was composed of four countries speaking three different languages, and their armies would have to work out their liaison on the spur of the moment on the field of battle. The Wehrmacht had the advantage of the initiative and of surprise, while the French army would leave its fortified hideouts and advance to meet it. In such circumstances, could the clash turn out to be anything else but a sledgehammer against a pin?

The Breakthrough at Sedan

I THE INVASION OF HOLLAND

ONCE the Germans had decided to direct their main thrust against Sedan, Holland moved out of the main orbit of battle. Her neutrality was still going to be violated at the request of Goering who was afraid that she might be used as an aircraft-carrier for the RAF.

The Dutch had an army of 400,000 men, short of officers, equipment and training. Half the population, the large cities and almost the whole of her industry lay between the three large rivers of the Meuse, the Waal and the Rhine. The Dutch were aware of the dangers threatening them, thanks to the intelligence supplied by their military attaché in Berlin, who had obtained it from the most reliable source possible—the Abwehr. Even before 1939, they had decided that only the vital area of the country would be properly defended; but they thought it possible to hold out there for several weeks, as the Belgians had done in the First World War. Reynders, the Supreme Commander, had even had hopes of giving battle outside this area, thus keeping open the possibility of linking with the Belgians. But the War Minister thought otherwise and when agreement with the Belgians proved impossible, Reynders was replaced by Winkelman.

The new generalissimo decided, in the event of German aggression, to abandon the north and east of the country entirely and the south in part. The Dutch Army would fight delaying actions on the Grebbe line, on the border of the provinces of Guelder and Utrecht; then it would retreat into 'old Holland' and protect it by the traditional method of flooding. The east to west movement of the Dutch forces would certainly not bring them towards the Seventh French Army which, according to the Allied plans, was coming to their help. On May 10, even before Holland had been handed the declaration of war, the German troops attacked. The Dutch had learnt what had happened in Oslo and, in expectation of parachute drops, had placed barriers on the roads and airfields; but these turned out to be not strong enough and too few in number. Thus, even though a daring surprise attack on the Royal Palace was frustrated, the German paratroops had little difficulty in seizing aerodromes around The Hague. General Winkelman succeeded in recapturing them but only by committing his reserves.

In the south, resistance became impossible after the bridges crossing the Meuse at Dordrecht and Moerdyk had fallen into the hands of German soldiers wearing Dutch uniform—some of them Dutch National Socialists trained in Germany. The disorderly retreat of the southern Dutch units towards the north and west caused a general collapse of morale. Also, German paratroops dropped over Waalhaven, close to Rotterdam, had succeeded in digging themselves in. They received reinforcements from gliders, transport aircraft and even seaplanes which landed on the Waal, in Rotterdam itself.

On May 13, the Panzer division of the Eighteenth German Army began its assault on the 'Dutch stronghold'. The night before, Winkelman had informed the Queen and her ministers that there was no chance of resisting. On May 13, Queen Wilhelmina embarked for England on a British torpedo-boat destroyer and her ministers followed suit. Like Norway, Holland would still remain in the war, together with her merchant fleet and the Dutch East Indies. General Winkelman had been given full powers to surrender when he thought fit.

On May 14, the German commander demanded the surrender of Rotterdam but the ultimatum was unsigned and rejected by the Dutch command, although the latter had decided to cease hostilities: a further ultimatum was then despatched; immediately afterwards, probably as a result of faulty liaison between the German services concerned, Rotterdam was bombed. The centre of the city became a mass of flames fanned by the wind; there were a thousand deaths and 25,000 houses were destroyed.

On May 15, at 9.30 a.m., General Winkelman ordered fighting to cease on all fronts, except in Zeeland. The promised Allied help that was expected proved illusory although the Dutch authorities had requested it in most urgent terms. General Vuillemin had not found it possible to detach one single squadron to go to the aid of the Dutch. The Seventh Army had indeed moved into Holland according to prearranged plan, occupying Walcheren and then pressing forward as far as Breda. But it was impossible to establish any link when the Dutch Army had ceased to exist and only a few small units were in fact able to join up with it. Moreover, the demolitions carried out by the Dutch had not been co-ordinated with the French advance. The Seventh Army's progress above all had to be halted because its headlong advance had jeopardised its right flank as a result of the withdrawal of the Allied troops that had moved forward into Belgium.

II THE BELGIAN FORCES AND PLANS

On May 10, the Belgian Army comprised 650,000 men, and rose to 900,000 after mobilisation. Amongst the 18 infantry divisions, there were only 6 regular ones; 2 of the cavalry divisions were motorised; there was one heavy artillery division but no tanks, little AA and only one regiment of fighter aircraft.

These troops were relying on a system of fortifications in depth. An emergency line with roads blocked or blown up ran from Antwerp to Arlon. The Albert canal position, depending on the fortification of Antwerp and Liège, consisted of fieldworks with machine-gun posts along the line of the canal, each containing two machine guns and a good 500 to 800 yards apart!

The fortified towns of Liège and Namur provided mutual support by means of a line of pill-boxes, equally rudimentary, on the left bank of the Meuse. But ever since 1930, the Belgians had thought of withdrawing to a line running from Antwerp to Namur. It was the shortest defence line; it could serve equally well as a second line of defence and as protection for a 'national stronghold', if the main French forces were committed elsewhere than in Belgium. It was this line to which the French had eventually decided to advance and had called it the 'Dyle plan'. The Belgians called it the 'kw line', after the names of the two villages at each end: Koningshoyet and Wavre. But even if flooding the Scheldt, the Lys and the Maulde might make some sectors of the 'national stronghold' difficult of access, there was no natural obstacle between Wavre-Gembloux and Namur. The Belgians had, in fact, started work in November 1939 on that part of the gap that ran from Antwerp to Louvain and had speeded it up after March 1940; two lines of pill-boxes had been built there. But they had overlooked the section between Louvain and Namur that the French were supposed to be occupying, although no previous agreement had been made with them, nor indeed any real contact. The final course of the line had not been settled until April 9. In all, on May 10, 520 pill-boxes had been built, only 20 for the British and 5 for the French; they had been planned for use by Belgian weapons and proved unsuitable for either the French or the British.

On May 10, the Belgian Army's order of battle was as follows: 4 divisions in covering positions; 12 divisions on the Albert canal; about 6 divisions could be detached for the defence of the kw line. It would seem, therefore, that the Belgian high command had not finally decided on its conduct of operations and that it was leaving its choice of defence positions open, to be modified according to the strength of the German attack, with the Albert canal defence line having the advantage of covering the whole national territory. But if there was to be a retreat, the whole Belgian Army was to withdraw into the national stronghold.

Even after the German attack, the Belgians, forced into a coalition against their will, were going to try to wage their own war. General van Overstraeten resisted any suggestion of subordinating the Belgian Army to any foreign army; it had merely been agreed, according to custom, that an Allied army fighting in any sector would incorporate the Belgian troops already in the line. Having made this concession, the Belgian command tried to safeguard the autonomy of its forces to the fullest possible extent. This gave rise to numerous misunderstandings, the first and not the least of which was caused by the behaviour of the *chasseurs ardennais*[1] who were unfortunately stationed at the very point chosen by the OKW for their breakthrough.

III THE 'CHASSEURS ARDENNAIS'

The Belgian plans included a 'K detachment', comprising one cavalry division and one division of *chasseurs ardennais*, to undertake demolition and blocking operations in the Ardennes before doubling back over the Meuse as soon as the enemy could no longer be contained; this detachment would then take up its allotted position on the KW line—that is to say, it would retreat north-westwards. The Belgians had expected a German attack in the Ardennes but they did not wish to protract the fighting there for fear of weakening the forces required for the 'national stronghold'. As a result, they were leaving this zone of operation entirely to the French.

The latter had received some warning of the intentions of their potential partners. General van Overstraeten had exchanged a few words on the subject with the French military attaché, General Laurent. But the fact was that on one hand the direction of the *chasseurs'* withdrawal made liaison with the French unit advancing to meet them impossible and on the other, General van Overstraeten had refused to disclose what demolitions were intended. Finally, the *chasseurs ardennais* had been given no orders to defend those points where demolition or blocking operations had been carried out, whereas the only way to delay the German advance was, in fact, to defend them. Acting in accordance with their orders, the Belgian *chasseurs* thus left without waiting for the French, whose morale was not a little shaken when they arrived and discovered that the allies whom they had come to help were no longer there.

1. Light infantry units.

This incident would have been of minor importance had it not happened at the exact spot where the German thrust was due to take place. For this reason, it provided the most significant example of the damage caused by the lack of co-operation between the Belgians and their allies. But it also shows that, without any consultation between themselves, they both overestimated the defensive value of the wooded mountain country of the Ardennes and underestimated the possibility of an enemy advance through that area. As General Wanty wrote: 'We were thus laying ourselves open to the biggest shock of all, being caught out intellectually.' As a start, 'being caught out' in this way completely invalidated, in the space of a few hours, all the plans laboriously drawn up in Belgium itself, by the Belgians as well as by the French.

IV THE FIGHTING IN BELGIUM

How was the link-up going to be made between the retreating Belgians and the French who were advancing to meet them? It had, of course, to be most carefully timed and its success depended on the combination of many factors. In order to cross the Ardennes—General Halder thought that the odds were ten to one against—the Germans needed to overcome with all possible speed the Belgian frontier posts. But the three bridges over the Albert canal were well defended as well as mined and the approaches to them were dominated by the impressive fort of Eben Emaël, which rose some 130 feet sheer above the canal and whose concrete defence works extended over an area of 1,000 yards by 750 yards. The whole position was all the more formidable since the Belgians had been in occupation as early as the night of May 9–10.

However, they were taken unawares by gliders which landed 300 German soldiers on the west bank of the canal, with such despatch that two bridges were captured intact. As for the fort of Eben Emaël, in the space of a few minutes a hundred or so pioneers, after landing from gliders, hurled explosive charges and bombs into its guns, against its protective covering and down its ventilation ducts. Not surprisingly these pioneers went to work swiftly and accurately, for they had previously practised the manoeuvre on a full-scale model. The fortress garrison was isolated but continued to keep the canal itself under fire. However, in the course of May 10, the Belgian forces, possibly deceived by a dummy parachute drop behind their lines, made no attempt either to recapture the bridges or to relieve the fort. On the morning of May 11, German assault parties clambered up into the fort and with explosive charges silenced the last batteries that were still firing. At noon the fort surrendered. This brilliant German exploit ushered in the Belgian campaign.

On May 12, the Belgians abandoned their positions on the Meuse and withdrew. Although harassed by Stukas, they had managed to avoid any catastrophic disaster and eight almost intact Belgian divisions took up their positions on the kw line between the Seventh French Army on their left and the British Expeditionary Force on their right. Perhaps the defensive battle planned by General Gamelin was to be fought in favourable conditions and on the positions anticipated.

Unfortunately, to enable the French operations to be carried out properly, the Belgian withdrawal should have been spread over four days whereas in fact it had taken only two. At the Gembloux gap, which was the critical sector, the French mechanised divisions were only just beginning to arrive, having been delayed because they had only started to move on the evening of May 10. It would perhaps have been wiser to withdraw to the Scheldt; but this emergency operation would have made the link-up of the Allied forces even more difficult. So battle was joined at Gembloux on May 13. Although inferior in tanks, without any good intelligence and insufficiently supported by their Air Force, the French held out, although some units, such as a Moroccan division, were thrown into battle almost immediately they arrived, and this was after forced marches. The battle was desperately hard but it finally enabled the First French Army to take up its position between Gembloux and Wavre on May 15.

Would the combined Allied forces have time to organise themselves, once having occupied their field positions? A meeting took place at Le Casteau, near Mons, between Edouard Daladier, Lord Gort's Chief of Staff, and King Leopold. Agreement was reached whereby General Billotte, commander of the First Army Group, would become the 'deputy for the Commander-in-Chief of the north-eastern front with the task of co-ordinating the operations of the Allied forces on Belgian territory'. This was not quite a single unified command but it was better than complete lack of unity and a free-for-all.

On May 15, the Germans attacked again. They were held at Louvain and at Gembloux. But in the afternoon the Allied armies received the order to disengage. They were threatened with being outflanked in the south. It was elsewhere, in the Sedan gap, that the enemy forced a decision.

V THE CROSSING OF THE ARDENNES

The Sedan sector was held by two French Armies; on the right, the Second Army under General Huntziger and on the left the Ninth Army under General Corap. The junction between the two Armies was down-stream from Sedan, where the Ardennes canal joined the Meuse.

The 'Dyle plan' had provided for the Second Army to remain where it was. Its task was the defensive one of resisting any attempt to thrust west-wards round the Maginot line. As for the Ninth Army, whilst its right wing was also to remain where it was, its left wing was to move up to the Meuse from Namur to Givet.

The battle started badly for the French: in the early hours of May 10, their airfields were bombed and many planes destroyed on the ground. At 8 a.m., French reconnaissance groups crossed the frontier; these were cavalry units whose task was to delay the enemy advance in order to give the main body of the Army time enough to move up into new defensive positions. It was considered that five days would be needed to reach these positions, as part of the Ninth Army was on foot. General Corap pro-ceeded with more thoroughness than despatch; he gave orders for the operation to proceed only 'after the Meuse was adequately held'. The French expected their opponents to move with equal deliberation. As General Georges had stated, 'on any assumption, whatever the concen-tration of enemy forces involved, operations are expected to develop com-paratively slowly by reason of the poor rail and road communications.'

In any case, contact was made between the French and the Belgians under General Kayaerts. But although the French were uncertain what at-titude to adopt towards their new allies—whether they should merely make contact or support them or incorporate them into their own forces—the Belgians had received very strict instructions which their leader carried out most religiously. Despite French objections, he gave orders for demoli-tion operations to be made according to plan and then beat a retreat in accordance with the timetable laid down, completely ignoring the exist-ence of the French. The first result of this demolition was to delay the progress of the French by cutting their road communications. The Bel-gians' object had been to hold up the German advance for one day, whereas the French estimated that they would need five days to come to their support. Lack of co-ordination could not be more damaging.

The whole operation was starting off on the wrong foot and the rapid and unexpected advance of the German armour was soon seriously to ag-gravate the situation. General von Kleist had ordered this group 'not to rest or relax; to move forward night and day, looking neither left nor right, always on the alert; the group must exploit its initial surprise and the enemy's confusion; take him everywhere unawares, harass him relent-lessly and have only one aim in mind: to get through.'

But it was not easy to put these vigorous instructions into practice, in view of the large number of vehicles—General Guderian's advanced units alone had 10,000—and the narrowness of the roads, which were few and far between. In fact, the von Kleist group stretched out like a long snake with its tail still trailing behind over the Rhine when its head had already reached the Meuse. This long winding body, forced to stick to the twisting mountain roads, could easily have been chopped to pieces by any air force that had control of the skies. But the Allied air forces were engaged elsewhere.[1] In this sector the sky was filled only with the throb of German aircraft.

Along all the roads there were countless gorges and many villages that could be converted into defensive 'plugs'; and the Belgians' demolition operations, both on the frontier itself and afterwards at Neufchâteau did, in fact, slow down the enemy advance. But with some exceptions, these demolished areas were not defended and the German engineers proceeded with the necessary repairs swiftly and quite undisturbed, so much so that Guderian made up one whole day on the timetable that he had set himself.

The fact remained that the crossing of the Meuse, which was the objective of von Kleist's group, was a tricky task. The river was deeply embanked. But the French were not yet firmly established at any point; they were neither in sufficient strength nor numerous enough to prevent the crossing. Two German Panzer divisions were facing one French light cavalry division—that is, one horse brigade and one motorised brigade, possessing thirty-three anti-tank guns in all.

Before they were even in position, the French were blown to pieces. At dawn on May 10, the Germans crossed the Our and the Sure without any difficulty. On May 11, the 5th Light Cavalry Division failed to blow up all the bridges over the Semois as it withdrew. In the night of the 11th–12th, the Germans crossed the Semois. Throughout, their air force provided cover for their armour and their complete mastery in the battle area enabled them to open up the way and demolish with devastating force any of their opponent's centres of resistance whose existence they detected or even suspected. The vertical dives and ear-splitting noise of the Stukas took the French soldiers by surprise and destroyed their morale.

By the evening of May 12—Guderian's timetable had been the 14th—the German troops had reached the banks of the Meuse. The eastern suburbs of Sedan had been captured but all the bridges over the Meuse had been blown up in time. The 'battle of the Meuse' was about to begin. What were the forces facing the Germans and what defensive positions did they hold? How were the French commanders going to react to this early defeat, serious and totally unexpected as it was?

1. The raids by French and Belgian aircraft on the Albert canal bridges had failed and all the aircraft engaged had been lost.

VI THE BATTLE OF SEDAN

The brunt of the attack fell on Huntziger's Second Army. It comprised 5 infantry divisions, some cavalry, 3 artillery regiments—and 3 tank battalions. Its front extended over fifty miles, so that, on average, each division had to cover a sector ten miles long. In addition, two of these divisions were B divisions and were not ready to be thrown headlong into hard fighting. While each division was planned to have fifty-two 25-mm and eight 47-mm anti-tank guns, the divisions stationed at Sedan each had a few dozen 25-mm guns to fight the German tanks—that is, eight per mile. It is true that they were in fortified positions but these were stronger on paper than in reality. The block-houses varied greatly in type and were incomplete; there were not enough steel doors, loop-hole shutters or trenches. By a strange paradox, the Second Army, much less well protected by concrete defence works, had received fewer anti-tank mines than the armies concentrated behind the Maginot line.

The task of the Second Army was of vital importance as it provided the hinge for the whole French Army, and if that hinge gave way, all the French armies on its left would be in danger of being attacked from the rear or even encircled. First and foremost amongst these was the Ninth Army that had advanced into Belgium. General Huntziger was well aware of the gravity of the situation; new plans had to be improvised at a moment's notice to meet the situation that had arisen; reserve units were hurriedly thrust into the front line without any organised means of communication while aircraft were thrown in regardless of heavy losses. The grave planning blunders of the French strategists were plain for all to see. The Ardennes which they had considered impassable for large motorised units had been crossed without difficulty. They had estimated that at least nine days would be required to mount any attempt to cross the Meuse and the Germans were there in three. However, it was not certain that the gravity of the situation had been fully appreciated by the French high command even as late as May 12. They had not halted the armies advancing into the plain of Belgium; obsessed by the lessons of the 1914–18 war which had taught the absolute necessity of a continuous front they were to endeavour to plug the gap at Sedan by committing units piecemeal. They also thought that, having covered seventy-five miles at one stretch, the German troops would be forced to regroup, that a slight respite would thus be gained and that the Germans would use artillery to prepare a fresh leap forward. On May 13 General Gamelin had, in fact, telephoned to General Georges that the cavalry which had been pulled out of Luxemburg were to be sent into Belgium in the rear of the First Army. At that time, he still saw the decisive fighting as taking place in Brabant.

General Guderian lost no time in disillusioning him. Drifting barges that were blocking the Meuse provided a convenient support for footbridges; and bridges on the canal which ran alongside the river were captured undamaged. At 11.00 a.m. on May 13, the German Air Force started bombing the French command posts, pill-boxes, gun positions and communications networks. In accordance with Guderian's directives, the raids were short and relatively light; but they were repeated over a period of several hours in order to protect the German sappers and infantry-men as they crossed the Meuse in rubber dinghies. The 1st Panzer Division broke through the French front line and established a pocket three miles deep at Chemery but the 2nd and 10th Panzer Divisions had greater difficulty in advancing. The engineers were hastily constructing bridges behind the infantry.

On the evening of May 13, the situation for the French was serious but not desperate. However, one alarming phenomenon was observed; at Bulson in the course of that afternoon some units were seized by panic and stampeded, as a result of fatigue, jarred nerves and the demoralisation caused by the overwhelming enemy air superiority which was turning the troops into sitting targets; also perhaps under the influence of the pitiful exodus of the civilian population which was now getting under way.

However, even though the Germans had achieved the bridgehead that they wanted, their situation remained difficult and even hazardous. Only the infantry had crossed the river; the armour was still on the other bank; their area of penetration into the French positions was a narrow pocket open to flank attack. It was true that the Meuse had also been crossed further north at Dinant and at Monthermé; but the left bank was not strongly occupied.

VII THE ALLIED COUNTER-ATTACKS

So on May 14 everything depended on the speed and weight of the Allied counter-attacks. The lack of bombers was cruelly apparent; the task of destroying the pontoon bridges over the Meuse was given to French and British fighter aircraft. They pressed home their attack and out of sixty-five British planes only thirty-two returned to base; even those were in bad shape. But only three bridges over the Meuse had been damaged and they were quickly rebuilt.

Would armoured divisions succeed where aircraft had failed? The 3rd Armoured Division was, in fact, thrown into the attack but in a way that plainly showed up the French command's inability to adapt to the new methods of warfare that they were now beginning to experience. First of all, the operations of the tanks and the aircraft were unco-ordinated. Next, in accordance with the lessons of the 1914-18 war, before counter-attacking, General Huntziger spent time taking steps to plug the gaps, even though the lightning speed of the German advance had made it impossible to do so. But as Colonel Le Goyet has written, consolidation and counter-attack are two mutually exclusive operations: 'In order to consolidate, you have to spread out, lengthen your line and disperse; to counter-attack, you must concentrate, group and act as one force; to delay counter-attacking until you have consolidated means wasting time and during that time, you will lose opportunities that will not occur again.'

A favourable opportunity presented itself, in fact, on that very afternoon of May 15. Carried away by his own daring, realising that his first task had been fulfilled before the date fixed and that he had broken through the French front line, General Guderian decided not to wait before carrying out the second part of his task, which was to swing round and thrust westward towards the sea. He did not know at that time that he was exerting pressure on the most vulnerable spot in the French defences; he struck while the iron was hot. He needed, however, to convince his superior officer, von Kleist, who thought him rash and was afraid of French counter-attacks. General Guderian condemned von Kleist's short-lived defensive reaction so vehemently—he said that it would amount to 'giving away victory on a plate'—that von Kleist allowed himself to be persuaded.

But it was a risky manoeuvre. To the south, Guderian had only the weak protection afforded by the Gross Deutschland regiment which had just spent an exhausting few days. Would General Huntziger seize his chance? He does not seem even to have realised that it existed; blinkered by the fear of leaving the road to Paris undefended, he carried out the defensive measures which he thought necessary. Of his own accord, he gave ground in order to regroup more effectively. Thus, without a fight he abandoned to the enemy a hundred or so small forts between the Chiers and the Meuse, in order to draw back towards the 'Inor junction'. This certainly had the advantage of shortening his line by a few miles, but this advantage was nullified by the greater weakness of his defence positions. By his own action, he had enlarged the German pocket south of the Meuse.

In these circumstances, would General Brochard's 3rd Armoured Division which was proceeding from Rheims be strong enough to deal with this pocket? As it turned out, this division was not sent into action. General Flavigny, the commander of the Tenth Army Corps to which the 3rd Armoured Division was attached, had been unfavourably impressed by

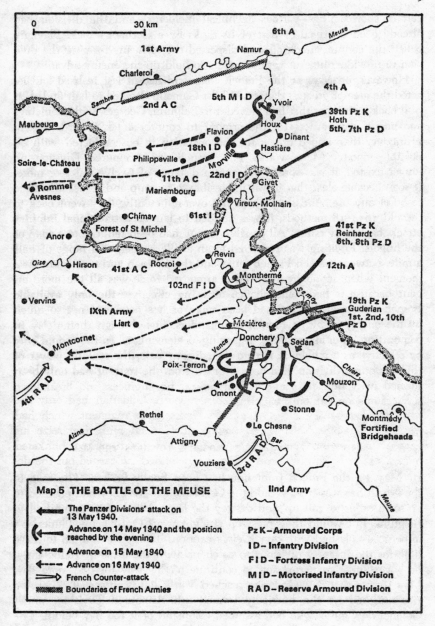

Map 5 **THE BATTLE OF THE MEUSE**

- The Panzer Divisions' attack on 13 May 1940.
- Advance on 14 May 1940 and the position reached by the evening
- Advance on 15 May 1940
- Advance on 16 May 1940
- French Counter-attack
- Boundaries of French Armies

Pz K – Armoured Corps
I D – Infantry Division
F I D – Fortress Infantry Division
M I D – Motorised Infantry Division
R A D – Reserve Armoured Division

certain shortcomings—various 'technical incidents'—and the division had
already been deprived of part of its tanks by a German attack. Flavigny
called the counter-attack off and dispersed the elements forming the division to provide 'plugs' at various points to hold up the enemy advance.

However, on May 15 the French command had at last realised and located the area of greatest danger. Whilst Gamelin decided to halt and then
pull back the armies that had moved into Belgium, Georges, with Gamelin's
agreement, gave orders for the armour to counter-attack towards Sedan.
Huntziger then issued orders for the operation to be conducted 'with all
possible vigour'. Mere words. The French 3rd Armoured Division no
longer existed; it was spread out over a distance of twelve miles or more.
It soon became clear that it was impossible to regroup and refuel it in time
to be of any use. And so, perhaps not over-reluctantly, they went back to
the old 1914–18 methods; it was decided to launch a traditional infantry
attack, backed by tanks. 'All possible vigour' had been reduced to a snap of
the fingers. Fighting was restricted to an artillery duel, at a range of half
a mile, between sixteen French tanks and the German anti-tank guns. At a
moment when action by a powerful armoured force was all the more urgent because it had some chance of being effective, the only available
French armoured division had been more or less destroyed not so much
by the enemy as by its French commanders, first through their delay in
committing it but above all by dispersing its elements when they could only
be effective as a whole. It is true that, in any case, the striking power of
this 'armoured division' had been blunted from the start: it had only been
formed in March 1940 and it had no AA, no engineers, no breakdown
services and no anti-tank batteries.

VIII THE WEHRMACHT'S PROGRESS TOWARDS THE SEA

By May 15, the French front line had been finally broken. The road to
the North Sea was free. Would the Germans take it? They had planned to
do so in order to 'roll up' and destroy the large Allied units committed in
Belgium. But would they press on straightaway? Once more, Guderian's
impetuosity clashed with von Kleist's caution. The latter wanted to leave
time for the infantry divisions to catch up with the armour. Reluctantly,
he gave Guderian permission to continue on his way for one more day,
May 16. On that day, Guderian reached Marle and Montcornet. There he
was attacked by the hurriedly formed 4th Armoured Division, under
Colonel de Gaulle, who had assumed command of it the day before. The
three tank battalions which composed it took up their positions during the
night, using their own resources. The infantry was unable to follow them,

owing to lack of transport. Action began before the terrain had been sufficiently reconnoitred and some of the tanks became bogged down. Nonetheless, there was hard fighting, but at nightfall, in view of threats to both flanks, the 4th Armoured Division had to pull back to its assembly points north of Laon.

Although Guderian's advance had not been seriously delayed, once again von Kleist would have liked to slow it down and Guderian had to appeal over his head to General List for permission to press on towards St Quentin. On May 19, he had reached Péronne and on the 20th he took Amiens and was thrusting towards Abbeville. The northern group of Allied armies—French, British and Belgian—was cut off from the rest of the French armies. The Allied forces were now all condemned to fight a defensive action on terrain that, on the whole, had not been prepared for it in any way. All the prearranged plans had to be revised on the spot, in a fluid situation. The complete futility of the Maginot line was apparent. It was a heavy, if not irreparable, defeat.

Yet the French weapons were not inferior in quality to the Germans'. General List has described how when captured French 25-mm anti-tank guns were immediately tried out against German armour plating, they went right through it. The morale of the ordinary soldier was not always as high as that of the preceding generation in 1914–18; but on the whole, the front-line troops fought well. The German successes were, of course, favoured by circumstances—misunderstanding between the Allies and the Belgians, the placing of weak French units just at the decisive point where they met the brunt of the German attack, the fact that Guderian, who played a vital personal role, was in command of the German spearhead.

In fact, the Germans had been allowed to fight in their own way; they combined speed and power; their rate of advance, the co-ordination of their forces—above all of their tanks and aircraft—their concentration of resources enabled them constantly to take the initiative and enjoy the benefit of surprise. They themselves seem sometimes to have been surprised by the extent and speed of their victory. In February 1940 General Halder had estimated that nine days would be required to cross through the Ardennes and over the Meuse, and this was the same time as the French high command had allowed.

In the event, the German Army had proved itself irresistibly superior in the field. Colonel Goutard was surely right when he drew attention to and deplored the 'lost opportunities' of the French command which, in E. Bauer's well-chosen words, was 'overtaken by events every day, throwing divisions about like small change on a card table and ordering consolidation at points generally too close to the point of breakthrough. Most of its orders were based on inadequate or belated intelligence for want of proper liaison and a communications system suited to the speed of the Blitzkrieg, and it seemed impossible to carry them out from the very moment they were issued.'

France certainly lacked an army to match her greatness and her policy. True, it was her governments—and their frequent changes were no help, either—which were mainly responsible for not having provided it. But basically they had provided the means required for the sort of army suggested by the general staff. And the general staff, all intellectually hidebound, could see no further than the 1914–18 war. No better proof of this arid and anachronistic attitude on the part of the French military pundits could be given than the use of reserves during the fighting. On May 16, Winston Churchill who had gone over to Paris because of the bad news, asked Gamelin: 'Where are your reserves?' And Gamelin replied: 'There aren't any.' Then he bitterly attacked General Georges whom he considered responsible for this piece of incompetence. 'I would never have thought,' he said, 'that a commander-in-chief defending a 500-mile front could have left it without a main striking force.'[1]

In fact, at the start some twenty divisions were available; but it was impossible to use them effectively at the right time. They needed at least four days to move anywhere and having achieved its success, the enemy had long since left the critical point where each division should have been thrown in. Thus the 14th Division under Delattre de Tassigny, which on May 12 had been ordered to proceed urgently to Sedan, did not reach Rethel until the night of May 16–17, by which time the German armour had already reached the bank of the Oise, fifty miles to the west. The French generals were still thinking in terms of moving foot-soldiers or horses; the German army, or at least its spearhead, was advancing at the speed of its motorised elements and its aircraft.

It is correct to say that this failure to keep up-to-date was just as much the fault of French industry as of the Army, and that the French people themselves had also failed to realise the danger in time. But this would not have prevented the Army from equipping itself for modern warfare—it had indeed partly done so—and above all, from adapting its methods to use modern equipment, if it had had a clear idea of what was required. But for want of armoured forces, of a powerful air force and of suitable planning, as Colonel Lyet rightly says, 'the battle of France was lost even before the surprise attack on Sedan'. In view of this, could and would the battle still be continued in France?

1. In his *Mémoires* General Gamelin wrote that his reply to the British Prime Minister was: 'There aren't any left.' This variant does not really make much material difference.

CHAPTER 3

The French Collapse

DURING these sad days in the history of France, Paul Reynaud had been steadily broadening his government in an attempt to provide the country with the widest possible spectrum of national unity—but not including the Communists. Camille Chautemps, Campinchi and Queuille, the Radicals surviving from Daladier's government, were joined, in minor posts, by Serol and Georges Monnet, two members of the Socialist party which had hitherto been content merely to support the government. On May 10 this opening towards the left was counter-balanced by the admission of two right-wingers, Louis Marin and Ybarnegaray—the latter a member of the *Parti social français* with Fascist sympathies and opposed to the republican régime. On June 5, another batch of politicians was added thereby making the government more cumbersome, without any apparent motive unless the change was based on arithmetical calculations that were now hardly relevant. More original was the invitation extended to certain experts, Dautry, Bouthillier, Prouvost, Paul Baudouin and General de Gaulle, who were all certain to support the French Premier and likely to strengthen his hand. But in fact, this very broad cabinet was lacking in homogeneity and did not add up to a proper team. Ever since Munich, if not before, all parties had been divided as to the necessity of the present conflict and the way to end it. In theory, Paul Reynaud, who throughout kept asseverating his determination and energy, had called on men who were as resolute as himself; but the course of events now split this conglomeration into warring elements.

In order to whip up public opinion, Paul Reynaud, justifiably worried, had called in Georges Mandel, Clemenceau's right-hand man, and, above all, Marshal Pétain; two names which recalled to every Frenchman the victory in 1918 and seemed to promise a repetition. Indeed, Mandel had never ceased advocating a firm attitude towards Nazism. Pétain's position was more ambiguous. At the age of 84, the Marshal had been appointed French ambassador to Spain by Daladier and Georges Bonnet, in order to try to patch up France's relations with Franco. He had never played an important part in politics or come to terms with any party, although, perhaps without his knowledge, a few trouble-makers had launched a campaign to bring him to power. After February 6, 1934, he had entered the Doumergue government but only in the cause of national unity. Later on he had refused to become a candidate to succeed Albert Lebrun as President of the Republic. Paul Reynaud announced that the Marshal 'was putting his wisdom and strength at the service of the country'—in fact, he had remained very vigorous despite his great age—and on May 21, the Senate rose as one man to give a prolonged ovation to the great soldier when he honoured them with a visit. What did Pétain really think of the situation? The despatches of the German ambassador in Madrid often represent him as being opposed to the continuance of the war but they were based on impressions and hearsay and not on actual statements by the Marshal. According to General Laure, his biographer, Marshal Pétain was convinced as early as May 18 that the war was lost and that all that remained was to try to conclude an honourable peace. But the Marshal, like a mysterious sphinx, said not a word. One thing is certain: he had not intrigued to get into the government but had been approached by them. If, in Paul Reynaud's mind, it was mainly a psychological operation, in the eyes of the public, Pétain was already assuming the role of saviour of the fatherland and his prestige and fame completely overshadowed his Premier.

The latter would have liked to dismiss the Supreme Commander Gamelin as soon as he came to power in March 1940 but Daladier had opposed this. The near-disasters now brought him down and General Weygand, another national hero full of years and glory—he was 72 years old—was recalled from Syria on May 19 to replace him. Weygand had been outstanding as Foch's right-hand man; he, too, was identified with the victory of 1918 in the eyes of the public. Nobody wished to be reminded that the two great military heroes who had in fact been in charge of the French Army between the wars, Pétain and Weygand, were largely responsible for its adoption of the out-of-date ideas and methods that had been at the root of its present setbacks and the misfortunes that had overtaken the country. Did Weygand have any illusions as to the military situation? It would seem not. But he accepted the difficult task offered him out of a sense of duty: 'To refuse,' he wrote, 'would have been cowardly.'

It seems that Paul Reynaud had not consulted the British over Weygand's appointment. And indeed, although his official titles were rather different from Gamelin's—Reynaud and Weygand were going to argue this point later on—the new French Supreme Commander wore more or less the same uniform as his predecessor. Even although he took the title of 'Commander-in-Chief of all theatres' and not merely that of 'Commander-in-Chief of the ground forces', Weygand still did not take precedence over Admiral Darlan or General Vuillemin. He was not an interallied commander-in-chief either; indeed, there was no interallied general staff. His appointment did nothing to improve the co-ordination of the Allied forces; yet this was more than ever necessary now that defeat, always a bad counsellor, was pulling the coalition asunder.

II WEYGAND'S PLAN

On May 19 General Weygand knew nothing about the front at all. He knew only that the enemy had penetrated deeply but he did not know accurately the forces or the movements and less still about the intentions of the British and the Belgians. On that day, he met Gamelin, who, in his own words, 'put him briefly in the picture', but curiously enough did not show him the report on the states of the armies that he had drawn up for the French Premier.

Gamelin, a very poor man of action but a remarkable armchair strategist —'we needed a soldier,' Jules Romains wrote, 'and we got a philosopher'— had sent General Georges instructions which, although he may have had grave doubts about their effectiveness, laid down the only obvious tactics, namely, for the armies in the north to break out of their encirclement and for a continuous front to be reformed along the Somme and the Aisne.[1] But these were the ideas of Gamelin the strategist; and in his capacity as Commander-in-Chief, this same man, even whilst stressing that 'it was a question of hours', was content merely to express them clearly on paper without ordering them to be carried out! Perhaps he wished to avoid committing his successor since he knew that he was in disgrace at the time. In any case, this strange behaviour serves to emphasise the extent to which this changing of horses at this moment of grave crisis was to increase rather than solve the difficulty of crossing the stream.

It was logical for General Weygand to wish to receive the fullest possible information from General Georges and General Doumenc—as Chief of Staff, the latter was able to reveal the Allies' shortage of tanks and aircraft and the wastage of their reserves. But the new generalissimo's notion of going by plane to discover the state of the encircled armies on the spot was not perhaps based on an accurate assessment of the speed at which the battle was developing. Finally, after having considered certain other possibilities, General Weygand adopted Gamelin's plan; but a good many 'valuable hours' had been lost and the situation had seriously deteriorated.

1. Amazingly, Gamelin also recommended an offensive 'towards the Mézières bridges'; which was completely unrealistic at that date but which would have been very useful—on May 14.

By this time, in fact, 27 out of the 137 large units of the Allied coalition as a whole had disappeared. In General Billotte's First Army Group, 13 French divisions, 9 British divisions and the whole of the Belgian Army were encircled. The British had formed a very accurate idea of the gravity of the situation and they had begun to take precautions to extricate themselves from the mess. The RAF had heavy losses; out of 474 planes operating in France, 206 were shot down in the evening of May 13. The Air Ministry calculated that at least 25 fighter squadrons must be kept on British soil in order to provide adequate air defence for the United Kingdom. So Churchill allowed Weygand only ten further squadrons for use in France; he refused to release the 600 fighters for which he was asked and which might perhaps have provided the only possible means of equalling the Luftwaffe in the critical battle that was about to ensue. This decision, based on national self-interest, may be thought to have saved Britain later on and, in addition, the whole Allied cause. But in the short run 'for the sake of an uncertain eventuality,' as E. Bauer properly points out, 'an effective fighting weapon was being held back from the main battle area'.

Britain was worried by the thought of her own defence and could not fail to be concerned at the fate of her Expeditionary Force on the continent—the only army that she possessed at that time and which could certainly not be replaced by the 'local defence volunteer' force which Eden had just decided to form. For his part, Lord Gort, realising that the situation was becoming hourly more serious and having little confidence in the judgment of General Billotte,[1] who had been his superior officer since May 12, had informed London via his CGS (Chief of Staff) that it was important to keep in mind a possible evacuation of the BEF under his command. In reply, on May 20, the British government, far from acceding to his request, instructed him, through General Ironside, his CGS, to move south-west, via Béthune and Arras, and place himself on the left of the French Army—a decision which was in line with General Weygand's wishes. But in anticipation of the worst, at the same time the British Admiralty began to assemble a large number of small craft and on that same May 20 held its first meeting to examine the urgent evacuation of 'very considerable forces' across the Channel. As Adrienne Hytier very properly points out, the French were not informed of this decision.

Lord Gort obeyed but without much conviction. His view was, in fact, that since he was outflanked on his right and his left flank was threatened, the only reasonable decision was to retreat towards the coast. The British

1. General Billotte had refused Lord Gort's request to replace British by French divisions on the Scheldt, suspecting that this request might be a hidden preparation for an evacuation.

general was aware that the Germans had reached Abbeville and Montreuil and that the 2,000 tons of ammunition and stores required by his army every day would now have to be shipped entirely through the North Sea ports. These supplies would be gravely jeopardised by the air attacks to which these ports were now being subjected. From May 20 onwards, Lord Gort was disinclined to undertake any actions of more than limited scope in the south. He was obeying but with mental reservations that made it only token obedience. Whether he decided on this himself or whether he had the more or less explicit approval of the British government is not clear. In any case, it was certainly neither willingly nor with any determination in his heart that General Gort took part on May 21 in the Interallied Conference called by General Weygand in Ypres.

III THE YPRES CONFERENCE

General Weygand has related the circumstances of his journey to Ypres, which might well have been dramatic. He wanted to meet King Leopold and General Gort in order to put forward his plan to them because, although both of them, through General Billotte, were in theory his subordinates, they were still in fact independent supreme commanders free to make their own decisions whenever they chose. Realising that for the moment the Allies still had numerical superiority in the Péronne–Abbeville–Cambrai triangle and anxious to take advantage of this while there was still time, General Weygand was, in short, adopting the broad outlines of Gamelin's 'personal and confidential order no. 12'. This provided for eight Franco-British divisions to attack from Arras–Cambrai southwards towards Bapaume; to protect themselves on the north, the Belgian Army would narrow its front by moving from the Scheldt to the Yser, where it would consolidate its defensive positions by opening the locks. General Frère's Seventh Army would advance northwards to link up with the encircled units. On the map, it seemed a simple and obvious manoeuvre; should it succeed, the Allies would once again have a continuous front line, the best of the Allied troops would avoid being either smashed or captured—and the British would continue to fight on French soil.

The Ypres Conference might thus have offered a last chance. In fact, a number of unfortunate incidents, together with the mental reservations of some of the participants, turned it into rather a confused and incoherent series of talks during which the necessary decisions were not taken as clearly and firmly as was desirable. First, General Weygand put his suggestions to King Leopold and General van Overstraeten, who pleaded the difficulties of the withdrawal and the tiredness of the Belgian troops. In reality, both of them shrank from the idea of relinquishing another square inch of Belgian territory.

With the arrival of General Billotte, commander of the First Army Group, another conference began. He painted a frankly gloomy picture of the state of the French armies that was not likely to allay King Leopold's misgivings or those of his military adviser. However, the Belgian ministers Pierlot, Denis and Spaak, who were not taking part in the military talks, were very keen for political reasons not to cut Belgium off from her allies. They even thought that the Belgian Army should simply withdraw south without further ado, something which for the moment was impossible. Their views were thus rather ahead of their sovereign's. The latter was shaken but unconvinced and accepted Weygand's suggestions.

The approval of General Gort, whose behaviour, to say the least, was surprising, had not been obtained. He claimed that he did not know the exact time of the meeting and it is true that communications were chaotic; he could never be reached personally, he was always 'out reconnoitring'. Van Overstraeten and Admiral Keyes, head of the British mission to the Belgian Army, were obliged to go and fetch him and when he eventually arrived, Weygand was no longer there! He had left without meeting the British commander who was to play the major role in the proposed operation and knowing nothing about his intentions. The Commander-in-Chief seems also not to have attached sufficient importance to Admiral Keyes' obvious hostility to his plans; the Admiral had not, of course, any real authority but his significantly cautious attitude increased the hesitations of the Belgians and the doubts of the British. The only thing we are told by Weygand is that the Admiral's knowledge of French had not improved.

Once Weygand had left, the real interallied conference began, without the Supreme Commander. Lord Gort made no secret of his lack of confidence in Weygand's plan; he is even reported as saying to King Leopold 'It's a bad job'. However, General Billotte and his deputy Fagalde insisted on decisions being taken in accordance with the Supreme Commander's wishes: the attack from the north southwards would take place as planned and the Belgians would withdraw to the Yser. So Weygand could prepare his equivalent attack from south to north.

But on his way back, King Leopold changed his mind. Perhaps he thought, on reflection, that the withdrawal to the Yser was not possible. Perhaps he was afraid that, with the English thrusting south, the Belgians would be left to fight a hopeless battle all by themselves. Or else, in accordance with his 'policy of independence', which was certainly a hardy growth, he wanted to create a purely Belgian bridgehead, as his Premier Pierlot accused him of doing. In any case, on May 22, King Leopold issued orders which limited the proposed withdrawal; only the first stage would be carried out; the Belgian Army would pull back, not to the Yser, but to the branch-canal of the Lys. This would leave a blank space at the southern end of their positions, at the point of junction with the BEF, through which the Germans would be able to pour. It is clear that this personal decision by Leopold was an extremely grave one.

To cap it all, General Billotte was killed in a car accident as he was on the way back to his headquarters; he was replaced by General Blanchard while General Prioux took over as commander of the First Army. But General Blanchard was obliged to find out about the plans and settle in, so that forty-eight valuable hours were lost—by the Allies, not by the Germans, whose own operations, though entirely predictable, do not seem to have received much attention from those taking part in the Ypres Conference.

IV THE EXECUTION OF WEYGAND'S PLAN

Weygand's plan was thus likely to get off to an inauspicious start, although, on May 22, the Interallied War Council meeting at Vincennes, with Churchill and General Dill present, gave it its blessing. Enthusiastically, Churchill sent Lord Gort instructions that even went beyond General Weygand's own scheme: he talked of an attack in the south by 'the Third Army Group'. Either because he was less optimistic or more realistic, General Weygand had fixed neither the date of the operation nor the size of the force to be employed, leaving this to the discretion of the commander concerned, General Blanchard.

But on May 20, Lord Gort had commented pessimistically on the proposed operations to Ironside: 'Neither the First Army nor the Belgians were in a position to fulfil their part in the operation . . . the supply position would make any prolonged operations difficult.' And in fact, from May 23 onwards, the British troops had to be rationed. It was plain that in these circumstances the British general, pressed for time, would be tempted to take his own decisions on the spot, whatever the results of talks 'at the highest level' might be. And on May 22, the Germans reached Boulogne which resisted for two days.

Meanwhile, on May 21 the limited operation agreed on by Generals Billotte, Ironside and Lord Gort at Lens, on May 20, as a sort of preliminary to the Weygand plan, had started. Although the forces involved comprised only one French light mechanised division, one infantry division and a tank brigade, the Allies advanced beyond Arras but were soon halted; the attackers had been counter-attacked by German Panzers, from the south, the west and the east. Despite its relative lack of success, this positive action had nonetheless caused the German command concern by showing the vulnerability of the flanks of its excessively and dangerously strung-out positions.

Weygand wanted to launch the operation a second time on a larger scale. But was this still possible on May 23? Would the English be able to deploy half their forces southwards whilst *at the same time* containing the Germans to the east? Would the French units, tired out by their marching and fighting and short of tanks and air-cover, have sufficient strength and morale for offensive action? The French command believed or made believe that this was the case, since on May 23 General Georges issued the order 'to continue to effect a link-up between the First Army Group and the Third Army Group'—a link-up that had not even begun. General Gort had, in fact, estimated that he could only throw in two divisions for this operation and not before May 26. In the south, at the other end of the pincer, General Frère had not yet been able to make any move.

So General Gort was thus forced to act on his own responsibility. Two of his divisions were surrounded in Arras and were in danger of annihilation. On May 24 a violent bombing raid on Dunkirk showed how frail and tenuous were the links on which the supply position of the BEF depended. On May 25, the Germans breached the Belgian lines at Courtrai. Thus threatened on his left, on his right and in the rear, obsessed by the fear of being responsible for the loss of the only army available to the British Commonwealth at that time, on May 25, on his own initiative, Lord Gort ordered the withdrawal of the divisions threatened in Arras. He took this decision without either asking or waiting for permission from the French command. Any hope of implementing Weygand's plan had now evaporated. It had never even been started.

V THE HALT OF THE GERMAN ARMOURED UNITS

Lord Gort had not taken his decision hastily or without knowledge of the facts; it was the result of a careful deliberation, based on a clear and accurate assessment of the deterioration in the situation. All the same, he did not know all the factors involved; he had moved a pawn on the board in the hope of saving it; but this affected a whole game of chess. He had made the first tear in the delicate fabric of the Allied coalition which Reynaud and Churchill were striving to knit together; and it led to its being slowly but inexorably torn to shreds.

To begin with, Lord Gort's decision condemned the First French Army to be annihilated or captured. He was also abandoning the Belgians to their fate for the British withdrawal forced them to provide their own protection both on the west and on the north-west, by throwing their last available forces into the melting pot. With one flick of his finger, Lord Gort had brought about a completely new orientation of the front lines. On May 26, Weygand as it were obeyed him by ordering a withdrawal towards Dunkirk, 'whilst fighting to save anything that could be saved', but the retreating troops were abandoning their heavy weapons and ammunition as they fled.

But Lord Gort had at least saved the BEF at the last moment, just when the German noose was about to tighten around its neck; he saved it but only by withdrawing it from the fighting; he preserved it for an uncertain future but in so doing turned the present situation that was merely alarming into a hopeless one.

If he had not taken this decision, would the BEF have necessarily been doomed? This is a question of vital importance, because the actions of the French, Germans and perhaps the Belgians were governed by those of the British. The French were, in fact, preparing to launch their V Army Corps into battle towards the north. On May 26, General Weygand gave the order to reduce the Somme bridgeheads and on May 27, the 4th Armoured Division under General de Gaulle launched a spirited attack on Abbeville on a ten-mile front; this time, it was supported by an infantry division. On the first day it achieved its objectives; on the second, it held off an enemy counter-attack. At the end of three days, the battle had been a partial success for the French. Next the 2nd Armoured Division took up the attack but it, too, was brought to a halt. The French were short of tanks; the 2nd Armoured Division was able to mass only 150 tanks on a front one and a half miles long. Above all, as always, the French command had failed to understand armoured warfare, by splitting up its forces and sending them into battle in successive waves rather than massing them for one concentrated attack.

But would this attack have succeeded had it been made towards Arras and if, *at the same time,* the British had taken the offensive in their sector on May 26 as arranged, even if only with two divisions? Would the Germans have continued their progress along the North Sea when they had, *before this,* decided to halt their armour? The reason for this halt is not very clear, since order no. 12 which, to judge by the war diaries of General Jodl and General Halder, probably issued the instructions, has not been recovered amongst Hitler's battle orders. But it is certain that the Führer was acting in agreement with the general in charge in the field, General von Rundstedt, and that he was merely underwriting the latter's decision.

Von Rundstedt had not taken his decision for political or even for general strategic reasons—such as Hitler's fear, based on his experience of the 1914–18 war, that the armour might become bogged down in Flanders or his desire to offer Goering's Luftwaffe a spectacular success at the expense of the Army, considered as being 'reactionary'. As Colonel Bernard rightly says, von Rundstedt had become aware of the need to give the tanks a breathing-space through the British attack on Arras on May 21 (which had pushed forward ten miles with three battalions and sixteen tanks), the French preparations on the Somme and the arrival of British reinforcements at Calais, a series of actions that would seem to make no sense unless it was intended to launch an attack in strength on the extended flanks of the German forces.

It is also known that the decision to renew the advance of the tanks towards Dunkirk was made on May 26 and implemented on May 27, *after* Lord Gort had ordered his troops to retreat north-westwards. In doing this, like a fish trying to slip away, Lord Gort was only inviting the fisherman to draw his net closer round him. He was thus dragging all the Allied forces in his wake—towards evacuation or surrender.[1]

VI THE BELGIAN CAPITULATION

After the German success at Courtrai on May 24, the Belgians had temporarily succeeded in restoring the situation by themselves. But as a result of Lord Gort's decision, their appeal for help to the British had remained unanswered. On May 25, the Sixth German Army, rested and refreshed, renewed its attack north of Lille. The Belgians succeeded in stopping them on the Scheldt but were unable to prevent a breakthrough on their southern front.

On May 26, the Allies were several times informed of the gravity of the situation. In particular, King Leopold warned Lord Gort: 'The moment is rapidly approaching when the Belgian troops will be no longer able to fight on.' That same day, an identical note, foreshadowing that the Army would capitulate to avoid a catastrophe, had been handed to General Champon, head of the French mission attached to the Belgian Army. In fact, the situation had become even more dramatic since there were 600,000 Belgian civilians caught in the fighting area and no evacuation by sea was conceivable. The only support from Lord Gort, as he continued his withdrawal, was to send two brigades, which were quite inadequate to plug the gaps in the Belgian positions and only sufficient to protect the rear of the British Army's retreat.

1. The idea that Hitler wanted to spare the British in order to come more easily to a settlement with Britain has never received an atom of proof. It was a hare started by Abetz' vivid imagination.

On May 27, King Leopold decided to surrender. He sent an envoy to parley with the enemy, without seeking the advice of the Allies and without even informing General Champon. The latter was in fact violently attacked by General van Overstraeten, who blamed the Allies 'for having deserted the Belgians' and concluded 'The time is coming when the strain is so great that the rope will break.'

Hitler made known his desires: he would accept nothing but an unconditional surrender. King Leopold gave in—and the French were only advised of his acceptance an hour after it had been communicated to the Germans. However, steps had been taken by the Belgians to save one French division, which was moved out of the Belgian battle area on Belgian lorries. The surrender became effective from 4 a.m. on May 28; the French had rather less than one night to deal with the new and serious situation that had arisen.

The Belgian surrender had, indeed, become inevitable and the Belgians had fought as long as they could. All the same, following in Lord Gort's footsteps, King Leopold, influenced by interests which were purely national interests, or at least considered as such, had taken a unilateral decision that spelled the doom of the coalition which, in fact, Belgium had never wholeheartedly supported. King Leopold, whom German pamphlets dropped over the Belgian lines accused of wanting to abandon his army, took the view, contrary to the King of Norway and the Queen of Holland, that he should consider himself a prisoner, like the soldiers he commanded. But why was he not content to play a purely passive role when he surrendered after the fighting? Perhaps he was anxious to avoid further suffering for his troops. Perhaps it was in order to avoid arousing the Germans' wrath that instructions were issued not to destroy all the equipment but to collect it and hand it over to the victors. But this surely was helping the enemy at the expense of the Allies.

VII THE DUNKIRK EVACUATION

On the same day that the Belgians surrendered, General Béthouart's troops took Narvik; this Allied success, the only one at this stage of the conflict, was to have no influence on its course; the divisions in Norway would have been better employed in France; in short, it proved that any operation on the periphery was of interest only if the main front was sound.

On May 28, the 'pocket' in which the Allied troops were shut round Dunkirk was rather less than sixty square miles. By the evening of May 26, the British Admiralty had given the signal for the evacuation—Operation 'Dynamo'. Churchill had informed Paul Reynaud; but Admiral Abrial, who was in charge of the Dunkirk defences, and General Blanchard did not receive official instructions to arrange for the French troops to be taken off until May 29, when the British troops had been embarking on the craft that had been coming to pick them up for the last three days. Moreover, Blanchard had made plans to hold the line of the Lys and he was still relying on British support. These misunderstandings and the resulting acrimony could not fail to make Franco-British co-operation more difficult at a time when it was more necessary than ever.

The preliminary calculations were pessimistic. 45,000 men seemed the maximum number that could be expected to be evacuated from the one single port of Dunkirk. This was why Weygand would have liked to retake Calais and Churchill even contemplated landing troops at Ostend. Both these plans had to be abandoned as impracticable.

From May 27 onwards, German bombers began to raid Dunkirk; but the RAF threw in all its reserves of fighters to defend the bridgehead, the embarkation points and the ships. If they took the shortest route between Dover and Dunkirk, at the end of the crossing the ships came under fire from the German batteries between Calais and Gravelines. Thus they were obliged to take a longer course by first steering north-east and their round trip took longer. Moreover, they were having to sweep for mines. On the first day only 7,700 men were landed in Britain, a disappointing performance.

By May 28, the operation was working more smoothly. Men were being taken off both in Dunkirk harbour and from the beaches; 17,000 men were saved; but 20,000 men were awaiting their turn, huddled together on the beaches and they had to be supplied with provisions by boat.

From May 29 onwards, the number of small craft rose considerably as yachts, launches, dredgers, trawlers and destroyers joined in; 47,000 men were taken off. But the arrival of the French troops produced some confusion, since in order to reach the sector allotted to them, they had to cross the approach paths being used by the British. Also communication between the various beaches was possible only by motor-car or motor-cycle. It was very fortunate that the weather remained fine throughout the operation.

By May 30 the whole of the BEF had withdrawn within the perimeter, which was now defended only by French troops who sacrificed themselves for their British brothers-in-arms. By now, 120,000 British had left as compared with only 6,000 French. The British government decided that from now on French and English should be taken off in equal numbers. The operation was to be concluded on June 1. At the request of the French government, it was extended until June 4.

Its success exceeded all expectations. In all, 330,000 men reached England—200,000 British, 130,000 French and a few Belgians—almost twice as many British as French. Two French divisions had been sacrificed; 40,000 French soldiers were captured after the last boat had left. The French had lost six torpedo-boat destroyers, sunk or damaged, while the British had lost nine. The British had left behind 1,200 artillery guns and 1,250 AA and anti-tank guns, 6,400 anti-tank rifles, 11,000 machine guns and 75,000 motorised vehicles—all their heavy equipment. The British Army would have to start again from scratch. One hundred and eighty RAF aircraft had been shot down in the course of the evacuation; but it was consoling to see, as a promise for the future, that the Luftwaffe had suffered even heavier losses and had been unable to prevent the embarkation. Its bombers had been an easy target for the British fighters, who had often won their dogfights with their German counterparts.

Though the result of Operation Dynamo was remarkable, it nonetheless represented the final act of a series of setbacks that would be difficult to reverse. To all intents and purposes, the British had vanished from the Continent with little idea of returning; the French would have to meet the second impending offensive on their own. And they were not very pleased with the British.

It is arguable whether the Allies could have acted in any other way. If the evacuation had been decided on earlier, several other ports would certainly have been available, in particular Ostend, Nieuport and Calais; some part of the equipment, at least the infantry weapons and perhaps some guns and lorries, would have been saved. But such a decision would have entailed abandoning the counter-attack that had been advocated by Gamelin and organised by Weygand.

It is true that it had not been possible to carry out the Weygand plan. But for a number of days it provided a sufficient threat to the German troops to make them slow down and even stop their advance. And when von Kleist's tanks in the von Rundstedt army group stopped, they were much nearer to Dunkirk than Lord Gort's infantry divisions and much better placed to occupy the whole of the North Sea coast than the tanks of von Bock's army group. The relative success of Dunkirk, or rather, its success in avoiding disaster, was, of course, due to the continued resistance of the Belgians until May 27, the competent logistical organisation of the British and the courage and self-sacrifice of the French. But what would have been achieved by all this if von Kleist had arrived at Dunkirk first? And if the Allies had not launched a counter-attack at Arras, however limited in extent, and if their units had given unmistakable signs of intending to embark, in other words if the Germans had not been worried about exposing their flanks, why should they have ceased their headlong advance, which, if successful, would have prevented any evacuation? The success of the evacuation was in any case not a victory; it enabled Britain, of course, to keep something of an army, although this army had hardly any weapons; above all, it meant that the French Army would stand alone against the impending assault by considerably superior forces.

VIII THE BATTLES ON THE SOMME AND THE AISNE

On June 4, General Weygand issued a terse and peremptory order: 'The Somme. To be held until June 15, by which date I shall have my reserves in position.' So the Commander-in-Chief did not completely despair of the situation. It seemed possible that a new 'miracle of the Marne' was on the cards. Weygand asked Georges to form 'two strike forces with the mechanised divisions and the majority of the reserve divisions, one in the area of Beauvais, the other in Argonne'; he was thus contemplating launching future counter-offensives, this time with concentrated forces.

But these forces no longer existed. In fact, Weygand had, on paper, only seventy-one divisions available, including four armoured divisions—in theory, at least, because they each had only fifty to eighty tanks apiece. The British still had one infantry division in France and one so-called armoured division, consisting of 3,000 men with 180 tanks, no artillery, no AA or anti-tank weapons, no ancillary services—and some of the tanks had no ammunition. Thus a fundamental difference between France's and Britain's conception of the meaning and conduct of their joint war was now apparent for all to see. France was fighting *her* battle which might be the last on French soil. Britain was only engaged in the first stage of the war; for her, France was merely the first line of her battle, the Channel was the second and, at a pinch, the Atlantic and her American cousins would be the final bulwark. Basically, Britain's attitude to France was rather like France's towards Poland; she urged her on and then dropped her to ensure her own safety since, at the end of the day, her own success would mean that of her ally.

The French saw things differently. The Germans noted an improvement in their fighting spirit. The French Premier took every opportunity of asserting his unconquerable determination, so much so that Churchill referred to him as 'indomitable'. However, this deliberate optimism was not shared by all the French leaders. While lunching with the American ambassador, Bullitt, on June 4, Pétain made no secret of his misgivings; he considered the war had been lost, through the fault of the British, who were willing to fight to the last Frenchman; then, safely ensconced behind the impassable anti-tank barrier of the Channel and protected by their fighter squadrons, which they had held back for their own selfish purposes, they would reach a negotiated peace at France's expense.

What was the true situation in the field? With 130 divisions, the Germans had overwhelming superiority; their armour had been regrouped into four corps of unequal sizes, according to the functions they had been assigned; now that its tasks in Flanders and Dunkirk were over, the Luftwaffe could concentrate on the one single objective of supporting the ground forces—and it had complete mastery of the skies. However, in order to demoralise the back areas, without encountering the slightest opposition, long-range bombers were raiding factories, aerodromes and communication centres in the Paris area, in Lyon, St Etienne and even as far afield as Marseilles, to the terror of the civilian population who saw them pass overhead. In France itself, the struggle was one-sided, if indeed the French had not already lost.

General Weygand had, however, restored a continuous front from Montmédy at the mouth of the Somme, along the Aisne, the Ailette and Crozat canals and the Somme. Defence positions had been built in depth. Would they hold out long enough? They had been improvised and to make up for the lack of anti-tank weapons, the French artillery—which in E. Bauer's words 'had an enormous technical and tactical superiority over its German counterpart and completely terrified the German infantryman'— had been dispersed to the various vulnerable points. On the other hand, the French counter-attacks had failed to eliminate the enemy bridgeheads south of the Somme.

At dawn on June 5, battle was joined on the Somme, in the area of von Bock's army group. On June 6, Weygand still showed a certain optimism, more stubborn than rational: the enemy had been held up by the 'French strongpoints'; but on June 7, the French defence line was pierced on the watershed between the Oise and the Somme. By June 9 Rommel had reached the outskirts of Rouen and the French Tenth Army had been 'rolled-up' at St Valéry-en-Caux—a second Dunkirk. South of Péronne, General Frère's Seventh Army had to pull back towards Paris as a result. On June 8, the Germans captured an important bridgehead on the Aisne round Soissons.

On June 9, von Rundstedt attacked in Champagne. On June 10, General Guderian succeeded in putting his armour across the Aisne; General Buisson's armoured group counter-attacked on the same day but it was held and then forced back. The battle for Champagne had been lost, as had the battle for Picardy; between the Maginot line and Le Havre, General Weygand had, at most, twenty-four divisions available.

On that same day June 10, Mussolini decided to enter the war. Roosevelt had vainly appealed to him on May 29 to 'save the Mediterranean

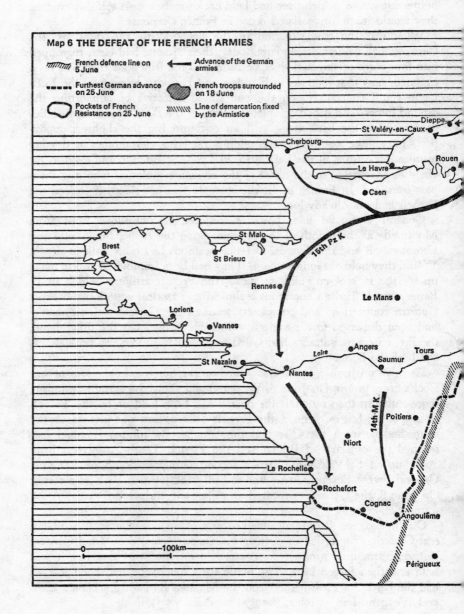

Map 6 THE DEFEAT OF THE FRENCH ARMIES

French defence line on 5 June

Furthest German advance on 25 June

Pockets of French Resistance on 25 June

Advance of the German armies

French troops surrounded on 18 June

Line of demarcation fixed by the Armistice

Dieppe
St Valéry-en-Caux
Cherbourg
Le Havre
Rouen
Caen
St Malo
Brest
St Brieuc
15th Pz K
Rennes
Le Mans
Lorient
Vannes
Angers
Tours
St Nazaire
Loire
Saumur
Nantes
14th M K
Poitiers
Niort
La Rochelle
Rochefort
Cognac
Angoulême
Périgueux

0   100km

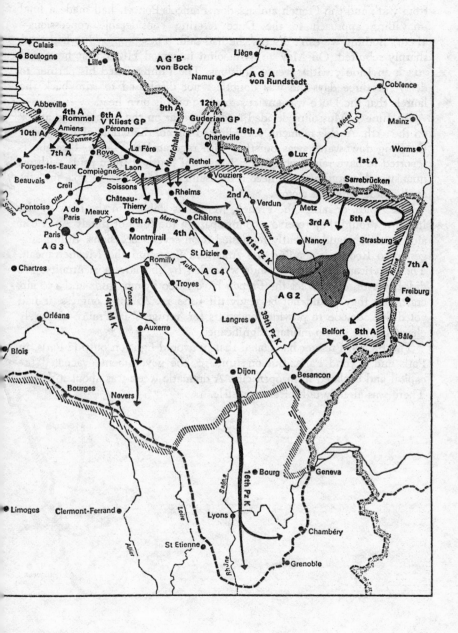

from war'; and the French ambassador, François-Poncet, had made a final unavailing approach to the Duce offering considerable concessions— 'there's nothing we can't discuss', he had said. These approaches had been sharply rebuffed. On May 30, Mussolini informed Hitler that he would attack on June 5 with seventy divisions. The Führer asked his partner to delay for three days—he was doubtless not displeased to trim back the laurels that the Duce was anxious to place on his own head.

On June 2, Mussolini decided to declare war on the 10th and to attack on the 11th. At this moment, according to Ciano, the whole of Italy, from the King downwards, was bursting with rage against France. Badoglio is reported to have raised objections; Mussolini brushed them aside with an unanswerable argument: 'I need a thousand dead in order to take my seat at the table with the victors.'

The Allies, or rather the French, were thus stabbed in the back by the Italians. Would they receive a counterpart in the form of timely American aid? Paul Reynaud urgently requested it on several occasions. Bullitt suggested to Roosevelt sending the American fleet into the Mediterranean. The American President's hands were tied by the law of neutrality. He did, however, offer to let the French have 2,000 75-mm guns and 150 aircraft. But they would not be ready till June 17. As for Congress, it had voted $50,000,000 to provide foodstuffs for 'refugees' in France—a purely charitable act, of no military significance.

The French Premier had stated that he would fight on outside Paris, in Paris and beyond Paris. But on June 10, the government evacuated the capital and declared it an open city. A dramatic week was about to begin. There was already talk of an armistice.

CHAPTER 4

The Armistice

FROM June 10, the French government was on the run, roaming and dispersing from one château to another, first in accordance with a prearranged plan but soon driven on by the enemy advance. It had expected to settle in Tours but it could only stay there four days. On June 15, it reached Bordeaux. During this fateful week, when the gravest of decisions had to be taken, the ministers were cut off from each other and from their staffs; they were no longer young, and suffered anguish and exhaustion on the roads or anywhere they could find to lay their heads; they were starved of news; sometimes they knew only what they could hear from the odd radio bulletins or the chance rumours picked up from their distraught compatriots; hardly had they taken a decision when it proved impossible to implement it, either because it had been overtaken by events or else because it had failed to reach the people supposed to carry it out.

The flight of the government was paralleled by the exodus of a whole nation. Starting from the north and from the north-east, from Belgium onwards, a flood of humanity, flowed in their millions towards the west and the south, people of every age and condition, flung headlong on to the roads by the dreadful fear of what the morrow might have in store. It was a vast tidal wave, washing away large swathes of humanity from the streets through which it poured; cars, motor-cyclists, cyclists and horse-drawn carts all moving at a snail's pace because of the congested roads. It dragged everything helter-skelter in its wake. The authorities went off either before or after those whom they had been appointed to govern; towns lost their mayors, councillors and clerks, their dustmen, policemen and firemen. Exhausted crowds camped out wherever they could, on guard against rioting and looting. When the enemy troops arrived they found a vacuum which their propaganda was not slow to exploit: 'We are coming in order to help civilians deserted by their leaders.'

At first this wave of panic caused a real collective trauma. France was deprived of any national or local government and the French left at the mercy of their obsessions and weaknesses. The sight was a demoralising one for the members of the government and President Albert Lebrun has told how deeply it affected him. On all sides the feeling was that everything was falling apart and that the state and all authority had ceased to exist. It would have been impossible not to be obsessed by all this when making these grave decisions.

The hordes of refugees mingled with the retreating army convoys. The chaos amongst the civilians infected the soldiers, and vice-versa; their panic rush took them along the same roads. Soldiers threw away their weapons and desertion became commonplace. German aircraft flew over and machine-gunned civilians and troops indiscriminately. The tanks forced their way through. In the general chaos, it was obvious that there was no longer any possibility of co-ordinated resistance.

II THE ROUT

Indeed, the German troops were advancing in all directions without meeting anything but local resistance. General Weygand—whom Paul Reynaud had thought of replacing by General Huntziger but then decided otherwise—had, of course, issued his instructions: the Tenth Army was to block the way west by digging in on the Perche hills; the Paris Army and the Seventh Army were to hold the Loire between Tours and Cosne; the Sixth, Fourth and Second Armies were to block the valleys of the Yonne, the Seine and the Marne; and finally the Second Army Group would leave the Maginot line and take up positions on the Swiss frontier. These positions were well dispersed but not continuous; and they were never to be held or even occupied, because the Supreme Commander no longer knew the whereabouts of the armies supposed to occupy them. All that remained were a number of isolated pockets of resistance under a few determined leaders at bridges, crossroads and communication centres. Some mayors were opposed to defending their towns for fear that they would be destroyed.

Premier Paul Reynaud conceived one last grandiose operation: the formation of a 'Breton stronghold' so that the struggle could be continued on some part of French territory and links maintained with his British ally; control of the seas would enable supplies to be brought in. Without great conviction, Weygand issued the necessary instructions on June 10. Generals Fagalde and Altmeyer were to regroup the divisions saved at Dunkirk and repatriated from England in order to man the stronghold. The collaboration of the British was obviously indispensable; on June 11, they began landing a Canadian division in France. On June 14, agreement was reached between Weygand and General Alanbrooke, the new commander of the BEF. Weygand made no secret of his pessimism to Alanbrooke; he called the stronghold a 'romantic idea' and confessed to him that the French Army was no longer capable of organised resistance. Alanbrooke was concerned at this and reported the real state of affairs to his government. The British government then took decisions which confirmed their intention to cease playing any part in the struggle on the Continent: they released Alanbrooke from his commitments, kept the BEF under their control, stopped sending reinforcements and prepared to re-embark the last British troops still on French soil.

On June 15, Sir John Dill, the British CIGS, informed Weygand that the BEF was no longer subordinated to him, but that he would help the French troops to embark if they so wished. In fact, the British now proceeded to undertake a second evacuation, this time very successfully (150,000 men including 20,000 Poles, and 310 guns). By June 18, there were no British soldiers left in France, except a few hidden stragglers looked after by French civilians.

By that date, moreover, the Germans had reached every objective within the range of their rate of advance. Guderian took St-Dizier, Langres and Besançon one after the other. On June 17, he had reached Pontarlier and had completely isolated the eastern army group. On the 18th, Belfort fell.

The Hoeppner group had crossed the Marne and then the Seine; one Panzer division had reached Auxerre, Avallon, the Jura and then moved on to Bourg, Lyon and the Dauphiné, where it was preparing to join up with the Italians; another, starting from Semur and Dijon, was fanning out towards the Rhône valley via Chalon-sur-Saône and Mâcon.

The Kleist group was making for Clermont-Ferrand via Provins, Sens, Montargis and Moulins. Finally, in the extreme west, the Hoth group with Rommel in the lead had captured the remnants of the Tenth Army in Rennes, took Cherbourg on the 17th, had almost reached Brest and was advancing on Niort.

Apart from a few isolated heroic feats, such as that of the Saumur cadets on a bridge over the Loire, the French had stopped fighting except in the north-east and in the Alps. According to General Prételat, General Weygand, against his advice, took too long to order the withdrawal of the Second Army Group. The latter had opposed the German attack in the Saar; when it pulled back, the enemy had been able to cross the Rhine; then it had been encircled by Guderian's advance; however, the struggle was still continuing and many units were offering stout resistance, particularly on the Maginot line—some of its forts did not surrender until ordered to do so, between June 25 and July 7.

In the Alps nothing happened on June 11, 12 or 13. On June 14, 'local' attacks were launched by the Italians on easily accessible points; these attacks were pressed home on June 15 and 16, but were halted by a French counter-attack on the 17th. Not until June 20 did the Italians attack in strength but only a few French advanced works were lost or bypassed on June 21 and 22. The struggle for Menton began in the evening of the 23rd, but the Italians succeeded in occupying only the old town. 450,000 Italians were pinned down by less than 180,000 French. The French considered that they had not been beaten by the Italians, in fact quite the reverse.

But in the pitiful state of France this was meagre consolation. How could the deterioration in the situation and the disintegration of the French Army fail to affect the determination of the members of the government and the military leaders?

III THE FRENCH GOVERNMENT'S DELIBERATIONS
(JUNE 13–16)

The government proved to be divided as to the answer to be given to the one question that faced them: should fighting continue or should hostilities be brought to an end by suing for peace?

This question, on which hung the present as well as the future of France, split the ministers into two groups, one led by the Premier, Paul Reynaud, the other by Marshal Pétain. The decision was taken in the course of discussions spread over four dramatic days and only after some violent clashes.

In the War Committee of May 25, 1940, the cessation of hostilities had been mentioned by the President and by Campinchi, the Minister for the Navy, as one of a number of possibilities that must be considered. In the Interallied Supreme Council held at Briare on June 11, Paul Reynaud informed Churchill that Marshal Pétain had expressed himself in favour of asking for an armistice but that he had not yet sent him a minute on the subject.

On June 12, at Cangé, it was General Weygand himself who, after reporting on the military situation, had concluded that fighting must be brought to an end, to the great consternation of the French cabinet, whose members had not imagined that the situation was so serious. Almost all the twenty-four ministers present rejected Weygand's proposal that Paul Reynaud described as 'completely inacceptable'.

The new factor in Weygand's approach to the matter was that he was speaking as much in political as in military terms. He considered that 'the country could not be allowed to drift; some troops would have to be kept in reserve in order to maintain public order which might shortly be gravely jeopardised; if an armistice were not requested without delay, the Army as well as the local civilian population and the refugees would get out of control.' In a word, the Supreme Commander was not confining himself to advising the government; over and above his very persuasive urgent military reasons, he was putting forward considerations of internal policy and even raising the question of defending a particular social order. He was going beyond his brief in order to indicate to the government the policy that they should follow. The only person to support Weygand was Marshal Pétain.

In face of this alliance of two great soldiers, what possible weight could the civilian ministers' opinions have, when their names were practically unknown to the French people and most of them were in any case incapable of forming an independent judgment for themselves? How could they avoid the natural inclination to cover themselves by siding with those who seemed to speak with indisputable authority and prestige?

And so, on June 13, Paul Reynaud's assistants, the 'experts' Bouthillier and Baudouin joined the ranks of those supporting an armistice. The politician Ybarnegaray followed suit, with the remark that he was a soldier and would follow his leaders.

Marshal Pétain now came out openly without reservation as the leader of the peace party. He read out to the Cabinet a memorandum whose contents went far beyond any request to cease hostilities. He brushed aside any idea of continuing the struggle beyond the frontiers of metropolitan France, not for military but for moral reasons: 'Abandoning French territory would amount to desertion. To deprive France of her natural defenders in a period of general confusion would mean delivering her into the hands of the enemy.' He wanted France's revival to be the work of the French themselves and not through 'the conquest of our territory by Allied guns'. Moreover, he did not see this French revival as taking place through military success but as the result of 'suffering imposed on the fatherland and its sons'. He concluded by describing an armistice not as a punishment for a defeat, with its incalculable consequences, but as the first stage in a fresh start, 'a necessary condition to ensure that immortal France should continue to exist for all time'. Thus while Marshal Pétain considered any military and political reasons for the government's decisions as clearly important, he took his stand on a quasi-religious level. As for the government, it may be wondered how far he recognised its authority; he had no desire to submit to a majority decision; his own decision had been taken once and for all: 'He would not leave France . . . and he would leave the government if necessary.'

No decision was reached that day. But Pétain's determination to act outside the government if he did not become its leader had already been shown when, without informing the Premier, he summoned General Weygand that afternoon to ask him to attend the cabinet meeting at Bordeaux on the following day. It was Weygand himself, correct to the last, who told Paul Reynaud of Pétain's request.

In Bordeaux, where the government arrived on June 14, two new-comers made their appearance on the scene. Laval, who was not a member of the government and who had hitherto played no part at all, had installed himself in the Hôtel de Ville. By exerting influence on the members of Parliament who were also in Bordeaux, he was able to provide the group of ministers who were behind Marshal Pétain with some incipient parliamentary support. In fact, a number of deputies informed Herriot, the leader of the Chamber of Deputies, that they wished to approach the government to suggest suing for peace.

Till now, Admiral Darlan had shown himself determined to continue the fight at the head of the Navy, whatever happened. The defeat of the Army had made the Admiral the senior French military commander and the Navy had become the last remaining organised force in France. His actions had thus suddenly become extremely important; but on June 12, Pétain succeeded in winning him over: he told him of 'his disgust at the government's wavering'; he emphasised 'the need to change the régime'; he forecast 'that a sort of Consulate would be necessary' and said 'that he saw him as a First Consul'.[1] Although on other occasions he still expressed himself in favour of continuing the fight—for example, on June 15 to Edouard Herriot—the Admiral had definitely made up his mind, so the opponents of an armistice could no longer rely on the Admiral of the Fleet. How would it then be possible to continue the fight overseas?

At the cabinet meeting on June 15, it was, however, still Weygand who held the limelight. Paul Reynaud asked him to put an end to hostilities, on land and in the metropolis, following the Dutch precedent, by surrendering the Army. In this way, the government would remain free to continue the war with the fleet and the Air Force in the French colonies. The general's reply gave a strange twist to the problem. He categorically refused to surrender, on the grounds that 'what was right in a monarchy was not right in a democracy in which governments follow one another in rapid succession'. When Paul Reynaud suggested giving the Supreme Commander a written order to cover him, Weygand replied that he would refuse to obey any such order. He considered that it would be dishonourable for the Army.

1. Darlan has given three roughly identical accounts of this meeting: one to Henri Béraud (*Gringoire*, May 5, 1941); one to Matteo Cornet, Campinchi's principal private secretary (Parliamentary Investigating Committee, vol. VII, p. 2188); and one in a letter to Marshal Pétain dated October 5, 1942 (Admiral Fernet: *Aux cotés du maréchal Pétain*, p. 282).

It was now no longer merely a question of a confrontation of forces, the sufferings of the civilian population or choosing the lesser evil. What had suddenly and dramatically emerged was the pre-revolutionary conception, held by a great Republican army leader, of his relationship with the French government. In reality, it was no more 'dishonourable' to order all the units which were continuing a hopeless battle to lay down their arms together than to let them surrender piecemeal, one after another, as had been the case with the 40,000 men who had been left behind at Dunkirk. Once again, it was a political or even an ethical point of view that the Supreme Commander was trying to force on the government; at the very least, he was intent on protecting the Army from any share in the responsibility for the disaster and ensuring that the government should assume full responsibility for suing for peace, which is a political act.

Supported by Frossard, Camille Chautemps now put forward one of those compromise solutions which were his speciality. He suggested that an armistice should be requested and Germany sounded as to her peace terms. These, he said, would be so outrageous that public opinion would refuse to accept them; this would restore unity in the government, which would thus be stronger and more able to continue the struggle in North Africa. According to Paul Reynaud, thirteen ministers voted for Chautemp's suggestion and only six against. This 'classical lobby compromise' as it was correctly termed by W. Langer, would in fact make Hitler 'the saviour of French unity', as Robert Aron pointed out. In any case, it could not really lead to much, since the 'unacceptable conditions' had not been defined. But some of Paul Reynaud's supporters had been lured away, although Chautemps afterwards denied that he had been in any way working hand in glove with the Pétain–Weygand faction.

In the morning of June 16, the ministers met again. Judging that further hesitation was impossible, Pétain brought matters to a head: he stood up and read a prepared letter of resignation, giving as his reason the delay in suing for peace. He even attempted to leave the room and President Lebrun was obliged to restrain him.

That afternoon, the government was informed of a staggering British proposal—in fact, thought up by General de Gaulle, Jean Monnet and René Pleven, the members of the co-ordinating committee for the purchase of armaments in London, and approved by Churchill. It suggested quite simply a complete political union of France and Britain. Its real purpose was, in fact, to gain time and prevent the supporters of an armistice from carrying the day. Paul Reynaud was the first to be surprised but he nonetheless put the proposal to his colleagues; they did not examine it closely. Chautemps and Ybarnegaray even thought that Britain meant to reduce France to the status of a dominion and expressed indignation.

That evening, without seeking the advice of any of his ministers, Paul Reynaud handed in his resignation to President Lebrun, proposing Marshal Pétain as his successor. When the leaders of the two houses, Jeanneney and Herriot were consulted, as is customary in a ministerial crisis, they concurred in the choice. To everyone's surprise, the Marshal pulled out of his pocket a readymade list of ministers. The new cabinet met at once and, in the night of June 16–17, Paul Baudouin, the new Minister of Foreign Affairs, asked the Spanish government to agree to act as intermediary with the Germans.

IV WAS THE ARMISTICE UNAVOIDABLE?

That the French Army, victorious in the First World War, had been crushed in less than forty days' fighting was an unprecedented disaster for the French nation, and as dramatic as it was unexpected. And the fact that suing for peace was also to involve occupation and resistance, collaboration and national revolution, was bound to lead to passionate heart-searching amongst the French as to its reasons and causes. Thus we find that those directly involved have offered long, often violently conflicting explanations—particularly Paul Reynaud and General Weygand.

On both sides, the arguments put forward were equally strong. Paul Reynaud, Mandel and Louis Marin have pointed out that France was bound to Britain by treaty and Hitler wanted the total destruction of France—as Paul Reynaud had said, 'he's Gengis Khan'; and, even although the army was beaten, France still had her fleet intact and an immense empire. Pétain and Weygand's retort was that France had done its utmost and that Britain had failed to do the same; that, on the other hand, it was despicable for those governing a country to leave it to its fate when the battle had gone against it. Weygand had added his personal interpretation of the honour of the Army and he had not disguised his apprehension that defeat might lead to social revolution.

In this way, the nub of the problem has frequently been strangely shifted so that the real question is concealed. This was to decide whether France could and should continue the fight outside metropolitan France, on the seas and in the colonies. In point of fact, no one had given the matter serious thought and no plans had been drawn up. General Weygand had never concealed his belief that any such project was doomed from the start because it was impracticable. But Truchet has shown that in French North Africa there were still 400,000 men and means were available to supply them with further manpower and equipment; that above all the whole population—Europeans, natives, civil servants and the military, with General Noguès at their head—were unanimous in wanting to continue the struggle. It is true that there were many unknown quantities, not least the attitude of Spain. But all in all, if no decision was reached, it was because no one had even begun to make any preparations for further fighting and the question was never examined, because after June 16 the new political leaders of France under Pétain and Weygand wanted nothing to do with it. What were their reasons?

V PETAIN'S IDEAS

The ideas which motivated the Marshal at this crucial time were communicated to the French people in a series of messages from June 20–25.

The prime cause of France's irretrievable defeat was, he stressed, the disparity of forces. Pétain considered that the British were especially responsible for this state of affairs.

To this inferiority in numbers there must be added a still greater inferiority in equipment. 'The French Air Force,' said the Marshal 'had to fight against odds of six to one.' Curiously enough, no mention was made of tanks, of tank–aircraft co-operation or of German Panzer tactics.

The truth probably was that for him the real causes went deeper, since they were moral rather than military: 'Love of pleasure was stronger than the spirit of sacrifice. People claimed things as their right rather than being willing to serve. They shirked effort and so they have fallen on evil times.' So it was the whole French people and no chance disparity between the armies involved that was responsible for France's defeat. By their bad conduct, the French people had called down condign punishment upon their heads. 'Our defeat had its roots in the laxity of our conduct.'

The conclusion followed inevitably from these premises: for the moment the harm was irreparable and the defeat irredeemable; by recognising this, 'the French were showing more greatness . . . than in meeting it with empty words and vain schemes'—a reference to Churchill's expressed determination that Britain would continue the fight alone and a reply to General de Gaulle's prophetic appeals from London.

There was nothing for France to do but to submit to her unhappy fate. That way lay wisdom and salvation, at least for what might still be saved. Seen from this viewpoint, it might moreover be a shrewd move to beat the British in the race to see who would give up first. For Pétain thought that Churchill's call for resistance at all costs was futile and perhaps even empty words.

This resigned pessimism had been expressed by Pétain even before the battle of the Somme had started. All that had happened since had only confirmed him in his conviction that Germany had won the war; so without losing a minute, the least unpalatable terms possible must be obtained so that no more French soldiers' lives should be uselessly sacrificed and also in order to preserve what little strength France still retained.

Thus when he took power Marshal Pétain was not concerned that fighting should stop, as he felt it must, for military reasons only, nor did France's diplomatic obligations towards her British ally weigh with him either. Looking beyond the catastrophe which, grave as it was, was only an accident in the life of a people, he was seeing into the future of France; and this future would only be assured if she could drag herself out of the morass into which she had been plunged by bad leadership and evil habits, and enter into the path of revival in which he would show the way. He did not look upon himself as merely taking over the tiller in a difficult moment but as the saviour for whom the country had been longing for many years. So it was pointless to consider continuing the struggle in Africa. Nor could France's task be dealt with by means of a mere suspension of hostilities which was always precarious and would inevitably be denounced. Moreover, since it was France who was responsible for the ills that had befallen her, it was for her alone to turn the tables on herself, in the due course of time.

VI REQUEST FOR GERMANY'S TERMS

It may thus be wondered whether it was really a truce that the Spanish government was to request from the Reich on France's behalf or whether it was not in fact Germany's peace terms.

Paul Baudouin relates in his memoirs that he handed M. de Léquérica, the Spanish ambassador to Paris, a handwritten note but he does not reveal its contents. He writes that the 'government had decided to ask Germany her terms for the cessation of hostilities'. Charles-Roux has come to his minister's help: 'It is possible,' he writes 'that M. Baudouin on one occasion used one word instead of another'—peace instead of armistice—'but the overall gist of his message left no doubt as to what request he was making.'

Paul Baudouin was a makeshift Foreign Minister and a novice, and his emotion at having such a grave step to take as his first act of diplomacy is understandable; but it is difficult to imagine that he displayed such confusion of mind and casualness of approach as to fail to distinguish a temporary armistice and a definitive peace, especially as he was implementing a vital decision which had been reached at a cabinet meeting that had only just ended.

In any case, the German ambassador in Madrid, von Stöhrer, had no doubts at all: Paul Baudouin had told Léquérica—the Spanish government had just informed him—that 'the French government wishes the Spanish government to transmit to Germany, with all desirable speed, a request for the immediate cessation of hostilities and that it should be informed of Germany's proposed *peace terms*'. When Léquérica asked the French minister if he was talking about an armistice or peace or both, Baudouin replied: 'Armistice terms were always, obviously, a temporary expedient and the French government was interested in knowing the peace terms.' So it is hardly a question of its being a slip of the tongue in a hurried conversation; Paul Baudouin had been perfectly explicit. And Hitler was not mistaken, either; in his order of the day to the Wehrmacht, he had stated: 'The newly formed French government has informed the German government that it intends to cease hostilities and wishes to be informed of our peace terms.'

Moreover, hardly had the request been made than Pétain made a solemn proclamation to the troops on June 17, that 'while recognising the heroic nature of their struggle', they must 'cease fighting'. A confession of this sort that he was abandoning the struggle, even if it was made 'with a heavy heart', not only placed the French envoys in an awkward position in their negotiations with the Germans over the conditions for an armistice and, if possible, peace terms; it also incurred the risk of encouraging the enemy to think that it was pointless to engage in talks with a government which, of its own accord, was ordering its armed forces to cease fighting, leaving the commanders to decide for themselves the best way to set about it; it considerably limited any possibility the French might have of rejecting or even of discussing the enemy's terms.

The first immediate result was that whole regiments of troops ceased fighting, since they had been ordered to do so.

What would have happened had Hitler demanded something 'unacceptable', that is, if he had made claims on the French empire and the French fleet? How could the Bordeaux government have been able to take up the fight again in view of the fact that it had deprived itself of any possibility of doing so? But Hitler did not place the Bordeaux government in such an embarrassing position, which would doubtless have caused its downfall. He was careful not to demand anything 'unacceptable' and he gave Mussolini his reasons.

VII HITLER'S IDEAS ON THE ARMISTICE

Whilst ordering the Wehrmacht to 'pursue the beaten foe energetically in every sector', Hitler was above all concerned to weaken Britain decisively by preventing the remaining French forces—the empire and the fleet— from casting their lot in with her.

On June 18 and 19, he met Mussolini and Ciano in Munich. The latter wrote: 'He spoke with a moderation and clearsightedness which were really surprising after such a victory . . . At that moment, I greatly admired him.' What was it Hitler said to his allies? He explained to them that it was important, during the negotiations, for a French government to continue to function in French territory. 'This would be far preferable to the situation that would arise if the French government fled to London to continue the war.' In addition, an agreement with a legal French government remaining in France would relieve the occupying powers of the 'unpleasant responsibility' of running the country directly. It was obviously more convenient to have the German decisions implemented by a government of French officials who would be more readily obeyed by their compatriots than foreigners, who were also their enemy. The Reich officials wanted to use again the methods which had proved their worth in Denmark and avoid the troubles they were encountering in Norway. The Bordeaux government knew nothing, of course, of these concerns of the Führer and had no suspicion that its decision to remain in France was playing directly into his hands.

Hitler was, above all, perturbed at the thought of what the French fleet might do. He had calculated that should it go over to Britain, it would in some cases double the strength of the Royal Navy. It was, therefore, necessary to come to an agreement with a French government that would remain in France and neutralise the fleet. 'This might be done by disarming the fleet in French ports under German and Italian supervision' with the guarantee that 'France's entire fleet would be returned to her when peace was finally concluded'. But Hitler doubted whether 'France would have the slightest confidence in any guarantee given by himself'. So he was thinking of impounding the fleet in a neutral country such as Spain or Portugal. In any case, it would be better to prevent the fleet from leaving for the United States, because they might, at a later date, hand it over to Britain; but he did not completely exclude the possibility of its going to America. A good solution would be for the fleet to scuttle itself.

Consequently, Hitler thought that, rather than the whole of France being occupied, the French government should be left with an area of theoretical sovereignty. Nor should any request be made to hand over the fleet; since it would be impossible to lay hands on it, it would escape and the French government would have no further interest in signing an armistice. Similarly, no demands should be made at the moment concerning the French colonial empire; this would be equally impossible to enforce and the only foreseeable result would be that France's colonial territories would go over to the British side.

Thus, far from being intoxicated by victory, Hitler was displaying surprisingly statesmanlike common sense. In a monologue which lasted for several hours, he had, in fact, given an outline of what his policy in France would be for the next four years: to exploit to the full, for Germany's benefit, a French government still retaining a semblance of authority. Graziani's notes report him as saying, 'all things considered, I prefer an enemy like France, whose forces are thickly concentrated, who can be got at and beaten, to enemies that are weaker but more dispersed.' But similar caution prevented Hitler from informing his opponents of his peace terms which the Bordeaux government was so anxious to learn.

Mussolini fully realised that his own views carried little weight since it was Hitler who had won the war. On June 22, he wrote to his colleague that he would make 'minimum' demands on the French. According to Ciano, Mussolini was even afraid that, by pressing his claims, he might compromise not only the current negotiations but even the good relations between Italy and Germany.[1]

But Hitler's 'moderation' did not include making France any gifts. He intended to take over the whole of the Channel and Atlantic coasts; to occupy France down to the Loire and the Swiss frontier; to include in the occupied zone the railway line to Spain in order to control the rail traffic with that country. Above all, the German economists had drawn up a plan for 'all the economic resources of France and her colonies' to be placed at Germany's disposal, an embargo on all cargo-vessels and German control of the press and the radio. Hitler had indeed been quite explicit to Mussolini: apart from the question of the French fleet and the French colonies, he was ready to make concessions on matters of detail 'which might seem of great importance to the French' but he would not concede any points of substance.

1. In the course of his talks with Ribbentrop in Munich, Ciano had informed him of Italy's claims: Nice, Corsica, Tunisia, French Somaliland; 'an outlet to the Atlantic' through French North Africa; redrawing the Tunisian frontier to include the Algerian iron and phosphate; Malta; and Italy should replace Britain in the Anglo-Egyptian Treaty and the Sudanese condominium! Not a bad price for ten days' unsuccessful participation in the war and hardly any fighting at all.

VIII THE SIGNING OF THE CONVENTION AT RETHONDES

Hitler wanted the signing of the armistice to be as spectacular and symbolic as possible; he ordered it to take place at Rethondes, where Marshal Foch had dictated his terms to the German delegates in 1918.

On June 21 at 3.30 p.m. the Führer received the French delegation in Foch's own carriage; he was accompanied by Ribbentrop, Goering, Keitel and the commanders-in-chief of the various branches of the Wehrmacht. After Keitel had read the preamble to the armistice terms in German, followed by a translation in French, Hitler stood up and left. For him, the matter was settled.

Keitel handed the French delegation the text of the German terms, emphasising that 'the basic conditions were not open to discussion and must be accepted or rejected as they stood'. It was a *Diktat*. The area for manoeuvre was not very large.

When the meeting reassembled, Jodl was in the chair. General Huntziger described the German terms as 'harsh and pitiless'. He asked whether the demarcation line of the occupied zone was unalterable.

To ensure the maintenance of law and order and to 'prevent the country drifting into Communism'—a phrase echoing Weygand's fears—Huntziger made it plain that France would need an army of 120,000 to 130,000 men. On this point Keitel gave his assent without difficulty 'for a provisional period'. Keitel then promised that the occupying troops would be limited to the needs of the war against Britain and that only 'a force sufficient to maintain law and order' would be stationed in Paris.

The Bordeaux government decided to request Germany to make some modifications to the original text. Two minor concessions were made by the victors: it was agreed that the French military aircraft need not be handed over to the Germans—General Bergeret considered this would be an insult to the honour of the French Air Force; the aircraft would merely be disarmed, under German supervision. Also, 'the German government would take into consideration the essential needs of the population of the non-occupied zone'.

But Keitel showed no flexibility with regard to another problem. When Huntziger made the point that the extradition of German exiles who were enjoying the right of asylum would be a shameful act on the part of the French people, Keitel replied unequivocally that they were 'warmongers and traitors to Germany' and that 'the extradition of that type of person would be demanded at all costs'. There was nothing further to be said.

The most important discussion, however, was on Article 8 of the convention. This laid down that naval vessels which were not under the control of the French government, that is, almost all of them, were to be disarmed in their pre-war home ports. Germany pledged herself not to seize them.

Huntziger proposed an amendment: 'After demobilisation and the removal of ammunition under Italian and German supervision, the French warships should proceed to French North African ports with half their peace-time establishment.' Huntziger gave as the reason for this request the fear of British air raids. For the proposed amendment to be fully effective, it ought also to have asked for the assurance that during the disarmament of the fleet under enemy supervision no attempt should be made to seize possession of it. But the question did not arise, for Keitel refused any discussion. He stressed the 'very generous' terms of Article 8 that the French did not seem fully to appreciate. The protection of the fleet against air attack was a question of detail that concerned the armistice commission. 'The German delegation rejected the French request'; Huntziger did not insist. So Article 8 placed the French fleet in danger of being seized by the enemy.

In the evening of June 22, orders came from Bordeaux to sign, which Huntziger did, as the only French signatory, after stating that 'the French government felt justified in expecting, having accepted such very onerous demands, that Germany would approach the ensuing negotiations in a spirit that would enable the two great neighbouring peoples to live and work in peace'. But although the Germans listened politely, they made no kind of pledge of this sort.

The French were very apprehensive about the Italians. But on June 23 in Rome, everything went off very well. The Italians put forward no claims likely to cause a breakdown in the negotiations. No mention was made of occupying the left bank of the Rhône or of occupying Corsica or Tunisia. They confined themselves to demanding the demilitarisation of a thirty-mile strip along the frontier and occupying those areas that had been conquered by the armies of the Prince of Piedmont. Instead of increasing their demands, as the French had feared, the Italians even made some concessions.

Admiral Le Luc tried to raise once again the question of disarming the fleet under Article 8. He asked for 'the idea of home port to be considered purely as a suggestion'. The Italians were conciliatory and said that they did not want the French ships to be exposed to the danger of being sunk. But these kind words did not lead to any change in the wording of the text. Neither in Rome nor at Rethondes was any improvement made in the wording of the armistice agreement and this article, if implemented, would seriously jeopardise the greater part of the French Navy.

France was beaten and had accepted her defeat. Britain was standing alone. Was she ready to withstand the blow?

PART III

BRITAIN STANDS ALONE

CHAPTER 1

The Battle of Britain

AT Rethondes, Hitler danced a joyful little jig on leaving Foch's carriage. There seemed no end to his hopes after such a swift succession of un-qualified victories.[1] Although he took great care not to reveal his war aims either to Mussolini, because of the slight rivalry between them, or to those he had conquered, in order not to arouse them from their paralysing stupor, to his intimates the Führer made no secret of his grandiose schemes; all the lands seized from Germany in the last 400 years would be handed back, not counting other gains.

In this immense plan to recover lost territory, Britain was only directly threatened with having to hand over some mandated territories, the former German colonies which she had been administering since 1918. Was it worth continuing the war for their sake? Chamberlain had dropped one or two hints concerning them on a number of occasions. Hitler con-sidered the British Commonwealth an institution worth preserving—after all, it was Aryan stock that was governing these vast territories.

So he was probably convinced that Britain would be quite happy at being asked for almost nothing and that, willy-nilly, she would accept the new situation that the Wehrmacht's victories had created in Europe. Ciano wrote: 'Hitler's desire to conclude peace as quickly as possible is obvious from everything he says.' On August 3, at the same time as he was giving orders to reduce the number of army divisions—and annexing Eupen, Malmédy and Alsace-Lorraine—the Führer made advances to the British government, through the King of Sweden.

Churchill's reply was an emphatic no. Possibly Hitler then had the thought of driving a wedge between the people of Britain and their Prime Minister. This may have been the meaning of the peculiar approach that was made to the Duke and Duchess of Windsor who were just getting ready to leave for the Bahamas, where the Duke had been appointed governor. Through the mediation of some Spanish friends, the Duke was

1. His prestige was enormous everywhere, even in Britain. The Afghan ambassador in Ankara had told von Papen that 'Germany had a large number of friends, more than she might think'.

warned that Churchill was planning to assassinate him; he was advised not to go and, in order to prevent him, his luggage was 'mislaid'; they even went so far as to hint that 'changes might possibly be made in the British constitution'—this is said to have made the Duchess 'look thoughtful'. But while not concealing the fact that he was no keen supporter of the war, the Duke refused to enter into 'negotiations against the instructions of his government': there was no fifth column in England.

II BRITISH DETERMINATION: WINSTON CHURCHILL

Nonetheless, the disparity between the two forces was discouraging. The British Army now had only 500 guns and 200 tanks; American arms were only just beginning to arrive, carefully packed in grease, because they dated from 1917–18. There were a few well-trained brigades but they had to defend thousands of miles of coastline. The Home Guard was being hurriedly drilled, using sticks and poles. The strike force consisted of 700 fighters and 500 bombers which were awaiting the Luftwaffe's onslaught. No one could say if and when Britain would take the offensive; for the moment and for a long time to come, she would have to 'stick it out' under attack from an opponent superior in numbers and free to choose the time, place and manner of its offensive.

It was at this dramatic moment that one morning, at breakfast, Winston Churchill, that amazing man who was leading the country, put forward the novel idea of 'prefabricated harbours' that would enable vast forces to be landed at any point on the coastline of the Continent. From this time onwards Churchill appears, in all his glory, as a unique personality, riding high above the storm. Journalist, serving officer, historian, MP and minister, his political career had hitherto been extremely controversial; in 1919, he had been one of the supporters of 'cordoning off' the Soviet Union; in 1925, as Chancellor of the Exchequer, he had been responsible for revaluing the pound, thus heading for the slump; he had been almost the only politician to side with Edward VIII at the time of the latter's abdication; as Colonial Secretary, he had crushed the nationalist movements; in 1935, he had disapproved of sanctions against Italy and as late as 1936 he had thought that Britain should keep out of any European war.

But the dismemberment of Czechoslovakia had opened his eyes to the peril of Hitler and from then on no one was more resolute in his determination to thwart it. With a touch of eccentricity in his dress, always smoking a cigar, a glass of whisky handy at crack of dawn, working to no systematic timetable, liable to go to bed at 2 a.m. and drag his advisers out of their own beds a couple of hours later, finding it hard to resist childish

pranks such as going for a bathe on a beach in Libya in front of all his
staff only a few miles away from the front line, Churchill displayed an
equanimity and optimism in the direst adversity that were of the greatest
comfort to his compatriots. He was able to hit on words and attitudes that
galvanised them into action and stung their pride: 'I can offer you,' he
said 'nothing but blood, sweat and tears.' But when announcing an impending German landing, he could make his hearers relax and laugh
when he said: 'We are waiting for the Germans'—pause—'so are the fish.'
In the smoking ruins of London, he would walk about making the V for
victory sign and with a word or a gesture, raise a cheer from those who
had been bombed out. Tireless, ubiquitous, a glutton for punishment,
imaginative, impulsive, with a gambler's pleasure in taking a risk, capable
of playing fair *and* of hitting below the belt, putting the safety of the
British Commonwealth above everything else, an orator, poet and man of
action, Churchill was also an inexhaustible source of ideas, anecdotes,
questions and schemes. Lloyd George used to say of him that he had ten
ideas a day but that he didn't know which was the right one. Marshall
considered that one of the main tasks of his general staff was to stop him
making strategic blunders. But this unorthodox visionary was able to build
for the future as well as living intensely in the present. The British people
felt at one with their leader; they admired his youthful spirit, his sturdy
vitality, his courage and even his childishness. An extraordinary man, a
specimen of humanity the like of which has rarely been seen over the
centuries, an anachronism fully in touch with his times, exasperating yet
irresistible, Churchill flourished in the dramatic atmosphere in which he
came to power and responded with all his bulldog pugnacity.

He had no intention of running the war through endless committees.
Within the government he formed a war cabinet of five members, includ-
ing the Labour opposition leader, Attlee. He himself was Prime Minister,
First Lord of the Treasury and National Defence Minister. It was he who
really directed the war effort and British strategy with the help of the
Chief of Staff's committee: John Dill and later Alanbrooke for the Army;
Dudley Pound for the Navy; Charles Portal for the RAF; his military ad-
viser was Lord Ismay.

III MERS EL-KEBIR

The Royal Navy was the most reassuring factor in the United Kingdom's
defences. But the defeat of France had deprived it of the co-operation of
the French fleet, whose future filled it with apprehension. If by some mishap the French fleet were to fall into the hands of the Germans, the Axis

powers would seize control of the Mediterranean; the Atlantic convoys—Britain's life-line—would be even more seriously jeopardised; a German landing would no longer be an empty threat.

Throughout those tragic days when France's request for German peace terms had first of all exaggerated and then shattered the relationship between the Allies, the British had been worried about the clauses imposed by the victors regarding the French fleet. Yet they had received every possible reassurance—from Reynaud, Pétain and Darlan; the French fleet, they had been told again and again, would never be handed over to the enemy; it would scuttle itself rather than fall into their hands. But the British had noted that the Bordeaux government had refused to allow the fleet to sail for British harbours and that the French Admiralty had taken certain steps to separate the two navies. They were doubtful whether the government of France would be able to prevent the enemy seizing the French ships; they wondered whether it might not be persuaded to hand them over of its own free will, if the Germans were to offer substantial advantages in exchange—the release of the prisoners of war, for example, as Churchill suggested.

In short, on July 1 the British government decided to eliminate the possible danger represented by the unknown quantity of the French fleet. It was particularly concerned about the implementation of Article 8 of the armistice convention, whereby the French ships were to return to their pre-war home ports—in the ports situated in occupied France they would be a tempting and easy prey for the enemy. The Bordeaux government had not transmitted to the British the veiled promises that it had obtained, suggesting that the dangerous stipulations contained in this clause might be judiciously modified.

On July 3 Operation 'Catapult' was launched. French ships at anchor in British harbours were treacherously attacked by British boarding parties, to the great indignation of their crews. Fortunately, in Alexandria talks between Admirals Cunningham and Godfroy led to an agreement to neutralise the latter's squadron without resort to arms. But at Mers el-Kebir where the bulk of the French fleet was at anchor a dramatic tragedy took place.

With the French Admiralty's full approval Admiral Gensoul rejected pointblank Admiral Somerville's four-point ultimatum. The British then launched an attack in which the odds were bound to be uneven; only one French battleship, the *Strasbourg*, managed to escape; the rest of the fleet was sunk or seriously damaged; and 1,300 French sailors were killed.

Although a reversal of alliances was only just averted—Marshal Pétain soothed Darlan's and Laval's wrath and decided to exercise a minimum of retaliation—the outrageous attack at Mers el-Kebir nonetheless set the seal on the break between France and England; it thus played into Hitler's hands and opened up the way for the French policy of collaboration.

However, these unfortunate consequences, plus the odium incurred by the aggression, were outweighed by the feeling that Britain was determined to fight to the last ditch, which impressed every country, not least the Axis powers. Churchill anticipated that this would be so and Ciano confirmed it when he wrote, 'this action by the British proves that their fighting spirit is unimpaired and that His Majesty's Fleet still has the toughness of the captains and pirates of the seventeenth century'. But the immediate danger to the British Isles from Germany was not in any way thereby reduced.

IV OPERATION 'SEA-LION'

In his directive no. 16, dated July 16, Hitler laid down outline plans for an attempted landing in England. It would be a surprise operation over a broad front stretching from Ramsgate to the west of the Isle of Wight. The air fleets based in Norway, the Netherlands, Belgium and France—3,000 aircraft in all—would overwhelm the defences, shoot down the RAF in air combat and neutralise the Royal Navy; under the protection of powerful coastal artillery, the German convoys would sail through a channel between mine-fields on either side. Hitler contemplated landing between twenty-five and forty divisions on the broadest possible front so that they would have an extensive field of operations. Von Brauchitsch and Halder meekly prepared the plans demanded by their Führer.

But Admiral Raeder, who would have the responsibility for the operation, quickly realised its risks and the inadequacies of its preparation. The German Navy had suffered heavy losses in Norway which were far from having been made good, even assuming that they could be; all the necessary shipping—barges, tugs, motor-boats—would have to be requisitioned in Germany and the occupied countries and brought up to the French Channel coast; this could not be done overnight.

The Army was asking the Navy to carry a first wave of 100,000 men with heavy equipment and AA weapons, followed by 160,000 men in the next three days.

The Navy had calculated that its preparations would not be completed before September 15; it considered that success could only be expected if air supremacy had been achieved in the first place and it asked for reassurance from the Luftwaffe on this point. Above all, it stated that it would be unable to provide effective protection for the convoys unless the landing area was narrowly circumscribed. But the general staff of the

Army, who would take over in the event of a successful landing, realised that where the Channel was narrowest, the terrain was ill-suited to tanks because of swampy ground and hills. Consequently, it hoped to land its troops over a wide front in order to make a broad enveloping movement round London, the nerve centre of the British defences.

These divergences of view between the Navy and the Army were matched by similar divergences between the Army and Air Force. Among other things, the Luftwaffe did not want to drop its paratroops until the bridgehead was well established, while the military considered that these paratroops must be dropped in order to achieve the bridgehead. In fact, Marshal Goering was not really interested in the projected landings; he thought that the Luftwaffe was strong enough to bring Britain to her knees on its own. As the British on their part were losing no time in bombing the ships concentrated on the French coast, Admiral Raeder found himself forced as a result of all these unresolved problems to suggest to Hitler that the operation be put back till October or till next year or indefinitely. In any case, since control of the sea was impossible, success would depend on control of the skies. It was up to the Luftwaffe.

V THE BATTLE OF BRITAIN

A battle was thus about to begin on the lines imagined by Douhet, fought out purely in the air, with soldiers and sailors playing no part, almost like spectators. The Germans had more aircraft but they had not had the time to set up airfields close to the British Isles in the occupied territories and the distance out and back had thus not been shortened; on the other hand the home-based British planes could carry out several sorties over the same period, so that in the air the balance was restored. In addition, the manoeuvrability and armament of the British fighter planes confirmed the experience of Dunkirk, and soon proved superior to those of their German opponents. As the Stuka dive-bombers were so vulnerable that they had to be withdrawn from the fighting and since the German bombers, because of the limitations of range of their fighters, were unable to receive the necessary fighter protection, the two sides seemed equal.

But the British were to turn the situation to their advantage by means of a completely new system of defence, thanks to a technical invention they alone possessed: radar. In fact, in addition to the easily penetrated barrage provided by 2,200 balloons and their excellent AA artillery which in July 1940, according to Churchill, consisted of some 1,800 guns, including 1,200 heavy ones, the British, thanks to the inventiveness of Sir Edward Appleton and Robert Watson Watt, were able to erect a chain of radar stations capable of detecting enemy aircraft and their strength, at a distance of sixty miles. In addition, they had decoded the control system of the German day and night bombers and had found ways of upsetting it. Intrigued by air photographs showing defence preparations along the British coast, the Germans had in fact sent the airship *Graf Zeppelin* on two reconnaissance missions but they had achieved nothing and Goering had decided not to attack the radar stations whose importance he failed to assess correctly. This blunder was the Luftwaffe's death warrant.

The Battle of Britain began on July 10, with attacks on Channel convoys and harassing attacks on south-coast harbours. The Luftwaffe wished to lure the RAF away from its bases and destroy it; but the British fighters refused to rise to the bait. To their great surprise, from July 10 to August 10, the Germans lost 286 planes and the English fighters only 150. August 15 was a decisive day; four successive waves, each of 100 aircraft, were launched against south-east England and the Germans lost 290 aircraft. Yet the radar stations were not yet completely ready and the aircraft were being located acoustically, that is to say, inaccurately and comparatively late.

At this juncture Goering decided to attack the British fighters on their airfields, in accordance with the old method that had shown its worth in Poland and France. But the situation was now very different. In eighteen days, the Luftwaffe made 7,500 sorties, 790 of them on August 31. The British AA proved powerful enough to disperse part of the aircraft before they reached their targets. The Spitfires looked after the rest and shot down nearly 500 enemy aircraft.

The Germans now realised that their aircraft were being lost thanks to some technical device of which they were unaware. A plotting and listening detachment between Calais and Boulogne succeeded in deciphering the riddle of the directional control system of Fighter Command and in reading the conversations between the British pilots and their ground installations. The Germans were thus enabled to discover the strength and location of British squadrons in the air and sometimes to warn their bombers that they were being stalked. In this way, by the end of August and in early September, the Luftwaffe's losses had dropped. From now on, the Germans' chances of success in the fighting depended on persistent jamming of their opponents' radio links.

Goering now decided on a 'terror offensive' against London, thus giving psychological warfare priority over the destruction of the enemy's armed forces. It is possible that, by giving it a short breathing space, this decision saved the British fighter force, whose planes were as worn out as their pilots. It was now the Londoners' turn to be sorely tried. They were to be pounded for two whole months; day after day, night after night, an average of 250 bombers came over and showered tons of high explosive and incendiary bombs over London; hundreds of fires were started and whole quarters devastated; this was the Blitz. Londoners took to sleeping in their cellars, while restaurants and night clubs opened up theirs, too. There was no lack of humour. A story went the rounds of a tailor who stuck up a notice on his door after every raid, reading 'Open as usual'. One night, the front of his shop was blown out and the notice read: 'More open than usual.'

Since the threatened destruction of their capital had not daunted British determination, the Luftwaffe turned to the industrial centres, with priority for aircraft factories. On November 15 Coventry was razed to the ground and Goebbels' propaganda machine found a new bogey word: 'coventry-sation'. But from October onwards there were radar stations all along the coast and what is more, thanks to the use of electronics, they were working perfectly in converting acoustic plotting into images on a tube. In addition, by December 1940, British AA consisted of 2,100 guns—more than before the air raids started. On October 12, Hitler drew the logical conclusion of his failure; the planned invasion of Britain was called off. According to Air Marshal Johnson, had the Luftwaffe persevered in its intensive attacks for another fortnight, the RAF would have had to admit defeat; but the British had won the first round.

VI THE MOBILISATION OF THE COMMONWEALTH

Before the war, the dominions made a point of leaving their defence in the hands of the metropolis; but now they found themselves in the position of having to come to its aid; they had been its debtors and they were now going to become its creditors. They were not prepared for this change; they had no soldiers, no armament factories and practically no metallurgical industry. Nor were they all equally aware of the gravity of the danger; some of them did not even feel themselves concerned. It is true that they had immense resources but exploiting them would be an extremely slow process. And for these resources to reach Britain or the various operational theatres, it was still necessary for Britain, having won the war in the air and thus saved her national territory, not to lose the war at sea.

Canada had declared war on Germany a few days after Britain, in order to obtain the greatest possible amount of American war equipment; but her army comprised only 4,500 men and her economy was a strictly agricultural one; reserve officers and men were forbidden by law to serve overseas. The French Canadians were against the war effort since they were not keen on being defenders of the British Commonwealth. But

Mackenzie King, who had been Premier for twenty years, looked on Canada as Britain's rear area. He put through Parliament a bill requiring 'all Canadians over sixteen years old' to sign on and in June 1941 this became military conscription for all men. Canada became the training area for pilots from the British Commonwealth. She linked her defences with those of the United States; she provided Britain with a merchant fleet of 300,000 tons which was to increase tenfold in the course of the war. From early in 1940, she began to build aircraft factories and naval shipyards and from 1941 onwards, Canadian troops were being sent to Britain and Hong Kong.

Australia and New Zealand were even less well defended than Canada and more deeply affected by the slump; and all activity in the military field had been suspended in Australia in 1929. The Conservative Prime Minister, Menzies, introduced compulsory military service as early as 1940. He forbade strikes and set up compulsory arbitration in labour disputes; consumption was restricted, starting with petrol. At the end of 1940, one New Zealand and four Australian divisions arrived in Egypt to guard the Suez Canal. Churchill had the shrewdness to keep Menzies closely in touch with the British war cabinet's decisions. Australian co-operation never wavered.

Things did not go quite so smoothly in South Africa. German propaganda had gained a lot of ground with the Afrikaner nationalists under General Herzog. Nazi racialism found supporters and Fascist organisations formed themselves into 'Grey shirts' or 'Black shirts'. In South-West Africa, the Germans had kept their nationality, while still being citizens of the Union. Nevertheless, Field Marshal Smuts succeeded in getting South Africa to declare war on Germany. But he was forced to accept one reservation: South African troops were not to fight outside Africa. Henceforth, Smuts, who had fought on the side of the Boers, was Churchill's faithful comrade in arms.

The nationalist leaders of India, whether they were members of Gandhi's Congress Party or of the Muslim League, were not pro-Nazi. But they were only willing to take part in the struggle against Germany if India would thereby achieve full dominion status as a pledge of future independence. Churchill refused: 'He would not dig the grave of the British Empire.' He was thus reduced to using strong-arm methods by imprisoning the nationalist leaders. As a result, some of them began to wonder if the way to liberate their country was by open revolt and alliance with the enemies of Britain. This climate of opinion made it impossible for Britain to raise large forces amongst the enormous population of India; only eight divisions were eventually sent to Egypt, from February 1941 onwards.

Furthermore, troops and arms were tied down in India in order to maintain law and order.

On her western flank, Britain was hampered by Eire's neutrality; this prevented her using Irish harbours and turning Ireland into an outpost in the battle of the Atlantic. In addition, a German landing was on the cards and British troops had to stand guard in Ulster in order to intervene swiftly if need be.

Despite these black spots, on the whole the enormous machine of empire had swung into motion to help the mother-country. She could thus consider the possibility of loosening the enemy's grip by opening up operational theatres on the periphery; this thought was to provide food for Churchill's fertile imagination.

VII THE EXILED GOVERNMENTS—FREE FRANCE

Other possibilities of action in Europe could well arise from the fact that London had become a sort of free capital of occupied Europe as a result of the arrival of the legal governments of the conquered countries. King Haakon of Norway, Queen Wilhelmina of Holland, President Beneš of Czechoslovakia and General Sikorski from Poland had found asylum with their governments, either because they had followed them there or had formed them in exile. Even if King Leopold III thought fit to consider himself a prisoner of war in Belgium, there was no doubt that Hubert Pierlot was the head of the legal Belgian government in London. The only exceptions were Denmark and France; the Vichy government had been recognised throughout the world as the legitimate French government; General de Gaulle had merely set up the dissident 'Free French' movement in London.

True, none of these governments could continue to exist without largesse from the British. None of them had much to offer, so their sum total did not amount to a great deal. However, the Dutch and Norwegian merchant fleets, the territories of Indonesia and the Belgian Congo and the Polish and French troops represented a substantial contribution and in her almost desperate isolation, England could not afford to turn away any ally in her struggle. From the psychological point of view, the presence in London of authorities from the occupied countries, albeit almost a token presence, was an encouragement for their peoples not to despair and not to submit passively to the occupying power's demands; it was to be hoped that, in the long run, this attitude would give rise to a whole network of underground resistance movements, like a Trojan horse in the heart of the enemy fortress.

However, the British did not recognise the right of the exiled governments to any real say in the conduct of the war; at the very most, they allowed them to sit on international commissions drawing up post-war plans of minor importance; all that the foreign leaders and troops had to do was to contribute to the British war effort by filling the role assigned to them.

Most of these governments, well aware of their weakness, accepted this control by the British without difficulty; but this did not apply to General de Gaulle. An advocate—unheeded in his own country—of tank warfare, a gifted writer, commander of the French armoured division that had fought most determinedly and with the greatest success against the Germans, a secretary of state in Paul Reynaud's government for a few days and one of the begetters of the plan for complete Anglo-French union, General de Gaulle had left for England on an English plane when Pétain had formed his government. From June 18 onwards, Churchill, who looked on him as the 'Constable of France', had encouraged him to use the BBC to appeal to the French to continue the fight. The general's appeals were prophetic in more ways than one, notably when he said: 'France has lost a battle, but she has not lost the war . . . because this war is a world war.' Few people heeded his words. General de Gaulle failed either to prevent the signing of the armistice or to arouse dissidence amongst the rulers and military leaders of the French colonies, or even to persuade anyone of the first rank or any large bodies of men to rally round him. Thus the British, anxious not to throw the Vichy government and the forces which it still retained into the arms of the Germans, refused to recognise General de Gaulle as the French representative, but merely as the leader of a group: Free France.

But General de Gaulle's view was that the Vichy government was the catspaw of Germany and that he alone would be capable of effectively defending France's interests, even against his own allies. There were thus frequent collisions: the General's stock was at its lowest when, in September 1940, off Dakar, he failed to rally French West Africa to his cause. Nonetheless, as considerable territories had come over to Free France (the French Pacific Islands, the Indian trading stations, French Equatorial Africa and the Cameroons) and he had a small army of soldiers, sailors and airmen under his command (the Free French merchant fleet amounted to 700,000 tons and French pilots took part in the Battle of Britain), General de Gaulle formed an embryonic French government called the French National Committee. A regular stream of volunteers joined his movement, although the attack at Mers el-Kebir considerably reduced the flow even if it did not make it completely dry up.

VIII THE INVOLVEMENT OF THE UNITED STATES

The exiled governments were keeping the flame alight, but the appearance of any national resistance movement in occupied territory was still only a hope and not yet a power to be reckoned with. So the help that Britain so sorely needed to withstand an enemy so much more powerful than herself was even less likely to come from the national resistance movements than from the Commonwealth. Possibly the United States would be willing to help.

American public opinion was shifting, though slowly. The defeat of France had caused great dismay and in the autumn of 1940, a survey showed that 75 per cent of Americans wanted to aid Britain although a greater number, 83 per cent, expressed itself as against taking part in the war. There were two minority groups that were trying to influence the mass of Americans. The members of the 'Committee for the Defence of America by Aiding the Allies', better known as the White Committee, after the name of its first chairman, were either pro-British through a feeling of kinship, or anti-Nazi, or else convinced that a Nazi victory in Europe would jeopardise the United States by placing them abruptly, and perhaps at too late a stage, in the front line of defence of democracy. Preparations must be made to meet such an eventuality.

But this committee was less powerful than its isolationist opponent, the America First Movement, founded in September 1940, which had as many as 850,000 members. America First considered that war must be avoided at all costs. It was not manoeuvred by the Nazis, it was not even pro-Nazi and the German ambassador to the United States urgently advised it not to compromise itself by organising sabotage or even pro-German demonstrations which would, in his view, have quite the opposite effect. America First was the voice of the strongly felt views of the Middle West of indifference towards Europe and suspicion of its tortuous Byzantine problems. Its centre was in Chicago. 'Ideas' it maintained 'cannot be destroyed by wars'; it was pointless to send 'Our boys' to their death in an attempt to prevent National Socialism from expanding in Europe. It showed the same lack of interest, moreover, in Russian Communism. America First was recruited mainly from Republicans but also included some Democrats. Its protagonists were industrialists such as Henry Ford, Catholic bishops, senators and state governors, well-known academics and personalities such as the pilot Charles Lindbergh, the hero of the Atlantic crossing.

Roosevelt had to show the greatest consideration for the divisions and lack of awareness in the American public. He was a complex character, paralysed and authoritarian, an aristocrat and a politician; a mixture of idealism and artfulness, kindness and obstinacy (he never spared his opponents), familiarity and earnestness. His co-operation with Wilson had left its mark on him; but he was above all anxious to avoid the older man's mistakes. He was deeply convinced of the evil nature of Nazism. The German ambassador to Washington deplored 'his determined and obstinately anti-German sentiments that would be unlikely to waver'.

Roosevelt was to act with consummate skill, showing perfect understanding of his powers and of his compatriots. There were no dramatic sessions in the House of Representatives or in the Senate, as in Paris and London; relations between Congress and the White House are traditionally based on distrust, if not hostility. The best method for a president was to reach agreement with a few influential leaders. But the most effective way of influencing the man in the street is to talk to him directly on the radio, using language he can understand. Roosevelt excelled in friendly little 'fireside' chats, almost as if talking to his family.

He stressed, above all, the defence of the United States, something to which no American would remain indifferent. Public-opinion polls had shown him beforehand exactly how far he could go. He had a freer hand after being re-elected in November 1940, when he took the unprecedented step of seeking office for the third time, although in order to succeed, his election campaign had contained solemn assurances that he would maintain United States' neutrality: 'As I have already said and shall repeat again and again, our boys will not be sent to fight in any foreign war'—a clever formula that did not exclude committing the United States to a war for the defence of their national interests, as this would then no longer be a 'foreign war'.

In simple language, Roosevelt kept putting forward three sorts of arguments to his compatriots, so that, in the words of his trusty lieutenant Hopkins, 'he would be pushed into war by them'. The Nazi leaders, he would explain, wanted to reduce Europe to slavery and then dominate the rest of the world; and the interests of the United States would be seriously jeopardised if Germany and Japan ruled the roost in the Atlantic and the Pacific; hence the need to help Britain, America's advance guard. On a more down-to-earth level, he would show how a victory of the Axis would be the Waterloo of the American economy; European markets would be closed to the American producers who would also have to meet at home the competition of lower-priced foreign goods produced by cheaper foreign labour. Finally, talking to people used to the Sunday sermons of their priests and pastors, Roosevelt would stress the moral values inherent in a firm attitude towards Fascist aggression; the defence of freedom, democracy and the American way of life thus became part of the defence of national and material interests.

One consequence of all these efforts with their very deliberate pattern of advance followed by cautious retreat, was the progressive rearmament of the United States. In July and August, two laws were passed doubling, on paper, the tonnage of the American war fleet; in September 1940, by the expedient of having 'selective military service' and army training, conscription was introduced. The President arranged for the necessary powers to be voted requiring industrial firms to produce manufactured goods, ordered by the Federal State, at predetermined prices in fixed quantities and with fixed delivery dates. Thus by July 1, 1941, the American Army numbered 1,400,000 men with thirty-three divisions, four of them armoured, supported by 6,000 aircraft. But, above all, the conversion of the greatest industry in the world had been started; E. Stettinius, Vice-President of General Motors, was made responsible for the mobilisation of industry. Roosevelt had succeeded in gaining acceptance for the idea that the United States was to become 'the arsenal of democracy'.

Churchill, whose mother was American, showed admirable skill in exploiting Roosevelt's favourable attitude and he maintained a regular correspondence with the President, increasingly cordial in tone. In September 1940, he asked for American destroyers: 'At the present rate of loss,' he wrote, 'we shall not be able to hold out for long.' Against the advice of Admiral Stark, who was the commander of the American Navy, Roosevelt, with General Pershing's public approval, decided to send fifty old destroyers in exchange for the lease of bases in the Caribbean—'to turn it into an American lake', in the words of Knox, the Secretary of State for the Navy. These bases were situated in Newfoundland, in Bermuda, the Bahamas, the West Indies and British Guiana. Aid to Britain was thus disguised as an improvement of the United States defence system.

On December 8, 1940, Churchill wrote Roosevelt a letter which he called 'the most important in his whole career'. In it he painted a broad picture of the military, political and economic situation. He ended with an urgent appeal for help: once her dollar reserves had run out, Britain would soon no longer be in a position to pay for the indispensable American equipment that she had been able to buy under the Cash and Carry law. Roosevelt showed ready understanding and seems to have hit on a solution to the problem, of his own accord. Stating that it was important to get rid of the 'superstition of the dollar', he explained to the Americans that war equipment must be lent to the British; they would return it at the end of hostilities. This was the 'Lend-Lease' bill, of incalculable importance for the course of the war. In theory, the system was based on reciprocity; in fact, the Americans were giving something in exchange for a theoretical deferred payment and were receiving nothing. Not only was the bill passed without difficulty by the legislative assemblies in March 1941 but Roosevelt managed to acquire at the same time a new and important power, that of distributing the war material produced in the States according to his own choice; a further shrewd move was that the bill did not contain the names of the countries benefiting from Lend-Lease, thus enabling the list to be extended as events might dictate.

This equipment still had to be shipped and the British Navy was in danger of not being equal to the task. Left to itself, it was even less able to prevent it all going to the bottom through enemy submarine attack. Ever since January 1941 the British and American general staffs had been examining together on a world scale their joint strategic problems. In April 1941, Roosevelt took a great step forward; he extended the 'American security zone' to the western part of the Atlantic from Greenland to the Azores. American vessels would report the presence of German ships to the British. By the end of May, the Americans were providing protection for their convoys all the way to Britain. In June, British ships were allowed to join American convoys. In July, the Americans established a naval base in Iceland.

So, little by little, Anglo-American co-operation became closer and closer. But although the United States were moving towards probable entry into the war, no date for this had yet been fixed, nor could it be guaranteed with complete certainty. Meanwhile, Hitler was extracting from the occupied countries of Europe the resources which he lacked at the outbreak of the conflict, in preparation for the long war that now faced him after the defeat of the Luftwaffe in the air by the British.

The Birth of Hitler's Europe

UNDER the *Führerprinzip*, in Nazi Germany nothing could happen unless Hitler had himself decided or approved it. But even though he had expressed in *Mein Kampf* and repeated in speeches a few slogans that he had inflated into political or military objectives—the overthrow of the humiliating Treaty of Versailles, the grouping of all the Germans together into one Fatherland, the acquisition of *Lebensraum*—Hitler and his lieutenants had never drawn up the appropriate detailed plans. Victory had, in any case, opened up unexpected vistas—the domination of Europe by Germany. How was this domination, based on conquest, to be reconciled with the needs of the war that as a result of Britain's obstinacy was now bound to be protracted?

Although Hitler often changed his plans, being a thoroughgoing opportunist who veered unexpectedly in accordance with the turn of events—Halder compared him to a 'political kaleidoscope'—there were still some constant notions influencing his behaviour: racial inequality and the supremacy of the Aryans; a system of education and upbringing that E. Vermeil described as 'soldierly'; an individual morality far removed from Christian principles and close to nature, subject to the overriding demands of the national good; the 'breeding' of human beings inspired by Darwinism; complete freedom of action for the strongest, based on a misinterpretation of Nietzsche's theory of the Superman.

But in the autumn of 1940 the very magnitude of his victory took Hitler rather by surprise; now he could indeed build for the future but he also had to look to more urgent matters. Diplomatically, he needed to isolate Britain and to extract the greatest possible benefit in Europe from his victory over France. Economically, he had to ensure a rational development of the conquered territories in order to provide for Germany's subsistence and the Wehrmacht's armaments.

Diplomatically, in accordance with the lessons taught by political geography, Hitler's aim in H. A. Jacobsen's words 'was to set up a regional system on a continental basis as opposed to the universal approach of the

Anglo-Saxons'. Such was the object of the tripartite pact of September 27, 1940, between Germany, Italy and Japan. The world was carved up at Britain's expense and to the exclusion of the United States: Japan's zone of influence was to be the Far East; Europe and Africa would be Germany's and Italy's. The latter was given the Mediterranean, although no very exact definition was given of the term; Hitler merely thought that below a certain latitude and outside a certain specified climate, conditions were not favourable for the establishment of a sound Aryan civilisation, although this did not prevent him from competing with Mussolini in certain areas; but the two partners in crime avoided mentioning this.

In this division of the world, a Greater Germany could arise in Europe. In Rosenberg's presence, Hitler once compared the birth of this *Grossreich* to that of Bismarck's Empire in 1860. He was, in a word, reviving Naumann's old conception of *Mitteleuropa*. On November 28, 1940, Himmler declared at a meeting of Gauleiters: 'I believe in a community of Germanic peoples, in which each will retain its own language and cultural heritage, which does not mean that they will be able to decide their own external economic or military policies.' Were one to look for the roots of such an empire, they would be found in the Germanic Holy Roman Empire. Thus Richard Ganzer, the Nazi philosopher of history, even though uncertain whether he was really expressing the ideas of the Master, who had been known to disown those who expounded his thought, saw it as a central nucleus (the Reich) around which would be grouped states in the process of being annexed, 'buffer' states, autonomous vassal states with specific tasks and independent states associated with the Reich.

One thing was certain: the exploitation of the entire resources of Europe could take place only under the system of autarchy foreshadowed in the Four Year Plan, which W. Schussler, another theorist, called 'returning to the Continental idea which existed before the discovery of America'. Germany would control production, technology and scientific research in every country; goods would be exchanged by a barter system so as to save the export of currency; working conditions would become uniform and this would lead to the appropriate movements of population.

Meanwhile—and this was not in contradiction to these gigantic plans— everything must be subordinated to satisfy the war industry's needs in order to complete and consolidate the victory. So the Steering Committee for Trade Policy was set up in Berlin, an organisation containing representatives from all the ministries concerned, to assess the contribution of each of the occupied countries, make an inventory of the raw materials and products most useful for the war economy, ensure increased production and protection and organise the financing of purchases and the movement of goods. The long-term policy was to keep heavy industry, the source of power, as a monopoly in German hands; the other countries were to be forced to become suppliers of foodstuffs and raw materials. In each sector of the economy, guile was to be used to achieve these ends: the velvet glove was to be used in preference to plundering or requisitioning and attempts were to be made to reach agreement with the political and industrial leaders of the occupied countries.

This was the overall political pattern of Europe under Nazi domination, both for the present and the future. While based on a unified conception, it was liable to variation in accordance with local conditions.

II CENTRAL EUROPE

Since March 1939, Bohemia and Moravia had become a protectorate of the Reich, with the diplomat von Neurath as the 'Protector'. However, the chiefs of police and of the ss were not subordinated to him but were directly under Himmler. This dual authority was to be the regular policy in German-occupied Europe. The running of the country had been taken over by the Germans; the Protector governed by decree. However, there was a Czech government with limited administrative powers.

In March 1939 Slovakia broke away from Bohemia and proclaimed her independence; although she had a treaty with the Reich granting her the latter's 'friendly protection', Slovakia ran her own affairs. Josef Tiso, a priest, became President of the State on October 26, 1939; he appointed A. Tuka as his Prime Minister. Slovakia was the launching pad for the German armies marching against Poland; she became a signatory to the 'tripartite pact' and voluntarily put her own economy at the service of the Reich's war economy and placed her press and radio at the latter's disposal.

Germany's exceptional role in the country was constantly being stressed by Bernard, the German ambassador in Bratislava, who considered Slovakia's status as a tempting bait for the smaller Slav nations, since it showed them, in his view, how they might themselves prosper by placing themselves within the German orbit. But if any Slovak minister chanced to imagine that he really was independent, Bernard took care to call him to order or denounce him to Berlin.

The situation in Poland was completely different. The 'incorporated territories'—containing 9 million inhabitants, 600,000 of whom were German before the war—had simply become German. Their government was in the hands of Germans from the Reich or the Baltic countries; the mark replaced the zloty, German law Polish law and so on. The problem was to discover who was or became German and who stayed Polish. To this end, a 'German national list' was drawn up containing the names of the ex-Polish German subjects and the Poles who were to be 'germanised' in the interests of Germany; they received total or partial citizenship. All the rest, that is to say the majority of the Poles, were placed in the category of 'protected citizens' and although enjoying some protection—apart from Jews and gypsies—they had no property-owning rights, no right to any education above primary level, no right of association, no right to go to theatres, museums or libraries, or to fill any posts or professions at managerial level.

Polish workers and employers were the least well paid—albeit better paid, in some cases, than in pre-war Poland—and then only for days actually worked and not for rest days or holidays. They could not sue their German employers—that would have been insulting behaviour. They received no family allowances and their rations were only about three-quarters of those of the Germans. There were countless police regulations restricting their freedom of movement—they had to have a special pass in order to travel by train or even bicycle. Very heavy penalties were inflicted for the various crimes they could commit; they could be condemned to death for showing ill-will towards Germans.

The status of the 'General Government'—12 million Poles, including Warsaw but with its capital in Cracow—was more amorphous. The Governor General, Frank, was directly responsible to Hitler and administered the territory through a government comprising 'divisions', which replaced ministries. Municipalities were in charge of German or Ukrainian and occasionally Polish mayors. Parallel to the German courts there existed Polish courts which were competent to deal only with civil cases between Poles and Polish law remained partly operative. There even existed a Polish police, strictly under German control, of course. The 'General Government' took over the Jews and Poles considered as undesirables in the incorporated territories.

The problem of the nationality of the inhabitants of the 'General Government' remained pending: the 'German national list' was not introduced there, even though excessive privileges were granted to the resident German minority—special residential districts, restaurants and railway carriages. The German authorities adopted the principle that, as a consequence of the war, the Polish nation had ceased to exist; as a result the inhabitants of the 'General Government' had become stateless. The consequence was that Poles living there retained certain benefits or liberties that were denied their compatriots in the incorporated territories. In the first few months, only the large firms were confiscated; and Poles could enter the liberal professions. But Polish associations were forbidden, education was restricted to primary level, racial discrimination was rife and the Gestapo ruled the roost.

Although not having taken part in the war, Romania was treated as a conquered vassal state. After receiving an ultimatum from the USSR she was forced to hand over Bessarabia and North Bukovina on June 26, 1940; while expressing some reservations about the Russian claims on Bukovina and watching over the lot of the Germans residing there, Hitler had advised King Carol to give in, although the latter had suggested 'co-operation in all fields' and stressed his willingness to 'speak the same language as Germany'.

Indeed, the Romanians, surrounded as they were by hostile neighbours, now saw German protection as their only salvation. They proclaimed their acceptance of Hitler's New Order in Europe. They expelled the French engineers working for the oil companies. But when Hungary claimed Transylvania from them and Bulgaria claimed Dobruja, Hitler and Mussolini both advised them to come to an agreement on these two requests directly, for, as Hitler wrote, 'Hungary and Bulgaria are old friends of Germany'. It was not as easy as that to join the winning side and there was a stiff entrance fee.

When direct negotiations failed, Ribbentrop and Ciano imposed their own 'arbitration' but Romania had to pay the piper. On August 30, Romania handed over to Hungary nearly 17,000 square miles and 2,300,000 inhabitants of Transylvania, including Cluj; and on September 7, 1940, it was Bulgaria's turn to be given Dobruja.

King Carol was forced to abdicate in favour of his son Michael, after having called on General Antonescu to form a government, with the approval of the German ambassador Fabricius. Antonescu took the title of 'Conducator'; he set up a Romanian Fascist movement, dissolved the political parties and included in the government Horia Sima's 'Iron Guard', which gave total allegiance to the German Nazi party. Their 'legionaries' immediately seized posts of power in the state and exacted vengeance on their opponents: house searches, arrests and forced suicides followed thick and fast. During the night of November 26–27, they massacred sixty-four prisoners held in their gaols; the well-known historian Iorga was also murdered.

Antonescu's authority began to weaken and in January 1941 he came into direct conflict with the Iron Guard. After standing by and watching this incipient civil war for a while, the Germans came down in favour of Antonescu against Horia Sima. They preferred their decisions to pass through a popular national leader rather than through someone only too well-known as dependent on them; but they held Horia Sima in reserve to keep Antonescu under pressure; this was another regular method of their policy in territories they occupied.

In any case, Antonescu was entirely subservient to them. He signed the tripartite pact; he applied the discriminatory measures against Jews demanded by the Reich; he allowed German troops into Romania on the pretext of training the Romanian Army and protecting the oil installations. He signed a ten-year plan of economic collaboration with Germany.

So the whole of central Europe, where Mussolini had been obliged to forego making any claims, had come under German sway. Either by direct control as in former Poland, by the expedient of protectorates as in Bohemia, or through puppet governments, Hitler's New Order reigned supreme; all the resources of every country were being fed into the German war-machine.

III WESTERN EUROPE

Germany's behaviour in the west was less harsh than in the east. Himmler recognised the Norwegians, the Dutch, the Swedes and the Flemings as branches of the Germanic race; Hitler was interested in Burgundy, the homeland of the fifth-century Burgundians, and in Normandy, the land of the Vikings. As for France in general, economic necessity required her to be granted special treatment for the time being.

In Norway the 'Administrative Council' set up by the Reich's High Commissioner, Joseph Terboven, which numbered amongst its members such important persons as the President of the Supreme Court and the Governor of Oslo, was striving to limit the powers of the Germans to the best of its ability, in the firm belief that King Haakon would approve. But Terboven refused to be taken in; he wanted a docile government to deal with. In June 1940 he asked the Legislative Assembly, the *Storting*, to replace the Administrative Council by the *Riksraad* or State Council. The *Storting* demurred for a few months and then gave in. But King Haakon refused to recognise the *Riksraad* and denied its legal competence to undertake the new responsibilities foisted on it by the occupying power.

With one accord, all the Norwegian political bodies and personalities now refused to collaborate with the Germans. Only Quisling approved everything; his newspaper *Fritt Folk* merely repeated German propaganda. Terboven had to acknowledge failure. He decided to dissolve the political parties and had some members of Quisling's party appointed to the *Riksraad*, although not Quisling himself as yet. Henceforth, Norway was allowed one single party, the *Nasjonal Samling*; Quisling remained its leader. This party tried to introduce its members into the various state, university and workers' organisations. The chance of a good job, the lure of power and various forms of pressure swelled the ranks of the party to some extent but it never achieved more than 100,000 members. For want of anything better, in February 1942 Terboven was led on logically to the next step of entrusting power to Quisling himself, though without altering the powers of the *Riksraad*.

Quisling revived the pattern of trade that existed in Norway at the time of the Hanseatic league, that is, Norwegian trade was exclusively directed towards the Baltic, and no longer via the North Sea. In any case, circumstances forced such a course; as a beginning, electrical power from Norway was fed to Germany.

Like Norway, Holland was for the Nazis a 'free National Socialist Germanic people'. It too had a National Socialist party whose leader was Mussert; it too was provided with a Reich High Commissioner, Seiss-Inquart. Like the Norwegians in their attitude to Quisling, the Dutch considered Mussert and his faithful followers as traitors. This was the reason why the Germans had felt it unwise to let them take over power.

Hitler had stated that Holland 'would remain politically and economically united so as to provide a gateway to the outside world'. There was thus no question of forcing a National Socialist régime on her nor of integrating her into the Reich, but it was hoped that she would join of her own free will. Executive power was exercised by Seiss-Inquart, assisted by four general commissioners—the one in charge of the police came directly under Himmler. But the government of the country was left to the Dutch, through the secretaries general in the ministries and the whole body of civil servants.

The Dutch people were wondering about their future and some important persons were not, *a priori*, averse to the idea of setting up a new government, distinct from the one in London. Their view was that people should accept the inevitable and adapt themselves to a long period of German domination. A very well-known politician, Hendrikus Colijn, expressed this point of view in a pamphlet entitled 'On the border of two worlds'.

But even though the membership of Mussert's party considerably increased, the population as a whole held itself aloof. Mussert took the view that Belgium should disappear in order to create a Greater Holland, closely linked with the Reich. The Germans used his supporters to spread their propaganda and to carry out their unsavoury police operations, but they kept Mussert himself in reserve.

The Dutch economy was nonetheless integrated with Germany's. Between December 1940 and April 1941, customs duties between the two countries were abolished and the Reich's wage-structures and conditions of work were introduced into Holland.

In Belgium, King Leopold's presence was both a hindrance and a promise. It prevented the Germans from forcing new institutions on the country but it was clear that if the King were to be won round to accept the occupation and speak out in favour of collaboration, he would be of inestimable value to the Germans. Leopold declared that 'he meant to avoid giving the Belgians the impression of wanting to reign at all costs under German pressure'. He proposed to withdraw to a small country house. Under the pretext that 'he ought to be granted special consideration', the Germans suggested, as a bait, the castle of Laeken as being 'more suitable and practical'. Leopold continued to consider himself as being held there as a prisoner of war.

Belgium formed a national government working under the responsibility of the military commander, General von Falkenhausen; it was administered by the secretaries general of the various ministries. Through resignations, lowering the age limit of retirement and the establishment of new posts, the Germans introduced into the administration people on whom they could rely. But the political, administrative and economic structures of Belgium were not changed.

IV THE VICHY GOVERNMENT

Of all the countries conquered by Germany, France was the only one whose legal government had signed an armistice putting an end to hostilities. The government had left Bordeaux and installed itself in Vichy because this small spa could provide accommodation for the administrative services in its many hotels and also because it was close to the occupied zone.

The Rethondes convention was harsh but it did not contain anything ignominious and it appeared to leave the French government with a number of not unimportant trump cards. The northern half of France was occupied by German troops but it had been agreed that the French government's authority should extend there—it being understood, of course, that the French authorities would act strictly in accordance with the directives issued by the Germans. The French government was even left free, in theory, to 'transfer its seat to Paris'.

In the so-called 'free' zone, the French government had, theoretically, complete authority. It retained all the attributes of a sovereign power. This meant that it could maintain diplomatic representation throughout the world and have ambassadors attached to it from every state, starting

Zone attached to the
German Command in Brussels
Arras
Amiens
Mézières
Banned Zone
Laon
Metz
Rheims
Annexed zone
Paris
Bar le
Duc
St Dizier
German Occupation Zone
Chaumont
Reserved
Langres
zone
Tours
Bourges
Dijon
Belfort
Döle
Poitiers
Châteauroux
Moulins
Charolles
Nantua
Angoulême
Vichy
(after the
Armistice)
Périgueux
Vienna
Langon
Valence
Free Zone
Italian
German occupied
occupation
(after Nov 1942)
zone (after
Nov 1942)
Mt-de-Marsan
Menton
Avignon
Aix

Demarcation line

Map 7
THE PARTITION OF FRANCE

0   100km

with the Soviet Union, the United States and the Vatican. On the other
hand, although the French troops had been demobilised, their weapons
collected up and handed over to the conqueror, the French government
had kept an 'armistice army' of about 100,000 men to maintain its authority in the territories that it still retained. The war fleet, almost intact before the British attack at Mers el-Kebir, was no longer a fighting force
because it was to be disarmed but it remained a valuable asset for any
eventual peace negotiations.

The economic clauses were very harsh; occupation costs were to be
charged to the French and France's external trade was blocked; to all intents and purposes the assets and stocks held in the occupied zone passed

into German hands, and their haul of captured goods was immense. But France still held on to her loyal colonial empire; some of the territories were of particular strategic importance—Tunisia, which had Bizerta, and French West Africa, which had Dakar.

After a number of reshuffles, the government under Pétain's leadership now contained no deputies from the former Third Republic except Pierre Laval. On July 10, 1940, the National Assembly meeting in Vichy unhesitatingly and by a large majority—only eighty members voted against—gave Marshal Pétain unlimited powers and the brief to provide France with a new constitution. At that time Marshal Pétain's popularity was immense; his dignity, noble bearing, unselfishness, plus memories of 1914–18 and the public conviction that he had saved the country from even greater misfortune meant that he had almost all the French people behind him. In fact, the Marshal was a capricious old man, easily tired, and his political experience was both recent and crude.

V THE APPLICATION OF THE ARMISTICE CONVENTION

The armistice terms were harsh and they were going to become even harsher because of the way in which the Germans applied them. The whole of the occupied zone was directly under the control of the military commander General von Stulpnagel; he issued directives to the *préfets,* he fixed prices, he requisitioned goods and labour, he gave direct orders to industrialists, he took over the French police and he interfered with the workings of justice; the press and radio were run by his departments. The Vichy government was, indeed, represented by a delegate in Paris but he was merely a go-between who passed information back and made known his government's wishes to the German military commander.

On their own authority the Germans modified the armistice convention in their favour. Thus they simply annexed the three *départements* that formed Alsace-Lorraine. After moving the customs posts back to the ridge along the Vosges, they introduced the German language and forbade the use of French: using the word 'bonjour' led to a fine on the spot. They expelled the French officials and replaced them by Germans; the French-speaking Lorrainers were forced to leave their district at a few hours' notice, taking with them only the bare necessities. The population of Alsace was organised into Nazi youth groups, labour groups and welfare groups; whole villages were transplanted into Germany. The Vichy government protested against this unilateral action but it did not think that its protests would have any effect except to arouse Hitler's wrath and so it did not make them public, thus rendering them quite ineffective.

Similarly, the Germans had joined the two northernmost *départements* (Nord and Pas-de-Calais) to their Brussels military command; this was done for military reasons—the Straits of Dover had great strategic importance—but no one knew what thoughts of dismemberment might lie behind the action and as a first result the coal of the area produced in such large quantities was now no longer available to the rest of the country. Another 'forbidden' zone was marked out in north-east France and it was disturbing to see that its borderline followed approximately that of the Holy Roman Empire.

The Germans turned the demarcation line between the occupied and free zones into a real frontier; neither goods nor mail nor travellers were allowed over it. Even Vichy ministers were turned back when they wanted to go to Paris. Thus France was cut into two sections, without any links between them, whereas in fact the one could not exist without the other. From the autumn of 1940 onwards, living conditions in the poor and mountainous free zone began to become difficult.

Finally, the Germans interfered in the southern zone; they sent many agents there and the members of the armistice commission poked their noses into everything; they tried to do business direct with the French living in the free zone; and they forced the Vichy government to submit its more important decisions, such as senior administrative appointments, for their approval.

VI THE EXPLOITATION OF FRANCE

On September 20 Keitel summed up Hitler's views thus: 'Upheavals in the French economy are a matter of indifference to us; any concessions granted to France must be balanced by deliveries from the non-occupied zone or the colonies.' Although left deliberately vague the intention plainly was to squeeze France till the pips squeaked.

Requisitioning of every sort continued in the northern zone after the signing of the armistice and the troops which had penetrated into the southern zone did not leave it without train-load after train-load of goods and industrial equipment. Thanks to a particularly favourable exchange-rate for the mark, the German soldiers throughout the occupied zone were able to strip all the shops on the cheap—with such eagerness that the Parisians called them 'Colorado beetles'.

The armistice convention provided the German authorities with more convenient and infinitely more effective methods. The occupation costs were fixed by the Germans unilaterally at 400 million francs a day. The French objected that such a sum would be enough for them to maintain

10 million soldiers and they tried to draw the distinction between occupation troops and those operating against Britain, who were more numerous and expensive. The Germans refused to accept any distinction or compromise and demanded payment of the indemnity in ten-day instalments. Such a constant drain on French finances could lead only to galloping inflation.

The armistice convention provided the Germans with many other means of extortion and further economic advantages. With the money which they did not spend they acquired not only goods and French assets but also shares in large French industrial and commercial firms. They were buying up the French economy with France's own money.

Thus the military Waterloo was completed by an economic Waterloo which became even more disastrous after the signing of the Franco-German compensation agreement. Its wording made it another *Diktat;* it provided, in fact, that the French Compensation Bureau should pay French exporters without taking any account of the receipt of German goods; and as the Reich was buying and not selling anything, very soon all the expenditure and transfer of funds turned into a one-way traffic, from France to Germany. The French protests fell on deaf ears; Hemming, the head of the economic section of the German Armistice Commission in Wiesbaden, was blunt and unbending: 'France declared war on Germany; any risks arising from the situation must be France's responsibility.'

VII THE POLICY OF COLLABORATION

Germany's harsh attitude had dismayed the Vichy government; but after having made some gestures of refusal and not without its delegates having disputed every inch of the way with the German Armistice Commission in Wiesbaden, it had duly knuckled under. The fact was that it considered that Germany had won the war and that the only thing left was to come to terms with reality. It had been greatly surprised that, left on her own, Britain had not surrendered; but Vichy continued to believe that even though Britain might still persist in fighting on she would find it impossible to return to the continent of Europe and win the war there.

Despite the British attacks at Mers el-Kebir and Dakar, and despite the support being given de Gaulle, who had been condemned to death in France as a traitor, Marshal Pétain did not want any reversal of alliances that would take France into war against her former ally. He wished to establish a *modus vivendi* with her in the hope that she would relax her blockade. However, he was anxious to recover the dissident colonial territories which had joined de Gaulle, and this operation did entail the risk of coming into conflict with Britain.

Pierre Laval and Admiral Darlan accepted this risk and even hoped it would come to pass. Their view was that, in the interests of France, the collaboration at administrative level laid down in the armistice convention and the economic collaboration that would be the inevitable consequence of that convention must be followed by political collaboration as the only way in which France could carve out for herself a less uncomfortable niche in Europe under German control, make Britain stand the bill for all the damage when peace came and perhaps replace Italy as Hitler's blue-eyed boy.

Pétain adopted this policy as his own and it was at his own request that he met Hitler at Montoire on October 24, 1940. At that time, Hitler was contemplating setting up a Mediterranean coalition against Britain. He thus needed the Vichy government's collaboration in order to gain a foothold in North Africa without trouble. At Montoire, the principle of collaboration was approved but no details of ways and means were worked out. Hitler very soon gave up his plan as a result of Franco's inflated demands and, above all, of Mussolini's attack on Greece. Consequently he felt no need to grant France any concessions; the armistice convention, interpreted as he pleased, was perfectly adequate to extract from her everything he wanted.

First Pierre Laval and then, after he had been ejected from the government on December 13, 1940, Admiral Darlan made repeated but fruitless advances; the only person to lend a favourable ear was Otto Abetz, who made Franco-German collaboration the mainstay of his policy. In May 1941, Admiral Darlan went as far as to grant the Germans bases in the French colonies, at Bizerta and Dakar, whilst German aircraft were permitted to land on airfields in Syria in order to help the Iraqi uprising against Britain.

VIII THE NATIONAL REVOLUTION

The new gentlemen of Vichy were for the most part old opponents of the Third Republic which they held responsible for their country's misfortunes. An intensive propaganda campaign was launched against the parliamentary system, the political parties and the leaders of the vanished régime. In order to 'restore' France and in the hope of currying favour with Hitler, the Vichy government set out to introduce certain reforms, some of them Fascist in spirit, under the name of 'National Revolution'.

One of the hobby-horses of this national revolution was 'the myth of the leader'. As leader of the country, Pétain became the object of a veritable cult, his messages were glossed, not discussed; the word went out 'think Pétain'. The premise was that power does not come from below and that the people need to be told what to do: 'schools of leadership' became widespread.

Marshal Pétain had not drawn up the constitution, as the National Assembly had requested; his political views were thus veiled in some mystery; but as a result of his past experience he had an entirely military conception of power, in the shape of a pyramid. He appointed and dismissed ministers as he pleased; it was he alone who took the decisions affecting the whole country—the policy of collaboration, for example. He declared: 'History will judge *me.*' In this way he established a monarchy in fact but not in name, to the great delight of Charles Maurras, the *Action française* political thinker.

However, the Marshal refused to accept those mainstays of Fascism, the single party and single youth movement. On the other hand, he grouped all the ex-servicemen into one 'Legion' and hoped that it would provide a body of disciplined, uncritical supporters. As for the machinery of state, elections were abolished; mayors were nominated, not elected. In the country, an important role was to be played by 'notables', and provincial squires deserted their manor houses in order to serve their country. Admiral Darlan appointed naval officers to many important posts; their loyalty would be guaranteed by their anglophobia and conservatism.

In theory the national revolution was anti-capitalistic. It rejected the class struggle and abolished all the syndicalist central committees of employers and workers. In practice, no serious action was taken against capitalist structures, even though their abuses were attacked; on the other hand, strikes were banned and wages frozen. The régime was not sympathetic towards the worker, who was considered revolutionary because he lacked roots, but towards the peasant, whose traditional virtues were praised. It was intended gradually to introduce a corporate régime to provide the framework of the whole economy.

The 'constructive' measures were matched by repressive and discriminatory action. Amongst the state corporations, the universities were particularly suspect and the subsidies to independent educational bodies, the reform of the syllabus and the influence given to the Minister of Youth were intended to limit their importance. From the French citizen himself, no opposition was tolerated; the press was strictly controlled; 'bad Frenchmen'—Communists, Socialists, Freemasons, free-thinkers—found themselves moved elsewhere, dismissed, placed under house arrest or interned. Those 'responsible for the defeat' were to be brought before a special court.

Finally, the Vichy government anticipated the Germans' wishes by issuing decrees against the Jews.

IX SPAIN

Despite a certain reluctance on some issues and occasionally digging in its heels, on the whole the Vichy government was moving in the direction that Hitler wanted, although this did not prevent him from greatly distrusting it—especially its military leaders; his pet aversion was General Weygand.

Franco's Spain had, on the other hand, in theory, been allied to the Reich since the Spanish Civil War. However, Franco refused to go to war when Hitler asked him to do so in Hendaye on October 23. Or rather, the Caudillo, while stating that he was ready to pay off his debt of gratitude, asked for time to prepare and put forward claims that Hitler considered excessive and in any case was not in a position to satisfy—wheat, artillery, Catalonia, French Morocco and the province of Oran. How could these ambitions be reconciled with France's participation in a Mediterranean coalition against Britain? Not forgetting that Hitler and Mussolini also coveted a share in Morocco.

Hitler did not like Franco; he identified him with his Wehrmacht generals and considered him lacking in the political sense and gifts of a real leader. For his own part, Franco had been deeply shocked by the German-Soviet pact: Moscow, he said, was the Antichrist with whom no compromise was possible. On the other hand, he was being both wooed and threatened by Britain, with the strong support of the United States; and only the Anglo-Saxons could supply Spain with the wheat and petrol she so urgently needed.

But above all, Spain had only just emerged from civil war and was still recovering from its effects; she was exhausted almost to the point of famine and incapable of embarking on a new conflict; remobilisation would be tantamount to putting weapons back into their opponents' hands; in the event of any conflict, moreover, the Canaries would speedily be occupied by the British fleet. Hitler saw what was happening; he thought that Franco was using Germany as a catspaw and afterwards, at the eleventh hour, just like Mussolini, he would do the absolute minimum necessary to win a seat at the victory table and pick up his share of the spoils from the losers.

Hitler took away a very bad impression from his Hendaye meeting. He told Ribbentrop that, rather than go through it again, he would prefer to have several teeth out. So he made little further effort to influence Franco and the ensuing talks between Serrano Suñer and Ribbentrop came to no practical conclusions. Satisfying Franco would in any case have certainly worried the Vichy government and perhaps prompted the rulers of the French empire to secede under the shadow of the impending threat, something that Hitler wished to avoid at all costs. Mainly, however, Hitler had not toyed for long with the scheme of campaigning in the Mediterranean, which Raeder had been trying to sell him. Ever since July 1940, he had been contemplating launching out once more on the age-old path of German expansion eastwards. From this viewpoint, it was certainly not desirable to open up another theatre of war. What the Führer needed was a western Europe where everything was quiet—and being suitably squeezed by Germany. A neutral Spain fitted in with these schemes; a belligerent Spain would raise more problems than it would solve.

CHAPTER 3

The Fighting in Africa and the Balkans

BOTH now and later, the war continued its course at sea, in Africa and in the Balkans.

I THE BATTLE OF THE ATLANTIC

The battle of the convoys was vital for Britain. There was no point in the Commonwealth's mobilising its resources and the Americans becoming actively friendly if the men and their weapons were going to Davy Jones' locker.

At the start of the struggle Britain was not really short of freighters. Even though entering the war had greatly reduced the number of foreign ships coming into her harbours compared with peacetime, since their owners were anxious not to jeopardise them, German victories since the summer of 1940 had had the happy result of increasing the British Merchant Navy by some 1,600 Norwegian, Dutch, French, Greek, Belgian and Polish vessels, comprising some 7 million tons in all.

But the advantages gained from this extra tonnage were greatly reduced by new difficulties. First of all the ships usually had to travel much longer distances; things which before the war had come from the occupied countries of Europe now had to be provided from outside Europe, round Africa via the Cape, rather than through the short cut of the Suez Canal. As it was impossible to use the east coast ports, the west coast harbours were heavily congested since they were obliged to accept types of cargoes which they were not equipped to handle. Such operations as unloading and despatching inland took much longer in rudimentary harbours like Freetown or others on the West African coast, for example, which were now in constant use.

With its centuries-old experience, the Royal Navy was indeed well placed to cope with any task, however difficult, thanks to its complex qualities of tradition, instinctive reactions and powers of decision, backed by a thorough knowledge of all the problems of sea warfare. But it had to face unforeseen dangers. Thus, in order to deal with the vast quantities of mines, in November 1940 it had been obliged to bring more than 700 mine-sweepers into operation. It was also suffering from certain shortages.

For example, for want of sufficient escort vessels, it was still very difficult for it to provide protection for convoys. These moved in cumbersome groups of thirty or forty vessels, at the speed of the slowest, that is at ten knots on average; sailing in four or five lines, they were defended against possible attack by only one corvette or destroyer to every ten freighters or more.

However, the question of air support had been satisfactorily solved as far as the Navy was concerned, since it had its own naval air force; moreover, it had been given priority in the use of the squadrons of Coastal Command. But the fighting in Norway had shown the vulnerability of ships to air attack; ship-mounted AA was an inadequate defence; in any case, there were not enough guns to arm merchant shipping. German bombing raids reduced the output of the naval armament factories and dockyards and hampered the working of the ports.

Also German submarines now had additional facilities which they would be able to exploit to the full. Their bases had been extended to Stavanger, Trondheim, Lorient, St-Nazaire, La Pallice and Bordeaux; they thus held the whole of the British Isles inside their net and they could go through the Straits of Dover with impunity. Whereas in June 1940, there were on average only twelve German submarines operating in the Atlantic, which were joined by some Italian submarines, in May 1941 there were forty. The largest of them was 800 tons and had a range of 15,000 miles.

Most of the submarines could go faster than the convoys, thus enabling repeated attacks to be made at different points. Since the Luftwaffe had provided Admiral Doenitz with an air force, spotting convoys had become easier.

Thus British shipping losses became alarming. From a maximum of 340,000 tons per month in 1940, they rose to 650,000 tons in April 1941, more than was being built by the British and Canadian shipyards combined. When Hitler extended the area of his blockade as far as Greenland, convoys were being attacked south of Newfoundland. In these circumstances, the fifty destroyers, old as they were, that were handed over by the United States, and the help given by the American Navy in protecting convoys were more than merely token gestures.

In accordance with Douhet's doctrine, the British tried to destroy the submarine bases by bombing from the air. While the towns all around suffered plenty of raids, the submarines remained unharmed in their massive concrete pens. So it proved more rewarding to seek them out close to the convoys round which they were lurking. For this purpose, from 1941 onwards the aircraft of Coastal Command were equipped with radar which could detect a submarine thirty miles away, although then sinking it was another matter.

A further hazard was that, in the winter of 1940, the German Navy again started despatching auxiliary cruisers and heavy vessels to attack convoys from Brest and Lorient. The Royal Navy was obliged to disperse its ships throughout the seven seas in order to hunt them down: in the Indian Ocean the *Admiral Scheer* was attacking British freighters on their voyage between Australia and the Cape. Even the heavy battleship *Bismarck* was put into service in May 1941. She was quickly spotted but succeeded in sinking the battleship *Hood*; she was then pursued by the British aircraft-carriers *Victorious* and *Ark Royal*; after being damaged, she was sunk by the guns of the cruiser *Norfolk*. It was then that their mistake in failing to build aircraft-carriers was fully brought home to the Kriegsmarine. Admiral Raeder was temporarily forced to stop sending his warships into the Atlantic. But the submarines continued to be very successful and things were no better for the British in the Mediterranean.

II NAVAL WARFARE IN THE MEDITERRANEAN.
THE ANTAGONISTS

'Thanks to aircraft, submarines, mines and small fast vessels,' wrote Admiral Assman, 'the Mediterranean had become merely an inland sea offering no possibility for deploying a powerful navy.' British possessions had become particularly vulnerable 'even for an opponent without a navy'. After the French fleet had withdrawn from the war, British control of the Mediterranean was all the more seriously jeopardised because the Royal Navy was heavily involved in protecting convoys in the Atlantic. And in the Mediterranean, Italy occupied a strategic position of paramount importance, by reason of her central geographical situation and her advanced bases in Sicily and Pantellaria. There was, however, one link missing in the Italian transversal chain running from north to south: Tunisia. Mussolini would have liked to occupy it as early as June 1940 but Hitler had persuaded him to leave it to the Vichy government in order not to create discontent in the French empire; in any case, Bizerta had been neutralised.

What place did the Mediterranean occupy in Hitler's overall conception of the war? Despite Admiral Raeder's suggestions, he refused to consider it an important operational theatre. According to General Halder, he thought that it would be impossible to prevent Britain from asserting her superiority there. All that could be done was to wage 'a war of attrition', taking care to ensure the 'greatest possible economy in the use of their forces', so as to postpone the day when British superiority would achieve its full effect—and it would then be pointless, because Britain would have been conquered elsewhere. In General Halder's view, the German Navy, which had different views on the matter, 'was dreaming in terms of continents'.

It was true that when the Axis partners were being assigned their specific tasks, it had been agreed that the Mediterranean would be Italy's preserve; Mussolini was very keen on this and he referred to it continually. These 'parallel interests' did, indeed, leave the two allies with one common 'enemy' but they prevented them from drawing up any plans for concerted action. Liaison had been established at staff level but each partner was jealous of his own independence and disinclined to reveal his schemes; the situation would need to become serious before the two dictators agreed to take joint decisions.

It was obviously Italy who had the greatest interest in driving the British out of the Mediterranean. Mussolini had frequently asserted that Italy was held 'prisoner' there and that she would only free herself by breaking open the two 'locks' of her prison, Gibraltar and Alexandria. And in fact, on July 11, 1940, the Duce had issued instructions in extremely determined and aggressive terms, to smash these 'locks'. But two days later these instructions had been withdrawn, with no explanation given. The fact was that the Italian Navy had confessed that it was powerless to carry them out and the high command had supported it; to seek out and destroy the British fleet was a task beyond their ability and any attempt to do so would be 'playing into the hands of the British'.

The Italian Navy was, in fact, gravely deficient in very many ways. Two promising additions had been made to it in August 1940, when the two battleships *Littorio* and *Vittorio Veneto* were brought into commission, because they were as good as any of the warships in the British fleet. But, like the older ships, these new ones were giants with hulls of clay, since they would be lacking any aircraft-carrier escort or effective cover by land-based aircraft. Experimental radar had been tried out in Leghorn but no ships had actually been equipped with it; so the Italian fleet was blind and deaf and while it could be spotted by the enemy, it would itself know nothing of its opponents until it was attacked. The lack of proper gun-laying equipment precluded any use of naval guns at night; at such times, they were not even kept loaded. The fleet also lacked submarine chasers and boats to undertake amphibious operations. Out of 108 submarines, 20 had been withdrawn from service as obsolete; 33 had been despatched into the Atlantic where 11 of them were lost in the space of a fortnight, from June 14 to 29. Barely 50 or so remained in service in the Mediterranean; their noisy engines made them liable to be picked up by listening devices;

they were unable to turn quickly; they dived slowly and were thus very vulnerable to enemy aircraft overhead.

If we add that its mines were old and inefficient and that the Spanish war had disrupted its logistics, it was clear that the Italian Navy was a second-rate force, able to play a part when supported by powerful allies but incapable of any independent large-scale initiative when left to itself. Moreover, its fuel-oil supplies were in a parlous state; it had been calculated that stocks would run out by June 1941; as a constant link with North Africa was essential to supply the troops fighting there, priority had to be given almost exclusively to the ships and the oil being used for convoy protection.

Accordingly, the Italian supreme command, and first and foremost the naval high command, saw the Italian war fleet as too valuable an asset to be lightly squandered. This fear paralysed any initiative because it induced the Italian Admiralty—*Supermarina*—to interfere in the most minor details thus depriving the executive officers of all chance of initiative.

Yet the British Mediterranean fleet, towards which the Italians felt something of an inferiority complex, was by no means unbeatable. It had evacuated Malta and divided its forces into two squadrons, based on Gibraltar (Admiral Somerville) and Alexandria (Admiral Cunningham). In many respects, the attack on Mers el-Kebir had been merely a confession of weakness and fear. However, unlike the Italian fleet, each British squadron formed a formidable fighting force, thanks to the combination of battleship and aircraft-carrier. The battleship with its escort of cruisers and torpedo-boats provided the aircraft-carrier with the support of its AA, and the latter's fighters gave overall air cover. But whereas the strength of the Italian Navy in the Mediterranean remained more or less constant, the number of units in the British squadrons were sometimes dangerously reduced by the requirements of other operational theatres. The Italian Navy usually failed to exploit this temporary weakness of their opponents.

The great problem for the British was to avoid the 9,000-mile-long voyage round the Cape for their convoys. Shipping was escorted by the Gibraltar-based squadron until off Bizerta; in the eastern Mediterranean, they were taken over by the Alexandria contingent, while in between, the island of Malta had the vital role.

III THE PROBLEM OF MALTA

Malta lies only about sixty miles away from Sicily. Even before the beginning of the war, the Italian Navy had realised that troop supplies to Africa could only be ensured by bombing Malta into submission or to destruction. The British for their part had considered that it would rapidly become impossible to hold Malta and as soon as the first Italian air raids were launched in June 1940, they had withdrawn their ground forces, submarines and aircraft; so the Italian convoys on their way to Libya passed by the island unmolested.

In November 1940, having realised that the Italian air raids were not serious, the British returned to Malta in force in order to use it as a sort of aircraft-carrier; the result was that Italian shipping suffered its first losses.

The Italian Air Force could deploy only about a hundred aircraft to raid Malta. But in December 1940, the Germans based a squadron of 400 aircraft in Sicily, which from January 1941 onwards started pounding the air and harbour installations of Malta. The result soon showed; fewer Italian freighters were sunk and for a while the Malta-based British bombers stopped raiding Naples, Messina, La Spezia, Tripoli and Benghazi; in addition, one British aircraft-carrier was badly hit. The 'Malta problem' seemed by way of being solved in Italy's favour.

IV THE NAVAL BATTLES IN THE MEDITERRANEAN

Although for Hitler the Mediterranean was a secondary operational theatre, Churchill had not taken long to realise that in view of the Wehrmacht's successes, the Mediterranean was now the only possible front where injury could be inflicted on the weakest of his opponents, to ward off the grave threat menacing the British Isles. The most immediate way to achieve this aim would have been for the French colonies to stay in the war or come back into it. But Pétain, Weygand and Noguès remained deaf to all Churchill's invitations and pleas and the attack on Dakar, intended to win French West Africa over to the Allies, had ended in failure.

Meanwhile, the Italian Navy was being vigorously harried by the British fleet. On July 9, a brush took place at Punto Stilio, south of Calabria; an Italian battleship and a cruiser were hit; the Italian bombers did not arrive until the fighting was all over and then dropped a few bombs on their own fleet. On July 19, off Cape Spada in Crete, there was another clash: one Italian cruiser was sunk; the Italian bombers arrived on the scene in time to attack the British ship that was picking up the survivors.

The British then tried a bold move. On November 11, 1940, a large naval force managed to sail right across the middle of the Mediterranean without being spotted. At night, from a distance of fifty miles, the aircraft-carrier *Illustrious* launched twenty-four aircraft in two waves against the Italian battleships anchored off Taranto and seriously damaged three of the six of them; in addition two cruisers were disabled. 'So all the pheasants had gone home to roost,' Admiral Cunningham wrote. At the same time, part of the British fleet had undertaken a related operation against merchant shipping in the Straits of Otranto. The British force had escaped observation by the Italian Air Force for the whole of November 12.

The Italians were forced to move the rest of their fleet to Naples which still allowed them to operate in the western Mediterranean but not in the eastern Mediterranean. The victory at Taranto was a great boost for British morale. The First Sea Lord wrote to Admiral Cunningham: 'Just before the news of Taranto, the Cabinet were rather down in the dumps; but Taranto had a most amazing effect upon them.' The balance of power in the Mediterranean had been completely transformed.

Encouraged by this first success, another British squadron set off from Gibraltar on February 6, 1941; after feinting to move out into the Atlantic, it sailed towards Genoa and on the morning of the 9th, without being detected, it shelled the harbour and the industrial area. Nearly 200 Italian aircraft searched for it in vain.

The only Italian successes were in transporting arms and ammunition to Libya by submarine without loss; but restricting submarines to such a role meant greatly diminishing their importance. Proof had been given that, without German support, the Italians did not constitute a very formidable threat. They had provided further evidence of this in Africa.

V THE WAR IN EAST AFRICA

On the map, the Italian armies could take Egypt and the Sudan in a pincer movement, starting from Libya and Ethiopia. Indeed, in August 1940, they had no difficulty in seizing British Somaliland, which was undefended, and then invaded the Sudan and Kenya. In Ethiopia, the Italians had large forces under the command of the Duke of Aosta but their antiquated equipment included very few anti-tank weapons, meagre stocks of fuel, six AA batteries and thirty Caproni fighter aircraft which, according to General Pesenti, were 'splendid museum pieces'. Some native units were armed with guns dating from the Austro-Hungarian Empire.

The natives were, on the whole, unreliable; under the Italian occupation little respect had been shown for local rank and this meant that general revolt was simmering below the surface, above all in Choa and Harar. The return of the Negus Haile Selassie in January 1941 galvanised the opposition; stirred up by the British, guerrilla warfare gradually spread and the Askari deserted *en masse* to join up with the 'patriots'.

In these circumstances, the Duke of Aosta's 70,000 men were placed in a situation that was all the more precarious because they were completely cut off from their homeland and throughout the whole course of hostilities received only one cargo of rice and fuel oil. Although protected by the neutrality of the Djibouti territory which General Le Gentilhomme had not succeeded in winning over to the Free French cause, the fastness of Ethiopia was invested from the Sudan and Kenya by a mixed force of British, Indians, Afrikaners and Free French. In the north, General Platt penetrated into Eritrea, broke Italian resistance at Keren in March 1941 and occupied Asmara and Massawa, picking up 15,000 prisoners. In the south, General Cunningham invaded Italian Somaliland, moved diagonally north-west, broke through the Italians' defences in February 1941, taking 20,000 prisoners, and reached Addis Ababa in April. The Duke of Aosta took refuge on the Amba-Alagie plateau, where he surrendered in May 1941.

The King of Italy had not been Emperor of Abyssinia for very long. Once again, the Negus sat on the throne of the King of Kings and a treaty was signed forging close links between Ethiopia and Britain. In this sector, the war died down except for the blockade of Djibouti, until that town went over to the Free French in December 1942.

For their part, a handful of Free French under Leclerc had set off from the Chad and after crossing 1,000 miles of desert had brought France back into the war by capturing, on their own ground, the better armed and more numerous Italian garrison of Kufra. In the oasis which he had just taken, General Leclerc made the vow not to lay down his arms until he had succeeded in having the French flag hoisted once more over Metz and Strasbourg. These seemed empty words, when the Germans were parading through Paris.

VI ITALIAN SETBACKS IN LIBYA

Egypt occupied a position of paramount importance for the whole of the Middle East: she controlled the Suez Canal, the British Commonwealth's major artery; any power occupying it could influence Arab opinion in its favour, though not perhaps Turkey. Thus Egypt had the power to provide access to the rich sources of oil which were crucial for motorised warfare and she was also the key to the Italian *Impero*.

The belligerents on both sides were aware of her importance. Even on the eve of a possible German landing in the British Isles, Churchill had despatched to Egypt one-third of the few tanks that the British Army had salvaged from Dunkirk. A Commonwealth army was gradually being assembled there, with Australians, Indians and New Zealanders predominating. In early January 1941, General Wavell had 150,000 men under him.

For his part, Mussolini had ordered Marshal Balbo to launch an offensive towards Egypt with the 175,000 men under his command and Ciano had confirmed this decision to Hitler on July 7, 1940. But Balbo's reaction had been unfavourable on the grounds of lack of motorised transport and of the inferiority of the Italian tanks, armed only with machine guns, in comparison with the British tanks. At this moment of time, the Wehrmacht clearly had ample means to make good these shortcomings. But Mussolini was most reluctant to ask for this and the OKW would not have been very keen to grant it. Even after the defeat at Taranto, at the Italo-German military conference held at Innsbruck on November 15, 1940, the first of its kind, the two Axis partners kept their distance from each other. The result was a statement by Ribbentrop announcing that Germany was seeking no political advantage in the Arab world and, secondly, a sort of neutralisation of the Wehrmacht, which was going to rest on its laurels for the next nine months; the result of this was to allow the Italians to give blatant evidence of their alarming weakness and the British gradually to recover from their original inferiority.

However, in the Middle East a vast anti-British Arab conspiracy was being plotted, with its centre in Iraq and the Grand Mufti of Jerusalem as its leader. The conspirators had informed Rome and Berlin of their desire to 'settle the Jewish question in Palestine in accordance with the Arabs' national and racial interests'. They were planning an uprising in Transjordan and Palestine and hoping to arm 10,000 men in Syria from French army depots.

But in order to spur the Arabs on, it was still necessary for the Italians to achieve some spectacular successes. In September 1940, General Graziani had finally grouped his forces and stocked up with supplies. But he found himself up against some inconvenient geographical facts; his reinforcements would have to move over hard ground, across a steppe-like semi-desert, with only one road and an occasional urban settlement along the coast. Accordingly Graziani made a slow, cautious and strictly limited advance.

He took Sollum and Sidi-Barrani where he stopped and built field fortifications and a pipeline for drinking water. By so doing, he dawdled for three months and the British used the time to their advantage. In December, it was they who attacked with a small motorised army of 30,000 men. The Italians were taken violently by surprise and their ensuing disorderly retreat was equally violent. Three of their divisions were put out of action and their air force disappeared completely from the skies. The British advanced some 450 miles, took Bardia in January 1941, followed by Tobruk, the strongest naval base in Cyrenaica, which was defended by a double ring of concrete fortifications. It surrendered two days after being attacked by the Australians on January 21. The British reached El Agheila on the Tripolitanian border, having taken 100,000 prisoners.

Here they halted for both logistical and political reasons. For the first time the 'law of desert warfare' clamped down on them with full force: at a certain moment one army must call a halt to its victorious advance because it has outstripped its supplies; on the other hand, the loser regains strength as his supply route becomes shorter. Thus the balance was restored. Another feature of the war at this time was that Britain was powerless to meet all her commitments; thus, paradoxically, Italy's other setbacks in Greece were going to palliate the full effect of those that she had suffered in Africa.

VII ITALIAN SETBACKS IN GREECE

On October 15, 1940, Mussolini decided, in fact, to attack Greece. This apparently trivial move was to turn out to be one of the most important decisions of the Second World War. Mussolini's motives seemed as petty as his ambitions were grandiose. It was plain that conquering a few bare mountains could not begin to solve the problem of Italy's over-population or the poverty of her economy. In terms of the war, passing through Epirus was not the shortest way to Alexandria. And finally, attacking Greece meant giving the British a chance of regaining a foothold on the Continent. Entirely absorbed in his schemes for crushing England, when talking with Ciano in July 1940, Hitler had made no secret of his anxiety not to see another theatre of operations in central or southern Europe. Similarly he had never ceased advising the hotheaded Hungarians to restrain their desire to have a go at the Romanians in order to recover Transylvania—advice that was as good as an order to sit still and do nothing.

Mussolini's action would seem to have been motivated by jealousy of Hitler's victories. He was anxious to achieve, like Hitler, on his own initiative and under his own steam, political and military successes that would rescue him from his passive, secondary role and give him a seat at the victory table in the final settlement. According to Count Ciano and the diplomat Alfieri, the monotonous series of failures that had hitherto greeted all his schemes had filled him with a morbid sense of humiliation that was beginning to turn into a chronic state of depression. He was particularly embittered by the dominant position of Germany in Romania —a Latin land and his private preserve—and by the moves that Hitler had made, though fleetingly, to establish closer relations with Vichy France, a beaten country. To break out of this evil spell, the Duce must gain glory in a parallel war, one that he would win on his own, thus making his dream of Italian supremacy in Mare Nostrum come true.

But the operation could not have been worse prepared. Whereas the Fascist party leaders saw it as a mere formality, Marshal Badoglio made reservations; he considered the proposed forces inadequate; he asked for time to examine all the aspects of the campaign; his first point was met, his second not—Mussolini insisted on its starting immediately. As for the Navy, according to Bragadin it had not even been consulted, although it was to be required to occupy the Greek islands and transport three divisions across the Adriatic in one single night. The first obstacle was the disparity between the amount of shipping space required, 10,000 tons daily, and the amount that could be handled by the Albanian ports, which was 3,500 tons at the most. On November 1, Durazzo harbour was completely jammed with more ships than quayside space and 30,000 tons of goods already landed which it was impossible to move inland. But nobody had dared to gainsay the Duce or even to point out that his directives and his calculations were based on a confusion between the various schemes that had been submitted to him.

The Italians threw eleven divisions into their first attack, later increasing them to sixteen and then to twenty-five. Against them the Greeks could at first put up only four first-line divisions. By the end of October, the aggressors won some early successes but they were soon brought to a halt by the state of the roads, which were narrow, few in number and washed away by the autumn rains. The whole Greek population rallied round its government; the mountain villagers, men and women, supplied their troops with provisions. In the middle of November, with their rear protected from any intervention on the part of Bulgaria by a statement from the Turks that would certainly preclude her entry into the war, the Greeks counter-attacked and forced the Italians to retreat all along the line. In less than ten days, the aggressors had been pushed back beyond their starting-point. Italian propaganda put out the story that the Greeks were unsuccessfully attempting to prevent the strategic retreat of the Bersaglieri; the whole of occupied Europe was splitting its sides with laughter. Placards were put up outside Menton, facing towards Italy: 'Greeks, please stop here: this is France.'

On December 4, the Greeks were pouring down towards Valona, one of the main Albanian harbours. Badoglio was made the scapegoat and replaced by Ugo Cavallero but this did not change the situation. While British submarines penetrated even into the Otranto channel and sank Italian ships and the Albanians were becoming restless, in January 1941 General Papagos was endeavouring to force the Italians to go back to

Italy. Thrashed in Epirus and thrashed in Libya, Mussolini could think of nothing better to do than to appeal for help to Hitler. He saw him on January 10, 1941, although he had at first put off the meeting in the hope that he could have arrived crowned with victory. 'I shan't have blood enough for all my blushes when I see him,' he said to Ciano. Hitler's pitying tone stung him to the quick and after he had left he showed his vigour —by sending ministers and high-ranking Fascists off to fight in Greece.

VIII GERMAN AND BRITISH INTERVENTION IN GREECE

The Duce's action had been an unpleasant surprise for the Führer. It was, indeed, difficult for him to show annoyance at his partner's not divulging his intentions, since he himself had behaved in the same way towards him previously. But he could blame him for not succeeding, and this he did not fail to do. He explained his fear that the British might bomb the Ploesti oilfields and he despatched fighter aircraft to protect them. He was not, however, very keen on sending troops to Albania and his generals did not urge him to do so. Nevertheless, consideration was given to an attack on Greece through Bulgaria, under the cover-name 'Marita'; such an attack would also serve the purpose of keeping the Bulgarians in hand who were rather disturbed by the Italians' lack of success.

In December 1940, when Mussolini's setbacks at sea, in Albania and in Africa had become obvious and even disastrous, Hitler felt that Axis solidarity and his friendship with Mussolini forbade him to remain passive any longer. The okw worked out a plan to inject mountain troops and armour into the Italian-Greek front, one army corps in all, to help the Italians stabilise their front and mount a counter-attack. Subsequently, if need arose, this army corps would support the German Twelfth Army in an attack launched from Bulgaria in the direction of Salonica. General Paulus, who was given the task of examining the project, concluded that the troops would not be ready until the middle of February; the fluctuating front as well as the mountainous terrain would preclude a war of movement and would require a frontal assault that would be so costly in men and equipment that the Führer hesitated. Eventually, he cancelled the scheme.

Churchill had been similarly most hesitant before deciding to help the Greeks. He felt that it was politically and morally impossible to leave in the lurch a brave little nation whose stubbornness was arousing the enthusiasm of the populations of the occupied countries and the admiration of the Americans from Roosevelt downwards. On the other hand, his War Minister, Eden,[1] as well as Wavell, considered that the defence of Egypt was paramount; they did not want the reinforcements intended for the African front to be diverted to Greece. The Prime Minister's impulsiveness and his eagerness to take risks, together with memories of Marathon and Salamis, made him decide in favour. The Greeks had appealed to the British on February 8; from March 4 onwards, at the rate of two convoys a week, 68,000 men were taken out of the Libyan front or from the reserves in Egypt and ferried over without mishap to Greece. It was a makeshift expedition and inadequately equipped.

Yet at the start everything went well. As there were indications that the Italian fleet was making ready to try to intercept the convoys on their way to Greece, the naval force stationed at Alexandria put out to sea and on March 28, 1941, having spotted an Italian squadron in the night, it moved in to within less than two and a half miles without being observed, close to Cape Matapan. The Italian guns were blown to bits before they had time to fire. Three Italian cruisers and two destroyers were sunk. 'You could see whole turrets being blown skyhigh,' wrote Admiral Cunningham, 'and great lumps of metal; the ships soon turned into flaming torches.' And yet before the action started the British admiral had been wondering whether the inferiority of his forces would not make them an easy prey for the enemy. But the damaged 35,000-ton battleship *Vittorio Veneto* had been happy just to get away without a fight.

IX THE CRUSHING OF YUGOSLAVIA

Returning more or less to Weygand's 1940 plans, the British wanted two things: to avoid involving the Germans in Greece—and so their troops remained strictly in central Greece—and, secondly, in the course of time to form a coalition combining Yugoslavia, Turkey and Greece. Eden undertook the preliminary diplomatic approaches. But the Turks were evasive and in Yugoslavia, the Regent Prince Paul refused to let himself be drawn by the bait of obtaining Istria, which the British angled in front of him. The only result was to worry Hitler who ordered Yugoslavia to become a signatory to the tripartite pact.

The Yugoslavs first turned to the British but on March 8 and 9 in Athens, Eden and Dill were unable to promise them any immediate help. Approaches to the Soviet Union were equally unrewarding; the Soviet ambassador in Belgrade went off to Moscow with lists of equipment that Yugoslavia would have liked to have but he did not come back. However,

1. When he became Foreign Minister, Eden changed his mind and sided with Churchill!

after momentarily toying with the idea of occupying Salonica, on which they asked the Germans their view without receiving any reply, the Yugoslavs began to help Greece by sending her food and ammunition.

Hitler then insisted on their signing the tripartite pact; and on March 25 Prince Paul and the government of Tsvetković and Marković gave way. In return, Germany and Italy pledged themselves not to send troops through Yugoslav territory and, in a secret clause, promised to hand Salonica over to Yugoslavia.

In Belgrade the news of the signing of the tripartite pact aroused popular indignation which was fanned by British and possibly American agents, even if they had not been entirely responsible for creating it. Eden moreover had not returned to London but was waiting in Malta. On March 27, a military coup got rid of the regency and the government. Young King Peter proclaimed himself of age and General Simović became Prime Minister.

If the British had hoped to provide an obstacle to Germany's advance southwards, Hitler lost no time in destroying their illusions. On April 6, 800 aircraft pounded Belgrade and the main Yugoslav communication centres with bombs. Using Bulgaria as their starting base, German troops swiftly cut Yugoslavia off from Greece. Before the Yugoslavs had even completed their mobilisation the Germans had taken Skopje on April 7 and Zagreb on the 11th. The Italians, Hungarians and Bulgarians all rushed in together for the kill; on April 12, Belgrade fell.

The British barely had time to pick up King Peter and the Yugoslav government and take them away to England, where the King joined the growing band of exiled sovereigns. Hitler decided to deal with Slovenia separately and set her aside for the moment. The Hungarians occupied part of the Banat; the Italians took possession of Dalmatia and the islands; Croatia and Montenegro were proclaimed independent; Yugoslavia was reduced to the tiny territory of Serbia and placed under German occupation. It was highly inadvisable for little states to rebel against Hitler's Reich or oppose it. Greece was about to learn the same lesson.

X GREECE CRUSHED

Only the RAF had fought in Albania and then with a mere fifty aircraft; the Greeks complained that even these were not used very freely. As for the Expeditionary Force, it had advanced no further than Larissa and was now marking time. It demonstrated the ambiguity of the Anglo-Greek alliance. The British merely wanted to set up a bridgehead in preparation for better days to come; they wished to avoid arousing too much alarm in

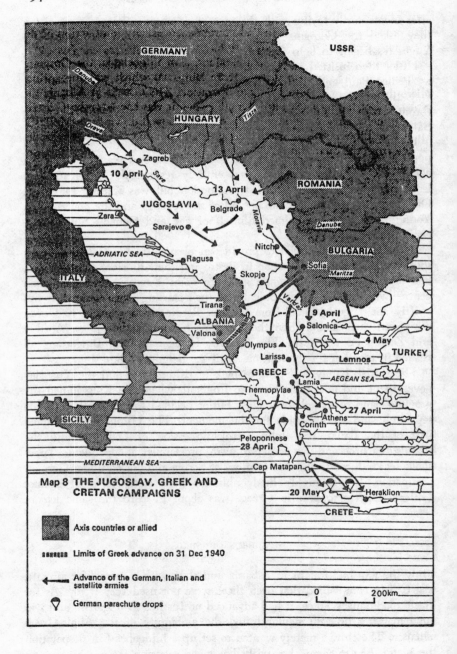

Map 8 THE JUGOSLAV, GREEK AND
CRETAN CAMPAIGNS

Axis countries or allied

Limits of Greek advance on 31 Dec 1940

Advance of the German, Italian and
satellite armies

German parachute drops

0   200km

the Germans so that the latter should not pounce on them before they were properly established, and they were encouraging the Greeks, who by this time had fifteen divisions, to fall back on to their positions. But the Greeks did not want to give up Thrace and Macedonia without a fight and they could not make up their minds to withdraw from the Albanian front, where they were winning and hoping to link up with the Yugoslavs. The British themselves had decided to move back as far as Thermopylae in the event of a German attack. In these circumstances, any joint action of the Allied armies was out of the question.

On April 6, the same day as the offensive in Yugoslavia, the Germans launched their attack on Greece from Bulgaria, which was the spring-board of the whole of this Balkan operation. The Greeks in Albania did not think of falling back until the 9th, when it was too late; the German forces, including an armoured division, had moved down from Monastir and were blocking their way. One after another the Greek units, under attack from the direction of Thessaly as well, were cut up, flung back into the mountains and ordered by their leaders to scatter. On April 20, General Papagos asked the Germans for an armistice; by then the Italians had still not succeeded in crossing the Greek-Albanian border and the Greek rearguards during their retreat had never ceased their local counter-attacks against them. But these minor successes could do nothing to affect the fate of Greece. On April 27 Athens was occupied and the swastika was hoisted on the Acropolis. While King George left with his government for Cairo and a large part of the Greek Navy and merchant fleet took refuge in Alexandria, the British were carrying out a difficult evacuation of Greece and the Peloponnese almost without a fight. Once again they had lost face in a repetition of Dunkirk, saving their troops but leaving their equipment behind. Once more they had shown that the available forces were not adequate for the vast schemes which were planned for them. Of course they still held the island of Crete; but for how long?

XI THE BATTLE OF CRETE

From the beginning of the war, the British had realised the importance of Crete for the control of the western Mediterranean; they were particularly attracted by the sheltered roadstead of Suda Bay, in the west of the island, which they wanted to turn into a naval base, a sort of Mediterranean Scapa Flow; but there had never been any serious attempt to defend Crete, nor had one ever been contemplated. In any case there were insufficient means to do so and the fleet seemed capable of ensuring the protection of the island. At the start of the intervention in Greece, Crete had been considered as an advance supply base; but it suddenly became a last strong-hold held by 22,000 Commonwealth troops, including General Freyberg's New Zealand division.

But the island was defenceless; all the harbours and airfields were on the more exposed north coast; in the south, a better protected plain which might have been used to provide an excellent airfield could now not be got ready in time. Crete became the scene of operations between the German Air Force and the Royal Navy—an uneven contest, as the Norwegian expedition had already demonstrated. In addition, recent precedent could have shown how the Wehrmacht would carry out its attack; paratroops had been dropped on the isthmus of Corinth to forestall British troops as they were withdrawing towards the Peloponnese. And the Luftwaffe was employing a vast concentration of forces: 716 aircraft, including 430 bombers which, with 500 troop-carrying aircraft and 72 gliders, dropped a whole airborne division, comprising three mountain-infantry regiments, one armoured battalion and a motor-cycle battalion. In one sudden move, the attackers established themselves in strength, in the heart of their opponents' defences, like some fifth column falling from the heavens. The defenders who had been facing outwards to the sea had been caught in the rear.

When every attempt to retake the airfields and stem the flow of reinforcements had failed, it was apparent that any attempt to remain on the island would be doomed to failure. But the evacuation proved difficult. In the first place, it was held up by Churchill's stubborn optimism. On May 20, 1941, while the paratroops were showering down on to the island, he cabled to Wavell: 'Victory in Crete essential at this turning-point in the war. Use every exertion to achieve it by all possible means.' Not until May 26 when the New Zealand General Freyberg announced that the struggle was hopeless, was the order given, once again, to evacuate the men without worrying about the equipment. But the British fleet had in the last few days been greatly weakened; for example, the aircraft-carrier *Formidable* had lost every single one of its fighters. The men could only be taken off at night, on exposed beaches, between midnight and 3 a.m. so as to allow the ships to avoid the German Air Force attacks under cover of darkness. During the four nights from May 28 till June 1, the tremendous feat of embarking 16,500 men was accomplished; but three cruisers and six destroyers were sunk and two battleships and one aircraft-carrier damaged and put out of action for several months.

The Greek operation ended in pitiful failure; in Admiral Cunningham's words, 'a disastrous episode in the history of the Royal Navy'. Britain's weakness had been cruelly exposed for all to see. 'To save Crete,' wrote Cunningham, all that was needed were 'three long-range fighters and a few bomber squadrons'. Mastery of the seas was clearly of no use without control of the skies. Moreover, while the New Zealanders and Australians who had borne the brunt of the fighting were showing their dissatisfaction, the depletion of the British units in Africa, plus the arrival of German reinforcements, was to lead to further galling setbacks for the British Commonwealth.

XII THE SUCCESSES OF ROMMEL AND THE "AFRIKA KORPS"

In January 1941, Hitler had decided to help the Italians in Libya as well as in Malta and Greece. He thought that the loss of North Africa, though acceptable militarily, would cause strong psychological repercussions in Italy that were better avoided. Against Admiral Raeder's advice, who wanted to 'clean out the Mediterranean in 1940–41', the proposed reinforcements for Africa were not intended to take the offensive but merely to stabilise the Italian front. Accordingly, first of all, a light division was sent; it was followed by a Panzer division; together, the two made up the *Afrika Korps* under the command of Rommel, one of the German tank commanders who had sped along the French roads in June 1940.

Hardly had Rommel arrived when, on his own initiative, he launched a lightning war which, once Cyrenaica was reconquered, was to take him right up to the gates of Egypt. Tireless, indifferent to hunger or climate, wilful and imaginative, equally swift to think and to act, always in the forefront, Rommel believed in pouncing without giving his foe a moment's respite. His rashness sometimes cut him off from his units and once nearly led to his capture; he was never at his command-post and he frequently embarrassed his subordinates by leaving them without instructions, especially when he went off with his chief of staff. But to compensate for this, he was in a position to exploit any favourable chance in the field. As he was constantly up with his men, sharing their life and all its dangers, he very quickly became extremely popular. His brilliant successes made him a legendary hero in his own lifetime; he became 'the desert fox'.

The British generals facing him gave the impression of being anxious not to miss their tea-break. They were having great difficulty in adapting themselves to desert warfare, in establishing close co-operation between the three services—the fighting was taking place in areas less than forty miles from the coast, so the Navy often intervened. They were outclassed in every field; they could only regain the upper hand if they achieved enormous superiority in equipment.

Taking advantage of the gap left by the departure of the British troops for Greece, Rommel hustled his enemy out of his positions. He pressed on, disregarding the objections of the Italian leaders to whom he was supposed to be subordinated. But he was unable to take Tobruk which remained as a thorn in the flesh of his north flank for 200 days. When he reached the Egyptian border, shortage of petrol and Hitler's orders, since the Führer did not wish to have to send large numbers of troops to Africa, brought Rommel to a halt when he thought Suez was in his grasp.

The British were able to organise their defence at Mersa Matruh, well in front of the vital zone of the Nile delta. The tables had, however, been totally turned in favour of the Axis. At the same time, Malta was neutralised by the Luftwaffe in Sicily and the British found their way across the Mediterranean barred. In addition, reinforcements were reaching Rommel, aided and abetted by the Vichy government and the use of Tunisian territorial waters by Italian freighters, in accordance with the terms of the 'Paris protocols'. In addition, encouraged by German successes, Arab nationalists were becoming restless and were making no secret of their hatred of the British, in Egypt as well as in Syria.

XIII THE WAR IN SYRIA

In April 1941, a military coup in Iraq had abolished the regency and brought General Rashid Ali to power. He had secretly formed an anti-British and anti-Jewish conspiracy with the Grand Mufti in Jerusalem. Rashid Ali dismissed Parliament, proclaimed Iraqi independence and on May 2 attacked the British garrison in Baghdad. The Germans did not want to miss the opportunity but, in order to help the Iraqi rebels, they needed to pass through Syria. In Berchtesgaden on May 11, 1941, Admiral Darlan who had been head of the Vichy government since Laval's dismissal accepted the terms of the 'protocol' dictated by Hitler. More convinced than ever of the invincibility of Germany, Admiral Darlan could at last see the possibility of achieving the collaboration with Germany which he had been pursuing in the hope of some relaxation of the harsh clauses of the armistice and of future benefit to France. The negotiations took a broader form. It was agreed that the Germans would use the Syrian harbours and airfields to send help to the Iraqi rebels, who would be given weapons stockpiled by the French in accordance with the armistice terms. In addition, Rommel would receive supplies via Tunisian territorial waters as well as by land, rail and road, with France providing the necessary lorries. Finally, the Germans would be granted bases in Dakar and Bizerta. Once again, the possibility of winning back the dissident equatorial African colonies was considered.

On his return to Paris Darlan signed the protocol, which was ratified by the Vichy government, and instructions were given to implement it. But this implementation required the collaboration of General Weygand, Commander-in-Chief in Africa, and of the Governor, General Boisson. On being summoned to Vichy, they protested vigorously and expressed the view that the army in Africa would not accept the terms of the protocol. They suggested that France should ask for concessions in exchange—the release of prisoners of war, a reduction in the occupation costs—to which the Germans could not agree. Implementation of the protocol which had already begun in Tunisia was now stopped, and, because of the swift defeat of the Iraqi rebels and of Rommel's successes, both of which rendered French collaboration no longer necessary, the Germans did not insist on its strict enforcement.

But in France there had been great indignation at the Vichy government's violation of the armistice. Pastor Basdevant, the legal adviser to the French Ministry of Foreign Affairs, vigorously condemned it. There had been even greater indignation in London where Free France violently denounced it as 'Vichy treachery'. There were hopeful indications that General Dentz's troops, who were opposed to the 'protocols', were only awaiting the opportunity to break away from Pétain. General de Gaulle persuaded the British to attempt to capture Syria; they did so rather reluctantly because they knew to their cost how limited their resources were. The attempt degenerated into a deplorable conflict between Frenchmen, because the hoped-for break with Vichy did not take place or at least only partially.

Despite American pressure—Admiral Leahy told Pétain that 'resistance to the English in Syria would work in Hitler's favour and not France's'—the Vichy government decided to fight. Pétain replied to Leahy: 'The British have attacked us. We know that we shall lose Syria but we are determined to fight to the bitter end.' After a few weeks' fighting in the course of which there were some thousand casualties on each side, General Dentz signed an armistice with the British. Contrary to General de Gaulle's expectations, only a small number of French officers and men joined Free France; the majority, on the other hand, showed him bitter animosity. General Catroux had proclaimed the principle of independence for Syria and the Lebanon; but this principle became a reality only after the war.

Meanwhile the British had recaptured Baghdad and put men on whom they could rely back into power in Iraq. The Middle East had been sealed off against Axis interference and British control re-established in the Arab world as well as over its vast resources of oil. It was a faint glimmer of hope in the gloom which enveloped Britain in June 1941.

XIV THE STATE OF THE WAR IN JUNE 1941

In June 1941, it was clear that, following her early successes in the Battle of Britain and then those at sea and in Africa, Britain had been striving to achieve a state of readiness that had been neglected so long that it could hardly be quickly attained. She had suffered one setback after another. True enough, her territory was now more adequately defended; she had raised and trained thirty-seven divisions, though they were short of tanks. But rather than a landing in the British Isles, the danger now seemed to lie in attacks in the direction of Gibraltar—whose defences had been hurriedly strengthened but still gave cause for alarm—but above all in the direction of Alexandria. The happy ending to the Syrian problem guaranteed Egypt's rear and excluded any possibility of attack from the north; but on the borders of Cyrenaica the situation was fraught with danger. Threatened with being cut off from her Asian empire, Britain was in the still greater peril of being cut off from the United States by the mounting curve of merchant shipping sinkings in the Atlantic. Even in the Mediterranean, the Royal Navy had its back to the wall.

Britain was without doubt going to be forced back on the defensive for a long time to come. Churchill chafed at this but what else could be done? The Wehrmacht's victories and the German submarine successes, together with the fact that the German-Soviet pact was working smoothly, had changed the blockade of Germany into a blockade of the British Isles. While the British fleet continued to keep watchful guard over the coastline of Europe and issued a niggardly quota of importation permits, the gain from all this was little more than the pressure it exerted on the Vichy government which, however, still continued to maintain an attitude of benevolent neutrality towards the Reich. True, Churchill had thoughts of showering tons of bombs on German territory and had called for an immense programme of aircraft production: 14,000 aircraft in two years. But these aircraft did not exist nor did he know when he would get them, and meanwhile the air raids on German towns, communications and synthetic-petrol factories had more a token effect than a real one. As for a British landing in Europe, it was just a pipe-dream.

In these circumstances, how could one escape the conclusion that, even if Britain could no longer lose the war, she still had no chance of winning it? This was the firm belief of the Vichy government's leaders. Although Italy had shown herself surprisingly weak, did Germany not seem more unbeatable than ever? Any initiative could only come from Hitler. What would he do? The Mediterranean offered him vast vistas; Alexandria and

Suez were within reach of the Luftwaffe; the unstable Arabs had only just settled down and could easily be roused again; with more tanks and petrol, Rommel could continue his victorious advance and this time reach Cairo. Even faced with such gloomy prospects as these, it is possible that Churchill would still not admit defeat; but how long could he hold out if the whole of the available German forces were then hurled against the British Isles?

But Hitler had chosen another path. There was now no going back on his decision to attack the Soviet Union; on June 1, 1941, the armoured divisions and most of the Air Force left the Balkans. On June 22, 1941, the USSR was invaded. At once, through Hitler's deliberate choice, the war assumed worldwide proportions. Full of self-confidence, Hitler seemed to have lost his fear of fighting on two fronts, although the diversions that he had been forced to make as a result of Churchill's enterprising operations all round the Mediterranean had cost him valuable time. The war was moving into a new phase; it was also going to change its scope, its nature and even its objectives.

BOOK TWO

THE WORLD WAR
(June 1941–January 1943)

THE GREATER REICH

CHAPTER 1

The Break Between Germany and Russia

THE German-Soviet war is one of the phases of the Second World War which raises the greatest number of questions for the historian. Not that he lacks sources, which are plentiful enough. On the German side, the most important documents are known; but in their memoirs the Wehrmacht generals are inclined to dissociate themselves from their Führer and lay at his door all the sins of Germany—after the war. On the Soviet side there is also a mass of publications, but they repeat each other; changes of government have modified the official approach to the writing of history, but without sharpening the writers' critical faculties or allowing them full scope. Dissension and weaknesses tend to be glossed over in a continual eulogy of the Soviet people, the régime and the Communist party, which finds convenient expression in propagandist slogans. With this goes a systematic suspicion and disparagement of works published in 'the West', whose authors they choose to regard as enemies of the USSR and describe as 'falsifiers of history'. Soviet historians of the Second World War, often epic or lyrical in tone, still observe strict taboos—for example, concerning the motives and working of the German-Soviet pact. Hence there are embarrassing gaps and omissions.

I HITLER'S DECISION

If we trace the development of Hitler's attitude towards the USSR through the diaries of Generals Halder and Warlimont, he seems to have shown a peculiar singleness of purpose. It all began on July 21, 1940, when Hitler ordered von Brauchitsch, the head of the Army, to prepare for an attack on the Soviet Union. At this time, the Battle of Britain had only just begun, orders had been given to attempt a landing on the other side of the Channel, and Hitler had recently decided to reduce the number of infantry divisions. A puzzling decision, if ever there was one, ascribed by E. Bauer to a 'sudden illumination'. However that may be, from now on Hitler's resolve was to unfold with faultless logic. On July 29, during a conference at headquarters, the date for the attack was fixed for the spring of

1941; it was to be another Blitzkrieg, a 'lightning war'. The task of drawing up the preliminary plans was given to General Marks, commander of the Eighteenth Army stationed near the USSR. The following day, Halder set to work himself.

The German military leaders do not seem to have raised any serious objections. Admiral Raeder voiced the fear that the operations under consideration might prejudice the submarine war by cutting down the submarine-building programme. Marshal Goering showed some anxiety lest the Luftwaffe's commitment in the east might rob German territory of some of its protection from British bombers. The sole aim of these reservations was to point out beforehand the possibilities of failure so as to anticipate any blame should the occasion arise. But those who were really responsible, the OKW and OKH, without raising any fundamental objections, confined themselves to demanding facilities for the immense task that they were called upon to perform at very short notice.

On August 9 General Warlimont, the general in command of the operations, drew up the preliminary directives. The plan was called the *Aufbau Ost* (reconstruction of the east). His aim was to prepare for the attack by setting up the necessary services: roads, railways, bridges, hospitals, stocks of equipment, provisions, etc.

On August 26, Hitler began to transfer infantry and artillery divisions to the east. The reason given—probably a pretext—was to protect the Romanian oil-fields, which were in no danger. In his instructions on the methods to be employed, General Jodl insisted on the need for concealing the operation: 'We must not give the Russians the impression that we are preparing for war,' he said.

The crucial conference of the general staff took place on December 5. Hitler gave his approval to the plan which von Brauchitsch and Halder put before him and which had been drawn up by Paulus. He pompously announced that 'he would not make the same mistake as Napoleon'. It was on December 18 that the immense operation was given its final codename of 'Barbarossa'. The same day, Hitler issued his 'order no. 21' which fixed the beginning of the operation for May 15. The Balkan campaign forced him to postpone it until June 21—like Napoleon, Hitler was setting out for Moscow later than he would have wished.

Thus, from the summer of 1940 onwards, the whole of Hitler's train of thought and consequently the whole of Germany's political, diplomatic and military activity seems to have been geared to one major, if not single target: to ensure the most favourable situation for a decisive battle against the USSR. The operations of the *Afrika Korps* in Yugoslavia and Greece were only minor ones, carried out more or less reluctantly as the occasion required.

II GERMAN-SOVIET RELATIONS

Hitler's decision was perhaps the result of a deterioration in German-Soviet relations. The pact was certainly not working entirely to his liking. The Russians were showing some ill-will towards Finland and they were at odds with the Germans over the exploitation of nickel mines at Petsamo. On both sides there were complaints about delays in commercial transactions.

Hitler had been annoyed by the USSR's unexpected annexation of Bukovina, and Molotov, for his part, was complaining that 'the arbitration of Vienna' had reshaped central Europe to the detriment of Romania, without anyone having consulted the USSR or even giving her proper notice of it.

On September 2, 1940, the USSR had also been concerned at the signing of the tripartite pact between Japan, Italy and Germany. Although obviously directed against the United States and Britain, did the agreement not perhaps include a few secret clauses against herself? Was it not, in fact, a revival of the anti-Comintern pact? But on this she had been given all possible reassurance since she had even been invited to join it and in the gigantic partition of the world outlined by the pact she had even been offered a vast area as her share—the Persian Gulf and India.

On November 12, 1940, Molotov came to Berlin to discuss these grand prospects. His response to the temptation of the wide open spaces of Asia was very down-to-earth: he asked about Finland, which he regarded as belonging to the Soviet sphere of influence; Bulgaria, to whom the USSR, in order to emphasise her dominant role, would have liked to give a guarantee similar to the one which the Reich had given Romania; and the 'convention of Montreux' on the Dardanelles, which the USSR wanted to modify in her favour, in a way which Molotov described as 'not just on paper'. Molotov also mentioned Swedish neutrality, the Danish straits and Japan—the latter might be a trifle less interested in China since Indonesia had fallen into her lap through the Dutch defeat.

In short, each talked about himself and turned a deaf ear to the other. But although he made no effort to convince him, Hitler paid no attention to his companion's *desiderata*. German troops entered Bulgaria to attack Greece, and Bulgaria joined the tripartite pact, without the USSR making any protest. Furthermore, the very day that the USSR signed a friendship pact with Yugoslavia the latter was attacked by the Wehrmacht and conquered in a matter of days: not only did the USSR make no attempt to go to her 'friend's' aid, but she allowed her to be carved up by her neighbours without breathing a word. The Yugoslav minister was expelled from Moscow, without ceremony, since Yugoslavia no longer existed.

The USSR thus seemed to have resigned herself to surrendering the Balkans to German influence. There was nothing in her behaviour to worry the Führer to the extent of provoking him to declare war.

III HITLER'S REASONS

So on June 22, when Goebbels' propaganda machine declared that the Wehrmacht's invasion was a preventive measure to forestall Soviet aggression, it was clear that these implausible reasons were meant for the record and it is difficult to see why Stalin should have gone to so much trouble to exonerate himself from the sinister schemes attributed to him unless it were also for the record. But what then were the Führer's real reasons?

It is probable that although Hitler had been examining it as a possible course of action, until the autumn of 1940 he had not taken any definite decision. But the development of the war had gradually forced him to do so. His failure in the Battle of Britain, the difficulties he had encountered in forming a Mediterranean coalition and above all Mussolini's initiative in Greece had shifted the 'map of the war' from western to south-east Europe. The British offensive in Greece and the Belgrade putsch finally determined Germany's choice of this area for her new victory. Beyond stretched the boundless horizons of the USSR.

To say that Hitler was seeking victory over Britain in Moscow does not seem quite true. It was from the United States that Britain was hoping for an injection of new blood; of course, though it was not a matter of indifference to her whether the USSR became a partner of the Reich or was attacked by her it was less important to her than whether or not her cause was taken up or deserted by the United States. But the withdrawal of Britain from the Continent and the obvious impossibility of beating her on her own ground automatically brought Hitler back to his familiar fantasies: the fight against Bolshevism and the conquest of land in the east. For the time being the overthrow of Britain took second place.

On March 30, 1941, at a conference attended by the generals of the three forces and lasting two and a half hours, the Führer fell quite naturally into the tone of *Mein Kampf*. 'The Communists,' he said, 'never have been and never will be our friends. The fight which is about to begin is a war of extermination. If Germany does not embark upon it in this spirit she may well defeat the enemy but in thirty years from now they will once again rise up and confront her.'

A few weeks earlier he had confided to his closest colleagues: 'The vast expanses of Russia contain inexhaustible riches. Germany must, if not appropriate them, at least exploit them politically and economically. In this way she will be able to present a triumphant challenge to the whole world.'[1]

The pact with the USSR did of course give the Reich access to this wealth but only a little at a time and on the humiliating condition that Stalin was agreeable. From this viewpoint, Fabry is correct in writing that the German-Soviet pact contained the seeds of its own destruction; it had blown up the Polish dividing wall which the treaties of 1918 had set up between Germany and the Soviet Union; it had brought into contact two opponents whose temporary readiness to come to an understanding had not overcome their fundamental hostility, while their possession of a common border now made a direct confrontation possible.

Moreover the moment seemed well chosen for the Reich; Britain's weakness made it improbable that she could create a second front for a long time; the opportunity must be seized to strike in the east as a continuation and extension of the Polish campaign. Hitler also had very little doubt about the USSR's weakness; had this not been unmistakably proved by her defeats in Finland and her failure to speak out when the German invasion of the Balkans threatened her sphere of influence?[2] Hitler wanted this new victory to be entirely his own; he did not inform Mussolini until the very day of the attack and it was only at the Duce's entreaty that he agreed to the latter's proposal to send an Italian expeditionary force to the USSR, for it was Mussolini's opinion that 'Italy could not remain out of the war against the USSR' and he promised that this would not result in any withdrawal of troops from the African front.

IV WAS STALIN CAUGHT UNAWARES?

We now know that Stalin did not lack warning. Cordell Hull tells us in his memoirs how the American commercial attaché in Berlin used to re-

1. On August 26, 1941, in a circular to the German legations abroad, Ribbentrop defined the importance of a victory over the USSR in the following terms: the control of the Ukraine would guarantee a permanent source of food supplies; Russian materials would bring about a considerable improvement in the German war economy; and victory in the east would enable the Reich to turn and face their last enemy, Britain.

2. In the controversies stirred up in the USSR by 'de-Stalinisation', great importance has rightly been attached to the 'purges' ordered by Stalin in the Red Army. They had convinced the French general staff that the Soviet forces were disorganised and they thus provided a partial explanation for the Franco-British reluctance to enter into a pact with the USSR. On the other hand, they had prompted Hitler to attack an army which he considered to be 'eighty per cent decapitated', and which he reckoned would take two years to recover.

ceive intelligence in a cinema from a quite high-placed anti-Nazi German. It was in this way that knowledge of the plan for the attack against the Soviet Union reached the USA; 'it was so detailed', said Cordell Hull, 'that at first I didn't believe it'. The plan was communicated to Moscow at the beginning of 1941. In March the USSR was provided with more information from the same source—including the indication that wads of ruble notes had been printed in Germany. On April 19, Churchill warned Stalin that German troops were 'massing in Poland'.[1] It seems that Stalin thought this intelligence was exaggerated or even invented in order to cause dissension between the USSR and the Reich.

Yet it was confirmed by other more confidential sources. The Russian authors of the *History of the Great Soviet War* write:

> From Soviet intelligence agencies—among them Sorge in Tokyo—from frontier guards, from diplomatic representatives, from foreign friends of the USSR, particularly from Poland, Romania, Czechoslovakia, Finland, Hungary and even Germany, there came indisputable information testifying to the extremely serious situation on the Soviet borders.

Even more explicit was the evidence disclosed in the USSR, where several hundred Abwehr agents were captured in 1940–41. Questioning revealed that spy-training centres had been set up in several German towns and that their members were provided by groups of Ukrainian, Baltic, Armenian and Georgian emigrants. In addition, battalions of exiles were being raised and trained to form embryonic national armies and civilian governments. The brain behind the undertaking was the 'Russian section' of the 'Geopolitical Institute'. Neither had the concentration of several million men on their borders escaped the notice of Russian intelligence; in April it was ascertained that there had been eighty violations of Soviet territory by aircraft, and the USSR complained to Berlin about it.

Obviously, all these reports were swamped by many others of a different and contradictory nature; their importance could be exaggerated or minimised, according to the way the facts were presented. And the Soviet intelligence chief, involved as he was, like all the Soviet top men at the time, in the 'personality cult', wanted above all else to please Stalin; he thus had his own reasons for describing as 'questionable' the intelligence concerning Germany's hostile designs against the USSR, since Stalin did not like to hear about them.

Perhaps Stalin was determined not to let himself be convinced. It seems difficult to believe that the wary Georgian should have placed absolute confidence in Hitler; even more difficult to accept that he had all of a sud-

---

1. Information confirmed by Sumner Welles, *The Times for Decision,* pp. 170–171, New York, Harper & Row, 1945.

den come round to the idea of coexistence with the Fascist states and that he believed that this coexistence could last, and Russia give up her revolutionary mission in the world. A certain number of decisions seem to show that Stalin had seen through Hitler's intentions or at least that he was uneasy about them; he became President of the Council of Ministers on May 7. In June, the port of Leningrad was closed. Above all, on April 13, 1941, when Matsuoka, the Japanese Foreign Minister, was passing through Moscow on his way back from Berlin, the USSR and Japan signed a non-aggression pact. Stalin attached sufficient importance to it to go to the station and bid farewell to the Japanese minister on the platform as he was leaving, a rare gesture which attracted a great deal of comment; the fact was that this pact covered the USSR in Asia, should she be attacked in Europe.

It seems therefore likely that, foreseeing the storm and knowing that he was not fully protected against it, Stalin worked things so as not to hasten its outbreak at his expense. This is why on March 20, after the invasion of Bulgaria by German troops, a circular from the Soviet Foreign Office to its officials, while asking them to warn the Balkan states against falling too completely under the German yoke, concluded that 'the German-Soviet treaty was essential to the successful achievement of the most urgent objective, namely, the destruction of the British Commonwealth'. This is why on June 13 the Soviet government recognised Rashid-Ali's government in Iraq, while the Tass Agency, in a communiqué widely broadcast by the whole Soviet and Communist press, denounced the British officials who, for purposes which were not difficult to fathom, were spreading 'false rumours' about disagreements between the Germans and Russians.

In any case the Wehrmacht's aggression was a complete surprise for the Russian people, just as it was for the Red Army, insufficiently on its guard; and also, it seems, for Stalin himself, who thought that he had at least gained time, if not even warded off the danger. According to Ambassador Maisky, he shut himself up for three days in the Kremlin, during which time the Soviet government remained without a leader and its members were given no instructions. The question now automatically springs to mind, what would have been the result if Hitler had sent an ultimatum to Stalin, if he was so anxious for peace? To what extent would he have stood his ground? But this time, although he had shown that he could win victories simply by brandishing dangerous threats, Hitler had announced to his generals 'that no agreement was possible with a Communist'. He was at last embarking on his war of religion and extermination. He was going to justify Paul Reynaud's assessment of him as the Gengis Khan of modern times.

V HITLER'S OBJECTIVES

In the east, Hitler's objectives were practically unlimited. It was not merely a question of destroying the potential threat of the Red Army or even of gaining possession of a certain amount of territory, however extensive it might be. He had to obliterate the ussr, wipe her off the map of Europe, like Poland, and split her up into independent states. In order to do this the Wehrmacht would have to reach the Volga and the Caucasus; from there raids would be launched against the most remote strongholds, as, for example, the Urals. Once this total victory had been won, Romania, the 'General Government' and Finland would be enlarged and 'buffer states', whose area could then be accurately fixed, would be set up in the Ukraine, White Russia and the Baltic countries. The rest would remain a Slav block, 'Muscovy', which they would take care to leave in a reassuring state of chronic underdevelopment.

These objectives were to be achieved in the first instance by military victories but also by a deliberate policy of terror. The aim was not only to protect the Wehrmacht's rear but to destroy the achievements of the existing Bolshevik régime root and branch and to exterminate the Jews and Communists who had accomplished them. The population would thus be brought to heel with a single blow and firmly established in a state of permanent bondage.

So the directive on 'the jurisdiction of an exceptional court in the Barbarossa region' ordered 'complete ruthlessness' towards the civilian population and the immediate execution of all individuals or representatives of communities suspected of hostility towards the invaders. Political commissars in the armies and top-ranking officials of the Communist party were to be shot as soon as they were captured. As the ussr was not a signatory to the Geneva Convention, Soviet prisoners of war would not benefit from its protective clauses and would be subjected to forced labour.

A programme for the economic exploitation of the conquered territories, called 'the Green File', provided for the German seizure of industry, raw materials, crude oil and food stuffs. The best land would be colonised by Aryan settlers—including room for the Scandinavians and the Dutch.

The *Aufbau Ost*, the eastern plan, looked further; after the war, German domination in eastern Europe would be established by a reign of terror—Hitler liked to forecast that it would last 'for a thousand years'. The subjugated peoples would receive only primary education, restricted to simple sums, learning how to write their name and to learning 'that, by divine ordinance, they should obey the Germans and be honest, hard-working and submissive'. Their state of health would be kept at a rudimentary level so that any population increase would be checked from time to time by epidemics. As for 'Muscovy', that sewage dump would be visited by punitive expeditions as a warning and a reminder to its subhuman inhabitants that the Germans were their masters. Seventy per cent of the Slav population would be transported to Muscovy, which could very well begin west of the Urals, although its exact location was not yet fixed.

Such were Hitler's grandiose and monstrous 'ideas'. Goebbels was to paraphrase them by brandishing the slogans 'crusade' and 'total mobilisation of Europe against Asian Bolshevism'. Himmler was to denounce any consideration shown to the Russians as a sentimental aberration. The war against the USSR was thus essentially an ideological and a racial war. But it required vast resources and, of course, most important, the victory of the Wehrmacht.

VI THE WEHRMACHT'S FORCES AND PLANS

On June 22, 1941, the German armies along the Soviet frontiers were concentrated in four operational areas: on the Finnish front, from Petsamo to north of Leningrad, General Dietl's mountain troops were fighting shoulder to shoulder with Marshal Mannerheim's Finnish army. Their target was Murmansk and the Carelian territory covering Leningrad. The northern army group, under the command of Marshal von Leeb, consisted of three armies, one of which was armoured; its target was Leningrad. The central army group under Marshal von Bock would advance on Moscow; it also contained three armies, but two of them armoured. In the south, the group of armies under von Rundstedt was to advance towards Kiev, Dnepropetrovsk and Odessa; this group was more heterogeneous; in addition to the four German armies, one of which was armoured, there were Hungarian and Romanian contingents—between which German units had had to be sandwiched—and later on the Italian expeditionary force. Each group of armies was supported by an air fleet. Naval support was provided in the Baltic.

In all, the German forces numbered 150 infantry divisions and 30 armoured divisions, added to which there were 15 Finnish divisions, 20 Romanian divisions, 10 or so Hungarian and the same number of Italian divisions; the non-German units were inferior in the quality of their officers, their training and equipment. About 60 German divisions were left to guard Norway, Denmark, Belgium, Holland and France; 7 were stationed in the Balkans; 2 were operating in Libya. Plainly, the Germans had not exhausted their reserves of manpower; but Hitler refused Halder's request for 40 supplementary divisions, so as not to jeopardise the output of the war industries.

About 4,000 tanks were engaged in the USSR; this included 2,400 heavy tanks—the Germans were convinced that their Mark IV Panzer was superior to any other. The Luftwaffe comprised 3,000 aircraft, two-thirds of its total force, 1,000 of which were bombers and 900 fighters. In point of fact, 3,000 aircraft on a front 1,250 to 1,900 miles long was hardly more than two aircraft per mile, whereas in the Polish and French campaigns the density was ten per mile. But the quality of the German equipment was superior to the Russians'; the majority of the Soviet fighters could fly only as fast as the Nazi bombers.

The OKH had realised that the great Russian plain between the Baltic and the Black Sea was divided from west to east by two areas difficult to negotiate by ground forces: the Pripet Marshes between Kiev and Minsk, and the Valday plateau between Leningrad and Moscow. These two obstacles left three wide corridors of approach to Leningrad, Moscow and Kiev, and this geographical factor had influenced the Wehrmacht's grouping and objectives. However, realising that the armies advancing on Leningrad and Kiev would have to cross numerous rivers and that Moscow was the point where most of the main Soviet railway lines converged—and rail was the only method of transport which could be used all the year round— General Halder had suggested that the Soviet capital should be made the chief target. Since the Russians were aware of this and would mass the bulk of their troops to its defence, the decisive battles would be fought and the Red Army destroyed in front of Moscow. But Hitler attached equal importance to the capture of Leningrad and Stalingrad, the names of which, wrote General de Cossé-Brissac, 'fascinated him'. It was in these 'sacred cities of Communism' that he wanted to 'overthrow the hydra-headed Red monster'. And Hitler had found little trouble in forcing his views on his generals.

VII HITLER AS WAR LEADER

For to an increasing extent, it was Hitler and Hitler alone who conducted the war, in the political and diplomatic field, in armaments production and in strategy. He alone took the decisions, disclosing them in dribs and drabs to small committees which were gradually extended in size as his decisions required a greater number of people to carry them out. At these meetings Hitler would of course, listen and try to understand, but above all he held forth and forced his wishes on his colleagues, whether they found them congenial or not. Since each of them knew only part of what was in the master's mind, they fell over one another to agree by paraphrasing his decrees. The generals were the last to offer any real criticism of the Führer's decisions, except when they had very serious objections to put forward on technical grounds; but these objections concerned only the execution, not the idea or the decision itself. 'The Führer had informed Jodl and me once and for all that politics were none of our business,' wrote Keitel; '. . . we were not always in agreement with his decisions at the operational level, yet we always carried them out to the letter.'

How good was Hitler as a strategist? It is a fact that he had studied the works of the great German war theorists from Frederick the Great and Clausewitz to Moltke and von Seekt. According to Speer, 'in matters relating to army equipment, the characteristics of weapons and various types of ammunition, he knew more than his chief of staff.' Guderian had often been struck by the Führer's extraordinary memory, his gift of persuasion and his immense will-power. He possessed in addition an outstanding sense of when to take strategic advantage of a situation and showed an amazing flair for discovering the most unorthodox and unexpected solutions.

He thought that the qualities which made up a military leader were intelligence, tenacity and iron nerves and that he possessed these qualities more than his generals. This conviction of his superiority led him to intervene in every detail; but he lacked the necessary professional knowledge and he paralysed his subordinates and caused confusion.

Above all, Hitler had become intoxicated with the extraordinary successes he had achieved. He believed quite simply that he was a genius. He wrote to Mussolini: 'Above the world of mediocrities, there is the fraternity of exceptional beings'; he considered himself irreplaceable and this filled him with a feverish desire always to see things bigger and better and to go faster and faster. He allowed himself to be taken in by the fulsome flattery of his lieutenants, who extolled him as 'the greatest military leader of all times'. But he was self-taught and his mind was often cluttered and confused. With the arrogance of the upstart, he would dismiss his opponents in a few contemptuous and peremptory phrases—as when he described the British soldier as 'so lazy that he would almost rather die of cold than build himself a shelter'. He was swift to abuse and swift to anger; he quickly lost all sense of proportion, whether he was talking about 'degenerate parliamentary scoundrels' or about the United States, whose 'production was the biggest fraud in the world'. He often allowed himself to be carried away by his emotions and he was superstitious: he advised Mussolini not to enter the war on June 7 because it was a Friday. He was thus often unable to distinguish between what was possible and what was not. His lack of moral sense, his cruelty, his instability, his morbid sensitivity and his manic reactions which made him pass from hysterical rage to blind obstinacy and despondency were to reveal their destructive nature when the tide turned against him. On the other hand, the boldness and originality of this novice were going to help the German Army as long as it retained its superiority.

VIII THE USSR'S FORCES AND PLANS

In June 1941 the German Army's superiority over the Red Army was beyond any shadow of doubt. With 170 million inhabitants, the USSR could of course raise larger armies than Germany and her economy would be able to equip them; but in 1941, the modernisation of the Red Army, although under way, was far from being complete.

There was, however, no shortage of soldiers; the age of conscription had been lowered and the length of service increased, so that in 1941 4 million men could be mobilised; what is more, nearly 10 million men, 6 million of them young, had undergone a course of intensive military training. The training of officers and NCO's was proceeding apace under Timoshenko, the new War Commissar; about a thousand officers had been initiated in modern methods of warfare at the Military Academy. Large numbers of militant Communists had been made to join the Army, in which 55 per cent of the cadres were card-carrying Party members; the political commissars had, however, been withdrawn, so as to allow greater responsibility to the military leaders. The Red Army contained 209 infantry and 32 cavalry divisions.

But in June 1941 a large number of the young recruits had not yet completed their training and above all the units' equipment was for the most part antiquated. Some excellent prototypes had been produced: a rifle with telescopic sights and automatic loading; a machine gun and an automatic pistol, anti-tank weapons. But the units had not received their full allocation; for example, the majority possessed nothing more than anti-tank grenades.

The artillery had the advantage over the German artillery, particularly with regard to their mortars; they were being equipped with recoilless guns; rocket-guns (*Katiuschas*) were already in existence before the war and aircraft armed with rockets had been tried out in the Finnish war. But only twenty per cent of the artillery was mechanically propelled and then only by under-powered agricultural tractors. The tanks were good and well armed, but the medium tank, the T.34, which Soviet military historians consider the best in the Second World War, was as yet being produced only in small numbers; above all, although some independent armoured divisions had been formed, the available equipment had been distributed amongst all of them, so that the majority of the armoured forces were not at full strength. Moreover, the Red Army did not have any large engineering unit; its ancillary services were inadequate and its means of communication unreliable because they operated through the peacetime telephone and telegraph systems. Finally, the 6,000 Russian aircraft belonged to a type that was now out of date—the I 16 fighter had a speed of 290 miles an hour and carried 224 pounds of bombs, while the Messerschmitt 110 could fly at 340 miles an hour carrying 1120 pounds of bombs. None of the new aircraft whose prototypes were still being developed were yet being mass-produced.

The USSR's military experience was confined to the civil war, the Spanish war, the fighting against Japan in 1938–9 and above all to the war against Finland. Theories based on inadequate experience led to serious blunders, such as the useless employment of large armoured units, or the use of the air force in purely tactical operations. The Russian strategists thought that the infantry still had the chief role in war and that armies could be mobilised and deployed long before the operations proper took place. They could envisage attacks only on limited fronts and never on fronts that might be 95 miles and sometimes more than 190 miles long. Basically, they were not so very different from the French generals of 1939.

However, by developing branches of industry linked with national defence—special alloys and machine-tools—and by moving centres of industry and armaments factories to the Urals, or establishing new ones there, the USSR had braced herself for a long war. The Comintern and the national Communist parties also provided her with effective 'revolutionary dynamite'. But the effectiveness of these methods would not show itself until later on.

So although the Germans had misjudged the Soviet forces by underestimating their manpower and the number and quality of their tanks as well as by their belief that the non-Russian population would revolt, at the beginning of the war they commanded great superiority, which was still further enhanced by the fact that their opponents were inexperienced and taken by surprise. The Germans were to achieve successes of such magnitude that any power smaller in area, population and economic potential than the USSR would have been forced to admit defeat.

The Wehrmacht's Victories in the USSR

I THE SURPRISE ATTACK

At the Nuremberg trials Generals Halder and Jodl asserted that in attacking the USSR, Hitler had done no more than forestall her; to justify this preventive war they adduced Soviet concentrations on the frontier, the distribution of maps of Poland to the commanders of the Russian tanks, the construction of airfields close to German territory, etc. Soviet historians have vigorously and indignantly denied these allegations and by way of refutation they stress the shortcomings of the Red Army, for which Stalin is today held responsible. Besides, these allegations are contradicted by the statements of other German leaders. On June 21, while inspecting his front-line troops—his task was to seize the stronghold of Brest-Litovsk—Guderian smugly noted that the Russians suspected nothing, for they were drilling and marching to the sound of military music.

In actual fact, on the first day the Germans' only unpleasant surprise was the power of the Soviet T34 tanks, which General Reinhard compared to 'great lumbering bears', which 'made his tanks flare up like tinder'. But it was the Russians who had the most painful surprises in store for themselves.

In the first place, since the Soviet airfields were not large enough to take the new types of aircraft, the latter had all been assembled on a small number of bases; and as the order to disperse them arrived too late, by noon on June 22 the Soviet Air Force had lost 1,200 aircraft as a result of raids on 66 airfields or of heavy air fighting.

Then again the German attack surprised the Soviet troops scattered along the frontier. Their guns had been removed from the fortified positions along the old line; along the new one, work was not yet finished and there were gaps of several miles sandwiched between solid fortifications. There were forty-four divisions, forty of them infantry, deployed along a 1,250-mile-long front; each division was therefore defending a sector thirty miles long on average—at best fifteen miles, at worst sixty—whereas in theory a sector was only five to eight miles long. The covering troops on the frontier were even occupying salients whose flanks were not manned. No operational units had been concentrated or positioned in such a way as to meet a surprise attack; the bulk of the covering units was fifty miles to the rear. These defence positions meant that the enemy started with a local superiority of four or five to one. The Soviet soldiers were sometimes extremely inexperienced: the drivers of some of the tanks had been introduced to their machines only a few hours previously.

Nevertheless, on June 21 the Soviet authorities had had wind of impending German aggression, without giving it too much credence. Precautions had been taken, but in some places—in the region of Kiev, for example, as General Purkaiev reported—the alarm had not been given until June 22 between 4 and 6 a.m., when the enemy onslaught had already begun. As in Poland and France, the Wehrmacht had benefited from a surprise attack which gave them a great advantage from the very beginning.

II THE GERMAN BLITZKRIEG

Hitler thought that the USSR would admit defeat in six months and the Red Army disintegrate in eight weeks. Counting his Moscow chickens before they were hatched, he forecast that from July 14, 1941 onwards he would be able to reduce the strength of the Army and transfer these extra resources to the Navy and Air Force, in order to launch them against Britain and, if need be, against the United States. At the end of September, he gave orders that forty infantry divisions were to be disbanded in 1942, with the appropriate reduction in the manufacture of armaments for the Army. His roving imagination was already mapping out a vast pincer movement against Suez and the Persian Gulf for the same year, via Libya and Turkey. Nor were these schemes mere bombast.

Indeed, in the USSR everything was working out according to plan. The lessons of the Polish and French campaigns were bearing fruit. Once again the Germans, after gaining mastery of the air, developed their attack by the combined action of very large forces in the first stage of the offensive; the attack was then intensified at the enemy's weak points by armoured columns supported by the Air Force; the breakthrough was enlarged by scattering the enemy forces and then surrounding them. The most frequent method of encirclement was that of 'pincer movements', whose claws would start more than sixty miles apart and join up in the enemy's rear to encircle a whole army, or what was left of it. Once again the day had been won by meticulous preparation, the rapidity with which the forces were able to regroup, the attempt to smash the enemy by breaching gaps more than sixty miles wide and the ability to change the direction of attack according to the way the fighting was going.

The Luftwaffe was fully engaged in every sector; its sorties amounted to some 2,500 or 3,000 every day, which meant several for each fighter. On June 25, the first raid on Moscow took place. The first unpleasant surprise here was that the city's air defence proved so effective that further raids could be carried out only at night, in reduced strength.

This partial defeat in the air was amply compensated for by the victories achieved on the ground. On the evening of June 22, misinformed about the state of the forces and the course of the fighting, the Soviet Chief of Staff had ordered counter-attacks based on a misunderstanding of the Red Army's offensive potential. Although lines of attack were well chosen, owing to hasty preparation these attacks resulted only in considerable losses, through lack of air cover, adequate artillery support and motorised traction. As a result, by the evening of June 25, the German troops had advanced 145 miles towards Minsk and 125 miles from Brest-Litovsk. On July 3, Halder noted in his diary that the campaign against the USSR had been won in a fortnight. The Soviet Chief of Staff then decided to give up fighting 'along the frontiers' and join battle on a Narva–Pskov–Polotsk–Dnepr–Kherson line, where the natural defences in several areas had been strengthened by fortified works. Would the retreating armies retain the necessary cohesion and strength to stand their ground there?

Though cut off from their adjacent units and sometimes surrounded, many Soviet units continued fighting on their own. The majority of them surrendered when their ammunition, food-supplies and fuel gave out; everywhere their stocks had been captured or destroyed. In the north Riga had fallen, although Tallin held out until August 15. In the centre, the enemy had crossed the Beresina on July 4, broken through the Stalin line and conquered Vitebsk. In the south, Lvov was captured on June 30 and the Romanians advanced as far as Czernovitz. On July 6, the Germans reached the outskirts of Zhitomir and von Rundstedt's right wing was advancing between Kiev and Mohilev. After a war lasting eighteen days, the German Army leaped forward 280 miles; Latvia, Lithuania, Byelorussia and a large part of the Ukraine had been conquered; the Russians had lost 2,000 lorry loads of ammunition, 300,000 prisoners, 3,000 guns, 1,500 tanks and 2,000 aircraft.

Although they had suffered widespread defeat, they were nevertheless not crushed; the large scale of the German operations, which was out of all proportion to the number of troops employed—as Jodl said at Nuremberg, 'We really needed 300 divisions'—left gaps through which a good many Soviet units escaped encirclement. The Soviet Chief of Staff then adopted certain measures which Marshal Yeremenko listed as follows: incompetent leaders were removed and replaced; discipline was restored; morale was boosted by a few local victories (for example, concentrated raids by the few available air squadrons); intelligence and fortifications were improved; better collaboration between the various services was organised; more concentrated use was made of armour; and the technique of tank-warfare was improved. In short, the Russians were being initiated into modern warfare in and through their very experience of defeat. Would they have enough time?

They anticipated that the Wehrmacht's chief target would be Moscow. Timoshenko was given the task of delaying its advance as much as possible outside Smolensk. The battle began on July 10 and lasted until August 10. As a result, in August the Germans advanced less rapidly. Another stiff delaying action was fought at Briansk. Whereas on July 23 the German commander was hoping to capture Leningrad and Moscow on August 25, and reach the Volga in October and the Caucasus in November, he had to change his tune and envisage a winter campaign which he had not bargained for. He thus realised that the size of the USSR was liable to turn what had been an unqualified triumph in France into a Pyrrhic victory.

The Russian resistance led Hitler to take a closer interest in the fighting. Unlike Halder, he considered that they should concentrate their main energies not on Moscow, but on the wings, Leningrad and Kiev. He preferred economic targets to the political objective of Moscow. He wanted to capture the Donetz basin before the autumn rains set in by mid-September. The centre group of armies should therefore halt their advance towards Moscow.

Events seemed to prove Hitler right. On September 2, the external fortifications of Leningrad were under German fire; on September 8 the Neva was crossed and the following day the Germans captured Tikhvin 125 miles east of Leningrad. The Finnish Army, for its part, had seized Viborg. But the most spectacular victories were in the south: at Uman, Boudienny's troops were encircled and left behind 150,000 prisoners; Kiev fell on September 24; in this operational area the Russians lost 600,000 prisoners and 1,700 guns. But autumn had arrived; the Red Army had suffered heavy defeats but she had not been crushed. The Soviet government had not the slightest intention of admitting defeat.

III THE BATTLES OF LENINGRAD AND MOSCOW

In the summer the German soldiers marched on and on, often without water and without a proper route, guided by maps which proved more and more inaccurate the further eastward they penetrated, until, as Hossbach relates, it reached the point where 'a place shown as a large village would turn out to be an industrial town of 60,000 inhabitants'. In the autumn, they came up against another enemy, the mud, which prevented supplies from coming through. Hossbach states: 'When they ran into the mud our machines had to admit defeat; infantry and mounted units were now the most mobile part of the army.' There was no longer any trace of the conditions so favourable to a Panzer Blitzkrieg. Besides, the tanks were much the worse for wear after their trek across the Russian steppes. One fact had emerged which was frequently to recur: the Wehrmacht's supply lines had been strung out and were sometimes cut off by Soviet troops who stayed behind, more or less organised and armed, in territories which in theory had been conquered. Fuel supplies were running short while consumption was rising.

It is true that Soviet economic potential had suffered tremendous losses which to all appearance were irreparable. The Germans had seized industrial areas producing 63 per cent of the country's coal, 68 per cent of the cast iron and 58 per cent of the steel as well as fertile land which produced 38 per cent of the wheat, 84 per cent of the sugar and 60 per cent of the livestock. On top of these losses, there was the systematic destruction caused by the Russians 'scorched earth' tactics, inherited from Kutusov and advocated by Stalin. Railways, bridges and factories were blown up, including the gigantic Dnepropetrovsk dam, the pride and joy of the first Five Year Plan; barns, stocks and warehouses were set on fire. Could the USSR hope to receive any help from outside? Since the German aggression Churchill, the man who had wanted to use the blockade to force the Bolshevik state into submission in 1920, had declared Britain's total solidarity with the USSR. 'Russia's danger,' he had stated 'is our danger, just as the cause of every Russian fighting for his home is the cause of free men and free peoples all over the world.' The British government had contemplated sending convoys via the North Cape to Murmansk, but it was at too low an ebb itself to be able to send very much and Stalin was very dissatisfied. Relations between the new allies showed signs of strain.

In the extreme north, in Lapland, fighting was between only isolated units, separated by vast, impassable areas cut off by forests and marshes. The only way of getting provisions through to the forces was on the backs of men or mules; a day's march of ten miles was an athletic feat. The Germans failed to reach the Murmansk railway line and in the autumn of 1941 the front settled down.

In Finland, Marshal Mannerheim's troops were carrying on their own war. No joint command had been set up with Germany and each stuck to his ideological guns. After winning back the part of Carelia which had been handed over to the Russians, Mannerheim refused to take part in

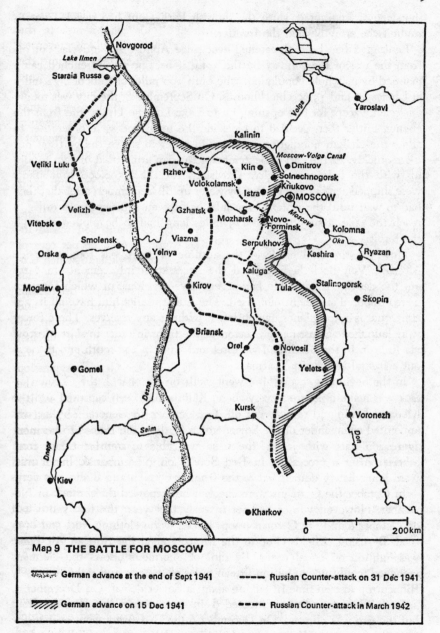

Map 9 THE BATTLE FOR MOSCOW

〜〜〜 German advance at the end of Sept 1941   - - - - Russian Counter-attack on 31 Dec 1941

▨▨▨ German advance on 15 Dec 1941   – – – – Russian Counter-attack in March 1942

the siege of Leningrad, since the Finnish Parliament had decided not to commit the army beyond the frontier.

Leningrad had been threatened ever since August 20, and was cut off from the rest of the country by the 30th; it became an entrenched camp manned by its whole population, who built 390 miles of trenches, 22 miles of barricades and 15,000 blockhouses. On September 8, the city was totally encircled, except for one opening on to Lake Ladoga. Under fire from the enemy, Hitler then decided to blockade the town and gave orders not to allow the civilian population to leave, in order to starve the garrison out more quickly. At the end of September a Russian army tried in vain to join up with the beleaguered city. Provisions for the 2,500,000 inhabitants were shipped across Lake Ladoga by water up till September; after that they had to wait until the water of the lake had frozen sufficiently; in order to reach the lake, a supply route 125 miles long had to be plotted through the forest.

However, the vital battle of the autumn of 1941 was fought outside Moscow. Von Bock had received the necessary reinforcements to carry out the decisive assault. He had seventy-five divisions, of which fourteen were armoured and eight motorised. The Luftwaffe let him have all its aircraft, that is 1,500 planes, which left it without any reserves. These forces were launched against narrow sectors of the front in order to skirt Moscow via Kalinin in the north and via Orel and Tula in the south and to carry out a frontal attack via Vyazma.

In the beginning, everything went well: on October 2, the German attack was making progress everywhere; Kalinin had been captured and the Moscow–Leningrad railway cut off. On October 10 General Zhukov was appointed commander of the Soviet troops in the west; thanks to her non-aggression pact with Japan, the USSR was able to transfer troops from Siberia. After a procession in Red Square on November 6, these units were immediately despatched to the front.

In October the Germans were checked but renewed their attack in November. However, winter had set in early that year; the first snows fell on October 6 and the German troops lacked warm clothing, fuel and even food. By using airfields close to the Moscow area, the Russian Air Force was fighting on equal terms. By dint of enormous efforts the Germans managed to advance to within fifteen miles of the city and rather unwisely Ribbentrop lost no time in talking about a Soviet defeat. On December 2, a fresh German advance succeeded in penetrating the Russian front but the gap was plugged. On December 6 the Red Army went over to the counter-offensive and recaptured Kalinin. Reluctantly, Hitler had to give the order for the Wehrmacht to fall back on the defensive. After so many resounding victories, why were the German armies defeated on this particular occasion?

The German generals blamed the early and bitter cold, for which their troops were unprepared; they had been defeated, in short, by the winter. But Soviet historians make the point that the Soviet soldiers were not all that well off either. Although the Russian troops were more accustomed to the cold and it was chiefly the attackers who were put out of action by the engines freezing up, it is a fact that even before the first snowfall, the German troops had shown signs of fatigue. It was on the field that they were brought to a halt. Whatever the cause, the German defeat, which was their first, came as a great shock and it left its mark. The results were not slow to make themselves felt; dissension was sown in the German camp. In quick succession Hitler dismissed von Rundstedt, discharged General Hoepner from the Army for having ordered a withdrawal and himself replaced von Brauchitsch as commander of the ground forces. The Führer thus became at one and the same time Head of State, President of the Council, Secretary of War, Supreme Commander of the German forces and Chief of the Army. Every soldier, sailor and airman was bound to him by an oath of personal allegiance. In addition, Hitler persuaded the Reichstag to bestow on him the title of 'Supreme Master of Justice'. But this accumulation of powers and responsibilities had no influence on the rigours of the Russian winter and the dogged resolution of the Red Army.

IV WINTER 1941–2

Hitler had pretended to treat the Russian cold with scorn. Basing his policy on his experiences in the 1914–18 war, he ordered Guderian to use gun-fire to dig individual holes for the front-line infantry. The frozen earth was so hard that it was impossible to carry out the order. Nevertheless Guderian was relieved of his command a few days later.

The cold caused the radiators of the tanks and lorries to burst, through lack of anti-freeze; the petrol solidified, for they had no apparatus to heat it before filling the fuel-tanks. The frozen oil no longer lubricated and the synthetic rubber lost its elasticity.

Because of the enemy or the bad weather, the Wehrmacht had been deprived of a large part of its resources. Halder stated that out of 500,000 vehicles, 30 per cent were beyond repair, 40 per cent needed a complete overhaul and 30 per cent required minor repairs. Rail transport was growing steadily more inadequate at the very moment when the roads were becoming impassable. The centre group of armies were receiving sixteen trains of provisions per day instead of the thirty-one it needed. With its 1,700 aircraft, the Luftwaffe could no longer provide air-cover for the retreating troops; the planes were forced to perform acrobatics, such as landing on frozen lakes; some squadrons had to be taken away from the Mediterranean front. The cold was making itself felt especially among the Italian troops, and their leader General Messe reported that their morale was seriously affected.

However, Hitler was obsessed by the fear that the loss of a few bits of land might demoralise his troops. On January 2, 1942, he refused von Kluge's request for permission to withdraw. On January 15, rather than disobey, Marshal von Leeb asked to be relieved of his command.

Life was hard for the Russians. In Leningrad the besieged inhabitants were eating bread made of 10 per cent cellulose, 10 per cent cattle feed, 2 per cent paper dust, 2 per cent flour dust, 3 per cent cornflour and 73 per cent rye flour; they ate it with sausage containing 40 per cent soya flour. In December 1941, they had to bury more than 50,000 dead; in order to obtain water they burned furniture and books to melt the ice.

The Germans worked out a plan for setting up small scattered centres of resistance in the occupied villages, covered by outposts and capable of defending themselves long enough for the tanks and aircraft to come to their support. The most important points formed self-contained independent fronts, generally where lines of communication intersected. These were the 'strong-points' of Staraya Russa, Vyazma, Orel, Kharkov, etc. But the Russians made the most of the vacant spaces which were left; they slipped in between the centres, surrounded them, shelled the mud-walled houses and captured whole regiments. The Germans tried to hang on to the river banks but the rivers were frozen and no longer provided an obstacle.

In the north the Red Army recaptured Tikhvin, to the east of Leningrad. Outside Moscow the Germans were driven back some sixty miles from the city; at the end of January they had been forced back to their starting points of October 15. In March the Russians penetrated the outskirts of Vyazma, some sixty miles from Smolensk; they skirted the 'strong-points' which were still holding out, as for example, at Rzhev. In the south Timoshenko, who had replaced Boudienny, had crossed the lower Donetz. While beleaguered Sebastopol continued to defend itself, the Russians, who held Kertch, had moved over to the offensive in the Crimea.

In April 1942 Halder totted up his winter losses: they amounted to 900,000 men, for whom his reinforcements of 450,000 men offered poor compensation; 74,000 vehicles were unserviceable and only 7,400 new ones had arrived; 1,847 new tanks were no replacement for the 2,340 put out of action. The southern group of armies now possessed only 50 per cent of its original fire-power and the centre and northern groups only 33 per cent.

It was in these circumstances that Hitler, after stating 'that the war would be won or lost in the south', decided to launch a crucial offensive in the spring.

V THE GERMAN OFFENSIVE OF SPRING 1942: OBJECTIVES AND DISPOSITION OF FORCES

However, Hitler lacked the resources to advance over the whole of the vast front. The objective was determined by one of the Reich's urgent economic needs: it was to be an offensive to obtain oil by conquering the Caucasus. At the end of 1941 the Reich's fuel stocks had fallen to 800,000 tons; that is, about one month's supply. Speer was hoping that the output of *ersatz* fuel would rise from 4 to 6 million tons in 1942. But stepping up the air and submarine war against Britain, which was expected to be resumed as soon as the Soviet Union had been destroyed, would require a considerable increase in the amount of oil, which Raeder estimated at 200,000 tons per month for the German Navy alone, whereas it was actually receiving only 84,000. Supplies of Romanian oil were now static, for the Romanian army in the USSR had to meet its own needs. In short, the dilemma was simple; according to the evidence of General Paulus at the Nuremberg trial, in June 1942 Hitler described it to the general officers of the southern group of armies as follows: 'If I do not get the Maikop and Groznyy oil, I shall be forced to stop the war.'

Hitler's orders on April 5, 1942, thus had the following aims: the capture of Sebastopol and mopping up the Kertch peninsula in order to protect the Germans' right flank from attack; to the north of these German defences, Voronezh, a key position, must be neutralised to protect the left flank; the destruction of the enemy armies between the Donetz and the Don, by a pincer operation starting from Voronezh on one side and from the Don estuary on the other; and, when these preliminaries had been successfully completed, an advance with all available forces towards the oil of the Caucasus. This time, although the Germans' plan was vast in scale it was simple and relatively limited in scope. If it succeeded, it would enable them to retain and exploit both the industrial basin of the Donetz and the wheat supply of the Ukraine and to add to these the oil from the Caucasus. Once this had been achieved, there would no longer be any fear of a long war.

Marshal von Bock, who was responsible for the operation, had about a hundred German infantry divisions, supported by 20 Panzer and 10 motorised divisions, in addition to which there were 22 Romanian, 13 Hungarian, 11 Italian, 1 Slovak and 1 Spanish divisions. The quality of

Map 10 THE GERMAN OFFENSIVES IN THE USSR

Countries occupied by or allied to Germany

Concentrations of German troops in June 1941

German advances from June to December 1941

Extreme limit of German advance on 15 Dec 1941

Front on 8 July 1941

Territory recaptured by the Russians in the winter of 1941-2

German offensive from June to Sept 1942

Extreme limit of German advance on 1st Sept 1942

these troops varied. The Hungarian Army, under the command of General Jany, had only rudimentary equipment and logistical resources, so much so that its supplies were uncertain from the start; it consisted mainly of poor peasants to whom this Russian campaign meant nothing, plus 20 per cent of foreigners who had settled in Hungary.

The Italian force, at first under the command of General Messe and then of General Garibaldi, comprised 11 divisions, one of them 'Black shirts'; although it had been given an *armata motorizzata*, fitted out with the best Italian equipment, its resources could not compare with those of the German units and it suffered in consequence. Messe had frequent clashes with von Kleist; the one complained that they were asking too much of the Italians; the other accused his allies of lacking aggression.

The Luftwaffe was in no condition to support the armies as it should have done. It had to leave a large number of fighters in the west to defend German territory against increasingly daring British raids. Instead of the 3,000 aircraft of June 1941 it could now muster only 2,000 to 2,500 in the east. Its equipment had not been substantially improved, apart from the emergence of a new Focke Wulf fighter. The Soviet Air Force, on the other hand, had made enormous strides; it had replaced nearly all its old aircraft, had received some British Hurricanes and was operating with Stormoviks which devoured tanks by the dozen. Far from merely surviving in the air, it could now even achieve mastery of the skies. Thus on the eve of its great advance, which Hitler hoped would be decisive, the German Army was in danger of being without air cover; this was hardly likely to strengthen the troops' morale.

VI THE GERMAN OFFENSIVE AND ITS VICTORIES

The German offensive began, as arranged on May 8, in the Crimea, a natural aircraft base which had to be neutralised in order to prevent possible raids on the Romanian oil wells. Von Manstein's Germans and Romanians 'mopped up' the Kertch peninsula and then launched an all-out attack against Sebastopol, which had been under seige since the end of October 1941. The fortress was defended by 600 guns and 1,000 mortars, which were able to take full advantage of the difficulties of the terrain and the large number of small natural positions. In mid-June the defenders were beginning to run out of ammunition. On July 2, the fortress surrendered; Soviet submarines managed to evacuate only a certain number of people. Sebastopol had held out for 250 days; the Russians had gained valuable time.

Timoshenko also attempted a delaying action by taking the initiative and attacking the Germans in the direction of Kharkov; after a few initial victories he was threatened with encirclement and had to withdraw.

But as a result the major German attack, the crucial one, could not begin until June 28, which was already late. According to the Germans, the Russians had guessed the enemy's plans: Halder said that the Soviet press had even published articles on the German intentions. They had prepared themselves by setting up a lightly occupied front, holding back powerful armoured and motorised units ready to move forward in support.

In the north von Weich was attacking on three fronts, Kursk-Voronezh, Byelgorod-Svoboda and Kupyansk-Rossoch. Hitler intervened in the conduct of operations. His orders were to not try to capture Voronezh at all costs, so as to concentrate the greatest possible weight of forces in the south, and he fell into a blind rage when he learnt that von Bock, whom he dismissed on the spot, had detached a Panzer division in order to capture the city.

Further to the south, Paulus, at the head of the Sixth Army, crossed the Don at Kalach and advanced towards Stalingrad; the Russians fell back systematically and Paulus was unable to press home his success as Hitler had taken some of his armoured and motorised units away from him in order to give them, logically enough, to Army Group A, whose task it was to carry out the great advance to the Caucasus. However, the Don was occupied along its whole length, although the Soviets retained a few bridgeheads on the south bank, which were to prove valuable. Nevertheless, the Germans had won a resounding victory, comparable to those of June–July 1941; the Russians had after all lost almost 600,000 prisoners.

Until now, in spite of a few inevitable hitches, the German plan had worked out as arranged; but once again Hitler became intoxicated with the taste of success; he now talked of a lightning advance towards the Persian Gulf. And even, according to Halder, of vague operations in the direction of the east coast of South Africa. Now that he had reached the boundless open spaces of Russia the Führer seemed to have lost his head; he was no longer able to choose one direction and stick to it; as on previous occasions, he wanted everything at once. On July 13, he dictated his directive no. 45, which laid down, *at one and the same time*, two equally important lines of attack: Army Group A, as agreed, would advance southwards towards Rostov and the east coast of the Black Sea, so as to seize the harbours; from there it would strike out for the mountains of the Kuban and the oil wells, including those of Baku, which meant crossing the Caucasus, another great leap forward; as if this grandiose scheme were not enough, Army Group B, instead of confining itself to protecting Group A's advance by tying down as many of the enemy forces as possible, would also advance, in order to take Stalingrad and the whole of the lower course of the Volga. Hitler was thus trying to do two things at once. He was dispersing his forces at a time when they most needed to be concentrated. He was waiting to see whether circumstances—or his mood—would require him to move his forces from one line of advance to the other. He had lost any notion of adapting the ends to the means. Colonel Bernard was quite right in concluding that it was his lack of moderation at that moment of time that 'clinched his downfall'.

VII THE CAUCASUS AND STALINGRAD

Army Group A under von List first of all advanced rapidly towards the Caucasus. Von Kleist captured Rostov on July 27 and Krasnodar on August 9. On August 22 the swastika was hoisted over the El'brus. The Russians had been overrun as in the heyday of the Wehrmacht. But once again the vast open spaces exhausted the assailant and gave the defenders a new impetus. The various Caucasian fronts had been brought under the single command of Boudienny, who set up defensive positions in depth on all routes leading to Transcaucasia: six outside Ordzhonikidze and ten outside Baku, the strongest ones in the immediately threatened sectors of the Groznyy and Maikop oil-fields. More large units had been raised in Georgia, Azerbaidzhan and Armenia. As everywhere else, the local population played an active part in defending its land.

The German armies had covered 500 miles in clouds of dust and in 50 degrees centigrade. Its supplies were taking longer and longer to get through; after all, the round trip from the Ruhr took eight weeks by rail. On the road, the tank-lorries consumed a considerable amount of their cargo of fuel on the way. Hitler was annoyed at the consequent slow speed of advance. But since he was even more exasperated by the Russian resistance outside Stalingrad and since he appeared to be obsessed by the name, he forgot the original objectives and after giving von List the Fourth Armoured Army, he took it away from him again to give it back to Paulus, and von List was unable to do anything about it. This did not prevent the Führer from dismissing him at the beginning of September—this really seemed to be Hitler's only way of solving his difficulties.

On the Stalingrad front the Russians had not in fact, been content merely to put up a stubborn resistance; they had made a successful counter-attack and driven back the weakest elements of the enemy forces —the Hungarians and Italians. General Messe concluded that it was time to cut the costs and told Mussolini so. Even the Germans were shaken; General von Wieterheim wanted to pull back the spearhead which he had pushed forward on the Volga; General Schmidt had ordered a withdrawal on his own initiative. 'The command had had all it could stand,' reported Halder.

In September, although Novorossiysk had been captured, the first snows put a stop to the German offensive in the Caucasus; an attempt to capture Ordzhonikidze failed. There remained the Stalingrad front. Hitler stubbornly insisted on pursuing the offensive there. A plan was worked out on September 11: the attacks would begin on the 15th, and last for ten days. After violent street fighting the German LI Army Corps succeeded in reaching the Volga at three points. But the Russians were fighting every inch of the way.

In October the line showing the extent of the German advance looked impressive on the map. From Leningrad, the Valday hills and the upper course of the Volga, it skirted Moscow and Tula to the west, followed the Don, touched the loop of the Volga and formed a large curve between the foothills of the Caucasus and Tuapse on the Black Sea. The proposed objectives, however, had not been achieved; the oil wells were out of reach and intermittent and half-hearted raids had done little to reduce their output. Above all, the German defences were strung out dangerously over a distance of 2,165 miles, where 220 divisions were fighting—an average of ten miles per division. These defences were open to enemy counter-attack for something over 625 miles. 'It was a strategic heresy,' wrote Colonel Bernard, 'for to an increasing extent this front also represented a thinly held flank.'

On September 24, 1942, Halder noted in his diary: 'After the daily conference, I was relieved of my post by the Führer; my nerves are worn out and his are not much better; it is time for us to part company.' The time was past when Hitler and his generals worked hand in glove to achieve victory. At the same time Goebbels, in his own diary, was expressing his anxiety about the abnormal life which the Führer was leading, always under strain; he noted his nervous tics and was alarmed at how quickly he was aging.

At least Hitler was not mistaken in thinking himself protected from attack in western Europe. Although Stalin was clamouring for Churchill to attack, the latter was in no position to do so, and the experimental Dieppe raid on August 19, 1942, ended in complete disaster, though offering a wealth of lessons for future attempts, for which no date could yet be fixed. It is true that the Anglo-Saxons were supplying the USSR with modern equipment, via the Arctic Ocean, Iran and even Trans-Siberia. But on his visit to Stalin, Churchill could only reply to his demand for a real second front with fine words, promises—and a treaty of post-war friendship.

So, it was in the USSR that the war was being fought. The problem for the Germans was to retain their conquests against the impending Soviet attacks; but they lost the initiative for the whole winter, which the troops dreaded for its harshness and dangers; but Hitler had lost none of his optimism. Were the Germans' minds at least at rest about their rear areas? How were they running the vast Soviet territories which their armies had conquered and how did they treat the population?

VIII THE GERMAN OCCUPATION IN THE USSR: PRINCIPLES AND ORGANISATIONS

The Wehrmacht's conquests enabled Hitler to orientate the German expansion in the direction he had indicated in *Mein Kampf*: the new Reich continued on the path mapped out by the Teutonic Knights so that 'the German sword shall guarantee the German plough its furrows and the nation its daily bread'. The USSR was merely an extension of the prospects opened up in Poland.

Hitler's intention of destroying the centre of international Communism, first of all eliminating its shield and buckler, the Red Army, and then exploiting its wealth 'for a thousand years', was plain and clear; but although certain ways and means had been tried out in Poland, they had not been worked out in every detail and now that the war was being protracted, it might prove inadvisable to implement certain decisions. There were a number of discernible trends in the generals' ideas as to the right attitude to take. One group of officers who were experts on Russian affairs (Gehlen, Herre, Stauffenberg, Kostring and Wagner), and who were apparently supported by Goebbels, considered it good policy to declare war on Communism but not on the Russian people; some of them were even convinced that Germany and Russia must be reconciled. For the time being, therefore, it was important not to take any excessively harsh measures which would force the Russians to put up a desperate resistance and to adopt an attitude of uncompromising hostility. These soldiers did not have the ear of the Nazi politicians nor even of their leaders, the Wehrmacht general staff.

Rosenberg, the Nazi theorist from the Baltic, the author of one of the régime's bestsellers, *The Myth of the Twentieth Century*, had reached similar conclusions by different means. He proposed splitting up the USSR into a certain number of 'buffer states', to prevent any recrudescence of a powerful Russia. This policy entailed giving support to the separatist movements of the Byelorussians, Caucasians, Ukrainians and peoples of central Asia and treating the conquered peoples with relative moderation.

For Himmler, however, the Slavs were a backward people, subhuman

(*Untermenschen*), Asiatics whose vast territories should be colonised by pure Aryans. Moreover, these subhumans were, by their very nature, criminals. An ss pamphlet accused them of 'aspiring to conquer the world', and concluded: 'Europe, defend yourself.' This 'point of view' was supported by Martin Bormann, who had Hitler's ear. The Führer was fond of saying that the frontier between Europe and Asia was not a geographical one but the dividing line between the Germanic world and the Slav. 'For him the Slav, whether he lived under the Tartars, Peter the Great or Stalin, was born to bear the yoke.'

In theory, it was Rosenberg whose responsibility it was to work out German policy in the east. When he announced the forthcoming attack against the ussr, Hitler received him in his office with these words: 'Well, Rosenberg, your great hour has come.' After being given at first a purely planning role, on July 17, 1941, Rosenberg was promoted Minister of the Occupied Territories in the East. But his powers became operative and grew only as the military government handed the conquered territories over to him. In the area called 'the army zone', the army retained all its powers and the extent of this zone was elastic, depending on how operations were going.

This duality, together with the Red Army's resistance, certainly did not much help the formulation of a definite German policy. Matters were to be further complicated by a third power: Himmler's ss. Both because the okw had given them the responsibility of establishing a Draconic order in its own zone and ensuring that it was observed, and because Rosenberg, too, was quite willing to let them take repressive action against Jews and Communists in his own territory, the ss became the virtual masters everywhere. Consequently, German behaviour in the conquered territories was at first characterised by a ruthless and indiscriminate terror; and later on, or, more accurately, at the same time, by economic exploitation in which the desire for output was hampered by the equal desire to destroy Communist institutions. In these circumstances, any policy could only be arbitrary and pretty incoherent.

IX THE ADMINISTRATION OF THE CONQUERED AREAS

The Minister of the Occupied Territories had his seat in Berlin. The territories under his administration were divided into Reichscommissariats, which were subdivided into *Generalbezirke* (general regions) and then into *Kreisgebiete* (districts). A German was placed at the head of each division, responsible to Rosenberg but virtually omnipotent. Two Reichscommissariats were set up, one for the Ukraine, the second for the other territories—it was christened *Ostland*, which was no indication of its real boundaries for the future and could only have temporary significance.

In the *Ostland*, Byelorussia, Lithuania, Latvia and Estonia formed relatively autonomous districts, each provided with a capital and an administrator under the supervision of the Commissioner-General, Heinrich Lohse. This method of organisation seemed to indicate that the different nationalities would be respected.

In Rosenberg's mind the Ukraine was to be the largest of the 'buffer states', with a population of 60 million, covering an area of nearly 400,000 square miles and combining the Russian Ukraine with the Polish Ukraine and Czechoslovakian Ruthenia. In actual fact, although established as a Commissariat of the Reich under Erich Koch, the Ukraine had been divided into four. North Bukovina and the Odessa region had been placed under the administration of Romania; Romanian historians had discovered, most opportunely, that the region between the Dniestr and the Bug had at odd times been under the domination of Moldavian princes; Odessa was thus merely a former Romanian city, so Romania received her reward for her part in the war against the USSR by annexing a new province, Transnistria, from which she immediately gained a considerable item of loot: the Odessa trolley-buses were dismantled and put into service in Craiova.

West Ukraine, with Lvov, was incorporated into the Polish 'General-Government', under Hans Frank; East Ukraine, with Kharkov, remained in the army zone, because of its proximity to the fighting area. The Reichscommissariat was therefore confined to central Ukraine, including Kiev; in addition there was the territory of Pinsk and that part of Byelorussia which was formerly Polish.

In the territories under Rosenberg's authority only the minor officials were locally recruited, and kept under close German control. In the towns, municipal corporations were in charge of rubbish collection, public order and the registration of births, marriages and deaths; the 'agricultural offices' and 'labour exchanges' made it easier for the Germans to exploit the available resources. Burgomasters and, in the villages, elders were appointed by the German authorities, to whom they were responsible.

In all the territories the German authorities pretended that there was no governing class. On principle, no 'native' was appointed to any political or economic, or even less to any cultural office of importance. Exceptions to this rule were made only in the case of the Baltic states, where nationalist elements had taken part in the Red Army's defeat and enabled the Wehrmacht to advance towards Leningrad.

The inhabitants were everywhere else subjected to systematic humiliation by the occupiers and had to register with the police. They were forbidden to leave their homes without prior permission; they had no right to use the water from the wells and tanks near the German garrisons; they were free to go out only in daytime; at night, the patrols automatically opened fire on anyone infringing these regulations.

All these measures were, of course, partly explained by the proximity to the front with all its fluctuations; they did not necessarily represent the policy which the Germans intended following or would have followed after the war, a policy which they did not have time to work out in detail or even less to put into practice. It was nevertheless in keeping with the ideas which Hitler had always expressed. For the time being, the inhabitants could scarcely see it as a war of 'liberation'; it was hardly calculated to make them friendly towards the Germans; it nullified the effects of the Wehrmacht's propaganda about collaboration. Moreover, its harshness was intensified by economic exploitation and repression which was both indiscriminate and systematic. The USSR gave the Germans the chance of extending the methods first used against the Poles to a greater number of potential slaves.

X ECONOMIC EXPLOITATION

The task of developing the occupied territories in the 'capitalist' manner was entrusted to experts and technicians formed into *Wirtschaftskommandos* (economic control groups). Soviet citizens were thus given the chance of seeing capitalist societies—of which they knew nothing—at work —the Eastern General Coal Board, the Eastern Iron Company, etc.

However, the rational exploitation, already complicated by the setting up of new structures, was first of all hindered by the destruction carried out by the Red Army as it withdrew and even more by the demands of the military, which was being forced more and more to live from hand to mouth in the occupied territories. In order to harmonise the points of view, the economic authorities appointed representatives—*Referenten*—to the military commands. But the standpoints were too diverse to make concerted action always possible.

The result was that plundering became the rule and the economy could not be restored, let alone transformed. The armies were the more inclined to use local resources as supplies were experiencing greater difficulty and delays in arriving from Germany. So the soldiers did not go short of meat and bread but they were provided by killing off livestock and sometimes by requisitioning seed crops. Thus agricultural production decreased. It was the same for industrial production. The factories were generally not reopened because future plans made no provision for them in vassal states reduced to a strictly agricultural economy. But when, as was rare, reparations were decided upon, they came up against power shortage and lack of raw materials or machinery, so the Germans confined themselves to seizing stocks and dismantling equipment that could be salvaged and sent back to the Reich. This practice of continually helping themselves to produce completely paralysed any commercial activity.

On the financial plane, German purchases caused prices to rise and the issue of an occupation mark brought inflation; officials and employees particularly suffered from this. New taxes were levied: per head, per household and according to the number of windows, as well as on dogs and cats. The few banks which remained open were aimed at siphoning off the inhabitants' savings towards Germany.

All these badly co-ordinated measures could but impoverish the population; in the long run they would have proved detrimental to the occupier himself by exhausting his source of supplies. It was probably this consideration which determined the Germans' agrarian policy. A few sovkhozes were broken up and the land given to German settlers. Russian historians mention the names of 'barons' of the former Czarist régime who recovered their estates—such as Baron von Bilderding in the Volodanskoe sovkhoze and the big landowner Beck in the sovkhozes of Gari, Vichenka and Iskra, in the Don regions. These ghosts from the past were given the freehold of thousands of acres and sometimes several villages. According to Soviet historians, they seized cattle and agricultural machinery and reintroduced forced labour.

Similarly, the first intention had been to break up the Kolkhozes and to distribute the land among the peasants, the amount depending on their degree of submissiveness. But to avoid the risk of poor harvests, it seemed wiser to follow an intermediate system, the *obscina* (commune). In actual fact, this organisation revived the kolkhoze under another name; it allocated seed, horses and agricultural equipment, and assigned the chief tasks. The peasants kept only their houses and a piece of land of something over an acre. These communes gradually changed into co-operative farms, supplemented by 'centres of agricultural progress' under the control of German agronomists.

This may have been a wise measure in order to avoid too rapid a change but it was not understood by the peasants: on the one hand, they had been promised land and not been given it; on the other hand, requisitioning took away their cattle and crops. General Messe tells how this disappointment was expressed in the disillusioned phrase: 'At least Stalin left us with a cow, but Hitler has taken that away from us.' Moreover, preserving institutions meant retaining the technical experts. By this device the Com-

munists who were formerly managers of kolkhozes or sovkhozes, retained
or regained a small degree of power.

However, the most serious and dramatic procedure and the one arousing
the keenest and most lasting resentment, was the requisitioning of labour.
Thus in Orel, in November 1941, horses and smithies were confiscated and
boilermen and carpenters commandeered to work to fight the cold. Then
special services, *Arbeitsämter*, were gradually set up everywhere to
organise forced labour. At the beginning they made attractive proposi-
tions to persuade people to go to Germany of their own free will. It very
quickly became apparent that a systematic mobilisation of labour was necessary by combing whole regions; each place had to supply its own contingent and the burgomasters or elders were made responsible for seeing
that they were provided.

Thus workers from Krivoy Rog and the Donetz were sent to the industrial centres of the Ruhr. To make up for the lack of tractors, peasants
from Northern Ukraine were transferred to Southern Ukraine. Places
left deserted by their inhabitants when they retreated with the Red Army
were forcibly repopulated by taking people from elsewhere. These compulsory migrations affecting millions of men and women were accompanied by brutal and coercive measures, including harsh sanctions against
anyone refusing to comply or against their relatives. They were in themselves already the first step towards a reign of terror.

XI TERROR AS A SYSTEM OF GOVERNMENT

Both before and after the invasion of the USSR, a series of decisions had
been taken by the highest authorities of the Reich to safeguard the troops
and also to exterminate Communists and Jews. To this end, in March
1941, before the invasion of the USSR, Himmler had been given 'special
responsibilities . . . arising from the final decisive struggle between two
opposing political systems'. This euphemism was a cover for the following
measures.

In May Keitel had ordered that 'no pity' should be shown to civilians
guilty of acts hostile to the German troops; they were to be shot on the
spot, at the discretion of the officer in charge. On the other hand, German
soldiers who committed offences against these civilians would be treated
with great leniency: 'They will not necessarily be liable to punishment,
even if they have committed a military crime.' On July 16, 1941, Hitler
had spelt out this unlimited power of arbitrary punishment with his usual
laconic ruthlessness: 'Shoot everyone who gives you a black look.'

On July 17 Himmler took over all security in the occupied territories.

Each high official in Rosenberg's ministry was given an SS deputy appointed by Himmler and answerable to him.

The same day the Gestapo issued the order to exterminate those Soviet prisoners of war who 'represented a danger to the Reich'. On the instructions of the OKW it had been clearly understood as early as May 10 that political commissars would not be regarded as prisoners of war: 'They were liable to the death penalty in transit camps . . . without worrying about unnecessary considerations.'

On July 23, Keitel added a gloss to his ruthless decision of May. 'The army,' he said, 'must spread terror so as to nip in the bud any temptation to resist.'

The territories near the front were not the only ones to be affected by these measures, which might have been explained there as a safeguard for the army. On August 22, Rosenberg extended them to the territories under his allegedly civil jurisdiction. 'Any crime against the Reich and its army,' he decreed, 'the creation of any sort of atmosphere hostile to the Germans or any refusal to obey the orders of the military authorities . . .' would be punishable by death.

Thus all the occupying authorities, civil and military, in all the territories were unanimous in setting up a reign of terror. In his order of October 10, 1941, General von Reichenau defined the reasons for it as follows: 'It is to obliterate Asian influence on European culture; it is in this way that we shall fulfil our historic mission by liberating the German people for ever from the Jewish and Asian peril.'

The system was now established. The man responsible for these odious tasks was Heinrich Himmler and his SS. He was to be a thoroughly efficient executioner of a people.

The Soviet prisoners of war were the first victims of the harsh treatment which had been decreed; they were crowded together into improvised camps where, dying of starvation, they were doomed to destroy, if not even to devour, one another; later on they were sent to Germany and many of them vanished without trace in concentration camps—notably in Auschwitz. But Soviet deserters were treated no better; instead of separating them from the other prisoners and giving them preferential treatment, the Germans looked upon them with the greatest contempt.

All the conquered regions were the scenes of coldly premeditated acts of extermination. Countless examples were quoted at the Nuremberg tribunal. The Gestapo had drawn up lists of people condemned out of hand. A 'special' battalion called 'Nightingale' and belonging to the Brandenburg regiment was put in charge of the executions. According to one witness, 'the men burst into houses, dragged out the inhabitants and killed them in the backyard. In this way 3,000 lawyers, engineers and doctors were massacred.'

Operations of this kind were entrusted to special units, the *Einsatzgruppen*, who had already learned their trade in Poland. These units were attached to the armies; they were not dependent on them but they received any help they required from them. Their leaders were men from the criminal police and the Gestapo, the soldiers of the ss. They had served their apprenticeship in a police barracks at Pretsch on the Elbe, near Leipzig. Heydrich, the chief of the security forces of the Nazi party, had given them his orders in person. The *Einsatzgruppen* were instructed to carry out the 'liquidation of Jews and political commissars'. They recruited 'local volunteers' on the spot.

It was these *Einsatzgruppen* who started the gassing of the 'Reich's enemies' in the ussr. R. Hoess, the commander of the Auschwitz camp, explained how they set about it. The victims were first of all suffocated in lorries by the exhaust gases from the engines. They then acted as guinea-pigs to try out the gas *Zyclon-B*, which had been developed by the Reich's chemists. 'The Russians,' wrote Hoess, 'were made to undress in an entrance-hall and then they went into a specially fitted-out room under the pretence of being deloused.' The bodies were afterwards burnt on huge pyres.

General Messe, the commander of the Italian expeditionary force, had watched the Germans' harsh behaviour in the ussr all the more closely because by denouncing it he could have the pleasure of revenging himself for the way in which his German colleagues had wounded his pride. He concluded a report to Mussolini by noting a 'clear split between the conquerors and those they were dominating'. But he added this justifiable condemnation:

If the will for power, perfect military organisation and a spirit of discipline enabled the Germans to conquer vast territories, only a sense of justice and an understanding of the needs and mind of the people could have guaranteed that they would consolidate them. Up to now, on the eastern front the German people has shown that it possesses the first qualities in the highest degree; they cannot be said to have given any sign of possessing the second to an equal or sufficient extent.

Although the Soviet peoples thus had the spectacular privilege of providing Nazi Germany with the greatest number of martyrs, the fate of the Poles and Yugoslavs was no better. To varying degrees, all the peoples of occupied Europe were realising, to their cost, what the future had in store for them at the hands of the master race, whose slaves they would become as a result of the Wehrmacht's victory.

CHAPTER 3

The Domination of Europe

THE German–Soviet confrontation involved numbers of men and quantities of equipment which were without equal in the Second World War and historically without precedent. It brought about a complete change in the character of the war because of the vastness of the operational area, the high casualties and the long duration and relentlessness of the struggle. It was goodbye to the Blitzkrieg, which had started off with such jubilation, and to total and decisive victory won at the cost of slight losses which were amply compensated for by the immense spoils obtained, the territories conquered and the opponents who had been defeated. Nowhere else had the German soldier been exposed to such intense and prolonged suffering against an opponent tougher than himself. If the corps of general officers had been alarmed by the difficulties encountered and initial failures, the German soldier was even more demoralised by the 'Russian hell', and envied his comrades who had remained in the west waiting for a hypothetical British attack against the 'fortress of Europe'. Replacements had to be found for those who had fallen in battle or were exhausted. It was necessary to renew, increase and improve equipment and weapons which were always quite insufficient for their needs and quickly became unserviceable because of the vast distances they had to cover in summer and the bad winter weather against which they were helpless. In short, it had become a war of attrition, uncertain in its outcome and of unforeseeable duration.

Germany could no longer depend on winning it in a short, sharp and successful sweep with irresistible Panzer divisions supported by an all-conquering Luftwaffe. She had to mobilise all her resources and send into action all her able-bodied men. She thus came face to face with a contradiction: every German worker in uniform and up at the front was now one less in the factory producing her armaments. There was only one possible solution: maximum exploitation of the territories which had been conquered by the Wehrmacht or which its victories had forced into the Reich's orbit. So much, then, for the great plans for the future and the

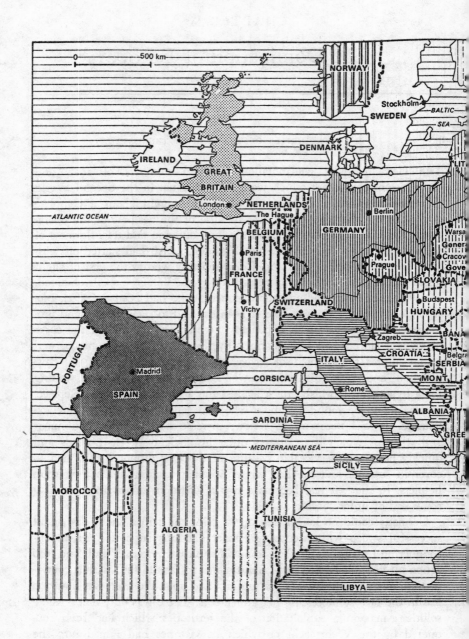

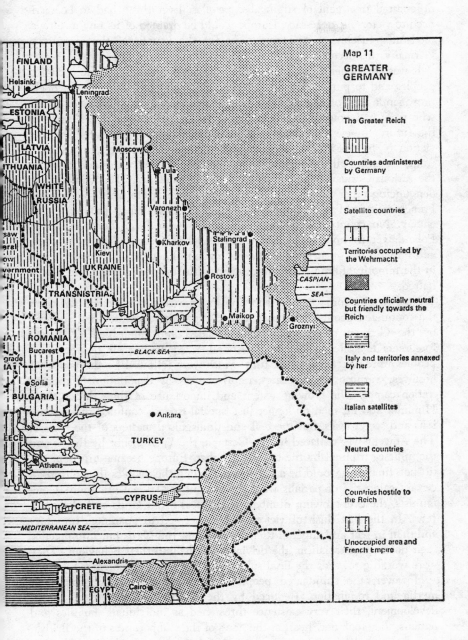

Map 11

GREATER GERMANY

The Greater Reich

Countries administered by Germany

Satellite countries

Territories occupied by the Wehrmacht

Countries officially neutral but friendly towards the Reich

Italy and territories annexed by her

Italian satellites

Neutral countries

Countries hostile to the Reich

Unoccupied area and French Empire

differential treatment of subjugated peoples. Everything had to be sacrificed to victory. If necessary, Europe would be drained of its raw materials,
foodstuffs, machinery and manpower for the benefit of the conqueror.
Germany was becoming an insatiable Minotaur.

It was consequently an inopportune moment to pander to the occupied
peoples and to put on a show of 'correctness' and benevolence. Goebbels'
propaganda was, of course, still trying to win over to the Reich volunteers
who were in favour of anti-Bolshevism, anti-Semitism and the Europe of
the future. In every country, groups of collaborators, motivated by conviction or by self-interest, were recruiting men to fight on the Russian
front, repeating all the slogans of the *Propaganda-Abteilung* and assisting
the various German police forces in their infamous tasks. Frenchmen were
denouncing other Frenchmen; French policemen were arresting Jews or
French resisters; French businessmen were offering French produce to the
enemy. No country in Europe completely escaped collaboration except
Poland; yet in no country did the collaborators succeed in convincing
and rallying the great mass of the population. They remained everywhere
in the minority, filling their countrymen with surprise, distrust and finally
hatred.

Nazi domination was now showing its true colours. It came down on
the conquered peoples with a system of repressive measures first suffered
by the German people, but now extended and intensified. The first
foreigners to suffer were the Poles and Russians but all the occupied
peoples were affected in their turn. Fines were followed by the taking of
hostages; warnings by shootings; imprisonment by deportation to concentration camps. The growing extent and importance of their duties made
Himmler and his men no longer just 'special troops', confined to ignominious and secret tasks, but the real and undisguised masters of the régime.
The Abwehr was replaced by the Gestapo, the Wehrmacht by the ss and
the military tribunal by the torture-chamber. Europe became a prison, until such time as it would be a graveyard. Among the peoples thus terrorised
certain categories of pariahs were singled out for special attention: Communists, the ever-growing numbers of resisters of all kinds and above all,
Jews. In the first flush of victory, which seemed to guarantee impunity
and then in fear and anger at their first defeats, the Nazis put into practice
their doctrine of racialism, the driving force behind their behaviour. They
were working towards the final solution to the Jewish problem.

However, the subjugated peoples were gradually shaking off their
inertia and resignation. Reduced by the occupier to a state of underdevelopment, their very existence threatened as individuals, families and
nations, they took new heart at the news of the stubbornness of the British,
and above all of the Soviets' unshakeable determination. All over Europe,

the Resistance was forming into groups, arming itself and preparing for action in the war of liberation. Europe was indeed being built but in suffering and in hope, not in accordance with the Nazis' orders but in defiance of them.

II POLITICAL DOMINATION

Hitler may have been clear in his own mind how the world would be organised as the result of German victory, but either deliberately or from expediency, he disclosed only fragments of his plans. Since they were often apparently contradictory, and even incoherent, there is every reason to believe that they were somewhat confused and far from being properly thought out. It is true that various German organisations set about drawing up plans, arguing fiercely about who had originated the ideas and what was to be gained from implementing them. In practice, everyone took part in a more or less co-ordinated way: Ribbentrop as Foreign Minister; Goering as Economic Director of the Reich; Rosenberg as Party theoretician and Minister for the Occupied Territories in the East; Himmler as the man responsible for ensuring the purity of the race; and also Goebbels, who had to give some substance to his propaganda arguments by providing tangible evidence of their application.

In June 1942, the ss Oberführer, Professor Dr Konrad Meyer, completed a very detailed plan to ensure Nazi domination in eastern Europe, the *Generalplan Ost*. The whole scheme was envisaged from the German viewpoint: rural colonisation and the creation of a 'healthy peasantry', involving the 'appropriate biological selection'; urban colonisation, leaving the Reich with 'complete freedom of planning'; and the creation of colonised districts in which the administration of justice was in the hands of German authorities and 'ss tribunals'. The estimated cost of the prospective 'reconstruction' took all possible factors into account, including removal, propaganda and 'supervisory' expenses. For example, 'the cost of providing space for one worker' was estimated at 'between 6,000 and 10,000 marks', depending on the type of industry. It is true that costs were to be met partly by 'reparations exacted from defeated enemies', and by 'the creation of a special capital fund formed from all the economic assets of the region to be reconstructed'—that is, from the contributions of the conquered people themselves. As for labour, a broad appeal was to be made to the forcibly tamed or naturally servile masses of prisoners of war, common-law criminals and those commandeered for forced labour. At no time were the rights of any communities or individuals to be taken into account and even less were their own requests to be met or even given a hearing. The whole thing was governed with pseudo-scientific rigour by a geopolitical law which Dr Meyer stated as follows: 'To reconcile the space to be colonised with the available human resources.' This would require a period of five 'lustres'.

This splendid scheme concerned, it is true, only one part of occupied Europe—the east. But Dr Meyer, in his far-sighted wisdom, stressed that it could be realised only if the whole Reich—including the countries of western Europe—worked towards it. What the Nazis wanted to impose on Europe was thus a colonial type of domination, systematised and based on the principle of deliberate toughness.

It is probable that on the whole Hitler shared this way of thinking, even if it had not been inspired by the ideas which he had expressed or was supposed to have expressed. But because of lack of time it proved impossible for this vast project to be fully carried out. The alarming way in which the war was developing was also forcing the Führer to give most of his time and thought primarily to the conduct of operations. In short, the political and administrative organisation of occupied Europe was, except in a few points, less the result of plans for the future than of present demands.

Thus, although generally convinced that it would be a source of strength and an advantage to Germany to expand eastwards, Hitler had not completely given up the idea of a colonial empire overseas; but apart from the Reich's recovery of the colonies lost in 1918, thus making reparation for the harm that had been unfairly inflicted on her, he avoided speaking about colonies, either because he did not wish to cause the French generals to defect to de Gaulle, or because in certain areas—notably in Morocco—he was competing with the ambitions of Franco or Mussolini or because he wanted to maintain the chance of a peaceful compromise with Britain.

Some light is thrown on the Führer's motives by, among other things, the monologue which he inflicted on some of his generals, as was his wont, on July 1, 1943. He put forward the principle that force was not enough to establish total domination; of course, it remained the crucial factor, but equally important was the intangible psychological factor *required by a tamer to dominate his animals*. This circus image showed Hitler's elevated ideas about the relationship between vanquished and vanquishers in their true light. At no time were the national interests of the conquered territories to stand in the way of the vanquisher's vital interests. For the Ukraine, for example, the Führer made it clear that if necessary he would say that he would build an independent state there; he would say it deliberately, but this would not mean that he would do it. Then, paraphrasing *Mein Kampf*, Hitler concluded: 'It is living space which is at stake in our fight.' According to him, it was not possible to have a great army and a powerful industry within a confined area. What constituted the strength of the Russian empire was not purely human strength, either in quantity or above all if one considers the personal quality of individuals; it was the strength of her gigantic empire. This nonsense did at least lead to one practical conclusion: Germany would not hesitate to seize those territories whose annexation seemed necessary for her greatness and power or simply for her well-being.

The inequality of rights and the temporary differences in status in Nazi-dominated Europe at the end of 1942, when it had reached its greatest extent, were not necessarily any indication of its future fate. They were nevertheless in keeping, as a whole, with views which had been expressed many a time by the Führer or his faithful henchmen.

III THE STATUS OF NAZI EUROPE

At the heart of Europe, as if its convenient geographical position was an invitation to her mission, lay the German Reich, that is the Germany which had emerged from the Treaty of Versailles, with the addition of Austria, the Sudeten Germans, the western part of Poland (Wartheland), Luxemburg, Alsace-Lorraine and Eupen and Malmédy; a small part of Slovenia had been taken from Yugoslavia and the former Polish district of Bialystok was again attached to east Prussia. All these territories were under German law and administration. They were both Germanised and Nazified. However, all the *Volksdeutsche* were not yet united; for those in Schleswig and Transylvania it was obviously only a matter of time; those in the Volga area would join the mother country once the USSR had been defeated. The Tyroleans had begun to leave their region; but after the Italian surrender it seemed more advisable to ask them to remain where they were and to annex their territory. As for those Alsatians who had taken refuge in France, even in the so-called free zone, the occupying authorities did not rest until the Vichy government had either handed them over or forced them to return to Alsace, whether they were Strasbourgers who had retreated to the Dordogne, young people from the work camps or legionaries. There were plans to make Brazilian Germans return to the bosom of the nation. On the other hand, foreigners who had settled on German territory without permission were expelled—Poles from the Poznan district and Silesia, or Lorrainers.

Hitler seems to have toyed with the idea of widening somewhat the concept of the Germanic race. In the course of a conversation with Goering on June 19, 1940 he had quoted Norwegians, Flemings and *Burgundians* as Germanic peoples. In his *Table-Talk* he one day added the

Normans. According to Dr Globke's cross-examination at Nuremberg, Hitler had given Stuckart, an official from the Ministry of Internal Affairs, the task of drawing up a scheme to divide France up in this way. Nazi geopolitics was not an exact science.

It was obviously to serve this German 'nucleus' of the master race that the territories without any clearly defined status, the 'General Government', Cracow, the *Ostland* and the Ukraine were 'kept in reserve', and marked out for German colonisation in the footsteps of the Teutonic Knights.

In theory, Italy was Germany's fully-fledged ally and equal. In fact only comparatively small and economically unimportant territories had been annexed by her and had come into her sphere: a few high French Alpine valleys and part of Menton; a section of Epirus and Thessaly and the Dalmatian coast and its islands. In addition the Italian armistice commissions dictated what was to be done on the left bank of the Rhône, in North Africa and the Near Eastern states. Croatia was to become a kingdom with a member of the House of Savoy as its king. But Hitler no longer had confidence in any Italian except Mussolini. And in most of Europe there was no part left for Italy to play.

Next to the Germans were the protected states: Bohemia-Moravia, Norway and Holland. In a Slav world doomed to slavery Bohemia-Moravia had a special place, for she belonged to Greater Germany; although it was intended that she should be progressively Germanised, she retained a diplomatic representative in Berlin and her president had the right to the honours accorded a foreign head of state. As for Norway and Holland, they had the privilege of governing themselves under the supervision of a German civil administrator, but they too were to play a part in the 'colonisation of the east'. The 'Dutch Company for the East' was set up in The Hague. Since 1941 peasants and artisans had been settled on the Vistula by a 'Dutch Company for providing Directors of Development for Eastern Europe'. In military-occupied Belgium, the Flemings, whose prisoners of war had been released, were recruited, to the same end, by the 'Belgian-European Syndicate for Agricultural and Industrial Expansion'.

However, as Quisling in Norway was most definitely not succeeding in winning the support and confidence of the Norwegians, Terboven was gradually induced to replace incompetent Norwegians in senior administrative posts by Germans. The same thing happened in Holland, where under the control of Seyss-Inquart, the Nazi system of compulsory grouping of peasants, fishermen, workers, etc., in one single corporation was introduced.

The territories of great strategic importance were answerable to the military authority. This was the case in the occupied zone of France, in

Belgium (to which the Nord and the Pas-de-Calais were attached),[1] in Greece (with control shared between Germans, Bulgarians and Italians) and in the Channel Islands, which were treated according to the laws of war since a state of hostility existed between Britain and Germany.

Denmark and the so-called free zone in France, even after its occupation in November 1942, retained governments theoretically independent but more or less subject to the German military authority.

The Greater Reich was surrounded by a circle of satellite states, which either by choice or by force had thrown in their lot with Germany in the war against the USSR. Slovakia, Romania and Croatia had slightly differing Fascist régimes—in Slovakia it was rather like Italian Fascism, in Romania there was no single party, and in Croatia the government was dependent on Italy until September 1943. The German minorities there enjoyed special rights. Only Hungary and Bulgaria had succeeded in retaining their own institutions, although there had admittedly never been anything democratic about them.

Finally, Spain was the ideological ally of the Greater Reich, and Sweden, which Rosenberg regarded as the Aryans' land of origin, had moved into its economic orbit.

Thus the Greater Reich was like a harlequin's coat tailored out of shreds and patches. The multiplicity of German authorities wrought the greatest confusion. In two particular ways, however, urgency brought about unity; throughout, the main factor was to achieve success for Germany and everywhere there reigned the same repressive system of supervision and punishments.

IV THE GREATER REICH'S FINANCES

In every country to which they came as conquerors, the German armies did not scruple to live off the inhabitants by levies, looting and commandeering. The occupying authorities did not continue these ruthless methods; they handled matters more subtly by making large purchases and then leaving the inhabitants to whistle for their money. On every occasion it proved a lucrative operation, and always ended by sending to Germany all those products which were considered useful while her own products never left the country. Psychologically, the occupied peoples were under the mistaken impression that they were not being plundered, and the behaviour of the Germans appeared to them correct in commercial and human terms.

1. In July 1944 Belgium was given a civil high commissioner—but not for long.

One of the first methods consisted in over-valuing the mark in relation to the currency of the conquered countries. Generally this rate remained stable, like that of a strong currency; but now and again it was regularly increased, as, for example, in Romania. One result was to restrict the purchase of German goods, which became more expensive; a second, linked with this, was to allow the Germans to purchase more at lower prices in the occupied countries. The German soldiers were the first to benefit and they were able to strip the shops with impunity.

The cost of supporting the occupation troops fell on the conquered countries (except in Denmark, which had not taken part in the fighting). The amount was fixed not in terms of the number of German soldiers in a country but according to her supposed wealth; in France, at 400 million francs per day, it was out of all proportion to the size of the occupation troops. Naturally, once the expenses of the troops' upkeep had been met, the occupiers still had considerable amounts left over. These they used to buy everything that there was to buy; what is more, they paid those foreign workers who had come to work in the Reich in the currency of their own country. Finally, with the national currency they bought shares in the national economy of every country. There was, of course, some awareness of the dangers of inflation; but the principle had been established that nothing should stand in the way of goods being sent to Germany; it was merely a question of making sure that inflation did not rise too steeply. At the end of February 1944 the Reich's Finance Minister, Schwerin von Krosigk, estimated that Germany had received about 47 thousand million marks through occupation charges alone—and of those about 25 thousand million came from France.

However, this was not the only way in which money was raised. Added to this were the costs of billeting the troops and of improving their quarters. In every country, for a mere trifle, fines were regularly inflicted on the occupied cities—in January 1941 Stavanger had to pay 100,000 crowns.

Unlike her opponents, Germany had entered the war without any currency reserves to finance her purchases. However, even before the war she had perfected an ingenious method of managing without them: this was the clearing-system. She continually extended it while at the same time distorting it so that it worked only one way—to her advantage. The purpose of the clearing-system was, in fact, to balance purchases and sales between two countries. Now, in all the occupied countries Germany quickly contracted widespread debts; the goods of the contracting party went to Germany but it received nothing in exchange; trains set off full and returned empty—assuming that even the engines and coaches returned at all. Germany promised to settle her debt but only after the war. In the meantime, the occupied countries had to find a way of paying their own exporters. In the summer of 1944 the same Minister of Finance, Schwerin von Krosigk, estimated the German debt at some 36 thousand million marks.

Finally, in order to nip inflation in the bud, or to prevent deliberate inflation in a specific country of the kind practised by the Weimar Republic, the Reich kept a watchful eye on the institutions issuing national currencies; sometimes, as in Holland, it appointed a fervent and reliable Nazi national at the head: sometimes, as for the Bank of France, it insisted on appointing a German comptroller with the right of veto.

As for private banks, either they played along with the occupier of their own accord in order to remain in existence, or else they came under his control. The Czech banks, for example, had to merge into four large institutions, in which German banks took over the majority of the shares. The intention was to restrict normal credit operations in order to keep them exclusively for fulfilling the needs of the Reich.

Thus in financial matters the whole of occupied Europe came under the same law, which looked forward to the post-war period when the mark would become international currency. The machinery for sucking the European economy dry was now ready.

V ECONOMIC EXPLOITATION

In every occupied country, the Germans' practice of requisitioning goods of all kinds by exercising the rights of the stronger continued virtually throughout the whole war. Generally speaking, it was more ruthless and cynical in eastern Europe. But on September 23, 1940, the French delegation to the Armistice Commission denounced the 'removal from factories and warehouses of plant or of goods'. At Pétain's trial a reliable witness estimated the number of French machine-tools which had been dismantled and taken away to Germany at 25,000.

Now that the financial machinery was working smoothly, looting of the occupied countries gave way to apparently normal trading. To pay for their purchases, the occupying authorities were able to add to the national currencies, which continued to swell their coffers, the assets in precious metals and jewels which they had seized from the banks, as well as the occupation marks printed by the *Reichskreditkassen*—in the summer of 1942 there were fifty-two in Europe—a currency which totally lacked any surety and could be increased indefinitely as the Germans wished, without the financial authorities of the occupied countries even being informed. Germany thus absorbed vast amounts of produce through the standard type of commercial transaction. All kinds of agencies and shady organisations, as well as many middlemen attracted by the profit, offered their services to German firms, so that the producers did not always realise who their real customers were nor their nationality.

To make the transactions even more profitable the occupying authorities fixed prices in such a way as to benefit Germany alone. Thus Romania let her have oil at the pre-war price but had to pay 50 per cent more for German imports.

All the economic transactions of occupied Europe were channelled into the Reich or her satellites. For France this meant a basic reshaping of her foreign trade. Germany had become dominant in central Europe even before the war, but this now turned into a monopoly. Thus Romania's exports to Germany rose from 63 per cent of her total exports in 1940 to 90 per cent in 1941 and 98.77 per cent in 1943; this included in particular the whole of her oil.

To the extent in which large-scale plans for the future were contemplated, it could be seen that Germany was aiming at a virtual monopoly of European industry after the war, especially in the field of metallurgy and chemistry; Berlin would also become the centre of the arts, letters, fashion and entertainment, radiating German culture. The remainder of Europe would be reduced to an agricultural economy and deprived of all intellectual prestige.

For the time being it was essential to direct the output of the various countries towards satisfying the needs of the German war economy and if possible increasing it. To this end, German experts were despatched more or less everywhere, particularly to Romania. All over Europe orders placed by the German authorities were eagerly sought after on the market, even in the so-called free zone of France. To avoid stagnation the manufacturers had to try to satisfy them before anything else, since they otherwise ran the immediate risk of not receiving the raw materials and the power supplies which they needed.

It was more difficult to command obedience from the agricultural producers, because there were so many of them. The occupying authorities encouraged them to form corporate groups, so as to have men at the head who would be answerable to them. In this way they bought up most of the foodstuffs; almost the whole of the poultry and dairy produce from Denmark and Holland made their way to the Reich. But it was easier for the peasants than for the manufacturers to use guile and trickery and keep a part of their crops for themselves.

The Germans' wealth of paper currency enabled them to attempt a vast programme of expropriation. In the field of agriculture, this was carried out by establishing settlers, a prerogative which was not restricted to eastern Europe, since huge experimental collective farms were set up in

Holland and in the Ardennes in France. In the sphere of industry, mining, banking and commerce, it consisted of buying large shares in industrial or other concerns. They began with foreign interests in the satellite countries—for example, French interests in the mines at Bor in Yugoslavia or in Romanian oil. But they quickly extended their interest to the largest and most varied concerns within the country itself. Thus in France German firms came to own 51 per cent of the shares of Francolor, the Société vinicole de Champagne, Carburants français, Gazogènes Imbert, and many others. The shares were paid for at above the quoted price in order to attract sellers. The biggest firms were 'sounded': Schneider, Westinghouse, Rhône-Poulenc, insurance companies, Saint Gobain and Hutchinson. The horrified General Huntziger one day remarked in the presence of the German Hemmen: 'You can buy up the whole of France.' To another Frenchman who was alarmed at German demands during some hard bargaining and who, in exasperation, eventually asked, 'Look here, what do you want?', another German replied, with the most brutal frankness, 'We want the lot.' So the German seizure of industrial and commercial property in Europe began.[1]

Naturally, the ever-increasing specialisation of the European economy along the lines desired by the Reich and the fact that it was so closely subjected to the latter's needs necessitated considerable movement of labour. The occupying authorities generally fixed wages and conditions of work—not always on terms unfavourable to the workers, if the comparison is based only on the nominal wages of the pre-war period. Besides, labour very quickly came forward of its own accord, for in the general slump almost the only guaranteed employment was with the Germans. The latter took advantage of this to send volunteers to work in Germany. Then, as the result of the enormous increase in the Germans' needs, volunteers were no longer enough, despite the appeal to humanitarian feelings by operations like 'relieving prisoners of war' which Laval engineered in France. It therefore became necessary to use force. This task was given to Gauleiter Sauckel. He set up 'Compulsory Labour Service' throughout Europe. Those commandeered were sometimes employed in their own country working for example, in the Todt organisation, on fortifications such as the 'Atlantic Wall'. But more often than not they were sent to Germany, where several million workers found themselves all living together—there were 600,000 from France—from every nation in Europe, with a majority of Soviet and Polish nationals. Most of them were workers and young men, but there were women also.

The exploitation of Europe, however disguised, was nonetheless tanta-

1. The 'Aryanisation' of firms for racialist reasons offered excellent possibilities for expropriation. Cf. the section 'The Fate of the Jews', page 271.

mount to actual looting. It had disastrous consequences for the people. Despite every effort to nip it in the bud, monetary inflation was inevitable; it resulted in an 'unofficial market' and a rise in prices. Scandalous fortunes were made through collaboration with the conqueror. But the majority of the population lived in increasing hardship: food was rationed and sometimes there was none at all. Vital products—medicines, for example—became scarce and as a result public health and hygiene suffered. It was the workers and employees with fixed salaries who were most badly affected. But the ruling classes were not always satisfied either; although certain businessmen were able to speculate and grow rich, many were capitalist property-owners who had been dispossessed or were in danger of being so. In every walk of life the occupiers' financial and economic policy thus aroused discontent which could only be increased by the severity and harshness of their police.

VI THE SECURITY OF THE REICH

As long as the people remained passive and resigned and the Germans continued to be successful in battle—these two factors were interdependent —the occupying authorities behaved correctly, at least in western Europe, for in the east they were brutal from the beginning. Things changed, or became worse, at the first setbacks and the first signs of opposition.

In order to forestall any danger, the Germans had taken the precaution of occupying solid positions of authority in the machinery of justice and the police services of each country. On the one hand, the German military tribunals had jurisdiction over everything concerned with safeguarding the German Army or the behaviour of German groups and nationals. On the other hand, the occupying authorities put pressure on the national judiciaries to take matters out of their hands or make them release protégés of theirs who had been charged.

In accordance with The Hague conventions, the police of the occupied countries were to maintain law and order: they were therefore serving the occupier. However, the latter employed them for unpleasant operations which aroused the inhabitants' indignation and hostility: for guarding military establishments, arresting Jews, suggesting hostages, identity checks, etc.

Above all, throughout every country, the Germans established their own police network and one which was particularly formidable and complex. The military commands had their own police services, whose task it was to maintain liaison with the national police—the *Geheime Feldpolizei* and

Map 12 THE WHOLE OF
FRANCE A PRISON

Each dot represents a political
prison or internment camp

Feldgendarmerie. For the purposes of intelligence and counter-espionage
they had 'special services'—the Abwehr.

However, the duality of the police services, which had been an established fact in the Reich since 1938, did not take long to emerge in occupied Europe, too. The RSHA (*Reichssicherheitshauptamt*), under Heydrich, which combined the normal state security police with the security
service of the SS (*Sicherheitsdienst*), wanted to establish itself in the
territories occupied by the Reich to carry out the racialist tasks required of
it. It intended supplanting the Abwehr and forcing itself on the Army.
Of the seven departments of the RSHA, two were particularly important;
counter-espionage, which included the teams of men who had the task of
tracking down those guilty of crimes against the security of the state
(*Geheime Staatspolizei*, or Gestapo), and the department (called *Amt VI*)
which claimed the sole right to obtain and exploit military intelligence, at
the expense of the Abwehr.

The nationals of the occupied countries who seemed indisposed to accept the new state of affairs soon discovered, to their cost, what the German police forces—who were agreed on this point—had in store for them.

Polizeihaft, or police detention, was the punishment for those who, by reason of their possible Communist, anarchist or Resistance—in France, Gaullist—activity, were considered so dangerous that their arrest and confinement in a German detention camp were necessary in the interests of the occupying power, it being understood that they could also be arrested as a form of reprisal. In France police detention took place in the camp at Compiègne.

Sicherungshaft, or security detention, was the punishment for acts jeopardising the interests of the Reich. This was a punitive and administrative measure, not a legal one; but at the end of legal proceedings it could be given to a man who had been accused and acquitted or to one who had been convicted and had completed his sentence.

Article 19 of Section III of the International Convention of Tokyo laid down that 'if, for exceptional reasons, the occupying state should find it absolutely necessary to take hostages, the latter should always be treated humanely. They should not, under any pretext whatsoever, be put to death or submitted to corporal punishment.' This rule of international law was unilaterally modified by the German authorities. As early as September 2, 1940, the military commander in Paris informed all *Feldkommandaturen:* 'Hostages are inhabitants of the country and their life is a guarantee for the good behaviour of the people. Their fate is thus in the hands of their countrymen. Consequently, the people must be clearly threatened that hostages will bear the responsibility for acts of hostility committed by anyone at all.'

The campaign against the USSR made these conditions worse. In December 1941, Marshal Keitel issued the decree poetically called *'Nacht und Nebel'* (Night and Fog). It laid down that persons arrested for hostility to the Reich's armies would be deported to Germany. They were to live there in complete solitary confinement and receive neither parcels nor correspondence. They were to be guarded by Himmler's ss.

In this way the practice of deporting the Reich's opponents to concentration camps was being extended. The ss and the Gestapo thus saw their responsibilities increasing and of course they did not demur. The Abwehr and the military tribunals were gradually deprived of power and the Reich's security ensured by more summary and brutal methods—the torture and immediate execution of suspects.

Amongst the groups of collaborators and from the prisoner of war camps the occupying authorities also raised special units to look after security, in their own way, in the occupied countries; there was a vast increase in the number of house searches and shootings and the burning of houses and villages. Sometimes these improvised policemen were given normal administrative powers, like Pavelić's Ustashi in Croatia or Darnand's militia in France. The militia was allowed to hold courts martial; in 1944, its leader became a member of the Vichy government with control of all the police forces and the responsibility for 'maintaining law and order'.[1]

VII POLAND'S MARTYRDOM

Of all the occupied countries, it was Poland, together with the territories of the USSR, which suffered most. In the eyes of the Nazis she was doubly guilty: she was peopled with Slavs, with a strong Jewish minority, and she had annexed German territories in 1918. Unfortunately for her, she fell under the Reich's yoke at an early stage and remained there for a long time. Hers was a true martyrdom, for in Poland there was time for some of the schemes for 'the eastern countries' to be carried out.

On May 28, 1940, in Hitler's special train, Himmler put forward to the Führer a few ideas which the latter 'found fair and reasonable'. It was a potted version of the great ss master's 'racial ideas'. After explaining that, in the 'little Slav tribes' of Poles or Byelorussians, it was essential not to create 'a national culture and a national consciousness', Himmler suggested 'breaking up this jumbled mass of people in the *Ostland*'. After this, 'racial screening' would begin, involving a 'racial examination' which would enable them to send to Germany all those children 'who proved to have some positive element from the racial point of view'. There they would change their name and it would be forbidden to treat them as 'Polacks', so that the Nazi ideal 'would find an echo in their soul'. After 'systematic application of these measures', all that would remain in the 'General Government' would be 'the lower elements of the population . . . human material without a Führer and fit to be navvies in Germany'. In short, a slave-dump.

However, the fact remained that, on the one hand, even the 'General Government' would become a land for Germanic colonisation and on the other, as Dr Wentzel, head of the Central Office for Racial Policy, expressed it in April 1942, 'the Polish people was the most hostile to Germany, the most dangerous and the most prone to conspiracy'. For the security of the Reich, it was therefore necessary to remove these undesirable Poles. And Dr Wentzel envisaged both an 'organised' emigration to South America, whence, in compensation, those Germans who had settled

1. Cf. the chapter entitled 'Collaboration', page 281.

there could come back, and the deportation to Siberia of 20 million Poles over a period of thirty years, at the rate of 700 to 800 trains per year, 'which was feasible from the technical point of view'. They would be 'slowly spread out over the expanse of Siberia'.

These loathsome plans could not be carried out, except in a few instances. The Polish historian Madajczyk has described how, in a few days, 100,000 Poles were driven out of the Zamosc region. Since a few Germans had settled there in the twentieth century, their presence was considered sufficient justification to call the country a 'Germanic land'. The expulsion of the Poles took place in the autumn of 1942, at the very moment when, on the Volga, other subhuman beings, Russians this time, were beginning to pin down the army of their lords and masters.

It is astonishing that the Germans, who were famed, and rightly so, for their organising ability, were so bemused by racial hatred that they succeeded in bringing nothing but chaos and poverty to Poland. They confiscated the possessions of Jews and 'absentees', or large estates and concerns which were important for the German war economy and the 'consolidation of Germanism'. Mines, foundries, various factories and large farms were taken from their rightful owners, with a view to being handed over later to German settlers, particularly ex-servicemen, who, however, never arrived. In the meantime, the system of 'temporary government' which had produced such chaos continued.

Dr Wentzel had foreseen that 'the Polish question could not be resolved in such a way that the Poles would be exterminated like the Jews'. However, 'in conjunction with the operation to exterminate the Jews', Gauleiter Greiser put forward his own suggestion of killing off 35,000 Poles who were suffering from consumption 'in order to eliminate the danger of contagion for the Germans'. We are thus led to wonder what would have been the ultimate fate in store for the Poles: to be reduced to a race of slaves in their own country, to be gradually exterminated or to be transferred to Siberia? Or all three at once?

In the meantime, every measure was taken to lop off the whole of Poland's élite. First of all, its members were systematically removed from positions of responsibility in the 'General Government' and elsewhere. Thus Vilna, which in 1943, according to German statistics, contained 104,000 Poles and 29,000 Lithuanians out of a non-Jewish population of 146,000, was administered only by Lithuanians and they alone had a cultural society. The Poles had only one primary school to which they could send their children and were not united in any organisation, even for charitable purposes. Even in the Wartheland the Roman Catholic Church was regarded as a possible source of resistance and treated with extreme harshness. In October 1941, out of 681 parish clergy and 147 monks in the archdiocese of Poznan, 451 were in gaol or in concentration camps, 120 had been 'expelled' to the 'General Government' and 74 had been shot. There remained 34 to minister to the Poles' religious needs.

The most extensive looting of works of art took place in Poland. Indeed, the Germans considered that non-Polish works of art were a product of the west and that those of any value produced in Poland were due to Germanic influence. So they carried off everything, since, to their mind, the Poles were fundamentally incapable of making any contribution to culture or art. In six months they managed to loot museums and palaces, collect the works of art together and list them in a voluminous carefully printed catalogue, bound in linen and decorated with a swastika. Watteau's *La femme polonaise* was found in Goering's villa at Berchtesgaden.

The Germans' behaviour became harsher and harsher, for with all the bludgeoning they received, the Poles still did not give in. Furthermore, all attempts to encourage a collaborationist movement among the leaders of political parties or the representatives of well-known families met with failure. As the battle front came nearer and the Wehrmacht's fortunes reached their lowest ebb, the military and political authorities became even more ruthless and the shootings and deportations increased.

The Germans had never been exactly gentle. The instructions of the organisation *Bund deutscher Osten* bore the reminder: 'Germans, the Pole is never your friend. He is inferior to every German on your farm or in your factory. Remember that you belong to the master nation.' When they were questioned after the war, the Polish workers employed by 'German masters' told how they were treated like cattle; their teeth were inspected and they were made to run and jump. After which the buyer, having weighed up his goods, paid a specified sum to the *Arbeitsamt* and took them away.

Forced-labour camps were set up in Poland very early on. The Polish Commission for War Crimes counted 435 of them. Living conditions there were very hard. In the camp at Skarzysko-Kamienna, for example, the effect on the workers of the chemical materials used was described by a witness in the following way: 'The men, dressed in paper held together by pieces of string, were yellow. Everything was yellow: the huts, the trees, the leaves. Women walked about, ginger-red from the action of the picric acid on their hair. Their bodies were yellow and even their eyes seemed yellow.'

But worse was still to come. Poland was to have the sad privilege of having the extermination camps of Auschwitz-Birkenau and Maidanek and the largest ghettoes in Europe set up on her territory. It was in Poland that the greatest number of Jews were done to death; it was she who, in proportion to her population, suffered the highest losses in human life from her merciless occupier.

The Germans who protested against these atrocities were few and far between. General Blaskowitz sent in a complaint which Hitler saw. General Ulex, the Governor of Cracow, condemned 'a situation which is dishonourable for the entire German people'. These isolated gestures made no difference when such ruthless behaviour was inspired by ethical and ethnic even more than by political motives.

CHAPTER 4

Concentration Camps and Genocide

HISTORIANS ask themselves what were the real motives behind Hitler's policy. Was he basically impelled by an urge for power as the Englishman Alan Bullock or the German Bracher think? In that case, the war would have been the Führer's way of extending his domination beyond the borders of Germany. As far as we can judge from the hotchpotch of ideas expressed in *Mein Kampf*, in his speeches and in *Table-Talk* in which, opportunist that he was, Hitler was swayed by current happenings and gave full rein to his fancies, that rapidly became ravings, it would seem that his ideas on mankind and nations were based on Darwin's notions of selection: in the struggle for existence the strong assert themselves; through their might, they achieve right; the weak can only acknowledge and accept their weakness. The law of life is thus the harsh exploitation of man by man and peoples by peoples. Woe unto the conquered, the degenerate, the weak, the decadent! Power was the sole driving force behind policy and it was to be achieved at the point of the sword. But what were its aims? The greatness of Germany, naturally, and the prosperity of the German people who would at last achieve their proper place in the world: on top. This objective required first of all that they rediscover their fundamental unity, that is to say overcome the various rivalries that had long hampered their power—the rivalries between parties, classes, religions and regions. But above all, it was necessary for Germany to remain pure, that is to say to avoid any contamination by impure racial elements—and first and foremost, by the Jews.

I NAZI ANTI-SEMITISM

Hitler's myth was the superiority of the Aryan master race (of which the Germans were the direct descendants) and the Aryan vocation for world domination; J. Billig rightly points out that the widespread firm belief in this myth grew out of exasperation which filled the Germans with wild rage and this rage would vent itself on any hostile elements until they were destroyed. There was no possibility of coexistence or coming to terms with them; the struggle must aim at their extermination. In the forefront of all these enemies, uniting them and personifying them, Hitler's mythology set the Jew.

Starting from Hegelian dialectics, which they transposed or deformed, Hitler and Rosenberg saw the Reich (of Hitler) opposing the Gegenreich (of Israel); one was the antithesis of the other and the two were irreconcilable. Nordic man was an imaginary type of man endowed with fictitious virtues (based on an intellectual content so feeble as to border on puerility)—courage, heroism, a simple way of life, loyalty, devotion to the community. The Jew is his opposite; he is to the Aryan what Satan is to God. 'The Aryan,' in E. Vermeil's words, 'is the German integrated into the national community and looking at race only from that point of view. The Jew is integrated into his racial community which he sets up in opposition to all the nations in which he exerts his disruptive influence.' For this reason, moreover, the Jew is not a race but the seed of racial destruction—in a word, anti-race.

Hitler's indictment created an imaginary Jew endowed with every physical, intellectual and moral shortcoming. In the loathsome caricatures of his *Stürmer*, Streicher popularised the image of the Jew as obese and flabby, his vices were written all over his face. In his propaganda, Goebbels described him as 'like pus in an abscess, ever ready to defile pure German girls'.

According to Hitler, the Jew was responsible for all the evils that afflict nations; it was he who had invented the false egalitarianism of democracy that emasculates the strong man. He excelled in pulling the strings of all movements of an international nature—Anglo-Saxon plutocracy, Manchester School Liberalism, Marxist Communism, Freemasonry; 'The Jew,' the Führer wrote, 'has always known how to unite princes, aristocrats and the bourgeoisie at the international level; it was he who first shouted: "Workers of the world unite."'

The Jew preached a purely destructive intellectualism which was like a poison. He deprived thought of its quickening elements without which it could only be arid and dead—race, the people, the soil. He epitomised rootlessness and used it as his stock in trade. When he settled anywhere, it was only to cause harm. He had only ceased being a wanderer over the face of the earth in order to make his home amongst the great nations like a canker and devour them from within for his own profit.

On the other hand, all the higher civilisations, including the Greek and the Roman, stem from the Aryan race 'which comes from the north'; in the twentieth century, this race had blossomed forth in the German people and had found a worthy setting in the Third Reich.

German power was only possible if the Jewish peril could be exorcised once and for all. Inversely, as its power grew, the German people would become better able to achieve immunity against this virus that was infecting it. Hitler's anti-Semitism was thus both an idea leading to action and a reality governing a policy. Racialism and power were basically one and the same thing.

II THE SS

Starting with the task of protecting leading National Socialist personalities and then of keeping other parties under observation, in fact as a sort of spy and counter-espionage organisation, the 'Protection Sections' (*Schutzstaffeln der Nationalsozialistischen Arbeitspartei*) were given responsibility for internal security in the Reich when the Nazi party came to power and became one with the state. By 1934 it already numbered 50,000. The logical conclusion of this conglomeration of tasks was the appointment in 1936 of Reichsführer ss Heinrich Himmler to be head of the entire Reich police forces, completely independent of the Minister of the Interior. From 1933 onwards, a special branch, the 'Death's Head ss', had been put in charge of running the concentration camps. The war was to give the ss ever-increasing powers and turn them into the architects of the Nazi world created out of Germany's conquests.

Himmler, a small, insignificant-looking man with a neat moustache and receding chin, was in fact a fanatic; he sought neither the satisfactions of power, fame as an orator nor worldly success; as a zealous and blindly obedient supporter of Hitler, he believed in the Messianic mission with which he was entrusted. He devoted all his energies to the formation of a Nazi élite, the ss, which was to be an 'order' within the party and the state.

It was to be a racial order. As early as 1937, Himmler asserted: 'Our Nordic blood confers on us an inventive genius far above that of other nations.' Preserving the purity of this blood demanded rigorous precautions: the ss had to obtain the permission of their superior officers before they could marry; bigamy, the kidnapping of children as well as procreating them outside marriage were considered legitimate means if they were felt to be necessary. The ss were educated in special schools of their own. The whole system reached its apogee in the organisation which Himmler pompously called *Lebensborn*, the fountain of life, the source of German expansion in the world.

The selection of the ss was governed by racial criteria, purporting to be scientific but containing a great deal of nonsense. Himmler described them in these terms: 'I started by requiring a certain height because I know that people who are above a certain height have the right kind of blood. I examined photographs of each one and asked myself the question: are there traces of foreign blood?'

Himmler also stated in 1937: 'The coming decades will see the extermination of the inferior beings who are fighting against Germany, the cradle of the Nordic race and torch-bearer of civilisation.' The conquered Slav territories enabled these words to become deeds.

Henceforth the ss would be able to operate not only as an instrument of orthodox racialism but as the founder of the Nazi social order on conquered soil. 'It was,' wrote J. Billig, 'the embodiment of the myth of the master race raised to its extreme pitch of violence.'

In this function, the ss was the protector of the German state and it had sole charge of criminal justice. But by its nature it existed on the fringe of the state. Its mentality was that of a devoted and ferocious servant ready to undertake any task it might be given. The ss relieved the state and its organisations such as the Wehrmacht of the responsibility for operations that were unworthy of them. Its role was to prepare the way, by violent methods, for the Nazi colonisation of eastern Europe and to reduce the 'sub-men' to the bondage for which nature had intended them.

Accordingly, the ss diversified its organisation. It was no longer merely a group of shock troops for internal political use. From the time of the invasion of France onwards, it included armed units. These divisions were under the orders of the Wehrmacht which considered them crack troops; but the Wehrmacht was also at the service of the ss when the latter had need of large numbers of men to enforce 'Nazi order in the rearward areas'.

The ss were answerable for their conduct only to their leaders. They set up their own courts which dispensed justice according to their own ideas of honour and duty. Thus, two ss men who had summarily shot down some fifty Jews in a Polish synagogue were condemned by a field court martial to a long term of imprisonment. But, like many others of a similar nature, the sentence was not carried out. The verdict was quashed on the grounds that 'at the sight of the Jews, the accused had become aware with extraordinary intensity of the hostility of the Jews towards Germany'. So their behaviour was quite excusable, if not even praiseworthy. The ss's only link with the rest of German society was the strict terms of the oath its members took to their leaders. The transformation of the ss into a state within a state was completed when it created its own economic services. However, Himmler had absolutely no intention of directing Nazi policy; he never intervened in discussions on major questions of strategy, war economy or diplomacy. He remained the faithful servant to implement Hitler's desires and he did nothing without the latter's approval. But in reality his role was much greater because he was shaping from within the German society of the present from which the society of tomorrow would spring.

So the ss had a triple task of combating those considered unworthy, exploiting their wealth and putting them to death; and they were given every licence to carry this out and, as it were, get it working smoothly, in the concentration camps which Hitler had placed under their control as early as 1933.

III THE CONCENTRATION CAMPS

Concentration camps started in Germany as soon as the Nazis came to power. At first they were intended for those Germans who were opposed to Nazism—Communists, Social Democrats, Christian Democrats and conscientious objectors—with the purpose both of ensuring that they could not harm the régime and of 're-educating them'. Thus Dachau in Bavaria was opened in 1934, Buchenwald near Weimar in 1937 and Mauthausen in Austria in 1938. At that time, the Nazis tended to look on these camps as model prisons and were proud of them—photograph albums of Dachau were distributed to affiliated Nazi parties in occupied countries as an example to be followed; Mussert's albums were discovered in Holland.

However, from the start the camps showed certain characteristics that were to be constant; on the one hand, political internees and common-law criminals were inextricably mixed, with the latter in charge of the former and holding all the minor administrative posts, thus bringing the detainees into immediate contact with them; on the other hand, 're-education' took the form of systematic humiliation and bad treatment, such as to break down all resistance by completely destroying the personality.

With the war, as foreigners were added to the internal enemies of the Reich, their number increased. Accordingly, new concentration camps were built in the conquered territories. The largest of them were set up in Poland: Auschwitz, Maidanek and Stutthof. A women's camp was built at Ravensbrück in East Prussia; other men's camps appeared at Neuengamme near Hamburg, Flossenburg on the Czechoslovak border and Natzwieler-Struthof in the Vosges. The central organisation was at Oranienburg-Sachsenhausen; this was where general directives were prepared and reports received from the camp commandants. Some of the camps were linked together: Buchenwald and Dora, Oranienburg and Grossrosen; and they all hived off large numbers of *kommandos* of various sizes, formed for varying lengths of time; teams of detainees would be sent there to carry out some particular job, while remaining under the administrative control of the main camp. The whole area of the Greater Reich

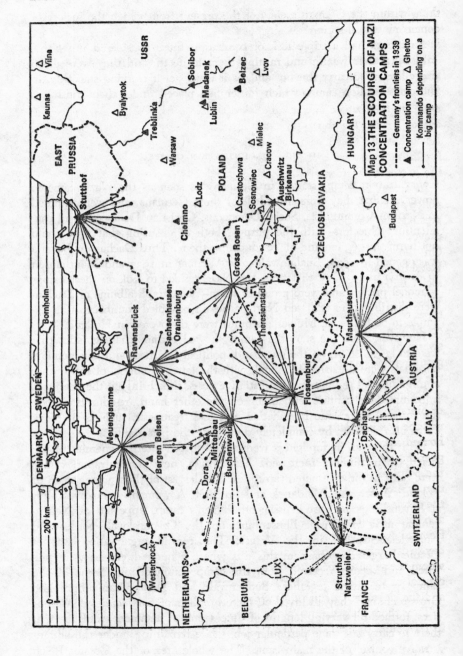

Map 13 THE SCOURGE OF NAZI
CONCENTRATION CAMPS

--- Germany's frontiers in 1939
▲ Concentration camp   △ Ghetto
▲ Kommando depending on a
•   big camp

thus became covered with a network of concentration camps and their dependencies; Buchenwald for example controlled a hundred or so *kommandos*.

In 1941, with Himmler's assent, Heydrich, the chief of the security police, classified all the camps into four categories: the first category was for *Schutzhäftlinge* (deportees) who were likely to mend their ways; the second, for those whose output in terms of work would be poor for reasons of age or health; the third, for detainees who were more dangerous for the Reich but still useful and capable of improvement; and finally the fourth, for those who were quite incorrigible and who as a result were to suffer the harshest treatment.

In actual fact, this division into special categories, based on a purely police approach, remained a dead letter. The fact was that, as the war progressed, the development of the camps was speeded up so fast that they proved to be chronically unable to cope with the work that they received. On the one hand, the camps became international towns, Towers of Babel in which detainees of all ages were living together, drawn from every social milieu and speaking every language under the sun; thus Buchenwald housed an average of 40,000 internees. On the other hand, the first types of detainee were joined by Communists of all nations, Soviet prisoners of war, Resistance fighters described as '*Nacht und Nebel*'[1] and the swarm of hostages or those picked up by chance or by mistake, not forgetting a few collaborators who had lost favour or fallen into disgrace with the occupying power.

Accordingly all the camps were provided with the same sort of system of hierarchy and organised on more or less the same principles. At the top was the *kommandantur*, comprising the camp commander and his deputies, housed in villas adjacent to the perimeter. ss units were responsible for guarding and employing the detainees; they comprised two main sections, the political section which held the prisoners' files and the economic section which looked after the commissariat and fixed the work required of the detainees. The ss were very few in number—at Mauthausen there were 260 for a population of 70,000. They stayed away from the detainees, apart from an occasional display of force to remind them of their presence. The day-to-day running of the whole camp was done by detainees, the *kapos* whom the ss entrusted with the subordinate posts which provided effective control of the blocks, barrack rooms, kitchens, workshops, secretarial staff and the sickroom (*Revier*). They were preferably common-law deportees.

Thus there grew up the closed universe of the concentration camp, with its own rules of living and social hierarchy. On their arrival, the deportees

1. Night and fog.

were shaved and stripped—in every sense of the word—dressed in cast-off clothing which made them look ridiculous, sometimes tattooed, given numbers and made to wear distinctive signs according to their nationality and the reason for their internment; these were different coloured triangles: green for 'common-law', red for 'political', pink for the anti-social, purple for conscientious objectors, and so on, with various letters on them, T for Czech, F for French, N for Dutch, etc. The *Nacht und Nebel* sometimes wore the letters NN; they were not allowed to receive any letters or parcels; they were forbidden to walk about the camp; and they lived in isolated blocks.

In fact, as the camps became more and more congested and their accommodation and services increasingly inadequate, the fate of all the detainees became very grim. At the mercy of their *kapos'* whims, liable to corporal punishment such as flogging on the slightest pretext, underfed, exhausted by unremitting toil, with little medical care, the wretched internees in order to survive were forced to resort to dreadful internecine strife which was only slightly mitigated by a few attempts at political organisation or group solidarity. Most of the time, these attempts came from the Communists, who formed the most homogeneous and disciplined element, and first and foremost from the German Communists who had been longest in the camps and were thus the most experienced, as well as occupying more of the minor administrative posts.

These living conditions, which became harsher and harsher as the war progressed, led to a high death-rate amongst the prisoners, which increased still further when they began to be employed in the German war industry. From 1942 onwards the organising of this employment was entrusted to ss General Pohl. It gave immense power to the ss: they could hire out to industrial concerns a labour force that cost them nothing, that was unable to make any protest and that could be continually renewed, as it was increased by recaptured prisoners of war or those unsuccessfully trying to evade forced labour. Several million men were thus taken on by the largest German firms—I. G. Farben, H. Goering, Krupp, Roechling; deportees were sent to work at Dora, Laura or Thekla in secret factories built underground to avoid enemy air raids. Some of them were even employed at Sachsenhausen in counterfeiting English pounds and American dollars that were put into circulation by an Austrian businessman, F. Schwend. These notes were used to buy men's consciences or other services such as those of the spy Cicero in Turkey, who was paid (and fooled) by them. Most of these fakes were good enough to be accepted by Swiss banks.

Through its concentration camps the ss thus managed to achieve all its objectives; the camps rendered Nazi Germany's opponents harmless and made them work for the glory of the Reich while condemning them to a lingering death; they became Germany's largest economic enterprise; as soon as war came, they moulded to their will the servile mass of 'sub-men' doomed to inescapable inferiority by reason of their racial or national origin or the fact that they had been defeated. The 'solution of the Jewish problem' increased their power still further.

IV THE FATE OF THE JEWS

Even before the war, the Jews in Germany, under the accusation of being stateless, had been subjected to discriminatory and humiliating measures; the Wehrmacht's victories now made it possible to extend these measures to the whole of occupied Europe.

The Jews were forbidden to work in the public services, to enter the liberal professions, to hold senior appointments in any organisation liable to influence public opinion—the cinema, radio, press, publishing, the theatre. Their names appeared on special census lists and they were forced to wear a yellow star; their identity cards and ration cards had to bear a distinguishing mark, as did their homes; they were not allowed to enter public places—cafés, parks, museums, theatres, cinemas or libraries. In Poland, they received reduced rations and required permission to move about.

The seizure of Jewish real estate steadily increased, on the pretext that they had themselves gained it by fraud from the countries in which they lived and which they would betray as a matter of course. This resulted in the immense swindle that went under the name of 'economic Aryanisation'; nationals of the various countries were put in charge of Jewish concerns. This transfer of property was a highly profitable business for the cover-men put up by the occupying authorities but also for the German firms which thus acquired considerable financial interests in the economy of the occupied countries.

The measures were accompanied by a campaign of vilification of the Jews through the medium of films—*Jud Süss*—lectures, exhibitions, pamphlets, newspaper articles and university teaching.

In addition to these measures designed to subject, expropriate or humiliate the Jews, they were made to form associations for the greater convenience of the German authorities. When they did not exist already, such associations were set up and the Jews were forced to join them—in France the General Union of Jews, in Holland the Jewish Council. They had the function of helping the occupying power in its decisions or implementing them. These associations sometimes published these decisions in special Jewish newspapers—the *Joodsche Weekblad* in Holland; they

collected the funds required to pay the fines inflicted on the Jewish communities; they drew up lists from which the occupier would select the
names of hostages to arrest, suspects to intern or those to be recruited for
forced labour. These associations controlled by leading Jewish personalities inspired sufficient confidence in their co-religionists to encourage
them to greater meekness but they had little power to alleviate their fate.

In the east, the *Einsatzgruppen* revived the tradition of the pogrom.
They stirred up the local population, denounced Jews for more or less
imaginary crimes and encouraged plunder, shop-looting and murder. They
hoped in this way to gain support for collaboration. In Poland, at Lvov,
in three successive pogroms organised by means of Ukrainian nationalists
and the dregs of the population, there were 10,000 victims. In Yugoslavia,
2,000 Jews were shot as reprisals for partisan operations. In Jassy on June
29, 1941, 8,000 Jews were wiped out either on the spot or after being
picked up and brought in. The list of crimes perpetrated in Poland, as
established by a special commission, is terrifyingly long. But this small-
town butchery merely offered the ss the chance to acquire the knack; it
did not offer a solution to the 'Jewish problem'.

V THE MADAGASCAR SCHEME

The purely German solution to the problem for a while consisted in letting the Jews leave the country more or less voluntarily. Whilst life in the
places where they lived was made increasingly unpleasant, no obstacle
was placed in their way if they wanted to seek asylum elsewhere, on the
understanding that they gave up most of their belongings. In this way,
several hundreds of thousands of German or Austrian Jews left their
country before the war and this explains the paradox that the proportion
of German Jews who disappeared during the war was the lowest in Europe.
The same policy seems to explain why, in the autumn of 1940, 7,000 Jews
were sent without warning from the province of Baden into unoccupied
France and why there were attempts to smuggle thousands of Polish Jews
over the demarcation line between Germany and the Soviet Union.

But the size of the Polish Jewish population caused Hitler embarrassment, as he explained in March 1940 to an American of German origin,
Colin Ross: 'It is the difficult question of finding enough room . . . I
would welcome any positive suggestion.' A solution had indeed been found
to the problem of cleaning up the annexed Polish territories by transferring
the Jews to the 'General Government' which became a sort of 'Jewish
reservation'. But this was only a springboard for better things, as Hitler

confessed to Colin Ross: 'In Lublin, the Jews are already packed as tight as sardines.'

For a while in the summer of 1940, the idea was toyed with of expelling all the Jews from Europe at the end of the war. This 'solution' would be written into the peace treaty. After some research Madagascar was chosen to receive the Jews after the 25,000 Frenchmen living there had been evacuated. Sea and air bases would be held by the Reich; the Jews would administer the rest of the island under a German governor dependent on Himmler; their European assets would provide the basis for the development of the country and for creating the appropriate infrastructures. The Jews would lose their original nationality without becoming Germans; they would be 'citizens of the mandated territory of Madagascar'.

Although this scheme was the subject of thorough discussion between all the ministries concerned, it does not seem to have been put to the Vichy government who, in accordance with the armistice convention, retained complete control of the island. Heydrich seems not to have been entirely enthusiastic. Moreover, the invasion of the USSR was to create problems that the 'Madagascar scheme' would have been unable to solve; at the same time, this invasion opened up new horizons which were to suggest other solutions to Heydrich, including 'the final solution'.

VI THE GHETTOES

One good way of segregating Jews so as to be able to strike at them more easily by cutting them off entirely from the outer world consisted in shovelling them into the ghettoes that formerly existed in certain Polish and Lithuanian cities. Those who had not lived in them before the war, as well as the small local Jewish communities, were all sent there. Thus each ghetto formed an entirely enclosed Jewish world, surrounded by a wall through which the Jews passed only when they went to work in other parts of the town. Outside, the Germans set about reviving the anti-Semitism of the non-Jews; inside there were all the horrors of promiscuity—ten people to a room—forced labour, under-nourishment, raids and reprisals. When no ghetto existed, they were set up; Heydrich, the 'protector' of Bohemia, shut his Jews up in the old disused fortress of Theresienstadt; in Belgrade, Rademacher chose the gypsy quarter for the Yugoslav Jews, after rejecting the idea of an island in the middle of the Danube. More than 435,000 people were crammed into the Warsaw ghetto.

Inside the ghetto there still remained some semblance of family life and independent administration. 'Jewish councils' (*Judenräte*), appointed by the Germans, ran the community rather like municipal councils, with the help of Jewish police. They negotiated work contracts with the Nazis and issued the regulations governing the punishment of offences. Their role has been the subject of extremely diverse judgments, many of them very critical. Some of these councils were even said to have gone as far as to draw up lists of Jews sentenced to be hanged as reprisals; most of them, by meeting German demands as well as they could, had hopes of saving their own skins and the lives of their loved ones. But Mazor stresses that many of these reluctant Quislings did rebel at great risk to themselves; some of them stirred up revolt, or, in despair, committed suicide.

In Lodz, Rumkovski, a man of philanthropic bent and a former small manufacturer now in his seventies, took his position very seriously. He set up various institutions, indeed almost a small court. His picture hung in every office, like the Führer's. He toured the schools, conducted marriage ceremonies, printed a local currency and stamp bearing his own effigy. But he did not succeed in saving either the Jewish community or some of its members or himself, for the behaviour of the Nazis condemned their victims to come to tragic choices, none of which led to anything but despair.

The ghetto formed an economically closed world. In Theresienstadt, the population was divided into 'hundreds' of men and women from sixteen to sixty years old, forced to work ten or twelve hours a day under the control of a 'prominent person'. It was a caricature of joint management of the means of production. In theory, each inhabitant received free board and lodging in exchange for his work; but the shops were often empty and the ration cards rarely honoured. These extraordinary business concerns which paid their staff no wages, were hotbeds of all sorts of illicit trading. The German bosses and the 'prominent persons' took all the profits; the clever ones, the dishonest ones and the better-placed ones amongst the detainees managed to live off the black market. After November 1942, the Jewish workers in Lvov became the property of the ss, who hired them out to firms, sometimes run by Jews who were individually employers but collectively slaves.

In these communities doomed to slow extinction, the state of health of the population was deplorable and epidemics rife. Informers flourished in the atmosphere of suspicion. Yet some cultural life went on, pursued with desperate eagerness as the expression of a sort of will to live; newspapers were printed, concerts and theatre performances took place and even a grim humour sometimes appeared. At times the ss fancied themselves as patrons of the arts and supported them, even if they did send the writers and performers off to be killed next day. The ghettoes were in fact, only one stage in the 'final solution to the Jewish problem'.

VII THE FINAL SOLUTION TO THE JEWISH PROBLEM

At the beginning of 1942, Hitler announced in two speeches that the Jews would be exterminated; the scheme to transport them out of Europe had thus been abandoned. This change of heart in Nazi policy was the logical consequence of the behaviour of the ss in the ussr. Had they not been invited to 'protect the Wehrmacht' by immediately executing Jews and leading Communists—since to the Nazi mind, these were only two forms of the same enemy? After mass shootings—34,000 in two days in Kiev— followed by cremating the bodies on vast funeral pyres, the ss had worked out a rough and ready system of itinerant gas-chambers; they asphyxiated their victims with the exhaust fumes from their lorries. But the ss found this method not very practical because the victims took too long to die and this restricted output. On request, the German chemists produced a gas called *Zyclon-B* and its rapid effect proved most encouraging when it was tried out.

It was in these circumstances that, at Wannsee, near Berlin, apparently at Heydrich's suggestion, the decision was taken to exterminate the European Jews, a decision communicated in a letter from Heydrich himself to the Wilhelmstrasse apparently without their raising any objection. The operation began in Poland, a testing-ground for the ss, and was entrusted to Globocnik, the ss chief of the Lublin district; it was given the cover-name *Aktion Reinhard* in memory of the 'great' Reinhard Heydrich who had recently been executed by the Czech Resistance movement in Prague.

The method consisted of installing, in certain camps, gas-chambers camouflaged as shower-rooms, together with giant cremation ovens. At Birkenau, in open country a few miles from Auschwitz, a complete range of buildings was constructed, after expelling everyone in the vicinity to exclude any indiscreet observers; Himmler came to inspect the building personally. The same precautions were not considered necessary at Maidanek; the camp could be seen from Lublin and Jews still alive could observe from their ghetto the smoke produced by incinerating the corpses of their comrades, in full knowledge of the fate awaiting them.

In November 1942, a few Gauleiters raised objections to the 'final solution' on the grounds that it was depriving the Reich's war economy of a valuable labour force. A middle way was found: the healthy Jews would be sent out to work until they became exhausted; the others, after periodical 'selection', would be exterminated; those who for some reason or other were not exterminated, would be sterilised—an operation based on frightful experiments on human guinea pigs taken from the concentration camps.

All that remained was to drive the cattle to the slaughter-house door. Jews were rounded up in their thousands all over Europe, with the more or less willing co-operation of the authorities in the occupied countries; in Romania Antonescu, to his credit, delayed implementing the measures until they had become difficult to apply. In France, the poor wretches were crammed into makeshift internment centres, in the *Vélodrome d'Hiver* after the 'big round-up' on July 16, 1942, at Beaune-la-Rolande, Pithiviers and Drancy. In Holland, it was the Westerborck camp. Thence they were transported 'eastwards'—the trains deposited them at the very gates of Birkenau.

Gradually the ghettoes emptied of their inhabitants. On July 22, the *Judenrat* of the Warsaw ghettoes themselves announced the beginning of the 'big operation'; by July 1943 there were no longer any Jews officially living in Lvov. On September 1 in Lodz, Rumkovski had the hospitals evacuated and the patients handed over to the Nazis. On June 21, 1943, Himmler ordered all the Jews in the *Ostland* who were unfit for work to be sent to concentration camps. In Hungary Eichmann, the man in charge of the operation, was particularly keen on sending Jews to the gas-chamber; from March to June 1944, helped by the diplomat Wesen-mayer, he succeeded in deporting 400,000 Jews, at a time when the Red Army was already approaching and the Wehrmacht was finding it impossible to obtain lorries to move their troops, whereas Eichmann had no difficulty at all. This same Eichmann tried to have Dutch Jews born of mixed marriages deported to Birkenau, when Himmler considered that sterilisation would meet the case. He even ordered 1,127 Jews to be trans-ferred from Rome to Birkenau when Hitler himself wanted them to be confined in Mauthausen as hostages. The ss had been possessed by a lust for murder.

How many Jews died in this 'final solution'? L. Poliakov and B. Mark, who are specialists on this question, are agreed with Israeli statisticians in placing the figure at 6 million, i.e. more than 40 per cent of the whole Jewish people. It is the most atrocious crime in the history of mankind, in its grievousness and its wantonness, because the death of these wretched people contributed in no way at all to the success of the German armies. They were killed as a result of an ethos based on the will to power and on racialism and applied by one of the most highly developed countries in the world with all the vast organising ability and scientific knowledge at its command, because its sense of discipline and its patriotism had been com-pletely perverted.

VIII DID THE JEWS ALLOW THEMSELVES TO BE MASSACRED?

The immense number of Jews who died raises the question of whether, in the vast majority of cases, the Jews allowed themselves to be massacred. Could they have done anything else? It is probable that a certain atavistic feeling based on memories of centuries and centuries of persecution, tended to produce meekness and resignation; they knew that a storm does not last for ever. By submission and prayer, the Jewish people lost many members of their race but they did continue to exist and hope for better days to come.

But in addition, the Nazis had taken all sorts of precautions. Fooled up to the very last minute, hundreds of thousands of Jews went to the gas chambers still not realising what was happening; earlier on, they had left their homes or their ghettoes convinced that once they had been transferred in accordance with the orders issued by their present masters they would be allowed to live in peace. The 'solution' was so unthinkably bestial that their minds were bemused; and when their eyes opened it was too late.

The Nazis were also very skilful in their use of 'collective responsibility'. Dvorjetzky has analysed what 'the call of the woods' meant for those who were detained close to the Russian front: the promise of freedom and fighting; but their families were left behind in the towns as hostages so during the journey or in the camps and ghettoes, any attempt at escape or revolt would bring out the informer, for fear of reprisals.

And finally, the inhabitants of the concentration camps were never free from observation. As Wellers reminds us: 'The detainees lived night and day in public, slept in public, washed in public, performed their natural functions in public and died in public. In this sort of congestion, secrecy of any kind was impossible.'

It is all the more remarkable that nonetheless plots and revolts did take place, motivated by bitter despair but sometimes systematically prepared. Group communities in apartment-houses or ghettoes and national or political affiliation in the camps turned into resistance organisations. Though the insurrection at Lvov proved abortive, at Sobibor on the other hand, on October 14, 1943, 300 detainees managed to escape after killing nine ss. In Cracow, Bialystok and Treblinka, the ghettoes were 'liquidated' after fighting that sometimes lasted several days. Above all, in Warsaw the first German attempt in January 1943 was successfully opposed by four Jewish combat groups, out of the fifty that had been organised. In

April they had to call in tanks, guns and flame throwers. Fighting lasted four weeks with the attackers compelled to reduce the underground bunkers one by one by blowing up blocks of houses with high explosive. Not until May 15 could ss General Stroop announce: 'The Jewish quarter no longer exists.'

So the Jews did fight their own war during the war itself and it was difficult for them to do more than they did. But there is another question: how much did the rest of the world know about the enormous crime that was being perpetrated and what did it do to try to stop it?

IX THE SILENCE OF THE VATICAN

In London, the Allies had been informed by the Polish Resistance of what was being concocted, albeit without realising its full horror, and through the BBC they had threatened the Reich with reprisals. Even during the war, they had decided to bring the war criminals before special courts when it was ended. These threats and decisions stemmed partly from considerations of psychological warfare.

It is a fact that nobody in Europe, and probably not even the German people, fully realised the immensity of the loathsome crime of genocide being committed against the Jews, as well as the gypsies, and which also threatened the Slavs. Such a crime was unprecedented and seemed incredible in the twentieth century. The International Red Cross said nothing and managed to gain entry into the camps only at the very end of the war; this inspection *in extremis* could not alter the state of affairs. The Vatican also said nothing, thereby incurring violent criticism as well as giving rise to extremely heated debate. Its policy towards Germany, wrote F. L'Huillier, 'has caused many Roman Catholics great qualms of conscience' and 'set a riddle for almost all thinking men'. What was this policy?

When he was papal nuncio in Germany, the future Pope Pius XII had been responsible for arranging the concordat whereby the Vatican gave the Third Reich international recognition at a time when the Nazi régime had not yet achieved, through its military successes, the prestige and power which made it unassailable. It is true that later on the encyclical *Mit brennender Sorge* condemned certain excesses of National Socialism but not the doctrine itself or its underlying racialism. Nevertheless, it aroused Hitler's wrath and was made the excuse for a violent anti-Catholic campaign in the Reich.

Ever since his election, Pope Pius XII had continually shown goodwill towards Germany by his constant display of affection for the German people, for whom he felt a particular regard. Between the lines, it was possible to read a distinction between the people and its régime but this distinction was subtle rather than overt. When war became imminent, the Pope asked the weaker power, the state that was threatened, Roman Catholic Poland, to make concessions to preserve peace. Later on, by appointing ecclesiastical dignitaries to dismembered Poland, the Pope seemed to recognise the *fait accompli* that had been achieved by violence.

If we add that the Vatican never directly intervened with the German government but always confined its approaches to the Italian government and that, while continually making peaceful declarations and canvassing in favour of peace, it refused to make any concrete proposals that could only lead to a condemnation of the aggressor, it is plain that the Vatican did little to stand in the way of Nazi policy. The invasion of Holland, Belgium, France, Yugoslavia and Greece touched the Pope's heart but called forth no protest. Faced by a constant stream of entreaty on behalf of the victims of Nazism, the Pope used every effort to mitigate the lot of the Roman Catholics, above all the priests and specifically those interned in Dachau; but he kept silent on the dreadful treatment that was being meted out to Jews. Yet it seems that by the end of 1942, he must have known all about it.

Pius XII thus showed the greatest caution in his relations with Hitler. True, this caution did not amount to pretending ignorance or, even less, showing approval. Many people who were threatened or persecuted, including many Jews, found asylum in the Vatican or in religious communities in Italy. Privately the Pope frequently referred to his concern and even to his distress. The voice of the Vatican was sufficiently outspoken in its broadcasts to inspire some of the earlier Resistance tracts circulated in France. And finally, Pius XII firmly refused to recognise the attack against the Soviet Union as any kind of crusade. But the fact remains that the only international authority that could raise its voice against the monstrous crimes of the Nazis was the Vatican, and the Vatican kept silent.

We can only surmise about the motivation behind such behaviour. Was the Pope imprisoned in a doctrine which forbade him to intervene in the affairs of another state—in fact, to give unto Caesar those things which are Caesar's? Was it this same doctrine that led him to give *de facto* recognition to the scandalous Ustashi régime in Croatia which professed Catholicism and set out forcibly to convert the orthodox Serbs living in the new state? Did Pius XII fear that he might aggravate the lot of the German Roman Catholics and priests? This meant putting the preservation of the Church before elementary principles of humanity that are fundamental to Christianity.

One is thus led to wonder whether the Vatican did not think that it was best to choose the lesser of the two evils. With his aristocratic temperament and social background and with the prevailing feeling in the Curia at the time, it is probable that Pius XII was led to find the true or most formidable enemy of Roman Catholic dogma and the Roman Catholic world in the materialism and atheism of Communism. By opposing it, in however wrong-headed a way, Germany represented western civilisation and was perhaps even its bulwark against Asia, since the Church still existed in Germany. After all, it was not all that long since the 'Red' barbarians in Spain had committed atrocities against churches and monasteries.

As for saying that the Pope's silence can be explained away as a calculation based on the likelihood of obtaining a 'real peace', this would mean expecting too much or too little from the international hearing that the Pope's utterances could command. Whatever it did, the Vatican was entirely powerless to establish a 'real peace'. On the other hand, a firm protest by Pius XII against the extermination of the Jews, published in the Catholic Press all over the world, would not perhaps have prevented or slowed down the massacre, although in this matter there can be no certainty. What is certain is that such a protest would have been a revelation for most people and that it would have turned Roman Catholics away from collaboration and perhaps made the German Catholics less submissive, quite apart from the relief that it would have provided for millions of troubled consciences.

CHAPTER 5

Collaboration

THE Hitler régime needed to keep the German people well in hand and to win the greatest possible support abroad; its prestige required this as did the successful conclusion of the war. Propaganda, inspired and controlled by Goebbels, was thus one of the pillars of its policy. Helped by the Wehrmacht's successes, the pre-war European Fascist parties gained many members, and hopes of victory as well as subsidies from the victor brought others into being. In the occupied countries, these parties acted as henchmen for the German authorities; in the satellite countries, if they were not themselves in the seat of power, the threat that they represented to their governments made the latter more ready to submit to the Germans' requests. Only in Poland and the Soviet Union did Nazi policy do nothing to play down its determination to exterminate its ideological and racial opponents and thus sow discord in their ranks. In those two countries collaboration was a dismal failure.

I THE 'VOLKSDEUTSCHE'

In various countries, the German minority, the *Volksdeutsche*, provided the spearhead for Nazi penetration. Hitler insisted on their being granted autonomous status, so that they should keep their 'Germanity' by retaining direct links with the Reich. Thus F. Karmasin in Slovakia made no secret of the fact that he was a German agent and took his orders from Ribbentrop. The Slovak Germans were represented in the government by a Secretary of State and they levied their own taxes for their own purposes.

In Croatia, Dr Branimir Altgayer had been granted authority in all matters concerning the Germans; but those Germans who were officials in the Croat state took their oath to Hitler. The Germans had the right to wear Nazi insignia, to use the Nazi salute and to sing Party songs.

In Romania, the status of the German minority in Transylvania had been settled on August 30, 1940, in Vienna by a special protocol. It was completed by an agreement between Antonescu and A. Schmidt, leader of the minority, which gave it the status of a public corporation having the right to issue its own laws.

In Hungary there existed a 'National League of Germans', with Franz Basch as its leader; it had its own schools and was proportionally represented in the government service. But the Hungarian government, jealous of its own authority, had refused to grant it special status and its members were not allowed to wear the swastika.

II GOEBBELS' PROPAGANDA

In theory German propaganda was shared between various organisations. The Führer had made foreign propaganda the preserve of Ribbentrop and the Wilhelmstrasse; Dietrich was in charge of the press; Max Amann, one of the Führer's most trusty lieutenants, was responsible for the Party press; and finally, the Wehrmacht had its own propaganda service. In theory, that left very little for Dr Goebbels, who bore the title of 'Propaganda Minister'—merely the cinema and the radio, for internal use only. But in fact, it was he who set the tone and in practice he finished up, if not in complete control, at least guiding everything along his own lines.

This half-failed intellectual—he had not succeeded in achieving fame despite having published thirty or so books and pamphlets—was one of Hitler's earliest companions. He had greatly contributed to fabricating Hitler's legend and the latter had to some extent modelled his attitude on the image of himself popularised by Goebbels. An efficient propagandist, a brilliant speaker and orator and a splendid actor, capable of pleading the most conflicting causes in quick succession, Goebbels had more cleverness and ambition than real conviction; he thought Rosenberg a complete and utter idiot. Cultured and intelligent, he was also a mass of complexes, vain and unscrupulous. He had defined his function in one sentence: 'I had to keep up German morale.' It was a good pretext for poking his fingers into every pie—the shortage of warm winter clothing for the troops in Russia, the size of the potato crop or racial purity.

Goebbels regularly wrote the editorial for the weekly *Das Reich*. But above all, he had the radio and he knew how to use it; his broadcasts went out for eleven hours every day to the North Americans; there were eight hours for Africa and a whole programme for the British in preparation for a landing in the British Isles. In the occupied countries he introduced propaganda services to replace those run by the embassies or the Wehrmacht. They purged the libraries; controlled the press—'an armful of directives every day', Bonnafous, the Vichy Minister of Information used to say; founded or backed newspapers; supervised the cinema news programmes; acquired interests in publishing houses, cinema and gramophone-record firms, news agencies and even printing presses;

formed large numbers of cultural associations to spread the good (Nazi) word; produced films and organised anti-Masonic, anti-Semitic or anti-Bolshevik exhibitions; spread 'German culture' by means of weeklies, reviews, concerts and lectures; invited scientists, artists and men of letters to tour Germany; nor did they neglect fashion.

Goebbels was the inventor of the Nazi ritual; it was he who had perfected the giant Nuremberg rallies with rolling drums, flags, spotlights and endless parades of troops in uniform. For him, a human being was a collection of passions and instincts and it was to these he appealed and not to reason. On this point he was at one with Hitler, who considered the masses devoid of any sense of freedom, toleration or decency; they were unintelligent and needed to feel themselves dominated; it gave them a feeling of peace and security.

The scene of the mass rallies was carefully chosen for its historical associations or the possibility of cramming it with people, thus making it easier to create a collective spirit. Noises off-stage, marching songs, inspired applause amplified by loudspeakers, the march-past in columns ten deep, aroused and sustained enthusiasm so that the individual sank into the mass and lost his ability to think or criticise, all turned into uniformed automata caught up in a lasting delirious hysteria.

There was no question of telling the masses the truth. On November 10, 1938, Hitler had told German journalists in these explicit terms what their duty was: 'The rightness of the leaders' attitude must be continually stressed as a matter of principle.' Accordingly no matter was ever thoroughly explored; arguments were replaced by slogans of an alluring simplicity; by the continual hammering home of the same associations of words all the time, people came to believe what they heard.

Consequently, in order to be effective, propaganda restricted itself to a few well-chosen themes: extravagant praise of the Führer, and emphasis on the obnoxious nature of his enemies, the Jews and the Marxists. Before the war, Hitler had been presented as the great friend and comrade, a hero combining charm and strength, the modern Siegfried. When war came, he became a national symbol, the skilled statesman able to handle any political, diplomatic or economic problem, the infallible leader. When setbacks began to occur, he remained the protector, the shield and buckler of the people, the saviour. Thus Goebbels praised him as being the 'watchword of all who believe in Germany . . . the redeemer . . . the leader who understands the people and fights on their behalf'. The NS Frauenwarte, the official organ of the association of National Socialist women, wrote simply: 'You owe everything to the Führer, your wages, the blue sky above, life.' Children recited a prayer with these words: 'Führer, my Führer, my Faith, my Light, it is to you I owe my daily bread.' Even the

Führer's style was considered as a model; Goebbels praised him as 'the cultivator of the German language'.

At first the Jew was put forward as a man without a country, a ferment of dissolution amongst peoples. Then, when the paradoxical alliance of the Communist Soviet Union and the capitalist Anglo-Saxon countries came into being against Germany, the Jew became the connecting link explaining this monstrous union. As part of its pretentious rubbish, German propaganda tirelessly brandished the spectre of the 'Jewish-plutocratic-Marxist-Masonic conspiracy.' There, too, Hitler had shown the way; he had the knack of tarring all his opponents, however different they might be, with the same brush so as to appear all the nobler by contrast. In *Mein Kampf* he had expounded his belief that the bigger the lie, the more likely it was to be believed.

III THE COLLABORATORS IN OCCUPIED EUROPE

The German 'New Order' was not without its attractions for various categories of people in the occupied countries. More than one captain of industry rejoiced in the elimination of social conflict, the banning of strikes and the vast market that might be expected from a German Europe. In every country anti-Semitism was glowing with a quiet fire that needed little to make it flare up anew. The property-owning classes and above all the petty bourgeoisie looked on Fascism as championing a social order based on private property. The Churches were tempted by the thought of the final elimination of atheistic and materialistic Communism. More than one aesthete was taken in by the virility, the martial look, the healthy physique and the splendid bearing of the victorious young German warriors: did not Drieu la Rochelle sing the praises of the 'tough Nazi fighter who can regenerate mankind and who is a combination of American gangster, Foreign Legionary and aircrew' in short 'a man who believes only in acts'? Even Nazi Germany's social achievements compared with those of the liberal democracies were not without attractions for trade unionists. And even when no ideological sympathy existed, the distribution of generous largesse by the occupying power was an excellent method of making converts and enlisting supporters. Thus the Gestapo found it easy to recruit auxiliaries sometimes even from the criminal classes. In a word, in every country groups of collaborators became legion, all fashioned more or less on the same model.

In all the groups the dominant figure was the leader, the infallible master of the masses; everywhere the attempt was made to enrol the whole of the population into territorial and co-operative organisations of a paramilitary type; everywhere there were by myths, rituals and slogans rather than ideas; everywhere appeal was made to violence, fanaticism and terror; the virtues of discipline, blind obedience and sacrifice to the good cause were praised to the skies. The gestures, the dress—the coloured shirt—the ceremonial, the hierarchy and the vocabulary were all copied from the Nazis.

Thus in occupied Europe there appeared a sort of anti-Semitism that was imported and imitated from Germany rather than properly indigenous —for example, it did not exist in Italian Fascism. So we find such strange perversions as nationalist groups whose members had joined out of fear or even hatred of Germany turning into fanatical supporters of a German-dominated Europe. The first result of which was their acceptance of the occupation, exploitation and obliteration of their own country.

Yet each of these groups proclaimed itself 'national'. Was it a relic of patriotism, at least in words, or their desire not to alienate conservative elements? In any case, the 'programmes' of the various Fascist parties were singularly close to one another. They all demanded: a 'strong government' led by a 'strong man'; social order within a framework of political and economic stability; the 'solidarity' of all classes that was jeopardised only by the demands of the people, supported or incited by the workers' parties and trade unions; precedence of national over sectarian interests and of collective groups over individuals. Europe became the theatre of a 'Fascist international' where the same play was performed all the time, imported from Germany and having the same mass methods of indoctrination, the same enemies to be fought and the same passionate fury in shooting them down. The only national differences lay in the relative roles that German policy assigned to its puppets in each country.

In Norway, Quisling had the sad distinction of giving his name to a whole category of traitors. In fact his Fascism was, if such an expression is possible, the purest sort of all, because it sprang neither from economic uncertainty nor national emergency nor even from self-interest but from belief, a rather naïve belief indeed, in all the tawdry myths with which Nazism had decked itself out. Quisling believed in the Aryans, in the Germanic racial community which was to bring together the Scandinavians and the Germans. He was a missionary rather than a politician.

Quisling provided the occupying power with its first experience of collaborating with local pro-Nazi elements. It helped it to work out the appropriate methods of behaviour: use the Nazis to infiltrate the government services and win them over by eliminating the hostile elements within them, thus avoiding a direct takeover, which would be not only tricky but burdensome and dangerous; thus the unpopular measures put out by the occupying powers had a better chance of being acceptable to public opinion since they would appear to have been agreed upon and applied by fellow citizens. But should the collaborators fail to fulfil the role allotted them they would be ruthlessly swept aside, however loyal they might be.

Quisling learnt this to his cost in Norway as did Mussert in Holland. Both of them were either brought on or sent off the field according to whether they were still useful.

Thus Mussert had the notion that the Reich would help him to create a Greater Holland stretching as far as Flanders in France and which would be a sort of western marches of Greater Germany while retaining a certain amount of independence. But he ran up against thinly disguised German designs to annex Holland and learnt the sad lesson that a Nazi can always find someone more Nazi than himself. His acceptance of defeat did not prevent Seyss-Inquart from subsidising dissident groups supporting a straightforward annexation of Holland, led by Rost van Tonningen.

In Belgium the defeat of the democracies had led the Flemish nationalists to think that the death knell of French influence, under which they considered that they had been suffering for many years, had finally tolled. This ethnic and linguistic group which felt politically and economically bullied made common cause with Nazism as much to satisfy its claims as through ideological sympathy. In fact, it was really the inherently brittle nature of Belgium that was being confirmed and aggravated by events.

Paradoxically enough, the Walloon Fascists, the 'rexists' who predated the invasion, found themselves led by the internal logic of their action to the blatant aberration of proclaiming Belgium's 'Germanity of blood and soil'. The point was that, in the Nazis' eyes, Quisling, Mussert and de Clerk were Germanic; but Degrelle was not. Therefore he had to go further and shout louder and commit himself more deeply than the others. In every country, the Fascists found themselves caught up in a sort of inevitable spiral; faced by the threat of those who were more extreme and servile than themselves, they had steadily to increase their offers to the occupying power.

French Fascism was more complicated because there was no French Führer and it had split up into rival groups; on the other hand, it comprised elements from the traditional Left, the radicals and Socialists and sometimes the Communists. Indeed, the Vichy régime had drawn into its orbit the French right-wing reactionaries. So in the northern zone, we find the anti-militarist G. Suarez's *Aujourd'hui,* the anti-clerical Socialist sympathiser and radical R. Château's *La France au travail,* the syndicalist G. Dumoulin's *Atelier,* all denouncing the clericalism, the paternalism, the militarism and the jingoistic nationalism of the Vichy rulers and all subsidised by the ambassador Otto Abetz who used them to exert pressure on the Vichy leaders. The most powerful of these groups was the *Rassemblement national populaire* of the former Popular Front minister Marcel Déat, who in his *L'Oeuvre* attacked the Jews, the Anglo-Saxons, the *Action française,* Communists and Liberals in the best Goebbels style and advocated a planned economy, the protection of the race, the integration of France into a German Europe and French participation in the war on the German side.

There were other groups more in line with pre-war French Fascism: the ex-*Action française* R. Brasillach and his team who ran *Je suis partout,* Deloncle's *Comité secret d'action révolutionnaire,* consisting of *cagoulards,*[1] Bucard's *Parti franciste* and above all, Jacques Doriot's *Parti populaire français* whose spokesman was the writer Drieu la Rochelle. Before the war, the PPF had tried to win over the mass of workers by demanding nationalisation of certain industries and calling itself socialist in order to thwart the workers' parties. Under the occupation it became more and more the defender of peasants and small property-owners, as well as small traders and artisans, by espousing their grievances against the large firms. It claimed that by doing this it was fighting against French decadence by attacking international capitalism or Marxism. But violence could not add up to a programme. The 'physical revolution' preached by Drieu la Rochelle—sport for all, holidays and back to nature—was not really adequate either to provide a programme for industry or society.

Rommel's advance towards Egypt had aroused certain hopes amongst the Arab nationalists. Hadj Amin al Husseini, the Grand Mufti of Jerusalem, had become a Nazi supporter and taken refuge in Berlin after the failure of Rashid Ali's revolt. The Germans had acknowledged his right to create a Palestinian state and solve the 'Jewish problem' there according to ethnical and religious criteria similar to the solution that was being achieved in occupied Europe. The Mufti delivered himself of fanatical propaganda on the Berlin radio; he was the mediator between the Reich and Italy on the one hand and Farouk in Egypt or Bourguiba in Tunisia on the other.

All these Fascist groups developed in similar ways. Hitler intended them to be his loyal henchmen or even slaves. They provided the men of action to do the occupying power's dirty work; they carried out police or reprisal operations against their compatriots—raids, arson or murder; they were the purveyors of the future inmates of concentration camps.

Thus they came to an ever increasing extent within Himmler's purview and they vied with each other in their eagerness to recruit volunteers for the anti-Bolshevik crusade. They became Waffen ss, 'the shock troops of

1. Literally 'hooded men'; an extreme right-wing group.

the new order'. In France the 'Legion of French Volunteers against Bolshevism' was formed in which Doriot served for a while. Twenty thousand supporters of Mussert served in the German Army and several thousand in the police; Mussert had suggested raising 300,000 men to be sent to Russia, but Hitler refused for fear that they might not be amenable enough. De Clerk became head of a 'Flemish Legion' officered entirely by Germans, and Degrelle of a 'Walloon Legion' which he took off to the Ukraine. Quisling divided the members of his anti-Bolshevik Norwegian legion between the Russian front and the internal front against his compatriots. The Grand Mufti recruited a Moslem Legion which goose-stepped in a Berlin parade together with Bosnians or Soviet prisoners of war from Azerbaidzhan and Turkestan.

All these volunteers wore German uniform and took an oath to Hitler, 'the Führer of Germanity'; the Flemings even took an oath to Himmler. These nationalists had become the mercenaries of the power that was occupying their country. The same fate was in store for the collaborators in the satellite states.

IV THE SATELLITES

In Romania, the Germans continued to maintain their trust in Antonescu, holding the 'Iron Guard' up their sleeve should need arise. Antonescu had set up a personal dictatorship accepted by young King Michael. His government consisted of officers, civil servants and experts, all of them responsible to him. But despite Goebbels' persuasion, the *Conducator* did not establish 'single party' rule, although the 'historical parties' remained banned—according to Mr Popescu-Puturi, Maniu and Bratianu, the leaders of these parties, had advised their members to accept the régime.

This régime was, however, in many respects a Fascist one. Popular assent was obtained by organised plebiscites. Freedom had been suppressed and there were thousands of arrests and internments. Nazi-type organisations—corporations, youth movements and 'Work and Light' cultural propaganda—brought the régime into line with that of the Reich.

Von Killinger, the new German ambassador, had been recommended to Antonescu by Hitler as an 'adviser'; in fact, no important measure could be passed without his approval. On the list of the staff of the German ambassador there was a 'police attaché'. The Romanian ministry of propaganda had been reorganised by Goebbels' 'experts', so that the press was tightly controlled and directed by the German ambassador and German culture became predominant in the theatre, music, literature and the fine arts. By meekly agreeing to send workers to Germany and allowing the

Romanian units in the USSR to be used as the Wehrmacht generals saw fit, Antonescu had turned Romania into the perfect satellite.

In Hungary, the Germans had allowed the pre-war political régime under the Regent, Horthy, to continue. They felt some affinity with it in view of the veiled dictatorship it had set up and its anti-Semitism. But the independent spirit of the Magyars did not fail to cause them some concern. Accordingly, they were keeping note of Ferenc Szalassi's Arrow Cross movement.

Szalassi recruited his supporters from the lower ranks of the army and the lower middle classes. But he also made an impact on the industrial proletariat, which lacked any political or trade union organisation—particularly amongst the miners and unskilled workers. The movement had obtained twenty-five per cent of the votes in the elections and returned forty-nine members of Parliament. Compared with the conservative Hungarian ruling classes, the Arrow Cross seemed like a revolutionary mass movement.

As such, the movement gave Admiral Horthy and his associates cause for concern. They made no secret of the fact that they would forcibly oppose any attempt on Szalassi's part to achieve power. Although the Germans openly supported and subsidised Szalassi and succeeded in obtaining his release from prison, they did not immediately try to force this issue. They did not need to do so as long as the Hungarian government showed its loyalty as an ally in the struggle against the USSR.

On the other hand, in Croatia it was the Fascist Ustashi party that took over power under its leader Ante Pavelić, who had been the instigator of King Alexander's assassination and who was proclaimed *poglavnik* of the Croatian state. This was because Matchek, the head of the Croatian peasant party, had rejected the advances of the Italian occupying authorities. Pavelić instituted a reign of terror against the Serbs living in Croatia, the Communists, the Jews and the gypsies. He set up concentration camps at Jasenovać and Stara-Gadićoka, in which the inmates were regularly slaughtered. The entire populations of some localities inhabited by Serbs were massacred, such as those of the village of Suvaja in July 1941.

Pavelić, who was protected by Mussolini, recognised the Italians as owners of most of the Dalmatian islands and coastline; he even accepted an Italian protectorate over Croatia and it was intended that a member of the house of Savoy should become its king; but the Duke of Spoleto never ascended his throne. The fact was that the Ustashi's atrocities had finally disturbed and aroused the indignation of their Italian protectors themselves, despite the help that they provided them in their struggle against Tito's partisans.

V COLLABORATION IN THE SOVIET UNION

Collaboration in the USSR is a question which Soviet historians seem disinclined to treat; they restrict themselves to a wholesale condemnation of it as treachery, while playing down its extent and its effects. However, although all the offers made to the Poles—apart from a few isolated neophyte Quislings, like the publicist Ladislas Studnicki—had been spurned, so much so that for example, even Poles fairly close to the Nazis ideologically fought against them in the National Military Forces (NSZ), it seems that on the contrary the Wehrmacht was not always entirely unwelcome in the USSR, especially in the western territories inhabited by non-Russians.

Thus a few thousand Estonians enlisted in the Wehrmacht or in the Finnish Army and fought outside Leningrad. In the Ukraine, national councils were set up which formed combat groups. Finally, in contrast to the fierce fighting spirit of most of the Red Army units, some of them, consisting of Armenians, Tartars, Caucasians and Moslems, proved much less keen, as was shown by the abnormally high number of prisoners captured.

On the initiative of General von Schekendorff, commanding the rear area of Army Group Centre, seven armed battalions and 200,000 auxiliary volunteers (Hilfswillige) were raised among the Soviet prisoners of war. The Hilfswillige were not armed but were employed in the Wehrmacht's auxiliary services, wearing German uniforms. In the course of the war, their number grew to 650,000 out of several million POWs; but these poor hungry wretches were impelled less by the idea of voluntary service than by the desire to escape their miserable fate.

By adopting these measures, the Wehrmacht was acting rather on its own. In the USSR the instructions of the occupying authorities were always to exercise extreme rigour to the point of collective extermination. The nationalists of other races were consequently caught between 'the hammer and the anvil'. Thus some Ukrainians, under A. Melnyk, continued to support collaboration despite everything; but others, such as Stephen Bandera and Mykol Lebed began to distrust Nazi Germany as much as Bolshevik Russia, the more so as their first moves—the proclamation in Lemberg of a provisional Ukrainian government combined with a sort of pre-Parliament—were disowned by the Germans. Some Ukrainian nationalists joined underground anti-German organisations, so that in June 1942 Hitler categorically forbade the formation of Ostbataillons and was reluctant to agree to the use of auxiliaries. He was afraid of putting arms into his opponents' hands.

However, some German leaders had the impression that a great opportunity had been lost. This was apparently Goebbels' view and above all, Sauckel's, whose efforts to recruit labour for the Reich were hampered by the severity of the occupation. In October 1942, Rosenberg's political deputy, Otto Bräutigam, who was in charge of relations with the branch of the Wehrmacht concerned with occupation matters, even spoke up against the way Soviet POWs were treated; he described it as 'a great tragedy'; he considered it the cause of 'the increase in the Red Army's powers of resistance' and as a result responsible for the 'death of thousands of German soldiers'. Bräutigam urged on Rosenberg the need to create a Russian 'anti-régime' consisting of native Russians of standing. He was backed by officers such as Colonel Stauffenberg and the head of the Wehrmacht's propaganda services, Colonel Martin. Then, at the end of the summer of 1942, General Vlassov was captured. This Soviet army commander had had a brilliant career. As a former deputy to Chiang Kai-shek's Russian military adviser, he had received the Order of Lenin at the age of thirty-nine and had ably defended Kiev in September 1941. Then he had been put in charge of the military government in Moscow when the capital was in grave danger. Finally, he had received the order to relieve Leningrad; his army had been surrounded and, famished and exhausted, had been forced to surrender. It seems that Vlassov had been revolted by Stalin's harsh directives and the great losses that they entailed; although he would not desert, he had refused to be taken out by the aircraft that had been made available for him after the rout of his army.

Vlassov accepted Colonel Martin's suggestion of forming an anti-Stalin 'Russian Committee'. At the beginning of 1943, he issued a manifesto from Smolensk containing fourteen points: the recognition of the freedom of the peoples composing the USSR, the reintroduction of private property and political and religious liberty, the return of the land forming the kolkhozes to the peasants; in a word, he was advocating something that was not Stalinism but not capitalism either. As for the Jews, Vlassov adopted Hitler's approach in all its severity and proclaimed that there would be 'no room for Jews in the new Russia'.

Vlassov was welcomed sympathetically by the German officers and often by the local population. Rosenberg gave him his support, albeit reluctantly, for he favoured the dismemberment of the USSR whereas Vlassov merely wanted to give greater autonomy to the various peoples, which did not win him the sympathy of the Baltic or Ukrainian nationalists.

At the end of the day, Hitler restricted his role to being an instrument of propaganda to increase the number of desertions from the Red Army. No important operation was ever entrusted to the Russian National Committee. Vlassov's propaganda was even kept under close watch: the Germans took the precaution of editing and publishing the newspapers representing his movement. Displeased by some of Vlassov's statements in the course of an official tour, Keitel even ordered the general to be transferred to a prisoner-of-war camp. The fact is that in the USSR, Nazi anti-Communism and racialism were not just propaganda but the expression, indeed the very heart, of German policy, even to the detriment of the military operations, where a Wehrmacht victory seemed, indeed, in hardly any doubt at the moment.

VI THE VICHY REGIME AND COLLABORATION

The almost limitless victories of the Wehrmacht reinforced the Vichy government in its conviction that Germany had won the war. It was true that the encroachments of the occupying authorities, such as the annexation of Alsace-Lorraine and forcible German participation in the French economy, still raised a tremendous stir, in Wiesbaden, however, rather than in Vichy. But the Germans had three infallible ways of bringing pressure to bear on the Vichy government: at the slightest hint of opposition, they closed the demarcation line, or used open blackmail regarding the fate of the million French prisoners of war, or set the subsidised press of the collaborators in the northern zone at the throats of the Vichy government.

Although he merely had the title of Vice-President of the Council of Ministers, Admiral Darlan had in fact been leading the government since February 1941. He had introduced three former members of the PPF into it—Pucheu, Benoist-Méchin and Marion; the first two made no secret of the fact that they were staking their careers on the success of collaboration and the third frankly advertised his Fascist views—and he was in charge of information and propaganda. As for Admiral Darlan, it would seem that he has, mistakenly, been considered as a sort of enigmatic sphinx. This naval man who had frequented Republican political circles—unusual behavior for one in his position and regarded with suspicion—was indeed cold and cautious, despite being a southerner. He possessed great organising ability but was lacking in general culture and political experience and above all, his mind was already made up: the United States would not be ready to make war before the Germans had completed their victory. As for Britain, the Admiral's personal enemy, she was exhausted and in her final death throes. Marshal Pétain was aging and his natural tendency to let his collaborators take over responsibility at awkward moments, even if he then disowned or replaced them at the appropriate moment, left Admiral Darlan in charge of French policy.

Internally, the national revolution was touched up somewhat to bring it closer to Fascism, although neither the single party system nor the single youth movement was ever adopted. First of all, police repression was stepped up; at the beginning of 1942, 50,000 opponents of the régime were imprisoned and 30,000 interned in improvised camps; the Communists, the Gaullists, the foreign Jews and the 'unorthodox' were the main victims; the first of these in particular were despatched to twelve Algerian camps to be subjected to exhausting hard labour. When the Socialist Marx Dormoy, the former Popular Front minister, was assassinated by members of the PPF in July 1941, although a police investigation was ordered, it proceeded with leisurely caution. The murderers were arrested but their investigation took so long that two years later their trial had still not started.

Justice moreover now took its course in ways that were very different from those under the Republic. When attempts on the lives of the occupying troops began, a law on 'Communist plots' was applied retrospectively; instructions were issued that Communists who were already in prison when the attacks were made and thus had nothing to do with them, were to be sentenced to death by special courts. The Marshal set up a political Council of Justice; it was to advise him on bringing those responsible for the defeat before a Supreme Court of Justice at Riom; but on his own initiative the Marshal condemned those alleged to be guilty—Paul Reynaud, Léon Blum, Edouard Daladier and General Gamelin—to be interned before the Court of Justice had pronounced any judgment, in fact even before it had met.

In Fascist style, an oath of allegiance to the person of Marshal Pétain had to be taken first of all by the military, then by the judiciary—only one member refused—and finally by every official without discussion. The organisation of the economy became noticeably more corporative in nature. The *Charte du Travail* (Labour Charter) in its final form was different from René Belin's earlier scheme; *syndicats* (trade unions) continued to exist but they were unified and militarised, because the trade union delegates were no longer elected but appointed. Although not acknowledged as such, a sort of state control arose, partly through force of circumstance, partly because of the 'young technocrats' that Darlan liked to see around him. Thus, it was the government that fixed the minimum wage and appointed the members of the governing bodies of the professional organisations. As a first step towards government by notables that the national revolution was theoretically committed to setting up, an appointed National Council was created to advise the government; to avoid any similarity between it and a republican assembly it was to meet only in exceptional circumstances and would work mainly through its 'departments'. On the other hand, a further step was taken towards a totalitarian régime by forming, within the Ex-Servicemen's Legion, a *service d'ordre* (SOL), to maintain good order and discipline, whose uniform and function were an unfortunate reminder of the way in which the ss had come into being.

These internal Fascist tendencies of the régime went together with an outspoken desire to collaborate. Marion instructed the press to publish nothing that might stand in the way of collaboration.

One sign of this tameness was the stricter application of the anti-Semitic laws. A quota was fixed for the number of Jews to be admitted into the liberal professions—for lawyers it was two per cent. The 'Aryanisation' of Jewish concerns in the occupied zone proceeded according to the rules laid down by Vichy and under the supervision of French officials. A 'Legion of French Volunteers against Bolshevism' was raised in the northern zone; it was a private foundation, the work of the collaborationist movements but it received the blessing and the encouragement of the French head of state.

Would matters reach the stage of military collaboration? Admiral Darlan was still tending that way, despite the abortive 'Paris protocols'; and Weygand's recall from North Africa reassured the Germans. In January 1942, Rommel was once again in difficulties in Libya and he withdrew; Benghazi was recaptured by the British. It seemed the *Afrika Korps* might have to retreat to Tunisia. The Vichy government showed concern and negotiations were started between Abetz and Darlan's envoy, Benoist-Méchin. On the French side there exists no written evidence about them and they are known only through remarks made by the negotiator. But on the German side, the matter appears quite plain: Abetz communicated to Berlin a proposal from the Vichy government that it would enter the war against Britain. He stated explicitly that this proposal had been unanimously approved. But Rommel's situation recovered and Hitler, true to his principle of not creating a running sore in French Africa or, more accurately, of not opening the door to the British Army, did not proceed further with Vichy's proposal; once again, he did not need to.

So Darlan failed to reap any benefit from his policy of collaboration; he succeeded neither in obtaining the return of any large numbers of French prisoners nor any relief from the financial and economic burden imposed by the armistice convention. It seemed this was perhaps because he was *persona non grata* with the Germans, and especially with Abetz. For in Vichy they did not realise that the Germans were neither able nor willing to grant concessions to France, whatever leaders she might have. It was thought that Pierre Laval enjoyed their trust and that he was the one man to meet the situation; so in April 1942 he returned to power. The German leaders were so unenthusiastic, however, that Goering even urged him not to accept, although Abetz was delighted. This return made up for his personal failure on December 13, 1940.

Pierre Laval made no secret of the fact that he would intensify the policy of collaboration. He would have a free hand because the Constitutional Bill no. xi conferred on him 'effective control of France's internal and external policy'. Pétain had finally become the 'figurehead' that Laval had wanted him to be as long ago as June 1940. Pierre Laval brought new blood into the government; the Marshal's earlier ministers either resigned or were dismissed by him; two convinced supporters of collaboration, A. Bonnard and Bichelonne were appointed, one to 'condition' French youth, the other to control the economy in the way likely to prove most satisfactory to the Germans.

With the same purpose in mind, Laval took four crucial decisions. He used the whole weight of Vichy's information and propaganda services to requisition labour by luring Frenchmen to volunteer for work in Germany; he thought up the idea of older prisoners being 'relieved' by young workers; when the supply of volunteers for Germany began to run dry, he threatened and punished defaulters and set the French police on to them. He changed the 'Legion of French Volunteers' into the 'Tricolour Legion', thus giving it an official status. He instructed the French police to carry out massive round-ups of foreign Jews, both in the southern and in the occupied zones. Finally, he allowed the Gestapo to track down French resisters in the southern zone, especially those passing clandestine radio messages to the British believing that they were safe from the Germans.

Pierre Laval was a loyal supporter of Nazi Germany, and his loyalty never swerved. He expressed it in the plainest possible terms: 'I want Germany to win' he stated in June 1942. The next clause provides the explanation of this wish: 'since otherwise Bolshevism will triumph in Europe'; but this clause in no way reduces the gravity of his statement nor does it make his intention less obvious.

VII THE FRIENDSHIP OF SPAIN

During the war against France, the Spaniards had shown themselves actively friendly towards the Axis. Franco had been anxious to preserve the neutrality of his country exhausted by civil war and despite his fears that if the war were protracted the Anglo-Saxons might carry it into Spanish territory, he was bound to Germany and Italy by obligations that were too recent for him not to oblige them in his turn. He had agreed to allow German submarines to refuel in Spanish waters and for radio and meteorolog-

ical stations to co-operate with the Luftwaffe. This had not prevented
the Germans from expressing their dissatisfaction and Goering had sharply
criticised the Caudillo for not entering the war.

After the defeat of France some Spaniards felt that the time had come
to help themselves to some of the French colonies. Serrano Suñer became
Foreign Minister instead of General Beigbeder, who was thought to be
too neutral, or even anglophile. But in October 1940, in Hendaye, Hitler
refused to pay the high price that Franco set as a condition of participat-
ing in a coalition to take Gibraltar from Britain and carry the war into
Africa via the French colonies. As a result the relations between the Axis
and their debtor cooled off.

The entry of the Wehrmacht into the USSR clarified the situation; the
focal point of the war was now definitely moving away from the Iberian
peninsula. Hitler was now no keener than Franco to see Spain turn into a
battlefield where her weakness, like that of the French colonies, could only
tempt the Anglo-Saxons to make a move.

This did not affect the question of ideological solidarity; the very day
that the German-Soviet war started, a mass demonstration took place in
Madrid in front of the British Embassy, shouting: 'Gibraltar'. Franco
raised no objections to transferring workers to Germany; he merely
negotiated on their behalf the most favourable possible terms. Since
Bolshevism was for him the implacable enemy of Christian civilisation, of
which Spain was the champion, in reply to Hitler's appeal for an 'anti-
Bolshevik crusade', Franco sent the 'Azul Division' to fight in the USSR; its
strength rose to 60,000 men. In addition, rare metallic ores, such as
wolfram, were reserved for the Reich.

All this time, the Anglo-Saxons were working out more or less realistic
schemes for occupying the Canary Islands; but at the same time, Churchill
did not hesitate to hint at a future settlement with Spain after the war, at
the expense of the French colonial possessions. Franco refused to be
tempted; he remained true to his ideological friends and made the theatri-
cal gesture of offering the 'breasts of a million Spaniards' to form a bulwark
in Berlin should the need arise. Such grandiloquence made no positive contribution towards collaboration that was of a sentimental rather than an
effective nature.

VIII SWEDISH SUPPLIES

The Swedes had been terrified to see the war coming closer as a result of
the Finnish and Norwegian campaigns. They had succeeded in preserving their neutrality by failing to respond to their neighbours' appeals for

help. Germany's victory had insured them against the risk of becoming an operational theatre but inevitably made them henceforth dependent on Germany. Being unable to refuse the Reich's requests, Sweden attempted merely to limit their extent and to obtain the best possible terms in return.

From 1940 onwards and throughout the whole of the war, Sweden supplied Germany with almost all the iron ore that she mined but did not herself smelt, that is, about 9,000,000 tons a year. After raising certain difficulties, she agreed that the Wehrmacht's equipment and troops on their way to and from Norway should be transported by rail over her territory or by ship through her territorial waters. Between July and December 1940, 130,000 men and more than 500 railway trucks passed through in both directions. In June 1941, when a whole German division with all its men and equipment went over Swedish territory to take up its positions in Finland on the Soviet tundra, Swedish neutrality became really nothing more than a polite fiction, particularly as German aircraft were flying over her air space without let or hindrance.

Nonetheless, Sweden set a limit beyond which she would not go; she refused to sign a political treaty with Germany and she would not accept the Reich's suggestions that she should become, officially and in writing, an economic unit in Germany's Europe, even if, in fact, she was one. Her policy brought her not inconsiderable advantages: she paid for German coal at one-third the price paid by Switzerland; although, as in other countries throughout Europe, her balance of payments with the Reich was in deficit, it was quite a bearable one.

In compensation, Sweden did not pursue the British agents operating in her territory with any great zeal; she gave shelter to Danish and Norwegian resisters; she gave asylum to Jews who were being hunted down in Denmark. In short, she endeavoured to give the least possible dissatisfaction to the Allies, who alleviated the blockade somewhat in her favour. This did not prevent the Baltic from becoming a German lake.

The same thing happened in the Black Sea. Although Turkey had been a creditor in her clearing account with Germany even before the war, and though she was afraid of supplying goods without receiving any equivalent return, she applied the clauses of the trading agreement signed in June 1940 with scrupulous exactness. She provided the Reich with grain, oil seed and scarce metallic ores. Von Papen, the German ambassador, was extremely active and he laid down the law in Ankara. As long as the Wehrmacht successes continued, it would be difficult for small states not to submit to the law of the conqueror.

Resistance Movements Begin

THERE was resistance to the occupying power throughout Europe. It could be found in every occupied country, but it was never unified or co-ordinated. This enormous Trojan horse in the heart of enemy territory was, of course, used by the Allies but with some mistrust. Yet in every country the resisters were much alike. First of all, they were anti-German; Italian occupation was relatively restricted and milder. All the resisters were motivated by two feelings: patriotism and the hatred of foreign or national Fascism; their war was at one and the same time a political struggle and military combat, ideological as well as patriotic. Consequently the resisters hounded down collaborators who were the friends of the enemy; resistance turned into civil war and sought to take over power.

Resistance warfare was ruthless; since the occupier had made terror a method of government, the partisans replied with counter-terror—the Germans, incidentally, called them 'terrorists'. It was a total war, based on a rudimentary sort of Manicheism: you were either for or against the occupier and those in between, the ones who were neutral or lukewarm, were fated to disappear because sooner or later they were forced to take a decision. Finally, the Resistance army was born under the sign of poverty; it lacked weapons, money and trained personnel; all it could do was to produce as many 'pin-pricks' as possible, without expecting to gain any real victory; it was incapable of winning the war and it was often merely an advance party that had to be sacrificed, doomed never to enjoy the victory for which its sacrifices had prepared the way; its losses were, proportionately, very high.

I THE METHODS OF THE RESISTANCE FIGHTERS

In every country the resisters found themselves in basically similar situations; they were all volunteers, often thrown entirely on their own resources. Their groups were always very unstable; for want of experience and precedents, they had to work out their own methods of fighting.

Passive resistance was an early form, before the resisters had gained any experience; it was shown in deliberately misunderstanding the occupiers' orders or by slowness in carrying them out, spreading witticisms or jokes which ridiculed the victor and cut him down to size. It was a spontaneous action of limited scope which worried the occupier because he sensed it rather than being able to weigh up its exact importance, except when it was shown by gatherings and demonstrations in places of historic importance—Wenceslas Square in Prague or the Arc de Triomphe in Paris.

This popular action fitted in with the psychological warfare that the Resistance movements discovered by experience. The distribution of occasional tracts, followed by newspapers that appeared more or less regularly, was another step forward, since it presupposed the existence of organised and stable groups—collecting news items, building up stocks of ink and paper, using printing machines, distributing the various broadsheets.

The underground press was in itself a form of action because though its aim was to inform, it sought even more to convince and stir up public opinion. The latter was also aroused by the behaviour of the occupying power, especially towards the Jews. Help for the enemy's victims—Jews and escaped prisoners—was highly dangerous for the helper; it thus implied a more determined commitment and it necessitated joint group action. One example of this was the escape channels which collected, sheltered and passed through to safety Allied aircrews who had been shot down over occupied territory.

All these early groups were formed by chance meetings, common sympathies or friendships, professional, ideological or family links. The networks were something different, especially the intelligence networks. They could not be satisfied with more or less active sympathisers; they necessitated learning a technique. The intelligence networks were rather like spy-rings, and their agents had to learn how to observe, select and pass on their information; but it was not professional spying nor was it practised in enemy country but in one's own national territory occupied by the enemy; many sections of the population were involved.

Informing the Allies as to the disposition, movements and intentions of the enemy was in itself a form of aggression against it. But sabotage and violence against persons were direct action; with the poor resources at its disposal, the subjugated population tried to paralyse the enemy war-machine. They began with acts that were in easy reach—cutting telephone wires, attacks on isolated soldiers. Later, sabotage became part of a strategy linked with the advance of the Allied armies. Thus in occupied territories, war turned to such things as destroying transport and factories working for the enemy. Corporate bodies such as railwaymen or post office workers were to play an important role in this because of the opportunities offered by their profession. Other forms of sabotage were working to rule or an open strike. The culmination of these tactics was the 'scorched earth' policy which caused the local population as much suffering as the enemy, if not more.

The logical outcome of all these operations was to take up arms again. It began with groups (called *maquisards* in France and 'partisans' in the USSR) which undertook harassing operations—attacks on depots, on patrols, on collaborators or raids against villages. These groups operated in inaccessible districts of the occupied territory, in mountains or forests. Their chief weapon was their mobility; the scope and force of the action depended on the amount of co-operation they found amongst the population itself; they could not exist if it were hostile. In this way the Resistance movements could form a proper front, as in Yugoslavia or Russia, or rouse a whole people, as in France and Poland.

II THE ALLIES AND THE RESISTANCE

In all their activities, the Resistance movements would be rendered powerless had they to rely on their own resources; they needed to receive arms, ammunition, money, instructions and sometimes even instructors from outside. They had to fit into Allied strategy and even more important not obstruct it; they were of tactical importance only and it was not for them to choose how they should be used. That at least was the view of the big Allied powers towards them; poor but proud, the Resistance movements felt restive under this control but were unable to shake it off.

Until June 1941, Britain was alone in the war; she carried with her all the hopes of the occupied peoples, as she was sheltering the legal governments driven out of their countries by invasion. Britain tried to inject something of her determination into the subjected peoples. Broadcasting thus proved to be a powerful instrument of psychological warfare. The BBC organised thirty-five hours' broadcasting a day, directed at eighteen countries in twenty-three different languages. In 1943, the German department of the BBC comprised more than a hundred people. Thus the populations of the various countries were no longer left in ignorance of the way the war was going; they learnt about British successes and German setbacks; they were told what was happening in their own countries, of the enemy's depredations at their expense or of the way in which they were threatened by its intentions. They no longer felt isolated and they could receive advice and even instructions. Resignation was replaced by hope and a feeling of impotence by the will to act. The skill of the BBC lay in not copying Goebbels' consummate technique of lying. The BBC showed complete and utter frankness; it did not hide British failures; it appealed to reason, to the critical faculties and the better feelings of its listeners. Its action was carried further by parachute drops of pamphlets, newspapers and miniature books, but the effect of these was infinitesimal compared with that of the radio broadcasts which at regular intervals spread the good word into every home.

But at the same time, Britain looked on the Resistance movement as a sort of rearguard on the Continent. They expected to receive intelligence information from them, as for example news of German preparations for a landing. Military intelligence sent agents over to the Continent to form intelligence networks by recruiting volunteers amongst the nationals whose position in society made them good sources of information—such as engineers working in naval dockyards. For its part, the Ministry of Economic Warfare had formed a subversive warfare branch—Special Operations Executive (SOE)—with the task of organising, in all the occupied countries, sabotage of the enemy war effort, limited in scope, at carefully selected places and with small groups of agents.

Britain thus perfected a whole technique of underground warfare: 'personal messages' on the radio giving direct instructions to agents hundreds of miles away, in language that could be understood by them alone; training camps for agents; despatching men or materials by submarine or air; the manufacture of the appropriate tools—explosives such as malleable plastic, devices for two-way radio transmission, clandestine transmitters that became more and more powerful and easy to handle.

But Britain's influence could be more easily and effectively exercised in western than in central and eastern Europe, because of the distances involved. On the other hand, she allowed the Resistance movements in each country only limited independence; she was even afraid that they might launch out prematurely; she counselled caution and warned them to await better days. The attitude of the USSR after June 1941 was quite different.

When the USSR was invaded, Stalin made an appeal for help to Communist parties all over the world. He wanted them to begin fighting the occupying power without delay by all the means in their power, however limited, so as to pin down as many troops as possible and prevent their being sent to Russia. Communists everywhere responded to this appeal. Until now, they had professed the belief that the war was being waged between two rival imperialistic powers and that whatever the outcome it did not concern the people. And now, suddenly, they were to preach a patriotic war, a war to the knife; the French Communist party took over the traditionally anti-German slogans of the nationalists: 'One man, one Boche.'

The Communists supported and practised what they called 'immediate action', consisting of violence and sabotage, without worrying about enemy reprisals and the losses they would entail. But at the same time, they found the right words to appeal to the mass of the people; they explained that their wretched state, although indeed brought about by monopolistic capitalism, had been rendered intolerable by Hitler's aggression. So the social revolution must be achieved through national liberation. Except in Yugoslavia, the Communists in every country stretched out the hand of friendship to all the enemies of the occupying power, even if overnight they had been their opponents. They advocated the formation of broadly based 'national fronts'.

With the Communists, the Resistance movements became more popular and more incisive; strikes, stoppages and sabotage increased in the factories. In return, the occupying power used sterner measures; it took to shootings and taking 'hostages'; the blood of these martyrs inspired further volunteers who were brought into the Communists' orbit. Despite this, they received no help from the USSR; the latter was too heavily absorbed in her own fight and too much concerned about her own fate to be able to share any of her own resources. Russia did not organise anything resembling the British SOE; she sent weapons and equipment only to her own partisans. She merely issued instructions via the Comintern and these instructions were obeyed.

III RESISTANCE IN WESTERN EUROPE

The legal governments of Norway, Holland and Belgium were in London and in the occupied territories nobody questioned their legality. But their weakness made them entirely dependent on the British, who practically controlled the Resistance movements in the occupied countries, and even sent them articles already written for inclusion in the underground newspapers. In all these countries the Communist party played little part. The situation in France was completely different.

In Norway, where a landing was one of Churchill's obsessions to which he gave a periodical airing, surprise attacks—notably on the Lofoten Islands —were carried out by Norwegian commandos from London, with information and help from local resisters. Since it was organised by officers the Resistance movement assumed a military nature and was formed into one single group, the *Milorg*, under the actual commander of the Norwegian Army, General Ruge. Communications were established with the Shetland Isles which functioned with such regularity that they became known as the Shetland bus. One of the exploits of the Resistance movement was the partial sabotage of the 'heavy water' factory in March 1943.

On their part, the Norwegian population offered unswerving moral resistance to Quisling's attempts to organise them in the Nazi manner; academics, officials, the young and the sportsmen all refused to be shepherded into single movements. The Lutheran Church spoke out condemning collaboration. The High Court ceased to function. The high commissioner, Terboven, retorted by mass arrests—1,000 officers and 1,200 students were picked up in a single operation.

In Denmark the situation was different, as collaboration was official, since the German invasion had not changed either the régime or its leaders. But the Nazis were not very successful; in the 1943 elections 97 per cent of the votes went to democratic parties. Resistance started through the operations of the SOE; information for the British was communicated to Sweden by secret telephone. Then, as the war proceeded, the Danes gradually changed their attitude, especially after the measures adopted against the Jews, and the Danish authorities followed suit. Underground papers were circulated and organised sabotage began. Seven thousand Jews were saved and sent to Sweden. But the country was flat and unwooded and did not lend itself to guerrilla warfare.

Holland was no more suited to this type of warfare than Denmark. Her isolation in the middle of occupied countries with no outlet to the outer world was hardly conducive to underground activity. Yet it is remarkable that an underground was formed despite the attentions of the Germans and despite the activities of Mussert's movement. It was the arrest of Jews in Amsterdam that sparked off the first large-scale popular reaction in February 1941; it took the form of a sympathetic strike and some universities had to be shut down.

An underground press which had existed since the summer of 1940 published newspapers running to 80,000 copies (*I shall hold on, The Word, Free Holland*); in 1941, 120 secret newspapers were circulating; in 1943 there were another 150. At about the same date the first intelligence networks began to function; reports and messages reached London via Sweden or Geneva; escape organisations linked up with Belgian and French networks. But this activity was brought to a halt by a remarkable success on the part of German counter-intelligence services, who managed to take the place of the resisters, collecting the parachute drops intended for them and for some months transmitting false intelligence to the British. The harm thus caused was not made good until the end of 1943. But before then, many students and workers had refused to go to work in Germany. There were frequent brawls between Dutch Nazis and resisters.

In Belgium, memories of the occupation in 1914–18 were still very fresh in men's minds and the first underground newspapers took the titles of earlier days—*Libre Belgique* was a notable example. Escape networks automatically picked up the threads of the First World War; they extended their activities into France; thus 'Comète' had branches in Montauban and 'Pat O'Leary' in Marseilles.

From 1942 onwards, contact had been made with the government in London and there were thirty-five intelligence networks in operation, employing almost 10,000 people, including 300 agents who had been dropped by parachute. The Belgian government decided to let the 'Secret Army' have sole control of military Resistance while the 'Independence Front' was in charge of civil action. But there were other fringe groups that remained independent. In contrast with Holland, armed action had been contemplated, in the Ardennes.

IV THE FRENCH RESISTANCE

The French had no experience of underground warfare; they were utterly crushed by the defeat of their reputedly invincible army, without arms and condemned to a state of underdevelopment that produced privation, physical suffering and lack of spirit, and they were more than divided by their misfortunes. They were thus inclined to inertia, and this was encouraged by the Vichy régime's propaganda which asserted that it was the duty of every good citizen to obey Marshal Pétain—'think Pétain' was their injunction.

In these circumstances, the first volunteers in favour of continuing the struggle gathered round General de Gaulle in London, and the volunteers who had remained in France were anxious to help or join him. General de Gaulle thus found himself commanding a small army which fought in the Atlantic, in the skies of Europe, in Ethiopia, in the Sahara and in Libya. This army was gradually increased by additions from territories that came over to his cause, either voluntarily, like Equatorial Africa, the Cameroons and the Pacific islands or else after a fight, like Saint-Pierre-et-Miquelon, Syria, the Lebanon and Madagascar. Now and again the British let General de Gaulle speak to the French on the BBC. They also allowed him to form a special organisation, the *Bureau central de Renseignements et d'Action* which was to make contact with the French underground Resistance movement and provide it with arms and officers.

Free France was a conglomeration of Frenchmen from every political and social sphere. Its intention was to be merely a fighting organisation and its leader pledged himself to leave the French to decide the fate of their country for themselves after the war. However, it categorically and vigorously condemned both the Third Republic, which they regarded as responsible for the defeat and which had now disappeared as a result of that defeat; and the Vichy régime which was considered illegal and guilty of abject and premature submission to the occupying power.

In France, the customary framework of society no longer existed—political parties, trade unions or societies such as the Freemasons. The French were thus open to form fresh allegiances. They discovered General de Gaulle through the British radio; few, however, followed him immediately; for a long time to come the French people continued to put their trust in Marshal Pétain, who was universally respected. In the 'armistice army', however, in violation of the terms of the convention, certain branches of the service were stockpiling arms and arresting German agents.

Meanwhile an underground press was developing spontaneously and attacking the occupier, though not always the Vichy régime; heterogeneous groups of 'Resistance movements' grew up round these newspapers. For a long time they were to remain rather weak, lacking both substance and experience, short of money and without any means of action. However, they differed according to the zones. In Alsace, which had been annexed, any opposition was considered treason by the Germans; if they did not want to return to their country, the Alsatians who were sheltering in France could only rely for help on the Vichy authorities. In the *départements* of Nord and Pas-de-Calais, memories of the 1914–18 occupation contributed to the early appearance of a Resistance movement; in December 1940 the Lille *Feldkommandantur* reported forty telephone wires cut and a dozen other acts of sabotage. But groups such as 'La Voix du Nord' could only find local recruits and could influence only a restricted area.

In the occupied zone, there was a good deal of enterprising activity and the presence of the occupying power was a constant provocation. Officers organised intelligence branches, in co-operation with the armistice army's own intelligence services. Young ethnologists at the Musée de l'Homme formed a Committee of Public Safety which started circulating a roneoed broadsheet, *Résistance,* as early as December 15, 1940. Students published and distributed the newspaper *Défense de la France.* 'Ceux de la Résistance', 'Ceux de la Libération', 'Pantagruel', 'Valmy' and 'Arc' were little groups that had difficulty in avoiding the attentions of the Gestapo. 'Libération Nord' and 'l'Organisation civile et militaire' were larger because the first of them drew its recruits from trade unionists and Socialists and the second from reserve officers' associations and government and industrial executives.

In the southern zone where the absence of any occupying power reduced the risk, there were three large movements that extended to every *département*: 'Franc-Tireur' and above all Emmanuel d'Astier de la Vigerie's 'Libération Sud' and 'Combat'. Henri Frenay, the leader of the latter, showed himself to be a remarkable organiser; he created the structures of underground Resistance—secret army, propaganda, intelligence, false papers, accommodation, parachute drops, help for those in trouble.

After June 1941, the Communist party as a whole joined the Resistance movement, whereas previously only isolated members had been active in it. The party started the 'Front national', widely open to the Right. It became solidly established in both zones and produced specialised newspapers for every trade or professional association and, in theory, welcomed into its ranks the Communist party's action groups—the 'Francs Tireurs et Partisans' who, while preaching and seeking the collaboration of all the opponents of the occupying power, in fact preserved their independence.

Thus the Resistance developed an even greater tendency to form rival splinter groups, because the reappearance of the Communist party as an active force gave new life to the Socialist party. General de Gaulle's achievement was to be to unify it. His agents had already created intelligence networks, the most active of which was the 'Confrérie Notre-Dame'. But the General entrusted Jean Moulin, a former *préfet* who had joined him in London, with a far bigger political mission. With stubborn determination that was crowned by success, Jean Moulin set out first of all to co-ordinate the action of the Resistance movements in the southern zone and then those in the northern zone. By the middle of 1942 the non-occupied zone had its 'United Resistance Movements', all of whose volunteers were enlisted in one single 'Secret Army', under General Delestraint, who was appointed by General de Gaulle. At the same time, Jean Moulin provided the Resistance with joint organisations: a 'Research Committee', a department in charge of parachute drops and landing grounds, an underground press service, and a 'Solidarity Committee'.

Thanks to Moulin's activities, the Socialists, Communists and various moderate politicians acknowledged General de Gaulle's authority. Moreover de Gaulle's attitude had changed. He had promised to introduce a certain number of social reforms after the Liberation and thus appeared as a leader of a broader 'Front populaire'. Correspondingly, Marshal Pétain's popularity declined, because of the policy of collaboration which he represented. The armistice army's Resistance activities were curtailed by Laval when he returned to power; in any case, it was the work of a few groups of expert technicians, with no appeal to the masses.

Thus 'Gaullism' arose in France. It was not obedience to a blind trust in one man, General de Gaulle, but acceptance of the cause he represented: a refusal to collaborate, a refusal to give in, a continuation of the fight by all possible means inside and outside the country and the liberation, rebirth and transformation of France.

V RESISTANCE IN CENTRAL EUROPE

The first country to experience German occupation was Czechoslovakia. After March 1939, the Resistance was directed by President Beneš from France, where he had taken refuge. The problem was to maintain or re-establish communications with the country from outside and this had been achieved by August 1939. The first underground resisters were Czechs, soldiers and Communists, in two separate groups that were unfriendly but not enemies. Opposition to Germany was shown by mass gatherings—a strike of tramway workers on the anniversary of the Munich agreement, boycotting the feast of St Mathias, in spite of a thousand preventive arrests by the Gestapo. By January 1940, a 'Central Committee for Internal Resistance' (UVOD) was circulating underground literature and broadcasting thousands of messages a month to Paris and London by secret radio transmitters. Czechs enlisted in the German Army acted as informers and others organized sabotage in Germany itself.

The defeat of France was a 'second Munich'. Then, after the German-Soviet pact, the Communists broke violently with President Beneš' supporters, whom they even accused of helping 'the British colonial magnates in their dirty war'. For its part, the provisional Czechoslovak government in London started talks with the Polish government to form, after the war, a Polish-Czechoslovak confederation which could only mean once again creating a sort of 'cordon sanitaire' round the USSR.

When the USSR entered the war, everything changed. The Comintern's directives were followed to the letter by the Czech Communists; they called for national unity against the occupier. The USSR recognised the exiled Czech government and pledged itself to restoring Czechoslovakia to her former state after the war. For his part, President Beneš had drawn his conclusions from what had happened; he was now convinced that Czechoslovakia could in future only live with the backing of Soviet friendship. The wait-and-see attitude, more or less neutralistic, represented by President Hacha and his supporters was roundly condemned, both inside and outside the country.

On May 27, 1942, agents from London executed the 'protector' Heydrich. The occupying power's reprisals were appalling: the villages of Lidice and Lezaky were destroyed and their inhabitants exterminated; 10,000 people were arrested in Bohemia, 2,000 of them underground workers. The UVOD never recovered from these blows and continued to exist only in small ineffective groups. London issued instructions to go warily. The Soviet setbacks also forced the Communists to restrict their activities. But despite these momentary handicaps, Czechoslovakia herself was making a fresh start with her underground movement. Everyone had come to recognise that its existence was dependent on two factors: the need for better internal understanding between Czechs and Slovaks and a reconciliation with the Soviet Union.

The German occupation was nowhere harsher than in Poland, nor was any other people more united in resisting the occupier. Every political party, of both left and right, resisted. In 1939 the Communist party had played a very small part, both because its leaders had taken refuge in Moscow and because the party had been abolished by the ussr in the part of Poland that she was occupying; also the Moscow exiles had been prohibited from undertaking any political activity. The Polish people thus unreservedly recognised the authority of the exiled Polish government, which had moved from Angers to London and was under the presidency of a Liberal, General Sikorski. The composition of this government reflected concern for national unity but some of its members were very reactionary, both anti-Semitic and anti-democratic. For the exiled Poles, as for most of the Resistance workers inside the country, Poland had two enemies, both more or less equally loathed: Germany and the Soviet Union.

After the defeat of France, distance made communications between London and occupied Poland difficult. Between February 1941 and April 1942, the Polish government requested 104 air operations; only twelve were authorised, nine of which were successful. The British allowed the Polish section of soe a certain freedom which the exiled government was able to use to good effect. But on the other hand, the difficulties of communication, even by radio—the relatively few receiving sets in Poland had been confiscated by the Germans—forced the underground groups to work out their own activities. The many early small groups mainly formed themselves into the 'Secret Army' (ak).

The Soviet entry into the war did little to change the Poles' feelings towards the ussr; but it did create a new situation for General Sikorski. He went to Russia to negotiate an agreement with Stalin whereby Polish prisoners of war interned in Russia would be released to form a new Polish army. Sikorski would have liked this army to fight with the Red Army in the ussr. But Stalin raised all sorts of difficulties; he refused to make any guarantee about the Polish frontiers; in December 1941 he formed Polish Communists exiled in Moscow, some of whom had taken Soviet nationality, into a 'Polish patriots' group which did not recognise the authority of the London government. In these circumstances, it seemed wiser to despatch the new Polish Army, on its release from Soviet captivity, to the Middle East where it would be trained under the command of General Anders.

The Polish underground Resistance showed great activity; it drew up schemes for widespread sabotage operations which it put into effect—particularly against the railways to hinder traffic going to the USSR. It transmitted information concerning very large areas, collected either by Poles who had been sent to work in the Ruhr or from Poles serving in the Wehrmacht and who accompanied it in its advance up to the Volga. But however hardy and determined the Polish Resistance might be, it could not ignore the fact that, geographically, it was in the Red Army's sphere of influence and that same Red Army had invaded Poland and dismembered her in September 1939.

VI THE RESISTANCE IN THE BALKANS

After the March 1941 putsch and the invasion of Yugoslavia, King Peter went to London with his government and they were entirely cut off from their country. But in this hilly country where communications were difficult, the Wehrmacht was content merely to disrupt the army without occupying the whole territory. In the mountains there still existed units that had barely had time to be mobilised. In the heart of Serbia, in the Ravna Gora, Colonel Mihailović was thus able to retain control of his troops; he called them *chetniks*, in memory of the struggle against the Turks. His reputation soon spread beyond the borders of his own country; the exiled Yugoslav government was glad to make him their representative, in the field, with the title of War Minister. The British wished to help him but he was a long way away.

However, when the USSR entered the war, the Yugoslav Communist party, in accordance with Stalin's instructions, formed a military committee headed by Broz, otherwise known as Tito; this Communist party had few members and those were mainly in the towns; but some of its members had gained valuable military experience while fighting in the international brigades in Spain. The leaders set out to spread the good word and to set an example by their actions; on July 4, 1941, they gave the order for a national uprising; they followed this by liberating towns and installing new officials, after executing those accused of collaborating. Far from sacrificing their revolutionary programme to national unity, Tito's supporters advocated it as well as practising what they preached. They made it known that after the war the new Yugoslavia would be a federal state, totally transformed economically and socially by the revolution.

Stalin was alarmed by this political propaganda, which he found far too flamboyant and likely to jeopardise the broad anti-German alliance that he was advocating. At his urgent suggestion, Tito tried, unwillingly, to come to an agreement with Mihailović. But the latter made no secret of his 'pan-Serbianism', following the tradition of Alexander 1, and this caused concern to Tito who was a Croatian. On the strength of his title of War Minister and in pursuance of the orders from his government in London, Mihailović tried to take over the partisans into his command. Consequently, agreement between the two did not last very long and internecine strife began even in Serbia itself, Mihailović's own territory, when partisans tried to establish themselves there. The *chetniks* came off second best.

From this time onwards, Tito was a lone rider, despite Stalin's calls to order. He raised a 'proletarian army', without ranks, where fighting went hand in hand with training in Communist doctrine. Wherever he settled and however short his stay, Tito abolished the existing institutions and left only the party structure intact. On November 26 and 27, 1942, he called together a consultative assembly at Bihac, consisting of fifty-four delegates representing every area and every nationality in Yugoslavia; the 'Anti-Fascist Council of National Liberation' (AVNOY), which was directing the partisans' struggle, decided to introduce communal control of property, popular political education and the establishment of revolutionary Committees of Liberation.

This spectacular success resulted in the 'National Liberation Army' (ALNY), now about 80,000 strong, being attacked by a combined force of nearly thirty German, Italian, Bulgarian, Hungarian and Ustashi divisions. During the winter of 1942-3, the partisans were forced to keep on the move from Bosnia to Montenegro, fighting hard though ravaged by typhus. They were also attacked by the *chetniks* under Mihailović, who was scared by their revolutionary programme. In Yugoslavia, therefore, the struggle against the occupying power was also a civil war and a revolution as well.

The same thing happened in Greece and Albania. In Greece, the King and the government had taken refuge in Cairo and no longer had any authority over their country, which was governed by a group of collaborationist generals. As in Yugoslavia, the Resistance was born in the mountains; sometimes it was started by officers, at other times by the Communist party. All of them were enabled to arm and equip themselves thanks to the stores left behind by the British and to the equipment relinquished or hidden by the Greek Army. But though they were agreed in continuing the struggle and repudiating the monarchy, the two main organisations soon started to fight each other. The largest non-Communist group was the EDES under General Zervas; but there were other small fringe groups, such as Colonel Psaros' EKKA. The Communists formed the ELAS group.

In October 1942, the British sent a mission to Greece. Churchill considered that it belonged to the British sphere of influence and he intended to re-establish the monarchy there, if necessary against the will of the Greeks. The British mission tried to co-operate with all the Resistance movements, indiscriminately; they helped them organise acts of sabotage to hold up the supplies going to Rommel. The sabotage of the Gorgopotamos viaduct on the Athens–Salonica line on November 25, 1942 made a great stir. But this sort of co-operation between ELAS and EDES was short-lived; the British were powerless to do anything but sit back and watch their bitter struggles.

Later on General Davies' mission to Albania met the same disappointing fate. Enver Hodja's Communist 'National Liberation Movement' was opposed by the right-wing party's 'National Front' or 'Balli'. The two groups were as keen to eliminate each other in order to seize power after the war as they were to fight the Germans. The violent British objections and rebukes had no effect.

*

So, by the end of 1942, the European Resistance movements, though not as yet very strong, were growing everywhere. Except in Yugoslavia, they did not create any actual new operational theatre but their progress and increasing support from the people worried the occupying power. At the same time the Resistance movements were bringing about fundamental modifications in the structures of the countries where they appeared. They stood revealed as a powerful factor of political and economic change. Their divisions mirrored those of the extempore coalition fighting against Nazi Germany; their internecine strife pointed forward to the divisions that later became apparent in post-war Europe.

PART II
JAPAN'S GREATER ASIA

CHAPTER 1

The Break Between Japan and the United States

JAPAN had been waging war against China since 1931; despite her successes, she was becoming bogged down. The defeat of France and Britain's almost desperate isolation were to open up unlimited vistas for Japanese imperialism which stemmed equally from economic necessity and xenophobic nationalism.

I JAPANESE IMPERIALISM

On her mountainous archipelago, Japan had difficulty in supporting her highly prolific population of 73 million inhabitants. She had looked for additional resources through industrial development copied from the West and she had been remarkably successful. But even in this direction, there were serious obstacles in the way of her expansion: on her own territory she could find neither the sources of energy nor the raw materials that she needed; in order to obtain them she was obliged to dispose of a large part, of her manufactured goods to other countries at a low price. As her economic stability and progress was thus bound up with the size of her external trade, which had to be shipped by sea, her economy was vulnerable. It had already suffered from growing pains in 1919 and had been very seriously affected by the worldwide slump of the 'thirties.

Japanese nationalism, based on the firm belief in Japan's divine mission, had been greatly increased by legitimate pride in the happy combination of a recently acquired western technology and an original, jealously preserved, traditional culture. Though the principles of Shintoism, the national religion teaching the divine origin of the empire of the Rising Sun, were no longer blindly accepted by the Japanese ruling classes and though they knew that their country's material civilisation still lagged behind that of the white races, they would accept no suggestion of spiritual inferiority. Without exception, they believed that one day they would catch up with their rivals and then irresistibly outstrip them. They disagreed only in the means of winning this race for supremacy.

The emperor Hirohito, more interested in laboratory experiments than in politics, and the immense trusts that had arisen through industrialisation, were both supporters of peaceful methods; was not the whole of east Asia open to economic and political penetration that would be all the more easily achieved because of their proximity and racial affinity? But some powerful nationalist groups held diametrically opposed views. Thus the Kokuhonsha, the 'Society of the Foundations of the Country', with 200,000 members, based its action on the following four principles: Japan's unique religious character; anything that was contrary to this outstanding originality should be reformed; its special nature gave Japan a special mission in Asia; and anything standing in the way of this mission must be forcibly crushed.

These secret societies contained civil and military personalities of the highest rank, but more and more they were joined by active and lively young officers who, having risen from the poorer classes, were aware of the difficult material conditions in which the Japanese people were living and wanted to put an end to this state of affairs by victories and conquests which would show that the Japanese were invincible, a fact sufficiently obvious to them since the defeat of Russia in 1905. Any Japanese leaders considered too timorous by these fanatics were fit only to be murdered; amongst others, two Prime Ministers had met the dramatic fate of being shot down in their offices at pointblank range in 1930 and 1932.

Thus Japan had gradually become steeped in a Fascist mentality suited to their national temperament: the political institutions had not changed but the control of the state had to all intents and purposes passed into the hands of the Army and Navy, where the 'Young Turks' gradually imposed their extremist views. They were xenophobes and not anti-Semites; but as in Italy and Germany they preached the cult of violence, unswerving obedience and the conviction that only war could provide the solution to the country's difficulties.

In what direction should expansion take place and on which opponent should the blow fall? In this matter the two main ruling forces, the Army and the Navy, disagreed. The Army was tempted by the vast spaces within its reach, the immense areas of Asia; there it would come up against the USSR. The Navy, by its very nature, yearned for vast horizons over the seas; the colonial empires of the British, French, Dutch and Americans barred their way or were ripe for elimination.

II THE CHINA WAR

With her vast size and supposedly inexhaustible wealth of resources, China offered both the reserves of raw materials and the commercial outlet that the Japanese were seeking. Since 1930 they had been penetrating into China in two ways: their businessmen had invested all their available capital there, and, in the country itself, after a more or less deliberately provoked incident in 1931, their Korean-based Army had, on its own authority, occupied the north-eastern provinces. From there, whether Tokyo liked it or not, it had the firm intention of occupying Manchuria and advancing at least as far as Inner Mongolia; its only fault was being more royalist than the Emperor.

The war had got off to a good start as a result of China's great military weakness. The Japanese always adopted the same procedure; they shelled the towns and then went in with their armoured vehicles; unable to defend themselves, all that the Chinese could do was to abandon the town and withdraw inland. Thus Peking, Chang-kia-kow, Tai-yuan, Canton, Hangkow, Shanghai and other towns had fallen without striking a blow. By 1939 the Japanese army had conquered the richest part of China, her ports, communication routes and her few industrial centres; but in fact, a million Japanese were lost in the vastness of China. The Army had believed that it could deal with the 'Chinese incident' in a few months; but it was able to push out in any depth only a few tentacles in order to 'mop up' a region and remained unable properly to occupy the whole country. With a few exceptions, they found themselves facing an opponent who was elusive because he was non-existent. Japan was nibbling at China without digesting her.

In face of the Japanese threat, the Chinese government of Chiang Kai-shek, a disciple of Sun-Yat-sen, the founder of the republic and leader of the single party of the Kuomintang, had in 1937 become outwardly reconciled with its Communist opponent Mao Tse-tung. The Chinese government had moved its capital out of reach of the Japanese to Chungking in the mountains of the interior. It had sent its officers to be trained in Europe and it was trying its hand at guerrilla warfare, something which only the Communists showed themselves able to do. Mao Tse-tung had summed up its principles in four lines of verse:

> *When the enemy advances, I withdraw;*
> *When the enemy withdraws, I advance;*
> *When the enemy settles in, I disturb him;*
> *When the enemy is exhausted, I fight him.*

In fact, complete anarchy reigned in China. The Japanese had been able to play on her internal dissensions and her superficial unity. They had created the theoretically independent state of Manchukuo and set up a 'Chinese Republican Central Government' under a friend of Chiang Kai-shek's, Wang Tsin-wei, who had deserted to their side. They had raised troops of mercenaries and employed terrorist methods that the Chinese called 'the three Alls'—fire, massacre and loot.

In this way, China had lost many men and most of the territories on which she depended for her soldiers and her money. This ordeal had disrupted government and caused corruption and anarchy. If left to herself China would be unable to drive out the Japanese; she would have to receive arms and the necessary instructors from outside and these could reach her only via the Yünnan-Tonkin railway line and subsidiarily via the Burma 'road', which ran over high mountains. For her part, Japan was floundering in an endless war which was hindering the exploitation of the part of the country that she had conquered. Her blatant ambition was becoming a matter of concern to all the powers with interests in China. Germany's victories in Europe were going to create a new situation, favourable to Japan.

III DEVELOPMENTS IN JAPANESE POLICY
(September 1939–June 1941)

Chiang Kai-shek was being supplied by Britain and France, from the latter via Indochina. The United States, by virtue of their axiom of not recognising any monopoly situation of any sort in China, which in their view should be 'free for all,' were also opposed to Japanese imperialism. But before the war, Chiang Kai-shek had found his main support in the USSR; in particular it was Russian pressure that had induced Mao Tse-tung to recognise his authority, in theory.

The Japanese had joined the anti-Comintern pact against the USSR in 1936. It is possible, as the Japanese ambassador in Rome has claimed, that this pact contained a secret clause with Germany in which the two countries pledged themselves not to sign any non-aggression agreement with the USSR. In any case, the signing of the German-Soviet pact had been considered by Tokyo as violating a promise. But once her representations to Berlin had been rebuffed, Japan calmed down very quickly and drew realistic conclusions from the incident: the Soviet Union was now to be left in peace by her forces alone—an undeclared war on the Siberian frontier in 1938 had already given warning of this. She therefore immediately suggested to the USSR a diplomatic settlement of the frontier dispute between Mongolia and Manchukuo. She even contemplated a non-aggression pact with the USSR, if the latter stopped supporting Chiang Kai-shek. Germany offered her good offices to help this rapprochement.

For Japan this represented a change in her foreign policy and a hint of its future course. The rapid defeat of France and Britain's forced inertia confirmed this. Japan suddenly found herself with a free hand in south-east Asia, where the United States were now her only serious rival. On September 4, 1940, at a conference of the four chief ministers, the territorial limits of Japan's 'New Order', the area of her self-appointed mission in the Far East, were fixed not just to include China and Manchukuo but also French Indochina, Thailand, Burma, Indonesia, the Pacific islands and India. Siberia, which had previously been included, no longer figured in the list. Ever since July, the GHQ had been stressing that war with Britain and the United States might prove necessary to achieve these objectives.

As a start, there was the possibility of cutting off the supplies that Chiang Kai-shek was receiving via the Yünnan railway, which was French property. An ultimatum to the Vichy government was accepted after it had realised the impossibility of offering any resistance without American help, which was not forthcoming. Operational bases, aerodromes and the port of Haiphong were granted to the Japanese though not before they had bared their teeth—in September the Canton army attacked the French in Langson and it had called off the attack only on the express orders of the Emperor.

After this success, however, Japan adopted a hesitant policy. She was weighing up the pros and cons of caution and peaceful advance, advocated by the Emperor, the diplomats, the businessmen and part of the Navy which was worried by the shortage of fuel oil in the event of a conflict with the USA and of a sudden strike, which now seemed possible owing to an exceptionally favourable combination of circumstances; convinced of its invincibility, the Army was urging immediate action on these lines and was warmly supported in the government by the War Minister, General Tojo. The Prime Minister Prince Konoye was striving to satisfy the military without going as far as open war; but the military leaders were thoroughly determined to go their own way, in the best interests of the country.

The anti-American trend of Japanese policy was confirmed by the signing of the tripartite pact in September 1940, whereby Japan received Germany's and Italy's agreement and support for the creation of a Greater East Asia Co-Prosperity Sphere in the vast area granted her in the proposed carve-up of the world. In October 1940, a Japanese mission went to the Dutch East Indies to arrange for supplies of tin, crude oil and rubber but found some difficulty in obtaining them.

Germany was very keen to reap the benefit of her agreement with Japan. By using the threat that Japan represented for the British Commonwealth in Asia, she thought that she might induce Britain to end the war. And by the prospect of a war on two fronts which this threat also offered, she hoped to persuade the United States not to abandon their neutrality. She thus encouraged Japan to confine her attentions to the weakest opponent, the British Commonwealth. In February 1941, Ribbentrop stated to the Japanese ambassador, Oshima: 'The Reich and Japan are both in the same boat. German defeat would mean the end of Japan's imperial ambitions, too. It would seem to be in Japan's interests to ensure that while the war is on she achieves the positions that she wishes to have when peace is concluded.'

This appeal did not fall on deaf ears; in January 1941, the Japanese General Staff was examining how to attack Singapore. But the German-Japanese agreement was not entirely free from suspicion and reservations. The immense expansion of a coloured people did not inspire great joy in the hearts of the racialist specialists amongst the Nazis. When Japan requested a completely free hand in Indochina and the Dutch East Indies, Germany expressed the wish that the *status quo* should remain unchanged: the German ambassador in Tokyo even described Japan's action in Indochina as 'a breach of trust'. Ribbentrop wanted to 'retain this bone of contention amongst the Pacific powers'.

On two occasions, a Chinese diplomat, followed by Kurusu, the Japanese ambassador in Berlin, and a Japanese general, asked for the Reich to mediate in order to settle the 'Chinese incident'. This idea was supported by Ott, the German ambassador in Tokyo. He considered that a peaceful bloc could be formed in Asia with Japan, China and the USSR. This would force the USA to remain very much on the alert in Asia and consequently reduce their freedom of action in Europe. But Germany refused to mediate between China and Japan.

Perhaps she was afraid that, once Japan had escaped from her Chinese wasps' nest, she would launch out on a war with the USA which would then inevitably fall back on to her. In any case, it is probable that the coolness of the support that she received from her ally confirmed Japan in her intention of pursuing her own policy alone by her own means. Failing peace with China, before embarking on any other venture, she needed to be covered in her rear by the neutrality of the USSR. Since Stalin was similarly concerned, the agreement which he and Matsuoka signed during the latter's brief visit to Moscow in April 1941, surprising as it might seem at first sight, stemmed very logically from the immediate interests of the two parties, as a not too remote consequence of the German-Soviet pact. It confirmed that Japan had chosen to direct her expansion towards the

South Seas. It left Japan and the USA a little more in direct confrontation, with the risk of a conflict accepted by the former. How, for their part, did the Americans see their policy in the Pacific and their relations with Japan?

IV THE DEVELOPMENT OF AMERICAN POLICY

The Americans had watched with concern Japan's takeover of Manchuria. They had condemned the treaty violations and had not recognised Manchukuo. However, they had carefully refrained from any gesture liable to lead them into a conflict for which they were unprepared. Businessmen were anxious for continued good relations with their Japanese customers or suppliers; before 1939, the Army was not strong and thinking only of defending its own continent, or at the most of defending the Philippines. The Navy, though better armed, wanted its strength to be increased and it did not want to fight on two fronts.

In these circumstances, the State Department followed a policy of extreme patience and caution. In spite of all their interests in China—capital investments, schools, hospitals, missions—which were jeopardised by the Sino-Japanese war, the United States confined themselves to making formal protests and advising their subjects to leave the country. The President even warned American citizens that they would transport weapons into China at their own risk. Passports were refused to airmen engaged as instructors by the Chinese.

Roosevelt was as conscious of the seriousness of the threat from Japan as of the danger from Germany. Grew, the American ambassador in Tokyo, recommended taking a tough line, to intimidate the Japanese, which was, in his view, the only way to avoid a trial of strength with them. Chiang Kai-shek's government was very popular in the States; it was spending enough money there to achieve that. Chiang was considered an American-style democrat and his wife's family, the Songs, as well as his wife herself, had a large number of friends in a wide variety of circles. In a word, it would have been quite easy to arouse American enthusiasm for China against the Japanese—the success of Pearl Buck's novels was a measure of this infatuation. In any case it would have been easier than arousing the Americans against Germany in favour of France. But Roosevelt was well aware of the worldwide nature of his obligations and he declined to make any premature or precipitate choice between Europe and Asia.

Accordingly Churchill's pleas in July and September 1940 that American ships should be sent to Singapore fell on deaf ears, as did Chiang's appeals for help or the suggestion of the Dutch East India authorities to hold a conference to organise the joint defence of the archipelago. The Vichy government's approaches at the time of the Japanese ultimatum over Indochina were equally unsuccessful.

Roosevelt was convinced that war between the United States and Japan was inevitable but he was endeavouring to delay it in order to be in a better position to meet it. He undertook limited and cautious retaliatory measures aimed at convincing the Japanese that America was taking a firm line. The entry of the Canton Army into Indochina was thus met by a partial embargo on goods indispensable for Japanese industry, starting with steel and scrap iron. The list of these goods grew gradually longer, with crude oil being kept as the final trump card. At the same time, considerable loans were granted to China, who was allowed to join the lend-lease club in May 1941.

However, the President was inhibited in this course of action by Britain's difficulties which he wished to remedy first. In January 1941, he came to an agreement with the British Premier that in the event of America's entering the war, Germany would be enemy number one; Japan would come later. This decision was not made known to the American public, which, even if it was not interested in Singapore, was concerned about Manila. But the decision did not prevent the Navy from keeping its eyes firmly fixed on the Pacific, although it did force Roosevelt to proceed more gently with Japan.

On April 9, 1941, the Secretary of State, Cordell Hull, informed the new Japanese ambassador of the American conditions for the maintenance of good relations between their two countries: respect for the territorial integrity of nations; equal rights and the principle of the 'open door' in matters of colonial expansion; non-intervention in the affairs of other countries; the *status quo* in the Pacific. It was not a very conciliatory attitude; but there was no threat of breaking-off relations and the door was left ajar for a diplomatic solution. Moreover, these rules were to be valid for the future only; the failure to mention the past was an implicit recognition of Manchukuo. 'If the Japanese government accepts these principles,' concluded Cordell Hull, 'they can serve as a basis for fresh negotiations.'

Prince Konoye's view was to accept these proposals and start talks; 'the Chinese incident' he thought, could be settled only by agreement with the USA; any advance southwards by force of arms would be fraught with immense danger; successful talks would enable Japan's stocks of raw materials to be peacefully replenished. But the Foreign Affairs and War Ministers, Matsuoka and Tojo, had different views from the Prime Minister's and they carried the day. Japan merely offered the United States a non-aggression pact, which, considering the offer inadequte, they rejected.

Attitudes were hardening on both sides. However, on June 21 the Americans moved a step forward: if the Chinese matter could be settled satisfactorily for both parties, they said, normal trading could be resumed between the two countries.

V THE JAPANESE-AMERICAN NEGOTIATIONS
(June–December 1941)

Germany's attack on the USSR on that same day opened up a new phase in Japanese-American relations. Once again, Germany had acted without consulting and without even informing Japan. And now here she was inviting Japan to start a war against Russia too, when only a few months earlier she had been persuading her against it! Although the ink on the non-aggression pact with the USSR was hardly dry, Matsuoka was tempted by the prospect of an easy conquest of Siberia. But there the Japanese would find neither the raw materials nor the commercial outlets which they were seeking. The Army pointed out that it was an unhoped-for chance to lay hands on them where they could be found; Britain had her back to the wall and the Soviet Union, too, for the moment; the United States were not ready. Its decision was irrevocable and it carried the day. Japan would expand, by force of arms, into the South Seas.

Negotiations now began between Japan and the United States. It is difficult to say whether they were sincere or whether on both sides their only purpose was to gain time with each party hoodwinking the other. It is possible that they may have been complicated by misunderstandings that have been analysed by the American historian Butow: the inexperience and ignorance of English of Admiral Nomura, who did not communicate to his government until May American proposals that had been made the previous month; the intervention of certain officious emissaries who led the Japanese to believe that negotiations had started and thus that the Americans were prepared to be conciliatory whereas the latter were making the start of actual negotiations conditional on a mimimum agreement on principles. One certain thing was that each side hoped to influence the other by a show of toughness and considered that the best way to bring the other round was to be highhanded. Was it not being said in Washington that Prince Konoye had a photograph of Roosevelt in his room?

However, in July 1941, after Konoye had got rid of the tiresome Matsuoka, a sort of compromise was reached between the opposing Japanese factions; it was decided that as a concession to the Emperor, Konoye and the Navy they would continue to negotiate but that at the same time certain precautionary steps must be taken in order to be in a favourable position should negotiations break down. The generals did not fail to take advantage of this. The importance of the views of the Army in the field had been frequently demonstrated by its tendency to act on its own initiative, so much so that before going to Washington Admiral Nomura had felt compelled to go the rounds of the Korean and Chinese headquarters. But the order to send troops into southern Indochina in July 1941 came from Tokyo. The Vichy government knuckled under all the more easily because this time it was under pressure from Germany who was anxious to see Japan going on the warpath. In addition, after urging the Siamese to claim part of Cambodia, Japan had placed herself in their good books by insisting on acting as mediator to ensure that they obtained it, despite the fact that their fleet had been smashed by a tiny French naval force from Indochina. It was clear that this new step was aimed at Malaya and Singapore and possibly Burma as well.

Coming as it did in the middle of the negotiations, this step persuaded the Americans of the bad faith of the Japanese, the more so as their secret services had succeeded in deciphering the secret code used by Tokyo in its messages to the Japanese embassy in Washington. Sumner Welles therefore informed Nomura that 'such acts were opposed to the spirit of the current discussions and would make any further negotiations pointless.' A few days later, Roosevelt took the gravest step that had ever been contemplated: he froze Japanese assets in the United States and imposed an actual embargo on fuel oil. At the same time General MacArthur was appointed commander of a new operational theatre, the Far East, the creation of which, as well as MacArthur's appointment, hardly seemed inspired by thoughts of peace. The revelation of Japan's duplicity appears to have made Roosevelt switch round completely in the space of forty-eight hours; he had just had the suggestion made to Nomura that Indochina should be declared neutral when he learned that the Japanese troops had established themselves there with the agreement of the Vichy government. His threefold decision caused the situation to deteriorate without hope of recovery. In particular the Japanese leaders were convinced that being deprived of dollars amounted to a blockade and would doom the Japanese economy to bankruptcy within two years. A decision must therefore be taken without delay: should it be peace or war?

However, the German suggestion of attacking Vladivostok was dismissed by the Japanese cabinet. Prince Konoye obtained permission to make one further attempt; he would ask for an interview with Roosevelt in person. General Tojo agreed to this only on condition that this approach should not stand in the way of opening hostilities with the USA if it emerged that 'the President of the United States was unable to understand Japan's intentions'. And as speed was essential in order to avoid 'economic strangulation' on September 5, the Japanese cabinet took some very grave decisions: it would reach a state of readiness for war by the end of October and if, by that date, it had not received satisfaction, it would make 'the decision to prepare for war'. The Emperor showed some reluctance but allowed the Army to convince him that the Pacific would be conquered within three months.

From this time onwards, the bogus negotiations in Washington were to be paralleled by real preparations for launching a campaign, which, moreover, were kept from the Japanese negotiators Nomura and Kurusu, the latter having been despatched specially to assist the former; both of them were keen to continue the talks and bring them to a successful conclusion. But they had been instructed to communicate to the Americans proposals that were so uncompromising as hardly to be acceptable: nonintervention in China; closure of the 'Burma road' by the British; no further aid to Chiang Kai-shek; a pledge not to undertake hostile action against Japan; agreement to hand over to Japan 'the necessary raw materials'; American support for the 'establishment of close economic relations between Japan on the one hand and the Dutch East Indies on the other'. In a word, Japan was asking the USA to acknowledge her supremacy in the Pacific and in return for these enormous demands, Japan made no concessions whatsoever; she would evacuate Indochina, the cause of the increased tension, 'only after a fair peace has been established in the Far East'.

Did the Japanese think that, in their concern over the major German successes in the USSR, the United States would show themselves more conciliatory in Asia? If so they had made a big mistake: Cordell Hull's reply merely recalled 'the fundamental principles that the American government and people had made their own'. It was clear, after such a reply, that Roosevelt would not now agree to meet Konoye and meanwhile the autumn deadline was approaching. Yet Konoye spoke out in favour of continuing negotiations; he then received a clear ultimatum from Tojo: 'Decisions are needed that can be taken only by another cabinet.' At the same time, as if fortuitously, an attempt was made on Konoye's life. He resigned and on October 18, General Tojo formed a government, seven of whose fourteen members were either generals or admirals; Admiral Tojo became Minister of Foreign Affairs. Ribbentrop urged them to be firm but they needed no urging.

On November 3, having obtained the assurance that, in the event of war with the United States, Germany would follow Japan, Tojo sent Nomura 'the final Japanese proposals'. At the same time, on November 5, without waiting further, Secret Operational Order no. 1 was transmitted to the Navy; its instructions were that the American Far Eastern Fleet should be destroyed as soon as hostilities began. What was the point then of Nomura's suggestion of evacuating the south of Indochina in exchange for unfreezing the Japanese assets? Cordell Hull replied that, in any case, the United States wished to be assured that 'Japan was adopting peaceful ways without any ulterior motive and was relinquishing her warlike aims.' This blunt refusal matched the Japanese hypocrisy.

The dialogue was at an end. Roosevelt sought the advice of his military leaders; the Joint Army and Navy Board as well as General Marshall and Admiral Stark were for pursuing the negotiations with a view to gaining a few more months, whilst reminding him, however, that Germany was the main enemy to be brought down, something of which Roosevelt was in any case personally well aware. The President had perhaps reached the conclusion that war was inevitable and that every effort must be made to saddle Japan with the responsibility for breaking off negotiations. He probably thought that the American public, whom he wished to convince that the present war was *their* war and who were still rather reluctant, would prove more keen on going to war if their first enemy was Japan. In any case, between November 22 and 26, his attitude hardened and he seems to have been aware that this hardening would probably lead to a surprise attack by the Japanese. And anyway, although General Tojo had couched the last proposals passed on by Admiral Nomura in the form of an ultimatum expiring first of all on November 25 but then postponed till November 29, he had not waited for the American reply to give Admiral Yamamoto the order to take up the positions required for a state of impending hostilities.

It is difficult to imagine a breakdown more easily accepted by both sides. Cordell Hull handed over his reply to Nomura on November 26, when he knew perfectly well that the ultimatum had expired. In his memoirs, Cordell Hull wrote humorously: 'The sword of Damocles hanging over our heads was fixed to an alarm-clock.' On the same day, Tojo was of the opinion that it was not possible to continue negotiations, whereas Nomura thought that a new date had been fixed for the ultimatum, November 29. The Japanese negotiators, who had been kept in ignorance until the very end, were only informed of the breakdown on December 7. The Emperor had advised strongly against attacking without warning; but by the time the memorandum considered as a declaration of war was handed in at Washington on December 8, the Japanese fleet had started operations and the British were attacked in Malaya without receiving any document notifying the opening of hostilities.

Both parties seemed to be glad to be going to war, which each either wanted or thought inevitable. But the Japanese military leaders had chosen their own time and place and they would benefit immensely from their surprise attack. As for Roosevelt, he had indeed achieved the awakening of the American conscience which he had been seeking; but at the cost of a tragic disaster, the destruction of the American fleet at Pearl Harbour. It is true that Japan's partner, Hitler, had not been informed of the decision by his ally any more than had their joint opponents. And so, after starting a war with the firm resolve to fight only one front at a time, the Führer had launched his people into a fight to the death with the three greatest powers in the world.

VI THE ATTACK ON PEARL HARBOUR

The idea of an attack by carrier-based aircraft against the American fleet in Pearl Harbour in the Hawaiian Islands came from Admiral Yamamoto, who in 1941 commanded the 'combined fleet', the highest operational command in Japan. He had great difficulty in obtaining agreement for it. Indeed, earlier Japanese plans had provided for the quickest possible occupation of areas rich in raw materials—the Navy was thinking particularly of crude oil which was in very short supply. The means were not available to launch major attacks in two directions and for different, if not divergent, purposes.

In addition, an attack in strength on Pearl Harbour seemed an extremely risky operation to the naval general staff and their head, Admiral Nagano. It would indeed mean committing all the large aircraft-carriers in one single operation. Were it to fail it might prove an irreparable disaster. Or more simply, the American fleet might be at sea and the lengthy expedition, deprived of its target, would result only in delaying the rich conquests that were earnestly desired. Success also required complete surprise; how could one guarantee that the fleet would not be detected during the 2,800 miles that it would have to cover?

In Admiral Yamamoto's view, as long as the United States possessed a powerful fighting fleet, it would provide a formidable threat for the new Japanese empire; thus it was necessary to begin by rendering it harmless; in this way, there would be time to fortify a whole ring of islands before the fleet could be repaired or built up again; to these arguments Yamamoto added the threat of resigning if they were not accepted.

His stubbornness was rewarded; suddenly, in October 1941, the Navy adopted his plan. It was known that, during manoeuvres, the American fleet was accustomed to put in at Pearl Harbour on Friday and sail again the following Monday; this was why the attack was fixed for Sunday, December 7 (December 8 in Japan). The Navy kept its secret to itself; since it had decided to make war, its plan of campaign was its own affair and it is probable that the Prime Minister, Tojo, was not completely informed until the decision had been taken. The Emperor, the other ministers, the army leaders and the Japanese people learnt about it, like the Americans, once the attack was over.

The raid raised a number of problems. Its success depended on the use of air torpedoes, but the water in the Pearl Harbour roadstead was shallow; the torpedoes would explode if they hit the bottom; it was not until October 1941 that a method was developed of stabilising air torpedoes by means of special ailerons. On the other hand, all the ships engaged would need to have an extremely long range of action, greater than that of some of the aircraft-carriers and most of the destroyers. It was decided to refuel them at sea on the outward journey as close as possible to the target area and let them make the return trip under their own resources by using petrol containers carried as cargo. The major obstacle to this procedure and one which was solved only after much discussion and cutting a good deal of red tape, was an article in the Navy regulations forbidding the use of bilges as cargo holds.

As the Americans often anchored their vessels in pairs in the Pearl Harbour roads, it seemed wise to supplement the torpedo operation with dive bombing. But there was a shortage of heavy bombs and so they had to be improvised by converting armour-piercing shells. All these preparations were concluded only at the last minute.

In addition, the aircraft-carriers taking part in the operation were short of aircrew and they could only be brought up to strength by calling on the pilots left in Japan. Once all these problems had been settled, the fleet had only one month in which to practise; it made use of it in the best possible conditions, in a stretch of water in the south of Kyushu which was shaped like the Pearl Harbour roads. The attacking technique of the torpedo-carrying aircraft and their height and speed were most carefully worked out.

And so, in a venture that was not devoid of danger, the Japanese deployed a combat fleet of unprecedented power, consisting of 4 battleships, 2 heavy cruisers, 6 aircraft-carriers and 10 destroyers; they had sent on ahead 22 long-range submarines and 5 midget submarines, armed with scaled-down torpedoes, each manned by one man which could penetrate into the outer harbour despite anti-submarine netting. It had been decided not to use landing troops, as much in order to avoid the extra burden and delay for the convoy as not to weaken the expeditionary forces intended for the Philippines and Malaya. The Pearl Harbour operation was thus, if complex in its detailed execution, extremely simple in its conception; it was merely a bombardment, lasting some hours, of a predetermined target by aircraft and warships; once the operation was completed, they would withdraw. It was a raid but on a massive scale and only of value if it proved decisive; in a word, a gamble.

What were the American defences? Lying some ten miles from Honolulu, Pearl Harbour is a roadstead entered through a narrow channel. As it was barely deep enough for large vessels, the latter were moored together at the most suitable spot. There was so little room that any manoeuvring could lead to a collision and the congested harbour could turn into a trap if a large vessel were sunk in the channel, some two miles long and a quarter wide. The anti-submarine detecting installations, the warehouses, arsenal, airfields, docks, workshops and oil-storage tanks, were completely uncamouflaged. From the top of the hills surrounding it, the outer harbour was clearly visible and nothing would be hidden from any close observers, of whom there was no shortage amongst the 100,000 Japanese on the island. So Admiral Yamamoto's squadron knew the enemy's defences with extreme accuracy; through observations transmitted by radio in an agreed code, he had learned that the Americans were not flying barrage balloons and had not put out any anti-torpedo netting; less pleasant was the news that three aircraft-carriers which had been expected to be at Pearl Harbour had left. But the attackers knew that at 7 o'clock every Sunday, the radar team left its post and was not replaced. The attack was timed to the minute.

It came as a complete surprise and achieved complete success. Out of 8 American battleships in the harbour, 7 were sunk and 1 damaged; 10 other ships were lost. Of the 394 aircraft in Oahu, 188 were destroyed and 159 others damaged. American casualties totalled 3,581 of which 2,403 were killed. In two whirlwind waves of aircraft, of which a mere 29 were shot down, the Japanese eliminated both the defences of the harbour and the major ships in the American Pacific surface fleet. Within the space of two hours naval superiority in the Pacific had passed into the hands of Japan.

The immensity of the disaster filled the American public first with stupefaction and then with anger; after the war, Roosevelt's opponents used it to blacken his memory. The ensuing large-scale inquest revealed incredible incompetence. First of all, it was discovered that Admiral Richardson had continually repeated his warnings against crowding the fleet into Pearl Harbour and had recommended its return to the us Pacific coast. In this, he came up against his superiors who were anxious to intimidate Japan; President Roosevelt had decided against Admiral Richardson's advice.

But in that case, since, against expert advice, the fleet was remaining in Pearl Harbour for diplomatic rather than military reasons, why was it not better protected? After the war Admiral Theobald undertook the role of public prosecutor. He drew attention to the many indications pointing to a raid on the harbour. In particular, it was known that twice a week the Japanese consul in Honolulu informed Tokyo regarding the ships' movements. On December 7 a Japanese midget submarine had been sunk in the channel. Was the incompetence of the naval and military authorities on the spot at fault? Admiral Kimmel and General Short pointed out that they had certainly been kept informed of the gravity of the situation but had never been warned that an attack was imminent. They had thus been unable to prepare for it; it had been detected at the very last minute and too late by two soldiers who had remained rather later than usual at their radar sets.

Responsibility, if responsibility there was, thus lay with the men at the top. When interrogated by the Investigating Commission, the Secretary of War, Stimson, and the Chief of Staff, General Marshall, stated that although they did indeed suspect a Japanese attack to be imminent, they were convinced that it would be launched against the Philippines. Accordingly they had given only a guarded warning to those responsible for the defence of Pearl Harbour on November 27 in order to avoid revealing to the Japanese that their intentions had been discovered because their diplomatic—but not their naval—code had been broken. All this demonstrated a rather alarming lack of preparation and excessive optimism on the part of the Americans.

Could one go further and imagine that President Roosevelt had knowingly let the Japanese have their head in order to shock American public opinion into awareness? He might, in a word, have been subtly provoking the Japanese who had then merely gone rather too far. The upsurge of American isolationism after the war lent force to the attacks on these lines which the Republicans made on their Democrat opponents, with the dead President providing the stick with which to beat his successor. But though there is no doubt that Roosevelt had very skilfully built up a pattern of acts irreconcilable with neutrality, above all against Germany, without declaring war, leaving the potential enemies of the United States the responsibility for the ultimate step, it cannot be proved that he had considered it necessary to expose the American fleet to such danger in order to set a trap for the Japanese. As M. Latreille has written, 'ever since politicians have been seeking means of preventing war, it has never been known whether it is better stubbornly to pursue a compromise that might be construed as weakness or to display very firm determination which might become foolhardiness.'

The Pearl Harbour attack did nonetheless have incalculable consequences. Militarily, the outcome proved less disastrous in the long run than might have been feared. Morison has pointed out that the departure of the three American aircraft-carriers and the fact that fortunately the dockyard was not destroyed still left the Americans with their most effective means of retaliation and the possibility of making good the losses. On the other hand the raid had revealed the Japanese's remarkable qualities of ingenuity, boldness and courage; but its success only partly disguised a relative weakness inherent in Japanese naval power, which had had to be mobilised almost in its entirety for this one single operation.

On the American side, this aggression roused public opinion much more than the loss of the Philippines would have done. The activities of the 'America First' committee stopped abruptly. Helped by racialism, national unanimity was reached much more easily and completely against the cowardly hypocritical Japs than against the Germans. President Roosevelt declared: 'We have to realise that modern war, as waged by the Nazis, is a repulsive business. We did not want to join in. But now we are in and we are going to fight with all our resources.' And the American nation backed him up completely.

Thus began the process which was to turn the greatest economic power in the world into the world's greatest military power. With his wide-ranging view of the world situation, his infallible understanding of his compatriots and his supreme skill in the choice of the appropriate means and arguments, President Roosevelt had succeeded in leading the United States exactly where he wished them to go. The United States was going to war without any predetermined aims; she had no territorial claims to make, no historic defeat to avenge and no hereditary enemy to destroy. She would, of course, be fighting in defence of her long-term national interests but above all for a certain conception of society, of freedom and of international law and morality. Her bitter initial defeat was not going to divert her from her main objective: the defeat of Germany. This view of the war, added to her lack of experience and inadequate preparation, was going to lead to a succession of disasters against Japan.

CHAPTER 2

Japan's Lightning War

WITH the advantage gained by her agression, for almost two years Japan was going to show herself superior to her opponents, on land and sea, and she used this superiority to carve herself out an immense empire.

I THE JAPANESE FORCES

With her 100 million inhabitants, 73 in the islands and 27 in Korea and Formosa, Japan possessed vast reserves of manpower; her troops were both well-trained and fanatically indoctrinated.

Her war fleet was almost as strong as the British Royal Navy. It consisted of some 15 battleships, 5 of them of more than 40,000 tons, 10 aircraft-carriers, 50 cruisers, 110 destroyers and 80 submarines. But the only really new warships were some of the aircraft-carriers; most of them —and in particular all the escort vessels—were converted passenger-ships or tankers; though the former were fast, the speed of the latter was less than 20 knots. The war fleet had 1,350 aircraft; the 450 shipborne aeroplanes were a formidable but limited striking force.

Despite the million men tied down in China the Japanese had large and formidable ground forces available; these men had experience in numerous landing operations and they were equipped for mountain and jungle warfare as well as being accustomed to monsoon conditions and great heat.

The land-based air force comprised 3,000 aircraft, rather few in view of the remoteness of the targets. A programme did exist to build 30,000 aircraft for the Army and 30,000 for the Navy but construction had been delayed and the Japanese aeronautical industry did not have the necessary equipment for mass-production.

These shortcomings throw light on the future difficulties of the Japanese war economy. It was true that mining output had increased threefold and steel production doubled between 1919 and 1939; the industry was highly concentrated and often modernised but by world standards, it was not very powerful. In addition, the country could not be fed from home production alone.

Moreover, all this potential had not been completely devoted to the war effort. While state control of foreign trade, currency, prices and wages had existed since 1937, the essential factor, that is heavy industry, remained outside the government's authority because of the immense power and the independence of the large trusts.

Above all, the Japanese economy was completely reliant on its shipping; it had to import 60 per cent of its raw materials, including 75 per cent of its iron ore, 60 per cent of its copper, 84 per cent of its lead and tin, 89 per cent of its bauxite and the whole of its rubber and nickel. In anticipation of an embargo, enormous quantities of crude oil had indeed been stockpiled, amounting to 43 million barrels which, it was estimated, would cover two years' consumption; but it was calculated that 16 million barrels would have to be imported in the second year of the war and 30 million in the third year.

If it is remembered that communication between the countless, unequally developed islands of the archipelago could obviously be maintained only by sea, the extent of the immense burden resting on the shoulders of the Japanese Merchant Navy can be fully appreciated. With a tonnage of six million, the merchant fleet was indeed largely modern—38 per cent of its ships were less than ten years old; their average speed and uniformity of construction were the highest in the world; their quality was excellent—in particular, their enormous fuel capacity enabled very long distances to be covered.

This merchant fleet was entirely under the control of the Army and the Navy, thus ensuring that it would be used to the best possible advantage for the war effort; but on the other hand the war fleet had requisitioned a large number of freighters in order to convert them into auxiliary cruisers or transport vessels for men and equipment. In December 1941, only 37 per cent of the normal fleet remained available. It was questionable whether this would suffice to cover the enormous amount of freight transport required. One Japanese shipowner had estimated the need at 20 million tons.

Like Germany, Japan was thus condemned to win a war only if it was short. Her earlier successes, the raid on Pearl Harbour, the advantage of having the initiative, the discipline and self-sacrificing qualities of her troops, in addition to the inadequate preparation, dispersal and divided objectives of her opponents, seemed an earnest of victory. But her tasks were as many and varied as they were immense. She had to do the following and do them quickly: conquer an empire, organise it, protect its internal lines of communication, fortify its outposts against American counter-attacks, fight and win in defence of these outposts, convince the conquered peoples that their future must lie with their conquerors and harmonise their economies with Japan's. All this had to be done before the Americans had converted their unlimited industrial potential into armament factories. And since Pearl Harbour, no new strike of any size could be made against the USA; now in their homeland, the Americans were out of reach of the Japanese forces; the latter, on the other hand, or at least, their forward positions, were not out of reach of the Americans.

II CONDUCT OF THE WAR IN JAPAN

The powers controlling the Japanese war effort consisted of a sham and a reality.

The sham was the theocratic and theoretically unrestricted authority of the Emperor as the combined political, military and religious head of the nation. In theory, he was assisted by advisers who, according to the constitution, bore the entire responsibility of the Emperor's actions and were answerable to the Diet. In fact, the latter had no authority; its functions did not extend beyond legislating and passing the Budget. Although free to behave as an absolute sovereign, the Emperor had chosen to be a constitutional monarch and follow the advice of his counsellors. He was, of course, kept informed and important decisions were taken only when he was present and with his approval; in fact, he listened and said nothing; he had the semblance of command but instead followed his subordinates who were the real holders of power. Bowing obsequiously they would present reports to him and he approved their conclusions, even when he sometimes expressed some reservations. Authority belonged to him and he could always recover it but he had relinquished his responsibility and took no active initiative.

The real power thus lay in the hands of the Emperor's advisers. In theory also, these were of two kinds: the government and the high command; in practice, they tended to form one only, the high command. Even before the war and more so throughout its whole course, Japan was subject to a military dictatorship and the general staff was, in fact, the government.

How had this come about? First of all, according to the constitution, the Army and the Navy were responsible only to the Emperor, which gave them considerable independence and shielded them from government interference. In consequence, the Prime Minister and his colleagues played no sort of role in working out the strategy and conduct of operations; they only knew what their military and naval colleagues saw fit to tell them; and these colleagues were never civilians but always an admiral and a general. They were appointed only with the approval of the high command and almost always at its suggestion. Thus there was no risk of disagreement between a minister and the Supreme Commander, as in most countries. But the result was that the conduct of a war became in practice the responsibility of the experts of the specialised military departments, above all the operations division, and even more of the military affairs division, which was in charge of national defence, mobilisation and international affairs.

This complete independence of the supreme command was personified, after Prince Konoye had been ousted, in General Tojo, at one and the same time Prime Minister, War Minister and the brains of the Army. Almost always he succeeded in getting his way. But he was hampered, if not sometimes even hamstrung, by having under him as colleagues not one proper combined general staff but two separate ones, the Army's and the Navy's. Co-ordination between the two was always difficult and often non-existent. On occasion, for want of agreement, an operation had to be delayed or cancelled. When agreement had been reached, the operation, necessarily an amphibious one, was not entrusted to one single leader but to two, of equal rank, a sailor and a soldier, and the two services each received their supplies in different ways. Similarly, in each operational theatre, covering enormous geographical areas, there would be found a naval and a military commander.

Japan's whole organisation for the conduct of war was thus faulty and badly co-ordinated; its efficiency could not fail to be adversely affected. But the full gravity of these weaknesses did not appear immediately.

III THE ALLIED FORCES

With 132 million inhabitants the United States was industrially an exceptionally powerful country, despite the aftermath of the slump of the thirties and a slight recession in 1938. In 1940, their level of production had caught up with that of 1929. The United States provided Europe with large quantities of cotton, cereals and oil; they had a near monopoly of rare metals, except for aluminium; they produced as much iron ore, cast iron and steel as the rest of the world put together. By means of capital investment and the political agreements they had concluded, they were able to carry Canada along in their wake, as well as the countries of Latin America where the 'Monroe doctrine' was not regarded as an empty phrase.

But for the moment, this extraordinary potential, estimated at more than one-third of total world industry and supported by unrivalled gold reserves and financial capital, was not yet adequately represented by the size of its armament industry, output of weapons or its armed forces.

At sea, though the Atlantic fleet was intact—but needing to be kept available for its own operational theatre (and the decision to help Britain would ensure that it must remain there)—the Pacific fleet had been reduced to the three aircraft-carriers which had escaped the disaster of Pearl Harbour and fifteen cruisers or destroyers in the Philippines. To these could be added the three Dutch cruisers at Surabaya and two British battleships that Churchill had decided to send to Singapore though they had no air cover. For an indefinite period of time therefore, the American fleet would be forced back on the defensive; its only possible aggressive action would have to be confined to submarine attacks on Japanese convoys. Their small number and remoteness from base would make defence difficult for the moment and attack difficult later on; the Hawaiian Islands were 2,500 miles from San Francisco, the Philippines were isolated to the west and the small Midway Islands of Wake and Guam were some 1,000 to 1,250 miles apart and none of them could be protected. Once they were lost, the Japanese archipelago would be invulnerable for many a long day.

The British flag flew over vast territories which were, however, practically cut off from the metropolis, and India and Australia had sent their best troops to the Middle East. The Hong Kong base was surrounded by Japanese-occupied Chinese territory. At what was likely to be the extreme limit of the Japanese advance, Free France provided Tahiti, the New Hebrides and New Caledonia; but the French forces were ludicrously small. The Dutch forces in Indonesia amounted to 100,000. The Americans had the same number in the Philippines.

After the Munich agreements, President Roosevelt had worked out ambitious plans for aircraft production; but the American aeronautical industry was still something of a cottage industry, despite the slight stimulus afforded by orders placed by France. Construction of the first batch of 5,500 aircraft had only just begun in July 1939. On December 8, 1941, the American air forces consisted of something over 2,000 land-based aircraft and 2,500 intended for the Navy.

So potentially the United States were enormously powerful; but they had to convert this power into a similarly powerful war-machine; the industrial realignment required to do this raised immense problems which would have to be solved as need arose. Time would be necessary and success depended on a complicated series of hypotheses: first and foremost, that the war should not be lost beforehand in Europe and Asia; that the hastily raised and hurriedly equipped armies should cohere to form a sound fighting force; that they should be wisely deployed; that the efforts of the Anglo-American coalition should be, if not jointly controlled, at least co-ordinated. Meanwhile, the only possible attitude was defensive; but how extensive would the withdrawal have to be and where could it be stopped?

IV AMERICAN STRATEGY AND HIGH COMMAND

The US general staff found itself faced by three possibilities: defending the Pacific at all costs, whatever the consequences for Europe, now that Japanese aggression had upset all the earlier plans; accepting the inevitable by resigning itself to the loss of the south-west Pacific and concentrating the maximum number of forces in Britain in order to achieve victory in Europe first of all, leaving the return match with Japan to some later date, as yet undetermined; or else defending the south-west Pacific using the greatest economy of means so as to proceed with the concentration of their forces in the British Isles.

The American military leaders chose the last solution—a compromise—for logistical reasons: evacuating the South Pacific would have been as complicated as reinforcing it. The British let themselves be easily convinced because they could glimpse the possibility of once again seizing the initiative on the continent of Europe without thereby relinquishing their Asian empire.

Thus a defensive position would need to be organised in the Pacific and this raised the problem of command, first of all with the Americans themselves and secondly with the Allies. Before Pearl Harbour there existed dual control, naval and military, of the American forces both in the Philippines and in the Hawaiian Islands. President Roosevelt decided that from December 17 all the Hawaii forces would come under the Navy and the Philippines forces under the Army.

The USA, Britain, Australia, New Zealand and the Dutch East Indies now found themselves suddenly all fighting in the same war together without any previous agreement other than general staff talks in April and these had ended in a discussion of offensive operations which were no longer valid. To deal with what was most urgent first, a unified Allied command was set up called ABDA; General Wavell was put in charge, assisted by deputies from the other nations in the alliance—an American for the Navy, an Englishman for the Air Force, a Dutchman for the Army; the French, whether they had joined the Free French or remained under Vichy, were left out in the cold. Wavell's authority was somewhat theoretical since each of his subordinates could appeal to his own government against his decisions. The fact was that interests differed: the British were primarily concerned with defending Malaya and Singapore, the Americans with maintaining their lines of communication, the Dutch with defending Indonesia and the Australians with defending their own country. This combination of weak partners could in any case never add up to one strong force.

On General Eisenhower's suggestion, General Marshall decided that a convoy of seven ships, bound for Australia, would be the nucleus of a force called, in anticipation, US Army Forces in Australia. Accordingly, during the first three months of 1942, Australia received 55 per cent of the troop transports and 33 per cent of the shipments of equipment from the USA. Indeed, though Australia and New Zealand were rich in cattle and agricultural produce, they were poor in tools and manpower; the north Australian harbours lacked docks and cranes; there were few inland roads and they were not really suitable for heavy lorries while the railway network was small and had the added inconvenience of five different gauges. As the American soldiers were more difficult to please than the Australians —the standard rations of the former contained thirty-nine items as against the latter's twenty-four—they had to be sent large quantities of food— spaghetti, rice, fruit, milk, cocoa, etc.—in addition to the arms, vehicles, ammunition and other items necessary for a campaign.

At the very moment when it was important to support the USSR, who had been granted the benefit of lend-lease by sending them convoys via Iran and the Arctic Ocean, the situation that had arisen in the Pacific, even on the basis of a strictly defensive policy with minimum outlay, demanded an enormous effort from the American Merchant Marine. Boats had to be taken off the most important civilian services. But the American authorities were handicapped by their respect for free enterprise and reluctant to place the whole of their private shipping under military control, so that it was not used as rationally as might have been desirable— in May 1942, there were on average seventy-eight ships immobilised and practically useless in the South African area.

The war in the Pacific thus set the Americans problems that were almost insuperable. The Japanese had similarly difficult ones to solve.

V NATURE OF THE WAR IN THE PACIFIC

The belligerents had first of all to overcome enormous distances. The war was waged in the western half of the Pacific, that is over an area comprising one-eighth of the earth's surface. Tokyo was over 4,500 miles from Hawaii and more than 3,000 miles from the Solomon Islands; from Midway to Burma was well over 6,000 miles and from New Caledonia to the Aleutians just under 4,500. It took twice as long to go from San Francisco to Brisbane as it did to go from New York to Liverpool. American experts estimated that 100,000 troops could be shipped to Great Britain with the same tonnage that could carry only 40,000 to Australia. As the distances increased, the number of problems and the difficulty of solving them grew in geometric proportion.

On both sides, the first priority was to get convoys safely into harbour. The American convoys had to leave from Pacific ports, which were fewer in number and less well equipped than those on the east coast. San Francisco was crammed to bursting point and the produce shipped from there had to come from thousands of miles away, food from the Middle West, arms and machinery from the Great Lakes and New England. As a rule, all troops sailing from America had to take with them a two months' supply of food; each soldier needed five to ten tons of equipment when he left and one ton per month afterwards.

The logistical services thus assumed paramount importance on both sides. Transports required long preparation, because it was important to work out how they should rotate, receive protection and then be replenished. Inevitably things arrived at the wrong destination and nothing could be done about it. Troops unaccompanied by their stores were as good as useless. Sometimes, a transport company would arrive safely but without its lorries, or bakers minus their ovens. But by adapting their big industrial techniques to the war, the Americans soon showed their superiority in assembling such delicate mechanisms, keeping them running easily and improving them.

In the Pacific war problems of equipment would thus be more complicated than elsewhere and the fighting troops correspondingly smaller in manpower. Above all, shipping was of paramount importance; but not just any kind of shipping; special craft of all shapes and sizes would have to be invented and then manufactured and despatched to their destinations. If one adds that the enormous size of the Asian continent was made even more formidable by the climate, the rugged nature of the terrain, the jungle, the lack of roads and railways and that, in a word, the sea was the shortest distance between two points, then clearly final victory must depend on victory at sea.

The Pacific war would thus be primarily an air and naval war, requiring organised fortified bases, closing in gradually on the enemy's strongholds and long-range naval and air transport and methods of warfare. To avoid dispersing their air forces after their widespread gains, the Japanese chose to fortify islands, thus turning them into unsinkable aircraft-carriers. In a few hours, aircraft could be fetched in from other bases in order to defend them. The Americans preferred mobile forces, squadrons in which battleships and aircraft-carriers gave each other mutual support. But on both sides, any offensive operation was an amphibious one, combining naval, ground and air forces. In such operations, surprise, minute attention to detail, secrecy and accuracy of execution were essential, and success depended on controlling the skies and the sea. This is the context in which this war was waged, a war rich in episode, when almost uninhabited islands were fought over ferociously and won at the cost of heavy casualties.

The furious, even ferocious nature of the fighting was going to be aggravated by a more or less overt racialism. The Japanese showed little respect for the provisions of the Geneva Convention governing the treatment of prisoners of war. H. James, an American historian and eye-witness, wrote, 'In my 40 months' captivity I cannot recall one single example of a Japanese civilian or soldier showing disgust or even sorrow when an act of brutality was committed in his presence.' The American and Philippine prisoners captured by the Japanese at Bataan—72,000 in all —had to walk long distances on foot under a tropical sun. Sick and wounded were finished off by their guards at the roadside, hundreds at a time. Out of 50,000 prisoners of many nationalities employed by the Japanese on the construction of a railway in Siam, 16,000 died of illness, exhaustion or torture; the celebrated film, *The Bridge over the River Kwai*, describes such an episode. When these horrors became known in the United States, they came as a bombshell; public opinion demanded merciless revenge. The Americans would often drive Japanese soldiers out of their shelters with flame throwers, turning them into human torches. It is not anticipating events to recall that the first atom bombs were dropped on Japan, certainly with less compunction than if they were to have been dropped on a white population. The fanatically indoctrinated Japanese soldiers preferred to be killed on their little islands rather than let themselves fall into enemy hands.

VI THE JAPANESE PLANS

Although waging the same war against the same adversaries—except the USSR—as Germany and Italy, Japan never concerted her actions with her Allies. She waged her own war to achieve her own objectives, which were both grandiose and detailed in their conception. The Japanese leaders, and first and foremost General Tojo, were all convinced of the legitimacy of their aspirations: Japan was suffocating in her islands and only powers who were opposed to her in principle would want to stop her breathing more freely. She was thus driven to break forcibly out of the vice in which she was being held. But at no time did the Japanese imagine that they would have to force the United States to their knees and that they would be able to dictate their peace terms to the White House. They wanted to build up their empire and were prepared to brush aside anything that stood in their way, first of all the American fleet; and then, once Japan's new position was well established and proof had been given that it was impossible to take her gains away from her, they would negotiate. The success of these schemes depended on a German victory in Europe or at least on Hitler's continuing for a long time yet to make the USSR incapable of any effective action in Asia; it also presupposed either that the United States would commit the bulk of her forces to the fighting in Europe or else that she would accept the situation as it was after her first defeats in Asia—a situation which entailed in fact losing only the Philippines, to which she had promised independence—rather an inadequate reason, surely, for waging a long and difficult war.

Having established these principles, the Japanese modified the extent and the limits of their future empire according to events. They also hesitated between several different schemes of how to conquer it. For the moment they had given up any designs on Siberia east of Lake Baikal and they had remained deaf to Germany's appeals to reach out towards her by a vast attack in the direction of India; nor had they any intention of occupying Australia and New Zealand, merely of isolating them. They thus had a threefold objective: to conquer the territories producing the raw materials which they lacked—oil, rubber and various ores which made the Dutch East Indies and Malaya particularly important; to fortify a line of small islands in the central Pacific so as to form a defensive barrier against the onslaught of the Americans; and to protect themselves in Burma and the key position of Singapore against a possible counter-offensive by Britain. After all this had been achieved, China would be completely isolated and her defeat and incorporation into the new political and economic area thus created would be only a matter of time.

The Japanese hesitated between three possibilities: a direct attack on the Dutch East Indies, considered too risky because it dangerously extended the lines of communication; a leapfrog advance from the Philippines to the Indian archipelago and Malaya, which was rejected because it was too slow; and a conquest of Malaya and the Indian archipelago both together, leaving out the Philippines as no longer necessary by reason of the decision to attack Pearl Harbour. The Japanese adopted a plan finally involving simultaneous advances towards the Dutch East Indies, the Philippines and Malaya. The element of surprise would compensate for the dispersal of forces. The remoteness of the objectives required careful timing for the troop landings, the advance of the Air Force, the allocation of shipping and the bringing up of supplies. The vast scope of the scheme made it very bold and very hazardous, but as it suited the book of each of the parties concerned, the government, the Army and the Navy, it was adopted. And the Japanese knew all about their opponents' weaknesses.

The operation was to be carried out in two phases. In the first phase, Hong Kong, Wake and Guam would be occupied and troops landed in the Philippines and Malaya; in the second phase the Dutch East Indies, Singapore and Burma would be conquered. In the east, no advance would be made beyond a line joining the Kurile, Wake and Gilbert Islands, the north coast of New Guinea, Timor and the northern Solomon Islands. In the south-west, the main stronghold would be Rabaul.

In these plans the attack on Pearl Harbour was in fact considered merely as an hors d'oeuvre, a preliminary tactical operation on a grand scale reserved for the Navy, the success of which would make it easier to carry out the rest of the scheme. And indeed for the first few months, everything took place as planned.

VII THE EARLY JAPANESE SUCCESSES

The Japanese repeated their tactics in almost identical fashion everywhere with the same success: enemy bases and airfields were bombed; troops were landed at selected points, never in great strength but sufficient to guarantee local superiority and ensure a swift victory; next, airfields were set up or brought back into action on the conquered territory; a fresh leap forward some hundreds of miles ahead was then made from this starting point with the least possible delay.

These combined operations imposed a great strain on the naval and air forces; but they carried out their tasks with extreme competence. The strike force of six fast aircraft-carriers, skilfully grouped and deployed, provided, whenever they were employed, air superiority of four or five aircraft to one. Between December 7, 1941, and April 1942, this force operated over an area extending from Hawaii to Ceylon, one-third of the circumference of the earth. In turn, they launched successive attacks on Pearl Harbour, Rabaul, Port Darwin, Tinjilap, Colombo and Trincomale, without losing one single ship.

The land-based air force showed similar mobility. Its 700 aircraft were divided into two air fleets; the first, based on the homeland, with advanced bases in the central Pacific, had the defensive role of covering Japan. The second had an offensive role: based at first on Formosa, Indochina and the Palau islands and later using island bases, its 350 aircraft and seaplanes flew from island to island, opening up the way for landings and destroying the enemy aircraft—300 in all—that were launched against them in small batches.

On December 8, Guam and Wake were attacked; the 500 defenders of Guam surrendered thirty-six hours later. Wake, about 1,500 miles from Guam, was only an atoll; the garrison, without food or water, surrendered on December 22. The Gilberts had already been conquered since the 9th.

Hong Kong was defended only against attack from the sea. On December 8, the bombing raids began and the Japanese 38th Division crossed the border into the peninsula. The 15,000 Australian, Canadian and Indian defenders were forced back into the suburb of Kowloon and then, on the 17th, to the island of Hong Kong, where the Japanese landed on the 19th; having run out of water, the garrison surrendered on December 25. These were Japan's first great successes; there were to be others.

VIII THE CONQUEST OF THE PHILIPPINES

The American government had shown indecision in its policy towards the Philippines. It had granted them independence in principle, to start in 1946, but it still kept them somewhat under its wing. It realised that they would be impossible to defend by reason of their remoteness but it could not bring itself to abandon them to their lot. As a result of this half-hearted attitude the archipelago was inadequately defended.

Thus in December, the army, 100,000 strong, of whom 75,000 were Filipinos, was supported by only about 100 fighters, 34 bombers and some 100 tanks; for want of adequately equipped airfields, it had not proved possible to disperse or camouflage them; radio communications were very slow and, as at Pearl Harbour, the presence on the island of large numbers of Japanese had made spying easy. Although as a result of incompetence, on which American historians have had little to say, perhaps because General MacArthur's responsibility is involved, the attack on Pearl Harbour became known six hours after the opening of hostilities, the Japanese Air Force destroyed half the American aircraft on the ground at Mindanao without having been in any way detected or even, it would seem, expected.

On December 10 the Japanese began to land on the north coast of Luzon and at Lingayen on December 24. The Americans were able neither to repulse them nor even to delay their advance. Soon there were 150,000 Japanese on the islands. MacArthur withdrew to the Bataan peninsula and it was a miracle that the endless columns moving along the single road were not disrupted by Japanese bombing.

It was clear that the Philippines could no longer be defended, although

MacArthur asserted the opposite. The few remaining aircraft were brought back to the Dutch East Indies; Admiral Hart's fleet received the order to seek refuge behind the barrier of Malaya before it was too late. General Yamashita's Japanese troops took possession of the islands one after the other without much difficulty. Lacking any support from outside, MacArthur's tiny army's first line of defence was pierced on January 22 at Bataan. Successive lines of defence only delayed the inevitable withdrawal to Corregidor on April 9 where it continued to fight; but, decimated by malaria and having run out of water, the last American garrison surrendered on May 7 having suffered fifty-three air raids. MacArthur left to take command of the forces that were beginning to be organised in Australia. He was unhappy to leave the Philippines and swore he would come back.

Like the British in Europe, the Americans in Asia had shown themselves unable to provide effective defence for the territories they had taken under their protection. The British and the Dutch were in no better plight.

IX THE CONQUEST OF THE DUTCH EAST INDIES

The Dutch Army totalled about 100,000 men of whom barely 35,000 were equipped with relatively modern equipment. Since they were spread out over an immense area and supported by 200 aircraft only 60 of which were of recent type, they were incapable of offering effective resistance anywhere. The creation of a unified Allied command and the arrival of General Wavell in Java produced little change. No amount of preliminary training could overcome the confusion created by the diversity of languages and, where the ships were concerned, by the absence of a common signals code.

Nonetheless, it had been possible to bring up some reinforcements—the American fleet from the Philippines, some American aircraft from Australia and the advance guard of an Australian division coming home from the Middle East. It did not amount to very much.

In accordance with their invariable tactics, the Japanese gradually invested Java, on the one hand by pouring down the Malacca peninsula towards Sumatra, on the other by landing in Borneo, in the Celebes and in the Moluccas, where from the island of Amboyna, they were able to start bombing the Dutch base of Surabaya. Wherever they went, they found the oil installations destroyed but this handicap did not hinder their advance.

Little by little the ring closed round Java, as the Japanese established their foothold in regions where no defence was possible. South Sumatra, Timor and Bali were occupied in February; so Java was cut off from Australia on the east while Singapore was falling on the west. At the same time, Batavia started to be bombed.

The battle for Java was waged at sea on February 27 and 28 and March 1, 1942. The Allied fleet under Admiral Doorman suffered an unfortunate mishap at the start of the fighting when the British cruiser *Electra* was sunk on the spot. Subsequently, the Japanese lost only one torpedo-boat destroyer but they sank two cruisers and three Allied torpedo-boat destroyers. It was a disaster, above all for the Dutch Navy, which had not fought for 150 years.

Without awaiting the outcome of a hopeless campaign, the Dutch authorities had evacuated Batavia. The Japanese landed on the plain in the north of Java and advanced swiftly. On the very first day they captured an airfield a few hundred miles from Bandung which had been made the capital. On March 6, they had reached the south coast of Java and entered Tjilatjap, which had been declared an 'open city'. Although fighting was still going on in Sumatra and on Timor, the Dutch authorities, having vainly attempted to negotiate a partial surrender, were forced to capitulate completely and unconditionally to General Hitoshi, who threatened to bombard the towns if they refused. The first thing that the Japanese did after their victory was to intern a large part of the white population of Java, in addition to the soldiers who had been captured.

X THE CONQUEST OF MALAYA AND SINGAPORE

For a long time the British had thought that the Japanese would not attack Singapore—this was the opinion of the Commander-in-Chief in the Far East. Churchill thought that at the worst they could not attack it before the spring of 1942. In any case, the British were relying on the American fleet to contain the Japanese, and the Pearl Harbour disaster was a bitter disappointment for them as well. All they could do was to face up to the situation with their own inadequate resources, that is about 90,000 men, lacking tanks, experienced officers and NCOs and even trained soldiers. To meet the Japanese squadrons based in Indochina the RAF had only 180 aircraft, most of them out-dated. The British government expected setbacks and was resigned to them because in their eyes the Asian theatre of war was a secondary one; but to save what it could, it nevertheless decided to send two modern battleships to Singapore. They arrived at the very last moment, on December 2.

The British high command had thought of moving into Siam to forestall the Japanese but was reluctant to violate that country's neutrality. The Japanese were less scrupulous. On December 8, they occupied Bangkok and the Siamese harbours close to the Malayan peninsula.

Could Admiral Philipps, the commander of the only respectable British force, possibly remain idle? He sailed to intercept the convoys that had been reported to him. He knew that the Japanese surface fleet was not there and that the danger would be aircraft and submarines. Warships had, of course, been sunk by aircraft in Norway and Crete but never a battleship. The British tended to underestimate their opponents and they did not know that the Japanese were the only people at that time to have perfected the technique of torpedo attack by aircraft. Completely without air cover or even reconnaissance planes, on December 10, despite their forty automatic AA weapons, the *Prince of Wales* and the *Repulse* were sent to the bottom in thirty-five minutes with all their crews. The British had now lost control of the seas as well as the skies.

With his lines of communication now protected, General Yamashita advanced into Malaya, both through the jungle and by means of a series of landings on the coast, along which ran both the railway line and the roads. The Indian and Australian troops, constantly attacked in the rear, could do nothing but retreat, until, demoralised, they finally took refuge in Singapore.

Well defended from the sea, where a number of little islands in the Malacca straits were powerfully fortified, Singapore was less well defended against the land, particularly since a causeway nearly two miles long joined it to the mainland. In the night of February 8–9 the Japanese made a surprise landing on the island, repaired the causeway and sent their tanks and artillery along it. On February 12, they were at the gates of Singapore; by the 14th they had taken the naval base and the water tanks. On the 15th, the garrison surrendered, handing over 80,000 prisoners. The Japanese had given themselves one hundred days to complete their programme and they had done it in seventy.

XI THE BURMA CAMPAIGN

Burma had separated from India in 1937 and the British had paid little attention to her defences, for one thing because the young Burmese intellectuals were very hostile. But it was important to protect the approaches to India and two divisions, one Indian and one Burmese, under General Hutton had been given this task.

For its own part, the Japanese general staff looked on Burma as a secondary operational theatre. But by despatching troops there, they were pursuing three aims: cutting China's last communications with the outside world (in January 1942 there were 100,000 tons of stores in Rangoon intended for Chungking), depriving long-range enemy aircraft of bases and guarding against an offensive from the direction of India. They possibly thought of making Burma a springboard for the invasion of India, but this is doubtful, although India did figure among the countries likely to form part of Greater East Asia Co-Prosperity Sphere. In any case, such a huge undertaking would have to be held over till later.

Burma was separated from India by mountains having no roads passable for vehicles; the lines of communication followed the valleys which lay north-south; from May to October the wet monsoon turned the tracks into torrents and the roads into quagmires; the only suitable season for campaigning was from October to May. These geographical conditions, aggravated by the low density of population and the paucity of resources, meant that though the fighting forces were small, the ancillary services were large and complex.

Now that they possessed airfields sufficiently close to Rangoon, the Japanese overran the hastily prepared British defences on the rivers and entered Rangoon in March 1942—an important gain because of its harbour installations, oil refineries and stores of commodities which were only partly destroyed.

The second phase now began. The Japanese moved up the Irrawaddy. They pushed back the British as well as the Chinese, who had come to their help—somewhat to the mortification of the British. They took Lashio, where the 'Burma road' started, then Mandalay and the oil wells, while their Air Force bombed Ceylon. The boldness of this operation intimidated the British so much that they recalled their ships as far as the east coast of Africa. As the Japanese fleet had not gone beyond the Andaman Islands, there were no ships left in the Indian Ocean. But feeling themselves threatened in the rear, the British made a landing at Diego Suarez and occupied the whole of the island of Madagascar, which caused them difficulties both with Vichy and Free France.

In a third phase, the British troops evacuated Burma, not without great difficulty and considerable losses, and took refuge in India, while what was left of the Chinese troops returned home. The wet monsoon put a stop to the fighting. But how was China to be supplied now? Where would the Japanese advance stop? And who was to stop it?

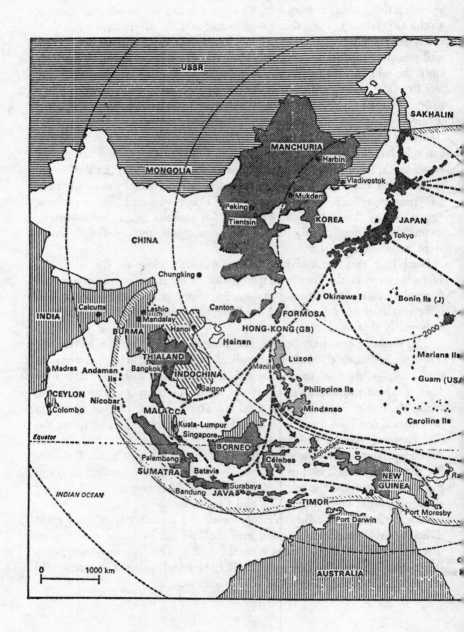

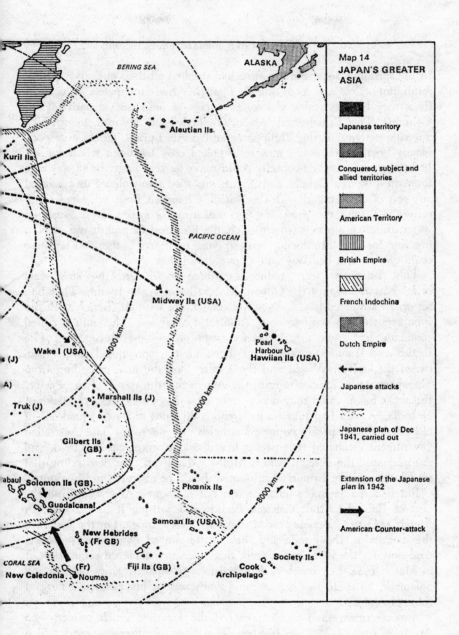

Map 14
JAPAN'S GREATER ASIA

Japanese territory

Conquered, subject and allied territories

American Territory

British Empire

French Indochina

Dutch Empire

Japanese attacks

Japanese plan of Dec 1941, carried out

Extension of the Japanese plan in 1942

American Counter-attack

XII JAPAN'S DEFENSIVE PERIMETER EXTENDED

In the spring of 1942, the Japanese had reached all their objectives with a minimum of loss and more quickly than they had anticipated. In each of them they had been able to take advantage of help from a native 'Fifth Column'. The British and Americans had been reduced to sporadic guerrilla activity in the Philippines and north Burma. China was completely isolated and could now be supplied only by air; a whole air lift had to be set up and its capacity could never be very large. India was in a ferment; although Gandhi and Nehru preached non-violence and refused any sort of co-operation with the British, Chandrah Bose, who had taken refuge in Burma, was preaching and preparing for armed revolt. Australia was withdrawing troops from the Middle East and Churchill was criticising her for not introducing conscription. In a word, the anti-Japanese coalition was in a bad way and its morale was low.

The Americans were reduced perforce to undertaking small-scale counter-attacks against the Gilbert, Marshall and Wake Islands. They had set up an advanced base in New Caledonia, not without friction with the Free French high commissioner, Admiral d'Argenlieu. The unified Allied command had come to an end for want of any useful function. The British and Americans decided to share out the operational theatres between themselves. Wavell and the British took the area extending from Singapore to the Mediterranean; the Americans, the whole of the Pacific. But what forces could they deploy over these huge areas? For the defence of India, Wavell had four under-strength divisions and two squadrons of old aircraft with poorly equipped airfields and no radar. The Australian government estimated that twenty-five divisions were required to defend Australia and the Foreign Affairs Minister, Dr Evatt, was demanding that six whole weeks of Britain's war output should be allocated to his country.

But had the Japanese advance run out of steam? After capturing the port of Rabaul in the Bismarck Islands and turning it into a base, in March 1942 the Japanese landed troops in New Guinea. For the first time the mountains, the jungle and the climate slowed down their advance. And now for the first time as well, the Americans achieved some success: in March 1942 their bombers damaged twenty Japanese ships off Lea and Salamalla. In itself, this was nothing really serious but perhaps a taste of things to come.

Another unexpected incident caused the Japanese much concern: on April 18, 1942, Tokyo was bombed. The American aircraft-carriers which had escaped the Pearl Harbour disaster were responsible for the raid, which had a considerable effect on morale. It was a cold shower to put a damper on their elation. The Japanese then decided to enlarge their defensive perimeter in order to protect their homeland. At the very moment when they had come to realise that they had reached the limit of their strength, they found themselves contemplating further advances towards the Solomon Islands and the south of New Guinea; while other moves would take them towards New Caledonia, Samoa, the Fiji Islands, Midway and the Aleutians. True, if they had succeeded they would cut the lines between the United States and Australia, they would remove the threat of any attack launched from Alaska and they would deprive the United States of any base for operations west of Hawaii. But in doing this, were they not over-extending their lines of communication? In the sweet intoxication of victory, were they biting off more than they could chew?

CHAPTER 3

The Sphere of Co-prosperity

How were the Japanese going to administer and exploit their huge conquests? If truth be told, they had not worked out many detailed schemes, even fewer than the Germans. On the whole, they had been welcomed by the native populations but these were extremely diverse in race, religion and standards of living. Also, the war would force Japan to exploit their wealth for her own purposes straightaway and this desire to appropriate for her own use might mean that she would slip into the shoes of the colonising powers whom she had supplanted, to the detriment of the individual and national freedom towards which these populations aspired—or at least one section of their ruling classes and their educated classes. Finally, more than the previous occupying powers, Japan tended to impose on others the military way of life that she had adopted for herself. In any case, she was going to have insufficient time to consolidate her ascendancy and build her empire. But through her works, south-east Asia was going to be unsettled in a way that long outlasted her brief period of domination.

I THE JAPANESE EMPIRE

The Japanese empire ran down the whole coastline of Asia, from Manchuria to beyond Rangoon; it included all the archipelagos of the western Pacific up to a line running from the Aleutians to New Guinea, passing through the Gilbert Islands. It covered one-sixth of the earth's surface, that is, more than 32 million square miles. Most of it had been conquered from the Americans, the British and the Dutch but Siam was an ally of her own free will; Indochina had been occupied by virtue of agreements with the Vichy government recognising French sovereignty; Manchukuo was already a protectorate in which in theory there reigned a descendant of the Manchu dynasty, Pai-Yi; finally China was only partially conquered and still at war with Japan. The vast area of such an empire, added to its scattered nature, might be a weakness; the distance between Tokyo and the Solomon Isles was well over 3,000 miles. The empire would last as long as the Japanese war fleet and Air Force could retain mastery of its seas and its skies; Japan would be able to enjoy all its wealth only if her Merchant Navy was large enough to ensure and increase the flow of goods.

Thanks to her empire, Japan now had all the sources of energy and raw materials which she had previously lacked; coal, iron, oil; 70 per cent of the world production of tin and almost all of the rubber; she had cut the US off from her supply of natural rubber. Conversely, the conquered nations formed a vast market for her manufactured goods. Her war economy was thus able to work flat out; but the rational exploitation of her empire would have to wait for the end of the war in order to expand, on the supposition that Japan then possessed the necessary capital, industrial potential and structures as well as the necessary number of competent technicians.

The Japanese—above all their soldiers—believed in their mission in Asia; their task was to put an end to the domination of the white over the coloured races, while borrowing the former's science and technology, and to uproot the seeds of materialism and moral disintegration introduced by colonialism. Being more highly developed than other Far Eastern peoples, Japan would lead them on to material progress while still allowing them to retain their own cultures. The Japanese cabinet had defined its political aims as early as July 1940: it would establish a new order in eastern Asia. In February 1942, Tojo set up a 'Greater Asia Council', composed of senior civil servants and industrialists. Then in November 1942, a 'Ministry for Greater Asia' was set up under Aoki.

But the liberated peoples were not to be granted complete or immediate freedom. Their strategic importance made it necessary for certain territories, such as Hong Kong, Singapore, Borneo, New Guinea and Timor to be purely and simply annexed. A second type of country was to be progressively led forward into theoretical independence, similar to that of Manchukuo; thus on August 1, 1943, Burma was proclaimed independent and, on October 15, 1943, the Philippines, both proclamations being accompanied by the signing of military, political and economic alliances, reducing them to satellite states—both countries declared war on the United States. The Malay states and the Dutch East Indies were also to be granted theoretical independence; but though the Ministry of Foreign Affairs was inclined to let them have it without delay, the Navy and the Army preferred it to be deferred till later on.

Finally, other countries became allies of the Japanese; thus Siam, when she declared war on Britain and the United States, received the high mountainous region of upper Burma in compensation, as well as the promise of Cambodia. The Chinese Nankin government under Wang Tsing-wei also declared war on the British and Anglo-Americans and it was likely to be given Tonkin. However, the future of Indochina was not clearly defined; the French administration was still functioning and the Japanese were afraid of creating unrest if they got rid of it; in this way, the French stayed on in an equivocal position, on the one hand as representing a certain amount of independence *vis-à-vis* the occupying power, on the other as a colonial survival opposed by local nationalist feeling.

As far as India was concerned, plans were fairly vague. The British would naturally be driven out; but the Japanese did not consider the Indians ripe for self-government, although not feeling themselves capable of ruling them directly. Moderate support was given to Chandrah Bose who, when he came to take part in a Congress of Greater Asian countries in Tokyo, found himself treated as a guest and not as an active member. Nonetheless Chandrah Bose, a former member of the Congress party, formed a 'League for Indian Independence' in Bangkok, with Japanese backing; then, on October 21, 1943, in Singapore, he formed a 'Free Indian Government' which was to raise a national army from amongst the Indian soldiers captured by the Japanese.

All these schemes, the product of propaganda or of ideas for the future, found difficulty in facing up to the harsh reality. Even had they not so wished, the Japanese had too pressing a need for all the wealth of the countries they had conquered not to take it for themselves. They made a clean sweep of their foodstuffs and raw materials, which they bought for a song; their businessmen simply replaced the colonisers who had been expropriated; they had recourse to paper money in order to buy everything on the cheap, although this did not prevent the occupying troops from extorting and commandeering from the local population. The abject poverty of the masses was merely increased and food rationing had to be introduced.

Nor were the Japanese free from a superiority complex towards the natives. They were imbued with the feeling that they were military conquerors, established there by right of conquest. They often showed arrogance, contempt and even cruelty towards the natives. One of the Burmese nationalist leaders, Ba Maw, protested to Tojo against the excesses committed by the occupation troops but General Kimura, the Commander-in-Chief in Burma, took several months before he could bring himself to put down his subordinates' 'mistakes'. In every country, the inhabitants complained of the harshness of the *Kempeitai*, the Japanese military police.

The Japanese military or civil authorities rarely appointed natives to any senior governmental positions and when they did agree to do so, they reduced their powers. They dismissed officials imbued with western ideas and methods as being guilty of 'collaborating' with colonialism. They replaced them by younger men whom they hoped to win over by promoting them and whom they trained in Japan. They intended to make

Japanese the standard language in south-east Asia. Even in religious matters, they were not free from a certain imperialism. In October 1943 they
removed the two 'living Buddhas' from Mongolia and Tibet, carried them
off to Japan, and set up a 'Greater Asian Society of Young Buddhists'.

Although the Japanese had no difficulty in rousing the native populations against their former white masters whom they systematically looted,
maltreated and humiliated, on the other hand, after they had raised great
hopes amongst the nationalist movements which were spurred on by their
arrival, they then caused them great disappointment and even aroused
antagonism against themselves.

II LOCAL NATIONALIST MOVEMENTS

In Indochina, the Cao Daist sect openly professed sympathy for Japan,
but in October 1941 the Indochinese Communist party under Ngugen
Ai Quoi, who was the son of a scholar and had studied in Paris, was
broadened to become the Independence Front or Vietminh. In 1943,
Ngugen Ai Quoi became Ho Chi Minh, 'he who brings light'. The expressed aims of the movement were two in number: to destroy 'colonialism' but to destroy 'Fascist imperialism' as well; while the enemy was
French colonisation, Japanese neo-imperialism was not necessarily the
friend, at least as long as it did not give independence to Vietnam.

In the Philippines the natives felt themselves superior to the occupying
Japanese. The latter found supporters amongst the ruling classes but met
with great hostility from the population of the interior, the Huks. President
Quezon had formed a 'free government' in the United States. Guerrilla
forces were formed, officered by Americans, some of whom had not left the
country, and were supplied by air or submarine; these gradually grew into
a 'People's Army', which levied taxes from collaborators and adopted violent action and sabotage in the towns. In 1943 the Americans estimated
its strength at 30,000 men.

In Burma the Buddhist-inspired *Wunthann*, the equivalent of the Indian Congress Party, was recruited from among the leading citizens; it
adapted itself quite well to the Japanese occupation. But the mountain
peoples in the north of the country were, by tradition, less docile. British
agents, trained in a special camp in Colombo, were dropped amongst them
by parachute to form guerrilla units.

In Malaya there was an aristocracy of recent growth based on the
mineral wealth and rubber plantations of their country; they turned their
back on the West, preferring to complete their studies in Cairo or Mecca.
They had formed the Malay Union which in 1940 had asked the British

authorities for their own minister, tax reform and the right of diplomatic representation. They welcomed the Japanese and provided the core of the 'Malayan Youth Movement'. However, the Sultan of Pahang refused to collaborate through fear of seeing his powers reduced.

Everywhere the Japanese came up against two groups who, because of their homogeneity, were particularly hostile: the colonies of Chinese and the Communists. In Malaya, they were one and the same thing. As soon as the Japanese attacked, the Malayan Communist party, led by Chinese, offered its services to the British who, however, were reluctant to give them arms, lest they might turn them against the British. The party seized them, however, from the stocks of arms left behind by the British troops during their hasty retreat. It formed carefully organised and strictly graded groups, patrols and regiments—seven anti-Japanese regiments—taking their orders from a 'guerrilla headquarters'. The British sent instructors whom the Communists accepted as advisers but without giving up hope of forming a Malayan Communist republic at the end of the war.

III INDONESIA

The situation was much more complicated in Indonesia, because of its considerable Moslem element, with which the Japanese endeavoured to ingratiate themselves.

Contrary to Dutch hopes, the natives had remained passive spectators of the Japanese attack and victorious occupation. The Japanese seemed in no hurry to talk of independence, even of administrative independence—Indonesia remained under military authority but it was divided; Java was controlled by the Sixteenth Army, Sumatra by the Twenty-fifth; Borneo, the Celebes and Timor were under the Navy. At the beginning, the Dutch administrative machinery was retained, no doubt in the interests of efficiency, in order not to introduce too rapid a change in an area so vitally important for the Japanese war economy.

The Dutch were all gradually interned, together with their wives and children, and replaced by Japanese and Indonesians both in the public and the private sector of government and industry. The main emphasis was placed on combating the aftermath of colonialism; foreign languages—Dutch and English—were banned and Japanese replaced them in the schools; the press was tightly curbed; all the professions and other collective bodies were organised as corporations in order to make stricter control possible. The Chinese, two million of them, who had shown signs of resistance, were forced to knuckle under after a number of them had been arrested.

Economic exploitation started at once. In order not to overburden their Merchant Navy, the Japanese had decided that the armies of occupation would live off the country; in addition, each one of the territories had the task both of exporting the maximum possible amount to Japan and of supplying its own needs by importing as little as possible. The result was that the country was squeezed dry of its wealth without receiving anything in return. This could not fail to disturb its economy and reduce the standard of living.

Ever since the eighteenth century most of the population of Sumatra and Java had been converted to Islam, an Islam adapted to the religious concepts already present; the Moslem priests and scribes were the spiritual leaders of the peasant communities and Moslem culture was retained by many of the élite who had no access to European education. The Dutch had done nothing to hinder the Moslem movement in so far as it was confined to religious, cultural or social matters; but they kept a very watchful eye on any possible political repercussions.

However, side by side with the traditional Moslem hierarchy, a nationalist party had grown up which wished for reforms in religious matters and independence at the political level. But it was torn between two factions according to whether the intellectuals who were its leaders had retained a Moslem culture, enhanced by study in Cairo, or else had acquired a non-religious, western culture.

The Japanese were not entirely without experience in Moslem matters. In 1930, for propaganda purposes, they had founded a Japanese Moslem Society which had organised a Pan-Moslem Congress in Tokyo in 1938 that had been attended by a delegation from Indonesia. The military government set up a 'Religious Affairs Bureau' whose members had spent some time in the Middle East.

The Japanese were aiming at winning over the enormous Moslem movement to their cause. They directed their effort towards the traditional hierarchy, rather like the French government in Morocco. Accordingly, they banned the two Moslem political parties which had been more or less tolerated by the Dutch and replaced them by new associations with themselves in control. The Moslems were formed into a 'Moslem Federation' which had existed earlier but had gradually disappeared. As for the small non-Moslem parties, they were also formed into a single organisation called *Putera*.

The Indonesian nationalist leaders were divided as to the attitude to adopt towards this Japanese policy. The most important of them, such as Soekarno or Mohammad Hatta, accepted it. Others, like the veteran nationalist militant Dr Tjipto Mangunkusumo, opposed it but were obliged to go into hiding and their insurrection never led to any subversive action or guerrilla warfare.

The two organisations *Putera* and the Moslem Federation were rivals, and this rivalry did not displease the Japanese, who wanted to divide in order to rule. But it did hinder the mobilisation of Indonesian resources for Japan's benefit. Accordingly, in 1943, the Japanese created an entirely new multi-racial mass movement *Djawa Hokokai* (Association for the Assistance of Java) which replaced all the others and in which they kept all the leading posts for themselves: at the risk of undermining their propaganda, they even introduced the cult of the Emperor into it.

It was not the best way to woo the Indonesians and this soon became obvious, especially as the granting of independence to Burma and the Philippines had aroused hopes in Java that quickly turned sour. In June 1943, General Tojo issued a decree allowing the Indonesians to participate, in a modest way, in the running of their country. A 'Central Consultative Committee' was set up in September 1943, with Soekarno as chairman; its power extended to the provinces in the form of local councils. This reform, however limited in extent, nonetheless strengthened nationalism at a time when it was still barely articulate.

Did the Japanese become aware of this and try to take back with one hand what they were giving away with the other? They doubtless felt closer in spirit to the traditional Moslem hierarchy than to the Europeanised nationalist leaders; they could see that the peasantry was still living in the social structures provided by its religious leaders and they considered these leaders more pliable as well as less dangerous than the nationalists. All these reasons led them to form in January 1944 a powerful Moslem association, *Masjumi*, covering the whole country, whereas *Djawa Hokokai*, as its name indicated, was restricted to Java. Control of *Masjumi* was placed in the hands of Moslems and not of the Japanese, as was invariably the case elsewhere. Moslems, too, formed most of the recruits of the volunteer force created by the Japanese as a sort of auxiliary military under the name of *Peta*.

Thus in 1944 Indonesia and especially Java became a Japanese protectorate, in which the occupying power allowed some say to national independence while basing its own authority on the Moslem hierarchy. Accordingly *Masjumi* loudly asserted that Japan's cause was the cause of Islam and its war a holy war. But the nationalists could find little satisfaction in a system which maintained and reinforced political, religious and social structures which they considered oppressive and out-moded and which made them serve a foreign power while indefinitely postponing any hope of independence.

Later, when Japan's military situation deteriorated, Tokyo considered it necessary to avoid unrest in Indonesia; the best method to achieve this seemed to be to gain the confidence of the nationalist leaders, who had moreover been actively and often successfully infiltrating and setting up cells in the mass organisations sponsored by the Japanese, including *Djawa Hokokai*.

IV CHINA UNDER THE CHUNGKING GOVERNMENT

Japan was thus experiencing great difficulties in organising and exploiting the vast empire which had come her way through the fortunes of war. It was clear that any military setbacks or slackening of her military or economic potential would only aggravate them. And she was still engaged in a war in China that seemed interminable.

True, she controlled the richest and most populous regions and even though she had not succeeded in arousing a really popular collaborationist movement, her authority was accepted there and was undisputed. This was not the case in the peripheral lands of the Middle Empire.

Now completely isolated in his mountains and deprived of all supplies from outside, Chiang Kai-shek had ceased to be a serious threat for the time being; conversely, the remoteness and height of his demesne meant that it was well-nigh impregnable. But his army, slowly starved of modern weapons, was falling apart. His administration was being reduced to anarchy and in the absence of any proper central authority each local potentate was acting as he thought fit. Corruption and muddle were rife from top to bottom.

Moreover, the Chinese state had no resources; taxes were collected only at irregular intervals and the provinces where they yielded most were under the Japanese yoke; before the war, half its revenue came from customs duties, which no longer existed. In contrast to this dwindling income, the outlay due to the war was ever-increasing. Most fortunately, the Chinese gold and silver reserves had found a safe haven abroad and they provided security for the necessary purchases. But in China herself, loans and the issue of government bonds had not prevented galloping inflation. By 1941, prices had risen tenfold since 1937. The growing increase in bank notes called for 150 tons per month of special paper and ink, flown in from Burma.

The middle classes, the intellectuals and civil servants, were hardest hit by this growing anarchy, even if some tradesmen and middlemen were making good profits. Chiang Kai-shek's popularity suffered a good deal as a result. And no aid was now being given to the Chinese by the Soviet Union since she had been attacked; nor was Britain in any position to replace her. Only the United States had the necessary means. But they were asking themselves if the game was worth the candle. Although practically at his last gasp, Chiang in fact continued to put forward the most exorbitant claims. He haggled bitterly over his price for continuing the fight and threatened to make a deal with the Japanese if he was not given satisfaction. He refused to allow the Chinese armies to be commanded by foreigners and he even requested that all the Allied forces fighting in Burma should be placed under his control.

In June 1942, despite misgivings and the immense difficulties involved in implementing its decision, the American government resolved to help Chiang Kai-shek. His collapse would indeed have grave consequences; Japan's prestige and aggressiveness would appreciably increase and considerable forces would be freed; she would be able to draw the resources she needed from China; it would never be possible again to bomb her from the continent of Asia; the defeat of China would also have the most unfortunate repercussions in the territories conquered by Japan.

In a word, without too many illusions, the Americans thought that China must be kept in the war. They suspected that Chiang or his associates would squander much of the aid supplied to him and that he would not use all the rest in the fight against Japan but would hold it back in order to appear stronger when peace came; perhaps he might even use it against his internal enemies? But a China that had relapsed into anarchy at the end of the war was not a very attractive proposition either. So President Roosevelt plied Chiang with friendly and flattering messages and endeavoured to calm him down when he was not able to satisfy all his requests.

From February 1942 onwards General Stilwell became Chiang's military adviser; he was an energetic and honest soldier who was appalled by the anarchy which he discovered and he was impervious to Chinese wiles. As a result he did not get on very well with Chiang, whom he called 'peanut' in his correspondence, and he was reduced to impotent rage when he learned that Chinese generals, suitably primed with dollars, were still not paying or feeding their troops.

As a first step—an expensive one and of limited value—60,000 Chinese soldiers were flown into India to receive modern training and equipment and, if possible, a better fighting spirit. It would, however, have been more valuable to despatch equipment to China so that the fight might be resumed. But how could it be done? One possible route started from Karachi and reached Sin-Kiang via Russian Turkestan; but this idea never went beyond the planning stage. Flying over the mountains of India would need heavy long-range aircraft and of these the United States had only a limited number.

As a bait for the countries occupied by Japan, and in order to make them realise that the victory of the Anglo-Saxons would not mean an automatic return to the *status quo*, in January 1943 the British and Americans gave up their extra-territorial rights in China.

Finally, in order to put the finances of the Chungking government on a better footing, it was granted a 500-million-dollar loan. The Chinese refused to pay any interest and resisted any suggestion of restrictions on how it was to be spent; as for repayment, that could be left for discussion after the war; for the moment, this American action was looked on by the Chinese as long overdue recognition of the sacrifices that China had made for the common cause in the last five years. The Americans had thus no sort of guarantee that this life-line that was now being offered China as a last desperate chance would be adequate to reactivate her economy or the fighting spirit of her troops.

V COMMUNIST CHINA

It is true that another China was coming into being, using her own resources, in the mountainous districts of Chen-si and Kan-su, a Communist China under her leaders Mao Tse-tung and Chou En-lai, with her capital in Yenan. She was initiating a new form of fighting and working out the principles of a fundamental revolution.

Chinese Communism had its roots in an agrarian society; since its adversaries were occupying the towns, it had developed in a very poor rural community; in contrast to Russian Bolshevism, it drew its support from the peasant masses, masses composed of small farmers as much as real proletarians. A few intellectuals, some of them of bourgeois origin, succeeded in organising a real Communist state.

Following Stalin's directive Mao Tse-tung considered that before the revolution could succeed, Japan must be defeated. Once China had been liberated, the Revolution would spread to all colonial or semi-colonised countries. Nothing must stand in the way of victory and all men of goodwill who were anti-imperialist, including even capitalists, were invited to co-operate in its realisation. Accordingly, the 'United anti-Japanese National Front' was set up, which implied an agreement with Chiang Kaishek, however great the cost and even if Chiang's armies attacked the Communist Red Army.

The Chinese Communist party was thus led by economic pressures to abandon the idea of confiscating land in order to hand it over to poor peasants and to confine itself to reducing farm rents and land taxes in the areas which it controlled. It even declared its support for co-operation with capitalist industrialists if this could strengthen the war effort. So Mao Tse-tung condemned in vigorous terms those whom he called 'leftist deviationists' who thought that revolution could take place in one single operation and begin without further delay. Their attitude, he said, only succeeded in frightening many Chinese and isolating the Communist party. It would thus be playing into the hands of enemy number one: Japan.

The Communist state was self-sufficient; from the Soviet Union it received kind words but no material aid. The United States ignored it completely, at that time not so much because of hostility to its ideas as because she failed to realise its significance and underestimated the contribution it could make. In 1941, Mao Tse-tung arranged for the lessons he had delivered to the pupils of the Soviet Red Army Academy after 1936 to be printed, distributed and put into effect. It was his doctrine of revolutionary warfare, which starts from nothing and must lead to the victory of the revolution. Its essence is therefore aggression. But it must be applied in the light of a full knowledge of the real balance of forces; subversive warfare cannot succeed by means of a few decisive battles; it requires a long struggle and considerable suffering.

In particular, the enemy must be induced to penetrate deeply into the territory controlled by the Communist state; it is true that it would cause great devastation but it would also come up against a hostile population, controlled by the Party and determined to resist, in which guerrilla units would feel themselves at home as 'a fish in water'. So the Red Army should give as much ground as necessary, not in order to dig in behind some fortified line assumed to be impregnable but in order to wait for the situation to turn round in its favour; if no opportunity presented itself, it should disappear into thin air, melt into the population or else reform somewhere else. The favourable opportunity would be provided by the dispersal of the enemy's forces, which might give the partisans a temporary local superiority in numbers; and the enemy's troops which had been exposed in this way would then not be captured or obliged to withdraw but completely wiped out.

While the Chinese Red Army endeavoured to manufacture the weapons it needed in the territories under its control, it relied even more on seizing them from the enemy by plundering its transports, ransacking its stores and attacking its factories and arsenals.

In this way Mao Tse-tung defined the type of war which was for him 'one of the highest forms of the struggle to resolve the contradictions between classes, nations, states or political groups'. Victory would mean setting the seal on the identification of people, Army and Party. After that, the second stage, the revolution proper, could begin; to tell the truth, it had already begun because the forces that would bring it about were already in position. In this way the dictatorship of the proletariat would come about through the Communist party; and land, the banks and the big firms would be socialised.

This economic revolution would, however, be incomplete unless it was cultural as well. In his *Talks on art and literature in Yenan*, Mao emphasised still more strongly Lenin's refusal to accept bourgeois culture. He developed the theory, which was also Lenin's, that 'all art, literature and culture belong to a particular class and depend on a definite political line'. The proletarian party must fight on 'the cultural front'; revolutionary art must be 'useful for the revolutionary masses'. It is true that the artist remains creative; his value must, however, be assessed not by aesthetic but by political criteria; it is no use his 'expressing himself' if he does not speak the language that the masses expect.

Thus in 1942, Chinese Communism began to follow a line of thought different from that of Soviet Communism. At this time, the USSR was rediscovering her own historical, Russian values and extolling them in order to provide intellectual nourishment for her fight. On the other hand, even though for tactical reasons he had come to an understanding with Chiang Kai-shek, Mao Tse-tung never ceased denouncing the political and intellectual attitude of the Kuomintang as reactionary. For him, the class struggle was taking place at different levels—economic, political and ideological—at the same time. It must go on and on and would never be complete on the ideological level, even when the economic basis of bourgeois society had disappeared.

PART III

THE WATERSHED OF
THE WAR

At the end of 1942 and beginning of 1943, the map of the war became stabilised and then went into reverse on every front; the Axis armed forces were first checked and then pushed back. Yet this happy result was in no way the result of Allied co-ordination. In fact, the three operational theatres were separate and distinct: none of the belligerents was fighting in all of them. The Atlantic and North Africa were the lists in which the navies and air forces and to a smaller extent the armies of the British and Americans faced those of the Germans and Italians; the Russian steppes were the scene of a colossal single combat between Germany and the Soviet Union; in the Pacific, the United States were fighting it out with Japan; in all these theatres, there were the weaker brethren trying to cover themselves by joining in the fight of the larger powers.

The war had reached a turning point, but this was not the result of better organisation or strategy on the part of one or other of the two coalitions. But after having achieved almost unhoped-for success and attained their objectives, entirely in the first case and more or less completely in the second, Japan and Germany after their long series of victories had run out of steam. As they had not destroyed their opponents, the latter had gradually reformed and increased their strength, so that a balance of forces was reached. Victory had not yet decided whom she would eventually favour, but from now onwards she seemed to be more fickle.

The fact was that the American armament industry was beginning to turn out tanks, Flying Fortresses, aircraft-carriers, freighters, lorries, guns, submarines and tankers in large quantities. For her part, the Soviet Union found her wide open spaces working in her favour and she had completed the reconversion of her industry in the Urals and beyond. Thus the chances were becoming more even.

And so the Japanese expansion was halted at Guadalcanal and Midway whilst in the battle of the Atlantic the graph of the amount of shipping built intersected with that of the amount sunk, and the production of German submarines was balanced by the number of those lost. In Africa,

Rommel was brought to a halt at the gateway to Egypt and then pushed back; at the same time, the Americans gained a foothold in North Africa. Above all, the Red Army inflicted its first sharp defeat at Stalingrad.

In every operational theatre, hope changed sides.

CHAPTER 1

A Balance of Forces in the War at Sea

AFTER March 1942, the American Army and Navy planners had turned their minds to the problem of the necessary co-ordination between the services; the Navy and the Army were rivals and their views so divergent that all parties were agreed that a single command for the whole operational theatre was out of the question. It remained only to apportion the responsibility for each separate geographical area.

General MacArthur was made Commander-in-Chief of the Southwest Pacific Area, which included Australia, the Philippines, New Guinea, the Solomons, the Bismarck Islands and Indonesia. The rest of the Pacific came under Admiral Nimitz. These two commands were co-ordinated by the Joint Chief of Staff in Washington, which thus acted as GHQ for the Pacific. In fact, this headquarters had no head, except the President of the United States, and all its decisions were the result of compromise. In consequence, there were close-fought tussles, with few holds barred, over the allocation of ships, aircraft, units and supplies. But the first condition for success in each of the operational theatres that had been thus created and which were sufficiently large and separate for there to be little possibility of interference, was that the Commander-in-Chief had the ground, sea and air forces under his command: he chose his own deputies, decided on operations and had complete control in action.

In late 1943 the great strength of the Americans began to show itself by the appearance on operations of the B 29 bombers, splendidly adapted to the enormous size of the Pacific since they were able to carry nine tons of bombs for more than 3,000 miles at over 350 m.p.h.; each plane was a small factory with its six generators, its 170 various sorts of motor and fifteen miles of electric wiring. The American Navy had 9,000 landing craft and their naval shipyards were churning out submarines at the rate of one every five days. The battleships damaged at Pearl Harbour, now re-equipped and in some cases modernised, were gradually being brought back into service.

This military efficiency was shown in the introduction of a combat weapon as effective as it was flexible: the Task Force. Of varying size and composition, each task force represented at sea the equivalent of a tank corps on land. Using destroyers as scouts and submarines as escorts, its battleships and cruisers could fire by radar on an enemy twenty-five miles away. The aircraft-carriers provided the ships with intelligence, prepared their attack and protected them against enemy aircraft. Troop transports, workshop and hospital ships and supply vessels of all kinds and sizes gave the Task Force considerable autonomy of action and enabled it to concentrate its attacks on selected targets.

The American naval industry produced floating docks made of elements welded together which enabled the largest battleship to be repaired at sea. The dock was submerged by filling ballast tanks; the damaged ship was floated into it; then the ballast tanks were pumped out and the whole thing lifted out of the sea like an authentic dry dock. Valuable time was thus gained because, except in cases of really serious damage, ships no longer needed to travel all the way back to the American dockyards where they remained out of action for a long period.

II THE CORAL SEA AND MIDWAY

The Japanese were given their first warning in the Coral Sea from May 4 to 8, 1942. For the first time in history, the only units really engaged were aircraft-carriers; the warships did not join in but merely defended themselves against enemy aircraft. One aircraft-carrier was lost on each side. This indecisive battle had the result of averting any danger directed from Japan against the north of Australia and of inducing the Japanese to abandon the idea of taking Port Moresby by sea.

Another, more considerable, naval engagement took place on June 4 and 5, 1942, at Midway, an atoll situated 2,500 miles from Tokyo and something under 1,000 miles from Hawaii. After the idea of an attack on Australia had been rejected, since the Japanese Army was against it, Admiral Yamamoto, taking advantage of the feeling aroused by Doolittle's air raid on Tokyo, had succeeded in obtaining approval for a plan with a double objective: the remaining American fleet in the Pacific would be lured to Midway and destroyed.

Admiral Yamamoto had considerable forces at his disposal: nearly 200 vessels, including eleven battleships and eight aircraft-carriers with a strength of 700 aircraft. In order to disperse the American ships, Yamamoto concocted a diversionary operation against the Aleutians; he could not know that the American intelligence service had intercepted Japanese messages which left Admiral Nimitz in no doubt as to the real Japanese intentions. There was time to strengthen the air defences of Midway, notably with B 17 heavy bombers. But even when concentrated, the American naval forces were inferior, on paper, to their opponents, since they comprised only three aircraft-carriers, seven heavy cruisers and seventeen destroyers—and this despite the fact that Yamamoto had despatched two aircraft-carriers and four battleships to the Aleutians on a fool's errand.

Unfortunately for himself, the Japanese general also drew up his forces in a way calculated to reduce his margin of superiority: he made the blunder of fragmenting his forces into small vulnerable groups. In addition, as his aircraft-carriers had the task both of destroying Midway's defences and of attacking the American fleet, they were tied to a very exact timetable, which meant that they had little freedom of action. Also, Admiral Yamamoto was relying mainly on his battleships; the aircraft-carriers and submarines were intended to act merely as their advance guard and protective screen, thus failing to take advantage of the benefit that might accrue from using the ship-borne aircraft; finally, by mischance, the Japanese submarines had not reached their stations by the proper time and the Japanese were in the dark as to the movements of the closely concentrated American fleet.

Battle was joined on June 4, when a Japanese air raid on Midway destroyed their installations; if a landing had been made at once the island would have had to surrender on the spot; but the Americans had shot down forty-three enemy aircraft and these were going to be needed in the air and naval battle a few hours later. Indeed, the American squadron's aircraft attacked the Japanese planes as they were on their way back from Midway and short of fuel and ammunition. Three Japanese aircraft-carriers were destroyed as against only one American aircraft-carrier. One further tactical blunder was committed by Admiral Yamamoto during the fight: he formed his aircraft-carriers into a compact group, thus making them a target impossible to miss, whereas their American opponents were sufficiently far apart not to be hit by the same attack but close enough to help each other.

Without having had the opportunity of committing his battleships, and despite his superior armament, Admiral Yamamoto turned back since he totally lacked air support. For two days he was pursued by the Americans; guided by searchlight, their aircraft sank another Japanese aircraft-carrier, a battleship, a cruiser and three destroyers. On June 7 the chase was called off.

The aircraft-carriers had shown not only the crucial part they could play but also their vulnerability. When one of them was hit, its aircraft had to land on another one; there were many accidents, for instance one aircraft's machine guns went off as it was landing and killed many of the crew. The Americans had lost a large number of torpedo aircraft which lacked speed but had won the day partly because of the proximity of Midway, the aircraft which were based there and its airfields where the ship-borne aircraft were able to land as required.

The battle of Midway was in the best tradition of naval battles and it was a decisive one. Admiral Yamamoto had let slip an opportunity that would not occur again. The Japanese fleet was now only marginally superior to the Americans'. Above all, the Americans had won in spite of being the weaker side; they owed their victory to their better techniques, tactics and organisation and this augured well for the future.

III GUADALCANAL

After insistent demands General MacArthur had received his reinforcements: one Australian division which had been withdrawn from the Middle East and two American divisions. Although he considered this inadequate, he adopted the principle that Australia would have to be defended outside Australia, which meant that he was intending to take the offensive. A scheme to occupy and organise a good airfield close to Buna failed when the Japanese forestalled the Allies by three weeks.

Backed by Marshall, MacArthur reckoned that if the Navy 'did their stuff', it would be possible to make a direct attack on Rabaul straightaway. He would have liked to try in July 1942, but as the 700 aircraft collected in Australia could not now attack Rabaul from New Guinea, MacArthur asked the Navy for two aircraft-carriers. Admiral King thought the scheme was too ambitious and risky. His view was that they should advance more slowly and cautiously, starting by occupying Tulagi and Guadalcanal in the South Solomon Islands; the next stage would be the North Solomons, and Rabaul would have to be kept for the third stage.

As a result of this procrastination, the Japanese retained the initiative and in July 1942 landed on Guadalcanal, which could serve as an aircraft-carrier for advancing to New Caledonia. But a land attack on Port Moresby failed and a tough and costly series of actions was started by the Australians and Americans as they pursued the Japanese vigorously when they retreated. Then, although the Australians were poorly trained and not well equipped and the American artillery was inadequate, on August 7, 1942, 19,000 men were landed on Guadalcanal.

Success on the ground depended on supplying the troops and this could be done only by sea. A series of air and naval battles took place from

August 8 to October 26, with fluctuating fortunes on both sides. The Japanese had naval superiority but the Americans were stronger in the air. As a result the outcome remained uncertain.

The most important naval battle took place from November 12 to 15. It began with an unexpected engagement, haphazardly, because of an error in the functioning of the American radar; there were serious losses on both sides and two American admirals were killed. Shortly afterwards, eleven Japanese transports steaming towards Guadalcanal with inadequate protection were sunk. Finally, in the night of November 14–15, in thick fog, Admiral Lee's Task Force used its radar to destroy three Japanese cruisers and a Japanese battleship from a distance of nearly nine miles. 'The guns had been laid automatically on invisible targets,' Colonel Bernard wrote; 'allowance was made for the force and the direction of the wind, the speed of the ships, the pitching motion of the targets and the guns and the shells struck home with tremendous speed and accuracy.' As at Midway, this was a decisive American victory.

On February 8, 1943, Guadalcanal was taken. The Japanese succeeded in withdrawing part of their troops but their advance had now come to its end.

IV AMERICAN SUBMARINE OPERATIONS IN THE PACIFIC

Being forced to give priority to naval battles, the Japanese Navy did not have adequate means of protecting the convoys—troop-carriers and freighters—plying between the Japanese archipelago and its empire. There was no central authority to organise such a protection. And as Reussner wrote, 'it is not possible to improvise a convoy protection system; one needs the appropriate equipment, a coherent theory and personnel well-trained in anti-submarine warfare.'

On paper, the Japanese did indeed possess 300 escort vessels but they were old, slow and unarmed; later on, when the decision had been taken to build such vessels, there were no prototypes; suitable escort ships did not begin to be brought into action until 1943. These inadequate resources were distributed amongst the various port-admirals in the homeland and the territorial commands in the conquered countries. In such circumstances, any joint action was out of the question and each authority did as it pleased; it was practically impossible to co-ordinate the movements of convoys, reallocate escort vessels or draw up a regular list of priorities. The local authorities did not always know the arrival dates of the ships supposed to be on their way to them; if escort vessels happened to be available, everything was all right; if there were none, then the ships sailed away unprotected.

Accordingly, although precautions were taken to defend troop-carriers, which were as a rule always escorted by naval vessels, merchant ships were reduced to forming convoys to escort themselves, so that they could take advantage of each other's experience. American submarines had never had it so good.

The Americans had relatively few flotillas, but they used them to the best advantage. The Hawaiian flotilla's operations extended as far as Formosa and, with something over a dozen craft, it began to exercise an increasingly tight blockade over the east coast of Japan. The group based at Brisbane supported the surface fleet in hindering the Japanese advance towards New Guinea. The Fremantle flotilla had the task of cutting Japan's links with the Philippines, Indochina, the Indian archipelago and Malaya—the main sources of raw materials.

On December 31, 1942, Japan had lost a million tons of shipping through American submarine action, a loss barely made good by captured or newly built ships. Thus, in the Pacific, the Japanese thrust had, on the whole, been contained; inside its defensive perimeter, though Greater Asia was indeed still safe, the shadow of an American threat was appearing both in the air and at sea.

What was happening in the Atlantic Ocean during this same period?

V GERMAN SUBMARINE SUCCESSES IN THE ATLANTIC

In the Atlantic, the situation was reversed. It was the Allies who were experiencing the greatest difficulty in protecting their vital lines of communication against German submarines, which were enjoying considerable success and creating a critical situation for their opponents.

The Germans had been steadily increasing the number of submarines in service. In April 1942, Admiral Raeder reported the following situation to Hitler: the German Navy had 288 submarines, 125 of which were operational—19 in the Arctic Ocean, 81 in the Atlantic, 20 in the Mediterranean, 5 at base. Since the beginning of the war, 304 new submarines had been brought into service and 105 had been lost; the average monthly loss was 2.9 per cent of the total number and 4.9 per cent of the number at sea; as the Reich's naval dockyards were turning out approximately 20 submarines a month at that time, the number of new craft was more than the losses. The future looked optimistic. By the end of 1942, there would be 400 U-boats actually in service.

In addition, the quality of the submarines had also been steadily improving. Trials of the *Walter*, with a gas-turbine engine capable of an underwater speed of 23 knots, had proved successful; an anti-Asdic device and a radar detector had been perfected; the submarines were armed with electric and acoustic T 5 torpedoes, with a range of 6,500 yards and a speed of 25 knots.

Methods of submarine warfare had also improved. From the beginning of 1941, Admiral Doenitz had ordered the general tactics of undertaking night attacks only; the submarines remained submerged during the day, surfaced in the dark, fired their torpedoes and then dispersed with all speed to reload their forward tubes. In order to counteract their weakness when submerged, they were grouped into 'packs' so as to launch an almost uninterrupted sequence of attacks against the convoys they had spotted. In March 1942, the introduction of 'milch-cows', large tanker submarines, enabled submarines to be refuelled at sea and doubled the range of the smaller craft. As a result, there was no part of the Atlantic now beyond their reach—they were even operating off the American coast, from Canada as far south as Venezuela.

Submarine reconnaissance was provided by long-range four-engined aircraft based on Trondheim, Cognac, Vannes and Mérignac. They reported convoys to the west of Ireland in time for submarines and bombers to go out and attack them. In 1941, 220 co-ordinated attacks of this type were made. They ceased in 1942 when the Luftwaffe's heavy commitments in the USSR prevented it from operating in the Atlantic.

All the same, the submarines' list of kills was impressive and its rising curve was alarming for the Allies. Between September 1939 and December 1941 nearly 8 million tons of Allied merchant shipping had been sunk and only one-third of this replaced. The gravity of these figures spoke for itself. The United States entry into the war, far from improving the position by adding fresh tonnage and considerably increasing the potential naval construction programme, merely made it worse. The German submarines calmly waited to pick off the American ships almost as they came out of harbour—the large urban centres along the coast had no blackout. The American Merchant Marine alone suffered losses described by Morison as 'terrifying': 500,000 tons from January to April 1942, 350,000 in May, 365,000 in June; it was like a second Pearl Harbour.

For the first seven months of 1942 the overall Allied naval losses amounted to 4,760,000 tons, that is 460,000 tons more than in the previous year. The month of June was particularly disastrous: 800,000 tons went to the bottom; one Allied merchant ship was being sunk every four hours. Things were not much better in the last five months of 1942, because more than 3 million tons of shipping were lost—400,000 in the first week of July, as Churchill cabled to Roosevelt. In return, the Kriegsmarine had lost about 50 submarines, still less than were being turned out by its naval dockyards.

In addition, German surface ships began their raiding operations again. Between the North Cape and Spitzbergen, lurking in fjords or hiding behind the countless islands off the Norwegian coast, the battleship *Tirpitz* and four fast cruisers were constantly threatening the convoys that were carrying the promised equipment to Murmansk for the Russians. Other ships of the German Navy dealt a resounding, spectacular and humiliating blow to the pride of the Royal Navy. On February 12, 1942, the *Scharnhorst* and *Gneisenau*, which had been shut up in the outer harbour at Brest for the last six months and regularly bombed without sustaining any damage, managed to break out. After having momentarily toyed with the idea of putting the ships out of commission and transferring the crews to Norway, Hitler, ignoring Admiral Raeder's advice that the operation was too risky, had decided in fact to let them try to pass through the English Channel. The British Admiralty had anticipated this operation and were on the watch to foil it; they received regular intelligence from a French Resistance network called the *Confrérie Notre-Dame,* one of whose members was a naval officer in the Brest dockyard. The German ships left in the night of February 11, moving slowly because mine-sweepers were clearing the way for them. They were in fact spotted but a radar failure in two British reconnaissance aircraft caused delay in launching the formidable force that had been made ready to pursue them—6 destroyers, 8 MTBS, 42 torpedo aircraft and 500 fighters. The attacks could not start until noon on February 12. Hampered by bad visibility, they were unable to prevent the *Scharnhorst* and *Gneisenau* from arriving safely at Wilhelmshaven, although each of them struck a mine. The British had been made to look ridiculous on their favourite element, the sea, in the Straits of Dover to boot, right under their very noses.

VI ALARMING OUTLOOK FOR THE ALLIES

It is not exaggerating to think, as does Chester Wilmot, that the gloomy prospect of steadily mounting shipping losses was to colour the whole of Allied strategy for many months to come and even dictate it. In fact, the German submarines—the Italians and the Air Force were of secondary importance by comparison—were jeopardising their entire war effort. Their hopes of success depended on their industrial superiority and these hopes would be reduced to nil if this industrial production was finding its way to the bottom of the sea. In assessing the total damage, as well as the actual loss of shipping, there must be added all its cargo which would never reach its destination, that is, for a 3,000-ton freighter, a score of tanks, a similar number of guns, thirty or so self-propelled machine guns and 1,000 tons of supplies and ammunition.

Britain's imports, indispensable if she was to be the springboard for a successful counter-offensive and without which she could only become progressively weaker, fell to 24 million tons by weight compared with 30 millions in 1941 and 54 millions before the war. Transporting troops also became more difficult now that units were more motorised and powerfully armed. Lorries and jeeps were shipped dismantled and men were crammed into transatlantic liners—15,000 per trip were packed into the *Queen Mary* as compared with the 6,000 previously; but a successful enemy attack made the losses all the greater.

The Americans even began to wonder whether they would be able to maintain the European war effort as planned. It seemed it might be better to look to their own defence, such as ensuring the safety of the oil tanker traffic, without which their industry would grind to a halt. Should not priority be shifted to the Pacific until things improved in Europe? The Navy still found this solution tempting.

In any case, it was plainly impossible to meet all the obligations of the war at sea: a choice had to be made. In the autumn of 1942, the whole convoy system in the Atlantic was altered; those intended for the USSR and the Mediterranean were temporarily suspended, which called forth bitter protests from Stalin and well suited Rommel's book. The Home Fleet whose task was the protection of the British Isles had its destroyers taken away for convoy duty.

The Admiralty was at variance with the Air Ministry as to the best use of heavy bombers. Would it not be better to cease using them in raids on Germany and put them on anti-submarine patrols since there were not enough of them to fulfil both tasks at once? Admiral Pound pithily pointed out the principle on which Britain's power was based: 'If we lose the war at sea, we shall lose the war.' The RAF replied that by bombing the shipyards and submarine bases, they would win the war, by eliminating the opponent—it was Douhet's doctrine all over again. To this the Admiralty replied—and the admission must have been a painful one—that control of the sea had become pointless and indeed impossible without control of the air. In order to solve the problem, Churchill set up an interministerial committee on anti-submarine warfare with himself as chairman. At their first meeting in November 1942, the committee settled the squabble: they decided to transfer thirty Halifax bombers from Bomber to Coastal Command. Britain was in fact being thrust back on to the defensive. But however significant such a measure was, it did not solve the problem of protecting convoys.

VII CONVOY PROTECTION

The first important thing to be done—though it was unlikely to be achieved quickly—was to step up the output of freighters; yet it would not be sensible to do this at the expense of naval construction. In 1942, British shipyards turned out 1,300,000 tons of merchant shipping; with the help of the Canadian and, above all, the US shipyards, it would be possible to launch something over 7 million tons—but this was less than the amount being sunk.

Another thing would be to change the type of ships being built. Thus in a moment of untimely optimism, the Americans decided to give priority to landing equipment over escort vessels. These priorities were reversed but the decision did not become fully effective until towards the end of the war, when the submarine threat had died down considerably. Out of a programme of 1,000 escort destroyers planned by the United States, 520 were completed, 420 fitted out and only 373 brought into effective service during the war.

So the most urgent thing was to cut down losses. A more elaborate co-ordination of convoys partly succeeded in doing this. Coastal shipping destined for New York was directed into two channels, with sailings at regular intervals, one from Key West, the other from Guantanamo, with branch lines for the Gulf of Mexico and the Caribbean; this enabled more effective protection and reduced losses, which were especially high for isolated ships. Thus between August and December 1942, 166 Allied vessels in convoy were sunk as against 256 sailing separately; between January and July, the respective figures had been 73 and 574.

The Atlantic convoys linked on to the coastal convoys with the punctuality and accuracy of a railway timetable. But there were vast areas of the Atlantic, off Trinidad for example, which were out of range of land-based aircraft; these 'air-gaps' left the enemy submarines free to surface and refuel; the Germans did not fail to discover them and concentrate their submarines there.

The only real solution, therefore, was to strengthen the convoys' defences to enable them to fight the submarines on equal terms and, better still, sink them. For a long time the measures undertaken to achieve this were rather tentative. Then the British fitted out their escort vessels with radar and this greatly reduced the attacks in 'packs', since the submarines were detected several miles away. Wellington bombers were fitted with a searchlight which enabled them to operate at night; the explosive power of depth charges was doubled by using a new type of explosive.

The fact remained that only aircraft were capable of detecting submarines easily, attacking them without risk and pursuing them for a sufficient length of time to put them out of action. Since they did not have an adequate number of escort aircraft-carriers, the Admiralty fitted out cargo ships with catapults for fighter planes; but the escort vessels then had to pick up the aircrews, because the aircraft were irrecoverable. The remedy cost as much as the disease.

The final and decisive solution was thus the aircraft-carrier, armed both with anti-submarine weapons and fighters. The first one, the *Audacity*, converted from a captured German liner, came into service in the autumn of 1941; she carried only eight aircraft and she was sunk by a submarine in December 1941; despite this unhappy beginning, in December 1942 for the first time the number of submarines destroyed was the same as the number of freighters sunk, whereas previously the proportion had been ten ships sunk for every submarine put out of action. The experiment was thus conclusive.

The first mobile protection group was formed in September 1942; it consisted of six naval vessels and a tanker; its task was to go to the aid of convoys under attack and to hunt down the submarines whilst the escorting vessels, the convoys' watchdogs, could only bark at their heels without moving very far away. But this sort of group could achieve maximum effectiveness only if it included aircraft-carriers and these did not come into general use until the spring of 1943.

VIII TOWARDS A BALANCE OF FORCES IN THE BATTLE OF THE ATLANTIC

On December 31, 1942, Hitler learnt through the BBC of the failure of a German naval operation on the Murmansk route. The heavy cruiser *Hipper*, one light cruiser and six destroyers had attacked a convoy without much effect. The Führer was furious and his rage was fanned by Goering, who complained at having to immobilise air squadrons in support of a navy which, he claimed, was not fighting with sufficient determination. Hitler echoed this complaint and held the Army up as an example to the Navy; when the former 'has once launched an operation, it sees it through to the bitter end'. In his irritation the Führer contemplated having the guns unbolted from the heavy naval surface vessels and installed on land. In the end, he took the decision not to send any more ships of the line out to sea; they would be restricted to operating in Norwegian waters and even in the Baltic.

Admiral Raeder bore the brunt of the Master's wrath; he was replaced

as Commander-in-Chief of the Kriegsmarine by Admiral Doenitz, hitherto
the Chief Submarine Commander. The logical conclusion was that submarine warfare was going to be intensified. But what with? On the one
hand, as the Allied aircraft received their radar equipment, so it became
more dangerous for the submarines to surface; in Doenitz's words, 'they
had to keep their heads under water'. In October 1942, thirteen submarines had been sunk and in November, fifteen as against only eleven
new ones built. The German naval construction programme was still
suffering from Hitler's earlier decisions in 1939 and 1940 to grant priority
in the allocation of raw materials to the Army's needs—Admiral Raeder
wrote that he had been reduced to obtaining copper on the French and
Belgian black markets. Doenitz worked out an improved production
schedule; thirty submarines were to be built per month—but not until the
end of 1944.

For their part, the Americans formed five mobile convoy protection
groups in March 1943. There were now also merchant ships coming into
service which had been converted into escort vessels and aircraft-carriers
each with a score of aircraft and a flying deck some 150 to 190 yards long.
The Kaiser shipyards in the States were being equipped to mass-produce
them.

Results were soon forthcoming. In March 1943 the Allied shipping
losses still amounted to 500,000 tons, 97 ships in all. But then these
figures suddenly dropped. In April, one convoy lost 13 ships but sank 5
submarines. The amount of shipping built matched the shipping sunk;
the number of German submarines destroyed rose above the number
brought into service. As in the Pacific, a balance of forces was reached in
Britain's life-line, the Atlantic.

And the expectations of the British and the Americans were all the
greater since the vicissitudes of the war at sea had not prevented them
from taking the offensive in Africa with great success.

CHAPTER 2

The Germans Halted in Africa

SINCE April 1941, Rommel and his *Afrika Korps*, together with the Italian allies to whom he was subordinated, had been occupying the Bardia–Sollum Halfaya line in Cyrenaica. To enable the troops to hold their positions and if possible to strike out towards Egypt, the vital problem was their supplies. The only way they could get through was by sea and the Malta-based aircraft and ships were a constant threat to the convoys. After the Wehrmacht's attack on the USSR, the African front became even more of a side-show for the Germans; both for Mediterranean shipping and vital reinforcements, the Axis troops had to rely above all on Italy. And, as time went by, it emerged that the latter was very weak.

I ITALIAN WEAKNESS

In order to hold on to the conquests which she had had such trouble in acquiring, Italy had immobilised thirty divisions in Yugoslavia and Greece; eight others, one of them armoured, was on guard between the Little Saint Bernard Pass and the Mediterranean; there were two defending Sicily; and finally, there were Messe's troops in the USSR, some ten large units adding up to a total of 200,000 men and 22,000 motorised vehicles.

This Italian Army, seriously weakened as a result of being dispersed, had been unable to mobilise in the way which it had anticipated and which would have provided it with eighty divisions. The armaments factories were turning out seventy tanks and twelve self-propelled tracked guns per month, barely enough to form two armoured battalions every three months. The shortage of coal and electricity as well as the lack of raw materials meant that only 300 aircraft could be produced per month, for the most part inferior in quality to British aircraft.

At sea, since Kesselring's Luftwaffe had abandoned the airfields of Sicily for those of the USSR, the percentage of Italian convoys lost rose from 12 per cent in July 1941 to 41 per cent in July and 62 per cent in November; according to Bragadin, at the end of 1941 the proportion of ships sunk rose to 80 per cent. These losses were due mainly to the British 'K Force' in

Malta, composed of light cruisers and destroyers supported by long-range torpedo aircraft.

After such a blood-letting, the Italian Navy was virtually defenceless; none of her ships was yet equipped with radar; only three destroyers possessed any device comparable to Asdic; there was only one escort vessel fit to carry out its tasks; the conversion of two liners into aircraft-carriers did not solve the problem. In December 1941, Mussolini drew the moral from his failure and wrote to Hitler: 'It is at sea that the outcome of the battle is being jeopardised.'

Indeed, from June to November 1941, even with less traffic than in the preceding six months, the Italian Navy lost forty-four ships, totalling 220,000 tons. On November 9, a complete convoy of nine ships was sunk; on December 14, ships totalling 100,000 tons were assembled to escort two ships carrying tanks—involving a prohibitive consumption of fuel, for a petrol shortage was looming up in the near future. Some ships were already having to empty their tanks to provide fuel for others.

It was in these favourable conditions that Auchinleck attacked in November 1941; in mid-December, after a tank-battle lasting a whole month, Rommel, unable to make good the gaps left by the fighting, was compelled to retreat as far as the Great Syrtis, abandoning Cyrenaica; he stopped on the El Agheila–Maranda line which he was able to hold thanks to the lie of the land and the opponent's exhaustion.

However, the Axis troops that managed to hold out there were in a sorry state. The *Afrika Korps* had lost 15,000 of its 45,000 men, 220 of its 250 tanks and some fifty guns. On the Italian side, things were much worse; their five divisions now numbered only 20,000 men, with 80 per cent of their tanks gone and half their artillery—120 tanks and 180 guns abandoned or captured by the enemy. It is easy to see how Churchill was able to predict in the House of Commons 'the thorough destruction of the German-Italian army in Africa in the very near future'. But Rommel was tough and Churchill was counting his chickens before they were hatched.

                    II ROMMEL'S 'RECOVERY'

In fact, a series of mishaps severely handicapped the British Mediterranean squadron; the aircraft-carrier *Ark Royal* and one battleship were sunk and two cruisers were damaged by mines. On December 18 the Italians sent manned torpedoes into Alexandria harbour and put two battleships on their beam-ends, where they lay for several months. These losses, added to those that the Royal Navy was suffering at the same time in the Atlantic and off Malaya, resulted in the British Navy's sudden disappearance from the Mediterranean. The Commonwealth troops in Egypt had to be provisioned via the long route round the Cape.

Then again the winter truce in the USSR enabled Kesselring's Second Air Fleet to return to Sicily. Once more Malta was heavily pounded; the Axis MTBS and submarines preyed on the approaches to the island, so that she was again reduced to impotence. In February 1942, by a strange and rapid reversal of the situation, not one single ton of the Italian convoys to Tripoli was lost.

Rommel was not a man to let such an opportunity slip through his fingers and he seized it even before he had time to ascertain whether or not it was favourable. Seeing that the British were hesitating and marking time—Australian divisions had had to be withdrawn from the Middle East and sent to the Pacific—he took up the offensive again on his own initiative, barely eighteen days after retreating, and without waiting or asking for the permission of his Italian commander or even paying any heed to his advice. The British were caught unawares and withdrew in disorder. Without firing a shot, Rommel reconquered Benghazi, whose population was now becoming used to changing its master every so often, and in seventeen days he reached the area of Tobruk. General Ritchie, commander of the British Eighth Army, somehow managed to establish himself on the Gazala–Bir-Hakeim line, having lost in his turn 130 guns, 280 tanks and 2,000 lorries. This was the round trip to Libya.

In order to consolidate this unexpected victory, the Axis clearly had to take precautions in case the British returned to the attack, that is they had to neutralise Malta. This could be done diplomatically if the Italian ships were allowed to move in the shelter of Tunisian territorial waters and if the Axis was given control of the base at Bizerta. This was the course advocated by Marshal Cavallero, the Italian Chief of Staff. He emphasised that in this way the war in the Mediterranean would be finally won; he believed that, at a price, the Vichy government would not raise great difficulties; since Italy was neither able nor willing to give up Corsica, could not Germany promise France the Walloon area of Belgium and even Brussels? But Hitler refused to commit himself; being completely taken up with the eastern front, he wanted at all costs to avoid creating new problems in the Mediterranean.

In these circumstances, the only alternative seemed to be to capture Malta. This was also suggested by Marshal Cavallero, supported by Admiral Raeder, who wrote to Hitler in February 1942: 'It is a matter of urgency to seize Malta as quickly as possible and to launch an attack against the Suez Canal before the end of 1942.' Mussolini was all enthusiasm for this idea but he knew that the Italian forces were incapable of carrying it out on their own. As for Rommel, he had no desire to find himself deprived of the resources he needed for his long-awaited final victorious advance towards Egypt.

The decision depended, of course, on Hitler and he proved to be both attracted by it and yet hesitant. Finally, he remained faithful to the principle of not doing two things at once and the OKW approved: the date for the great offensive towards the Caucasian oil was drawing near; what did the sinking of a few Italian ships matter compared with this crucial target? Easy though it might seem in view of the dilapidated state of her defences, the capture of Malta would nevertheless mean taking aircraft and men away from the Russian front; moreover, once the island had fallen, it would be necessary to set up a solid defence on it and this would require regular reinforcements and supplies. In short, Hitler was for postponing the attack.

Moreover, the German Air Force seemed quite adequate for the task. Out of the 150 British aircraft based in Malta at the beginning of January 1942, in February only thirty remained. The British tried to reinforce them by Spitfires, which took off from aircraft-carriers and landed on airfields which German bombs had turned into craters. But the island also had to be kept supplied and only ships were capable of doing this. However, in March 1942, out of a convoy of 26,000 tons, only 5,000 reached their destination. June was much worse: a convoy coming from Egypt had to turn back while one from Gibraltar lost four of its six freighters on the way, at the hands of German aircraft and Italian cruisers.

Inversely, the shipping intended for the Axis troops in Africa was crossing as regular as clockwork. In the first quarter of 1942, only 16,000 out of 190,000 tons went to the bottom; in April, 160,000 tons got through with losses of 1 per cent and in May 170,000, with 7 per cent losses. Surely one could conclude from this that Malta had become harmless and did not require much more attention? Hitler informed Mussolini of his view that it would be better for Rommel to strike against Egypt. Perhaps the Führer, still fascinated by vistas of grandeur, had been attracted by the image of a gigantic pincer movement seizing the Middle East from Libya on one side and Turkey on the other. In any case, the time was past when the Duce had an equal right to put forward his point of view and his criticisms. He meekly acquiesced in the opinion of his ally and protector. 'The historic moment had come to conquer Egypt,' he said.

III THE 'AFRIKA KORPS'' OFFENSIVE TOWARDS EGYPT

This was what Rommel had been waiting for. In the words of Bauer, 'the *Afrika Korps* had grown its claws again.' In January 1942 it had been reinforced by the arrival of 150 tanks followed by another 135; its strength had been increased by eleven battalions—ludicrous figures in comparison with those engaged in the USSR but sufficient to tip the scale of power in Africa. The kindly spring weather had enabled this amount to be tripled. So Rommel was able to convince Hitler, with whom he was in correspondence over the heads of the Italian authorities, that he would reach Cairo in no time at all; once he was master of the rich Nile delta, it would supply him with his provisions, and, having lost her function, Malta would fall 'like a ripe fruit'. Marshal Cavallero showed some scepticism, but this Piedmontese general, whom Ciano branded as having 'the mentality of a Neopolitan parliamentarian', was used to bending to the Duce's wishes; and the Master had spoken. The fact remained, as Admiral Assman stressed, that 'the attack on Malta would have ensured a solid base for one of the pillars on which the projected operation rested, while to go rushing off first to Suez was a major gamble which was completely unnecessary from the strategic point of view.' But the optimism and dash of Rommel, who had Hitler's ear and was liked by him, had won over even the OKW, which, following his example, suddenly changed from favouring cautious defence in Africa to a desire for an offensive at all costs. And Rommel was to come very close to winning his gamble.

His opponent, General Auchinleck, had a presentiment of the German attack. He insistently demanded replacements for the units which had been transferred to the Pacific and was promised eight divisions, though he estimated that he needed seventeen, or at the very least twelve. He vigorously denounced the behaviour of his troops, whom he described as 'amateurs', and of their officers, whom he saw as old style Bengal lancers. As he also considered his tanks and anti-tank weapons to be inferior to those of the Germans, Auchinleck was in no hurry to obey Churchill's orders, while the latter, seething with impatience, was urging him to take up the offensive.

But it was Rommel who attacked, on May 26. After a few days of indecisive fighting, the Eighth Army retreated, leaving the Free French brigade under General Koenig to delay the enemy advance and prevent it from carrying out an encircling sweep from the south, by clinging on to Bir-Hakeim for as long as possible; Koenig fulfilled his task. Nevertheless, after only fourteen hours of siege, Tobruk, which had held out for so long the previous year, fell on June 20, giving Rommel 40,000 prisoners, a large amount of equipment and above all stocks of provisions and fuel which there had not been time to destroy and which were very welcome to the *Afrika Korps* and its vehicles. A few days later, Rommel was at Mersa Matruh and then at El Alamein, where Auchinleck admitted that he was not sure of being able to hold on.

In London, emotion was running high. Egypt seemed lost and the fleet evacuated Alexandria. Egyptian nationalism reared its head at once. Fortunately Nahas Pasha, the head of the Anglophile group of the Wafd, who had been made Prime Minister by the British ambassador, Sir Miles Lampson, proved absolutely reliable, even though his old opponent Ahmed Maher did not conceal his hostility towards the occupier. In order to ensure law and order, the British took the precaution of disarming the Egyptian troops. Nahas Pasha placed the emphasis on defending democracy, expelled dubious elements from his ministry and even dissociated himself from the secretary general of the Wafd. British law and order reigned in Egypt.

Churchill, however, had to face criticism in the House of Commons. He launched a dramatic and passionate appeal which recalled the worst moments of the summer of 1940: 'Every man in uniform must fight as if Kent or Sussex was going to be invaded. Egypt must be held at all costs.' He dismissed Auchinleck, who was the scapegoat for the defeats and especially for the loss of Tobruk, whereas the general had warned London in January 1942 that no stronghold could be held beyond the Egyptian frontier.

However, the inexorable law of desert warfare this time played in favour of the British and saved them. At the gates of Alexandria, while his opponents were in complete confusion, Rommel now had only twenty-six tanks with which to deal the final blow, and these were short of petrol; his soldiers were exhausted; his supply lines, which were too far extended, were being bombed by the RAF. Sick at heart, he was forced to halt. It would perhaps have been wiser to retreat again in order to put 250 miles of desert between the *Afrika Korps* and the British Army, which was taking on a new lease of life and increasing in strength as it reached Egyptian soil. But this was not Rommel's temperament, nor was it Hitler's orders.

Since the fighting in the USSR had made it necessary to recall the four German squadrons from Sicily, Malta had begun to breathe again; from August 1942 onwards she suffered fewer and fewer attacks and in November none at all. The number of bombers and torpedo aircraft based there could be considerably increased. Once again the Italian convoys found themselves exposed to alarming attacks: from August 1942 to January 1943 fifty-three ships were sunk; in October losses reached 44 per cent and in December 52 per cent. Rommel was suffering from the fact that the fronts were mutually dependent and from the difficulties facing the Wehrmacht in the USSR. Would he be able to resist the new attack which the British were preparing?

IV THE PAUSE AT EL ALAMEIN. THE BRITISH PREPARATIONS

The *Afrika Korps* had come within forty miles of Alexandria. On August 31 its leader said to his troops: 'In three days we shall be at Alexandria.' In actual fact the battle lasted till September and the soldiers dubbed it the 'six day race'. It was the British superiority in the air combined with the *Afrika Korps'* lack of petrol which clinched the matter. The British aircraft made 18,000 sorties and dropped 930 tons of bombs on their opponents, who were concentrated in an area of less than sixty miles. Rommel had asked for at least 10,000 tons of petrol; he was promised 6,000 and received 600.

The only result of the German attacks was to make a small gap in the enemy lines which was gradually closed up again. Rommel did not like failure and for eighteen months he had spared no effort nor his health. He went back to Germany to rest. The first round of the battle had ended in a draw.

When he returned on October 24, he found a very different state of affairs. Churchill had completely recast the British command; in Cairo Alexander had replaced Auchinleck as Commander-in-Chief; Montgomery had been put in command of the Eighth Army. This son of a Tasmanian clergyman was a strange mixture of mysticism, austerity and careful determination; he had absolute self-confidence; in his mobile command post he kept a portrait of Rommel so that he could stare at it intensely in order to divine his opponent's intentions at his leisure. He demanded a great deal of himself and of his troops; he thought that they should lead a strict life and that comfort made them soft. No one was given home leave, only leave to go to Cairo. Some campaign veterans thus found themselves away from home for five years. Surprisingly, Montgomery enjoyed great popularity among his soldiers, who nicknamed him 'Monty'.

Despite his eccentricities, 'Monty' was a cautious and extremely careful leader. He had realised that the ups and downs which the Eighth Army had been experiencing since 1940 with their succession of victories and defeats, were demoralising the men. His intention was to muster enough resources to advance without afterwards being forced to retreat. He cancelled the orders involving further withdrawal, sacked some of his officers, supervised training and, in a way which was unprecedented in the British Army and seemed impossible in view of the independent traditions of each of the services, combined the Army and Air Force in a joint general staff. He formed an armoured force similar to the *Afrika Korps*. And he waited until a continuous stream of reinforcements had arrived in Egypt and given him ample and lasting superiority in men and equipment. Churchill, always impetuous, was irritated by this slowness and urged Montgomery to hurry. But the latter, although still unknown, was daring enough, according to his biographer Alan Moorehead,[1] simply to reply to the all-powerful Prime Minister: 'If the attack begins in September it will fail; if we wait until October, I can guarantee a great victory and the destruction of Rommel's army; am I still to attack in September?' And Winston, who liked men of character, approved the plan which Monty submitted to him.

The Nile delta was a far livelier jumping-off point for an army than the Cyrenaican desert. Montgomery received a further supply of American Sherman tanks and he soon had twice as many tanks as Rommel. He gained the mastery he needed in the air. Fresh troops, notably New Zealanders, put new life into his infantry. He united his various different units into a homogeneous force. At last, by the night of October 23-24, he considered that he was ready and he launched his offensive.

V THE BATTLE OF EL ALAMEIN

Montgomery's preparations had not gone unnoticed by the German-Italian command. They had wondered whether, after the fruitless attack of August 31, it would not be better to fall back to the west in order to reduce its line of communications and increase that of its opponents. Rommel had had several discussions with Kesselring about this. They concluded that the positions which they had reached, stretching from the sea to the Qattara depression, an area of many hundreds if not thousands of square miles which were completely impassable, were good and must be held. Kesselring had no difficulty in convincing Mussolini, who was obsessed with the long-delayed leap to victory in Egypt. Rommel, for his part, saw Hitler and he seems not to have suggested a withdrawal which he knew the Führer opposed on principle.

The lie of the land did not leave much chance for the opponents to show great imagination in their renewed attack; with one flank backing on to the sea and the other bordering on the desert, their only possibilities were a frontal attack on the flank or an encircling movement from inland, or to carry out both operations simultaneously or in succession. The tanks were hampered in their movements by dust and gravel, low-lying marshes, sandstorms and surfaces of jagged rock. The desert air was healthy but the

1. *Montgomery*, London, Hamish Hamilton, 1965.

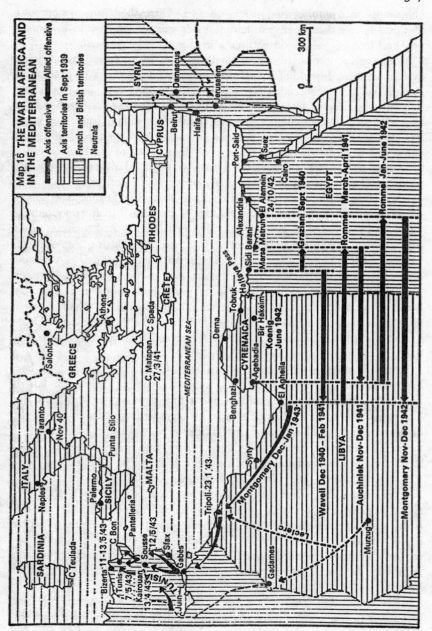

Map 15 THE WAR IN AFRICA AND IN THE MEDITERRANEAN

→ Axis offensive ← Allied offensive

Axis territories in Sept 1939

French and British territories

Neutrals

ubiquitous mosquito carried nasty diseases. Over the vast, monotonous expanses where there were no landmarks, it was all too easy to lose one's way and lack of water soon became a matter of grave concern.

Montgomery was not much of an innovator; he preferred to act with extreme caution. Instead of trying to destroy the enemy tanks all at once, as Rommel did, he proceeded by nibbling operations and by frequently switching his line of attack, in one of those decisive breakthrough battles which Churchill compared to a naval battle but which was even more like an air battle; thus one by one the bases essential for the enemy tank operations were destroyed; the tanks were then forced to fall back in order to escape destruction themselves. This was what Monty meant by his phrase: 'I'll make Rommel dance to my tune.'

Rommel had protected his defence lines by laying hundreds of thousands of mines. On the evening of October 24, one British armoured division had succeeded in breaking through but another had scarcely made any advance; the situation was not very satisfactory. During the night of October 24-25, Montgomery and his lieutenants had a council of war and decided to carry out their plan at all costs. But at the same time, in order to be ready for any eventuality, Monty positioned troops in reserve. 'A leader who can act like this,' he wrote with a self-satisfaction which he took no trouble to disguise, 'is on the point of victory.' On the morning of October 25 the 10th Armoured Division also succeeded in crossing the minefields.

When Rommel made a hasty return from Germany, the situation had taken a disturbing turn; his deputy, General Stumme, had been killed. Fighting continued on his positions for a few days longer and then the 'desert fox' had to make himself scarce. He signalled the OKW on the night of November 2-3. They waited until Hitler was awake to tell him the bad news. The Führer's violent anger surprised no one. How had they dared to disobey him, he exclaimed, when the previous day he had ordered Rommel to 'conquer or die'? However, Rommel's aide-de-camp arrived at the OKW to justify his leader's decision: one had to accept the inevitable. Despite his preoccupation with the situation in Stalingrad and although disturbing concentrations of ships had been reported at Gibraltar, Hitler decided to reinforce the African Army with men, tanks and aircraft, apparently without any concern about the delays they would encounter on their way. In actual fact it proved possible to send only a few thousand men.

After 'de-mining Rommel's garden', Montgomery took great care not to launch into a wild race to cover the greatest possible distance in the shortest possible time. He had fully realised that in desert warfare supplies must follow on so as to avoid Pyrrhic victories. After each advance, he did not extend his lines, however great the temptation or however favourable the opportunity. He waited for the enemy counter-attack in positions which he himself had chosen; he boldly set up stocks of equipment and food supplies as near as possible to the front; he formed a 'forward supply group', with the task of equipping harbours and bases as he advanced.

Hitler's orders forbade Rommel to disengage in order to have room to regroup; he was to fight every inch of the way, which was exactly what Montgomery was wanting. But he could not find any line to establish a foothold. Petrol was arriving in ever-diminishing quantities. He clashed with the Italian command which, under pressure from the Duce, did not wish to be pushed so unceremoniously out of Cyrenaica and intended offering resistance at Sollum, then at Mersa el-Brega, short of the Great Syrtis, and finally at Bouerat outside Tripoli. However, these intentions were cancelled and contradicted by the Italian units which, after fighting bravely at El Alamein, became demoralised in retreat and broke up. And how was it possible to hold on firmly to a specific point with defeated troops who were not receiving any replacements either of equipment or ammunition?

Despite his steady succession of victories Montgomery was not free of anxiety; he could solve his supply problem only by capturing harbours which were in good condition. In January 1943 he wrote that if he did not reach Tripoli within ten days he would have to halt or even withdraw. But he arrived there before the fateful date and by a symbolic chance was joined there by the small Free French unit, ragged and wretchedly armed, which Leclerc had brought victoriously across the Sahara from Lake Chad. Nothing could now stop the Eighth Army. The conquest of Cyrenaica was followed by that of Tripolitania. Both Churchill and Montgomery noted it in their memoirs; 'Before El Alamein,' wrote one of them, 'we never had a victory; after El Alamein we never had a defeat'; which the other echoed when he wrote: 'For seventeen months we did not have one single failure.' The British victory in Africa was a replica of the American success at Midway; it was not due to a lucky chance, to a temporarily favourable combination of circumstances or to the genius of a military leader but to the superiority which the Allies had gained in armaments, manpower and organisation. And so the Mareth line, the gateway to Tunisia, had now been reached and other Allied troops, Americans this time, had come from the other side of the Atlantic to join hands with the Eighth Army.

VI OPERATION 'TORCH': THE ALLIED DECISION

In April 1942, the British and Americans had agreed on Operation 'Bolero', by which a powerful American force would be assembled in Britain, capable, at the earliest possible moment, of launching the full-scale attack across the Channel for which Stalin was continuing to clamour. If it were further delayed, there was a risk that either the Russians would be defeated or they would cut their losses with the Germans in order to put an end to the fighting in the east. A limited operation ('Sledgehammer') had been contemplated for the summer of 1942 but calculations had shown that a landing would not really be possible before the spring of 1943 at the earliest (Operation 'Round-up').

However, Churchill had mapped out another plan which he had christened 'Gymnast'. Why not strike while the iron was hot and take advantage of the flourishing state of the North African front in order to gain victory by a landing in French territory? Churchill had a bee in his bonnet about bringing the French colonies back into the war; he saw all sorts of advantages in it: it would ensure the protection of Gibraltar, regain control of the Mediterranean, economise on shipping by avoiding detours round the Cape and very quickly bring down Italy, the weakest opponent.

The Americans, however, and Marshall particularly, were of a very different opinion. With their industrial power and their inexperience in military matters, they saw an offensive as an immense rationalised operation which would bring enormous amounts of equipment together at the right place and at the right time, thanks to meticulous planning and an exact timetable against which the Germans would have no adequate reply. The British, who were more empirical and wanted to husband their strength, were amused by this youthful impetuosity; for them the landing could only be the last and crucial blow against an enemy already worn down by a series of previous attacks.

It quickly became apparent that it was impossible to attempt to do anything across the Channel during the summer of 1942, because of the earlier delay in assembling men and equipment in Britain. The plan was to have a million men ready to embark in 2,200 special landing craft in the autumn of 1942; in fact, there were only 250,000 men and 400 craft. This was the result of the support given to MacArthur in the Pacific and Alexander in Egypt. Plans had to be revised.

Seizing his chance, Churchill, whose besetting sin was stubbornness, brought up 'Gymnast' again and since Marshall was still reluctant, he appealed to Roosevelt. On July 30, after several weeks of discussion, Roosevelt resigned himself to following his ally, on condition that the plan for a landing in Europe in the spring of 1943 was not abandoned.

Churchill, however, knew that his most authoritative military leaders were of the opinion that a landing in French North Africa in 1942 would make another landing in Europe in 1943 impossible. His silence on this point, as d'Hoop writes,[1] leads one to assume 'both an inveterate optimism and blatant dishonesty'. The experimental Dieppe raid on August 19, 1942 seemed to prove that he was right. Carried out with 6,000 men and one tank regiment, it needed 237 ships and landing craft and although a good deal was learnt from it, it ended in failure after revealing the full complexity of large-scale amphibious operations. Nevertheless, some Americans, in particular Admiral King, did not draw the same conclusions from it as the British Premier: since it was impossible to attack in Europe, they said, they might just as well reinforce MacArthur in the Pacific, and since King was in charge of the allocation of ships, it needed all Roosevelt's authority to prevent Operation 'Torch'—the code name given to the landing in North Africa—from being deprived of essential shipping from the outset.

The fact nevertheless remained that 'Torch' was a makeshift operation, for which time was even more short because the date was fixed for the autumn, in order to prevent the Wehrmacht from taking advantage of the semi-truce in winter in the USSR by reorganising its troops in the west. Both the diplomatic and the military preparations—and the two were linked—would be bound to suffer from this.

Indeed the first problem which the preparations for 'Torch' had to solve was what kind of welcome the Allies would receive from the French troops and authorities; they were known to be loyal to Vichy—this they had proved at Mers el-Kebir, at Dakar, in the Middle East and in Madagascar—and very much against the British and the Free French. In order not to jeopardise the chances of coming to an agreement, it was therefore decided that it would be strictly an American operation, at least outwardly; it would be under an American general and, failing Marshall, whom Churchill suggested but whom Roosevelt wanted to keep by him, the choice fell on Eisenhower. It was also decided that General de Gaulle and Free France and even more the internal French Resistance should be kept out of the way and in ignorance—a decision which was all the more agreeable to Roosevelt because he denied that Free France had any right to represent France and because the American authorities had been greatly annoyed by the incidents of St-Pierre and Miquelon, which had been 'freed' by Admiral Muselier against the United States' wishes, and of New

1. 'Les Problèmes Stratégiques de la Grande Bretagne, juin '41–juillet '42', *Revue d'histoire de la deuxième guerre mondiale*, July 1965.

Caledonia, when the French commissioner Thierry d'Argenlieu had briefly taken to the jungle on the arrival of the Americans. Cordell Hull referred to them as the 'so-called Free French'.

But how were they to approach the Vichy troops in such a way as to neutralise them without at the same time divulging the secret of the expedition? The American diplomats made some discreet inquiries as to how they stood, with Murphy, the Consul-General at Algiers, playing the chief role. It seemed impossible to approach Pétain directly and dangerous to bring Admiral Darlan into it—even though he was Commander-in-Chief of the Vichy troops and even though he had made a few timid advances to the Americans after being removed from power in favour of Laval in April 1942; but he was the man of the 'Paris protocol' who supported French collaboration with the Axis. And the French Navy's hostility to the British was common knowledge. General Weygand continued to enjoy great prestige in French North Africa but he no longer had any official post and he declined the surreptitious advances which were made to him—he was above all else, he said, a disciplined soldier.

The Americans' choice therefore fell upon General Giraud, a man with a firmly established reputation in Africa as a good fighter, who had made a glorious escape from the fortress of Koenigstein and who had dared to stand up to Otto Abetz, the Reich's ambassador, when he came to ask him on behalf of the Führer to go back to his German prison, since otherwise he would make the French prisoners of war pay for it. The American diplomat Murphy had several conversations with Giraud, which ended in a vague agreement whose ambiguity was going to give rise to serious misunderstandings and tiresome confusion. The Americans recognised Giraud as the leader of the French Resistance; between de Gaulle the outcast and Pétain the untouchable they were, in fact, backing a 'third man'. They were relying on him to rally the French North African troops to the Allied cause and to avoid any bloodshed between the French and themselves. But whether he was intoxicated with his popularity or whether he had been deceived, General Giraud had completely different ideas; he thought that he was going to be put in charge of all the Allied troops in North Africa; he advocated a landing on the French Mediterranean coast, and no one told him bluntly that it was impossible; he set up a complete semi-clandestine network in the Armistice Army which he intended sending into the occupied zone. Sure that the Americans would support him, he had nothing but contempt for the French underground Resistance and he evaded the approaches which they made to him. To him, General de Gaulle was merely a brigadier-general, whose respect for discipline and rank required him to submit to his command. Some of Giraud's remarks give the impression that he saw himself as the head of the whole European

Resistance movement. In fact, having been away from France for nearly two years, General Giraud had not gauged the development of French public opinion; he disapproved of collaboration for patriotic reasons; but he did approve of the National Revolution, for he had said so and put it in writing; he had complete and utter respect for Pétain.

VII THE PREPARATIONS IN NORTH AFRICA

Every step was taken to keep Giraud's arrival in Algiers till the last moment, so that it would cause the psychological shock that was hoped for; a British-controlled network in France, 'Alliance', was given the task of transporting him on a British submarine. In North Africa itself, the field had been prepared both by the Americans and by the General's emissaries; American consuls, who were sometimes nothing more than disguised special service agents, had established themselves in the big cities after an agreement with General Weygand at the time of his proconsulate in Africa and had for some months been enlarging the number of necessary contacts. The Office of Strategic Services itself had set up a powerful branch in Tangier and established contacts with the intelligence and counter-espionage services of the Armistice Army which had rallied to Giraud. So a whole conspiracy could be set afoot in Algeria and Morocco.

The American consuls had found that on the whole the people of North Africa—officials, French settlers and natives—were loyal to the Vichy government. Free France had succeeded in recruiting only a small number of supporters in an offshoot of the metropolitan Resistance movement 'Combat', consisting primarily of academics. As for the army, its patriotism was as certain as its hostility to General de Gaulle; but since it was imbued with the official neutralism of the Vichy government, summed up in General Weygand's formula of 'fighting anyone who threatened the rights of France', there was no doubt that it would regard the Allied landing troops as aggressors and would open fire on them, unless their leaders gave them other orders in due course.

This barrel of gunpowder had therefore to be defused. The plot centred on a 'Group of Five', people of importance in favour of General Giraud, consisting of General Mast, the industrialist Lemaigre-Dubreuil, a leader of the Youth Work Camps, Van Hecke, an extreme right-wing journalist, Rigault, the officer Henri d'Astier de la Vigerie (two of whose brothers were on the side of General de Gaulle but who was himself a royalist), and the diplomat Tarbé de Saint-Hardouin. 'The Five' recruited accomplices in most of the services and in the large towns of North Africa. A double plot was hatched; in Algiers a putsch would neutralise those Vichy leaders who were assumed to be hostile, so that the American landing could be safely carried out; at Rabat, General Béthouart—the only leader who had achieved a French victory in 1940 at Narvik—would prevent any opposition from the Resident General Noguès, the GOC unless the latter were warned at the very last minute and joined the conspirators. In the meantime General Giraud would arrive in Algiers, take over command of the troops and the trick would have worked.

General Eisenhower sent his deputy, General Clark, by submarine to make contact with the Group of Five in the region of Cherchell in Algeria. The Five submitted to him their plan, which he approved, and presented him with a whole list of suggestions and *desiderata* which he did not exclude. They asked him for the arms they needed for the success of their attempt and they insisted on the landings taking place in the whole of North Africa, including Tunisia. Clark listened carefully and showed himself to be understanding but took good care not to give his companions the slightest inkling of the Americans' real plans, for fear of letting the cat out of the bag. The conspirators were to be forced to act alone, and virtually in the dark. From this point onwards a difference of views was apparent but no one thought it wise to emphasise it in case this made it worse: the resisters were acting from a specifically French point of view and with political aims which the Americans refused to go into or to understand; for them the only thing which mattered was the success of the military operation.

Indeed, the Allies had had some difficulty in deciding on a final plan. The British proposed simultaneous landings in Casablanca, Oran, Algiers and Bône; Admiral Cunningham, who was anxious to put an end to his trouble in the Mediterranean, wanted them to go as far as Bizerta, thus cutting off Rommel's rear, and the Axis would find it impossible to establish itself in Tunisia. The Americans, however, were more pessimistic; they were responsible for the operation and they knew that their resources were limited. They did not feel completely reassured about the behaviour of the French troops and they were afraid that they might continue offering strong resistance; finally, they were worried by Franco's attitude and by the possibility of a German reaction in the direction of Gibraltar. It was therefore important not to make the lines of the expedition too long.

In the end, the plan was not fully decided on until September 20. Three landing areas were fixed on, Casablanca, Oran and Algiers. The force operating in the west would be purely American; the one in the centre, against Oran, would be made up of American troops, convoyed by the Royal Navy and supported by an Anglo-American air force; the one in the east, against Algiers, would consist of troops from both countries, protected by the Royal Navy and supported by the RAF. They would all be under an American commander. There would be no landing east of Algiers until there was absolute certainty of success in the capital; only then would they advance towards eastern Algeria and if possible to Tunisia.

This was a wise but at the same time a complicated scheme; putting it into practice proved difficult. It required a great deal of time and it was precisely time that was lacking: there were only ninety days instead of the 360 which were deemed necessary. If one adds to this the fact that half the American troops had to be provided by the contingents which had arrived in Britain and that almost the whole of the available supply of troops had to be used, any large-scale operation across the Channel in 1943 became impossible.

Besides, the lack of experience of those carrying it out, especially of the Americans, gave rise to numerous problems. They have been carefully listed by Morison: some of the landing craft did not receive their engines until the day before they were due to sail; the crews had been recruited in a hurry and were bad at handling their craft; the aircraft-carriers which were to escort them came almost straight from the shipyards; the troops had not been trained to transfer at sea from the troop-ships to the landing craft which had been provided to land them; the co-ordination of Army and Navy was far from perfect; on September 9 Admiral Hewitt still did not know what naval forces he would have at his disposal, and so on. In short the chances were that this experimental interallied amphibious operation would not be a brilliant one.

VIII THE LANDING

The American convoys had to cover 3,000 miles; those which had come from Britain had the task of shipping men and provisions to Gibraltar—they had been taken there by 340 troop-ships in the course of the previous weeks. Miracle number one: neither the Axis powers nor the Vichy authorities detected these gigantic armadas until later: at the time, everyone thought that there was going to be an operation in the area of Dakar or Malta.

The okw's log-book mentions that on November 4, even though the Germans knew that forces were being concentrated at Gibraltar, they were not yet worried by it. On November 6 the convoys were sighted at sea; Mussolini and Kesselring then expressed the opinion that they were heading for North Africa; but those in charge of German naval operations thought that the landings which could now be expected would probably take place in Tripoli, perhaps in Sicily and Sardinia and, as the last hypothesis, in French North Africa. Besides, what could be done? Commitments on the eastern front were so heavy that all of the Wehrmacht's forces were needed and a rapid survey made it plain that it was impossible to send air forces to the Mediterranean. They therefore had to resign themselves to strictly defensive measures—to putting into practice the 'Attila plan' for invading the unoccupied French zone, while in contradiction of this the shock units, notably the 6th Panzer Division, were transferred from France to Russia. Besides, an operation on French territory did not seem such an alarming possibility; with their ears still ringing with Laval's and Darlan's suggestions of collaboration, the Germans considered—as General Jodl said to Hitler on November 7—that an Allied landing on French territory 'would finally drive France into Germany's arms'.

The landing troops' opponents, real or feared, were therefore taken utterly by surprise. The first fortunate result of this was the complete success of the Algiers putsch. On the night of November 7–8 a few hundred young men, virtually unarmed, mostly Jews who had been joined by a small handful of Arabs, took over the city without bloodshed. Most of the officials were captured in their homes, notably General Juin, who commanded the troops, and Admiral Darlan, who had chosen an inopportune moment to come to Algiers to the bedside of his son who was suffering from poliomyelitis. The city's defences were thus disorganised and the Americans took advantage of this to land without difficulty. But they did so later than planned and at points known only to themselves. This removed any possibility of co-ordination with those who had carried out the putsch; at daybreak, the VIPs were freed and fighting broke out. As a last straw, General Giraud was not there; he was in Gibraltar arguing with General Eisenhower, for he had been greatly disappointed to learn that he was not the interallied Commander-in-Chief; a radio broadcast of a communiqué supposedly issued by him was inadequate compensation for his absence.

At the other end of the operation in Casablanca, the putsch, after a good start, had taken a bad turn. General Béthouart had used rebel troops to cut off the Residence; but General Noguès, who had been held prisoner for a short while, had succeeded in giving his orders through an uncut telephone link and loyal troops had come to free him. It was now General Béthouart's turn to be arrested and threatened with court martial. There, too, it had not been possible to prevent fighting and the French naval forces, under Admiral Michelier, were by no means negligible. Finally, at Oran a British attempt to force the harbour had failed and there was fighting there, too.

All the precautions which had been taken to avoid a Franco-Allied clash had therefore failed; the Americans' prime concern was to put an end to it as quickly as possible; but being unable to dictate their terms or to rely on General Giraud to make sure that they were accepted, they found themselves obliged to enter into discussions with the Vichy authorities, whom in any case they had nothing against, and they were forced to realise that Admiral Darlan alone, as Commander-in-Chief, had the power to call a cease-fire. So it was with him that an armistice was signed in Algiers at 6.45 p.m. on November 8.

But the fighting was continuing at Casablanca, where General Noguès, furious at his humiliating mishap, was even less disposed to put a stop to it because Marshal Pétain had appointed him commander of the troops, after disowning Admiral Darlan; the struggle was to continue until November 11, causing 2,000 casualties among the French, who lost all their fleet, among them the battleship *Jean-Bart*. The Americans' clumsiness had prevented them from achieving a rapid victory; their aircraft-carriers were so lacking in training that one of them lost twenty-one of its thirty-one planes, all as a result of accidents, except for one which was shot down; this same lack of experience cost them 150 landing craft out of the 347 intended to land on the Fedhala beach; the land fighting at Mehedia lasted longer and caused greater bloodshed because General Truscott, who had little knowledge of the capabilities of naval gunnery, failed to ask for its initial support.

When the cease-fire came, the landing had, however, been everywhere successful, although at a higher cost than had been anticipated. But politically the situation had taken a completely unexpected turn. When General Giraud arrived in Algiers, the dice were already cast and the other French military leaders refused to recognise his authority; they even severely criticised his behaviour. General Giraud accepted this state of affairs with equanimity; he was not interested in politics; he would be satisfied if the French Empire came back into the war and he was given command of an army. Admiral Darlan, on the other hand, the man of the 'Paris protocol' of May 1941, had made a spectacular comeback.

The fact was that he had succeeded in receiving Marshal Pétain's blessing, thanks to the French Admiralty's having kept a direct line with Vichy, thus allowing a certain amount of communication by telegram. One of these messages mentioned a 'secret agreement' of the Marshal's; the Admiral took advantage of it to explain away his sudden change as being authorised by the Head of State. He was not a rebel since Pétain approved of him and he claimed that he was only acting in accordance with the latter's secret intentions, which he was not in a position to divulge.

The exact meaning of this telegram has been hotly disputed; the Marshal's apologists have made great use of it in their campaign to rehabilitate him; they even draw attention to a task which Pétain was supposed to have given Darlan on August 4, 1940, which was obviously without any bearing on the totally unexpected situation of November 1942 and to which Admiral Darlan himself had never referred. General Schmitt and Dhers, by tracing the sequence of events very closely, have shown that this telegram was sent after they had taken place; not only did it arrive after Admiral Darlan had put an end to the fighting on his own initiative without being ordered to do so by Vichy, but it also referred to a previous phase, when the Admiral had informed Vichy of his intention of resisting the landing troops by force of arms. The 'secret agreement' thus concerned Darlan's original desire to fight and not his sudden swing over to the Allies; moreover, the Marshal's real thoughts had been expressed when he subsequently publicly disowned and formally condemned the Admiral.

This debate is important only from the strictly French viewpoint of the death-sentence passed on Marshal Pétain by the High Court of Justice in 1945 and the atmosphere of discord and passionate feeling which it continued to arouse in France. The important thing for the course of events is that Admiral Darlan, with the Marshal's consent, either real, assumed or invented, had reaffirmed his personal authority, forced an end to the fighting and retained power, which was reinforced by a *de facto* recognition of the Americans. The result was utter chaos.

One thing that does seem to be true is that the American landing put the Vichy government in a very difficult situation—even if some of its members and probably Marshal Pétain himself were delighted, in their heart of hearts. It gave no promise of a liberation of France in the near future and it exposed her to stern German reprisals. By losing control over the colonies, the Vichy government lost one of its chief assets and almost one of its *raisons d'être;* it looked as though it might deal the death-blow to the policy of collaboration advocated by Laval. Darlan's sudden swing could only confirm Hitler in his fundamental distrust of the French and his hostility towards them. What disasters might now be in store for France? The Marshal's policy, 'the gift of his person', had been dictated by the desire to reduce the misfortunes of the French and the firm belief that he was the only one who could do it. This was why he had refused to leave France in June 1940; this was why he refused again in November 1942, despite the urgings of some of those close to him, among them Admiral Auphan, and at the risk of upsetting a good many of his followers. His extreme caution, combined with the circumstances, prevented him from speaking his mind. It was therefore probable that the Marshal confined himself to accepting the *fait accompli* by letting Admiral Darlan follow a course, which he was in any case no longer in any position to prevent, and by remaining in France himself to save what he could from any possible disaster.

A 'secret agreement' with Admiral Darlan's sudden volte-face would have had some real meaning only if it had been accompanied by concrete measures which, it is true, would have had to be kept secret by reason of the circumstances. But no such measures were taken, either in Tunisia or in Toulon. The consequences of this were going to be very tiresome and even disastrous; yet it was not time which was lacking.

Indeed, no German reaction to the landing had been organised until November 10; it took the form on the one hand of the invasion of the southern zone by German and Italian troops and on the other hand the setting-up of a solid 'bridgehead' in Tunisia. There could be no serious objections to the first operation but the second was very risky and as the OKW had pointed out, it demanded a 'close and friendly' liaison with the French military authorities. This liaison worked perfectly, and no 'secret disagreement' occurred to disrupt it; furthermore, Vichy sent out a special envoy, Admiral Platon, the Colonial Minister, to negotiate it. In the face of this mutual determination, the Algiers discussions and the uncertainties arising from them reduced the French forces in Tunisia to inactivity, including those of their leaders who were sympathetic to the British and Americans.

So German transport aircraft were able to land on Tunis airfield without a single shot being fired against them; 'defence against anyone' did not operate against them at all. The French troops withdrew to the mountains west of Tunisia, as if their job had been to oppose a possible Anglo-American advance. Without meeting any opposition, the Germans were able quite happily to reinforce their advance-guard units by air and sea, to the point of despatching three German and two Italian divisions to Tunisia. They extended the perimeter of the occupied territories in the north by seizing Bizerta without firing a shot and capturing Admiral Derrien's small flotilla there; in the south they went to the aid of the *Afrika Korps*, which would thus be certain of being able to retreat westwards. It was not until November 19 that the French commander in Tunisia, General Barré, rejected the German ultimatum—in the meantime instructions to this effect had been received from Algiers, eleven days after the 'secret agreement' between Marshal Pétain and Admiral Darlan.

IX RESULTS OF OPERATION 'TORCH'

The Allied landing in North Africa therefore ended in semi-victory. It had clearly lacked boldness and breadth of conception but this was not realised until General Franco's complete inactivity had been confirmed. Above all, the American armies had shown how badly prepared they were for the enormous tasks awaiting them; all in all, Operation 'Torch', which had been restricted both in its area and in its risks, had been a good preparation for the crucial offensive across the Channel and the difficulty in carrying it out left one to suppose that a similar offensive in 1943 would very probably end in costly failure. It could therefore be argued that it was not just a huge waste of time, indeed quite the reverse.

In North Africa, on the other hand, the failure of the 'Giraud scheme' was creating a somewhat confused political situation. The recognition of Admiral Darlan, even though presented by President Roosevelt as a 'temporary expedient', nevertheless came as a shock to Allied public opinion, both American and British, and even more so to the French. It seemed that some kind of prize was being offered to the men who had upheld the policy of collaboration at the expense of volunteers—such as General de Gaulle—who had never given up fighting with the Allies even in their worst hours. In Africa, the Vichy government did not change its supporters or its laws—some of them inspired by Hitler, such as the abolition of the Crémieux Decree which had granted Algerian Jews French nationality. General de Gaulle made violent protest in London and the whole French underground Resistance followed suit; any contact with Darlan seemed to them dishonourable. Besides, did not Darlan disown those responsible for the Algiers conspiracy and anyone involved in it for disobedience to him, by demoting them from their posts and even imprisoning them? The ease with which the Admiral had obtained the support of West Africa and as a result the reinvolvement of the whole of French Africa in the war were small compensation for the troubled political situation which had been created and in which General Eisenhower struggled on as best he could but without always quite understanding the ins and outs of it all.

In France herself, the chief victim of the operation was the Vichy régime. A visit by Laval to Hitler's headquarters was unable to prevent the invasion of the southern zone, against which Marshal Pétain made a formal protest which had no practical effect. The plan drawn up by General Giraud was not carried out and the Vichy authorities ordered the Armistice Army not to resist the invader. Only General Delattre de Tassigny, in Montpellier, tried to take to the maquis, but scarcely anyone followed him and he was disowned by the government and imprisoned. The occupation of the southern zone was shared between the Germans and the Italians, with the Rhône as a boundary. All the cities were occupied without any difficulty. The Armistice Army which had at first been withdrawn to its barracks, was disarmed and then dissolved, except for one division which, together with the Navy, was given the task of defending the fortified port of Toulon, coming under the orders of the German formation called the 'Felber Group'.

The German authorities purported to regard the southern zone as still free; they did not set up any new districts within the zone of the kind which existed in the north. This was pure fiction; the semi-independence which the armistice had given the Vichy government was well and truly over. Robbed of its colonies, its army and its home territory and forced to break off diplomatic relations with the United States, Marshal Pétain's government could no longer even pretend to have a policy of its own, for it no longer had the means. This was the end of the experiment which began with the Rethondes armistice of a French government theoretically retaining a little independence and hoping to set the country on its feet again thanks to military neutrality offset by political and economic collaboration with the conqueror, and to the plan of reform called the National Revolution. There were only two possible cards left for the French to play: either full collaboration or Resistance. Most of the officers of the Armistice Army opted for the second; they did not, however, join the existing Gaullist Resistance movements; they tried via Spain to join the ranks of the new French army being formed in North Africa; those who stayed on in France made up the Army Resistance Organisation (ORA) which also wanted to depend only on this regular African army.

What would the Toulon fleet do? Admiral Darlan's invitation to come and join him in Algeria met with a resounding and vigorous refusal from its commander, Admiral de Laborde. Between their direct leader and Marshal Pétain, the sailors chose to obey the head of state. But there was the risk that they would allow themselves to be wholly or partly tempted by the call to arms. From November 16, Hitler decided, as a precaution, to neutralise the fleet and if possible to take control of it. The strictest secrecy was observed in order to prevent the Vichy government and even the Italians from learning about it. To reduce the risk, the French troops were withdrawn from Toulon, which the German shock units were stealthily approaching to the apparent unconcern of the French Admiralty. After all, Hitler had promised not to try to seize any ships.

At dawn on November 26, 1942, the German attack was launched. The French sailors were caught completely off their guard—Admiral Marquis, the port-admiral, was captured in bed. Since no sailing orders had been given, very few of the ships' commanders decided to make their escape, although it was not fuel that was lacking but only the orders or the will to do so. Only five submarines escaped, one of which was scuttled when it got out to sea while another went on to be impounded in Spain.

The other ships conscientiously obeyed the orders to scuttle which Darlan himself had issued a long time before. Thus four battleships, two of which had survived Mers el-Kebir, 7 cruisers, 17 torpedo-boat destroyers, 1 aircraft-transport ship, 6 sloops and 16 submarines were deliberately sunk—a total of 220,000 tons. In addition the Kriegsmarine took over in the Mediterranean ports 159 merchant ships amounting to 650,000 tons.

All that remained of the French fleet which had emerged unbeaten and intact from the fighting of 1939–40 had thus gone to the bottom without any benefit to France at all. It is true that Admiral de Laborde considered that honour had been saved. He had no difficulty in proving that Hitler had broken his word; why had he not given more thought to earlier cases when the Führer had similarly broken his word? This gentlemanly language had an anachronistic ring when referring to the men, the aims and the methods of Nazi Germany.

The Battle of Stalingrad

In 1942 Stalingrad was a city of 600,000 inhabitants, extending for nearly forty miles along the right bank of the Volga; it was a great industrial and communications centre. At this point, there was no bridge across this great Russian river, which was from half to one and a quarter miles wide and could be crossed only by ferries and boats. Hitler had ordered the Wehrmacht to capture and destroy the city. The strategic purpose was to cut the great connecting link from north to south formed by the Volga. But the very name of Stalingrad and its role in the Bolshevik revolution seem to have obsessed the Führer to such an extent that he attached a symbolic and almost mystical significance to conquering it. Since the Russians, for their part, were equally determined to retain the city, its approaches and later the centre itself were to be the scene of hard fighting for nearly five months followed by the most sensational reversal of any situation in the whole of the Second World War.

I THE GERMAN OFFENSIVE

Whereas the Germans—Halder, for example—say that the targets of the German summer offensive of 1942 had become known to the Russians, the latter claim that they were expecting it to take place in the direction of Moscow; according to them, it was this error of judgment which was responsible for the Wehrmacht's initial victories; but the Soviet Chief of Staff set about rectifying it as quickly as possible. As early as July 1942, he transferred two of the reserve armies to the Stalingrad front, which had been entrusted to General Yeremenko, with Nikita Khrushchev as party delegate and member of the Military Council.

In mid-July, when it became obvious that the attacker's aim was to capture the city, a line of defences was set up in the suburbs of Stalingrad, using a work-force of about 20,000 people. At the same time some of the city's inhabitants were taught how to handle AA guns and thousands of workers enlisted in a people's militia to defend the factories. As the only railway line on the left bank was under enemy fire and the Volga itself was not safe, since the Luftwaffe had it covered, Stalingrad's industry was adapted to manufacture arms for its defenders; thus the tractor factory went over to assembling tanks which were sent straight from the testing bench to the front. But Stalingrad had still not become an entrenched camp nor a really fortified city.

In the first few months the Germans showed themselves almost irresistible, even though the Fourth Armoured Army had been withdrawn from the sector to be used in an attack on Rostov in the south. The Sixth Army, under Paulus, with two armoured and two infantry corps, was given the task of capturing Stalingrad and then of striking out towards Astrakhan in order to paralyse all traffic on the Volga. At the beginning of August it had reached the outer perimeter of the city's defences; some of their advances were most spectacular; thus the 14th Division advanced thirty miles in three days, from the Don loop to north of Stalingrad, reaching the Volga on August 23.

Instead of attacking the front at each end, so as to take the city from behind, the German command chose a frontal attack; it was letting itself in for a street battle. On August 25 the Soviet military on the Stalingrad front declared a state of siege, which did not prevent the Russian troops from having to be brought back inside the defensive perimeter on September 2. Paulus had eleven divisions, three of them armoured, against which Yeremenko could put up only five infantry divisions and two tank brigades. The Soviet command sent five divisions as reinforcements. In order to relieve the city it launched an attack in the north against the enemy units which had reached the Volga; this did not achieve any great success but gave the city a little breathing-space.

The Soviet reinforcements were being ferried across to the right bank of the Volga by the army flotilla; in this way 65,000 men and 24,000 tons of ammunition were convoyed across protected by armour-plated motor boats and floating batteries of artillery and AA guns; 35,000 wounded soldiers and 200,000 civilians who were of no use for the purpose of defence were taken back in the reverse direction.

However, on September 12 the front ran along a line varying from one to six miles from the built-up area. On the 13th the assault on the city began. Until the 26th the fighting took place chiefly in the centre and southern quarters; most of the industrial quarters in the north were not yet directly threatened. But the factories came under fire from the Germans and had to stop work and be evacuated. Since the Volga could no longer be used as a north–south communication line, the objectives fixed by Hitler in his directive of April 5, 1942 had been won. Thus any continuing attempts to capture the whole city were now only a matter of prestige.

However, on the Führer's orders the OKW decided 'to finish off the Battle of Stalingrad after mopping up the last parts of the city occupied by the enemy'. Hitler seems to have been irritated by the effect on world opinion of Stalin's communiqués extolling the heroic defence of the city which bore his name. Motives of vanity and propaganda thus took precedence over strictly military aims. The Germans also probably thought that the city's defenders, who had been driven back to the Volga, were in desperate straits. They had not calculated what quantities of men and equipment they might lose for every square yard they won in fierce fighting in a ruined city.

On September 27 fighting took place in the heart of the giant factories 'Red October' and 'Barricades'; every house became the scene of relentless fighting which took place with hand grenades and bayonets on every floor, in the rooms and in the lift-shafts; gaping holes in the walls enabled the defenders to pass from one block to another without being caught. In defying the enemy in this way, the Russians, fired by the feeling that they were fighting in their homes and for their belongings, showed unparalleled morale.

In fact, twelve German divisions wore themselves out in these exhausting battles, while thirty others were forced to cover their flanks, and yet in October the Russians still remained in control of most of Stalingrad. The Germans had not succeeded in preventing reinforcements from crossing the Volga. Their supply lines had become greatly extended while those of the Russians had shortened to their advantage. However, at the beginning of November, misinformed by their Air Force, whose inadequacies had become alarmingly obvious, Hitler and the OKW considered the Russians incapable of a counter-offensive. In his directive of October 14 Hitler decreed: 'The Russians will not be able to bring as many forces into the winter campaign as they did last year; whatever happens, the winter will not be a harder one.' A rash forecast!

II PREPARATIONS FOR A SOVIET COUNTER-OFFENSIVE

The Russians, wrote Marshal Yeremenko, had turned their setbacks to their own advantage by accumulating a wealth of experience; they had learnt to dispose their defences in depth, perfected the tactics of attacking the flanks of advanced enemy points and speeded up the transfer of reserves from quiet areas of the front to those sectors which were threatened; tanks had been better co-ordinated with the artillery and infantry and command of the large units simplified and streamlined by cutting out the intermediate echelons; the constant enemy attacks were blocked by concentrations

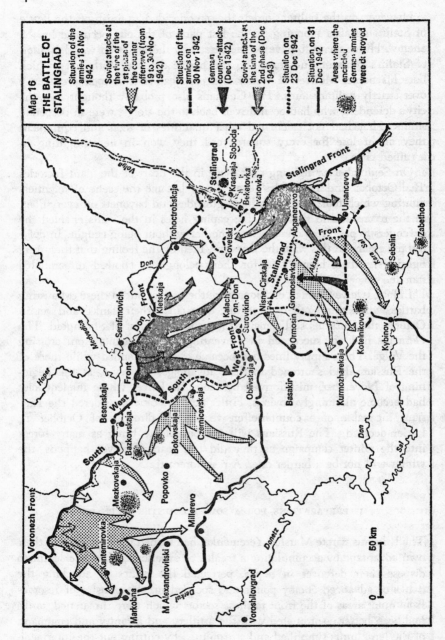

Map 16
THE BATTLE OF
STALINGRAD

Situation of the armies 18 Nov 1942

Soviet attacks at the time of the 1st phase of the counter offensive (from 19 to 30 Nov 1942)

Situation of the armies on 30 Nov 1942

German counter-attacks (Dec 1942)

Soviet attacks at the time of the 2nd phase (Dec 1943)

Situation on 23 Dec 1942

Situation on 31 Dec 1942

Areas where the encircled German armies were destroyed

50 km

0

of guns, so-called 'fists', concentrating as many as 200 guns every 1,000 yards or so. Above all the Soviet general staff were determined not to confine themselves to a static defence; any enemy advance must be checked by an immediate counter-offensive.

Since September 1942 a plan for a vast Soviet counter-stroke had been worked out in conferences at which Stalin met Zhukov, Voronov, Yeremenko and Vassilievskg. In October the weak points of the German positions, which had now become stabilised, had been detected. The German positions were based much more on the Don than on the Volga, which they had reached only at a few points. But even on the Don their situation was not favourable. Indeed, the Russians had retained or acquired bridgeheads on the right bank of the river, notably in the Serafimovitch sector; they had remained in control of the outlets of passages through a string of lakes. From some of the heights to which they had been clinging they could threaten the Sixth Army's flank. Above all, the corridor created by the advance of the German tanks between the Don and the Volga formed a narrow isthmus where any defence in depth was impossible. In short, the Soviet forces were enveloping the Fourth Armoured Army and what is more, the Sixth Army; and the latter was protected on its flanks only by satellite armies which were not very sound. Operation 'Stalingrad' rested on shaky foundations.

The plan for the Soviet counter-offensive provided first of all for the destruction of the German forces which had ventured directly into Stalingrad. The attacks were to be launched from the north by the army group from the Don in the direction of Kalach; from the south in the direction of Abganerovo by the group of armies from the Stalingrad front; this double enveloping movement would close like a vice on Paulus' Sixth Army. The battle to achieve this encirclement was to take four days; it was to be supported by minor diversionary attacks at Kalinin and Vyazma. The objective was therefore strictly limited and clearly defined.

The Soviet Armies found themselves facing the Italian Army, two Romanian Armies and the German Sixth and Fourth Armies, that is, fifty divisions, of which five were armoured and four motorised; but their reserves were dispersed as well as reduced in number. On the front as a whole the Russians did not have any real superiority, either in manpower or in armaments; the quality of their Air Force was even distinctly inferior. But in the Stalingrad sector they had mustered 25 per cent of their large infantry units and 60 per cent of their armoured and mechanised forces. They thus obtained a local superiority of two to one in men and eight to one in tanks. On their lines of penetration their superiority was much more marked and indeed overwhelming; thus the Fifth Armoured Army was attacking with odds of seven to two in manpower.

From June to December 1942, according to Marshal Rokossovski, the forces engaged by each camp changed as follows:

	June 1942			September 1942			December 1942		
	Men	Tanks	Air-craft	Men	Tanks	Air-craft	Men	Tanks	Air-craft
Soviet	187,000	360	337	590,000	600	389	854,000	797	1,035
German	250,000	740	1,200	590,000	1,000	1,000	846,000	770	1,066

The task of dispatching Soviet reinforcements became more difficult when the autumn rains caused the waters of the Volga to rise six and a half feet above normal and then a little later on when the river began to freeze, Russian engineers had to construct ten crossing-points.

On three occasions German raids damaged the cables on the left bank which were supporting the three footbridges by which pedestrians crossed the river. The steppe-like character of the terrain and the fact that built-up areas were few and far between meant that it was difficult to conceal the Russian troop concentrations; accordingly the units moved about only at night; in clear weather all movement was held up for twenty-four hours; during the day the men hid in the villages or, where there were none, at the bottom of gullies. This huge effort seems to have been badly assessed by the German general staff, although the Romanian general, Dimitrescu, several times expressed anxiety. But Paulus did not worry much about it and when the Soviet Army took up the offensive with considerably larger resources, it came as a disagreeable shock to the Wehrmacht.

III THE ENCIRCLEMENT OF THE GERMAN SIXTH ARMY

The Soviet attack began on November 19 on the Don front under the command of Rokossovski and continued on the 20th on the Stalingrad front under Yeremenko.

The movement along the Russian lines extended for more than 185 miles but the breakthrough was achieved over less than 125 miles. In order to destroy the enemy forces in depth the Russians had arranged their attacking troops in four successive echelons. After some eighty minutes of intensive artillery preparation, short but sharp, they launched their shock and mine-clearing units and the units of heavy tanks and self propelled guns, supported by the Air Force. These paved the way for the mobile groups of medium and light tanks and of motorised infantry, whose task was to exploit the initial success as quickly as possible by attacking the enemy's communication lines in order completely to disorganise its defence positions. Simultaneously, groups of all arms with mortars and flame-throwers were destroying any centres of resistance likely to provide a basis of local enemy counter-attacks. Finally, the light infantry, engineers and anti-tank groups widened the gap on the flanks and organised defence positions at suitable points to hold up any enemy counter-attack. The Russians moved over from the defensive to the offensive in all sectors with the result that they gained the enormous advantage of surprise. Their success was overwhelming.

In the north, by the evening of the 19th, the armoured forces of the Don front had advanced twenty-two miles; after destroying the Romanian 1st Armoured Division, they reached the region of Kalach on November 22 and moved across to the left bank of the Don, while on the right bank they seized the most important enemy operational base at Kalach. On November 23 a Romanian group which had been encircled in the Raspopinskaya region was taken prisoner with all its 27,000 men.

For their part, the troops on the Stalingrad front in the south broke the enemy resistance in four days and on November 23 joined forces with the troops of the Don front at Sovietski.

Thus within the time laid down the Soviet offensive of November ended by encircling the German Sixth Army and part of the Fourth Army eighty-seven miles west of Stalingrad, that is, twenty-two divisions in all, numbering more than 300,000 men. In addition, the Romanian Third Army was smashed and the Fourth was in a bad way. From November 24 onwards the attack on the encircled forces began.

On November 19 Hitler was at Berchtesgaden; he was informed of the attack by the OKW's new Chief of Staff, Zeitzler, the successor to Halder, who was himself at the Rastenburg headquarters in Pomerania. Although his information was inadequate and he was unable to assess the seriousness of the situation, the Führer's reaction was immediate and characteristic. He did not hesitate for one second to interfere in the details of operations. He notified Paulus that he should at all costs hold the western and southern ends of his positions. At the same time Hitler placed von Manstein, who was several hundred miles away in Vitebsk, in command of the armies on the Don. Von Manstein was held up by bad weather and was to be several days taking over his new command. As yet, Keitel, Jodl and Goering were entirely of the Führer's opinion: the Stalingrad position was much too important not to be held at all costs.

As for the Soviet general staff, they were hungry for more. In order to exploit to the full the success which had been achieved, a very large-scale operation had been devised. Golikov's armies on the southern Voronezh front and all Vatutin's on the south-west front would launch a large-scale offensive in the direction of Rostov in order to destroy the entire south wing of the German defences.

But in December the tired Soviet troops momentarily came to a halt. It was then that von Manstein took up the initiative again to free the German troops which had been encircled.

IV VON MANSTEIN'S COUNTER-OFFENSIVE

Von Manstein had the remainder of the Fourth Armoured Army and the two Romanian Armies, four fresh Romanian divisions and one motorised division; he divided them into two mass formations, each linked at the rear by a railway, on both sides of the Don, at Ormosin and Kotelnikovo. But he was not ready in time to take advantage of the tiredness of the Russian troops. On December 3, according to Samsonov, he had a four to one superiority in tanks; he decided, however, to wait for the LVII Armoured Corps which was in the Caucasus. By the time he made up his mind to attack, on December 12, the Russians had had time to be reinforced; the balance of forces had been restored.

At its most northerly point von Manstein's Don army was thirty miles away from von Paulus' Sixth Army, which came under his command. But realising that the Russians were firmly ensconced at this spot, von Manstein decided to attack further to the south, at Kotelnikovo, seventy-five miles from Stalingrad. He was going to use a more distant springboard, to give him greater impetus.

The German Don army's attack advanced until December 19 first as far as the River Aksazh and then to the tributary of the Volga, the Mychtov, which it crossed, but was then held up.

At this moment a serious danger was beginning to threaten its rear. The Soviet general staff had launched its huge operation. Once again it put pressure on the satellite troops. On December 16, cut to pieces on the south-west front, the Italian Eighth Army retreated and in eight days the Russians advanced between 60 and 125 miles. Aware of the danger, the German high command had to remove troops from other sectors and send to France for the shock units which had now finished occupying the southern zone. But the first result of this new Soviet offensive was to make any further advance by von Manstein impossible. There was even a risk of danger to the positions of the German units which had advanced into the Caucasus.

Accordingly on December 23 General Hoth, who was in command of von Manstein's tanks, realised that it was impossible for him to advance. Worse still, on December 24 Yeremenko launched the Soviet Fifth Army, under Popov, in an attack on Stalingrad. Hoth had to withdraw to his starting-point, Kotelnikovo, which he lost on December 31. Von Manstein's counter-offensive had not succeeded.

V THE CAUSES OF THE GERMAN DEFEAT

What was the encircled Paulus doing in the meantime? After the war the Stalingrad disaster gave rise to long and lively controversy, both among the Germans who had taken part and among German and Soviet historians. Several German generals, including Zeitzler, vainly tried to take credit for having had the shrewdness to warn Hitler of the danger of clinging to Stalingrad at any price. Their clear-sightedness and courage in contradicting their Führer seems to have been greater after the event than at the time. Soviet historians vehemently criticise the German argument that by ordering a 'gradual withdrawal' in good time Hitler would have saved the Wehrmacht from the Stalingrad disaster; they showed that the Soviet offensive was strong enough and on a large enough scale, in the new circumstances which this withdrawal would have created, to advance just as quickly and successfully in other sectors, in Voronezh, for example; besides, if the German forces which had ventured towards the Volga had retreated, those which had advanced a long way into the Caucasus would have been exposed and forced into a hasty and more hazardous withdrawal. As for von Manstein and Paulus, they each, in their Memoirs, threw the responsibility for the defeat on to the other. Is it possible from these contradictory statements to determine what actually happened?

At the source of it all was Hitler's pigheadedness in regarding any withdrawal as a defeatist operation; it is certain that the Führer, who was in communication with Paulus over the head of the latter's superior officer, von Manstein, had ordered the commander of the Sixth Army not to abandon any of the positions he was occupying, in what he called the 'Stalingrad fortress'. But it seems equally certain that even in the autumn of 1942, the Wehrmacht's general staff, probably misled by the great successes of the summer, did not think that the Red Army was in a position to launch any major winter operations; after all, why should the Sixth Army not set up in the part of Stalingrad which it had conquered a strongpoint capable of offering lengthy resistance to Soviet attacks?

The problem, then, was whether the encircled Sixth Army could be sufficiently well supplied to withstand the severe winter and to hold its own against the enemy. As there was no question of bringing supplies up by

land, the task could be given only to the Luftwaffe. This was where
Goering's personal responsibility came in. In his usual boasting way, the
Field Marshal undertook to arrange for the daily lift of the 300 tons of various items which careful calculations showed to be the minimum needed
by the Sixth Army in order to keep going. Did Goering, as Rohden writes,
express this opinion against the judgment of the experts and air fleet commanders who argued that they now had a reduced number of aircraft,
that the machines were the worse for wear and that the Russian winter
presented unforeseen hazards? At all events, it is clear that Hitler, who
wanted nothing better than to believe Goering, trusted him blindly, in
spite of the unfortunate precedent of the failure of the Battle of Britain
and the well-known boastfulness of the Luftwaffe's Commander-in-Chief; it
is also probable that Goering, like a good courtier, had eagerly anticipated
his Führer's wishes.

In these circumstances what else could Paulus do but obey? The head of
the German Sixth Army did not lack character. In his sector he had of his
own accord cancelled the orders for the execution of the Red Army's political commissars and the systematic extermination of the Jews. He was also
an experienced tactician, conscientious to a fault. But this fine German
general was imbued by tradition and by nature with the doctrine of respect
for discipline; in addition, he did not have the overall view of the situation which could have enabled him deliberately to take initiatives which
in any case went against his nature.

Accordingly on December 19, when Hoth's tanks came to within thirty
miles of his own, Paulus did not move, since he had been refused permission to attempt a break-out which would have meant abandoning advanced
positions which both the Führer and the OKW—the head of the German
nation and his superior officers—ordered him to hold at all costs. To explain
his failure to act, Paulus put forward psychological and technical arguments. Although the army corps generals had all been in favour of a sortie,
he said, the officers and soldiers of the Sixth Army preferred to try to hold
on to their positions. Furthermore, there was not enough petrol for the
tanks to cover more than three-fifths of the distance separating them from
those of Hoth. In short, Paulus could not have attacked even if he had
wanted to, since the soldiers' reluctance and the lack of fuel made any
advance very risky. Von Manstein refuted these arguments; an advance
of a mere twenty miles or so, he wrote, which Paulus admitted to be feasible, would have enabled Hoth, by dint of a tremendous effort, to join up
with him; however narrow, the corridor thus formed would have made it
possible either for the Sixth Army to escape or for it to receive the supplies enabling it to keep going afterwards.

Manstein had told Paulus all this by telephone on December 23. The head of the Sixth Army therefore knew perfectly well how he stood and it was a struggle with his conscience which prompted him to act as he did. However much he sympathised with his soldiers' sufferings and despite his anxiety about their future fate, Paulus did not think it possible to disobey orders which he was told were necessary in order to prevent the south wing of the Wehrmacht's front from collapsing and to allow a new front to be established later on. He wrote: 'Is a responsible leader, when faced with the prospect of his own death or of the destruction or capture of his army, thereby released from his duty to obey orders?' And in his heart of hearts his answer to this question was 'no'. In these circumstances, von Manstein hardly had a right to criticise Paulus for not disobeying. He himself, who was his superior officer, had never given him any orders to this effect, since this would have involved an act of disobedience on his part. Paulus' drama was, in fact, at this moment that of the whole Wehrmacht which thought it its duty to obey the Führer of the German people *perinde ac cadaver*, despite the objections which everyone was beginning to raise in his own mind but which few had the courage to express.

VI THE DEATH THROES OF PAULUS' ARMY

Paulus had set the daily amount of supplies he needed first of all at 500 and then at 300 tons; this he never received. At the beginning, the aircraft were flying night and day and since the take-off areas were not very far from Stalingrad—about 125 miles—the load amounted to 137 tons per day for as long as Hoth's attempt to join up with the Sixth Army lasted. But when, following upon Hoth's withdrawal, the air bridge became longer, flying conditions grew more difficult because the pilots were hampered by fogs and storms and were subjected, in addition, to Russian AA fire which was becoming continually more powerful the closer it came. The Russians also raided the take-off bases and landing-strips; they sent up rockets similar to those used by Paulus to mark his landing-grounds, so as to throw the relief aircraft off course and shoot them down. The Sixth Army, for its part, lacked competent staff and its reception areas were becoming more and more restricted and dangerous as the Russian vice closed round them.

At the beginning of January, cold, fighting and disease had deprived Paulus of 80,000 men. The troops' rations had been reduced to just over five ounces of bread and one ounce of fat per man per day. The wounded could no longer be evacuated and on January 28 Paulus gave orders not to feed them any more so as to help keep up the strength of those who were fighting. In the second fortnight of January the amount brought in by air continued to decrease; it dropped to 70, 60 and even as low as 40 tons per day. It became more and more necessary to resort to parachute drops, for the planes could no longer afford to take such extreme risks; many containers were lost, either because they broke as they hit the ground or because they fell outside the reception area.

As its struggle to survive grew harder and harder, demoralisation set in in the Sixth Army and dissension in the German camp. Letters written by officers and soldiers shortly after Christmas and held back by order of the OKW showed that 57 per cent of the men no longer believed in victory; 33 per cent displayed indifference to the régime; 34 per cent were hostile. A general's son whose father had refused out of a sense of duty, to evacuate him from Stalingrad, violently reproached him and threatened to desert; a pianist was in despair because his hands were frostbitten; one officer wrote that this hell had caused him to lose his faith; fathers and husbands made known their last will and testament; perhaps through fear of the censorship, only one soldier dared to express his revolt; the rest sank into despair, which resignation did little to mitigate. The Sixth Army's general staff and Paulus himself had the feeling that their colleagues, and especially the Luftwaffe, had abandoned them; the Luftwaffe turned on the Wehrmacht and Hitler came down like a ton of bricks on both of them.

During this time the Russians did not remain inactive. Voronov was in charge of operations. On January 8, he sent an ultimatum which was rejected by Paulus on Hitler's orders. On January 10, more than 7,000 pieces of artillery, well over 400 to the square mile, started a massive softening-up process which was then completed by the bombers. In the evening, the first German line was broken through and the Russians advanced three to four miles. But it took two Soviet Armies three days to dislodge the second line of defence.

On January 17 Paulus' units poured into Stalingrad, some of them in disorder. On January 24, in order to spur the defenders on to greater efforts, Hitler showered them with titles and decorations; Paulus was promoted to field marshal. Goebbels' propaganda machine sang the praises of the men's heroism: 'The Red hordes smashed against their granite resistance.' This did not prevent von Seydlitz, Paulus' second-in-command, from suggesting that they accept the new Russian ultimatum. Disciplined to the last, Paulus rejected it, but he informed von Manstein that 'there is no longer any sense in prolonging the struggle; the catastrophe is inevitable; in order to save the men who are still alive I request immediate permission to surrender.' This permission was refused him; Hitler was categorical: against the Reds it was a case of conquer or die.

On January 25 street fighting began. Paulus gave permission for shock detachments to be formed and gave them a free hand to try to break out from their encirclement; but most of them failed. The area of resistance, the 'cauldron of Stalingrad', was gradually shrinking; on January 31 the last section surrendered in the south. On February 1 a report by the German VIII Air Corps read: 'Five aircraft have just returned from their mission; three did not find our troops; the fourth thought it caught sight of something; the fifth saw some lights.' A few hours later another message signalled: 'The course of our lines can no longer be made out; the enemy is on our former landing-ground.' On this day the German Sixth Army ceased to exist.

On February 2, the last section in the north surrendered, including Paulus. Ninety-one thousand men, among them 2,500 officers and twenty-four generals, were captured with hundreds of guns and tanks; 20,000 wounded came out of the cellars; since January 10 the encircled units had lost 100,000 men.

Germany declared three days of national mourning. But Hitler, in his funeral speech, had one last dig at Paulus: 'He could not succeed in crossing the threshold of immortality.'

VII THE SOVIET WINTER OFFENSIVE 1942–3

The victory of Stalingrad was the most outstanding episode of the Soviet offensive in the beginning of 1943 but in fact the whole of the front had been shaken, either simultaneously or sector by sector. The Wehrmacht had given ground everywhere.

Faced with being cut off, the German Armies whose task it was to seize the Caucasus had to make a hasty withdrawal of 375 miles in forty days. The Russians could not check their retreat until they had captured Stalingrad and restored rail communication out from the city. The German troops thus succeeded in withdrawing as far as Rostov; those which could not manage this were evacuated by sea. In this sector the Wehrmacht's order to withdraw had been given in good time, so as to avoid a second encirclement which would have turned the Stalingrad defeat into an irretrievable disaster. This success had been achieved in the nick of time, for Rokossovski's Don group of armies had advanced 125 miles southwards and on February 14 recaptured Rostov.

Further to the north, Vatutin, at the head of the south-west group of armies, had crossed the frozen Don and advanced as far as the Donetz.

On the Voronezh front, Golikov's group of armies had cut the poorly equipped and already demoralised Hungarian troops to pieces. In a matter of days one division had been destroyed and two more had to be withdrawn from the front. The first Soviet objective—to open up a gap in the

German defences—was achieved in the course of two weeks in January 1943. The Hungarian Second Army had lost 140,000 men and eighty per cent of its equipment; the survivors were sent back to Hungary. In February, the Soviet line of advance had reached Kursk in the west, Kharkov further to the south and then ran along the Dnepr near Dnepropetrovsk. At the end of February a German counter-attack pushed the front line back to the Donetz but did not succeed in crossing it.

On the Moscow front the USSR capital was finally freed; the pocket held by the enemy at Rzhev and Vyazma was mopped up. Although the northern sectors remained quieter, on the Leningrad front Schlussenburg was reconquered.

Thus the Red Army had dealt a crushing blow to Hitler's hopes, to the OKW's calculations and to Goebbels' propaganda. Despite its losses, not only had it not been forced to remain on the defensive during the winter or compelled to restrict itself to small attacks but it had launched an almost all-out offensive more powerful than the previous year. One very good German army had been captured and four satellite armies destroyed; a considerable part of the Wehrmacht's artillery, engineering and reserve units had been obliterated. In spite of the particularly severe cold, the total advance was 125 miles on average and had sometimes attained 375 miles. An immense territory of 7,500 square miles—almost the area of France—including the northern Caucasus, Stalingrad, Rostov, Voronezh and most of the districts of Krasnodar, Voroshilovgrad, Smolensk and Orel, had been liberated.

VIII THE IMPORTANCE OF THE VICTORY OF STALINGRAD

The name of Stalingrad resounded all over the world, and Soviet historians rightly see the Red Army's brilliant success as the most crucial victory of the Second World War and one which marked its turning-point.

True, this was not yet final victory. Von Manstein was not entirely wrong in stressing that the Wehrmacht's southern wing had not been destroyed; to which Yeremenko replied that the Russians' hopes did not extend that far. The German Army had shown that its remaining forces were still formidable when, taking advantage of a somewhat hasty Soviet advance which had not been consolidated because of insufficient reserves, it had gone over to the offensive again at Kharkov. With the Nazis, you couldn't count your chickens before they were hatched. Nobody could foretell how the struggle between the armies would develop when the summer returned and which of the two would be in a position to take up the initiative.

It had nonetheless been proved that the Wehrmacht was not invincible and Hitler was the cause of its first great defeat. He had taken all the decisions privately with Zeitzler, the OKW's Chief of Staff, and he did not seem to grasp the full seriousness of the setbacks. At a conference of the OKW on January 23, 1943, while everyone was expecting Paulus to surrender at any minute, Hitler spoke of everything except Stalingrad; he seemed to be concerned only with future party meetings at Nuremberg and with the need to build a new hall. This lack of response to reality was not compensated for—quite the reverse—by the Führer's direct interference in the details of operations when he had neither the technical experience nor the necessary information to reach a decision. In short, although Hitler and his generals were not yet at loggerheads, the military leaders' confidence in him was beginning to suffer a few hard knocks.

Germany's allies were particularly affected. At the very moment when she was losing the last of her colonial empire, Italy had left her best equipment and her crack units in the USSR. Hungary had no army left and could not hope for any compensation for her defeats. General Antonescu wrote to Hitler that the Romanian Army, 230,000 strong in November 1942, had been reduced to 75,000 in January 1943. Both Count Ciano and the Romanian Foreign Minister, Mihaïl Antonescu, had begun to toy with the idea of breaking loose from the German yoke. Turkey, who had been both attracted and alarmed by Germany's great successes in the summer and was on the verge of rushing to help her to victory, crept back into her shell of neutrality.

It was not, of course, only at Stalingrad that a balance of forces had been reached which gave promise of a new era. But in the battle of the Atlantic convoys, this balance could well be upset by some technical invention of one of the belligerents and although it was full of promise for the future, the effects had not yet made themselves felt. At El Alamein the British victory showed yet again that the Italians were incurably weak and perhaps also that Germany had not sent sufficient forces to Africa. But at Stalingrad it was the full power of the Wehrmacht which had been beaten; the fact that tactical errors had been made did nothing to detract from the Red Army's extraordinary recovery. It had realised how to use the vast spaces of the USSR to the best advantage, how to retreat in order to come back more strongly and how to seize or create favourable opportunities. Its victory was due not only to 'General Winter' nor to the Russian soldier's dogged qualities and capacity for suffering. It had been able, at the right time and place, to provide manpower and equipment superior to those of its opponent; a new team of strategists had worked out the plans most appropriate to the circumstances and had carried them out in the field. The Soviet victory was the Red Army's victory, but it was also the victory of the Soviet economy and of the Bolshevik régime.

For the Communist party had completely identified itself with the Russian nation in order to give it leadership and train it for battle. Contrary to the hopes of the invaders, even after the first setbacks rebellion had not broken out either amongst the non-Russian population or among the peasants. Victory was going to knit the Russian people even more closely to its leaders who no longer appeared as having achieved power through a revolution stemming from national defeat but as the rightful heirs of the men, régimes and social classes which had built up the greatness of Russia.

Finally, this victory was Stalin's victory. Neither the failure of the policy of compromise with the Reich nor the setbacks of the first few months of the war had shaken his authority or weakened his determination. He had taken all responsibility, both political and military, upon himself, and had proved himself capable of shouldering it. His calm self-assurance, his nerves of steel, his realistic way of looking at things and his deep-seated cynicism, which was not bothered by principles or scruples, had enabled him to combine determination and efficiency.

The USSR gained enormous prestige throughout the world from a victory which she had achieved entirely on her own. The memory of the dubious era of the German-Soviet pact was fading away like a passing accident. She alone among the great Allied powers identified her cause with that of the oppressed peoples. She offered everyone the example of steadfastness in adversity, and by resisting the occupier she was pointing the road to victory. In every country she became a source of strength and pride to the Communist party, which was the spearhead of the underground struggle. The workers' strikes in northern Italy in March 1943 and the unification of the Resistance forces in France in the spring of the same year were not entirely unconnected with Stalingrad.

In short, the USSR seemed set to take advantage of any German defeat by filling the large vacuum that it would create in Europe. True, this defeat was not yet in sight; the Nazi Reich even strengthened its position by setting itself up as the champion of the struggle to oppose any revival of the threat of Bolshevism.

But the USSR, for her part, had earned the right to be more demanding with regard to her Anglo-Saxon allies. How was the 'strange alliance' which had been born out of the Nazi peril going to work?

BOOK THREE

THE DEFEAT OF ITALY

THE ALLIED WAR-MACHINE

BRITAIN, the United States and the USSR were associates in the same coalition by the fact of possessing common enemies rather than by mutual inclination. Britain and America had laid the foundations for close co-operation even before the war started and had built them up and defined them since, but Russia was exploring quite new ground in joining them —she had for twenty-two months been closely linked to their chief enemy, the Nazi Reich, and had even provided it with part of its fighting resources. It was obvious that, when added together, the human, economic and military potential of the three allies far surpassed that of the Axis powers, as long as they were entirely applied to the war effort and the armed forces thus produced were committed not in extended order but according to comprehensive plans based on mutual co-operation and jointly applied.

There were very powerful obstacles to the realisation of this indispensable co-operation. The USSR was not taking part in the war in the Pacific, but she was bearing the whole brunt of the Wehrmacht's attacks in Europe and her only concern was her struggle to survive. On the other hand, the United States had been attacked by Japan at a time when they were reserving their strength to strike, in the first place, against Germany. Britain, who had stood alone in bearing Nazi Germany's assault, was hoping to have a little breathing-space. How were these three rather reluctant allies going to harmonise their aims, co-ordinate their resources and conduct at one and the same time their own war and the common struggle? In short, how was the Allied war-machine going to be set up and put into operation?

CHAPTER 1

The Anglo-American War

I THE BRITISH CONDUCT OF THE WAR

BRITAIN had been holding the fort since September 1939; she had gained experience which would benefit, but also put pressure on, the United States. The British conduct of the war was the result of one of those compromises, of which British history offers so many examples, between respect for tradition and forward-looking empiricism, as well as between the normal working of democratic institutions and that concentration of powers which produces efficiency.

For the whole of the war, the government remained responsible to Parliament and public opinion. Churchill thus from time to time had to face motions of censure from MPs, challenging the Cabinet. In point of fact, since the latter was composed of representatives from the two main political parties, it was practically certain not to 'fall' unless a large majority of public opinion came out against it.

The 'War Cabinet', consisting of five members, in a ministry which numbered sixty, was, with the consent of all the ministers, alone responsible for the conduct of the war. At the beginning, it met every day and any urgent business was immediately put before it while all important papers and telegrams were communicated to its members.

But little by little, this daily meeting seemed less and less necessary. In the end, there came into being what Churchill called the Monday parade which was attended, in addition to the members of the War Cabinet, by those ministers whose presence was required by the agenda, and the military leaders; weekly situation reports were then presented. The rest of the time, and very soon for the whole of the time, all the ministers, including those who belonged to the War Cabinet, confined themselves, as Churchill wrote, 'to relieving the Prime Minister of the burden of internal affairs and of party problems'. So, while the principle of collective responsibility of the Ministry for every decision remained sacrosanct, the whole conduct of the war was left to the Prime Minister. Churchill developed the habit of dealing directly with heads of foreign governments or of the dominions, and especially with Roosevelt, through messages which he himself drew up and only rarely communicated to the War Cabinet. He likewise formulated British strategy and took the appropriate decisions directly with the Chiefs of Staff of the three services.

The fact was that the Prime Minister was also Minister for National Defence; his deputies, the Secretaries of State at the Admiralty, the Air Ministry and the War Office, confined themselves to administrative tasks, and did not attend either the meetings of the War Cabinet or those of the Committee of Chiefs of Staff. Since the members of these scarcely changed at all in the course of the conflict, a remarkable continuity in the conduct of the war was thus ensured.

The Chiefs of Staff—Army, Navy and Air Force—would study the situation in all its aspects and suggest solutions to the Prime Minister. When the latter had reached a decision after taking advice from his own general staff—which was at the same time the military office of the Secretary to the War Cabinet—the decisions adopted would go back for the Chiefs of Staff to carry out; they would give their instructions to the commanders of the British forces in the various operational theatres, to whom, as a general rule, they would allow a certain freedom of action by refraining from interfering in matters falling within the latters' province but without allowing them any power of initiative.

Thus the three levels of responsibility were clearly defined and graded; the government directed the political, diplomatic and military action; the general staffs drew up the overall strategy; and the commanders of the armed forces conducted the operations in their respective theatres. In actual fact, although there was nothing in writing to this effect, Churchill, with general agreement, intervened and imposed his will at every stage. The country's dramatic situation suited him down to the ground. Throughout the whole war his role of driving force was of incomparable importance. Although sometimes rash and impulsive, he was never downhearted, for he was immune to fatigue and never at a loss to concoct the boldest schemes.

II THE AMERICAN CONDUCT OF THE WAR

The same three grades of authority were to be found in the United States. At the top was the President whose powers were even greater than the British Prime Minister's, since, according to the Constitution, he was at one and the same time head of state, head of the government and commander of the armed forces.

Indeed the conduct of the war did not require any structural alteration in the peacetime government of the country. The White House remained a family residence, without formality and with no visible official staff. The team of cabinet officers continued to lack uniformity, any differences of opinion being settled by the President. The President was still without any direct control over the congress and in order to put through his budgets and laws in the House of Representatives or in the Senate he had to negotiate with the leaders of the parties, whose considerable power remained undiminished. Above all he had to handle public opinion very carefully, for the state of war did not prevent the Constitution from operating in the normal way and the President's mandate expired at the end of his four years in office.

The American Chiefs of Staff corresponded almost exactly to their British counterparts. Their committee was presided over by Admiral Leahy but dominated by the personality of General Marshall, Chief of Staff of the Army. Their relationship was rather strained, owing to the old rivalry between the Army and the Navy. Moreover, the us Army Air Force, while theoretically part of the Army, was reluctant to let its squadrons be incorporated into the combined forces, where it would have no control over them and where they ran the risk of receiving orders which would not always take into account its special characteristics and approach. It wanted to be assigned only missions in general terms, so that it could then carry them out in its own way. As a result there were frequent clashes, both with the Army and the Navy.

Finally, in the field there were the commanders of each operational area; but the extent of their responsibilities and their remoteness from Washington often gave them a real independence to which their superiors took no exception, whereas the British found it excessive and were perturbed by it.

The actual conduct of the war therefore fell upon President Roosevelt. He was a complex person, a mixture of authoritarianism and familiarity, a man of great experience yet naïve. Eden used to say of him that 'he reminded him of a man deftly juggling with sticks of dynamite without realising their danger'. Everyone, indeed, fell under the President's spell. Roosevelt was less keen than Churchill on military affairs, a fact which led him to give a freer hand to his Chiefs of Staff than the British Prime Minister. Nevertheless, he knew quite well what he wanted, even though he disclosed little of what was going on in his mind, and he was both shrewd and skilful in achieving his aims. But he was not without his personal whims, and his dislikes were even stronger and more lasting than his likes. So he tended to play his own game, which he had carried out by people picked by himself outside the administration; for his missions, he chose men on whom he could rely, letting them deal with the most important issues directly with the authorities to whom they had been sent as delegates. Thus his friend Harry Hopkins acted secretly and efficiently as the power behind the throne; his opponents called him 'the Rasputin of the White House'. Hopkins was in poor health, like Roosevelt, but activated by the same sort of energy and intelligence as the President. He had not been one of the 'Brains Trust' of the 'New Deal', but he had served as Secretary of Commerce and director of the Public Works Administration and Federal Emergency Relief Administration; nevertheless it was only as Roosevelt's friend that during the war he accomplished his most important missions to Churchill and Stalin. It was he who distributed American equipment to Europe and Roosevelt hoped to make him a sort of economic dictator with the task of exploiting all the resources of the coalition.

III ANGLO-AMERICAN CO-OPERATION

Churchill and Roosevelt got on very well together. They were drawn together by a common culture, an identical religious attitude and a lofty and completely aristocratic sense of their office and authority. Both of them showed themselves determined to work hand in glove and they made no important decisions without prior agreement. Moreover, by means of a special code, they were in continous communication by direct cable between Washington and the American embassy in London. Churchill reveals in his Memoirs that by this method he sent 950 messages to Roosevelt and received 800 replies. It was Churchill and Roosevelt who together took the main decisions committing the Anglo-Saxon coalition; their meetings were therefore of the utmost consequence and they attended them accompanied by such a considerable staff that in fact, their respective states travelled about with them.

To assist them, they set up a Combined Chiefs of Staff, with permanent headquarters in Washington. The American Chiefs of Staff were members; their British counterparts, compelled to remain in London with their government, were represented by general officers, of whom the most outstanding was Sir John Dill. But they remained in daily, and often hourly, contact with their superiors in London, so as to be certain to represent their views. The Combined Chiefs met often—200 times in all, according to Churchill; first of all, each national committee sat separately; then the two groups met to compare their points of view and reach their conclusions. They then submitted them to Roosevelt and Churchill, who either endorsed them or settled any points of difference.

Co-ordination of this sort between two great states was unprecedented; to be sure, it was made easier by the common language—although sometimes words took on a different meaning in English and American, giving rise to misunderstandings, which might start rather tartly before they ended in laughter.[1] In every area where British and Americans fought together, combined staffs were appointed, sometimes not without trouble and after very careful apportioning of the rights, powers and responsibilities of each one; on the whole, they operated satisfactorily. The economic resources were likewise managed by mutual agreement, in an unusual way. Thus, in January 1942 the Combined Shipping Adjustment Board came into existence; its task was to allocate Allied shipping according to the civil and military supply requirements. It had charge of a 'pool' of Allied merchant navies flying about twenty flags and its decisions were enforced by two subcommittees, one residing in London and the other in Washington. In 1944, this organisation found itself controlling a merchant fleet of 65 million tons and a tanker fleet of 20 million tons—that is to say 90 per cent and 95 per cent respectively of the current world total at the time.

Obviously this complicated machine sometimes seized up and it did not function without some squeaks and groans. At first it moved slowly; the Allies were carrying on the war through external lines of communication over vast distances; the movement of troops took a long time, especially from the Atlantic to the Pacific operational theatres. Prolonged delays were involved before things could be made to run easily, for plans had to be carefully examined by both sides, frequently compared and were then subject to the agreement of the two leaders. They had to be very precise since the deployment of any forces required a very elaborate timetable which was too complicated to be easily altered once it had been decided on.

There was often a difference of view between the two partners because their war aims were not the same. The main subjects of disagreement were the fate of the colonial empires, relations with the USSR, the role and future of France, and the place and date of the landing in Europe—to mention but a few of the main problems which gave rise to animated discussions and misunderstandings and lasting friction.

However, opinions were also divided on purely military matters. Britain had to defend a Commonwealth that spread over the five continents; even by concentrating all her forces on one single point, she was unable to win a decisive victory over Germany. She would have run too great a

---

1. Churchill tells how a long and animated discussion was started one day about the expression 'to table it'. In English, it meant that the plan in question would be considered immediately but in American it meant that they would shelve it. There ensued a sharp argument for some time which was dissolved in laughter when the mistake was realised.

risk of losing everything at once by 'putting all her eggs in one basket'. She therefore formulated an Allied strategy in keeping with her weakness and her interests, that is to say a peripheral strategy; its trump cards were the blockade and the Air Force but also repeated operations in remote minor areas, where German power would gradually be worn down until it could be dealt a decisive blow with less effort. But although the Americans had accepted the premise that the protection of Britain was essential for the defence of the United States, they had no desire to fight for her Commonwealth; they were furious that forces should remain unused, or, as they saw it, misused, to recapture Burma or to take possession of the Dodecanese Islands; according to them, this meant jeopardising the success of a concentrated attack, which the superiority of their united resources would make irresistible; backing the British at every point meant a dangerous and pointless dispersal of their forces, thus protracting the war.

In short, the British accused the Americans of thinking only of military victory and not concerning themselves enough with the political consequences of the war. The Americans were afraid of becoming involved in the Byzantine quarrels of old Europe and of playing into the hands of British imperialism.

These differences of conception were sufficiently serious to break up even the most solid alliance but they never prevented the British and Americans from always managing to reach agreement by means of mutual concessions and this owed a great deal to Roosevelt's understanding approach. In short, never before had two great nations been united by so close an understanding in a war of such magnitude. However, as the Americans progressively passed out of their novice stage and took an increasing and eventually predominant part in the combined operations, they were able to force their point of view more and more frequently on to the British who had no alternative but to accept it.

The Anglo-American alliance was so weighty, so carefully balanced and its united resources so considerable that the other nations fighting against Germany—with the exception of the USSR—could do nothing but submit to its decisions; General de Gaulle and the Polish government in London, among others, were to discover this to their cost.

At least in the Atlantic Charter they found no difficulty in agreeing amongst themselves upon the principles for which British and Americans were fighting.

IV THE ATLANTIC CHARTER

Off the shores of Newfoundland, to which they had each come on board a battleship, Churchill presented Roosevelt with the draft of a solemn joint declaration, in order, he said, 'to direct their policies on the same lines'. Roosevelt accepted the idea and introduced a few slight modifications into the text which, when signed by the two statesmen on August 12, 1941, became 'the Atlantic Charter'.

The United States and Britain first of all drew attention to the contrast between their own idealism and the ambitions of the Axis states; they asserted that they were not seeking any territorial or other aggrandisement and that they were opposed to 'any territorial change which did not conform to the wishes, freely expressed, of the peoples concerned'; expressed in broad terms, the statement meant that any annexations by the Axis states would not be recognised; it did not, however, imply any commitment to re-establish the territorial integrity of any conquered countries —Churchill had not even made this promise to de Gaulle with regard to France. The Allies went on to recognise 'the right of all peoples to choose the form of government under which they wish to live'—this was a condemnation of dictatorships.

Article 4 went even further, for, taken literally, it would have implied the sharing of world resources. Indeed, in it was stated that they would 'favour the access of all states, great or small, conquerors or conquered, to world trade and the raw materials necessary for their economic prosperity' —a reply to Axis propaganda which represented the war as the struggle of proletarian against wealthy nations.

For this to be achieved, 'the fullest international collaboration in the economic field' was necessary, as was also a lasting peace giving to all men 'the certainty of being able to end their days free from fear and want'. The freedom of the seas was a condition of such a peace and the renunciation of the use of force guaranteed its preservation. Finally, reference was made to 'a broader and more permanent system of general security', without making any mention of the existence of the League of Nations.

The Atlantic Charter, conceived in very general terms, might at times sound hollow. Yet it sounded a note of human solidarity and brotherhood and of national equality which stood out like a ray of hope against the violence, racial discrimination and exploitation of the weak perpetrated by the totalitarian régimes.

The document was signed by all the Allied nations, with some reservations on the part of the USSR, and became the programme for the peaceful reconstruction of the world; but respecting it and putting it into operation would be a different matter and more difficult than proclaiming it.

V THE ADOPTION OF A COMBINED STRATEGY

Immediately after the attack on Pearl Harbour, anxious about the turn United States strategy might take as a result of the disaster that had befallen their fleet, Churchill had gone to Washington to have discussions with Roosevelt. From December 22, 1941, to January 14, 1942, the two men and their staffs examined all the problems with which they were faced and reached complete agreement on the solutions. This conference, called 'Arcadia', was therefore of paramount importance for the conduct of the war, for from it dates the close co-operation between the British and Americans.

It was then that the decision was taken to set up the Combined Chiefs of Staff and to pool all the military and economic resources of the two countries. They were to take joint responsibility for the conduct of operations, the distribution of forces and equipment, the co-ordination of means of communication, the utilisation of intelligence and the administration of the conquered areas.

Churchill was afraid that Roosevelt might be more anti-Japanese than anti-German. He was completely reassured; the Nazi Reich remained the United States' enemy number one. Without going into too much detail about the significance of this proposal, it was decided as a result of this to leave in the Pacific only those forces necessary to defend points of vital importance: Hawaii, Alaska, Australia, New Zealand and India, likewise Singapore and the Philippines—but the Malayan peninsula had already been nibbled at and the Philippine archipelago was half lost. Japan's hour of reckoning would strike after Germany's.

Against the latter, the Americans, conscious of their weakness, had provisionally adopted the British plan of wearing her down progressively by air raids, the blockade, commando raids and minor attacks on the periphery of Europe; it was contemplated making an operation in Tunisia in 1942. Churchill succeeded in adding help to the subversive movements in the occupied territories—a subject about which the Americans had absolutely no notion. During this time, invasion bases would be gradually established round the Reich and in 1943 a return to the Continent would prove possible from several directions, either simultaneously or in succession.

In the course of 1942 the Americans changed their ideas. They put forward, and the British reluctantly accepted, the 'Bolero–Round-up' plan of landing in Europe in the course of 1943, with Britain as its launching pad. Churchill fought hard to make them give up views which he considered over-simple and which proved to be premature; all that remained of 'Bolero' was the ill-starred raid on Dieppe. Returning to their peripheral strategy of 'Arcadia', the two allies, at Churchill's instigation, began a landing in North Africa: this was Operation 'Torch'.[1]

This time, however, the Americans had followed their allies with grave misgivings. Marshall was no more keen to send Sherman tanks to Auchinleck than Hitler to send Tiger tanks to the Italians. Admiral King and Secretary of War Stimson did not hide the fact that abandoning 'Bolero', together with the serious losses sustained by the convoys across the Atlantic, would in their opinion be bound to lead to a revision of American strategy and give priority to the Pacific. On two occasions, supported by Marshall, they approached Roosevelt to request this. But the President then showed that he was able to take vital decisions alone—if need be. Against the judgment of almost all his advisers—Eisenhower spoke of 'the blackest day in history'—he supported Churchill and insisted on Operation 'Torch'.

In the course of 1942, at Roosevelt's suggestion, the two allies had carried out a worldwide division of responsibilities. They were agreed that the Pacific would be an American operational area; Australia and New Zealand would therefore leave the British zone of influence to place themselves under the protection of an outsider; the two dominions raised no objection but asked to be represented on the Combined Chiefs of Staff, a request which was refused to avoid overburdening the organisation. The Middle East and the Indian Ocean remained British theatres. As for Europe and the Atlantic, they were equally divided, which in the ordinary course of events would lead to an American command, in view of the growing disparity between the Allied forces as the United States took the lead.

However, this logical division of duties and responsibilities brought to light deep differences of opinion. Outside the metropolis, the chief British interests were in their Commonwealth, which area had been assigned to them; inevitably, they would make the most strenuous efforts to interest their partner in them. The Americans, however, were particularly drawn to the Pacific, although they had given priority to the war against Germany. They had to find the means of reconciling these two contradictory demands; both would obviously be jeopardised if they followed the British and sent their forces in yet another direction—the Mediterranean or Burma. The result was endless and sometimes heated discussions.

For the moment, however, the success of Operation 'Torch', which ought

1. See pp. 390–402.

to be exploited to the full, was pointing in the direction which the British wanted. In their meeting at Anfa near Casablanca in January 1943, (called the Casablanca conference), Churchill and Roosevelt drew the appropriate conclusions. First of all, they could not avoid taking a very close interest in the French problems in French North Africa; each summoned his 'favourite', and Giraud and de Gaulle had to overcome their mutual dislike and shake hands in public for the record. Delighted at having got Roosevelt where he wanted him, Churchill did not conceal from de Gaulle that he would not support him against his American ally—'Between Roosevelt and you,' he told him, 'I pick the big one.'[1]

On the other hand, it was confirmed that Germany remained the Allies' chief enemy. But how could she be reached from the shores of Africa? It was decided that a great anti-submarine offensive would be launched to protect Atlantic shipping and increase its flow, a necessary prerequisite for any offensive. In the meantime, the Reich's territory would be relentlessly pounded by 'carpet bombing'. This was an admission of semi-impotence for an indefinite period. Was it in order to conceal this fact that one day, to the amazement of the journalists present, Roosevelt launched his great idea of 'unconditional surrender' of the Anglo-Americans' opponents, Germany, Japan and Italy?

VI UNCONDITIONAL SURRENDER

Thus, on January 24, 1943, in Churchill's presence, Roosevelt stated:

> 'The President and the Prime Minister, after considering as a whole the operations of the world war, are more convinced than ever that the world can return to peace only by the total elimination of German and Japanese war power, which enables us to reduce the aims of the war to a very simple formula: the unconditional surrender of Germany, Italy and Japan. Unconditional surrender implies the firm intention of ensuring that peace reigns in the world for generations. It does not imply the destruction of the German people, nor of the Italian or Japanese peoples; but it does imply the destruction in Germany, Italy and Japan of a philosophy based on the conquest and subjugation of other peoples.'

Churchill's embarrassment during Roosevelt's speech was abundant proof that he was in no way its co-author. With a rather forced smile, he confined himself to a brief word of approval and proposed an unenthusiastic toast to unconditional surrender.

1. Translator's note: in Churchill's pidgin French: 'Je choisis le large.'

This declaration had therefore been thought up by Roosevelt alone; it was certainly not the result of a sudden illumination during the course of a meal, as his son Elliott relates, but of slow and mature reflection, as Hopkins confirms. Perhaps it was even a last fruit of his collaboration with Wilson, to which he was so fond of referring. He had set his heart on it, for he repeated it on several occasions; in Christmas 1943, he made it even clearer when he stated that 'the United Nations had no intention of turning the German people into slaves', but it was not until May 1944 that he toned it down and then only in favour of the Axis satellites in eastern Europe, whom Stalin was very anxious to placate as the Red Army approached them.

As it stood, the call for unconditional surrender, together with the disaster of Pearl Harbour, formed one of the stalking-horses of Roosevelt's opponents after his death. They blamed it for the unsatisfactory conclusion of the armistice with Italy, for Nazi Germany's willingness to go on fighting right up to the last minute and for Japan's delay in capitulating. In short, they laid at its door all the sins of Israel.

It is likely that Roosevelt was wanting to please Stalin, who was only half-satisfied by Operation 'Torch', for in his eyes it did not really open up a second front. He also had in mind to give reassurances as to the American war aims to the resisting nations of Europe, who must inevitably be worried by Darlan's promotion and the policy of co-operation with all kinds of Quislings that this seemed to represent. Also, as Calvet was right in stressing, there was the important role played by Roosevelt's recollection of the conditions imposed upon the Southerners by General Grant and the religious and moral motivation, always dear to the American heart, which gave the current war the character of a crusade. We must also remember that it was essential to remind American public opinion that now that it was involved in the war it would have to see it through to the end.

But whatever Roosevelt's reasons, they are less important than the consequences of his decision. It is hardly true that it deprived the British of all diplomatic freedom of action. To believe this would be to forget that negotiating with Germany and Japan meant recognising the whole or a part of their conquests and probably of their political régimes. Nor did it doom the Resistance movements in the Axis countries to failure. The Italian Resistance at all events continued; and no one had ever discovered the existence of any Resistance in Japan. As for German opposition to Hitler, it had hitherto proved most disappointing; and Roosevelt's decision did not prevent the assassination attempt of July 20, 1944, from coming within a hair's breadth of succeeding: besides, there was nothing in it likely to discourage possible German Resistance, indeed quite the reverse, since the United States President differentiated very clearly, much more clearly than the Pope, for example, between the régimes on which he was making war and the peoples to whom he was offering peace. To state, as Liddell Hart has, that the call for 'unconditional surrender' was 'the biggest blunder of the war' is, in my opinion, to make two mistakes: it forgets the existence of national Resistance movements swamped by the occupation, to whom Roosevelt was throwing a life-line; and it also misunderstands the essential nature of the Nazi régime and the Japanese faction then in power; whatever the Allied proposals, they were led by fanatics who were utterly determined to fight to the bitter end and to be destroyed, preferring to drag their country down with them if necessary rather than surrender.

VII ITALY, THE NEXT ALLIED OBJECTIVE

At Casablanca, the Anglo-American strategists were forced to realise that they would not have enough shipping for an attack across the Channel in 1943. They therefore reverted to the alternative of Mediterranean or Pacific.

Within the Chief of Staffs' Committee, Admiral King aggressively supported the second solution: while forced to accept that major operations against Germany should receive priority, he refused to release ships for minor operations in Europe. He considered that the war there should be concluded within a reasonable period of time in order to leave the United States sufficient forces to beat Japan. He was afraid that with the help of the jungle and the ferocity of her men, the latter might have time to build up an impregnable position. He suggested making use of available resources to open up the route to Burma so as to prevent the collapse of China.

Admiral King was supported by General Marshall, to whom he returned the favour by giving him his backing for an offensive across the Channel; and both of them were strongly against an extension of operations in the Mediterranean area.

They were, however, compelled to acknowledge two things. The first was that the Allies were involved in campaigns which it was essential to bring to a successful conclusion: the conquest of Tunisia, the offensive in Tripolitania of the British Eighth Army reinforced by American equipment, and additional aid to the USSR. It was impossible to send men as well as equipment to Britain without jeopardising the success of these campaigns. Secondly, there were the prospects opened up by the success in Africa: pressure on neutral states such as Turkey and Spain; retaining the strategic initiative; keeping the Suez Canal permanently open; the possibility of putting Italy out of action; forcing Germany to disperse her forces or transfer them from one front to another.

President Roosevelt was particularly alive to those prospects. He was also anxious to consolidate the friendship with Britain by showing regard for her vital interests—and the Middle East fell into this category. After guiding his advisers along the lines he desired, he excelled in giving them the impression that they were the ones who had made the decision and he was equally skilful in bringing them back to his chosen path when they showed signs of straying from it. He arranged for very careful examination to be given to all the possible consequences of the successful landings in North Africa as, for example, an invasion of Spain, which was supported by Admiral Leahy but opposed by General Marshall, or the idea of a landing in the Balkans across the Adriatic which Churchill was beginning to put forward. In short, he was, or pretended to be, convinced that major successes in the Mediterranean would make the final offensive across the Channel easier, even if they were not its necessary prerequisite. And when Marshall and King returned to the charge and suggested shifting the centre of gravity of American strategy to the Pacific, he gave a categorical refusal. One of his chief concerns was probably that if the Americans moved out of Europe, this might pave the way for German success in the USSR or drive Stalin to a reconciliation with Hitler.

In May 1943, a new interallied conference took place in Washington under the code-name of 'Trident'. The Americans were now very worried about the way the war was developing in the Pacific; they had no difficulty in eliciting the concession that the fighting there should be slightly stepped up. Since there could be no question about Hitler's continuing to remain enemy number one, the only alternative was to cut down operations in the Mediterranean. So Marshall agreed to their being continued but on that condition only. The British gave way, or pretended to. They accepted the date of the spring of 1944 for the landing in north-east Europe; by then, they would have had time to see how things were going. For the moment, even the smallest Mediterranean operations were important: the conquest of Tunisia and Tripolitania, the landing in Sicily and the free movement of shipping in the Mediterranean. If the Italian tree were given a thorough shake it might not be impossible to bring down Mussolini and perhaps even uproot him. After all, the defeat of even the weakest of the Axis powers was not an aim to be spurned. And Churchill had more than one trick up his sleeve when he wanted to bring up for a second time matters which, theoretically, had been already settled but to which he had not given his full approval.

In any case, there was ample proof that a grand Allied strategy was possible only with vast equipment; the construction of troop-ships and freighters, for example, was of paramount importance. A huge output would be necessary to cope with every eventuality—the great distances, enemy submarine attacks, blocking of ports, diversity of cargoes, the need to operate simultaneously in very remote areas—and to draw up in advance the complicated plans for putting the necessary men with their arms and supplies in the right place at the right time. It was to this end that the United States, following the policy laid down by Roosevelt, were in the process of becoming, as he put it, 'the arsenal of democracy'.

CHAPTER 2

The American Arsenal

In the course of the war, the United States provided the Allied coalition with more than half its armaments—thirty-five per cent of those employed against Germany and no less than eighty-six per cent of those used to force Japan to her knees. However, this enormous industrial effort did not prevent her from mobilising twelve per cent of her total population, as high a percentage as Britain and lower only than the USSR; in 1944, her armed forces numbered 12,000,000 and more than 5 million of them were fighting thousands of miles from their homeland in almost every operational theatre except eastern Europe. While providing the British Commonwealth, the USSR and Nationalist China with arms and loans, at the same time she more than doubled her industrial output and her national income, and the individual standard of living rose. In the well-known formula, in contrast to Germany which had produced guns instead of butter, the States produced guns and more butter as well. Yet no fundamental change in their economic ideas or structures was needed to produce these truly extraordinary results.

I CHOICES AND PROGRAMMES

However, the war caught the United States almost completely unprepared; she had no army—190,000 men in 1939, 50,000 of them overseas, and 329 light tanks—no stocks of arms or ammunition and barely a war industry, which represented only 2 per cent of the total output and labour force.

It is true that she had unlimited potential. In 1939, in Néré's words, 'She represented nearly 42 per cent of total world production of capital goods, as against 14 or 15 per cent by Germany, 14 per cent by Great Britain and less than 5 per cent by France.' But although she had come out of the deep slough of the depression, the American economy was still experiencing its aftermath; it was not working full out and was using only part of its potential raw materials, plant and labour force—there were almost 7 million unemployed; orders for armaments could thus be met and, as in the early years in Nazi Germany, provide a stimulus for the economy. On the other hand, this vast, thinly populated continent, as yet not being fully exploited, contained reserves of raw materials, energy and space that Europe, outside Soviet Russia, had long since lost. To these resources might be added the as yet untapped and little known resources of the States' geographical complement, Latin America.

But this peace economy had to be 'converted' into a war economy while not impoverishing the country. To do this, it was important to draw up armament production schedules, allocate orders, in proper priority, provide the necessary credit, ensure and increase the supply of labour to the right industries; and all this without giving rise to inflation or reducing the standard of living, in consequence by stabilising prices and wages. Now the American economy was ruled by the sacrosanct law of 'free enterprise'; how could production be co-ordinated and channelled towards the manufacture of armaments without imitating the rigid state-control of the totalitarian régimes, which was anathema to the American public, and when, moreover, these régimes were considered the complete antithesis of the American way of life and opposed on these grounds? The economic crisis had, however, induced the President of the United States, with his New Deal, to take certain tentative steps to increase the part played by the state in the economic sphere. These pointed the way; as a result, President Roosevelt's role was to be crucial in transforming the American economy into what he himself called 'the arsenal of democracy'.

It was he who insisted—and everything followed from this—on helping Britain at the time of her direst need, when the military were afraid that any such help might prove useless. The British in fact agreed that part of the new divisions that they were raising should use American equipment, thus providing the first boost to American war industry.

Later, this development in American industry came up against opposition both from the conservatives who disliked the increasing public expenditure and from the 'progressive' elements who had come to the fore through the New Deal and who thought that unproductive military expenditure could not fail to damage the economy or else cause an artificial boom. Roosevelt had to manoeuvre between the two trends and always got his way in the end.

Once the decision had been taken to help the democracies and, later on, just Britain, by providing arms, at the outset a choice had to be made: should such help have priority or should the American forces be rearmed first of all? Roosevelt's decision was emphatic: they should both be done together. 'We shall,' he said, 'allow the opponents of force the use of the material resources of our nation; and *at the same time,* we shall provide ourselves in America with equipment capable of meeting any defence needs.'

As a logical consequence of this, on July 7, 1941, the Secretaries of the War and the Navy were instructed to 'explore the overall needs of production necessary to defeat our possible enemies'. From the mass of reports which he received, Roosevelt extracted a programme which he called the 'Victory Program'; it fixed the size of the expenditure on armaments and the number of divisions that the American Army would need. These estimates were almost entirely guesswork, because they had not been drawn up with any specific strategy in mind; they took no account of the resources of a possible enemy, as yet unknown, which would need to be met with superior resources; and they added together hypothetical needs without really assessing America's ability to meet them all. But Roosevelt particularly wanted to fire people's imagination and stimulate their energy; his decisions on economic matters were at one with the determination which he was at the same time showing against Japan.

Accordingly, after the attack on Pearl Harbour, the 'Victory Program', with Churchill's agreement, was expanded at the 'Arcadia' conference. At the beginning of 1942, Roosevelt announced a compulsory programme in words that brooked no discussion: 'Let no one say that this cannot be done; it must be done and we are committed to doing it.' The schedule for 1942–3 was laid down as follows:

	First estimates	1942	1943
Combat aircraft	31,000	60,000	125,000
Tanks	29,500	45,000	75,000
AA guns	8,900	20,000	35,000
Machine guns (both years)	238,000	500,000	
Merchant ships (tonnage)		6,000,000	10,000,000

But it still remained to work out the means of achieving these astronomical figures and then putting them into operation.

II ECONOMIC MOBILISATION

As early as 1939, Bernard Baruch, Roosevelt's trusty adviser, had worked out a plan for a complete economic mobilisation and state-controlled war economy. The President did not adopt it for technical, moral and personal reasons. Technically, the military were not in a position to draw up an overall programme when they did not know what war they would have to wage and against whom. Psychologically, American public opinion was not ready to accept such a straitjacket as long as 'their boys' were not yet under fire—and Roosevelt knew full well that he must not try to rush things. Morally, since the United States did not possess a body of senior civil servants free from personal interests and trained to serve the state, the men capable of running such a cumbersome machine would perforce have to be borrowed from the large concerns which would themselves be involved and they would be exposed to the danger of being unable to forget their origins and former links. And finally, Roosevelt disliked the thought of relinquishing some of his own powers.

Jean Monnet and Arthur Purvis, the heads of the French and British purchasing commissions, had vainly pleaded for a minimum amount of co-ordination of American industrial production in order to facilitate their task. In 1941 and 1942, complete anarchy reigned; expenditure had no sooner been authorised by Congress than the orders poured out, simultaneously if not in self-contradiction, without the military authorities who placed them showing any concern as to their feasibility or having any means of meeting them. As a result there were long delays, shortages of raw materials and transport bottlenecks. It was impossible to cope at the same time with the demands of the American Army, the war against Japan and of lend-lease, even when they were as urgent as supplies for the USSR, and all this at a time when the Allies were suffering one disaster after another in the Pacific, Africa and eastern Europe. The allocation of the arms produced could be settled only month by month and for each item separately; the beneficiaries never knew in advance what they would receive, which made it impossible for them to draw up advance plans; a unit under training would suddenly lose its equipment to a division embarking for England or to a convoy leaving for Murmansk. In the midst of all this chaos, Roosevelt imperturbably continued to issue orders that every need must be met, convinced that the US economic machine, once launched, would prove inexhaustibly powerful through the determination and drive of the American people.

However, the early results did raise the question of whether the President's programme was not too ambitious; experts asked themselves if it was feasible and concluded that, on a number of points, it was not. For their part, the military were demanding that priorities should be worked out after a more thorough examination of their plans and they were taking steps to acquire the means necessary to satisfy them. In a word, the authorities in Washington were gradually taking over control of the war industry, a process which reached its peak in 1943.

The chief role of the organisations created for this purpose was the purchase of products and services—what the military called procurement—and channelling and directing productivity. In fact, however large the margin of control allowed, deliberately and as it were on principle, to the manufacturers, it was still necessary, in order to achieve the intended aims, to allocate the raw materials and labour force required and to keep an eye on the wage and price structures, the amount of profit and the question of taxation. After all, prices governed the movement of raw materials and by affecting profits, spurred on productivity. In order to make raw materials available where they were most needed, it was in fact necessary to ban their use in other sectors of the economy. Finally, coercive measures, ranging from compulsory orders to buying out businesses, could be expected against those firms which refused to toe the line or proved inefficient.

In short, at the end of the day the Federal authorities were poking their nose into everything and first of all providing themselves with the necessary bodies to do so. Thus, when a problem became urgent, they created, *ad hoc*, the appropriate agency to deal with it, without always worrying about the existing machinery. This led to permanent confusion and endless rivalry arising from conflicts over terms of reference; but another result was overall flexibility which left a great deal of scope to the initiative and imagination of those in charge. Moreover the various bodies gradually sorted themselves out and found their right level of importance.

Thus the Production Executive Committee, under Charles E. Wilson's chairmanship from September 1942 onwards, was given the job of supervising the orders placed by the military in order to assess their effect on the economy. The Controlled Materials Plan set up in November 1942 had the task of keeping an eye on essential raw materials—the ones most in demand were always the same, steel, aluminium and copper. The CMP would intervene to prevent industrialists from excessive stockpiling and thus 'freezing' a raw material for months on end. On the instigation of the trade union leader Walter Reuther, at the beginning of 1942 Roosevelt had already cut back production of cars for civilian use and restricted the production of refrigerators.

But the most important agency was the office of War Mobilization which came under Donald Wilson in the spring of 1943; it did not concern itself with the day-to-day running of the economy but it suggested to the President at the highest political level the long- or short-term decisions deemed necessary for the war economy and thus for the economy as a whole, since an adequate output of arms could no longer be reconciled with unrestricted 'civilian' production. A commission presided over by Senator Truman investigated cases of fraud and examined contracts.

Thus every branch of the American economy gradually fell under state control. For example, ports were placed under the authority of a high-ranking officer, generally a peacetime transport expert dressed up as a general.

But these were temporary structures, created solely by the state of war. From February 1944 onwards, the Baruch-Hancock report prepared for the reconversion to a peacetime economy. Shortly afterwards, the Office of War Mobilization added to its title the significant words 'and Reconversion', heralding a not too distant future for which everyone earnestly longed.

III ECONOMIC STABILITY

Being good disciples of Lord Keynes, the American economists had great confidence in the effectiveness of indirect controls in maintaining economic stability, that is by financial and monetary means and restricting purchasing power. Threatened inflation was thus held in check first of all by traditional means.

From 1939 to 1944 state expenditure rose from 13,000 to 71,000 million dollars. The switching of part of the civilian production to war production could not fail to lead to an excess of demand over supply, which was assessed at 17,000 million dollars in 1942. In 1944, it rose to 93,000 million. The first thing was to increase taxes, relying on the public spirit of the Americans. During the war federal revenue rose sevenfold almost entirely thanks to a steady increase in income tax. Another measure was to withdraw excess cash from circulation by directing it towards savings that at times were practically compulsory; the result was an increase in the public debt of 230,000 million dollars, although the rate of interest on the loans never exceeded three per cent. Such policies could be followed only if wage-earners retained a decent standard of living and if price stability and confidence in the dollar led subscribers to hope that after the war their savings held in war bonds would enable them to buy more goods than during the war.

Nevertheless inflationary pressures were not removed but only held temporarily in check—the same thing happened in occupied France. The massive sums taken out of circulation by taxation and loans were never sufficient to meet the increasingly massive expenditure on the war; from 1939 to 1945, the deficit on the Budget was greater than the sum total of Federal expenditure for the previous 150 years. Individual savings and the inflated cash liquidity of firms succeeded in holding in check an inflationary movement that proved irresistible after the war.

Galloping price increases were another inevitable danger. In the course of 1941, the consumer price index rose ten per cent and food prices twenty per cent. Price control had to be instituted and this automatically entailed the fixing of wages; the first measure was opposed by most of the members of Congress, usually the defenders of private interests, particularly those of farmers. The workers' trade unions opposed the second on the grounds of existing legislation.

On April 28, 1942, the Office of Price Administration fixed a price ceiling for most current consumer goods. Fraud became so widespread—especially by bringing out new articles slightly different from those falling within the regulations—that the Office of Price Administration found its task of inspection and price-fixing becoming more and more complicated. In the second half of 1942 it did, however, succeed in holding down price increases, which had risen sharply at the beginning of that year.

But wages were following an exactly opposite curve; from the first to the second half of 1942 the index of increase rose from 0.6 to 1 per cent. President Roosevelt then put through the Stabilization Act empowering him to publish before November 1, 1942, 'a general order stabilizing prices, wages and remuneration affecting the cost of living' at the level of September 15 of that same year. The Office of Economic Stabilization was set up to implement this decision under the chairmanship of the Supreme Court judge James Byrnes.

Rising prices and their race with wages were temporarily halted. In April 1943, the increase in prices reached four per cent and in wages three per cent. On April 8, 1943, Roosevelt issued the order to hold the line and froze prices and wages and forbade the Office of Price Administration to increase the former. In the summer of 1943, there was further federal intervention; a subsidy of 400 million dollars was offered to farmers to reduce commodity prices. At the same time, sugar, meat, fats, coffee and petrol were put on ration. These measures were effective and the rise in the cost of living was almost completely checked until the end of the war, with wholesale prices being held down rather better than retail prices. After the end of hostilities their upward curve began again until by 1948 they were double those of 1939, the increase being most marked in textiles and foodstuffs and least in fuel and rents. This did not, however, prevent the gross national product—after adjustments for price and tax increases—from rising by fifty per cent during the same period.

The fact remained that where one was dealing with new models continually being improved, the prices of arms and war equipment could not be fixed in the abstract without grave risk of error. In order to prevent firms from making excessive profits, the Army drew up contracts with them that were flexible enough to enable prices to be fixed in the course of manufacture, based on actual costs. The obverse of this was that firms had no incentive whatsoever to reduce their prime costs. President Roosevelt

introduced the revolutionary measure of revision of contracts, thus
contravening the principle of non-retrospective legislation. This was called
renegotiation, which meant going into prices again after they had previously been fixed, thereby restricting the firms' profit margins. In this way
nearly 10,000 million dollars were saved. This curbed the more scandalous
fortunes being made by war profiteers; but firms working on national
defence contracts were still doing sufficiently well on the one hand for the
United States war costs to be markedly higher, proportionately, than Britain's and secondly to justify the workers' trade unions in protesting against
the discrepancy between the increase in employers' profits and the blocking
of wages and salaries.

IV MANPOWER

In the autumn of 1943, full employment had been practically achieved;
the seven million unemployed had filled the places left empty by those who
had joined the armed forces or taken the new jobs created in the armaments industry; there was already a noticeable shortage of skilled labour,
particularly in New England and California.

Once again a number of members of Congress raised the old question
that had been settled by one of Roosevelt's earlier decisions; isolationism
reared its head again under the formula: 'weapons not men'—based on
Churchill's statement: 'Give us the tools and we shall finish the job.' The
campaign was led by a former President, Herbert Hoover, who had a reputation as an economic pundit. He was afraid that production might fall
because of labour shortages; he pointed out that the enemy had been
weakened; he thought that lack of shipping made it impossible to send
large numbers of troops overseas. Many congressmen and senators followed in his wake, for electioneering purposes—one provisionally exempted
conscript meant one extra vote.

Stimson, the Secretary of War, backed the general staff who were opposed to any reduction in manpower in the armed forces. He advocated
'national service', empowering the government to control all civilian employment. After seeking advice from various committees of 'wise men',
Roosevelt ordered a reduction in the armed forces of a few hundred thousand men, which turned out to be an opportune measure, since the Army
could not manage to enlist all the men whom it theoretically had the right
to.

However, perhaps owing to the trade unions' reluctance—the mistake
had been made of not associating them sufficiently closely with the war
effort—or else out of respect for the rights of free citizens, Roosevelt did

not introduce the 'national service' requested by Stimson, which was under consideration in 1944 but had been opposed by bodies representing the interests of the family as well as feminist organisations. Consequently, the employment of manpower and experts was never subject to one direct control, in fact not even handled in accordance with any definite policy. Responsibility was spread out between many bodies—the Civil Service Commission, the War Manpower Commission, the Department of Labour, etc. The result was that neither the military nor industry were ever fully satisfied and at the end of the war there were 44 million American men and women without a job or not looking for one.

The government confined itself to *ad hoc* remedies which turned out to be barely adequate: employing blacks—in 1941, Roosevelt set up the Fair Employment Practices Committee to prevent any discrimination against coloured people in the labour market; taking on 60,000 Mexicans in the agricultural sector; setting to work 125,000 of the 425,000 German and Italian prisoners interned in the United States; bringing retired people and invalids back into employment. The proportion of women employed did not increase as much as it might have done.

Another grave concern was the strict observance of social legislation in order not to cause strikes. Powerful employers like Ford refused to have anything to do with this in their factories and the Army was hesitant to give them contracts for fear that social strife might cause work stoppages. In fact, in 1941 a big strike almost paralysed the aeronautical industry; the government was reluctant to use legislation to restrict the right to strike and preferred to offer to mediate.

Pearl Harbour brought an outburst of national feeling. The trade unions patriotically pledged themselves not to stir up further strikes. Yet some did occur, which were blamed on 'irresponsible elements' and in 1943 called forth a reaction from the government in the form of a law insisting on thirty days' notice of withdrawal of labour and giving the President the right to take over factories needed for national defence purposes.

V AMERICA'S MIGHT

Despite the Army's needs and the unproductive expenditure that this entailed, America's output of goods of every sort continued to rise throughout the war. Within the space of three years, more industrial plants were built than during the ten previous years. Bauxite mines were discovered and exploited and production of aluminium increased sixfold; that of synthetic rubber went from 50,000 to 70,000 tons; the wheat harvest rose 33 per cent and coal output by 32 per cent. For that matter, civilian consumption rose continually as well, despite a slight reduction in motor cars and domestic appliances.

Throughout the war, national unity was the rule although there were outbreaks of racial violence, notably in Los Angeles and Detroit. The foreign policy was approved by both parties and Wendell Willkie, Roosevelt's unsuccessful opponent in the presidential elections, became his trusty representative on foreign missions. However, civil rights were fully respected; the press remained free; elections took place as in peacetime. The United States was an example of a democracy that did not turn its back on its principles whilst overcoming totalitarian régimes.

At the same time she provided herself with the most powerful army in the world, even though she had to create it from scratch within the space of a few months and recruiting, training and equipping all had to be undertaken simultaneously. Those who were called up were allocated to posts most suited to their intellectual ability and civilian occupation; the better educated were fed into the Air Force and the ancillary services; as a result difficulty was experienced in finding the 136,000 officers needed for the Army, 112,000 of them in 1942 and 1943; quality was often sacrificed to quantity and the problem of training the higher-ranking officers was never completely solved.

A man's initial training lasted only thirteen to seventeen weeks, including enlisting, medical examination, basic training and specialised training; once he had joined his unit, it became painfully obvious how inadequate his preparation was; the remedy was to set up military training establishments in Britain and, later on, in France. Training also suffered from shortage of arms and equipment and the lack of experienced officers and NCOs; it proved necessary for equipment to be used according to a rota system and to recall officers from fighting units.

When a new division was being formed, its commanding officer, his deputies and 200 senior officers were detailed three months in advance; they followed various courses; then they joined up with a thousand men who had already been trained in a parent division; next they were joined by the remaining officers and NCOs, who for the next fortnight or so took over the divisional equipment and prepared to receive the 13,000 to 15,000 other ranks. The group then had thirty-five weeks to turn itself into a fighting unit; but it did sometimes happen that divisional commanders went into action without ever having had the chance of taking their unit on manoeuvres.

As a rather rough and ready guess, in 1940 Lieutenant-General Wedemeyer at Roosevelt's request had estimated the American Army manpower requirements at 8,800,000 men, including the Air Force. He turned out to be just about right. On the other hand, planning errors occurred in the structure of the Army; for example, AA had been overplayed and there had to be a massive reallocation of AA crewmen. Above all, out of the 200 scheduled divisions, sixty-one were supposed to be mechanised and fifty-one motorised. It proved necessary to reduce this somewhat, as such a task was beyond the powers even of American industry.

Eventually, by the end of 1940, 23 divisions were operational; 13 were raised in 1941; in 1943, their number had risen to 91, comprising 67 infantry, 3 cavalry, 16 armoured and 3 airborne divisions.

Their equipment mirrored America's economic power. In all, the Army had at its service 96,000 tanks, 61,000 field guns, 7 million rifles, 2,300,000 lorries, 1,200,000 radio sets, 20,000 radars. More than 5 million men went overseas, including 2,700,000 to the Pacific, together with 11 million of the 21 million tons' total output of munitions. At Christmas-time 1944, the post handled 2,600,000 bags of Army mail via New York and 750,000 via San Francisco.

In particular, the Air Force had started from nothing. After the Munich agreement, Roosevelt had asked Hopkins to undertake a broad investigation of the possibilities of the American aeronautical industry. He wanted it to reach a productive capacity of 20,000 aircraft per year and an actual output of 10,000. But the American officers had no idea of air warfare; when the new Air Force commander General Arnold asked his deputies to assess their demands, they asked for 1,500 aircraft—but between 1940 and 1945 more than 300,000 were going to be built, as well as 800,000 engines.

As usual, Roosevelt wanted to stimulate output by drawing up a huge manufacturing programme: 18,000 aircraft and one million men by October 1, 1942. But a great deal of time elapsed between choosing a prototype, manufacturing it and going into mass production; the B 17 was on the drawing-board in 1938 and not delivered until 1941.

Roosevelt gave his approval to the plan put up by the Air Staff to create a Strategic Bomber Command; it had to be built, armed and trained entirely from scratch. By the end of November 1941, the Air Force comprised 300,000 men and 9,000 aircraft; by the end of the war, there were more than 100,000 planes being serviced by one million mechanics and flown by 200,000 pilots, including 1,500 women pilots on transport and meteorological flights.

As for shipbuilding, in less than two months, from June 1941, in order to counter the havoc caused by submarines 140 shipyards were started up in Delaware Bay, round Puget Sound, on the Mississippi and along the shores of the Great Lakes. They were assembly yards which put together parts that had been produced by factories in all the states of the Union and delivered by rail. By the maximum use of standardisation, it proved possible to halve the number of hours required to produce some

types of craft—Liberty Ships, for example. The output of boats rose from
746 in 1942 to 2,242 in 1943 and 2,161 in 1944.

This immense achievement was, on the whole, the result of the usual
American method of the 'profit motive', combining massive government
expenditure, widespread purchasing power and price-fixing that encouraged production; the correctives were restraint on excessive profits, a
restriction of competition through compulsory co-operation and the establishment of priorities in raw materials and credit facilities. The Americans were, of course, a very rich people at the start and their impetus was
not slowed down by the privations inflicted on Europe; nor did they ever
suffer any war damage and they were never under any threat of invasion.

Yet they still seem not to have exploited their economic and demographic
potential to the full. They could perhaps have gone further by adopting
at the outset an authoritarian system of state control on the lines advocated by Bernard Baruch. They would doubtless have thereby avoided a
great deal of confusion and gained time. But it would have meant going
against their convictions and their traditions of voluntary co-operation
and free initiative—what Mossé has called 'America's Promethean spirit'.
It is not certain that other methods, appealing more to a sense of discipline
and obedience and less to joy in action and creativeness might not have
damped their enthusiasm and their eagerness to produce.

There is, however, the opposite view: although it had become the dominating factor in the economy, the War Department had changed neither
structures, social relations nor people's mentality. The New Deal and its
left-wing trend were not revived. If the underprivileged social strata—
coloured people, workers, farmers—did benefit somewhat from the war, it
was more as a result of the strains on the labour market than of any deliberate action on the part of the authorities. At the end of the day, the
boom created by the war basically benefited the richer regions and better
off social classes.

All the same, economic analysis progressed to everyone's benefit; prosperity was based on monetary expenditure and Budget deficits which before the war would have been considered as heading straight for
bankruptcy; the lessons thus learnt greatly helped full employment and
the handling of economic crises after the war. Finally, whereas the pre-
war years of depression had stifled scientific research and prevented inventions from being developed, the 'mobilisation of brain-power' brought
about scientific advances, the most spectacular of which and the most
fraught with consequences for the future was the discovery of the use of
nuclear energy in the atom bomb.[1] So technology prospered and, as a result, the welfare of the American people.

1. Cf. p. 767, et seq.

VI LEND-LEASE

President Roosevelt certainly did not consider his slogan 'America, the arsenal of democracy' as mere propaganda. At the end of 1941, he decided that three-quarters of American armament production would be sent to the countries benefiting from lend-lease—the American general staff considered this proportion too high and felt that it might jeopardise the arming of the American forces. The attack on Pearl Harbour forced a change of outlook and it proved necessary after all, within certain limits, to fall back on to the formula 'America First'.

Lend-lease aid rose progressively from 189 million dollars in 1941 to 3,200 million dollars in 1942, 6,600 million in 1943, 7,300 million in 1944 and then went back to 3,000 million in 1945.

The chief beneficiary was Britain; but the Soviet Union also received a not inconsiderable share[1] and the new French Army raised in North Africa was fitted out with American equipment.[2] In 1941 the Americans provided the British with 1,000 tanks and 5,194 aircraft; in 1942 with 4,389 tanks and 6,847 aircraft. Total lend-lease aid represented 16 per cent of American production but it was as high as 38 per cent of their output of tanks. Arms were the main item supplied but aid also included raw materials, industrial plant, food, charter shipping and services such as ship repairs, etc.

VII LATIN AMERICA

As early as the spring of 1940, Roosevelt had stated: 'For the United States to maintain their security and political and economic position in the western hemisphere' it was necessary 'to ensure economic prosperity in Central and South America and establish this prosperity within the framework of co-operation and economic interdependence within that hemisphere'. In fact, the United States imported from Latin America 90 per cent of their coffee, 85 per cent of their sugar, 78 per cent of their bauxite, 70 per cent of their tungsten, 39 per cent of their tin, 25 per cent of their copper and lead and 30 per cent of their crude oil. It was important to keep this important source of supplies and to make sure that the Axis powers had no access to it. At the military level it was not out of the question that Nazi Germany might stir up trouble or even gain a foothold in some South

1. Cf. p. 485.
2. Cf. p. 511.

American republic, thanks to a dictator sympathetic towards Fascism. With the lapse of time the Monroe doctrine had not become merely a distant memory; it still lived on in the minds and hearts of the Americans; in recalling and even magnifying the danger of economic, political and military penetration into South America by Germany, Roosevelt was sure of striking a sympathetic chord with his compatriots; the 'Victory Program' had included the formation of an armed force equipped to take part in any hostilities that might break out in that part of the world.

German propaganda lent fuel to these fears. It was stressing the exploitation of South America by American capitalists and distributing quantities of literature and film strips in Spanish on the theme of the struggle for liberation of states under Yankee oppression, particularly Puerto Rico and Cuba. It was clever enough not to attack democracy but American plutocracy and imperialism. The German propaganda services had acquired a radio station in Montevideo which was intended to broadcast to the states bordering the River Plate.

There were, moreover, a number of countries which were already in difficulties with the United States. Mexico had expropriated the American oil companies and the United States was proclaiming the existence of 'Communist and National Socialist plots' in that country; in May 1940, the American naval attaché wrote that the Mexican government was ready to expel any American agents who might be reported to them and that it was expecting a German victory to strengthen Mexico's position vis-à-vis the United States. In Brazil, in June 1940, President Vargas had informed the German ambassador of his firm intention of maintaining Brazil's independence, his personal sympathy for the totalitarian states and his dislike of the democratic system. In the Argentine, British interests and French cultural influence were predominant; but German propaganda appeared on the radio, in the cinema and in the newspaper Pampero. However, the Foreign Affairs Minister, Cantilho, was very anti-German; but after the defeat of France, through fear of falling too closely under the control of the United States, the Argentine government assured the Reich that it intended to follow a purely Argentine policy, maintain good relations with all the belligerents and in particular retain Germany's friendship.

The United States thus had to overcome the handicap of latent hostility and a backlog of distrust, although this was not everywhere the case; her relations with Chile, Uruguay and Panama were excellent. She set out to develop both political and economic solidarity between the two halves of the continent; on November 15, 1939, she set up a body of experts, the Inter-American Financial and Economic Committee, in Panama; then she called a series of pan-American conferences, held in Rio de Janeiro in January 1942, in Washington in June of the same year and in Mexico in February 1945, when the 'Chapultepec act' laid the foundations for effective joint co-operation.

Roosevelt appointed Nelson A. Rockefeller the 'co-ordinator for inter-American affairs'. Between September 1939 and December 1941, the Import-Export Bank authorised loans of 225 million dollars to sixteen Latin American countries who were admitted to the lend-lease club. Purchases by the United States rose to 2,300 million dollars and in 1945 their sales reached 3,000 million dollars, that is one-third of their total exports. American technical experts were sent out to modernise the economy of various countries. Spectacular projects took shape, such as the Inter-American Highway, a pan-American road joining Alaska and Patagonia.

In fact, the grip of American capital on Latin America merely grew tighter. It was American capital that provided Brazil with her first large metallurgical concern, Volta Redonda, situated in the heart of the forest. In Chile, it ousted European interests and secured for itself a monopoly in copper, as it did also for lead in Peru. Standard Oil provided up to 72 per cent of Venezuela's national income and 95 per cent of its exports; it built steel works and railways. American investments in Mexico tripled; 90 per cent of her imports came from the United States and 72 per cent of her exports went there. In Cuba, the Americans had the monopoly of sugar production and iron ore. In Central America, all the exports of agricultural produce were in the hands of the United Fruit Company.

Some difficulties were not smoothed out. In February 1944 the United States refused to recognise the Farrell government in the Argentine. They froze Argentine credits and recalled their ambassador; Colonel Peron became leader of a national socialist movement which was Fascist but socialistic in inspiration, and bought out the foreign owners of the public services. An undercurrent of nationalism persisted throughout the whole of Latin America.

On the whole, however, the United States maintained and increased her control. The South American states benefited from this; Brazil's industrial output increased fourfold; new sources of wealth were being exploited everywhere; the Yankee firms brought high wages and improved hygiene and health. But the essential problem had not been solved; indeed, it had become more difficult: the new profits went into the hands of the ruling class, of European origin, and the native population remained primitive and wretched.

The Americans remained indifferent if not hostile to any attempts at social reform, such as the distribution of land to Indians in Colombia organised by President Lopez or the workers' buildings put up by President Medina Angarita in Venezuela. They even viewed them as a dangerous

Communist influence. In fact, true Communism did take root in Latin America during the war; a Communist central office was opened in Montevideo as early as August 1942; the Confederation of Latin American workers was infiltrated by Communist parties; in Guatemala, the government passed into the hands of trade unionists in 1944; in Cuba, three Communists joined the government in 1945.

Thus the United States had aroused two kinds of opposition, one based on social grounds, the second on xenophobia; they had also not always succeeded in obtaining the support of the ruling classes while being identified with them in the eyes of the oppressed classes. However, during the war this dual hostility did not give rise to any serious incidents. On the contrary, the various countries of Latin America, in their haste to support the winning side, meekly declared war on Germany and Japan with varying delays—Mexico in May 1942, Brazil in August 1942, Bolivia in April 1943, Colombia in November 1943, Paraguay, Ecuador, Peru, Chile and Venezuela in February 1945. Only the 'colonels' government' in the Argentine under Peron proved somewhat obstreperous, so much so that the USA and Britain withdrew their ambassadors from Buenos Aires; Peron decided to join the war in March 1945, so as to earn admission to the UN.

VIII BRITISH WAR PRODUCTION

Between the wars, as early as 1929, academic economists and Treasury experts had worked out a doctrine for a war economy, complete in every point; it was based on the principle that inflation must be curbed at the outset by means of ruthless taxation, a system of loans and, above all, as its principal novelty, sharply different from the American system, by widespread government control in fixing prices and wages, cutting down profits, introducing rationing and directing foreign trade. On the economic level, Britain was thus ready for war and the theory only needed to be applied.

But it was not applied at the right time and here, as in the diplomatic sphere, Neville Chamberlain's leadership proved disastrous. Right up to the declaration of war, the government showed reluctance to demand too great an effort from the country; for fear of financial difficulties, it slowed down and postponed the conversion of industry to armament production as an urgent priority; only seven per cent of the national income was devoted to the rearmament programme after the Munich agreements, when the full danger from Hitler could surely have been easily assessed.

When war broke out, the government gave itself three years to mobilise the resources of the country completely; its chief concern was to ensure

financial stability and conserve the dollar reserves, which looked likely
to run out rather rapidly. Accordingly, orders for armaments from the
United States were restricted as much as possible. It was not until January
1940 that merchant shipping was requisitioned; in June 1940 there were
still one million unemployed.

Once Winston Churchill was in power, financial concerns moved into
the background; like Clemenceau, he made war in order to win and everything else was subordinated to victory. But there was a good deal of
leeway to make up. In June 1940, industrial conscription was introduced
by law. The number of people employed in the war industry increased by
2,000,000 in the space of six months and by July 1941, forty per cent of
the active population were either mobilised in the Army or else conscripted
for industry. The nation was committed to the war more resolutely than
in any other country and the public spirit and patriotism of the British
meant that the government had no need to employ coercion, as there were
enough volunteers to satisfy every need. The system of direction of labour
was organised in such a way that a worker could avoid military service
only by being employed in the war industry; thus becoming a miner was
an alternative to having to join the armed forces.

Scientists were not forgotten. They were grouped into a Directorate of
Miscellaneous Weapon Development, otherwise known as the 'wheezers
and dodgers', under the Canadian engineer Charles Goodeve. For five
years they worked under constant prodding from Churchill; most of their
inventions were practical—machines for producing drinking water for
troops fighting in the desert, methods of camouflaging ships and rivers,
artificial harbours and floating roads. But some of them belonged rather
to science fiction, such as an enormous rocket-propelled drum full of high
explosive to destroy the Atlantic wall, which was abandoned because of
the grave danger to those actually using it.

This immense effort of a whole people deriving more from their whole-
hearted devotion than from their resources and economic potential, produced results that were sometimes excellent but frequently inadequate.
Thus the struggle against inflation almost achieved perfection thanks to
taxation, the reduction in imports and also to a fall in the standard of living—fourteen per cent overall compared with 1938 and twenty per cent
in food consumption.

These restrictions and the ensuing privations were spread equally
throughout the whole population thanks to rationing, price control, taxation, the development of utility articles and subsidies to stabilise the cost
of living. There was no under-nourishment nor any increase in the death-
rate, not even any deterioration in health. Social justice and the absence
of any organised black market were the distinguishing characteristics of

the British economy in time of war; wages kept up with prices; even while the war was still on, wide-ranging social reforms were worked out, such as the Beveridge plan of national insurance in December 1942, which was going to provide the model for more or less all the systems of social welfare introduced into various countries after the war.

To meet the food requirements of the nation, arable farming was given priority over sheep and cattle breeding. Seven million acres of pasture were put under the plough; grain production doubled. Production of iron and bauxite increased and, despite the destruction caused by German air raids, industrial output continued to rise, at least until 1943, without causing any very marked fall in the production of consumer goods.

However, these positive results were offset by three failures, in the spheres of employment, coal-mining and armament production, which showed that their leader Winston Churchill was asking the British people for an effort beyond their means, however great the need for it in the critical situation in which they found themselves.

In 1941 a shortage of skilled labour became apparent; from 1942 onwards, this shortage became a general one; it proved necessary to fix a ceiling for the Army of roughly 2 million men. The lack of competent manpower became worse and worse, although in 1944, fifty-five per cent of all the active adult population were working in the war industries. The low birthrate reduced the number of young men liable for national service every year; it proved necessary to increase working hours, introduce compulsory national service for women between twenty and thirty years old, employ Irishmen in spite of their dislike of the English—a dislike that was heartily reciprocated—and put 200,000 German POWs to work.

However, the shortcomings could not be made good in every important sector and output ceased to rise after 1943. The fact that Bevin, a member of the Labour Party, was Minister of Labour had ensured the greatest possible co-operation of the trade unions. Bevin disliked authoritarian methods of forcing workers to switch jobs in accordance with the needs of the war industry but he was obliged to resign himself to the official direction of labour. He did not succeed in satisfying every need nor did he prevent strikes from occurring, although the number of hours lost in this way was lower than in 1914–18.

At the moment when Britain needed the greatest possible supply of power, she went through a serious crisis in the coal industry owing to antiquated mining equipment and the erroneous calculation that the disappearance of exports would always ensure an adequate output for internal needs. From 1940 to 1945, coal production fell from 224 to 180 million tons and the danger of shortage was looming as early as 1941. Till then the government had only exercised indirect control through professional organisations. It had to change its methods. In June 1941 it set up the Ministry of Fuel and Power which increasingly intervened in matters of technology, wages and social questions; mechanisation, open-cast mining and coal rationing were some of the methods used. Mines were requisitioned and placed under government control but the owners continued to draw their dividends.

Indeed, feeling amongst the miners remained very strained. Thus the idea of nationalising the coal industry made headway. In 1944 Bevin, himself a miner's son, suggested this, at the same time as establishing state control of urban development and the main public services. In March 1945, the Reid Report, a technical examination of the matter by engineers, reached the same conclusions.

Manpower shortages, difficulties in the coal industry and in transport, the increasing size of the armed forces and their ever-increasing needs; all these weaknesses and contradictory requirements could not fail to affect the armaments industry. Moreover, in the Purvis Programme, similar to the American 'Victory Program', in order to provide an incentive for itself the industry had set its sights very high, indeed too high. Nor was it ever organised in a completely satisfactory way, for the equipping of each of the three services came under three separate government departments. Planning errors also occurred such as building long-range bombers, on the basis of a 'peripheral strategy' which proved to be impossible owing to lack of the necessary industrial potential and was partly overtaken once the Americans' strategic plans were adopted; but the mistake caused harm to 'combined operations' which were now becoming the rule. Above all, unlike the Americans, the British had too little time to work out a long-term armaments programme; they were always having to cope with emergencies—small ships to counter the submarine danger in 1940, tanks for Libya in 1941. The repeated changes in types of weapon, plus the small number of large factories, made mass-production methods difficult.

As a result, an output of only 626 tanks a month was reached in 1941, far fewer than the Army wanted. In 1942, an ambitious production schedule of 2,300 aircraft per month was drawn up but no more than 2,000 were ever built. The factories turned out 8,611 tanks in 1942 but only 7,476 in 1943 and still fewer in 1944. Similarly, aircraft-production reached its ceiling of 26,000 in 1943 and 1944.

From 1944 onwards, it became more and more obvious that industry was running out of steam, to such an extent that the government's chief concern was to obtain America's agreement to start reconverting the economy even before the war was over and turning it over to peacetime needs during the period between Germany's and Japan's surrender, which was assumed likely to be lengthy. The atom bomb curtailed this period; in September 1945, President Truman cut off Britain's lend-lease aid. Not only had Britain not obtained results proportionate to the immense effort, she was going to be hurled into a sea of trouble in which it proved impossible to keep her footing.

IX THE COMMONWEALTH

However, aid had not failed to be forthcoming from the Commonwealth, although it had turned out to be far less than had been anticipated at the beginning of the war and in the long run it was counter-balanced by the irresistible movement tending to draw the Commonwealth away from Great Britain.

In Canada, indeed, Prime Minister Mackenzie King proclaimed unswerving attachment to the mother country. A Canadian army was raised which was on active service from 1942 onwards, took part in the Dieppe raid, in the fighting in Italy, the Normandy landings and the ensuing campaigns in France and Germany. Canada also provided herself with a merchant fleet by building shipyards on the Great Lakes; in 1945 this merchant navy was as large as France's in 1939.

But loyal though he was, the Canadian Premier saw the Dominions' partnership in terms of free consultation and not of rigid centralisation, which was still the ideal of two such unabashed inperialists as Churchill and Alanbrooke. On occasion, problems of internal policy adversely affected Anglo-Canadian co-operation. Thus the French Canadians were opposed to the principle of conscription; seventy-two per cent of them voted against it on April 27, 1942, whereas eighty per cent of the rest of the country voted in favour. French Canadians who did join up were unhappy about the small number of French Canadian officers, as commands were given in English. It was in order to satisfy this French-speaking minority that the Canadian government maintained links with Pétain and a diplomatic representative in Vichy.

The Pacific coast provinces on the other hand felt themselves almost part of the United States, who, quite logically, sought to utilise Canada's resources for their own industrial effort and invested enormous capital there; new factories grew up all around the Great Lakes and in the Vancouver district, without too much regard for the national frontier. In August 1940, Canada linked her defence with that of her powerful neighbour; on April 20, 1941, by the Hyde Park Convention, it joined its economy to the United States. Since Britain was so far away, henceforth almost all Canada's trade transactions were with the United States; many French Canadians went to work in New England, particularly in Vermont.

However, Canada was constantly concerned to retain her own charter and preserve her national unity in the American world of which she was becoming part. Marshal Smuts' statements that after the war the world would be ruled by the Great Powers caused alarm in Canada. The Atlantic Charter had also offended her susceptibilities by the way in which it seemed to represent an Anglo-American bid for supremacy.

All the same, Canada remained entirely loyal and she participated most actively in the war; on December 31, 1944, her armed forces had risen to more than 1 million men, that is forty per cent of her male population between eighteen and forty years old. But war meant emancipation for Canada and was leading her to wish for greater flexibility in the organisation of the Commonwealth.

Despite her earlier reluctance, South Africa nevertheless fought in the operational theatres in Africa but in these alone. After the capture of Ethiopia, two divisions won fame in the Eighth Army against Rommel; one brigade occupied Madagascar; twenty-seven squadrons were based in the Middle East in 1944, which was more than Britain's contribution. South African losses were heavy: 13,000 prisoners were taken in Tobruk. In 1945, 220,000 volunteers were demobilised. But this effort was largely the personal achievement of Field Marshal Smuts as Prime Minister, Defence Minister and Foreign Minister. Public opinion was not wholeheartedly behind him because there was a powerful nationalist party in favour of taking South Africa out of the Commonwealth; moreover, the army contained two-thirds Afrikaners against one-third British.

Australia was more loyal; Prime Minister Curtin even wanted to strengthen the Commonwealth by setting up a permanent secretariat. Australia raised an army and built eighty ships of 700 to 13,000 tons. But after Japan's aggression, the Australian forces were kept for defending their own country; they fitted into the American defence arrangements and fought under American generals; it was also United States plant and equipment that enabled Australia to modernise and enlarge her industries, harbours and means of transport.

The situation was similar in New Zealand, except that Prime Minister Savage was anxious to be consulted and not be reduced merely to an executive role in the Commonwealth. When it became clear that Britain could no longer guarantee her defence, New Zealand provided herself with diplomatic representation in Washington. However, she took part in the common effort to the fullest extent of her powers; in July 1942, her

US WAR ECONOMY AND PRODUCTION

	1939	1941	1942	1943	1944	1945
Gross National Product (in 1,000 million dollars)	91.4	126.4	161.6	194.3	213.7	215.2
Industrial Production (1935–1939 = 100)	109.0	162.0	199.0	239.0	235.0	203.0
Retail prices (1935–1939 = 100)	99.4	105.2	116.5	123.6	125.5	128.4
Wholesale prices (1926 = 100)	77.1	87.3	98.8	103.1	104.0	105.8
Workers (in millions)	45.7	50.3	53.7	54.5	54.0	52.8
Working hours (per week)	37.7	40.6	43.9	44.9	45.2	43.4
Stock Exchange (prices of 416 shares; 1935–1939 = 100)	94.2	80.0	69.4	91.9	99.8	121.5
Budgetary income (in 1,000 million dollars)	6.7	15.7	23.2	39.6	41.6	43.0
Budgetary expenditure (in 1,000 million dollars)	9.0	20.5	56.1	86.0	95.6	84.8
Public debt (in 1,000 million dollars)	42.0	58.0	108.2	165.9	230.6	278.0
Purchases of goods and services by the state (in 1,000 million dollars) including:	13.1	24.7	59.7	88.6	96.5	82.8
National defence (in 1,000 million dollars)	5.2	13.8	49.6	80.4	88.6	76.0
Personal income (in 1,000 million dollars)	72.6	95.3	122.7	150.3	165.9	171.9
Strength of the armed forces on January 1[1] (millions of men)	0.4	1.5	5.0	6.8	7.2	7.4
Production: of ships (in millions of tons)	1.5 (1940)	2.5	7.0	16.0	16.3	
of tanks	346 (1940)	4,052	24,997	29,497	17,565	20,000 (approx)
of aircraft	2,141 (1940)	19,433	47,836	85,898	96,318	46,000 (three-quarters)

1. Army and Air Force only and including only actual armed fighting personnel; including Navy and various ancillary services, 12 million men were mobilised.

armed forces numbered 154,000 men, that is one-tenth of her population.

Only in India did Britain meet really serious failure. Yet in the hour of danger, the Indian nationalists had sown sympathy. 'We are not seeking,' Gandhi had said, 'to base our independence on England's ruin.' But the Congress party's request in July 1940 for a provisional national government to be formed under the control of a viceroy met with a flat refusal from Churchill. It needed the fall of Singapore for Sir Stafford Cripps to be entrusted with reopening talks; the suggestion that the British government should issue a statement promising India dominion status was compared by Gandhi and Nehru at that time to 'a postdated cheque drawn on a bankrupt Empire'.

However, the British played on the rivalry between the Congress party, the Moslem League and the princes, as well as on the ethnic, social and regional differences in that enormous country. In 1939, the Indian Army totalled 353,000 men; on October 1, 1944, it had reached 2,641,000 men; but with a few exceptions, the Indians were never promoted to the higher ranks. At the same time, India was being exploited by the British in a shocking and even tragic manner; India's scanty rolling-stock was used to equip the railway running from Iran to the Caspian Sea and when, in 1942, the British halved their shipping traffic in the Indian Ocean, which was 100 ships a month before the war, famine ensued which caused the death of 1,500,000 people in Bengal in the summer of 1943.

*

Thus it was apparent from 1943 onwards that, left to herself, Britain would not be capable of winning the war. She was maintaining her position in the Allied coalition thanks only to lend-lease and to Roosevelt's kindness in pretending to continue considering Britain as an equal partner with the United States. History could hardly seem less moral, for Britain had held the breach, courageously and alone, against Nazi Germany; she had fought on by herself in order that peoples might be free. As a reward she had to face the sight of her capital and customers melting away all over the world, her empire crumbling, her industrial potential weakened and the admission of an irretrievable diminution of her power.

On the other hand the war was surely leading the United States to the summit of power; she had joined in after everyone else, after others had foundered in her absence; she was picking up the pieces of the legacy left by Britain; it was clear that she was becoming the *deus ex machina* to resolve the world drama that had started in 1939; Britain's dependence on her, her growing strength, military as well as economic, could not fail meanwhile to give her the most important voice, first of all in the interallied discussions on the conduct of the war and later at the conference tables where the world would be given its post-war shape.

But in 1943, her time had not quite come; it was still the Soviet Union that was bearing the brunt of the Wehrmacht's attacks.

The Soviet War

I THE CONDUCT OF THE WAR

IT is not easy to find out how the war was directed and conducted in the Soviet Union. It is true that Soviet historians offer a good deal of detail as to the nature and role of the bodies that exercised the real power within the structure of Soviet institutions. But they are very sparing of information regarding their functioning; when reading them it would seem that these bodies were never split by dissension, that their members always knew unhesitatingly what needed doing and that, in fact, they were uplifted by such strong patriotic feeling that they saw everything with complete lucidity and were inspired by unswerving determination and mutual understanding. Soviet historians are even more discreet about the personal part played by the men in charge of these various bodies; more accurately, until Stalin's death, they showed them as all completely dominated by the giant figure of Lenin's successor, who became a legend in his own lifetime; once the campaign against 'the personality cult' started, Stalin's role was discussed more but still not closely examined or assessed and, apart from Khrushchev for a few years, his colleagues still remain overshadowed by Stalin. On the other hand, the Soviet Communist party always comes in for unstinting and undifferentiated praise; every single success is attributed to it but it is referred to as an anonymous mass and the individuals who formed part of it remain completely unidentified; its exact role is all the more difficult to analyse as some of its constituent bodies—the Comintern for example—are locked in impenetrable secrecy, not to mention the secret police and the intelligence services.

Thus, in the Soviet Union more than anywhere else, there is appearance and there is reality. In principle, Soviet institutions remained in force and continued to function: the Supreme Soviet of the USSR approved the Budget and ratified agreements but it does seem that, in essential matters, it had practically been reduced to inactivity; its Praesidium promulgated a large number of resolutions; the Councils of the People's Commissars of the various republics took countless decisions but only in the civilian sphere, in short, in routine matters.

The conduct of the war and the solution of its enormous problems were entrusted to new bodies, set up as early as June 1941 by the Central Committee of the Party. It is not easy to see the reason for these bodies because in the USSR the Communist party was solidly established in every senior post, at every executive level; in fact, even before the war, in every sphere of government, every avenue led back to Stalin, who was leader of the Party as well as of the government. Nor does it seem as if the Party which had suffered numerous purges in consequence of the suspicious and spiteful nature of its ambitious Secretary-General, was in any way basically reshuffled during the war by dismissals as a punishment for individual failures. The new bodies probably enabled more efficient centralisation of the new tasks into fewer hands and gave increased power to a few carefully selected leaders, chosen in accordance with principles which escape us but, in all probability, mainly because Stalin trusted them.

In any case, the conduct of the war in all its aspects was the responsibility of the State Defence Committee under Stalin's chairmanship. It had the power to issue edicts having the force of law for the duration and its authority extended to all state and party organisations. One cannot fail to be reminded of the French Revolutionary Committee of Public Safety, but minus the *Convention*: the State Defence Committee was answerable only to itself.

All the other bodies were restricted to a purely executive capacity. However, the SDC did not set up any new services of its own; it exercised its authority through the normal machinery of state; thus it controlled the planned economy, directed towards war production by means of the Commission of the Plan (Gos Plan); but it took direct decisions on matters which it considered urgent and which in normal times might have seemed of minor importance—for example the laying of an oil pipeline over Lake Ladoga to supply Leningrad during its siege.

The State Defence Committee also controlled the armed forces with the help of the General Headquarters (*Stavka*) on which there sat officers representing the forces but also high party officials, promoted to be Marshals of the Soviet Union for the purpose—for example, Bulganin. This CHQ worked out strategy, allocated units to the various fronts and controlled the strategic reserves; its decisions were carried out by the armed forces' general staff, composed entirely of service representatives.

The State Defence Committee poked its nose into everything. It sent plenipotentiary delegates to the various republics, to the different fronts, to industrial concerns—for example, to settle a crisis in the coal industry in Karaganda in 1943; here again, one is reminded of the 'special missions' of the representatives of the *Convention*.

The other new bodies were given only minor tasks of local importance, or morale-boosting missions. Thus, in areas where the situation was becoming dangerous—for example, at Stalingrad—local defence committees were set up. When the need was felt, the SDC formed fresh people's commissariats or ministries, as for the production of tanks and mortars.

At grass-root level, the local soviets, trade unions, Komsomols and production co-operatives had the task of providing the necessary official backbone for the population and spurring it on to satisfy the war needs. Thus the soviets, with a million members in all, collected warm clothing for the troops, helped to look after their families but also to maintain law and order and good discipline. The trade unions worked to increase output; and the Komsomols, with 9 million members, were the constantly replenished rearing-ground of half-trained recruits. Other new bodies with special aims but with the same general purpose were set up—for example, the body 'for the defence and advancement of aeronautics and chemistry'.

II STALIN'S ROLE

What part did Stalin play in all this? For an accurate assessment we would have to discover what share he had in planning the decisions taken by the SDC and determine those which he approved and accepted responsibility for when others had provided the idea; this is impossible to assess in the present state of knowledge, at least in France. He was certainly a very clever man, indeed a crafty one, but within a tightly closed world which he had been able to organise to his own advantage and bring under his thumb: the Russian Communist party. Outside this world, he was astonishingly lacking in knowledge; he had never been outside the Soviet Union; he knew no foreign languages; his ideas were as dull as his style; in a word, he seemed to deserve the title of the 'most insignificant of Lenin's comrades' which had earned him the post of Secretary-General of the Party, because of the fears aroused in his colleagues by Trotsky's strong personality. From this central position, he had patiently spun his spider's web and he controlled all its threads from the confined space of a few rooms in the Kremlin where he lived in austerity and from which he ruled the greatest empire in the world—the USSR and her Communist partners. To achieve this degree of power and stay there, Stalin had had to show few scruples and great gifts of guile, deceit, intrigue and brutality; by bringing them into disrepute with his astounding accusations, Stalin had gradually eliminated all his opponents, real or imaginary; he had placed men whom he could trust in every important post in the machinery of government. His efficient management and the terror which he inspired had thus consolidated his authority by ensuring that it would be permanent.

But his policy had now suffered a setback of the utmost gravity; he had proved unable either to foresee or to prevent German aggression; his policy had led to such major reverses that his authority seemed in danger of foundering and the Bolshevik Revolution of disappearing; the Soviet Union herself was threatened with disruption. It seems that Stalin was able to manoeuvre so that at one and the same time he managed to establish his power even more strongly, protect himself against any backlash from either his enemies or those who had suffered at his hands in the Party and rally the whole population behind himself and the Communist régime.

He was and remained head of government and leader of the Party; in addition, he became Marshal Stalin, head of the armies of the Soviet Union and Chairman of the State Defence Committee. Thus, everything that took place began or ended with him. Not one important measure was taken without his having inspired or approved it. It was he who dealt, directly and personally, with Roosevelt and Churchill. It is, incidentally, a somewhat surprising fact that, in the British parliamentary democracy as well as in the American presidential democracy and the Soviet socialist democracy, the conduct of the war and thus the leadership of the nation fell to a civilian leader issuing his orders to the military, as in the totalitarian régimes of Germany and Italy; paradoxically it was only under the Japanese military dictatorship that some corporate authority existed. In any case, in the Soviet Union Stalin's role was certainly predominant. But although, in Churchill's or Roosevelt's actions, it is possible to distinguish the proportion of mistaken and successful ideas, any similar analysis of Stalin is impossible.

The new bodies seem to have had a triple function; they allowed Stalin to gather round himself the indispensable professional advisers, scientists for example, even if they were not long-standing Communists, without having to go through the cumbersome and slow governmental, administrative or Party channels. They put the ordinary Soviet institutions into a state of suspended animation; these were possible sources of opposition or rivalry and, however slight their importance might have been, they needed no longer to be taken into account; and now these new organisations removed any hope of playing a larger part in affairs as they might have been tempted to do in view of the new situation arising from the Russian setbacks. Finally, these new bodies seemed to show that the régime was changing its nature; it was identifying itself more with the nation; it was ceasing to be tyrannical and revolutionary in order to become merely the voice and instrument of the will of the peoples of the Soviet Union to repel the invader.

Accordingly, a superficial façade was created to inspire confidence in the Soviet leaders, both inside and outside the country—a confidence which the latter had good reason to believe was far from widespread. So we find a determined propaganda machine installing loudspeakers even in the depths of the country, to blare out Stalin's reassuring fatherly voice, giving advice and instruction at times of crisis or real danger. One particularly widespread image of him represented him as an amiable, smiling, confident 'Father of his People', full of quiet strength. This conception seems even to have misled the British and Americans who met him; they expected to see a despot with cruelty written all over his face and they discovered a jolly good sort, a hard drinker, shrewd but accessible and frank, in short, a very likeable man. This is the picture and impression that Eden and Hopkins conveyed in their reminiscences. Churchill and Roosevelt expressed the same idea in their war correspondence by the familiar nickname 'Uncle Joe'.

It was important for the international Communist party to achieve, like its leader, in its internal as well as its external image, the greatest possible support by disarming the animosity that it had aroused hitherto.

III RUSSIAN NEO-NATIONALISM

In any case, even before the war, the danger from Hitler had induced the Soviet political leaders, in contradiction with the early days of the régime, to stress national unity and patriotism. Thus a sort of mythical pantheon of illustrious Russians had been created: Alexis Tolstoy had extolled the work of Peter the Great; Eisenstein had recalled that of Ivan the Terrible. Tolstoy and Tchaikovsky were rehabilitated because they had written about and celebrated the story of the Holy War against Napoleon. In France, the Communist party had ceased to advise people to refuse to fight for their country; they no longer condemned outright the illustrious deeds and works of the past as being for the benefit of a small number of people at the expense of the workers but claimed that the people as a whole could take credit for them. Thus Thorez had shown that French cathedrals or the Château of Versailles belonged to the people because, after all, it was the people who had built them.

This trend had been momentarily brought to a halt by the German-Soviet pact; but the break between the signatories gave it fresh vigour and urgency. On November 6, 1941, Stalin told the troops massed in Red Square: 'The war you are fighting is a war of liberation, a just war, in which you can seek inspiration from our great forefathers, Alexander Nevski, Dimitri Donskoy, Alexander Suvorov, Michael Kutusov.' On July 29, 1942, the Supreme Praesidium decreed that the Kutusov and Alexander

Nevski decorations should be reinstated, and to these was added the Order of Lenin as their normal and natural successor in the history of the one and same Russian people.

Inversely, if the invaders continued to be described as 'Fascists', a word that incidentally became synonymous with bandits, they were above all accused of wishing to seize the USSR's wealth—especially her wheat and oil —and turn her inhabitants into slaves; so that the citizens of the Soviet Union were fighting for their possessions as well as for their self-respect and these included the Bolshevik régime that had given them the one and the other. It was, of course, Soviet national feeling but, above all, it was Russian: at the end of the war, Stalin, a Georgian, sang the praises of the Russian people and gratefully recognised it as the principal element and instrument of Soviet victory.

The power of religious feeling was not neglected; the Metropolitan Serge exhorted the Orthodox Russians to fight for Holy Russia, whereas the Bolshevik régime had been against religion. The 'Internationale' ceased to be the USSR's national anthem. In one of his poems, Simonov spoke of 'the Fatherland . . . country roads traced by our forefathers with wooden crosses on Russian graves'.

In the Red Army, old traditions were revived; the ranks of general and marshal made their appearance again together with the epaulettes that in 1917 the revolutionaries had torn off the uniforms of the Czarist officers. In the thick of the battle of Stalingrad the 'political commissars', whose task was to ensure that the Army remained subordinated to the Party, be-came 'deputy commanders in charge of political matters', and so were less embarrassing for the military commanders.

Laran has analysed a whole popular literature written by 'soldier authors'—M. Sholokhov, B. Polojov, A. Tvarkovskiy, M. Tikhonov—who extolled the qualities of the Russian fighting man; there were many songs celebrating the exploits of the 'Katyushas'; 'the bogatyrs of the Russia of Kiev have been roused from their long slumber to fight once more against the invader'; the jet rocket-gun was nicknamed 'Ivan the Terrible'. The government sponsored and encouraged this upsurge of feeling through the 'Pansoviet House of Popular Creation'. In a word, an immense patriotic fervour, half spontaneous, half officially inspired, filled the hearts of all the peoples of the Soviet Union.

IV THE DISSOLUTION OF THE COMINTERN

On May 15, 1943, a long resolution was passed by the Praesidium of the executive committee of the Communist International dissolving the body commonly known as the Comintern which had been directing from Moscow the action of Communist parties all over the world. Although not the first in date—it had been preceded by the International Association of Communist Trade Unions, Profintern, and The International Peasants' Association, Krestintern—the disappearance of this body was completely unexpected and it caused a sensation. Annie Kriegel has pointed out that though the members of the executive committee of the Comintern learned the news on reading *Pravda,* the decision had been maturing since the German-Soviet pact when Stalin was taking care not to alarm Hitler. So it was Stalin who had taken the decision, after a minimum of indispensable consultation.

It was Stalin himself who explained the event for foreign consumption in an interview which he granted to Reuter's correspondent.[1] He pointed out that this step put an end to 'the lie according to which the USSR interfered in the internal affairs of other states'; the decision would show how unfounded were the slanders describing 'the Communist parties of the different countries as not acting in accordance with the interests of their own people but obeying instructions from abroad'; it would enable 'patriots in freedom-loving countries to bring together all the progressive forces of their country . . . against Fascism'; as between nations themselves it would facilitate the establishment of 'an international front against the threat of Hitler'. But the decision had such a symbolic significance that, despite Thorez's vain attempts to justify it by reference to Marx's and Engels' dissolution of the 'League of Communists', according to Marty old revolutionaries 'shed tears as they signed it'; but they all submitted and gave their acceptance.

This measure seemed to put an end, at least for the moment, to the Soviet Union's aims of world revolution. Although it could partly be explained by certain difficulties in the functioning of the Comintern, it had certainly been taken with a view to reassuring foreign countries and first and foremost the Soviet Union's allies, the British and Americans and the non-Communist Resistance movements in occupied countries. It represented, in fact, the Soviet Union's contribution to the National Fronts. Goebbels was not mistaken when he denounced it as yet another monstrous act of collusion between Bolshevism and plutocracy. Although Churchill evinced some scepticism as to Stalin's intentions, Roosevelt and Hopkins certainly interpreted it in this way. As for the French Resistance, here are some of the views of its underground organisations, non-Communist and in some cases anti-Communist, on this sudden switch in USSR policy. 'Dissolving the Comintern,' wrote *Défense de la France,*

1. A. Kriegel, 'La Dissolution du Komintern', *Revue d'histoire de la deuxième guerre mondiale,* Oct. 1967.

'means that the USSR has given up the idea of issuing revolutionary directives to the Communist parties of the various countries; these parties will now be able to fit in with the ordinary lines of internal policy.' *Franc-Tireur* drew attention to Stalin's statements that 'the USSR wanted to let the liberated peoples have the right to rule themselves as they chose'. A 'Secret Army' paper, *La Quatrième République,* criticised those who persisted in thinking that 'Stalin wants to bolshevise the world, for the Soviet statesmen are too intelligent to follow such a will o' the wisp'. In short, the Resistance considered that there was no longer any obstacle to a lasting alliance between France and the USSR; it was even highly desirable.

Stalin wanted the Soviet Union to cease being a bogy in the world, just as he wanted Communist parties to become respectable in their own countries; and he had achieved his aim. But the disappearance of the Comintern for purely tactical reasons did not mean that the Kremlin's hold over international Communism was in any way weakened; it was merely an internal transfer of responsibility.

V THE SOVIET UNION AND THE COMMUNIST PARTIES

In fact, even before the Comintern was dissolved, the Communist parties in the various countries had already taken up 'national' attitudes in accordance with instructions received from Moscow. Ever since July 1941, the British Communist party had organised lectures and meetings to stimulate war production; it proclaimed that British workers should group themselves solidly behind the coalition government and the colonised peoples should play down their claims and realise that the immediate task was to beat Hitler. It deplored Gandhi's obstinate persistence in his narrow-minded attitude, a criticism echoed by an Indian Communist party manifesto which in the course of the party's first non-clandestine meeting in September 1942 proclaimed that 'India was ready to serve the Allied cause'. The British Communist party failed to join the Labour Party after having asked to do so only because the latter refused to let it in.

The US Communist party advised the blacks to put an end to their campaign for 'equal pay for equal work' in the war industry which, if implemented, would have jeopardised production. The Socialist leader Norman Thomas who called on the blacks to continue their struggle for equal rights was accused by the Communist newspaper, the *Daily Worker,* of advocating Fascism. One American Communist leader wrote that there were no longer any economic classes in the USA, but merely the American people. The 'America, Peace, Mobilisation' movement was merely changed to 'American People's Mobilisation'—the initials remained the same and the message was reversed.

All over the world, instructions from Moscow continued to be transmitted by radio to the Communist parties of various countries; thus Maurice Thorez, André Marty and Jean-Richard Bloch addressed the French people on Radio Moscow; but other more secret messages were picked up by the central committee of the underground French Communist party.

The groups of exiled Communists remained at Stalin's beck and call in Moscow. He kept them out of the way or brought them into the limelight as pawns in his game of chess. Although the Finn Kuusinen was put back into his box after his failure in Finland, Bierut the Pole, the Romanian Anna Pauker, Rakosi the Hungarian, the Italian Togliatti, the Germans Pieck and Ulbricht, Gottwald the Czech and the Bulgarian Dimitrov were all kept in reserve, to bide their time. The Comintern had not really disappeared, it had been naturalised as Russian; the directives addressed to the various Communist parties were no longer issued by a theoretically independent international body but by an office of the Soviet Party's Central Committee; and these instructions were no longer issued on behalf of world revolution but of the Soviet Union; her salvation offered the only hope that one day the fight to achieve world revolution might start again.

The role of the non-Russian Communist parties was to encourage national Resistance movements likely to relieve the pressure that the Wehrmacht was exerting on the Red Army and, in each country, to form teams to share or take over power at the Liberation. Greater importance would be granted to those parties in territories which the Red Army itself reconquered. But except for Yugoslavia—and there with certain reservations only—every Communist party approved wholeheartedly and at all times the Soviet Union's policies and loyally supported her *vis-à-vis* her allies, in particular for the opening of a second front.

The French Communist party's underground press, for example, never ceased supporting the Soviet Union on every issue, whatever changes in policy she might make. *L'Humanité* sang the praises of the Russian soldier as 'a citizen defending his land, his liberty, his life and his mother-country'. The war being waged by the USSR was a 'holy war for the freedom and dignity of mankind'; the 'Fascist' argument that the Bolshevik régime was attacking private property was 'bad propaganda which should not deceive anyone'. As for the liberty of nations, the USSR had 'no territorial ambitions with regard to other nations . . . she had more than once shown her respect for the right of nations to self-determination'. From all this, Jacques Duclos drew the conclusion that 'France, with one voice, wants a treaty with the USSR similar to the one signed by Czechoslovakia'.

The fact remained that, in taking part in this patriotic struggle, in re-cruiting new members more on the basis of their participation in the Re-sistance than of their political convictions, in placing in the forefront those who owed their fame to their militant partisan activity, and in preaching and practising the principle of the broadest possible national unity, it was impossible for the Communists not to change their nature somewhat. The military leaders in the occupied countries were not always going to be in agreement with the exiles who had lived too long in the Soviet Union not to have rather lost touch with their own country. As a sign of the shape of things to come, Kriegel has drawn attention to an appeal by Togliatti, which he made as early as July 1943, for 'polycen-trism', called for co-operation between Communist parties after the war and suggesting regional agreements that could be developed only at the cost of weakening the links with Moscow. But could the Russian Com-munist party itself fail to be affected by the patriotic struggle in which its members were unstintingly giving their all with the deep satisfaction of identifying themselves with the most fundamental aspirations of the peoples of the Soviet Union? In particular, it had played a preponderant role in ensuring that the high-quality armaments needed by the Red Army were produced in the right quantities and at the right time.

VI SOVIET ECONOMIC LOSSES THROUGH THE OCCUPATION

In 1940, the USSR produced nearly 30 million tons of iron ore, 15 million tons of cast iron and more than 18 million tons of steel, 166 million tons of coal, 31 million tons of oil and 48,000 million kilowatts of electricity. In certain sectors—the mechanical and machine-tool industries—plant was modern and output high; the enormous reserves of iron ore, coal or oil opened up unlimited possibilities.

But in the period immediately preceding the war, this economic poten-tial was not being used to manufacture sufficient armaments to equip the Red Army properly. Nowadays Soviet historians blame Stalin for this, since they claim that it was not until June 6, 1941, that he issued a pro-gramme for the mobilisation of war production, which was not ready to start before the end of 1942. So in 1940, Germany's output of modern air-craft was 10,250 as against a few dozen by the Soviet Union. Soviet tank production was better—nearly 2,800 in 1940—but still less than what was needed. Production of the 47-mm anti-tank gun had been stopped and Stalin has been held responsible for this, too, whilst the 57-mm gun which had been approved was still in the manufacturing stage.

Most of the Soviet Union's metallurgical industry was concentrated in factories in the western areas of the country, chiefly round Leningrad and Moscow, and in the Ukraine; their occupation, the fighting that took place there and the deliberate demolition undertaken in the course of the 'scorched earth' policy, cost the USSR 31,000 industrial concerns—factories, workshops, warehouses—over 40,000 miles of railway, 175,000 machine tools, 34,000 power hammers and forging presses, 62 blast-furnaces, 213 Martin furnaces and 45,000 looms. In towns held by the enemy, fifty per cent of the apartment blocks had been destroyed or badly damaged; 98,000 kolkhozes, 1,800 sovkhozes and 2,890 machinery and tractor depots had been devastated.

In six months, from June to November 1941, total industrial production fell to forty-eight per cent of the pre-war level; in particular output of ferrous and non-ferrous rolled sheet metal and of ball-bearings, indispensable for armaments, had been almost entirely brought to a stop in the turmoil.

This disastrous drop in production was accentuated in the course of 1942. Coal output fell from 142 million tons in 1941 to 75 million; production of cast iron from 18 million tons to 5; steel from 13.8 to 4.8 million tons.

The usual deliveries between regions or from coal mine to factory came to an abrupt stop; some factories outside the enemy's reach were no longer receiving any coal; others were unable to despatch their product for lack of transport. In the country there was a return to primitive methods of agriculture: hand-ploughs, home-made equipment; everywhere the most trivial articles and the most ordinary products became worth their weight in gold. In this catastrophe, the USSR was saved by her geography, her leaders' decisions and the courage and long-suffering nature of her inhabitants.

Her enormous size put large areas of the country beyond the reach of enemy operations, from the Urals and beyond; the problem was to have time enough and find the way to move men and machines into these areas and to enlarge the industrial concerns already sited there as a result of the Five Year Plans. Her population gave the Soviet Union equally unlimited reserves of manpower but it was necessary to turn women and peasants into skilled workers—in 1937 the active population still included 40 million rural workers. The government doubled its loans to discover raw materials in non-occupied areas; it gave priority to certain sectors of industry —special steels, for example; it sited new factories close to mining areas. In short, it sought to channel and direct production; but there remained two immense problems: the evacuation of workers and their machines eastwards and the mobilisation and training of manpower.

VII THE EVACUATION OF FACTORIES EASTWARDS

On June 24, 1941, only three days after the start of the war, the Party's Central Committee set up an Evacuation Committee, under Kaganovitch and later Svernik, helped by Kosygin; on June 27, the general outline of the programme was laid down by government decree and the first measures promulgated. The rapid anticipation and speed of these decisions are somewhat surprising; factories began to be evacuated well before they were threatened. As Girault remarks, 'Either the government organisations quickly became aware of the collapse of the front lines and reacted with great speed . . . or else they were following deliberate tactics . . . of fighting far back in the interior of the country.' It is certain that such far-reaching and complicated decisions could not have been deliberately worked out in the space of a few days; the vast amount of planning required must have been devised and worked out in advance; so one is led to wonder whether the Soviet counter-attacks in July 1941 had the purpose of enabling these plans to be carried out; in this respect therefore, Stalin seems to have acted wisely and he must be given a good mark despite the chorus of disapproval which now surrounds his memory.

It is true that the evacuation was made easier by the lines which the Soviet economy had been following before the war, the Five Year Plans, the development of natural resources and their conversion on the spot, in the Urals, Siberia and Turkestan. 'Twins' of factories sited in the west— in the mechanical, chemical and oil industries—had been built there; so some concerns found vacant places ready and waiting to fit them in; for example, the Kirov factory in Leningrad and the diesel engine factory at Kharkov merged with the tractor factory at Cheliabinsk to become the largest tank factory in the Soviet Union.

All the same, a gigantic effort was required. The Evacuation Committee split into three groups, each responsible for the transfer of the factories, the despatch of personnel and transport respectively; but in fact, the three sectors were inextricably linked. When the decision was taken to evacuate Moscow on October 16, 1941, the evacuation of government departments and 150,000 people had to be organised within twenty-four hours, using even Underground trains.

Between July and November 1941, 1,500,000 railway carriages were used to move 1,520 firms, including 1,300 very large ones, to the east, as well as 10 million people, more than 2 million of them from the Moscow region; 450 firms were set up in the Urals, 210 in western Siberia and 250 in central Asia. During these six months, the main factories in Dnepropetrovsk, Zaporozhye, Krivoy Rog, Kharkov, the Donetz (at times under enemy bombardment), Byelorussia, Leningrad and Moscow were dismantled and set up elsewhere; it is impossible to say how many fell, more or less intact, into German hands. A second, smaller wave was set off by the German offensive in the summer of 1942; it affected the centres of Stalingrad, Voronezh, Rostov and Krasnodar. When the new arrival was grafted on to an already existing factory, production restarted rapidly; Soviet historians quote the example of a factory from the Dnepr which was functioning again twenty days after being dismantled; one aircraft factory began to turn out aircraft again a fortnight after it had arrived, dismantled, at its new site; towards the end of 1941, the Leningrad factories in the Urals were sending heavy tanks to the front. But some of the industrial complexes were too large to be transported as they were and they were split up into specialised sections; thus, the Moscow ball-bearing factory, the largest in Europe, was set up at Kuibychev, Saratov and Tomsk; each section was intended to provide specific finished products, but the period of adaptation was bound to be that much longer.

Building new factories obviously took longer but it took place at a speed unknown before the war; thus, blast-furnaces which would have taken two and a half years to erect before the war, took only eight months at Magnitogorsk.

Results were not slow in coming. By March 1942, war production had caught up with that of June 1941; by the end of 1942, it had overtaken it. By that time, the Soviet Union was building more armaments than Germany; only slightly more tanks and aircraft but four times as many artillery guns; more than 6,000 miles of new railway lines had been laid. It was an undoubted success; as an American journalist put it, 'Magnitogorsk had defeated the Ruhr.'

This immense effort was to modify enormously the economic geography of the Soviet Union according to the programme drawn up by Voznessenski, chairman of the 'State Planning Commission' (Gos Plan) and as such the man best qualified to adapt current changes to the former or intended state of affairs. If, by reason of their remoteness, progress was quantitatively rather limited in Siberia and central Asia—although local production increased more than tenfold—by the end of the war the Urals were completely transformed. The old factories, some of them dating back to the eighteenth century, had been modernised; nearly a dozen blast-furnaces and dozens of other new furnaces and rolling-mills were erected; the output of cast iron in the Urals almost doubled; steel output rose sixty-five per cent and sheet iron fifty-five per cent.

This economic victory certainly owed a great deal to government organisations and Soviet scientists; it had been made possible only by the sweat and suffering of the people; it had exacted a very heavy toll of human effort.

VIII THE HUMAN EFFORT

Soviet historians certainly do not minimise this effort; on the contrary, they magnify it and see it as a demonstration of the gratitude and affection of the people of the Soviet Union towards the Soviet régime at the same time as an affirmation of their unquenchable patriotic feeling. However, they stress the productive exploits of the Stakhanovites rather than the sufferings endured by the human beings involved, where the picture they paint would seem rather to conflict with the good conduct marks which they very properly allot to the organisers of the evacuation and consequently to the Party, which is given the credit for every success.

Certain facts do exist which enable us to form some idea of these sufferings, and Girault has very efficiently collated and drawn attention to them. There was the Party meeting at Zlatoust on December 13, 1941 when the secretary was accused of incompetence for not supplying adequate provisions for the workers; there was the decision of the Party's Central Committee in April 1942 which shared out the agricultural production of sovkhozes to various factories whose workers went out to work on the land on their rest-days; there was another decision authorising workers to undertake market gardening on their own account—doubtless many of them had not waited to receive this permission; at the end of 1942, 5 million new gardeners were listed. The number of working hours was increased and holidays cancelled; thus the number of working days per year for an adult kolkhoze worker rose from 255 in 1940 to 350 in 1944; to stimulate production, considerable differentials in wages and rations were introduced.

If one accepts the statement of the Soviet historian Cadaev that in the Soviet Union prices dropped by 230 per cent between 1943 and 1945, one is impelled to ask oneself what rises there had been earlier and to imagine that they must have been so steep that wages had found it impossible to keep pace. Material living conditions—accommodation, hospitals, food-supplies, heating, schools—were all the less likely to be satisfactory, at least until 1943, because they had not been given priority in the existing schemes, because 10 million people were involved and because the proportion of unproductive elements amongst them was considerable—there were 600,000 children from Moscow and 300,000 from Leningrad. As Girault wrote, an honest account of these inevitable sufferings would 'in no way detract from the heroism of the Soviet people, in fact quite the reverse'.

The problems involved were, in fact, colossal and they had to be solved both quickly and in a co-ordinated manner. It was not sufficient just to transfer labour; it had to be allocated in the best possible way—switched from one type of activity to another—employees in the tertiary sector became workers in factories engaged in war production, the gaps in the essential industries had to be filled by taking on whole social categories; this makeshift labour force then had to be adequately trained to ensure that the product was of the required quality.

The requirements were immense. In September 1940, there were 20,-500,000 workers and employees in the Soviet Union; 6 million of them lived in the areas that were invaded; skilled workers were evacuated to the east in order of priority, but in insufficient numbers. Thus qualified manpower was in short supply in those activities where it was most needed; in heavy industry the number of specialist workers fell from 450,000 to 240,000; in the aeronautical industry, skilled manpower was no more than one-third of what it had been at the beginning of 1941. At the end of 1941, the 'Committee for the Census and Allocation of Manpower' spelt out its needs thus: there was a shortage of 215,000 workers in the evacuated factories, including 45,000 in the tank factories and 64,000 in the ordnance factories. This shortage could not fail to grow worse in view of the increased manpower demands of the Red Army and its losses which would require the mobilisation of civilian workers as the only means of meeting the first and replacing the second.

This shortage remained a constant factor in the Soviet war economy; in 1945, the numbers working in the economy as a whole were still only 27 million as against 30 million in 1940, that is 87 per cent; industrial workers and employees 9.5 as against 11 million, that is, 86 per cent; ordinary workers 6.3 as against 8.3 million, that is 76 per cent. In 1942 the drop was particularly steep and alarming: the number of workers and employees in the heavy metallurgical industry fell to less than half that of 1940 and the shortage of trained personnel—engineers and technicians—was even greater and more serious than that of workers. The situation did not begin to recover until 1943 and it never became entirely satisfactory.

Increasing the number of working hours had been a temporary remedy at first but its inevitable consequences had been a falling-off in individual output. The movement of employees from the tertiary to secondary sectors was also of some help but its scope was bound to be limited. Directing labour to work of special priority was another remedy: thus the labour force employed in the armament industry was increased at the expense of the consumer industries; although at the end of 1942 the number of workers in the aircraft industry was moving towards that employed in 1940, in the textile industries it was only fifty per cent; that is to say, the standard of living was being forced down. True, the workers' enthusiasm and competitive spirit were stimulated by an intensive campaign in which the Komsomols played the leading part; but its effects were bound to be moral rather than practical; there is a limit to human strength.

The solution was thus to bring new social categories into the labour force. Here too the movement had started before the war when the Ukraine kolkhozians had been switched to the mines. We must leave aside the forced-labour camps and resign ourselves to ignorance as to their number and size, as Soviet historians are very discreet on the subject and although they are no longer taboo as a subject for discussion, they are still taboo as a subject for study. On February 13, 1942, a decree mobilised all the able-bodied urban population; it applied to men from 16 to 55 years of age and women from 16 to 45. They were put under the control of the 'Labour Force Statistics and Allocation Committee'. Twelve million new workers thus became available for productive work, most of them women and young people. In 1940, women represented 38 per cent of the entire labour force; at the end of the war this proportion had risen to 55 per cent; in agriculture it had reached 71 per cent by 1943. Three million women became factory workers; they formed nine-tenths of the textile labour force but they also worked in the mines, in the petro-chemical industries, turning, welding, etc. As for the young people, the proportion of under-18s employed in the economy was 15 per cent in 1942; 750,000 girls were directed to the mines, railways and metallurgical industries.

This labour force was not mobilised in their home towns but assembled in certain urban and industrial centres; most of the time, to save transport, this labour force was made up from those living in the vicinity of the towns, but sometimes the call-up concerned one particular branch of activity—the whole population of one region, for example, was directed into coal-mining. By the end of 1942 nearly 800,000 urban workers had been called up for full-time employment; but there were in addition more than 1,400,000 seasonal workers; 800,000 young men had been directed into technical schools since it was clear that the qualifications of this makeshift labour force left a good deal to be desired.

Building huts, digging and working in the fields was relatively easy. But when a factory had been rebuilt and had received and reassembled its plant, you still had to have workers capable of running it; and in the Moscow factories in January 1942 out of 280,000 workmen, barely 15,000 had received adequate professional training; so in 1942, the Moscow Central Party Committee opened eleven schools of metallurgy and thirty-nine of various other trades in Moscow itself.

The result was a mixed success. Overall, between 1941 and 1945, 2,500,-

ooo skilled workers, or described as such, received training. In fact, it had not been possible always to set high standards; the newcomers had often merely been put into a gang and the foremen or older workers undertook to teach them the practice. In the schools, theoretical training was limited to six months; the rest was picked up in the factories. In certain branches of industry, where the work was of a particularly delicate nature, the shortcomings of the training were never made good.

Organisation was not everything and enthusiasm even less. It is difficult to agree with Rascate when he speaks of 500-per cent or even 1,000-per cent increases in production. But perhaps he is talking about special cases and levels that were particularly low in 1940. But it is a fact that war production in the USSR did increase considerably and that its workers did succeed in producing, at the right time 'the steel that wins a war'.

IX WAR PRODUCTION IN THE USSR

Soviet war production thus falls very clearly into a series of phases of development. After war was declared, the year 1941 was spent in the gigantic evacuation of factories to the east; it was thus bound to be marked by a sharp fall in output; factories had to be built or adapted and machinery reassembled; the necessary power resources were often lacking. It was from this point of view that 'General Winter' saved the Soviet Union; it is true that he made reconstruction slower and more difficult but he did not stop it, whereas he had put a stop to the Wehrmacht's all-conquering advance which, had it continued, would have made any reconstruction impossible—or pointless as a result of the defeat of the Red Army.

The evacuation continued in 1942 but the factories that had been moved were now beginning to go into production and an enormous labour force had been mobilised, trained and set to work. However, at the beginning of the year, production reached its lowest point; it rose in the spring and by the summer it had reached the 1940 level. Barring grave military setbacks—and this was the great importance of the battle of Stalingrad—economic victory was in sight.

From 1943 onwards, the impetus had been given and development was swift and steady. But overall the economy was stagnant, if not indeed in regression; certain losses were irretrievable; the switch to the east was no wonder-cure and would never lead to a revival; it was merely a last resort to ensure essentials.

And the essential thing was the output of armaments, and this continued to rise. To begin with, improved methods or greater skill on the part of workers frequently shortened production schedules: a fighter aircraft which took 20,000 hours to produce in 1941 needed only 12,500 in 1943 and a howitzer 2,400 hours compared with 4,500; the T 34 tank, 3,700 hours as against 8,000. These do not seem to be exceptional figures but they cannot have been the rule.

But an increasing number of weapons for the services certainly was the rule. By 1942, the USSR was producing 25,400 aircraft, 24,600 tanks and almost 30,000 field guns, as compared with the German output of 15,400, 9,300 and 12,000 respectively. Above all, the output of Stormovik tactical aircraft and T 34 tanks, both of which had proved their worth, moved to top priority—from July to December 1942 the T 34 tanks represented sixty-one per cent.

In 1943 production figures rose to 34,900 aircraft (11,193 of them Stormoviks), 24,000 tanks and 130,000 guns. In 1944, these figures were 40,000 aircraft, 29,000 tanks and 122,000 guns.

According to Colonel Kravchenko, between 1941 and 1945, the USSR thus produced 142,800 military aircraft, 102,500 tanks or armoured cars, 490,000 guns of which 92,000 were of more than 75-mm calibre. These figures are second only to those of the United States; they greatly exceed Britain's and Germany's. From 1943 onwards, the Red Army not only possessed superiority in numbers over the Wehrmacht but also a superior quantity of equipment of equally good quality. As there was no lack of fighting spirit and high competence amongst young Russian marshals either, the way to victory lay wide open.

It is clear that Russia's immense size and climate had prevented her from being smashed by the German Blitzkrieg as France had been. But these were only positive assets inasmuch as they gained time for the Russians. The Soviet leaders undoubtedly took maximum advantage of them. If Stalin is to take his share of blame for the setbacks it seems only fair to give him his credit for the successes. But the Communist party probably deserves the greater share: one Soviet writer after another says this and keeps on saying it, and although propaganda may play some part, there is truth in what they say. However, it is not Marxist-Leninist doctrine which was the cause of their success; that had been temporarily shelved. And it was only partly the earlier achievements of the régime because these had been largely conquered or destroyed by the invader. But the Party had provided the perfect framework and the enthusiasm needed by the whole population; more accurately, the economic machine began to function as a whole once the Party had been completely reformed after the losses caused by mobilisation. This was the result of the immense propaganda effort and the fine example of the 3 million Communists

SUMMARY TABLE OF SOVIET WAR PRODUCTION

	1940	1st half of 1941	1942	1943	1944	1945 (10 months)
Cast iron (millions of tons)	14.9	9.1	5	5.5	7.2	8.8
Percentage from the east	28					
Steel (millions of tons)	18.3	11.4	4.8	8.4	10.8	12.2
Percentage from the east	37					
Rolled sheet (millions of tons)	13.1	8.2	5.4	5.6	7.8	8.4
Military aircraft (modern)	A few dozen	3,950 (2nd half of 1941)	25,437	34,900	40,300	26,478
Tanks (and machine-gun carriers)	2,794	4,742	24,668	24,000	29,000	22,590
Artillery (guns)		29,561	29,561	130,000	122,000	77,000
Labour force (in millions)	30	26.2	18.4	27.5		

scattered throughout the Soviet Union, preaching the good word as well as showing the way.

The Party was able to share out the various tasks and by appealing to national feeling ensure that everyone gave of his best. The Soviet people learned to work in suffering, to hope in disaster and to build while fighting. Not only were no scandalous gains made from the national misfortune—economic collectivisation saw to that—but it is difficult to see how anyone could have failed to bear his share of the national burden either by suffering under the occupation or as a soldier at the front or as a producer on the home front. Greater equality began to exist between the regions, between Russia in Europe and Russia in Asia. But above all, as Girault writes, 'the peoples of the Soviet Union were united in their suffering and their struggle, their troubles and, in the end, their joys.' In the eyes of the Russian people both the régime and the Party benefited by being identified with the salvation of immortal Mother Russia.

CHAPTER 4

The Strange Alliance

HITLER turned the Soviet Union first into Britain's ally and then into the ally of the United States. These reluctant allies were all aware of the need to maintain their agreement throughout the war and to continue it after it was over. But their reasons for fighting and their aims were as entirely different as their mentality and behaviour. Hence understanding was difficult and there was deep distrust, mutual suspicion and frequent clashes.

The alliance required constant adjustment and it never functioned with perfect smoothness. Moreover these reluctant allies did not all have the same opponents. Stalin had to press Churchill for several months to make Britain declare war on the Axis satellites; he himself waited until 1945 before declaring war on Japan; the United States never broke with Finland, and the Soviet Union only intervened in Bulgaria in order to divert her from the Anglo-Saxons. By its very existence, therefore, the alliance set permanent problems and the leader of the American mission in Moscow, General John R. Deane, well placed to see how it worked, called it the strange alliance.

In view of the individual role that each leader played in his own country, the proper working of this strange alliance would clearly depend first of all on Churchill's, Roosevelt's and Stalin's conception of it, on their aims and on the relationship that they managed to establish between themselves.

I THE RELATIONSHIP BETWEEN CHURCHILL, ROOSEVELT AND STALIN

Their correspondence, which deals with all sorts of subjects, enables us to see this relationship from inside. Churchill and Roosevelt were attempting to bring Stalin into their circle of trust and friendship; they wrote to him on a personal note and they spared no pains to win him over. 'I consider our personal relations of the greatest importance,' Churchill wrote to him, and he passed information on to him which he described as confidential and which he asked him to keep to himself, as if the request had some chance of being met. Roosevelt was so convinced of his persuasive charm that in May 1943 he suggested a private talk between the two of them, with only an interpreter and a typist present. Whenever they met him, the two Anglo-Saxons were convivial and unceremonious, and the Georgian cleverly responded; thus he made the impression, particularly on Roosevelt, of being a 'good fellow' who could be trusted and whose frankness was attractive, even if tinged with toughness; in any case, pleasanter and more open than that Siberian block of ice, Molotov.

Churchill and Roosevelt were convinced—like Hitler and Ribbentrop before them—that the time when the Politburo was preparing world revolution was past and that patriotism would henceforth be stronger than Communism in the USSR—Communistic patriotism seemed a contradiction in terms. Roosevelt went furthest in this direction; he believed that his personal relationship with Stalin would put an end to the Soviet's distrust of capitalism—a happy result which, in his view, Churchill would be unable to achieve since he was the champion of imperialism based on a system of monarchy. Consequently, the President of the United States considered that the clever thing to do was to maintain a balance between his partners; thus the appearance of the Soviet Union on the scene sometimes threatened the good understanding existing between Britain and America. Wendell Willkie, his unsuccessful opponent in the presidential elections who became his envoy in the USSR, also stated, after being two days in Moscow, that 'there was not all that much difference between the American and Russian viewpoints'.

So in their correspondence we can see the two Western statesmen persistently wooing their heaven-sent ally, towards whom they felt a certain embarrassment because they were leaving him to bear the brunt of Hitler's attack on his own and they were prepared to accept and bear with his perpetual dissatisfaction; they took care not to rake up his recent shady associations but they were frequently brought up short by Stalin's cold realism. The latter never minced his words; he reminded Churchill that 'Britain would never have been able to continue the war without the help of the USSR' and when the British Premier complained of his correspondent's rather uncharitable criticisms of him, Stalin replied: 'It's a matter of personal contacts, so I speak my mind and you cannot regard it as an insult.' Stalin constantly displayed a touchy national pride and he persistently brought the correspondence back to the points which concerned him and to meeting his requests.

Consequently, little by little, mutual distrust grew up between them, irresistibly. A political and social rift separated the two Allied camps; it was made deeper by religious feeling: American Roman Catholic circles had expressed themselves against any collaboration with atheistic Communism. For his part, Stalin misjudged the importance and the role of American public opinion. The head of the American mission in Moscow, General Deane, very quickly realised the deep lack of understanding between the three leaders, despite the superficial cordiality of the correspondence which merely skated over the surface; he did not succeed in establishing personal relations with the Soviet military leaders with whom he had to work; in two years not one of them dared to invite him to his home; he did not even meet them except on very special occasions. This is how he described his disappointment to Marshall: 'We never make any request or suggestion that is not greeted with suspicion; the Soviets have absolutely no idea that any one can give without wanting to receive, with the result that even our gifts arouse their distrust.'

In fact, their reasons for lack of understanding and for distrust were deep-rooted. The Soviet Union, which had suffered invasion and which was for a long time the underdog, or even at bay, believed that her allies were not averse to letting her grow weaker, indeed were perhaps even doing it deliberately in order to impose their own terms on her when peace came. Even though they did not mention it, the British and Americans had not forgotten the German-Soviet pact; they were afraid that Hitler and Stalin might think it in their interest to revert to it and conclude a separate peace or at least reach a compromise to put an end to their hostilities. Against this sufficiently gloomy background, the Polish problem was going to cast so heavy a shadow as to make any permanent sweetness and light between the two parties impossible.

However, there was one point on which the three great powers were in agreement and this was that the decisions which committed the Allies must be taken by the three of them alone, like members of a sort of exclusive club. They exchanged envoys with each other who enjoyed their complete confidence; they paid visits to each other; and they met in conferences to take the major decisions required by the defeat of Germany and the advent of peace—at Teheran, Yalta and Potsdam. Thus the alliance jogged along until the surrender first of Germany and then of Japan.

II THE ANGLO-RUSSIAN ALLIANCE

At the time of the Wehrmacht's invasion, Stalin had been afraid lest Britain might have been notified of Hitler's peace proposals and jumped at the opportunity of extricating herself from the conflict on honourable terms. For their part, the British wondered whether the USSR would really fight and Lord Beaverbrook asked Maisky, the Soviet ambassador in

London: 'Won't what happened in France happen to you?' Churchill immediately reassured the Soviet leader's fears; on July 3 he wrote to Stalin: 'We shall do everything to help you that time, geography and our growing resources permit' and on July 12 an alliance for the duration of the war was agreed upon in principle. The stubborn fighting of the Red Army provided the British with the reply to their question.

But Stalin would not be satisfied with words: he called for the signing of a properly drawn-up treaty of alliance. He thought that Britain could despatch forty or so divisions to the Continent without further delay, to France, Archangel or the Balkans, since the Wehrmacht had denuded western Europe of troops, and he told Churchill so in a letter of July 18. He demanded supplies of equipment and gave a detailed list of his requirements, not only to the British ambassador, Cripps, but also to Roosevelt's envoy, Hopkins, at a time when the United States had not yet entered the war.

The Americans were hesitant about cutting down their supplies to the British in favour of the Russians, and the first convoy for the USSR did not leave for Archangel until August 12. As for the British, seeing the speed of the German advance, they wondered whether the Soviet Union had not already lost the war in Europe; this was doubtless what Churchill had in mind when he suggested sending Wavell, the Commander-in-Chief of the Indian operational theatre, to Moscow—would they not be reduced to planning for Anglo-Russian co-operation in Asia?

The fact remains that when they signed the Atlantic Charter the British and Americans systematically ignored the Soviet Union; certain clauses as to the 'right of self-determination of peoples' and 'the renunciation of territorial advantages' seemed to apply just as much to their ally as to their enemy. A trip to Moscow by Eden in the second half of December 1941 did not clear up all the misapprehensions. True, Churchill had previously written to Stalin that 'the fact that Russia was a Communist state did not present any obstacle to working out a proper plan to ensure our mutual security and legitimate interests'. But, at a time when the German offensive against the capital had barely been halted—and nobody knew how long for—Stalin had already listed to Eden in Moscow some of his peace claims: restoring Russian influence in the Baltic countries and redrawing the Polish frontier along the 'Curzon line'—which meant recognition by the Allies of the territorial gains acquired by the Soviet Union as a result of the German-Soviet pact (in return, Stalin recognised Britain's right to establish and maintain bases in France, Belgium, Holland, Denmark and Norway).

However, realising that he had done the wrong thing, Stalin did not insist on this delicate point. At the beginning of 1942, he signed the

United Nations Pact, a new version of the Atlantic Charter. But in exchange he asked for the immediate opening of a second front and remained unconvinced by Churchill's arguments that he lacked the necessary shipping, aircraft and manpower.

The United States' entry into the war opened up new prospects but brought no immediate change; in Washington, the British and American military leaders realised that there was no possibility of landing in Europe in 1942. It was poor consolation when on May 26, 1942 Churchill signed an Anglo-Soviet treaty of co-operation for twenty years with Stalin. The first part of the pact confirmed the alliance signed on July 12 for the duration of the war, plus the pledge that neither party would open separate negotiations with Hitler's Germany—this was the great fear that each had with regard to the other. The second part foreshadowed post-war co-operation to preserve peace and ensure their mutual security against any further German aggression.

However, there were two articles which showed that there were limits to the trust between the two countries; each of the contracting parties pledged herself not to make any territorial acquisitions on her own account and not to intervene in the internal affairs of other states. Churchill offered his own paraphrase of the articles in a statement he made to Eden in October 1942: 'It would be a disaster if Russian barbarism swamped the culture and independence of the countries of Europe.' Yet it was necessary to help the Soviet Union not to succumb beneath the hammer-blows of the Wehrmacht; so the USSR was admitted to the lend-lease club.

III LEND-LEASE AND THE USSR

Harriman, Roosevelt's special envoy in Moscow, somewhat incautiously promised Stalin 400 tanks and 300 aircraft to be delivered in two convoys per month, starting in July 1942; but the difficulties of shipping them were enormous and the risks very great.

First of all there was the shipping problem. As the Soviet Navy was in no position to provide the necessary protection, the Royal Navy had to take over the task, although Britain had accepted no commitment on this score. The Admiralty declared itself unable to guarantee more than two convoys of twenty-five ships a month or three convoys of twenty-five or thirty-five ships every two months. This had to be accepted as a beginning. Thus, at great cost to themselves, the British and the Americans intended to deliver to the Russians' own ports equipment that the recipients always considered to be inadequate or unsuited to their needs and while never ceasing to clamour for it, they denied that it had any beneficial effect on the course of the fighting.

The shortest way was the Great North Circle although New York was separated by 4,500 miles from the Soviet port of Murmansk, which was ice-free in winter. But as it passed through the Orkneys, the Phaeroes, Jan de Mayen and Bear Island, this shipping route ran along the southern limits of the ice-pack; the cold, the fog, the Arctic night and the icebergs made it arduous and dangerous. In the spring, danger came from German submarines and warships—the *Scharnhorst,* the *Gneisenau,* with their escorts, were sent up north after escaping from Brest. After being promised since August 1941, the first of the tanks—twenty of them in all—did not arrive until October; far from being effusively grateful, Stalin complained that they were badly crated and came in dismantled form.

At the end of May 1942, a convoy carrying 125,000 tons lost a fifth of its cargo—7 ships out of 35,147 tanks and 77 aircraft. At the end of June, out of 36 ships, only 11 reached their destination, with 164 tanks, 37 aircraft and 896 vehicles of various sorts. The fourteenth convoy which sailed during the period of the midnight sun, which acted as a magnificent searchlight for the submarines, had to turn back; and in view of this Churchill preferred to cancel the next one. At the end of 1942 results were rather disappointing; either because he failed to appreciate or refused to see the difficulties Stalin let loose a flood of recriminations especially attacking the reductions in some supplies—in particular tin and copper—which had been needed for the war in the Pacific.

There was another safer route joining the Persian Gulf with the Caspian Sea via Iran, a neutral state; but it was much longer—the Iranian ports were 13,000 miles away from the ports on the American Pacific coast. In addition, there were a large number of active and influential Germans in Iran—according to Israelian they maintained 4,000 agents there. On August 25, 1941 the Russians and the British asked the Shah to expel the Germans; on his refusal to do so, without any ultimatum troops of the two Allies converged on Teheran, forced the Shah to abdicate and leave the country and signed a treaty of alliance with his successor guaranteeing his independence.

Anglo-Russian co-operation had proved satisfactory. Later on, difficulties arose; when tribal leaders revolted against the central government, the British suspected the Russians of supporting the Kurdish independence movement in the north of the country. Next, after the British had obtained oil concessions in the zone they were occupying, it was the Russians' turn to claim equivalent privileges in theirs and they unleashed their propaganda against the Iranian government when it refused.

As for transporting American equipment to the ussr, which was the prime aim of the occupation of Iran, this met with enormous obstacles. Building a road was beyond the capacity of the British; there was only one railway and it was a single line from Teheran to the north of Iran. The British commandeered rolling-stock from India, where it was in short supply anyway, thus providing plenty of fuel for the Indian nationalists' anti-British propaganda. It was quite plain that this route was too slow and complicated to be used effectively by the Anglo-Saxons to supply the USSR.

However, the former thought that it could be used to provide the Soviet Union with military assistance, an aspect which was strongly stressed by the British ambassador, Stafford Cripps. One way would be first of all to relieve the USSR of the task of occupying Iran; Churchill suggested to Stalin taking over the occupation entirely with British troops, thus releasing some four to six Soviet divisions; Stalin saw this suggestion as the desire of the British to take the whole of Iran under their protection and a refusal to fight except vicariously through their allies. The second way consisted of sending troops to the Caucasus; Churchill suggested two divisions at the beginning of 1942 and Roosevelt a few squadrons. Stalin again refused; he wanted no foreign western troops on Soviet soil; this reluctance showed itself in constant tiresome interference with the British sailors at Murmansk, which caused great resentment. The only exception he made was for Free France; after having suggested sending a brigade which was kicking its heels in the Middle East waiting for the British to use it, de Gaulle sent the *Normandie-Niemen* Air Force regiment to the USSR.

Far from solving the difficulties between the Allies, lend-lease only added to them. Soviet historians play down the generosity of their allies; Israelian has written that the rate of delivery was ridiculously slow and that the Anglo-Saxons were less keen on helping to strengthen the Red Army than in letting it exhaust itself against Germany. Colonel Kravchenko assessed Anglo-Saxon aid at 8.9 per cent of the Soviet's own production of tanks and 1.5 for all other supplies; during the last year of the war, the percentage reached a level of less than 3 per cent.

Nevertheless, Allied supplies to the USSR, almost entirely from America, amounted in the course of the whole war to the not inconsiderable total of 11,000 million dollars, a sum never repaid. By the northern route alone, from July 1943 till March 1944 5,000 tanks, 7,000 aircraft and 7,000 cars and lorries were shipped; by the southern route, 2,000 locomotives. In addition to armaments, munitions and vehicles, there were all kinds of products which were in short supply in the Soviet Union—medical supplies for example. This aid did not save the Russians in their moment of greatest crisis—they had restored the situation on the Moscow front before it reached them and its use set them certain problems; by itself, it could

not ensure their victory; and it was not a great deal compared with the
giant effort of their own population. While all this is true, nonetheless it
was of value to them, above all during the difficult summers of 1942 and
1943, although its usefulness declined in 1944. Stalin was not merely being polite (this was not his habit anyway) when he told Roosevelt at the
Teheran conference: 'Without American supplies we should have lost the
war.' Previously, in February 1942, he had already expressed his gratitude
for the two 1,000 million dollar loans that the us had granted the ussr.

IV THE PROBLEM OF THE SECOND FRONT

As early as September 1941 Stalin had made an urgent request which from
then onwards was the leitmotif of his whole relationship with his two
allies. 'The ussr is fighting on her own and is in mortal danger; the only
thing to do is to pin down thirty German divisions elsewhere'—something
which the tiny operational theatre of Cyrenaica was plainly incapable of
doing. His double statement was amply confirmed by facts and figures.
According to captured German documents, Soviet historians estimate the
number of German divisions committed in the ussr as follows: in June
1941, 190; on November 1, 1942, 266; on July 1, 1943, 232; on May
1, 1944, 259; on May 1, 1945, 206. This meant that, on those dates, the
percentage of enemy forces opposing the Red Army alone was respectively:
70, 72, 66, 53, 60. The pressure relaxed somewhat in the course of time but
never completely; from the beginning to the end of the war, ever since
she had joined in, the ussr bore the heaviest share of the joint struggle.

True, Stalin was quite happy to forget that before June 1941 Britain and
France had faced Germany alone, whilst the ussr was congratulating the
latter on her success and providing her with equipment; and that France
had foundered in the uneven struggle. Once and for all, he had adopted
the attitude of a creditor claiming his due. It was quite obvious that he had
no conception of the difficulties of a landing and the enormous resources
needed for its success. Churchill was forced to tell him: 'You have so much
land that you do not find it easy to understand that we can only live and
fight as our sea-links permit.'

Although he told Cripps that, after all, 'Stalin was only reaping what
he had sown', Churchill was keen to relieve his exacting partner; as early
as the summer of 1941, he was contemplating an operation in Norway
and his military advisers were hard put to it to prove how impossible it was.

In April 1942, Roosevelt asked Stalin to send Molotov to Washington.
All that Stalin's right-hand man could talk about was the second front.
But when Roosevelt suggested cutting down on the equipment being sent

to the USSR in order to increase the resources needed for a second front and hasten its opening, Molotov was annoyed; he wanted both together. After consulting Marshall, Roosevelt promised that the second front would be opened in the course of 1942; the 'Bolero–Round-up' plan was then worked out to satisfy Stalin.

When the plan proved not to be feasible and was replaced by Operation 'Torch', Churchill, who was responsible for the decision, had the unwelcome task of informing Stalin. He went to Moscow in the course of the summer of 1942. Stalin made no bones about his displeasure; he realised the strategic importance of 'Torch', but 'in the plainest possible terms, he could not agree that the opening of the second front should be put off till 1943'.

When the situation of the Soviet armies at Stalingrad became critical the Americans proposed a scaled-down version of 'Bolero' which they called 'Sledgehammer'. But the British were afraid that even this reduced version might jeopardise the success of 'Torch'; they were also scared of a costly failure which would have serious consequences and the indifferent results of the Dieppe raid seemed to justify their view. However, when the landing in French North Africa proved a success, Stalin was generous in his congratulation of the Allies; he approved everything they did, even the 'exploitation of Darlan'; 'you must know how to use the Devil and his grandmother', he wrote to Roosevelt.

But with his success at Stalingrad to support him, he quickly returned to the charge: when was there going to be a real second front? He demanded that it be opened by the spring of 1943 at the latest. It was partly in order to satisfy him that in Casablanca Roosevelt invented the formula of the 'unconditional surrender' of their common foes. But Stalin was greatly disappointed that the only direct attack against Germany was going to be an intensification of the bombing; he considered that the Tunisian campaign and the subsequent landings in Sicily were not really the second front that was required, any more than 'Torch' had been.

So in February 1943, Churchill promised that the landing across the Channel would take place in August or September 1943. But by that date, although the fall of Italy seemed near, preparations for 'Overlord' were far from complete and once again the promise had to be cancelled. What was Stalin's attitude going to be when faced by this fresh evasion? Roosevelt and Churchill were worried, and to straighten things out, they suggested meeting Stalin.

The Russians had no doubt about the intentions of the Anglo-Saxons; they were administering just enough oxygen to prevent the Russians from suffocating without making them really strong. Thus Ambassador Maisky wrote that after the Soviet successes at Stalingrad, the Allies estimated that

the USSR was out of danger and could look after herself. This was certainly
not in Roosevelt's mind or in those of his military advisers; but it is not certain if it was not in Churchill's mind. In any case, the British Premier
was a past master in the art of diverting the Americans from their own
plans in order to lead them on to objectives more in line with British interests. His behaviour did not escape the notice of the Russians who began to look to Roosevelt to satisfy their wishes. But any closer understanding between the British and Americans and the USSR presupposed a
satisfactory solution to the deep rift between the Polish exile government
in London and the one in Moscow.

V THE POLISH PROBLEM BEFORE STALINGRAD

Britain had entered the war to defend the integrity and independence of
Poland and after the defeat of their armies, the Poles had continued to
fight, within and without the frontiers of their country. Now Poland had
been dismembered, oppressed and depopulated as much by the Russians
as by the Germans. Hitler's aggression against the USSR had abruptly
brought the Poles and the Russians together into the same camp; but it
very quickly became apparent that although they were allies, their war
aims and specifically those concerned with Polish territory were so diametrically opposed as to make them irreconcilable enemies. The British
and Americans were thus caught between two of their allies; in addition,
the British were bound by their pledges towards Poland; the Americans
were freer in that respect; but how could Roosevelt reconcile his crusade
for every sort of freedom with the sacrifice of a small state to the ambitions
of a larger one because it was an ally of the United States—in a word, to
let Stalin have something that he had refused Hitler?

The Polish-Soviet rift was as simple as it was dramatic: Poland wanted
to return to her 1939 frontiers after the war; Stalin intended to hold on
to the eastern Polish territories that he had been able to annex through
the German-Soviet pact.

General Sikorski's government in London was composed of representatives of the four democratic parties that had opposed Marshal Pilsudski's
dictatorship; but this did not make it pro-Russian. However, Sikorski
realised that the entry of the USSR into the Allied camp was an important new factor that had to be reckoned with. He therefore set about trying to reach an agreement with Stalin; he felt that he was being sufficiently
magnanimous in not claiming any compensation or reparations for the
damage caused by the Russians in Poland and demanding only his rights:
recognition of the eastern frontier of Poland as laid down in the Treaty of

Riga—the 1939 frontiers—and the release of all the Polish citizens captured, deported or interned in the USSR, which he calculated at 1,500,000.

Stalin would accept only a vague formula that the 'Soviet-German treaties were no longer valid'; this did not amount to a guarantee; but, under pressure from the British, the Poles pretended that it was satisfactory, though not before three ministers had expressed their disagreement by resigning. However, in August 1941 a military agreement between Poland and Russia provided for the raising of a Polish army from amongst the Polish prisoners taken by the Red Army, which the USSR would equip and supply with the American equipment granted to Poland under lend-lease.

But in December 1941, the Russians showed their hand. Stalin suggested to Eden that a protocol should be added to the projected Anglo-Russian agreement, recognising the rights of the Soviet Union to the Baltic states and east Poland. Churchill's reaction to this was extremely sharp: 'this transfer of territories', he wrote to Eden, 'would be contrary to the aims which we are fighting for; there can be no question of drawing up frontiers before peace is signed.' Stalin did not insist—after all the Germans were at the gates of Moscow: he even signed the Atlantic Charter, but with a significant reservation which was expressed verbally by his delegate, the Soviet ambassador in London, who signed on his behalf, 'that the Charter would necessarily have to be adapted to historical conditions, needs and particular circumstances.'

General Sikorski was realistic enough not to apply pressure at the sore points. During a visit to Moscow he confined himself to emphasising by the way, as something self-evident, that 'the 1939 borders must not be revised'. But the implementation of the military agreement was not all that easy. Stalin quite plainly had no great liking for this Polish army that was being released in rags and tatters from Soviet prisons and camps in order to be armed by its gaolers. Instead of the Polish units fighting in Europe with the Red Army and one day returning to Poland with them, Sikorski was forced to agree to their being transferred to Iran and trained and equipped by the British. The commander of the new army, General Anders, was surprised to find so few officers among the 180,000 released prisoners of war. Sikorski expressed his amazement to Stalin who merely replied that they had all, in fact, been released. Despite the chill caused by Anders' discovery, an assistance pact was signed between Poland and Russia providing in vague terms for 'friendly collaboration after the war'. It was not perfect harmony but neither was it a breakdown of relations between them.

However, the exiled Polish government in London had put forward to the Czech government under Beneš a proposal for a Polish-Czech federation as a first step towards the later amalgamation of the two countries, thus putting a stop to the old enmity which had been further fanned by Poland's participation in the dismemberment of Czechoslovakia after the Munich agreement. Beneš agreed only to a confederation of the two separate states, provided, however, with certain joint organisations such as a committee of ministers, general staff, foreign policy and parliamentary delegations. In January 1942, the two governments issued a joint declaration of agreement in principle and called on other European nations to join them. The Soviet government immediately evinced their hostility to what seemed to it to be a resurrection of the *cordon sanitaire* that had been set up immediately after the First World War. Beneš did not succeed in pacifying it by proposing tripartite collaboration between the Soviet Union, Czechoslovakia and Poland; on the contrary, this broader proposal met with opposition from the Poles. This veto by the Kremlin nipped the confederation in the bud; Beneš retreated to his tent and Polish-Soviet relations were manifestly not improved.

But if the Soviet Union's intentions towards Poland were so blatant at a time when the Wehrmacht was threatening Russia's very existence, what would they be after Stalingrad, when the danger seemed to be over?

VI THE POLISH PROBLEM AFTER STALINGRAD

In fact, at the beginning of 1942, Stalin took two further measures. On the one hand, he issued a decree whereby the hundreds of thousands of displaced Poles from eastern Poland who had moved into the Soviet Union became Soviet citizens—and the Polish government, under pressure from the British, decided not to protest. On the other hand, he formed the Union of Polish Patriots under Wanda Wasilevska, a Polish Communist writer married to a Soviet Ukrainian and herself a colonel in the Red Army. A Polish organisation in Moscow functioning independently of the legal Polish government could only mean a threat to set up a dissident movement. This time the Polish government complained bitterly to its British and American allies; but they seemed relatively unmoved.

The fact was that, impelled by an obvious sad but inescapable necessity, their views were gradually changing: how could they continue to demand that the USSR bear the brunt of the German onslaught almost alone and not keep their promises with regard to the opening of a second front, yet still refuse her any satisfaction with regard to her future frontiers in the west—a satisfaction which might in any case be given at the expense of Germany, since the latter was by definition excluded from benefiting from the Atlantic Charter? In this web of opposing interests, it was hardly possible that the weakest of all, Poland, should fail to be the scapegoat.

Moreover, the British themselves were beginning to find the attitude of the Poles in London rather tiresome. Their press was continually attacking the USSR; they confessed to Eden their hope and ambition that with the Soviet Union weakened and Germany crushed, Poland might become the most powerful central European western state. When he went to visit Roosevelt at the beginning of 1943, Sikorski made no bones about his wish to abolish the Polish corridor and the east Prussian enclave for the aggrandisement of Poland; he spoke of the Oder as Poland's western frontier without relinquishing any of his claims in the east.

In March 1943 Eden and Roosevelt came to an agreement that after the war the Soviet Union should keep Bessarabia and the part of Finland which she had conquered in 1940; true, Romania and Finland were enemy countries and Roosevelt vigorously refused to make any concession regarding the Baltic states; nevertheless, it was a first step towards recognising the Soviet's June 1941 frontiers.

But in April 1943, there came a bombshell. After the discovery of the corpses of several thousand Polish officers buried at Katyn, the Germans launched a big anti-Soviet campaign. Were they the bodies of the officers that Anders had been vainly looking for in Russia? Polish diplomats had previously been arrested in Moscow; two leaders of the Polish Jewish Socialist Party, the Bund, who had taken refuge in the USSR and, at the Soviet Union's request, had founded an anti-Fascist Jewish World Committee, had been accused of complicity with the Nazis and executed—covered with abuse and murdered, like all Stalin's enemies. General Sikorski asked for an investigation by the International Red Cross which the Soviet Union rejected. However, an investigation did take place, conducted by the Germans; it concluded that the Soviet Union was guilty and the Poles accepted its findings. *Pravda* replied by accusing Sikorski of being Hitler's accomplice—an accusaton for which no evidence was offered—and Stalin broke off relations with the Polish government in London. For the British and Americans, as for neutral public opinion, there was hardly any doubt that the horrible crime was the work of the Russians, committed either by Stalin's deliberate wish to destroy the Polish officer class or by subordinates who panicked at the time of the German attack.

Stalin now raised the Kosciusko Division in the USSR, which received Polish uniforms and was officered by Poles from the annexed Polish territories who had served in the Red Army—in fact, a sort of rival to Anders' army. He granted official Soviet support to Wasilevska's Union of Polish Patriots, which was joined by a number of Polish Communists who had hitherto been reduced to silence when not interned—an embryonic Polish government for the future and perhaps the only one that the Soviet Union would one day recognise.

The British and Americans realised that they must at all costs achieve some compromise. But on July 4 Sikorski was killed in an air crash. His successor, Mikolajczyk, was a moderate but he lacked his predecessor's authority and his War Minister, Soznkovski, was an obdurate anti-Communist.

Accordingly, when in September 1943 Eden put forward the compromise proposal agreed between the British and the Americans in Quebec, giving the Russians the Curzon line as their frontier in the west but offering Poland the compensation of east Prussia and part of Silesia, Mikolajczyk turned down the bargain; he had no right to lop off part of Poland by a revision of her eastern frontiers; such a plan, he said, not without foresight, would only lead to Poland's becoming a Soviet satellite.

The Polish problem, together with that of the second front, was to be in the forefront of the discussions that the three great powers decided to hold at Teheran in the autumn of 1943.

VII SECRET NEGOTIATIONS?

However, the 'strange allies' were mutually suspicious that each was trying to negotiate with the enemy behind the other's back. In February 1943, Moscow had been disturbed at contacts made in Geneva by a high-ranking ss officer, the Prince of Hohenlohe, with Allen Dulles, the head of the American intelligence services in Geneva.

In March 1943, the American State Secretariat was made aware of vague proposals coming from Romania via the Argentine ambassador in Paris—a circuitous route. These referred to Hitler's desire to come to terms with the British and Americans so as to conserve his forces for the struggle against Communism. Cordell Hull made no attempt to follow them up; but no mention of them seems to have been made to the Russians.

On roughly the same date, Himmler is said to have enquired of the Americans, via the Swedes, as to the exact meaning of the formula 'unconditional surrender'; he received no reply; and although this step is authenticated by a despatch sent to Roosevelt by Harrison and published by the Americans, the Swedes deny it.

On their part, at the beginning of 1943 the Hungarians had begun to bargain with the British to negotiate their withdrawal from the war, save the régime and protect Hungary from a Soviet occupation by joining in the fight against the Germans. One cannot say whether the Russians were informed of these approaches.

But as a rule they were kept very well informed by their agents. They themselves had been sounded by one of Ribbentrop's collaborators, Peter

Kleist, who had confided in a businessman called Clauss of undefined nationality, who frequented the Soviet embassy in Stockholm and whom Kleist has described as a Soviet agent. The Germans are said to have informed the Russians, via Clauss, that they were prepared to come back to the 1914 frontiers in the east—another way of settling the Polish problem by private arrangement between Germany and Russia. Molotov informed Harriman of these contacts but only some months later and describing Clauss as a German agent.

In January 1944, it was the Russians' turn to be alarmed. We find *Pravda* referring to talks between Ribbentrop and the British in Cairo. Churchill had to write to Stalin categorically denying these rumours.

Were these really attempts at 'secession' or merely the sort of contacts that countries at war always maintain even in the thick of the fighting, by means of more or less official agents, in order to keep their finger on their opponent's pulse? In any case, none of these attempted negotiations came to anything; that they should be known and should continue could, however, only aggravate the third reason for disagreement between the Allies, in addition to the second front and the Polish problem. This was the fear of each of the parties that one of them might negotiate a separate peace and leave the other holding the baby and compelled to settle their joint account with Hitler's Germany all alone.

PART II

THE ITALIAN SURRENDER

CHAPTER 1

The End of the War in Africa

BOTH because of their own lack of daring and because of their reduced strength, for which they blamed Operation 'Torch',[1] the Allies did not manage to seize the whole of French North Africa at once, and this enabled the Germans to send an expeditionary force first by air lift and then by sea and succeed in establishing themselves in Tunisia and joining hands with the *Afrika Korps*. Far from being brought to an end by the two brilliant operations of El Alamein and the American landing, the war in Africa was thus going to be continued at the point of intersection of these two great successes, by a difficult and costly campaign in Tunisia. Then again, Eisenhower's acceptance of Admiral Darlan, with Roosevelt's approval, was going to disturb the French and cause further dissension amongst them at the very moment when everyone capable of fighting was siding with the Allies, thus wiping out the memory of the Rethondes armistice. The shortlived reign of Admiral Darlan and then General Giraud's government, both supported by the Americans, were characterised by a very sharp opposition between the Algiers authorities and General de Gaulle in London; but the latter was relying on the underground Resistance. In the absence of any real reconciliation between the hostile elements of the French forces, it was going to take months of bitter discussion to bring them together in a French government under General de Gaulle in Algiers. At least this strife did not prevent a French army from being reborn and fitted out with modern equipment by the Americans. But it had lent fuel to a vigorous upsurge of local national feeling strong enough to undermine the French Empire, which up to now, despite the setbacks suffered by the mother country, had remained quiescent.

I FRENCH 'INDECISION' IN TUNISIA

The best that one can say is that the behaviour of the French troops in Tunisia was ambiguous. They were probably motivated by contradictory feelings; on the one hand, the spirit of revenge against Germany certainly still lingered on; but on the other hand, they were steeped in the

1. See p. 395.

Vichy mystique, according to which France no longer had any allies, since the British in particular were suspected of wanting to seize her colonies. This mystique was expressed by the slogan 'France and France alone' and in North Africa by Weygand's orders to 'defend the Empire against all comers'. In Tunisia it was obviously the Germans who were the aggressors; but they were only replying to other aggressors in the rest of French North Africa, the British and Americans. An admiral is said to have asked out loud the question in everyone's mind: 'Who's the enemy?' Since the leaders had not been given any information or instructions, they decided to wait and see; they took no action against the Germans until the situation in Algiers had been cleared up and until they had received unequivocal orders to do so. Time was thus lost that would never be recovered and the Germans took the fullest possible advantage of this.

General Barré, the commander of the armed forces, took great care not to collaborate with the Germans as he was ordered to do by Admiral Darlan on the morning of November 9 and also by the civil authorities under the Resident General, Admiral Esteva, and yet again by the commander of the Bizerta base, Admiral Derrien—seven destroyers and nine submarines were captured undamaged by the Germans. But he took no action against them. He had withdrawn from Tunis without fighting, so that German paratroopers and later the transport aircraft were able to land on El Aouina airfield without a shot being fired against them. Barré had taken his troops up into the mountains which dominated the Medjerda in the west in order, he wrote, to 'hold the road for the Americans'; but none of the enemy forces was in a position to seize this road, which did not need holding and this operation had not in any way been prearranged with the Americans. In other words, it could just as well have been directed against them to block their approach to Tunis, according to how the situation developed in Algiers.

General Barré also wrote that he had 'left' his rearguard in Tunis under Colonel Le Couteulx de Caumont with the task of 'waiting until the night of November 13–14 for reinforcements which it was hoped would come from the west'. But what forces were left in Tunis? What were they supposed to do? In any case, what action were these units capable of now that they had been left behind by their main forces? And why not leave all the units in Tunis? With orders to fire on 'all comers'?

It is true that General Barré referred to 'a plan which had been in existence for several months', according to which Tunis had been considered indefensible. The question was: against whom? Against a powerful Allied landing force supported by a strong fleet, certainly; but not against a few German paratroopers who could be picked off in mid-air.

To justify the Vichy troops' withdrawal, General Koeltz, who knew all about these events because he had played an important part in them, painted a telling picture of the troops' weakness and shortages; they had no anti-tank sections, no AA guns and no heavy batteries; there were not enough European officers and NCOs to lead the native troops; for want of petrol, engines were running on alcohol; there were no spare parts or even tyres. But the entire African Army was in the same parlous state; this had not prevented it from fighting against the British and Americans in Algiers, Oran and Casablanca; but it had stopped it from resisting the Germans, who were much less strong, in Tunis and Bizerta.

Moreover, another contradiction now emerges. Vichy propaganda had always presented the armistice as the only solution enabling France in June 1940 to keep an army which would one day be able to resume the fight against the Germans. On the other hand, General Weygand had managed to get round the clauses of this armistice and he was rightly given the credit for keeping more troops and weapons in Africa than he had a right to. What was the point if, when the time came, these troops were unable to defend a position as important as Tunis on their own and if they could not resume the fight against the Germans—the very fight for which the Vichy leaders had had the foresight to keep and train them —unless the Allies immediately flew to their aid those same Allies whom they had fought in Algiers, Oran and Casablanca, with the unfortunate result of hindering and delaying the advance eastward which they were supposed to be so eagerly awaiting?

For their part, General Anderson's British troops, which had been given the task of forestalling the Germans in northern Tunisia, had not advanced very quickly; although Bougie had been captured on November 11, the Djidjelli airfield was not taken until the 13th; owing to lack of air cover at Bougie many Allied boats were sunk by Axis aircraft; the lines of communication were very long, the terrain was mountainous and roads were few and narrow. No co-ordination with the French had been possible: General Giraud had not wanted to place his troops under British command. If, then, the British had advanced very quickly, as General Barré wished, in what circumstances and with what instructions would Franco-British liaison have been established with a view to their later mutual co-operation for the recapture of Tunis? No one knows.

General Anderson noted that the French mayors and leading French officials made no secret of their hostility to the Allies; the Arabs were indifferent; the French population was sympathetic but passive. Once Bône had been captured on November 12, both by sea and by paratroopers, on the 13th Anderson was joined by reinforcements from Algiers, but his whole command never amounted to more than one brigade. He occupied

Tabarka but on November 18 he had to face an enemy attack at the Djebel Abiod. Till then General Barré's 12,000 men do not seem to have given him the slightest assistance; it was not until November 19 that Barré rejected the German ultimatum. At that time there were still very few German troops; 1,000 men in Tunis, according to Anderson, and 4,000 in Bizerta; but they were near to their airfields, which the French had abandoned without a fight, and this gave them air superiority. At the end of November, Anderson was relieved to see French officers whom he considered to be sympathetic to the Axis leave General Barré's staff; he noticed that the older French officers were either hesitant or hostile, while the younger ones were keener and more sympathetic to the Allies. By this time it was too late; at the end of November, British dilatoriness and French 'indecision' had enabled the Italian and German troops to occupy the whole of Tunisia and join hands with the *Afrika Korps*; a hard campaign was going to be needed to make up for the great opportunity which they had lost, even though the German operation had been carried out with meagre resources and for a limited objective—the evacuation via Tunisia of the forces which were retreating from Tripolitania.

II THE TUNISIAN CAMPAIGN

On December 1 and 2, General Anderson was at last in a position to attack in the direction of Tunis; he was repulsed. The Germans, under von Arnim, even counter-attacked, but their forces were inadequate and they were checked. Another Allied offensive was planned for December 22 and 23; torrential rains made it impossible; the roads were impassable. General Eisenhower finally cancelled it on December 24, and it was replaced by an operation in the south in the direction of Sfax, where the roads were wider. The Allies had lost the first round.

However, the French had formed a line in the centre of Tunisia. Starting from Tebessa, under the command of the coc General Juin they had occupied the passes in the mountain ridges which run across Tunisia, in order to seize the outlets on to the Kairouan plain. As a result of this operation they might be able to cut off the German forces in Tunisia from those of the *Afrika Korps*.

In the course of January, in order to check this danger, General von Arnim launched his tanks against the French positions; for a month the French withstood the attack virtually on their own and with inadequate resources; they had heavy casualties—5,000 men—but they lost only the eastern ridge. General Giraud then agreed to incorporate the French troops into the Allied defenses—which he had to do in order to receive a

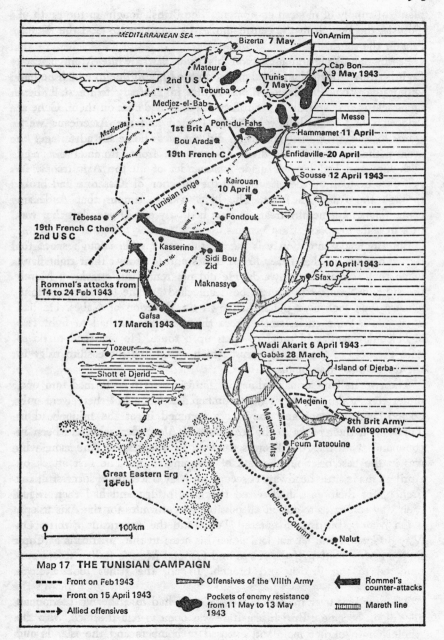

Map 17 **THE TUNISIAN CAMPAIGN**

- - - - - Front on Feb 1943

———— Front on 15 April 1943

- - -➤ Allied offensives

▨▨➤ Offensives of the VIIIth Army

◆ Pockets of enemy resistance
from 11 May to 13 May
1943

⬤ Rommel's
counter-attacks

▥▥▥▥ Mareth line

Labels on map:

MEDITERRANEAN SEA

Bizerta 7 May

VonArnim

Mateur

2nd U S C

Teburba

Cap Bon
9 May 1943

Tunis
7 May

Medjez-el-Bab

Messe

Pont-du-Fahs

1st Brit A

Hammamet 11 April

Bou Arada

19th French C

Enfidaville 20 April

Kairouan
10 April

Sousse 12 April 1943

Medjerda

Tunisian range

Tebessa

19th French C then
2nd U S C

Fondouk

Kasserine

Sidi Bou
Zid

10 April 1943

Rommel's attacks from
14 to 24 Feb 1943

Maknassy

Sfax

Gafsa
17 March 1943

Tozeur

Wadi Akarit 6 April 1943

Gabès 28 March

Shott el Djerid

Island of Djerba

Medenin

Matmata Mts

8th Brit Army
Montgomery

Foum Tataouine

Great Eastern Erg
18 Feb

Leclerc's Column

Nalut

0   100km

plentiful supply of modern equipment. The British fought in the north of Tunisia, the French in the centre—under General Koeltz—and the Americans in the south.

Fearing an American attack on his right flank, while Montgomery's Eighth Army launched a frontal attack on the Mareth line to which he had withdrawn, Rommel persuaded von Arnim in February to forestall them by attacking first and the latter inflicted a serious defeat on them. General Anderson had to withdraw both the French and the Americans westwards to Kasserine. But von Arnim did not press home his advantage; he even withdrew one of his divisions from the front. Rommel disagreed with him and had himself made commander of all the Axis troops. In February he took up the offensive in the direction of Kasserine and broke through the American front. The blow was so serious that Anderson contemplated a general retreat; he now had only one brigade left that was in a fit state to oppose the Germans.

But Rommel's intention was merely to clear a wide enough space for the withdrawal of the *Afrika Korps* troops and to protect their right flank when they retreated northwards. He did not renew his attack; in March the situation seemed to him to be deadlocked and he left Africa. Montgomery then took over the initiative in the direction of Gabès. He had envisaged a wide encirclement from the west but he had to fight two eighteen-day battles in order to open up a route. He managed to do so with the help of the French corps, which recaptured the eastern ridge in the direction of Kairouan.

The two Italian-German armies in Tunisia were now formed into one, under von Arnim; on paper they numbered 250,000 but there were only 90,000 combat troops and they were hemmed in at the bridgehead in Tunis, with their backs to the sea. General Alexander, who had been in command of all the Allied forces since 14 February, gave Anderson, who was in the best position, the task of mopping it up. The first attack on April 22 made little headway. A second on May 6 was more successful; the French, for their part, had seized the Fahs bridge and had then edged their way eastwards to cut off all possible retreat routes for the Axis troops.

On May 7, the British entered Tunis and the Americans Bizerta. On May 9 General von Vaerst laid down his arms to the Americans at Cape Bon; on May 13 the *Afrika Korps* and General Messe's Italian troops surrendered to the British and French. In all, the Allies took 250,000 prisoners.

The war was over in Africa and the Axis had lost; the Mediterranean once again became a British sea; Italy was open to Allied attack, with the whole length of her mainland exposed to bombers and the islands and southern Italy to landing fleets.

III DARLAN'S REIGN

The scuttling of the Toulon fleet and the Tunisian defeats had been very damaging to Admiral Darlan's prestige and authority; it was a heavy blow. Yet he continued to wield complete power, civil and military, on behalf of Marshal Pétain, who was committed to stay in France by his promise not to leave the French and was said in Algiers to be in a situation where it was impossible for him to express his thoughts publicly. The Admiral claimed that he had been authorised to interpret them and was doing so faithfully. Although he had been disowned by Pétain and deprived of all his titles, while his photograph was disappearing from the many places in the Southern Zone where it had been displayed beside the Marshal's, the Admiral had received the allegiance of all the men in charge in North Africa—except for those in Tunisia. Governor-General Boisson had placed French West Africa under his authority; the only territories over which he had no hold—among those answerable to the Vichy government—were Indochina and the French West Indies, which were governed, however, by two admirals who owed their posts to him, Decoux and Robert. Admiral Godfroy, who was in command of Force x in Alexandria, was still hesitating about whether to join him.

Admiral Darlan had kept on all the Vichy officials, even those most heavily compromised by their collaboration. On the other hand, he had put the Algiers Gaullists in prison and banned their newspaper *Combat*; he had dismissed the ringleaders who, on behalf of Giraud, had organised the putsch of November 8, and some remained under threat of prosecution; but others had apparently joined him and he had given them important posts—for example Henri d'Astier de la Vigerie was put in charge of the police.

The Admiral governed with a council of colonial governors—the 'Imperial Council'. Although disowned by his peers, General Giraud's prestige and the American support earned him command of the armed forces, a post which fulfilled his every wish and to which he intended to confine himself. Relations between the French administration and the Allied forces were governed by an agreement which the Admiral had made with General Clark, Eisenhower's deputy, an agreement which was much more favourable to the Americans, especially as far as the rate of the dollar was concerned, than those which had previously been negotiated by Lemaigre-Dubreuil on behalf of General Giraud.

The American consul Murphy maintained his support for Darlan, who was being violently attacked by Free France, the underground Resistance and the American press, and whom President Roosevelt had half-disowned by treating him as a 'temporary expedient'. On December 23, 1942, the Admiral was assassinated by a young Gaullist, Bonnier de La Chapelle, perhaps influenced by the chief of police himself, after a chaplain had given him absolution. A wind of panic immediately swept over Algiers; Murphy and Giraud thought that they were threatened; Bonnier de La Chapelle was immediately brought before a council of war, deserted by his protectors and executed.

There was so much upset in men's minds that the Count of Paris thought that his hour had come; he had been bitterly disappointed in Vichy, where he had hoped for a moment that Marshal Pétain would become a French General Monk; he had supporters in Algiers, even in Darlan's government, and an actual conspiracy had been hatched on his behalf; in the first stage he was to be declared 'lieutenant of the realm'; his supporters and the Count himself considered that this was the only solution capable of uniting the warring factions which were splitting the French among themselves. But although General Giraud, whom the members of the 'Imperial Council' had quickly and unanimously named as Darlan's successor, showed himself very well disposed towards the Count of Paris, he held out no hope. Not that he was a convinced republican or a determined opponent of monarchy; these constitutional problems were of little importance to Giraud; but it was his firm belief that while the war lasted, they must not risk dividing the French even more by political reforms and decisions which would commit them for the future and which they would regard as having been forced on them.

IV GENERAL GIRAUD'S GOVERNMENT

Thus for six months the colonies which had re-entered the struggle were to be governed by a man with the strange title of 'Civil and Military Commander', who had accepted this reponsibility only out of a sense of duty and who regretted that he was now unable to confine his activity to fighting, which in his opinion was the only thing he was qualified to do. General Giraud was a very fine man and a brave fighter and he had a great reputation in French North Africa—the Arabs used to say that he had 'baraka'. But he had no experience of government and he quickly showed that he was unable to cope with political and social problems. Refusing even to examine them, he declared that he was pursuing 'only one aim: victory', but he could not prevent these problems from arising.

In actual fact, the General's origins and upbringing tended to make him a great admirer of the National Revolution—he had said so to Marshal

Pétain both verbally and in writing. He therefore preserved its legislation in Africa; the Crémieux decree was not restored, neither were republican laws and institutions; on the other hand, he retained the censorship, the corporate organisation of the economy, the ban on freemasonry and political parties and the Vichy organisations of the Legion of Ex-Servicemen, with its 'police force' (SOL). Giraud had freed the men whom Vichy had imprisoned for opposition to the régime; but on the other hand all the officials appointed by this same régime remained in office. In doing this, Giraud indubitably had the backing of the African Army and administration and in France of the officers and NCOs of the dissolved Armistice Army. But he clashed violently with General de Gaulle and Free France, which was supported by the underground Resistance. It is true that on the other hand he enjoyed the almost unconditional support of the Americans.

Indeed, President Roosevelt had a genuine dislike for General de Gaulle at whom he was always poking fun and making nasty digs, as well as telling racy stories about him which were untrue. He found the General's policy and behaviour 'intolerable'; he considered that he was afflicted with a 'Messiah complex'. As far as his exasperation allowed him to express political views, Roosevelt refused, as long as the war lasted, to identify France with any committee; from now on he would not discuss or even negotiate with anyone but local authorities. Giraud was in power in North Africa: he came to an agreement with him. In Equatorial Africa it was de Gaulle: he granted him lend-lease aid. This principle led him to the conclusion that all power in North Africa, both civil and military, should be in the hands of the Allied Commander-in-Chief; if a French Committee was set up it would be by agreement between himself and Churchill, without taking French opinion into account or even asking for it; at the Liberation, France would be under Allied occupation and military government for at least six months. In the meantime Roosevelt strangely dissociated de Gaulle not only from the French Resistance but also from Free France—and he suggested appointing him 'Governor of Madagascar'.

Churchill was too conscious of his debt to Roosevelt and his dependence on him to cross him and he made no secret to General de Gaulle that 'between the President of the United States and him he picked the big man'. But he did not make the same blatant mistakes as his partner about the situation in France and the attitude of the French; he knew that de Gaulle was 'the symbol of the Resistance'; although he said that he found him 'impossible' and even that he was 'disgusted' by him, he continued to support him and delayed dismissing him until later.

Each being backed by a 'Big Power', Giraud and de Gaulle had put up a show of being reconciled at Anfa and had established mutual liaison bodies. But their relationship remained touchy and tense. De Gaulle criticised Giraud for giving in to the Americans and for the fact that the aftermath of Vichy lived on in Algiers; above all, he ridiculed Giraud's indifference to political problems; 'is there a single country,' he said, 'which can make war without pursuing political ends?'

In this de Gaulle had the unanimous backing of the underground Resistance. At his instigation, Jean Moulin had succeeded in grouping together representatives of all the important movements of the two zones, of the political parties—including Communists—and of the two main trade union central committees into a 'National Resistance Council', over which he presided. In the course of its first meeting in Paris on May 27, 1943, the Council had come out unequivocally in favour of an agreement between the two generals which would give Giraud command of the armies but leave political control to de Gaulle. The fact was that de Gaulle had promised to let the French people decide their own fate after the Liberation; while waiting for this expression of opinion regarding any possible changes, the laws of the Republic would be brought back into force—this had been done at Réunion as early as the end of 1942. Giraud's behaviour caused the Resistance movements to fear that the Vichy régime, against which they were fighting and having to defend themselves, would continue after the Liberation.

Giraud's views themselves had changed in the course of these discussions; he had declared himself a believer in the Republic and recommended that at the Liberation they should bring in 'the Treveneuc law' which aimed at giving power to representatives on *Conseils Généraux* in the event of Parliament's being prevented from sitting—an arrangement which all thoughtful people in the Resistance considered to be impracticable. Giraud could also not go on indefinitely rejecting the advances of General de Gaulle, who was suggesting a meeting between them to achieve an agreement between Frenchmen on their own, independently of any protection or interference from outside. A mission by General Catroux in Algiers cleared the ground and General de Gaulle arrived in North Africa on May 30, 1943.

V THE FRENCH NATIONAL LIBERATION COMMITTEE

Together with General Giraud he formed the French National Liberation Committee under their joint chairmanship, in which they were each represented by an equal number of supporters, with Giraud retaining command of the troops. The strength of the two monarchs was, however, obviously far from equal; in population, troops, wealth or foreign sympathy and support, General Giraud had far and away the advantage over his rival who was now his colleague. Roosevelt persisted in choosing to recognise no one but him; he wrote to Churchill on June 10, 1943, that if de Gaulle managed to secure control of French West Africa he would contemplate sending 'several regiments and some warships to Dakar'; he regarded de Gaulle as a troublemaker 'who is jeopardising the Allies' war effort and constituting a very serious threat to them . . . the situation is intolerable; we shall have to break with de Gaulle'.

However, the armed forces of the two dissident parties were gradually combined and a joint general staff was set up. But apart from differences in mentality, the amalgamation was made difficult by the fact that the Free French had been equipped by the British and the North African troops by the Americans. In France the Army Resistance Organisation, which had developed out of the Armistice Army, did not join up with the other Gaullist underground movements and regarded itself as an offshoot of the North African Army. The most difficult of all to amalgamate were the secret services in Algiers—the London Central Intelligence and Action Office and the Armistice Army's Intelligence and Counter-Espionage Services, which had both gone over to General Giraud; the second of these regarded the first as amateurs while they, in their turn, despised the others as Vichyists. They were all combined in a new organisation, the General Directorate of Special Services (DGSS); but Giraud considered that this organisation was of a military nature and should depend on him, while de Gaulle regarded it as having a political role and wanted to make it answerable to the head of government. In the end, de Gaulle succeeded in having one of his own men, Jacques Soustelle, appointed as head of the DGSS.

Behind this bitter and unpleasant quarrel between two men loomed the future of France and this was the real significance of this clash of ambitions. If de Gaulle succeeded, the Resistance would take over power at the Liberation and the National Resistance Council set about drawing up an immense programme of economic reform; whilst Giraud would aim at bringing in a substitute for the Vichy régime or at all events conservative forces. The DGSS, whose task it would be to arm and officer the Resistance, had a vital role to play which was by no means purely technical.

However, even in North Africa itself public opinion was swinging over to General de Gaulle, who had won favour by the integrity of his behaviour since the armistice, the soundness of his views and the wide-ranging scope of his programme, to say nothing of the quality of his style. Beside a man of this stature, Giraud cut a poor figure. Many more were joining the Free French Forces, with the aura of their prestige gained at

Kufra and Bir-Hakeim, than the North African units; furthermore, soldiers were deserting the latter to join the former; in New York, the sailors on the battleship *Richelieu,* in a state of semi-revolt, enlisted to fight in the Free French Navy; a number of Giraud's right-hand men, such as Jean Monnet, deserted him; General Delattre de Tassigny, who had come from France after escaping from prison, also went over to General de Gaulle.

Accordingly, Giraud gradually ceased to take any part in politics. When called upon to choose between his office as co-president of the French National Liberation Committee and that of Commander-in-Chief, he opted for the latter; but in so doing he came under the orders of the government and its leader; the result was that he was given the title of Inspector General of the Armed Forces; he found this demotion intolerable and handed in his resignation; deeply embittered, he withdrew to Morocco; he even accused General de Gaulle of wanting to have him assassinated.

The French National Liberation had not yet become the French government and was not recognised as such by the Allies: but it was going to behave as if it were. It set up a Consultative Assembly to advise it, presided over by Félix Gouin and representing those territories which came under its administration, the Free French, those living abroad and all shades of the underground Resistance. In every field it repealed the Vichy legislation and brought back that of the Republic; the *Conseils Généraux* started meeting again in Algeria; the Jews regained French citizenship.

The Committee was actively preparing for the liberation of France. It formed a whole body of new officials—Commissioners of the Republic and Prefects—who were appointed by agreement with the underground Resistance. At the same time the latter set up departmental Liberation Committees to co-ordinate the underground Resistance and act as general councils at the Liberation; they worked under the aegis of the National Resistance Council which they took as their model. The French National Liberation Committee drew up a complete programme of sanctions to be applied to collaborators and Vichy officials at the Liberation; they ranged from suspension from duty to 'loss of civil rights' and being brought to trial in courts of exceptional jurisdiction; Pétain and his ministers were to be judged by a High Court of Justice. As a beginning, Pucheu, who was guilty of having sent Frenchmen to the German firing squad, was sentenced to death and executed in Algiers in March 1944.

The French National Liberation Committee protested against the Allied plans to have France run by a military government (AMGOT) after the Liberation and to force her to accept an occupation currency. It embarked on an independent foreign policy; it asked to take part in decisions on Italy. After first of all refusing to meet Marshal Badoglio, who was an enemy of his, General de Gaulle declared that Franco-Italian friendship must overcome past differences. To make this statement, he went to Ajaccio which had now been freed; this new 'Latin' emphasis was clearly aimed at preventing British and American control from becoming too overbearing.

The French National Liberation Committee went one step further and taking the view that the Allies really had no business to interfere in French politics, on May 26, 1944 it declared itself the provisional government of the French Republic. By that time it had a proper army with very modern equipment; this it owed to the Americans and it was to a large extent the work of General Giraud.

VI THE REBIRTH OF THE FRENCH ARMY

The operation offered immense difficulties; the diversity of the troops which had to be equipped—blacks from French West Africa, Moslems from French North Africa, French Africans, Free French, those who had escaped from France; the language barrier; the diversity of eating habits; the lack of shipping and the small number of harbours equipped to receive, store and redistribute equipment; the small number of French technicians. These difficulties caused delays, bitter discussions and feelings of lasting resentment. In addition, trainees, in particular pilots, had to be sent to American schools and British equipment exchanged for American equipment, and it was necessary to arrange for the troops' supplies which the French were unable to provide. The equipment which had been unloaded had to be assembled at French bases; thus a conveyor-belt system was set up on the Algiers parade ground, where 2,700 vehicles of various types were assembled in one week, but whole companies needed to learn the necessary techniques.

The channels through which the French demands were met were also very complicated. On the French side the requirements were determined by a permanent military committee; missions were sent to the United States to see that they were fulfilled—General Béthouart and Lemaigre-Dubreuil in December 1942 and General Giraud himself in July 1943. But on the American side, the machinery was intricate; the commander-in-chief of the particular theatre submitted the French plans to the joint Chiefs of Staff in Washington with his recommendations; when they had made their decision, the plan came back to the Allied Commander-in-Chief, who passed it on to the Secretary of War for execution; then began complicated transactions which went from the operations department to the equipment depots via the ordnance departments or the various branches of the armed forces and a number of specialist committees; all that then remained to be done was to find the necessary ships, choose the loading harbours and form convoys. On this complex and circuitous route, progress was slow; the process of passing on and studying the files was still further delayed by differences of conception and language difficulties.

However, the Americans wanted to please General Giraud, even though they had been a little disappointed by his outdated strategic views; they regarded him as 'the only military representative of French interests', a formula which once again showed their lack of concern for General de Gaulle. Although General Eisenhower was full of goodwill, for him the task of arming the French took second place to arming his own troops and would have to wait until normal communications had been resumed and the necessary arrangements made.

As for General Giraud, he made considerable demands, but his ideas belonged to the pre-1939 era. Convinced that when peace came, the success of the Allied nations in achieving their war aims would depend on the strength of their armies, he wanted to raise and equip as many units as possible. In Washington General Béthouart presented a plan on his behalf which made provision for forming one general staff at army level, three army corps general staffs, three armoured divisions and eight infantry divisions, with an air force of 1,000 aircraft—500 fighters, 300 bombers and 200 transport aircraft. In theory, the Americans accepted these figures; but Giraud then asked for two further divisions which they refused. Then, since the French National Liberation Committee had decided to turn Leclerc's division into an armoured division, Giraud suggested having four armoured divisions instead of three, that is to say a total of twelve divisions instead of eleven. And one armoured division required five times as much equipment as one infantry division. The Americans suggested looking at the whole plan again, so that in the course of the summer of 1943 the great divergence of views between the French and American nations suddenly burst into the open and there began the long discussions which have been called 'the battle of the services'.

The French were wanting to arm and send into the field as many men as possible; in addition, they wanted to obtain the maximum amount of resources from the Americans while at the same time retaining comparative freedom of action for their army, for example by allocating to it the air units which were arriving already equipped from across the Atlantic. The Americans criticised these suggestions for showing a lack of understanding of modern warfare. In their view the latter required very considerable logistical services; they had calculated that in the air force, aircrew did not amount to more than a tenth of the manpower employed on the ground and they had learnt in the Pacific that a large number of soldiers never went into action. They were thus going back to the medieval conception of an army: a small number of fighting men and a large number of ancillaries. They had set up the 'Army Service Forces', which was, in fact, a ministry for armaments, transport and all the needs of an army—recruiting, tests, finances, billeting, supplies, transport, chaplaincies, laundries, theatres, etc. In addition, they noted that because of the predominance of coloured troops, the French lacked officers and NCOs, in spite of the thousands of men who had escaped from France and arrived in French North Africa via Spain, and they lacked an even greater number of experts able to take care of the logistic services. Moreover, they refused to use their bases for supplying the French Army or to accept any responsibility for this task and for all the problems which it raised; the Army would have to work all this out for itself.

The squabble took a political turn when the French refused to be incorporated into the American Army. In this attitude the Americans thought they detected the influence of Free France and its touchy nationalism; they suspected it of lacking loyalty and gratitude to them and even of being undisciplined—they had been shocked by the 'desertions' to it from the African Army. In short, in December 1943 there was a distinct stiffening among the Americans at all levels. Even Eisenhower suggested cutting off supplies from the French unless they proved more amenable; Roosevelt was all the more inclined to agree with him because he was extremely angry that despite his intervention on Giraud's behalf, the latter had been gradually ousted. In his general report, General Marshall summed up the American point of view about the French when he wrote that they had fought well when there were no political questions involved.

In the end the French were forced to give in. They agreed to their Air Force becoming part of the Allied air 'pool'; they resigned themselves to the fact that the Americans would arm only five infantry and two armoured divisions, with a third armoured division—Leclerc's—to be formed later on. In these circumstances, the Americans agreed to provide France with equipment worth 3,000 million dollars, that is to say eight per cent of the lend-lease, and consisting of 1,400 aircraft, 160,000 rifles, 30,000 machine guns, 3,000 guns and 5,000 tanks. They refitted a large part of the French war fleet, equipping it with radar.

The French, for their part, were able to raise and equip 560,000 men outside their own country, of whom 300,000 were natives of North Africa, black Africa and the South Sea Islands; 163,000 were employed in ancillary services; there was a reserve force of 50,000 men; 256,000 went to form the various expeditionary forces. The French National Liberation

Committee decided to place the Italian one under General Juin, to send Leclerc's armoured division to England and to form a second army under Delattre de Tassigny to operate in the south of France.

VII TOWARDS A FRENCH RECOVERY

Thus in Algiers, the temporary capital of France, the French National Liberation Committee was recovering or acquiring all the attributes of sovereign power. It was going to have an army which, thanks to American equipment, was more powerful than that of 1939, in spite of its small numbers. A last blow was dealt to the myth propagated by the Vichy régime that France could have recovered from her disaster of 1940 completely on her own or even become an arbitrator between exhausted antagonists by adopting a wait-and-see policy with a hint of collaboration. This French recovery constituted a personal triumph for General de Gaulle—although most of this army's officers and NCOs were still hostile to him—for he had constantly stated his view that by staying in the Allied camp France could still play a part in the war; he had never stopped working for this and events were proving him right. Through his intransigence in defending French interests he was enabling France to find her place again while at the same time preventing her from being made into a satellite by her powerful allies.

With her new-found freedom France had to be modernised—she was not making war, said General de Gaulle, in order to become a 'whited sepulchre' again. The Consultative Assembly in Algiers and the National Resistance Council in France were working out vast programmes of reform; they were planning for a controlled economy, the nationalisation of sources of energy and credit, the switch from an agricultural rural society to an industrialised urban society; the extension of education by democratising the schools and raising the school-leaving age; better training and increased efficiency in the civil service; an increase in the active population; the mechanisation of industry; the improvement of public health through social welfare services, etc.

But many people feared that France might be permanently weakened by defeat and occupation and that the damage they had caused would be a further burden for outworn economic structures and the rigid mentality which had produced them. Surely there was some hint of this in the fact that the rebirth of the Army had been possible only with American aid? Already the old structure of the colonial empire was showing signs of creaking—a prelude, perhaps, to breaking up altogether.

VIII THE EMPIRE: ITS DEVELOPMENT

The population of the Empire had behaved with amazing calm after the defeat of 1940, for even the leaders of the weak nationalist movements had not fully appreciated its seriousness. But the fratricidal strife in Dakar and Syria and then the American landing and the resulting friendly but none-theless foreign occupation of French North Africa had made French authority lose face and for six months even removed it completely from Tunisia. The difficulties experienced by France had revived the ambitions and intrigues—thoroughly outdated, of course—of British authorities such as the Colonial Office and the Intelligence Service. Above all, the Americans, and Roosevelt in particular, set themselves up as the champions of decolonisation, which, through a strange historical error, they believed had begun with American Independence, forgetting the extermination of the Indians and the slave trade out of which the United States had grown. Roosevelt considered that the colonial system implied war and that one could not fight Fascist slavery while doing nothing to free people from colonial slavery. The United States would set an example by 'freeing' the Philippines. On this particular point American capitalism strangely coincided with the views propounded by Soviet Communism. Moreover, Roosevelt condemned the British Empire just as much as the French Empire. He had informed Churchill that America would not help Britain merely to enable her to continue her brutal domination of colonial peoples. But the British Empire was taking an active part in the war, so that this was not the moment to undermine it. This was not the case with the French Empire. Elliott Roosevelt has told how in the course of a dinner at Rabat, to the growing embarrassment of Churchill, his father had first of all surprised and then tempted the Sultan of Morocco by opening up vistas of a post-war period in which the resources of Morocco would be developed by American aid and colonial exploitation by the French would come to an end.

General de Gaulle and the French Resistance were of a very different opinion; they were fighting to save France and they had no intention of losing any of her possessions; they had criticised the Vichy régime for giving up territory to Japan in Indochina, and General Giraud for being too submissive to their American ally in French North Africa; to a large extent, the Free French volunteers were also officers of the colonial army, overseas administrators or colonial settlers; the Communists themselves, eager to blow Déroulède's trumpet in order to win over all possible support inside the nation, had toned down their anti-colonial propaganda almost to the extent of praising the civilising influence of France in her Empire and contrasting it with Nazi racialism.

However, a change was taking place. In Equatorial Africa which had joined Free France, the work of Governor-General Félix Eboué, a negro from French Guyana, had earned General de Gaulle's approval when he gave more scope to African-born leaders and showed respect for customs and traditional social structures instead of continuing the policy of imposing the French way of life. During his anti-Giraud campaign, de Gaulle, speaking from London, had given the French North Africans a promise that he would improve their lot. In the Middle East, although the mandate which had been given to France by the League of Nations remained in existence until the end of the war, Free France had committed itself to granting independence to Syria and the Lebanon.

In October 1943 the governments of these two countries, secretly stirred up by British agents who had dreams of an Arab world united under British rule, asked that public services which were under the direct management of French officials should be handed over to them. The French National Liberation Committee refused and pointed out that no change of status in the mandated territories could be made until after the war. Going even further, the Lebanese government had a bill passed by Parliament to modify the Constitution, which had been granted them by France. The chief French representative, J. Helleu, took a strong line; he had the President of the Lebanese Republic and three ministers arrested, dissolved the House and set up a provisional government.

This gave rise to a serious Franco-British crisis at the very moment when the French National Liberation Committee's difficulties with the United States about arming the French troops required it to stay on the best of terms with the British. While the Egyptian and Iraqi press were unleashing attacks on 'French oppression', in November 1943 the British government actually sent an ultimatum to the French National Liberation Committee; it demanded the recall of Helleu and the freeing of the imprisoned leaders; otherwise British troops would take over the government of the Lebanon and Syria. The French National Liberation Committee tried to find a way out of the difficulty but eventually caved in; having advised its representative to be 'firm', it now cancelled his decisions, reestablished the *status quo* and renewed its promise to grant independence to the two states.

In North Africa the nationalists were also beginning to stir again. In Morocco the leading personalities who had joined forces to form the traditionalist Istiqlal movement were becoming reconciled with the Sultan, to whom they had hitherto been opposed. In Tunisia Bourguiba, the leader of the Neo-Destour, had gone over to the Axis and had spoken to his countrymen over Radio Bari; after the capture of Tunis the French National Liberation Committee had dismissed the Bey and put someone else in his place.

But the most striking and alarming changes had taken place in Algeria. Until then the nationalists had restricted themselves to demanding greater integration of the natives, and in 1936 Farhat Abbas had even declared that there was no such thing as an Algerian nation and never had been. In May 1941 he had made only moderate demands to the Vichy régime: equality of Frenchmen and natives in the Army, the abolition of the military régime in the southern territories and agricultural reform. But he continued to militate in favour of 'assimilating' the natives, which met with opposition from the French 'settlers' who were anxious to keep their distance from the latter. Although the Ulemas' movement was more traditionalist, being Moslem and Arab orientated, and Messali Hadj's 'People's Party' which had been momentarily linked with the Communists, was more inclined to take violent action, no serious agitation had occurred.

The American landing sparked off an irresistible chain of events. The only response to an appeal to the natives by Admiral Darlan to take an active part in the war was a letter from Farhat Abbas on December 20, 1942, demanding the drawing up of a political, economic and social statute which would make the masses aware of their rights and their duty to take part in the war effort. On February 10, 1943, the matter was taken a step further in 'the Algerian people's manifesto' which condemned colonisation and denounced assimilation, which had been Farhat Abbas's objective up to then, as a 'lie'. The manifesto called for 'complete freedom and equality for all inhabitants of Algeria, the recognition of Arabic as the official language and real and immediate participation for Moslems in their country's government'. In June 1943 this first step was followed up by a programme which was presented to the French National Liberation Committee, with the aim of forming an Algerian government composed half of Moslems and half of Frenchmen, and of making all posts open to Moslems.

General Catroux, the State Commissioner for Moslem Affairs in the French National Liberation Committee, rejected the programme with the declaration that 'the French will never agree to grant independence to Algeria, which is an integral part of France'; the nationalist leaders then refused to sit in the 'Finance Delegation', which led to their arrest for 'stirring up unrest in time of war'.

But on December 11, 1943, the French National Liberation Committee decided to retreat and brought in a certain number of reforms in favour of the Moslems. These were announced by General de Gaulle on the following day in Constantine in a speech which excited worldwide interest.

The élite of the native population would be granted French nationality without, however, giving up their personal status as Moslems; Moslems would have increased representation in the Assemblies and play a greater part in government; an immense programme of legislation and public works would improve their social and material situation. The 'Constantine Programme' was rejected both by the nationalists, who denounced it as a revival of the outmoded 1936 'Blum–Violette Plan', and by the French Algerians, who made no secret of the fact that they regarded it as the work of people who knew nothing at all about Algeria and that they would make no bones about repealing it once the French had gone back to their own country. Even men who had been Gaullists from the earliest days, like the Dean of the Law Faculty in Algiers, Viard, declared that they disagreed with the Moslem policy of the President of the French National Liberation Committee. As a result, Farhat Abbas became reconciled with the Ulemas and Messali Hadj. The manifesto became the charter for Algerian demands. The 'Friends of the Manifesto' soon numbered some several hundred thousand supporters and they launched a weekly paper, *Egalité*. The Algerian nationalists were turning from the peaceful and law-abiding development which they had been advocating hitherto to plans for violent action.

Black Africa was not moving so quickly. The French National Liberation Committee decided to hold a huge conference in Brazzaville to study its future. At the beginning of 1944 it was under the chairmanship of René Pleven and General de Gaulle took part in the final session and announced its conclusions. The conference had worked out a vast programme of social and economic reform to ensure gradual advancement for the natives; this programme aimed at africanising the administration and granting internal autonomy to territories for the future by providing them with assemblies which would gradually take over the running of the country. But there was no thought of granting any of these territories independence; in any case, the only people attending the conference had been colonial administrators.

*

Apart from its military consequences, the end of the war in Africa had thus brought France back into the concert of nations. At the same time this comeback was the beginning of a profound change in the political, economic and imperial structure of France. In the midst of her misfortunes, France was turning over a new leaf; her liberation would also be a rebirth. Nevertheless, the meaning and purpose of this development were not yet very clear, nor were they unanimously accepted; the only definite conclusion to be drawn was that the Vichy régime had been condemned, its laws abolished and its leaders punished. On the other hand, the Allies still did not look upon France as an equal, nor did they regard the French National Liberation Committee as her legal government. The Italian campaign was going to enable the Committee to establish itself rather more firmly and set its sights a little higher, thanks to the expeditionary force which was to have a share in the Allied victories.

CHAPTER 2

Italy Surrenders

I THE SICILIAN CAMPAIGN

In May 1943 in Washington, at the suggestion of the British and in spite of American reluctance, the Allies decided to follow up their success in Africa by putting Italy out of action. However, because of shortage of shipping and lack of experience, in order also not to jeopardise the major landing across the Channel, which still had priority, an operation of minor importance was planned; any landing near Rome or even at Naples was considered too risky and the idea was ruled out; an operation in Sardinia would have had the advantage of making it possible to follow up by bombing the industrial centres of northern Italy; but since it was open to converging counter-attacks both from Corsica and from the Italian coast, it seemed too hazardous.

They therefore settled for a landing in Sicily; this would have the main advantage of ensuring a completely free east–west passage through the Mediterranean. Throughout June there were raids on both Sicily and on the little island of Pantelleria, fifty miles from Tunisia and some sixty miles from Sicily. Mussolini loudly boasted that Pantelleria was impregnable; but on June 12, 1943 the garrison's 12,000 men surrendered merely as a result of air raids, after losing only 56 dead and 196 wounded. This hardly showed a strong will to fight on the part of the Italians.

Operation 'Husky', the code name given to the landing in Sicily, needed very intricate gearing, for it involved the Army, Navy and Air force, and both British and American troops—the French did not take part. The dispersal of the general staffs showed how complicated it was: the American General Eisenhower, the interallied commander, was in Algiers; but the British General Alexander, who was responsible for the operation, had established himself in Tunis, while the naval general staff were based on Malta and the Army set up its own base in Sicily as soon as the landing started. All this did not make communication any easier and caused delay in making the decisions. But the Allies were sufficiently well coordinated for an American naval officer, for example, to take command of a sector which had been allocated to the British fleet.

The landing took place during the night of July 9–10, 1943, and although it could not achieve any surprise effect, it was nevertheless virtually a complete success. An army of 160,000 men, half Americans under Patton and half British and Commonwealth troops under Montgomery, set foot on land without meeting any great resistance. They were covered by 1,000 aircraft and transported by 3,200 ships—among which use was made for the first time of landing craft, flat-bottomed boats which could be beached without damage and were provided with a swing-door in the bows. They also were supported by 1,700 guns and 600 tanks, while paratroopers seized airfields inland. The timing of the convoys had been so well co-ordinated that a Canadian division from Scotland took over its landing barges which had come from Tripoli at 1.30 a.m. as planned, within sight of the Sicilian coast. The only difficulties arose from 'false beaches' which they had failed to detect or banks of pebbles not properly reconnoitred, on which some craft were smashed; some paratroopers were dropped too soon and fell into the sea.

But there was virtually no reaction from the enemy. And yet the Italians had ten divisions in Sicily; it is true that their strength had been reduced and that half of them belonged to the type called 'coastal', that is to say that they consisted of older men. The Germans had sent 70,000 men to northern Sicily, one of which was a crack division, the Hermann Goering ss Division. However, the coastal batteries did not open fire; the Italian headquarters were destroyed by raids and the base of Augusta was abandoned the day before the British arrived.

Accordingly, the troops landed and advanced without much trouble. In the west, on July 22 the Americans occupied Palermo; in the east, the British seized Syracuse on the 12th, but were stopped outside Catania; nevertheless on the 21st they joined up with the Americans. In his usual presumptuous and boastful way, Mussolini had declared that 'no enemy will leave the island alive'; in actual fact the Italian troops had stampeded; only the Germans clung on to Etna long enough to enable their troops to be evacuated from the island, a move which for once Hitler himself had decided upon, since he was anxious not to let the enemy coils close around them as in Tunisia.

On August 5 the British entered Catania; on the 16th the Americans entered Messina. Although they achieved their objective, their success was not complete because the Germans managed to bring back almost all their troops and equipment to the Italian mainland, that is to say 50,000 men and 10,000 vehicles; the 200,000 prisoners were Italians.

Being unable to prevent this evacuation was the only comparative failure of the Allies in this Sicilian campaign. Once again they had proved over-cautious; they had thought it impossible to land in the north-east of

Sicily, which was the only way they could have reached the Straits of
Messina before the Germans could cross it. They had also not dared to
send their battleships to the straits in case they came under fire from the
powerful batteries on both sides. In addition, they made mistakes which
with better co-ordination could have been avoided; for example, the big
bombers which would have done a great deal to hinder the evacuation
had not been concentrated in time; General Alexander had not even called
his subordinate commanders together to make an overall plan of action.

In short, the Allied force proved irresistible only against the Italians;
with the Germans it was a different matter. Hitler made no secret of his
apprehensions to Mussolini, whom he met at Feltre on July 19. It was absolutely necessary that Italy should hold on, he said, now that the Soviet
offensive had been launched. The Duce promised everything the Führer
wished; but he was no longer in a position to prevent the collapse of Fascist
Italy. And his days were numbered.

II THE COLLAPSE OF FASCIST ITALY

By July 1943 there was no longer any shadow of doubt that the war was a
disaster for Italy. Not only had she not achieved any of the objectives for
which she had entered it but she had lost her empire; her Navy had been
driven out of Mare Nostrum and was not safe even in the bases in
the northern part of the country where it remained immobilised; the industrial centres were being flattened by increasingly massive raids; the
enemy had conquered Sicily and the whole length of the peninsula was
vulnerable and open to attack; the enemy's only difficulty was to choose
where to thrust home.

From the economic point of view, industrial output had dropped by 35
per cent since 1939 and agricultural output by 20 per cent; imports had
decreased by 78 per cent and exports by 54 per cent; the national debt had
risen from 146,000 million lire to 405,000 million and currency circulation
from 28,000 to 79,000 million. The state budgetary deficit, which reached
12,000 million lire in 1939, had risen to 87,000 million in 1943 and income now covered only 36 per cent of expenditure. Thanks to strict control, prices had theoretically only doubled, but a black market in every
commodity was flourishing in all regions; and the population was suffering
from a growing scarcity of foodstuffs. Corn was being sown in public
squares; by this symbolic gesture, which those in power extolled as an as-
sertion of the will to fight, the country was proving the depth of misery
created by inefficiency and neglect.

This disaster was shown in the Duce's physical condition. His stomach ulcer made him anxious and nervous and necessitated a debilitating diet and long periods of rest which were not really compatible with a position of absolute power. He had less will-power and even his reflexes seemed to have slowed down; his relatives were astonished to see a strange inertia, an almost complete apathy come over the old warrior; he seemed to be more and more indifferent, as if resigned to what was happening to him and to what lay in store for him. He retained the demagogue's confidence in words; he continued to believe that a speech was action; he took refuge in commonplaces and superficial judgments; he excused his failures by lashing out against the Italian people who had to be 'driven into battle by kicks up the behind'.

The régime which Mussolini had created had fallen into a similar decline; the sixty-year-old Duce was setting an example of moral corruption by flaunting his love affair with the young Claretta Petacci, who was burdened with a family greedy for honours and wealth. All around him things were breaking up. Senise, the chief of police, painted a picture of permanent public despondency, of impotence and chaos among those in power and of disobedience at every level. Only the militia and some young Fascists still believed in the régime and its leader; the most intelligent officials turned from ironic criticism to scepticism and moral defection; they were wondering how to desert the sinking ship in time with their weapons and kit. 'Fascism was dead long before 1943,' wrote Guido Leto, the chief of the Fascist secret police, the OVRA.

Everyone was full of grievances against Germany and these were frequently justified. She had not kept her promise to provide Italy with coal and the Romanian oil which she had agreed to send her had arrived only in driblets; for her the war in the Mediterranean had always taken second place and she had refused to provide the resources for the capture of Malta, which could have had far-reaching consequences; in the USSR the Italian Eighth Army which had had 220,000 men when it had arrived now numbered only 80,000, and the Wehrmacht had no scruples in assigning it dangerous tasks, at the same time covering it with sarcasm. The humiliating thing was that both in Greece and in Africa it was only the last-minute intervention of the Germans which had saved the Italian troops, and this the Italians found difficult to swallow. Relations between the two armies were characterised by a display of arrogance, brutality and contempt on the part of the German officers which the Italians' pride and sensitivity found impossible to tolerate. Personal diplomatic relations were no better. And on top of that the Germans no longer made any bones about their designs for annexing the Italian Tyrol.

Mussolini chafed because he had become Hitler's henchman, no longer had any active say in joint decisions and had to dance attendance on the

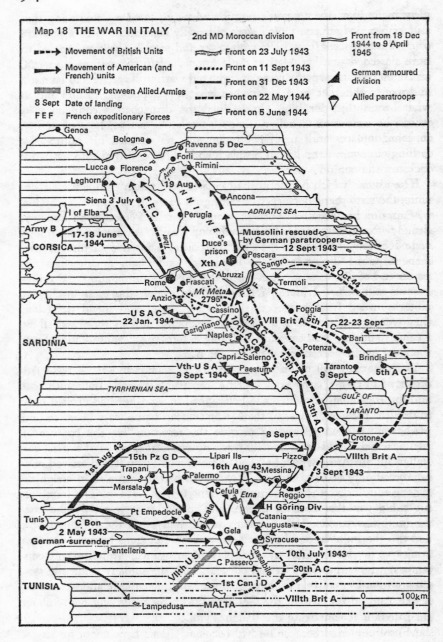

Map 18 **THE WAR IN ITALY**

- ▪--▶ Movement of British Units
- ──▶ Movement of American (and French) units
- ▨▨▨ Boundary between Allied Armies
- 8 Sept Date of landing
- FEF French expeditionary Forces

2nd MD Moroccan division
- 〰〰 Front on 23 July 1943
- •••••• Front on 11 Sept 1943
- ─── Front on 31 Dec 1943
- ▪─▪─ Front on 22 May 1944
- 〰〰 Front on 5 June 1944

── Front from 18 Dec 1944 to 9 April 1945

◤ German armoured division

♙ Allied paratroops

Führer. However, the personal bonds between the two men remained firm; disaster had not impaired their friendship nor affected their trust in each other. They realised that their fates were sealed. Hitler, in spite of the Duce's setbacks and his own irritation at some of Mussolini's decisions which had been particularly inappropriate, continued to admire his ally; he wrote to him that 'by carrying on his heroic struggle he had become a symbol for the whole world'. But their staffs were coming to hate each other more and more, whether it was Ciano and Ribbentrop—the former described the latter as a criminal—the general staffs or the leading officials of the two parties. And for the Italians themselves the word *tedeschi* was once more taking on a pejorative meaning.

How could Italy continue the fight? She was desperately short of resources. Mussolini had decided to raise a million men; national service was made compulsory for men between the ages of fourteen and seventy and for women between fourteen and sixty; but these measures were carried out rather unenthusiastically and they would have been effective only if the Italians had been willing to fight; but they were weary and becoming more and more indifferent to the 'Fascist war', from which they dissociated themselves. The government had been reshuffled by the dismissal of those ministers who took least trouble to hide their dissatisfaction— Ciano and Grandi; but those who had been ousted were quite naturally turning to open hostility. The Party had been given a new secretary, Carlo Scorza, a man who was devoted to the Duce. But what could he do about the fact that Allied submarines were making it difficult to transport lead and antimony from Sardinia, that tank production had dropped almost to zero and that the metallurgical industry was short of ore and electrical power?

The only obvious solution was *sganciamento,* a breakaway from Germany. Could Mussolini persuade Hitler to agree to Italy's becoming nonbelligerent again? How would he even dare to ask him, when the war was *his* war and the alliance with Germany *his* alliance? To withdraw from the one or to break the other would be tantamount to a denial of himself. All that he could do was to try to persuade Hitler to put an end to the fighting in the USSR. On March 25, 1943, he wrote to him to this effect: 'I think I am right in saying that the Russian chapter can now be brought to a close, if possible by a separate peace or by setting up a strong wall in the east which the Russians would be unable to cross. . . . We cannot carry on summer offensives and winter retreats without reaching a state of exhaustion which, even if mutual, will in the end benefit no one but the British and Americans.' The Duce was encouraged in this course by the Romanian Foreign Minister and by the Hungarian government. In Salzburg, where he had met Hitler in April 1943, he had tried to convince him without success. In Feltre, on July 19, he was so overcome by a feeling of shame at the Italian setbacks and of resignation at his power-lessness that he had not even dared to repeat his suggestions.

Was there any hope of the Allies being more understanding? As early as December 1942 Franzoni, the Italian minister in Lisbon, had made dis-creet approaches to Eden and Cordell Hull, with the approval of Ciano, who had not consulted his father-in-law; this contact had been maintained up to July 1943 without any result. In July 1943 Bastianini, the Under-Secretary of State for Foreign Affairs, had returned to the attack; he thought he was acting with the tacit approval of Mussolini, since the latter had not replied to his request for permission. It was a matter of saving the Duce. The British categorically refused; what other answer could they have given after the decisions reached in Casablanca?

Moreover, in the Allied camp it was the British who were keeping up 'the hard line' towards Italy; they did not think that there was any other solution to Fascism; they wanted the disturbances in Italy to be sufficiently serious to warrant the intervention of the Wehrmacht; it would thus help the British 'peripheral strategy'. For the same reason, they were in favour of intensive air raids, which Allied propaganda said were caused by the presence of the Germans in Italy, so as to stir up the Italian population against the *tedeschi*.

The Americans were said to be in favour of less hostile measures, in or-der to make it easier for Italy to join the Allied camp; they would have liked to restrict the bombing and to reassure the Italians as to their inten-tions once the Fascist régime had disappeared. This was the point of view expressed by Roosevelt, who was more inclined to be well-disposed towards Italy, the foe, than towards his ally, Free France.

The USSR was happy to stir the pot in this discussion. She intended hav-ing her say in the decisions about Italy; she continually accused her part-ners of wanting to present her with a *fait accompli* and on the whole she had much in common with the British point of view. The debate ended with the Allied bombing of Rome on July 19; it aroused intense emotion in all Italian circles. It proved that the approaches made by the Fascist régime to the Allied side had no more chance of success than Mussolini's suggestions to Hitler. It was up to the Italians and the Italians alone to find a solution to the two interrelated problems of the existence of Fascism and of Italy's participation in the war; and as a necessary prerequisite, Mussolini had to be ousted.

III THE ITALIAN RESISTANCE

Since the King, the aristocracy, the Church, the industrialists, the big landowners and a large part of the liberal middle classes had given their support to Fascism, for a considerable time the opposition had been confined to a few thousand scattered refugees leading a precarious existence in France, England and the United States. For a long time Mussolini's successes made the Italian people turn a deaf ear to their propaganda; their action was limited by the French and British policy of friendship with the Duce before the war; and the final factor which paralysed them completely was their own internal divisions.

However, three factors had helped them to regroup. The first was the work of a group of intellectuals led by the Rosselli brothers—who were murdered near Bagnoles-de-l'Orne by hired assassins of OVRA. They founded a movement called 'Freedom and Justice' whose aim was to use anti-Fascism to bridge the gap between Marxists and liberal democrats. The second factor was Stalin's anti-Nazi policy during the years 1935–8; this brought the Communists—who, moreover, in Italy, with Gramsci and Togliatti, had constantly displayed a certain amount of independence with regard to Moscow—closer to other political parties. The Spanish war was the final melting-pot in which they mingled together; 3,100 anti-Fascist Italians fought in the International Brigades; fighting in a sort of civil war on foreign soil, it was they who repulsed the 'black shirts' at Guadalajara; 700 of them were killed and 1,000 wounded.

'The Popular Union of Exiles' in France comprised 70,000 supporters and its newspaper, *La Voce degli Italiani,* even penetrated into Italy, where hitherto only the Communists had maintained an underground network which OVRA had not succeeded in breaking up. Communists, Socialists and supporters of 'Freedom and Justice' joined together to form an 'Action Front'; the Christian Democrats with Dom Sturzo remained on the fringe, since the behaviour of the Pope and the high Italian clergy made things awkward for them—Dom Sturzo had advocated peace in Spain. While the Action Front declared itself republican, since the King was both upholding Fascism and profiting from it, the Christian Democrats and the liberals who were hostile to the régime but had remained in Italy set their hopes on the monarchy and the Army to overthrow it.

The Action Front was broken up by the German-Soviet pact; some Socialists, like Saragat and Tasca, became irreconcilable opponents of the Communists. Then Italy's entry into the war plunged everyone into a moral dilemma: was opposing the government not the equivalent of trea-

son? France's defeat was nothing short of a disaster; the exiles who had
settled there were imprisoned or had to hide or even escape to America.
There as elsewhere the Wehrmacht's invasion of the USSR brought the
Communists back into the paths of righteousness; three times a week on
Radio Moscow, Togliatti urged the people to unite with the Allies in the
name of peace, freedom and independence. Once again, notably in France,
common fronts were formed between Communists and Socialists like Pietro
Nenni or Silvio Trentin. In all the Allied countries the anti-Fascist exiles
worked to persuade the governments and public not to confuse the Italian
people with the régime which was oppressing it. They tried not to restrict
themselves to purely destructive action; in New York Count Sforza drew
up an 'Eight-Point Manifesto', a programme for post-Fascist Italy, which
had the unanimous approval of the 'Pan-American Congress of Free
Italians' which met in Montevideo in August 1942.

Italy's defeats brought the exiled leaders back to their own country. All
were agreed that if Italy retained her ties with Germany she had lost the
war in any case, for a victorious Germany would bring her under her yoke.
The only way out was first to get rid of Fascism and then to side with the
Allies. But how could this be done? Some Christian Democrats continued
to hope that the King would recover his constitutional powers and bring
about a legal revolution which would cut the losses and avoid chaos by
making the whole of Italy swing over to the Allied cause in the hope of
not losing any of her territory.

But this was not the opinion of the Socialists and the new Action party
which had been formed by the merging of 'Freedom and Justice' with
young liberal intellectuals, and had a republican and socialistic programme. The Communists took up a more flexible line; they were trying
above all to unite the anti-Fascists. In 1943, on their initiative, a liaison
committee of the six anti-Fascist parties was formed—Communist, Socialist,
Action party, Christian Democrat, Liberal and Democrat Labour—this
last party consisting merely of a few of Bonomi's friends. The programme
was simple: to destroy Fascism and to hold over the solution of political
problems until after the Liberation.

Thus in Italy, unlike France, the Resistance was not formed into new
bodies of separate Resistance movements but incorporated into the former
political parties, with the addition of the Action party. The strength of
these parties varied greatly. Only the Communists had any sort of military
organisation; the Christian Democrats could count on the lower clergy
and 'Catholic Action'; but the Socialists had greater difficulty in re-
forming their party, while the Action party was only a skeleton structure
made up of intellectuals; as for the Liberals, virtually their only asset was
the prestige of having Benedetto Croce as a member. Although the strikes

in northern Italy in March 1943 had shown that anti-Fascism was becoming popular, in July 1943 the Italian Resistance was not a force to be reckoned with; it had not taken root throughout the country; it had no institution similar to the National Resistance Council in France; it had no armed forces; it had not really infiltrated the Italian civil service; and if one adds to this the fact that it was not known to the Allies and that it had not played any part in Sicily, it is obvious that it was incapable of overthrowing and replacing the Fascist régime on its own, however shaky and discredited the latter might be.

IV THE PLOT AGAINST MUSSOLINI

Since the underground Resistance was not in contact with other organisations, three groups were going to endeavour to bring down Mussolini. They made no attempt to co-ordinate their action; they each had only a few scraps of information about the plans and programme of the others; as a result, though the operation succeeded it was going to cause chaos all over Italy, split the country up between various authorities and lead to civil war.

The first and weakest group was the one formed by former politicians from pre-Fascist days; in actual fact there were two of them, Orlando and Bonomi. The former still had a great reputation abroad but in his own country his prestige had fallen considerably; the King referred to him as a 'ghost from the past'; but he had a great name which was likely to win the Allies' confidence; he was also only one man. Bonomi, on the other hand, had woven a spider's web; he was linked with the underground Resistance—he was relying especially on the Christian Democrat de Gasperi— but he was equally welcome at the royal palace and he had not broken with a few Fascists who were on the road to repudiating their party, realising that the cock would soon be crowing for them.

King Victor Emmanuel had the constitutional power to dismiss Mussolini—after all, the Duce was only the president of the Council summoned by him—and he was the titular commander of the armed forces which, if they followed him, would be capable of controlling any possible violent reaction by the last hard core of Fascists. But Victor Emmanuel had seriously compromised himself with the régime and he had never at any time protested against its excesses. On the other hand, he was a very cautious and secretive man; he would advance only by stealth, after making sure that all the odds were on his side and without revealing anything of his intentions. Amongst his entourage, Duke Acquarone, the minister of the Royal Household, was a safe and loyal henchman, more resolute than his sovereign.

On the military side, the ringleader was General Castellano, the Deputy Army Chief of Staff, an excellent look-out man who was aggressively anti-German. His first successful move was to get rid of Cavallero, the new scapegoat for Italy's failures, and to replace him by General Ambrosio, who had not compromised himself too much with Fascism, had a well-established reputation for honesty and was highly thought of by the King; the Duce's dismissal would depend on his resolution. It is true that at the very top of the military world there was still Marshal Badoglio, who was no longer playing any active part but his prestige remained great; if he took sides, the Army would follow him.

The third group was formed by anxious Fascists who had been ousted—Ciano and Grandi in the van, supported by the 'principal secondary characters' Bottai, Federzoni, Farinacci. Ciano was the most active, and also the most rash; he was in contact with General Castellano. Grandi, who had been ambassador in London, thought he enjoyed the confidence of the British and Americans; he was hoping to become Foreign Minister of the new government and thus make it easier for Italy to change sides. These Fascists were, of course, relying on benefiting from the national union which would follow their leader's downfall; they would thus save their skins and perhaps their portfolios.

The King had tried to contact the Allies. In the summer of 1942 the Italian consul in Geneva had spoken to his British counterpart, on behalf of the Duke of Aosta. As proof of the plot against Mussolini the British demanded that a prince of the House of Savoy should set up a government in Sardinia ready to collaborate with them. It is not known what Victor Emmanuel thought of this condition but it was not followed up. The Princess of Piedmont, the wife of the heir to the throne, had for her part approached the British Minister to the Vatican. Then she had asked Salazar to act as mediator, which the Portuguese dictator had agreed to do. The Allies had remained very cautious towards these advances, no doubt because the decisions they had taken in Casablanca compelled them to be firm; but they had not turned their back on a change of government made on the King's initiative; although they had not wanted to disclose their intentions and had not co-operated in any way, their silence was calculated to encourage Victor Emmanuel.

The defeats in Sicily speeded things up; urgent action was necessary before the war set the whole of Italy ablaze. This was what Bonomi went to explain to the old King: they must dismiss Mussolini and arrest him, he told the King—Castellano had worked out a plan to this effect—to form an anti-Fascist cabinet under a military man, denounce the German alliance and make contact with the Allies. If Germany did not react, Italy would return to a state of neutrality; if Germany attacked Italy, the latter would go over to the Allies. Half-convinced, the King took a few more days to think it over; on July 15 he summoned Badoglio; he seemed to be merely sounding him but the two men understood each other without spelling things out.

The failure of the Feltre interview on July 19 had caused Ambrosio to make up his mind once and for all and he controlled the Army, which was the engine-room of the plot. The Führer had continued to insult the Italians, while at the same time refusing them the aid they were pleading for—besides, he did not know where to get hold of the 2,000 aircraft for which they were asking. The Italians, said Hitler, had to decide to make war like the Germans, 'with a fanatical will to win'. Bastianini, Alfieri and Ambrosio had vainly laid siege to the Duce to make him admit to Hitler that Italy could no longer continue the fight; Mussolini said not a word. He could definitely not be relied upon to rescue Italy from her hornet's nest; the only answer now was to get rid of him.

The bombing of Rome on July 19 acted as a spur. On July 22 Grandi visited the Duce; he tried to persuade him to resign of his own free will; he found him convinced that Germany was soon going to win the war with the aid of a new weapon. That same day Acquarone and Castellano met: the King had decided to act. On July 24 Acquarone, Ambrosio and Castellano visited Badoglio on his behalf and told him that the King had decided to place him at the head of the government. They handed him the declaration which he had to read and which Orlando had drawn up at the King's request. Badoglio approved and said: 'Everything's all right.' The die was cast.

Two distinct plots were thus developing simultaneously, each only partly aware of the other; true, one alone was enough to bring down the Duce, who was both gullible and overcome by inertia. But what about afterwards? They had at one and the same time to avoid civil war, prevent or forestall the wrath of the Germans and win the confidence of the Allies. Was this not attempting the impossible? Hypocrisy and secrecy could not be the complete answer, even though Victor Emmanuel seemed to be establishing a kind of record for duplicity; on July 22, having already decided to have Mussolini arrested, he told him that he would be 'the last person to desert him'.

V THE FALL OF MUSSOLINI

On July 23 the Fascist rebels drew up the motion which Grandi presented the next day at the meeting of the Fascist Grand Council; Mussolini had been warned. It was clear that if this text was adopted the time had come for him to disappear from the scene. Yet he passively waited to see what would happen.

At 5.15 p.m. on July 24 the members of the Grand Council met attired in Fascist ceremonial dress—the dress of the political movement whose demise they were plotting—black tunic, grey-green breeches and boots. Mussolini's statement was a long, rambling lukewarm speech in his defence; those present were struck and perhaps encouraged by the Duce's weariness, his ashen face and his obvious resignation. Mussolini's conclusion, however, was quite clear: the grave failures had been due to the fact that the Army had not always obeyed him.

Grandi replied with an indictment of the way in which the régime, which, he said, was completely out of touch with the country, was slowly collapsing and disintegrating. He held Mussolini responsible; he accused him of failing to give any real direction to his policy through having taken on too many minor tasks. He then read his motion, which suggested 'a return to the Constitution' in order 'to unite all Italians morally and materially in this hour of crisis for the nation's future', that is to say that the King should again take over actual command of the armed forces and 'complete initiative in any decisions'. Mussolini would devote himself solely to being leader of the Party; he would make it once again into a 'block of granite' which would one day be able 'to overcome their difficulties'.

The régime's senior officials were therefore not bent on self-destruction; they were trying to extricate themselves from dire straits by changing their navigator. It was not for them but for the King to decide whether or not Mussolini continued to be Prime Minister; they probably reckoned that the King could not break completely with a régime to which he owed so much. Moreover, they all solemnly protested their friendship for the Duce whose burden they said they merely wished to lighten. Mussolini could have proposed an amendment to the motion and even refused to let it be put to the vote. He did no such thing; the result of the vote, which was taken verbally, was nineteen in favour and eight against with one abstention. Mussolini did not seem to have any illusions about its meaning. He stated: 'You have plunged the régime into a state of crisis,' and he refused the traditional 'Salute to the Duce' when he closed the meeting after ten hours of dramatic discussion. It was 2.30 in the morning and July 25; what was he going to do?

This was only the first act. After all, an opposition group of nineteen people—even if important figures—was still not the whole party. One faithful supporter, Galbiati, the commander of the Fascist militia, suggested having the nineteen arrested—a few of them had taken fright and gone back on their vote—calling in the Germans under Himmler and moving the front back to the lower Alps; he produced this surprising formula: 'Just as France, by fighting on, will save the honour of the French, so a Mussolini movement will save the honour of the Italians.' Mussolini refused. In the afternoon he meekly answered the royal summons; he was therefore placing his fate in the hands of his King, who owed him so much and had always continued to show him friendship—even though he took a malicious pleasure in humiliating him by taking precedence over him when they were both present at official ceremonies.

Victor Emmanuel knew what had happened at the meeting of the Grand Council—Grandi had told Acquarone about it. He knew that from now on Mussolini was alone, abandoned by everyone and weary of everything, and that he could now strike at him without risk. To make himself look taller, this dwarf of a man put on military uniform for the occasion. Mussolini trusted the King implicitly and came without any special protection; he had completely failed to grasp what was happening that day; he was not only paralysed but blind. The interview lasted twenty minutes. The King informed the Duce that he was dismissing him and replacing him by Badoglio—the Grand Council meeting had put him one day ahead of his schedule. Then, under the pretext of ensuring his safety he had him arrested in the Quirinal gardens by a captain of the *carabinieri*; the Duce meekly got into the car which left the Quirinal by a back exit while his escort was waiting calmly at the main gate, convinced that the King had invited his Prime Minister to stay to dinner. For his 'safety', Mussolini was to be imprisoned first in one of the Lipari Islands and then in a chalet in the Gran Sasso in the Apennines.

What were his followers going to do? At 11.30 Galbiati learned that the Duce was no longer in office, that Senise, who had previously been dismissed by him, had taken over again as Chief of Police and that Scorza, the party secretary, had fled. The chief of the militia summoned his friends and collaborators; only two of them suggested 'punitive action' which Galbiati brushed aside with the simple question: 'Against whom?' And without even trying to call together or even warn the members of the militia who were scattered around Rome, without appealing, as he had one moment thought of doing, to the armoured division of the militia, which was considered to be absolutely loyal to the Duce and was stationed some twenty miles from the capital, Galbiati meekly allowed Badoglio to oust him from his command. Fascism was well and truly dead.

For the nineteen it was a Day of Dupes. For Grandi, who thought that he was back in favour with the King and did not know that the latter had decided to call Badoglio, there was nothing to do but flee. Ciano did the same but had the unfortunate idea of taking refuge in Munich, right in the mouth of the German lion. Both men were doubtless afraid of bearing the brunt of the people's anger after the outburst of joy in the working-class districts of Rome at the announcement of Mussolini's fall. They had not collected their thirty silver pieces and several of the nineteen were going to pay for their betrayal with their lives.

The King had successfully brought off his palace conspiracy. But Italy was at war and it was no longer up to him to decide her fate; this depended on two formidable unknown quantities: how were the Germans going to react and what did the Allies want?

VI THE ITALIAN SURRENDER

Mussolini's fall was a great moral and political victory for the Allies; it had considerable symbolic significance—had not the Duce, the founder of European Fascism, declared that the twentieth century would be Fascist? The Italian Resistance had achieved its objective; it was in the logic of events that Italy should once again become a democracy in which the political parties would alternate in power. But the King did not wish to move so quickly; he confined himself to freeing the anti-Fascists who had been imprisoned and to restoring the trade unions, freedom of the press, freedom of assembly. Badoglio formed a purely military ministry which could be no more than a caretaker government and bore no resemblance to the face of post-Fascist Italy; besides, its members had been instruments of the fallen régime.

On the military plane, Mussolini's fall brought no benefits, for the Allies failed to take advantage of it. In order to appease the Germans and gain time, Badoglio declared that the war would continue; he wanted to avoid any violent German reaction which would be impossible to fend off and 'back out' only once he was sure that the Allies would be able to land considerable forces and reach Rome first. So on August 6 in Tarvis, Guariglia, the new Foreign Minister, met Ribbentrop who made no secret of his anxiety—according to the interpreter Schmidt he was even afraid of being kidnapped. Unruffled, Guariglia gave his companion his word of honour that Italy was not negotiating with the Allies and was remaining on Germany's side; yet he knew quite well that it had been decided to send an Italian emissary, General Castellano, to Lisbon to 'contact' the Allies. He added, however, that Italy was at the end of her tether. Badoglio just as bravely gave the same reassurance to Kesselring.

But Hitler was not taken in. Even before the Feltre interview, in the course of a naval conference on July 17, he had not concealed his distrust with regard to 'undesirable Italian elements'; a sort of court martial, he said, would have to be set up in Italy. And he laid down what measures were to be taken if the worst should happen. He regarded the fate of his friend Mussolini as a personal insult. Without more ado the German troops replaced the Italians guarding the railways and bridges—a sign of how quickly they would intervene if the occasion arose; one Panzer division crossed the Brenner. Hitler had contemplated abandoning the south of Italy but the Allies' inactivity made him decide to hold on there.

Badoglio, however, had succeeded in gaining time. On August 5 secret negotiations with the Allies had begun in Sicily. On August 18 in Quebec, Churchill and Roosevelt had drawn up the Allies' policy and strategic plans with regard to the new Italian government; Eisenhower was to seize Corsica and Sardinia and secure air bases close to Rome and if possible beyond; but at the same time, paradoxically, units and boats were taken away from his command, the former for the great attack across the Channel and the latter for the Pacific. In these circumstances Eisenhower thought it impossible to achieve the objectives which he had been set.

On the diplomatic level, there was a difference of views between Americans and British. The Americans would have liked to leave Eisenhower a free hand to impose a military armistice on the Italians as he thought fit, in order to retain the possibility of securing their help and to ensure the most favourable conditions for landing on the peninsula. But the British, who agreed with the Soviets on this point, attached scarcely any importance to Italy's contribution to the Allied war effort; they wanted to inform Italy straightaway of the harsh punishment she deserved—the desire to secure control of the sea in the Mediterranean was not far from British minds.

They compromised. Eisenhower was to deliver a brief and strictly military text to the Italians. A second document consisting of forty-four articles and containing the political and economic terms would be communicated to the Italian negotiators in Malta on September 29; in the meantime the landing would have taken place and the Italians put to the test.

But in any case, whether long or short, the armistice was a *Diktat* in which the Italians had no say and which was presented to them on August 31 in the form of an ultimatum; it was take it or leave it. This was a blow for the King and the Badoglio government: they were being no better treated than Mussolini would have been; however, they submitted; they were hoping that the Allied landing would take place north of Rome and that the capital would be occupied by an airborne division. The Allied general staff insinuated that this would be the case; but it mistrusted these Italians who had changed sides so easily and refused to lift the veil on its intentions; yet it knew perfectly well that with the forces at its command, there was no hope of reaching Rome.

On September 3 the armistice was signed in Cassibile; the terms remained secret; they would not be disclosed until the day of the landing. The Italians thought they had several days in which to find their feet and make preparations; they hoped particularly to separate the Italian troops from the German troops who were around Rome and to take control of the airfields on which the expected Allied division would be dropped. And on September 8 the Allied general staff suddenly informed Badoglio that they would announce the armistice that very evening and invited him to do the same on his side. During the night the landing took place, but a long way from Rome, south of Naples, in Salerno.

It was obvious that the Allies had merely wished to avoid being fired on by the Italians, but they were in for a nasty shock, for they found the Germans forewarned and firmly ensconced. As for Badoglio's government, it was caught off-guard and as far as it was concerned the affair was a failure. It considered that it was in no position to defend Rome against the Germans, who occupied it immediately; Badoglio himself left for Brindisi with the King. Worse still, on September 16 ss commando went to free Mussolini in the Gran Sasso: the *carabinieri* who were guarding the Duce let the planes land and the ss advance towards them without firing a shot. With German support Mussolini was to try to reunite the last followers of Fascism on the side of the Germans in a movement which he called 'Fascist, Republican and Revolutionary'. Italy was going to be ravaged by civil war.

Guariglia was not wrong to hold the Allies responsible for the failure of the Italian 'secession', and it quickly proved a total failure. The hundreds of thousands of Italian workmen who had gone to work in Germany became so many hostages; suspects were imprisoned; those presumed to be dangerous were confined in concentration camps.

Almost everywhere the Italian troops, demoralised and abandoned, allowed themselves to be disarmed and captured; in Toulon several thousand soldiers were made prisoner by a handful of German sailors. But on the Greek island of Cephalonia, the Italian units, when consulted by their leader, General Gandin, decided to break with the Axis; fighting broke out between the former allies, with the Germans gaining the advantage after seven days, thanks to their air superiority. All the Italian officers, including General Gandin, were massacred after they had surrendered; nearly 3,000 soldiers were packed on to pontoons in an area that was mined and died in the resulting explosions.

The hardest fighting took place in the Dodecanese. In Rhodes the 7,000 Germans, who were better armed and concentrated in a main striking force, overpowered 36,000 Italians, though not without a fight and not until after the Italian ships had left the island. On Leros the British were able to land 4,000 men; they were bombed without being able to defend themselves properly and in November they surrendered to enemy paratroopers. The British also sent small garrisons to Cos and Samos; they fared no better. The British were putting into practice their conception of peripheral strategy, hoping in this way to influence Turkey. But General Eisenhower was against using large forces; by the end of November 1943 all the Cyclades were occupied by the Germans; Campioni and Mascherpa, the two Italian admirals who were in command there, were handed over by the Germans to the special tribunal of the Fascist Republic, which sentenced them to death for desertion.

Only the Italian war fleet was able for the most part to escape from the Germans because as early as September 6 the admirals knew the clauses of the armistice and the part they were supposed to play; the large ships were ordered to go to Malta, the smaller ones to Palermo. The Germans captured a few units which were tied up in harbour, under construction or being repaired—3 cruisers, 8 destroyers, 22 torpedo-boats and 10 submarines. Their aircraft attacked the large ships which had set out from La Spezia and sank the battleship *Roma*. But the ships based at Taranto and Pola came into harbour safe and sound—that is to say, two 35,000-ton battleships, three 24,000-ton cruisers, 8 fast cruisers and 10 destroyers, in all 126 units, plus 90 merchant ships, one of which was a liner, 300,000 tons of shipping in all. Except for the cruisers, all these ships that had escaped were to be used by the Allies in the Atlantic.

Italy was too heavily committed in Hitler's war to withdraw from it without loss. For her, the armistice brought anything but peace; for eighteen months, throughout its length and breadth, the peninsula was to be the theatre of desperate fighting between the Allies and the Germans, but also between the Italians.

VII THE WAR IN THE ITALIAN PENINSULA

On the same day on which the armistice with Italy was made known, two divisions of the British Eighth Army had crossed the Straits of Messina under the protection of four battleships and 400 guns, which started firing as soon as they left the coasts of Sicily; they occupied Reggio and gained a foothold in Calabria. Other units landed in Taranto and advanced on Bari and Foggia.

But it was further to the north in Salerno that the main Allied effort took place, with General Clark's American Fifth Army; this spot had been chosen because it was at the limit of the radius of action of the fighter air force based in Sicily. In theory Clark should have found himself confronted only by Italian units which had been neutralised by the armistice; he was reckoning on having no difficulty in making his way to Naples—a large port which was vital for receiving supplies—and in cutting off the enemy's route to the heel and toe of Italy. But this time the Germans had detected the convoys at sea and had dug themselves in; the landing troops were greeted by a hail of gunfire and were counter-attacked before they had taken up their positions.

On the 10th Clark nevertheless captured Salerno; but on the 13th, because of the raids by the German Air Force based in Foggia, things had come to such a pass that he was almost compelled to re-embark; Admiral Cunningham's fleet had to come in very close to support him and commit the whole of his naval air force. However, the Germans had been tied down by the running sore of Salerno; they had withdrawn in the south and on September 27 the Eighth Army occupied the Foggia airfields—from where raids could be carried out on Austria and south Germany. On October 1 the Germans evacuated Naples.

Once again the attack had not been a surprise; but the Allies had had a little more practice in amphibious landing operations. In Tunisia and Sicily, the commander of the ground troops had complained at the belated arrival of support from an air force which was not under his control and with which communications were rather unreliable. After the Salerno landing, where this lack of co-ordination could have been fatal, a first attempt towards a solution was made by bringing the Army and Navy headquarters closer together; this was developed further by placing a certain number of aircraft at the armies' immediate disposal but with most of them remaining under the overall command of the Air Force.

The successive stages in the tactical use of the Air Force had now been worked out: up to D-day—7 the attacks were concentrated on the enemy airfields in order to achieve mastery in the air; from D-day—6 to D-day—1 their aim was to isolate the area under attack and rain bombs upon the enemy positions; on D-day all the available air forces supported the landing units; a varying percentage wrecked the lines of communication leading to them. From D + 4 onwards only twenty per cent of the aircraft continued to support the landing; the rest were engaged in tasks required by the extension of operations.

The Italian campaign thus became a test for the crucial operation across the Channel; but in Italy itself the Allies were going to make slow progress because their plan was to attract and tie down as many German troops as they possibly could; and these troops were able to dig themselves in very skilfully on the mountain barriers and behind the deep valleys which had been cut by the rivers at right angles to the coast. The Allies had only two tactics to choose from: a frontal attack, which would not make the most of their tank superiority, or a landing behind the enemy lines; but the narrow beaches and steep coastline prevented them from deploying their troops in great numbers and breaking through. In both cases their advance was slow and very gradual. However, by October 14 the Fifth Army had captured Capua, established its lines on the Volturno some thirty miles north of Naples and joined hands with the British Eighth Army on its right. It was going to be a long, long way to Rome.

VIII THE LIBERATION OF CORSICA

The Germans had regrouped their troops at the crucial spot in order to meet the danger; as early as September 9 they had begun to evacuate Sardinia via Corsica and Leghorn. The French were not going to let a chance like this slip through their fingers.

In Corsica public opinion was unanimously against the Italians, who had had 80,000 men occupying the island since November 1942. The Corsicans did not consider themselves in the least as Italians and had no wish to become so. Fred Scamaroni, one of General de Gaulle's envoys, had been sent from London to work on this grist to the Resistance mill; he had been arrested by OVRA and had either committed suicide in prison or else was tortured to death.

It was easier to help the Corsican Resistance from Algiers than from London, and General Giraud took over the task. The submarine *Casabianca* under Commander Lherminier, which had escaped from Toulon when the fleet had been scuttled, carried out several missions to put agents and weapons ashore. Without referring the matter to the French National Liberation Committee, since he considered it to be a military operation which depended on him alone, General Giraud armed only one Resistance organisation, the National Front, without realising that it was Communist-inspired. At the same time he had formed a 'shock battalion' under Commander Gambiez, as the advance guard of a French Army landing which he had asked General Juin to plan—without referring the matter to General Eisenhower and knowing full well that the latter did not want it.

On September 9 the National Front announced the Corsican uprising;

it set up a Liberation Committee in Ajaccio; the Corsicans laid a few ambushes for the German troops who were retreating northwards from the south; they were obviously not very strong. It is true that the *Casabianca* had transported a few hundred men and that the 'shock battalion' was at the ready as early as September 14. But General Eisenhower refused to deplete the Allied pool of ships in order to transport to the island the expeditionary force which Giraud had placed under General Martin; he also refused to lend any aircraft.

The liberation of Corsica was therefore a purely French affair. The French troops arrived without any heavy equipment in merchant ships and also in warships—which, in the Allies' opinion, could have been put to better use by keeping watch on the area round Bastia in order to hinder the Germans' evacuation of the island. The latter had recaptured Bastia; they held the whole of the route across the plain; they had tanks. All that the *maquisards* and shock battalions could do was threaten them from the passes of the mountain ridge. One thing in their favour was the attitude of General Magli's Italian troops who, without attacking the Germans, helped the French by placing lorries, radio links, mules and ambulances at their disposal.

The landing troops advanced towards Bastia through the mountains, guided by the whole population; not until after September 24 were they supported by a few aircraft. The Germans were blocking the Golo valley and defending Bastia to protect their evacuation. Preparations were made to attack the town, with the French and Italians co-operating; the American Air Force then intervened at the last minute to make things easier— and destroyed Bastia just as the enemy was abandoning it; only the harbour was captured undamaged before demolition of it had begun.

The liberation of Corsica was only a minor feat of arms—the French lost 70 dead and 270 wounded. But it had considerable repercussions in France; the island had been liberated, symbolically, by the joint effort of internal resisters and French forces from outside; the BCRA immediately made it a base for sending agents to the south of France.

In Algiers this personal initiative on the part of General Giraud did not improve his relationship with General de Gaulle, even less so as, to everyone's surprise, Corsica, which before the war had had only a tiny minority of Communists, woke up to find that the National Front had given it provisional Communist municipal councils voted in by acclamation in the public squares. Communist propaganda used Corsica as an example of how a popular rising could be successful at very little cost.

On the military plane, thirteen airfields were equipped, and although the island had very few plains, and these were small ones, she became a springboard for air raids against northern Italy and Bavaria; she was also a base for the landings on the French Mediterranean coast.

Corsica, moreover, was not the only region in which the Italian armistice had helped the Allies. In Yugoslavia Tito's followers had seized many of the stores belonging to the Italian occupation troops; they thus grew into an army of more than 200,000 men; they had been joined by a few Italian units and many individual volunteers. Tito now felt that he was strong enough completely to overthrow Mihailović, whom the British decided to desert; in November 1943, in Jajce in Bosnia the second session of the Yugoslav Anti-Fascist Council decided that the future state of Yugoslavia would be a Socialist democracy organised on a federal basis; it conferred the title of Marshal on Tito and forbade King Peter II to return to his country until the people had made up its mind about his fate. The Yugoslav Resistance felt that it had come of age and acted accordingly.

From November 1943 the Italian troops were evacuated from Albania via Valona. There again Communist supporters had taken advantage of the fact that they had been disarmed and had enlisted a few of them in their ranks; it was the same in the Greek maquis with a few survivors from Cephalonia.

Italians were thus showing that they had not changed sides merely out of opportunism; they were taking up their positions on the battlefield itself. However, the situation in Italy had become too confused for any common line of conduct to be adopted throughout the country.

IX THE DIVISION OF ITALY

By the autumn of 1943 the whole of the southern part of Italy was clear of Germans. It was under Allied military control, but administered by the legal Italian authorities: the King and Marshal Badoglio's government. Although this government had been reshuffled in November by the admission of civilians, it continued to consist of top-ranking officials and technical experts, without any representatives from the political parties. However, these parties had built up their strength again in the area and were asking to be admitted to the government; but they were pursuing their propaganda in the politically and socially least developed part of Italy and it was not fostered by the xenophobia and patriotism which the presence of the Germans aroused behind the front line. By definition there cannot be a Resistance in an area where there is no Occupation; Naples, moreover, was the only place where from September 27 to October 1 the people had revolted at the news that the Germans wanted to deport male adults and destroy the harbour. Nowhere else had any action been taken to prepare the ground for the Allied troops or make it easier for them to advance.

In these circumstances the Liberation Committees which had been set up by a coalition of anti-Fascist parties could take action only in internal politics; with varying degrees of enthusiasm they attacked the King and the government, whom they saw as the aftermath of Fascism; they thus made the impression of being revolutionary organisations in the eyes of the local population who had remained very much under the thumb of a conservative Church and over whom the big landowners had a great deal of influence. They also worried the Allies, particularly Churchill, who was anxious for Italy to remain a monarchy. Concerned above all to avoid disorder and ensure security, the Allied military command had formed a body of officers, 'the Allied Military Government of Occupied Territories' (AMGOT), which administered the territory and took care of the essential matter of supplies for the population. The Allies had drawn up a list of eminent Italians whom they considered to be deserving of a political role, but their choice was not always to the liking of the anti-Fascist parties.

Since the King and Badoglio were continually proclaiming their goodwill and giving increasing proof of it, they were gradually granted more and more actual power. On September 30, the Allies formally recognised the new Italian government's position as 'co-belligerent in the war against Germany'; and on October 13, 1943, this government declared war on Germany. How could it now be refused the attributes of a sovereign power? The Allies granted it permission to raise an army of limited strength, without, however, making any promise about Italy's future; and they allowed it to extend its powers equally to occupied Italy.

But in this region the government's departure had left room for the Resistance. Because of the presence of the Germans, the Resistance no longer confined itself to internal political action: its first objective, the fall of Fascism, had been achieved; from now on it was fighting to liberate the country from foreign occupation; it thus resembled the other national Resistance movements of occupied Europe. The anti-Fascist leaders had remained in Rome and they formed the 'National Liberation Committee' under the chairmanship of Bonomi, representing the Action party, the Christian Democrats (Gasperi and Gronchi), the Socialists (Nenni and Saragat), the Workers (Ruini), the Liberals (Soleri) and the Communists (Amendola). Regional Liberation Committees were set up in all the occupied provinces.

The resisters had taken up the struggle against the occupier more or less everywhere; when the Germans had occupied Rome, fighting had broken out even in the city streets and civilians had taken part. In the Abruzzi, in Umbria, the Marches, the Ligurian Apennines and the Slovenian Carso, groups of supporters had been formed by disbanded soldiers and anti-Fascists freed from jail, joined by young men from the towns.

The National Liberation Committee could feel that it was representing the living forces of the country; moreover, it had its seat in the capital. On October 16, 1943, it demanded that the struggle be directed against the Germans and the Fascists; this was tantamount to calling for the King to step down and the dissolution of the Badoglio government. But the Allies did not see it in this light; they fully accepted help from an Italian Resistance but on condition that it restricted itself to military action which was in keeping with their views and did not encroach on the political sphere. They did not sympathise with the Liberation Committee's revolutionary designs and since they considered that it was itself illegal and had only the authority which it had arrogated to itself, they did not grant it recognition. In addition, they wanted the Resistance to confine itself to carrying out small acts of sabotage on their instructions and they distrusted a general uprising, which in their eyes was synonymous with weakness and anarchy.

The King and Badoglio also had no intention of giving up their authority; they created a 'Military Intelligence Service' (SMI) which was set up in the centre; in Rome itself an underground military group under Colonel Montezemolo continued to be attached to the regular Army and not to the Liberation Committee. Finally, the latter's prestige was diminished by the authority of the Holy See; the Pope was making great efforts to have supplies provided for the population. He gave refuge to many anti-Fascists who were being pursued. He intervened with the Allies to prevent the city from being bombed. The people were growing used to the idea of Rome being governed from the Vatican.

Thus although Bonomi was a judicious chairman and was attempting to reconcile all Italians, the National Liberation Committee was not the major authority in the city, despite its title. Its counterpart in Upper Italy, which had its seat in Milan, was not at all the same sort of thing. True, it had the same structure as the one in Rome and in theory it agreed to take its orders from it; but the situation and social context were completely different.

Northern Italy was in fact the seat of the great Italian industrial centres. Here Communism and Socialism had long been firmly rooted. What they did could influence the masses, who followed them faithfully. Whereas the great Italian political movements, starting with the Risorgimento, had been the work of the bourgeoisie alone, for the first time workers, artisans and peasants became aware through and in the Resistance of the part they had to play.

This was going to make a tremendous difference to the Resistance. As far as the fighting was concerned it was going to be able to assert itself even in the cities, by means of mass demonstrations, acts of industrial sabotage, attacks on the enemy and strikes. But it did not limit its objectives merely to freeing territory; it had social and economic revolution in mind, the first stage of which was the struggle against the republican Fascists. In southern Italy the Resistance castigated the government; in Rome it claimed to be the government; in the north it was engaged in a patriotic and revolutionary civil war. It is true that the Liberation Committee of Upper Italy, whose authority extended as far as Florence, was joined by men of all views and from all walks of life; but it was not moderates like Bonomi who were in control of it but Communists and revolutionary intellectuals of the young Action party; and although some of the military continued to look to the Brindisi government, it was too far away to be able to govern effectively; and as for the Allies, at the end of 1943 they were preoccupied above all with their fighting in central Italy.

Thus not only did the Liberation Committee of Upper Italy become the leading wing of the Italian Resistance but it provided the framework for a vast revolutionary movement which was rousing the masses in Florence, Milan, Turin and Venice and laying the foundations for an Italy very different from the pre-war one, which in the south of the country continued to exist unchanged.